THE CONSUL AT ROME

In modern times there have been studies of the Roman Republican institutions as a whole as well as in-depth analyses of the senate, the popular assemblies, the tribunate of the plebs, the aedileship, the praetorship, and the censorship. However, the consulship, the highest magistracy of the Roman Republic, has not received the same attention from scholars. The purpose of this book is to analyse the tasks that consuls performed in the civil sphere during their term of office between the years 367 and 50 BC, using the preserved ancient sources as its basis. In short, it is a study of the consuls 'at work', both within and outside the city of Rome, in such varied fields as religion, diplomacy, legislation, jurisdiction, colonization, elections, and day-to-day politics. Clearly and accessibly written, it will provide an indispensable reference work for all scholars and students of the history of the Roman Republic.

FRANCISCO PINA POLO is Professor of Ancient History at the Departamento Ciencias Antigüedad at the Universidad de Zaragoza. He is co-editor of *Coloquios de Historia Antigua Universidad de Zaragoza* (I, 2001; II, 2003; III, 2005; IV, 2007; V, 2009; and VI, 2010), and his recent books include *Marco Tulio Cicerón* (2005) (German translation, *Rom, das bin ich. Marcus Tullius Cicero, ein Leben*, Stuttgart, 2010).

THE CONSUL AT ROME

The Civil Functions of the Consuls in the Roman Republic

FRANCISCO PINA POLO

CAMBRIDGE UNIVERSITY PRESS

Cambridge, New York, Melbourne, Madrid, Cape Town,
Singapore, São Paulo, Delhi, Tokyo, Mexico City

Cambridge University Press
The Edinburgh Building, Cambridge CB2 8RU, UK

Published in the United States of America by Cambridge University Press, New York

www.cambridge.org
Information on this title: www.cambridge.org/9780521190831

First published 2011

Printed in the United Kingdom at the University Press, Cambridge

A catalogue record for this publication is available from the British Library

Library of Congress Cataloguing in Publication data
Pina Polo, Francisco.
The consul at Rome : the civil functions of the consuls in the Roman
Republic / Francisco Pina Polo.
p.   cm.
ISBN 978-0-521-19083-1 (hardback)
1. Consuls, Roman.   2. Rome – Politics and government – 510–30 B.C.   I. Title.
DG83.5.C7P56   2011
937′.02–dc22
2010032405

ISBN 978-0-521-19083-1 Hardback

For Romana,
the best conceivable fellow traveller
on the voyage of life

Contents

Illustrations

Acknowledgements

This work is the result of two research projects funded by the Ministerio de Educación y Ciencia del Gobierno de España. The first, entitled 'Cónsules, consulares y el gobierno de la República romana' (HUM2004–02449), was carried out between 2005 and 2007. The second, 'Cónsules, consulares y el gobierno de la República romana entre Sila y Augusto' (HUM2007–60776/HIST), was conducted between 2008 and 2010. Thanks to them, I have been able to pay long visits to the University of Münster (Germany) and, in particular, to the Classics Centre, Oxford, where I was able to work in their magnificent libraries, especially the Sackler Library and the Bodleian. I would like to thank my hosts, Wolfson College, Oxford, for their assistance, and Professors Johannes Hahn, Alan Bowman, and Fergus Millar, who opened their doors for my research and with whose friendship I am honoured.

Rosa Anía and Noel Murphy translated the original Spanish text into English. The English text has been revised and improved by Charlotte Tupman. Some colleagues have been kind enough to read parts of the book and have contributed their ideas as well as correcting some errors: Silvia Alfayé, Hans Beck, Antonio Duplá, Frédéric Hurlet, Martin Jehne, Francisco Marco, Michael Peachin, Jonathan Prag, and John Rich. In particular, I would like to express my gratitude to Fergus Millar, who patiently read most of the manuscript and provided valuable suggestions which greatly contributed to enriching its contents. To all of them, my most sincere thanks. Of course, any mistakes that may remain are solely my responsibility.

Introduction

Studies both ancient and modern have been written on the Republican institutions as a whole, as well as in-depth analyses of the senate, the popular assemblies, the tribunate of the plebs, the aedileship, the praetorship, and the censorship. However, the consulship has not received the same attention from scholars. In fact, there are no monographs that deal specifically with the functions and activities of the supreme magistracy of the Roman state during the Republican period.

Of course, there are prosopographical studies which have shaped the chronology of the Republican consuls. Amongst these, Broughton's prosopography is absolutely essential, and without it this work would have been almost impossible to undertake.[1] With a more limited scope, Albert Neuendorff completed a prosopography of the consuls from 78 to 49, focusing mainly on the candidates for the annual consular elections, and Adolf Lippold specifically studied the political role of the consuls in the period between 264 and 201.[2] As a basis for consular prosopography, the *fasti consulares* have also been the subject of studies such as that of Fabio Mora, amongst others.[3]

To the best of my knowledge, the first doctoral thesis on the Roman consulship was written by the Utrecht scholar Heinrich Gabriel Römer. It was published in 1841 with the title *Dissertatio historico-antiquaria de consulum romanorum auctoritate libera* in Utrecht, as stated on the first page of the copy preserved in the Sackler Library, Oxford. This was deposited in 1950 by Brasenose College in the Ashmolean Museum Library. The book had previously been owned by Henry Francis Pelham, Camden Professor of Ancient History at Oxford from 1889 to 1907. Römer's thesis, written in

---

All dates in the book refer to the period BC. Any exceptions are noted where necessary in the text.

[1] Broughton 1951–86. See also the prosopography of the consuls between the passing of the *lex Villia* and the beginning of the civil war: Badian 1990.

[2] Neuendorff 1913; Lippold 1963.   [3] Mora 1999. See also Drummond 1974; Pinsent 1975.

I

Latin, is a worthy effort to understand the powers and functions of consuls in the Republican period. In just over one hundred pages, Römer studied the origin of the term consul, the form in which the consuls were elected, their relationship with the people through their presence in assemblies, their ability to convene the senate and discuss different questions with the senators, their authority in religious matters, and their role as commanders-in-chief of the Roman legions.

Römer's book, nowadays completely forgotten, is hitherto, as far as I know, the only monograph that deals exclusively with the Roman consulship in the Republican period. Obviously, this does not mean that there are no other works in which the consulship has been treated, more or less comprehensively, along with the other institutions of the Republican era, such as Theodor Mommsen's *Römisches Staatsrecht*, which was originally published in 1887.[4] Soon afterwards, Ettore De Ruggiero also dedicated a good number of pages to analysing consular activities in his *Dizionario epigrafico di antichità romane* in 1892.[5] Other authors, such as Jochen Bleicken and Francesco De Martino in the twentieth century, studied the Roman constitution and the evolution of the supreme magistracy of the Roman state throughout its history.[6] More recently, Wolfgang Kunkel followed suit with his *Staatsordnung und Staatspraxis der römischen Republik*, an encyclopaedic work completed by Roland Wittmann.[7] To this brief list of publications on the institutions of Republican Rome in which the consulship has been considered, a list which is by no means intended to be exhaustive, we can add the recent volume by Andrew Lintott on the Roman constitution.[8] And, of course, there is the important book by Adalberto Giovannini on the *imperium* of consuls, which is an attempt to unravel the characteristics of consular power, particularly during the late Republican period.[9]

In the introduction to his book on the Roman constitution, Lintott highlighted the fact that Mommsen's great study, which is still a work of reference, was to a large extent a theoretical rather than an empirical analysis: 'It is significant that the best known and fundamental modern attempt to give an account of the constitution, Theodor Mommsen's *Römisches Staatsrecht*, is highly theoretical, in spite of the assembly of source-material in the footnotes.'[10] Lintott's statement is not only completely accurate, but it also applies in general terms to the publications mentioned above. From the point of view

---

[4] Mommsen 1887–8, on the consulship vol. II 74–140.
[5] De Ruggiero 1892. See also Kübler 1900.   [6] De Martino 1990; Bleicken 1995.
[7] Kunkel and Wittmann 1995: esp. 311–37.
[8] Lintott 1999b, on the consulship 104–7. See also Brennan 2000: 31–64; North 2006: 256–77.
[9] Giovannini 1983.   [10] Lintott 1999b: 8.

of specialists in Roman law, the aforementioned studies are directed mainly towards determining the nature of the *imperium* with which consuls were invested, and thence establishing the functions that they must have fulfilled as magistrates. Some of these functions are illustrated by alluding to passages from ancient authors; others are simply presumed despite the fact that ancient sources do not mention them.

In contrast, this monograph intends to have an entirely empirical rather than a theoretical approach. My primary objective is to determine which functions were assigned to the consulship in political practice, with the preserved ancient sources taken as reference material. In short, it is an attempt to study the consuls 'at work', in their actual activities during their term of office.

In his reflections on the Republican constitution, Polybius[11] emphasizes the power of consuls as typical of a monarchical government, balanced by the aristocratic counter-power exercised by the senate and by the prerogatives of the people that were typical of a democracy, thus forming what the Greek author considered to be the balanced political regime that was the origin of the growing Roman hegemony across the Mediterranean.[12] According to Polybius the consuls were, on the one hand, the commanders of the Roman army, with full decision-making powers, which was their function when they left Rome to lead the legions; on the other hand, they were the heads of the Roman administration, which was their function while in Rome.

In the military field, Polybius claims that consuls had absolute power during war in recruiting both citizens and allies, in the appointment of military tribunes, and in the punishment of their subordinates. The Greek historian adds that consuls were also entitled to spend public funds as they deemed appropriate, with the co-operation of a quaestor at their service during military campaigns. The reading of the surviving books of Livy unquestionably confirms the largely military nature of the consulship during most of the Republic. As commanders-in-chief of the Roman army, the consuls spent long parts of their year as supreme magistrates away from Rome. Significantly, when Polybius refers to the consuls, he refers to them more frequently as *strategoi* rather than as *hupatoi*, thus highlighting their role as *imperatores* derived from their mainly military tasks.

On the other hand, during their stay in Rome before leading the legions, consuls were the heads of the Roman administration. In this respect, Polybius mentions a series of tasks assigned to them regarding both the

---

[11] Polyb. 6.12.   [12] Cf. Walbank 1957: 673–97; Nicolet 1974: 209–58; Lintott 1999b: 16–26.

senate and the people: the presentation of foreign embassies to the senate; deliberation within the senate on questions of interest to the community; the execution of decrees issued by the senate; summoning and presiding over popular assemblies; presentation before the people of measures to be taken and bills; and application of the laws passed by the people.

My purpose is to analyse precisely those consular tasks to which Polybius alludes that were not strictly military. My objective is to determine which civil functions were part of the *officium consulare*, both in the *Urbs* and outside it. I shall not, therefore, analyse the consuls as military chiefs, but it should be borne in mind that military tasks took up most of the work of the consuls during the consular year and that, obviously, most ancient sources refer to their military tasks much more frequently and in more detail. Information on consular civil tasks is consequently much less common than that on the consuls as commanders-in-chief of the Roman army, although the evidence is sufficient to reveal the complexity of consular activities, whether mandatory or occasional, in such varied fields as religion, diplomacy, legislation, jurisdiction, colonization, and elections.

The legal power of the consuls in the Republican period continues to be debated, and, to a great extent, the discussion still revolves around the theses put forward by Theodor Mommsen. Mommsen's starting point was that *imperium* defined the supreme power within the government of the Roman Republic, which as such represented the supreme authority both in the military sphere and in legal jurisdiction.[13] Mommsen distinguished two spheres of application of *imperium*, differentiating between *imperium domi* and *imperium militiae*. The former concept would have referred to the civil powers that a consul had exclusively within the city of Rome, whereas the *imperium militiae* would have been wielded exclusively outside the *Urbs*. The limit between both areas would have been geographical, marked by the sacred boundary of the city (*pomerium*).[14] Mommsen's thesis has generally been accepted in its main points by most scholars studying the matter.[15]

In his *Consulare imperium*, Giovannini offered a comprehensive critique of Mommsen's theories. In Giovannini's opinion, the definition traditionally given, following Mommsen, of the contrast between *imperium domi* and *imperium militiae* is incorrect, since such a contrast would not have been linked to the *pomerium* and would have been not a territorial but a qualitative contrast, depending on the tasks performed by the consuls. The formula *domi militiaeque* in fact distinguished civil and military activities,

---

[13] Mommsen 1887–8: i 22.   [14] Mommsen 1887–8: i 61–75.
[15] See now also on the concept of *imperium* Beck, forthcoming.

regardless of the place where they were carried out.[16] These domains of consular power were not incompatible, but were simultaneous and complementary. A consul had one *imperium*, both civil and military, and he exercised civil power over civilians and military power over the soldiers under his command.[17]

Recently, Fred Drogula has suggested a radically different scenario in regard to the powers held by the higher magistrates of the Roman Republic. In his opinion, Mommsen was correct in differentiating between the powers of a magistrate inside and outside Rome, but was wrong in assuming that the two spheres were governed by means of *imperium*.[18] Drogula argues that the distinction between *imperium domi* and *militiae* must be eliminated and that it never existed as such because the *imperium* was exclusively a military power wielded outside Rome.[19] There was certainly a marked difference between the exercise of civil and military powers, but such a difference came from *potestas* and *imperium* respectively.[20] Inside the *pomerium* consuls and praetors did not have *imperium*, since the *potestas* which was attached to their office and to all Roman magistracies was sufficient for the exercise of their civil functions.[21] The *imperium* as military command was banned inside the *pomerium*, and its use was permitted only in extraordinary circumstances: the celebration of a triumph, the appointment of a dictator, or the proclamation of the so-called 'ultimate decree of the senate' (*senatus consultum ultimum*).[22]

The debate therefore revolves around several questions which complement or exclude each other: whether from the very moment of their appointment consuls had *imperium* or simply *potestas*; whether *imperium* was exclusively a military command exercised outside Rome or was a single power within which a military and a civil command could be distinguished; whether the exercise of civil and military power depended on the physical location of the consuls, so that they could only wield their civil power inside

---

[16] Giovannini 1983: 7–15.   [17] Giovannini 1983: 27–30.   [18] Drogula 2007: 451.

[19] Drogula 2007: 430: '*Imperium* was the right to exercise military command – outside the *pomerium* – and no more.'

[20] Drogula 2007: 431: 'The divide between military and civilian powers at Rome was strong, and it is reasonable to believe that these powers derived from separate sources, *imperium* (military command) and *potestas* (civilian magisterial authority), rather than from a single military source (*imperium*)'; 451: 'The tremendous power of *imperium* was carefully limited by the sacred boundary of the *pomerium*, into which *imperium* (except in exceptional circumstances) did not extend. *Imperium* remained outside the city with all other things military, while within Rome magistrates functioned by right of their *potestas* to undertake their assigned duties.'

[21] Drogula 2007: 422: '*imperium* was not necessary within the *pomerium*, because *potestas* provided all the power and authority magistrates needed to perform the duties of their offices.'

[22] Drogula 2007: 442–51.

the *pomerium* and their military power outside it; or if the differentiation between *imperium domi* and *militiae* was not spatial, but depended on the tasks performed by consuls at each specific moment.

This monograph aims to make a practical contribution to the debate by means of the verification of the tasks that consuls performed during their term of office in the civil sphere. In this sense, most of the civil functions of the *officium consulis* which are set out in this book were definitely performed in the *Urbs* (religious, diplomatic, legislative, and electoral tasks, as well as communication with the people, etc.), and these are the activities that are fundamentally relevant for this book. But other tasks were carried out outside Rome once the consuls had left the city, and these must be included as consular civil activities. For example, a consul wearing the military cloak (*paludamentum*), acting as president over the electoral process, could call an election for a specific date by means of an edict issued from his province or during his return journey to the *Urbs* (*ex itinere*), where he was to preside over the elections. This was plainly a civil task performed by a consul without leaving his military command.[23] Likewise, the consul who was entrusted with presiding over the annual elections did so while wearing the *paludamentum*, and he usually returned to his province afterwards. But in cases where censorial elections were necessary, that same consul presided over them at the beginning of the consular year before leaving Rome to go to his province.

Outside Rome certain consular tasks were occasionally performed, such as the control of the use of the public land (*ager publicus*) and its apportioning in the colonization process. In 173, the consul Postumius was sent to Campania by the senate to recover public land that was being used improperly by some private individuals. To conduct this task, Postumius would not have left Rome wearing a military cloak and with the pomp of the procession with which a consul usually left the city to take command of the legions. Also, the consuls were occasionally entrusted by the senate with extraordinary investigations of matters of particular relevance, both within and outside Rome, as for example in the case of the Bacchanalia in 186. For a good part of the Republican period the consuls were great promoters of public works, many of them outside the *Urbs*, such as certain water works and most of the roads in Italy. In summary, this book deals with consular civil functions in a broad sense, especially, but not only, those performed in Rome, and it does not include the otherwise predominant role of the consuls as military chiefs on the battlefield for most of the Republican period.

[23] Giovannini 1983: 30.

The period selected for this analysis is from 367 to 50, from the approval of the Licinio-Sextian laws to the beginning of the civil war between the Caesarians and Pompeians. The date of the beginning of this study is justified by the fact, generally accepted although debated by current scholarship, that the approval in 367 of the Licinio-Sextian laws actually represented the start of the consulship as the supreme Republican magistracy, after the long period of experimentation which had taken place from the beginning of the Republican period. The study has been divided into two parts: the first concerning the period from 367 to Sulla's dictatorship; the second from 80 to 50. Between the fourth and second centuries the two consuls generally spent most of their term of office outside Rome, commanding their respective armies in their allotted provinces. However, during the first century, the consuls remained in Rome during most or all of the consular year. This means that, if the function of the consuls until Sulla's period was essentially, though not exclusively, to act as the supreme commanders of the Roman army, from the year 80 onwards their work focused mainly on their executive duties of government in Rome.

Since Mommsen, it has traditionally been considered that this substantial change in the institutional role of the consuls was the result of a law introduced by Sulla, who would thus have removed military command from the consuls, limiting their power to civil matters in the *Urbs*. Giovannini, however, demonstrated that the supposed *lex de provinciis ordinandis* attributed to Sulla never existed. It is therefore evident that there was a substantial difference between the political role played by consuls who spent a short period of time in Rome before setting off for their provinces leading their armies, and that of those who were the centre of Rome's political scene in the late Republican period. While this is true, we do not know for certain that this important change can be attributed to a Sullan law. Nevertheless, for practical reasons this book maintains that the alteration occurred during Sulla's dictatorship, although it must be recognized that his intervention in the change of the consulship as an institution is questionable.

For the historical period analysed in the first part of this monograph, Livy is, of course, our main source. In fact, in most cases he is the only available source for the years 367 to 167, and even when texts of other authors exist, they are based on Livy's work. In Books 21 to 45, which deal with the Middle Republic from 218 to 167, Livy structured his narrative following a pattern based on the movements of the consuls (and to a lesser extent those of other magistrates) between Rome and the provinces, differentiating between the activity deployed within the *Urbs* and that beyond it, essentially following the polarity between civilian and military matters. As Rome expanded her control over further territories, Livy overlapped the usual chronological sequencing based on the consular year with a new polarity: military activities in the East and the West of the Mediterranean. Whereas this applies between 218 and 167, there is no fixed structure for the books on the fourth century, and the loss of Livy's work after 167 prevents us from determining how he organized his account.[24] All other sources for this period (Polybius, Plutarch, Diodorus, Valerius Maximus, etc.) are secondary and only provide brief pieces of information which corroborate or complement those given by Livy.

It is clear that the sources for the mid-Republican period sometimes present problems of credibility, along with the fact that information on most of the third century is scarce due to the loss of the second decade of Livy's work. Nonetheless, the reading and analysis of ancient sources clearly continues to be the only appropriate method for the reconstruction of the institutional history of the Roman Republic in the pre-Sullan period, for which the available epigraphy is extremely scarce.[25] Although certain episodes narrated by the annalists, and later collected by Livy, generate reasonable doubts as regards their historicity (as noted when necessary), Livy's account as a whole allows us to produce a fairly accurate picture of the activities engaged in by the consuls, both within and outside Rome, throughout the period for which the work of the Latin author is preserved. It therefore enables us to determine with a certain amount of precision the actual role of the consulship in the government of the Roman Republic in the pre-Sullan period, including its duties, powers, functions, and tasks.

From the moment from which the books of Livy are no longer available, this picture fades considerably, to the point that for the second century, from 167 until the beginning of the first century, we have in many cases only very rough sketches. The period of time between Sulla's dictatorship and the beginning of the civil war between the Caesarians and Pompeians, which occupies the second part of this book, is no exception. This is rather paradoxical, since we have the preserved works of contemporaries who were directly involved in the Roman political scene, such as Cicero, Sallust, and Caesar.

---

[24] See Rich 1997, who suggests that the structure used by Livy for the mid-Republican period may have derived from the work of Valerius Antias (see also Rich 2005). In general, on the layout of Livy's work, see McDonald 1957; Luce 1977; Mineo 2006.

[25] Lintott 1999b: 7: 'We read the texts of laws and decrees of the senate, we study the fragments of learned commentaries to be found in antiquarian sources, but frequently our best guide to constitutional practice is to read in ancient narratives what actually happened over a period, and, where there was conflict, to discover, as far as we can, in what terms the issues were formulated at the time.'

We also have the texts of Greek authors, such as Appian, Cassius Dio, and Plutarch, along with other minor sources. However, we do not have a detailed account of the activities carried out by many of the consuls from 80 to 50, and it is at times particularly difficult to determine the routine of consular work. Exceptions to this are the years in which some of the great protagonists of the period were consuls, in particular Pompey, Cicero, and Caesar, on whom the ancient sources focus and provide abundant information. The limitations of the sources must be taken into consideration when tackling the study of the evolution of consular functions during the first century before the successive civil wars which led to the establishment of the Principate.

The structure of the first part of the book, on the pre-Sullan period, is inspired by the pattern provided by Livy for the development of the consular year in the mid-Republican period. The chapters are presented successively so that it is possible to follow approximately the usual order of the tasks undertaken by the consuls in this period, from the moment they took office and performed their religious and diplomatic duties in Rome at the beginning of the consular year to their presidency over the elections, usually held in the last few weeks of the consular year; also included are other tasks (public works, inquiries, etc.) which occasionally also fell to the consuls during their term of office and could be carried out both within the *Urbs* and outside it. The short stay of the consuls in Rome, and their habitual absence from the city because they were commanding their armies, set the pattern of the consular year in the pre-Sullan period and determined consular functions.

The second part of the book deals with the period from 80 to 50, for which we have no ancient sources that reflect, as Livy did, the structure of the course of the consular year; nor were the political circumstances the same. The habitual presence of the consuls in Rome during their time of office altered their participation in the political life of the city, making it more conspicuous. Although certain consular tasks continued to be mandatory at specific times of the year, increased flexibility meant that the consuls combined various functions; however, these remained similar to those of the pre-Sullan period. A chapter in the second part of the book describes the civil consular functions in the late-Republican period, preceded by a much-needed discussion on the existence of the supposed Sullan law on provincial government and its consequences for the consulship. Each of the two parts of the book concludes with an analysis of the activities carried out by the consuls during the consular year, in the first place for 190–189, and in the second place for the year 63.

PART I

The consular functions in the pre-Sullan age (367–81)

CHAPTER I

The consuls taking office

The day on which the consuls took office varied throughout the Republican period. Livy's *periochae* report that from the year 153 onwards the consuls took office on 1 January, and not on 15 March as had been the case until then, a change that may have been caused by the Celtiberian rebellion in Hispania.[1] According to Mommsen, the date of the Ides of March was designated as the beginning of the consular year some time between 233 and 217, although he favoured the year 222 as the most likely, given the dates of consular triumphs reported by the *fasti triumphales*.[2] More recently, Hans Beck suggested plausibly that, as in the case of the new regulation of 153, there may have been a military reason for beginning the consular year on 15 March, and that this may have taken place in 218, linked to the beginning of the Second Punic War.[3] The outbreak of the conflict may have made it advisable for the consuls to take office earlier in order to see to preliminary military actions as soon as possible, once they had completed their compulsory civil tasks in Rome. Nevertheless, the first time Livy mentions the consuls taking office on the Ides of March is in his account for the year 217, and from then on he provides the same information on a good number of occasions, which indicates that this was indeed the norm until 153.[4] The single known partial exception occurred in 210, when only Marcellus took office on 15 March, whilst his colleague M. Valerius Laevinus was forced to do so at a later date due to illness.[5]

There is only occasional evidence in written sources for the date on which the consuls took office before the Hannibalic War, or, as may have been the

---

[1] Liv. *per.* 47: 'mutandi comitia causa fuit, quod Hispani rebellabant.' Cf. Cassiod. *Chron.*: 'Q. Fulvius et T. Annius. hi primi consules kalendis Ianuariis magistratum inierunt propter subitum Celtiberiae bellum.'

[2] Mommsen 1887–8: I 599. In the same sense, Broughton 1951–86: II 638.   [3] Beck 2005: 409–11.

[4] 217: Liv. 22.1.5–7; 215: 23.30.17; 209: 27.7.7; 200: 31.5.2; 199: 32.1.1; 195: 33.43.1; 188: 38.35.7; 183: 39.45.1; 180: 40.35.2; 177: 41.8.4; 168: 44.19.1.

[5] Liv. 26.26.5–9.

case, for the date the supreme magistrates of Rome prior to the consulship took office. In fact it is probable that the date was variable, at least at an earlier stage; the ancient sources provide very different dates for the consuls taking office, generally in the second half of the year during the fifth and fourth centuries. Almost all the available sources refer to the fifth century, which certainly creates doubts about the reliability of the information: in the year 493 the consuls took office on the Calends of September;[6] in 476, in the month of Sextilis;[7] in 463, on the Calends of Sextilis;[8] in 462, three days before the Ides of the month of Sextilis;[9] in 451 and 450 they took office on the Ides of May;[10] in 443, coinciding with the full moon of December;[11] in 423, on the Ides of December;[12] and in 401, on the Calends of October.[13] For the fourth century only the date for 329 is known, when the consular year started on the Calends of the month of Quintilis.[14] In 321, both consuls abdicated, and their substitutes took office on the day of their election,[15] apparently starting a series of consulships which began at the end of autumn or at the beginning of winter.[16] Mommsen, once again on the basis of the known dates of the triumphs celebrated between the war against Pyrrhus and the end of the First Punic War, considered that by the third century the consular year always started on the Calends of May.[17]

We know therefore that the consular year started on the Calends of January from the year 153 onwards, a practice that remained unchanged until the end of the Republican period; that it started on the Ides of March possibly from the beginning of the Hannibalic War, and certainly from 217 onwards; and that before this date, during the third century, it may have started on the Calends of May, although it is also possible that there was no fixed day for the new consuls' taking office, which seems very likely at the beginning of the Republic.[18] The fact that the official date of the beginning

---

[6] Dion. Hal. 6.49.1. Cf. Broughton 1951–86: II 637–9.   [7] Dion. Hal. 9.25.1.
[8] Liv. 3.6.1.   [9] Liv. 3.8.2.   [10] Liv. 3.36.3; 3.38.1.   [11] Dion. Hal. 11.63.1.   [12] Liv. 4.37.3.
[13] Liv. 5.9.8.   [14] Liv. 8.20.3.   [15] Liv. 9.7.12–8.1.   [16] Broughton 1951–86: I 151.
[17] Mommsen 1859: 101–2. Cf. Morgan 1977: 90–1.
[18] Soltau (1888: 59) gave a table with the fluctuating dates at which, in his opinion, the consuls had taken office up until 222 and 153, when they started their office on the Ides of March and on the Calends of January respectively: 446: Ides December; 398: Calends October; 388: Calends July; 386: Ides March; 372: Calends December; 371: Calends July; 364: Ides March; 356: Calends December; 339: Ides October; 328: Calends July; 320: Calends December; 293: Ides July; 278: Calends May. See also the reconstruction of the dates of beginning of the consular years made by Leuze 1909: 350–75. Cf. Broughton 1951–86: II 637–9. On the other hand, Brind'Amour (1983: 175–6 and 361) believes that, after the decemviral reform of the middle of the fifth century, the magistrates always took office on the Ides of March, except for the military tribunes with consular power, who did so in December like the tribunes of the plebs, and except for those magistrates who had to abandon the magistracy before their year of office expired, in which case their substitutes may have taken office before the traditional date.

of the consular year varied until 153 is complemented by the fact that the official year and the consular year did not necessarily coincide with the astronomical year in the period before the Caesarian reform of the calendar. This means that, depending upon the inclusion of the necessary intercalary months, as well as upon their duration, the official year and the consular year could be ahead of, or behind, the astronomical year. The taking of office by the consuls on the Ides of March in the first third of the second century, when we have accurate data from Livy, in fact corresponded at times to the astronomical winter of the previous year, or the summer of that same year.[19]

Consequently, the consular year varied throughout the Republican period. If Mommsen's hypothesis is correct, then only from the beginning of the third century is there evidence that the consular year began and ended on a precise date, the Calends of May. Therefore, only from that moment onwards could we truly refer to the consulship as a magistracy which was strictly annual, between 1 May and 29 April, the dates when the consuls entered and left office. This annual duration endured throughout the successive changes, so that from the Second Punic War the consular year lasted from 15 March until 14 March the following year, and from 153 onwards the consular year started on 1 January and ended on 29 December. From then on, the date of the beginning of the consular year did not change, but the date of its ending did, logically becoming 31 December when Caesar ordered the introduction of changes to the calendar. Before the third century, the consulship – or the supreme magistracy of the Roman state preceding it – must therefore have had a variable duration, even longer than a year on some occasions,[20] since the highest magistrates did not take office at a predetermined date but on the basis of military and other needs that the Roman state might have had at the time.

This evolution of the consular year poses some problems regarding the eponymy of consuls.[21] It is undeniable that Romans associated events with the names of the consuls for the year in which they took place, and used the annual consular pair as a relative chronological marker for the history of Rome during the Republican period.[22] The preserved *fasti consulares* are

---

[19] See Holzapfel 1885: 341–4. For correspondences between consular year and astronomical year in the period between 218 and 168, see Derow 1973 and 1976.

[20] This can be gathered from the dates that Livy provides for the years 463 and 462, which are naturally subject to doubts about their reliability in view of the sources concerning this period in the history of Rome. Cf. Feeney 2007: 22: 'The consular year is a fuzzy chronological unit, not corresponding necessarily with the civil calendrical year.'

[21] Lucan 7.441: '... annos a consule nomen habentis'.   [22] Cornell 1995: 401; Feeney 2007: 171.

evidence of this practice.[23] However, we must differentiate the consular year from the official year, the former being variable and the latter being fixed.[24] Throughout the Republican period the consular year did not coincide with the official year, whether we consider that the latter started on 1 March or on 1 January. The rituals of the new year which were celebrated in March indicate that the official Roman year originally started in this month, linked directly to the spring season.[25] At some point there was a change from 1 March to 1 January, and it was possibly this latter day upon which the official year started during the entire Republican period, or at least for most of it.[26] Until 153, it would not have made any sense for the official Roman year to be subject to the multiple variations that the consular year underwent, both in its duration and in its beginning and end dates. Nevertheless, the modification in 153 of the date the consuls took office did not involve a change in the beginning of the official year.[27] On the contrary, it was the consular year which was adapted to the official year, and from that moment on, for the first time in the history of Rome, the consular year and the official year coincided completely in their dates.

However, when Livy talks about the beginning or the end of a given year before 153, he always refers to the consular year, not to the official year.[28] See, for example, how, when describing the new consuls taking office on the Ides of March 168, he claims that this event took place 'at the beginning of the following year' ('Idibus Martiis, principio insequentis anni . . . ').[29] He asserts that in 187 the consul M. Valerius went to Rome to preside over the elections 'almost at the close of the year' ('exitu prope anni').[30] The elections were indeed held on the twelfth day before the Calends of March,

---

[23] Nevertheless see the remarks of Wiseman 1979: 13–25: 'The assumption that an authoritative consular list was available as a public document is probably anachronistic for the second century BC – and indeed perhaps even for the first until Augustus had the so-called "Capitoline Fasti" inscribed for public view in the Forum' (p. 13).

[24] Michels 1967: 98: 'The consular year defines the period during which a particular pair of consuls was in office. It can begin in any day of the calendar year and it may be shorter than a calendar year if the consuls leave office before their full term has expired. The consular year is used to identify years in sequence . . . The calendar year, on the other hand, contains no variable elements, but is valid for any year. Its function is to provide dates within any one year, or dates which recur in a regular cycle.' *Contra* Brind'Amour 1983: 130, for whom the consular year and the official year were always the same year. In his opinion, in the year 153 'on revenait à une vieille pratique d'origine albaine, abandonnée à Rome depuis la fin de l'époque royale, mais dont l'entrée en fonction des tribuns en décembre et le culte de Janus en janvier conservaient le souvenir'. Cf. Feeney 2007: 171–2.

[25] Var. *L.* 6.33; Cic. *Leg.* 2.54; Ovid *Fast.* 1.39–44; 3.135–52; Fest. p. 136 L.; Plut. *Quaest. Rom.* 19. Cf. Michels 1967: 97.

[26] Michels 1967: 99.   [27] Michels 1967: 97–8. Against Michels' viewpoint see Brind'Amour 1983: 130.

[28] Michels 1967: 98. Cf. Mommsen 1859: 84–5.   [29] Liv. 44.19.1.   [30] Liv. 38.42.1.

approximately one month before the end of the consular year 188/7.[31] The following year, Cn. Manlius Vulso celebrated his triumph at the end of the year ('extremo anni') once the new magistrates had been elected, specifically on the third day before the Nones of March, which was once again almost at the end of the consular year 187/6.[32]

The taking of office of the new consuls was always accompanied by a series of rituals, ceremonies, and public events, which seem to have been maintained for centuries without significant changes.[33] According to Dionysius of Halicarnassus, the new consul took the auspices, which had to precede any important act in public life, at dawn.[34] The popular election and the *lex curiata de imperio* implicitly entitled the magistrate-elect to perform the auspicial ceremony, since his taking of office had to be sanctioned by the will of the gods. In fact, taking the auspices did not involve a consultation with Jupiter on the suitability of the day when the consul was to take over his magistracy since, as we have seen, this was already a fixed day, certainly since the Hannibalic War and perhaps before.[35] These were investiture auspices,[36] which were intended to seek Jupiter's approval of the man who was to become the new consul. The positive response of the deity meant that the consul was invested with *imperium* for the entire duration of his office. Nevertheless, when the magistrate was about to leave Rome to take command of his army, a new auspicial consultation was performed.

After taking the auspices, the new consul was dressed in the *toga praetexta* in his house in front of his Penates.[37] The salutation (*salutatio*) followed, still in his home, attended by those who wished to congratulate the new supreme magistrate of Rome. After that, a procession, in which the consul was accompanied by senators and friends, progressed through the city towards the Capitol.[38] The larger the retinue, the more significance the act had, and the greater the prestige afforded to the new magistrate. It is likely that the consuls met on the way to the Capitol, perhaps in the Forum or on the Via Sacra. Once they were at the Capitol, each of the new consuls

---

[31] Liv. 38.42.2.
[32] Liv. 39.6.3.Cf. Liv. 39.23.1: 'cum iam in exitu annus esset . . .' (consular year 186–185); 42.28.1: 'exitu prope anni C. Popilius consul Romam redit . . .' (consular year 172–171).
[33] Cf. Göll 1859: esp. 586–90.
[34] Dion. Hal. 2.5–6; Gel. 3.2. Cf. Cic. *Div.* 1.16. See Magdelain 1968: 36–43.
[35] This is the opinion of Catalano 1960: 43. *Contra* Magdelain 1968: 38 n. 3.
[36] Specifically stated in Dion. Hal. 2.5.1. Cf. Scheid 1985: 50.   [37] Liv. 21.63.
[38] Ovid *Fast.* 1.81; *Pont.* 4.4.27–9 (the text of Ovid comes from a poetic letter written in the year 13 AD from his exile in Tomis, in Ponto, to Sextus Pompeius, where he describes the ceremonies that the latter was to perform on his first day as consul).

had to sacrifice an ox to Jupiter, the animals having the same characteristics as the sacrificial victims used in the triumph: that is, they had to be white and young.[39] Afterwards, the consuls made the customary vows for the welfare of the community (*vota pro salute rei publicae*), and this act was followed immediately by a session of the senate.[40] The magistrates then returned to their homes, again probably escorted by senators and citizens.[41] The day may have ended with a meal to which the consuls invited the senators and other magistrates of the year.[42]

The first meeting of the senate in the consular year was held on the Capitol. This fact is attested from the Second Punic War onwards,[43] and can be explained on the one hand for practical reasons, since the senators had already attended the rituals of the taking of office of the new magistrates in the same place, and on the other hand, as a way of adding more lustre to an act of great political significance. In this first senatorial session, the consuls had to deliver a speech,[44] and a debate followed on the state of the *res publica*, where current matters were dealt with as well as issues of great interest to the Roman state, in both the political and the military sphere.[45] The normal practice was that both consuls went to the senate and presided over the session, and it is logical that it was compulsory for both to attend, since the usual debate that opened the new political year was the source of many decisions that concerned both consuls. This is apparent from an event in 210, when M. Valerius Laevinus could not take office due to illness. His colleague Marcellus, however, did take office: he summoned the senate as normal and spoke there. Nonetheless, the usual questions could not be dealt with due to the absence of Laevinus.[46]

---

[39] Liv. 21.14–15 (year 218); 41.14.7 (year 176). Cf. Ovid *Pont.* 4.4.30–34. From the reform of the year 153 onwards, when both the consular year and the official year started on 1 January, the god Janus may have been the recipient of the sacrifices conducted by the consuls on the first day of the year (Cic. *N.D.* 2.67). Cf. Taylor and Holland 1952: 138; Feeney 2007: 168.

[40] Ovid *Pont.* 4.4.35–6.   [41] Ovid *Pont.* 4.4.41–2.

[42] Cf. Cic. *Tusc.* 4.2; Plin. *Nat.* 14.17 (about Caesar).

[43] Livy specifically reports that the first senatorial session of the year took place on the Capitol on various occasions during the Second Punic War and at the beginning of the second century: 215: 23.31.1; 214: 24.10.1–2; 211: 26.1.1; 205: 28.38.12–14; 202: 30.27.1; 198: 32.8.1.

[44] Cf. Liv. 23.31 (speech of Ti. Sempronius Gracchus in the year 215); 26.26.5–9 (Marcellus speaks before the senate in 210).

[45] Liv. 26.1.1: 'Cn. Fulvius Centumalus P. Sulpicius Galba consules cum Idibus Martiis magistratum inissent, senatu in Capitolium vocato, de re publica, de administratione belli, de provinciis exercitibusque patres consuluerunt'; 28.40.20: 'de re publica, de exercitibus scribendis, de provinciis relatum'; 38.42.8: 'de provinciis et de re publica'. Cf. Briscoe 1981: 290: 'It was, it seems, unusual to begin the year with a debate on a specific subject: usually there was a general debate *de re publica*.'

[46] Liv. 26.26.5–9. Cf. Kunkel and Wittmann 1995: 194.

Along with this general debate, specific practical questions could be discussed in this first session of the senate, in particular the distribution by lot (*sortitio*), or more rarely by agreement (*comparatio*), of the provinces between both consuls, and the number of soldiers that each one was to levy and command depending on the needs of their particular province.[47] Livy's account suggests that the common trend was that the first question dealt with in the senate, and therefore the first decision taken by the senators in the new consular year, was the allotment of provinces to the consuls. This was no doubt due to the interest of the magistrates in knowing their immediate destination, and in order to begin as soon as possible to make the necessary preparations for the levy and for their departure.[48] In the case of the year 210, once Laevinus finally arrived in Rome a debate immediately took place in the senate on the state of the Republic and the distribution of the provinces.[49]

However, it can also be deduced from Livy that other questions could be dealt with in this first session, and that the order in which they were discussed could be changed depending on the priorities for each particular year, without any strict rule on the senatorial agenda. Thus, in 215 the senate decreed in its first session that taxes had to be doubled in order to meet the expenses of the war,[50] whereas in 214 the first decree passed by the senators urged the consuls to agree or to draw lots to decide which one of them would be in charge of presiding over the election of censors before taking command of their army.[51] In 205, along with the allotment of the provinces, the senate decreed that Scipio was to celebrate the games that he had promised during the mutiny of his troops in Hispania.[52]

At times, priority was given to the introduction to the senate of foreign embassies. In 177, the distribution of provinces between the consuls was dealt with on the day they took office, but a final decision was not taken at that point. Livy relates that on the day after the Ides of March, the

---

[47] Cf. Kunkel and Wittmann 1995: 306–7. The allotment of provinces at the beginning of the consular year remained unchanged during the entire Republican period until the year 123, when C. Sempronius Gracchus introduced the *lex de provinciis consularibus*, which set forth the obligation for the consular provinces to be decided before the new consuls were elected. On the Gracchan law see Vervaet 2006, with supplementary bibliography.

[48] In general, the allotment of provinces seems to have taken place on the same day as their taking office and to have been the first question dealt with: Liv. 27.7.7 (for the year 209); 28.38.12–14 (205: Scipio Africanus obtained the province of Sicily 'with his colleague's consent and without recourse to the lot', 'extra sortem, concedente collega'; in this case Livy reproduces the debate on this question much later on, 28.40–5); 30.27.1 (202); 31.5.3–7 (200); 32.8.1 (198); 33.25.4 (196); 33.43.1 (195); 38.35.7 (188); 39.45.1 (183); 40.18.3–5 (181); 41.14.8–10 (176); 43.11.12 (170); 45.16.1 (167). See Rosenstein 1995: 51–6; Vervaet 2006: 627.

[49] Liv. 26.27.17.   [50] Liv. 23.31.1.   [51] Liv. 24.10.1.   [52] Liv. 28.38.14.

ambassadors of Sardinia, who had already been waiting for some time to be heard, were received in the senate along with L. Minucius Thermus, who had fought in Histria as a legate under the consul Manlius. It was only after hearing all of them that the senate decided that Sardinia and Histria were to be the provinces of the consuls of that year.[53] A similar case was that of the Aetolian ambassadors in 190 and 189, whose reception at the senate also preceded the debate on the provinces. The priority was obvious, since the attitude of the ambassadors would have influenced whether the Roman senate decided to consider the Aetolians as friends or foes and, if the latter, to declare war against them, as eventually happened.[54]

Mommsen stated that the senate began its deliberations every year with religious resolutions.[55] However, as we have seen, this was not the usual procedure according to Livy, although occasionally it may have happened in cases where the reported prodigies were perceived as particularly serious. When in 193 land tremors were constant and caused panic amongst the population, the consuls were for some time almost exclusively occupied with performing the rites of expiation, to the point that the senate could not even be convened to deal with other matters of public interest. Apparently only once the question had been resolved, and the fear of divine wrath had dissipated, were the provinces allotted to the consuls.[56] Similarly, in the year 200, on the same day he took office, the consul P. Sulpicius Galba put forward a successful motion in the senate, according to which both consuls were to perform sacrifices with a specific prayer that the war which was about to start against Philip V be beneficial for Rome. Only when it was communicated that the sacrifices had been successfully completed was the question of the allotment of the provinces dealt with.[57]

Nevertheless, whatever the order in which they were raised, along with the distribution of the provinces and the provision for the necessary recruitment of troops, two other activities that were part of the responsibility of the consuls were usually also discussed in the first senatorial session or during the days that followed: religious matters of interest to the community and international diplomacy.

---

[53] Liv. 41.8–9. Embassies of the Latin allies were also received in the senate (41.8.6).

[54] Liv. 37.1.1; 37.1.7 (year 190); 37.49.1; 37.50.1 (year 189). On the Aetolian embassy Polyb. 21.2.3–6; Diodor. 29.4. The term *religiones* used by Livy does not refer to the prodigies, which the Latin author mentions later on, but to the taking of the auspices, which had to take place when the consuls took office and which preceded the first session of the year of the senate. Cf. Briscoe 1981: 289.

[55] Mommsen 1887–8: III 1059.   [56] Liv. 34.55.   [57] Liv. 31.5.

CHAPTER 2

Consuls and civic religion

Paradoxically, Polybius does not mention religious duties amongst those performed by the consuls,[1] despite the fact that some of these tasks were compulsory and according to Roman belief their fulfilment was of great importance to the welfare of the community.[2] In fact, the religious duties conducted by the consuls during the first few weeks of office were amongst their most important functions. Roman religion was national and civic, and its practice was a political issue since it concerned the entire community.[3] Most religious activities were performed in public following stringent rules, and their main purpose was to maintain or to restore the peace of the gods (*pax deorum*). Experts grouped into various priestly colleges served as essential, qualified advisers, but the management of religious affairs was in the hands of the senate, and the direct relationship between the community and the gods was assigned to the magistrates, especially to the consuls as supreme magistrates of the *civitas*.[4]

The first public ceremony conducted by the consuls consisted of visiting the temple of Jupiter on the Capitolium, to make their prayers to the supreme divinity of the Roman pantheon for the welfare of the community. The vows taken by the consuls on the day they assumed their duties must be seen as public vows (*vota publica*). The exact content of the vows is not known, nor whether there was a fixed formula set out by the senate or by a priestly college, in particular by the pontiffs. However, the consuls did not act as individuals but as supreme magistrates, and, as a result, they did not plead in their vow for the success of a specific venture that they might have to undertake, but for the welfare and safety of the Roman state in general during their term of office.[5] In modern historiography there is the

---

[1] Polyb. 6.12.   [2] Mommsen 1887–8: II 135–7; De Ruggiero 1892: 742–7.
[3] Cic. *Flac.* 69. Cf. Scheid 1985: 20.
[4] Scheid 1985: 29–34; Beard (1990: 31–4) emphasizes the leading role of the senate in Roman religious life (42: 'the Senate was the centre of religious power'); Beard, North, and Price 1998 I: 29–30; Rüpke 2006: 230.
[5] Cf. Orlin 1997: 36–8.

widespread idea that consuls, on their first day as magistrates, performed sacrifices in order to fulfil the vows taken by their predecessors.[6] However, more recently, Orlin has argued that the purpose of these sacrifices was to obtain favourable auspices for the coming year, rather than to perform the fulfillment (*solutio*) of the vows of previous consuls.[7]

Just as the consular year started with the rituals at the Capitolium, the stay of consuls in Rome before leaving for their respective provinces concluded with their delivery of new public vows in the same place, wearing their military uniform.[8] Between these actions, as guarantors of the *pax deorum*, their main task upon taking office was to deal with the expiation of all prodigies that had occurred in Rome and in Italy in the previous months, as well as to appoint a date for the celebration of the *feriae Latinae*, a festival which, in any event, had to be celebrated compulsorily under their presidency prior to their departure for their respective provinces.

Livy refers to these activities when he describes how the consul C. Flaminius left Rome hurriedly in 217 without performing his religious duties.[9] According to Livy, Flaminius left for his province without pronouncing the compulsory vows in the Capitolium either on the day of his taking office or on the day of leaving the *Urbs*. Nor did he attend, as was customary, the meeting of the senate for the opening of the consular year. He did not appoint a date for the celebration of the *feriae Latinae*, nor did he preside over the sacrifice to Jupiter Latiaris at the Mons Albanus, as was mandatory for a consul before taking military command. The senate decided to demand his return to Rome.[10] The legal outcome of the impiety of these contraventions was that Flaminius could no longer be considered a consul, but a mere *privatus*, a private citizen. The result for the *civitas* was divine punishment in the form of the great defeat suffered at Trasimene, where the consul himself died.[11]

Apart from these usual religious duties, from time to time the consuls had to carry out other duties that were not their exclusive concern but that of all magistrates with *imperium*, consuls and praetors and dictators. Amongst them was the task of taking, by order of the senate, the vow of public games (*ludi publici*) and presiding over the games if they were in Rome.

---

[6] Mommsen 1887–8: I 616; Bouché-Leclercq 1931: 59; Latte 1960: 152–3.   [7] Orlin 1997: 37.
[8] Liv. 21.63; 41.10; 45.39.11.   [9] Liv. 21.63.7–9. Cf. Meißner 2000: esp. 100–4; Beck 2005: 244–68.
[10] Liv. 22.1.5–7.
[11] The hostile ancient source tradition has stigmatized Flaminius as a bad example. For this reason the factual value of the sources about him is at least doubtful. See Broughton 1951–86: I 242; Beck 2005: 245. Flaminius may, in fact, have presided over the *feriae Latinae* of that year, as attested by the *Fasti Feriarum Latinarum* (*CIL* I[2] 1, p. 57).

In exceptional circumstances, consuls were also in charge of conducting the rite of *ver sacrum*.

THE EXPIATION OF PRODIGIES

To the Roman mentality, *prodigia* were all those phenomena considered supernatural or unearthly. They were perceived as an expression on earth of the gods' wrath.[12] Thus, the prodigy generally[13] meant that the peace of the gods had been breached by some impious human action, or expressed a warning for the future.[14] The misdemeanours committed or mistakes made by the citizens were not solely of a private nature. On the contrary, they had an impact on the community and imperilled its very existence. It was therefore necessary to re-establish the appropriate relationship between the *civitas* and the gods of Rome by means of suitable expiatory ceremonies, and such a task could only be performed by the magistrates who were the representatives of the citizens and who could thus act legitimately on their behalf.

In his first ten books Livy does not provide long lists of prodigies, simply isolated references,[15] and only after book 21 does he regularly register the reported portents.[16] The change could, however, have taken place towards the middle of the third century. We do not have Livy's text for that period, since the second decade is lost. But we do have a compilation made in the fourth century AD by Iulius Obsequens containing the lists of prodigies included in Livy's work.[17] This compilation goes back to the year 249, and therefore to book 19 of Livy's history. Thus it is reasonable to presume that this was the moment when Livy regularly started to include the lists of portents. However, we do not know the reason for this change, which may have been caused by a modification to the expiation of prodigies, but which

---

[12] On prodigies in Rome, Wülcker 1903; Luterbacher 1904; Händel 1959; Bloch 1963; Liebeschuetz 1979: 7–18; MacBain 1982; Sacchetti 1996; Rosenberger 1998; Rasmussen 2003; Engels 2007; Rosenberger 2007: 293–8.

[13] See however Luterbacher 1904: 5: 'das Wort *prodigium* kann auch ein gutes Zeichen bedeuten'. Cf. Engels 2007: 44–5.

[14] Engels 2007: 45–7. Rasmussen 2003: 35: 'A prodigy is a peculiar event described in the sources as a sign that the *pax deorum* has been disturbed, and this type of portent calls for expiation to be performed in public.'

[15] In his book 10 Livy mentions three prodigies between 296 and 293 (10.23.1; 10.31.8; 10.47.6). For the whole of the fifth and fourth centuries Livy collects scarcely twelve prodigies.

[16] Cf. De Saint-Denis 1942; Bloch 1963: 113; Sacchetti 1996: 210–27. See the summary of prodigies throughout the Republican period in Rasmussen 2003: 53–116; Engels 2007: 343–723.

[17] Cf. Schmidt 1968; Rasmussen 2003: 21–2.

may also have been due simply to better preservation of the data from that date and to its availability to later historians.[18] This means that we are not certain that during the first years of the Republic the registration of prodigies and their expiation followed the same process as from the Hannibalic War, a time from which testimonies are numerous.

We therefore have information on prodigies and their expiation for the period from 218 to 167. Livy does not make systematic listings of portents for each year – although he does so for many years, especially during the Second Punic War – and when he does include them, he generally mentions them at the beginning of each consular year – with some meaningful exceptions[19] – along with a description of the process followed.[20] Prodigies could be observed by any individual: an ordinary citizen, a priest or a magistrate. In principle, since it meant an alteration in the normal course of events, a prodigy generally had a negative nature and portended danger.[21] But the mere observation of a phenomenon considered as supernatural was not enough for its automatic consideration as a *prodigium*. For that purpose it was essential that the senate consider it as such and also that its expiation involve the state. For this reason, all the alleged prodigies that occurred throughout a year were compiled so that one of the new consuls, either on the first day of his office or immediately afterwards, could bring a list of portents before the senate. The consul produced his report on behalf of the people, including all details collected on each of the phenomena. If he deemed it convenient, he could even complement the report of events with an introduction before the senate of eyewitnesses of the occurrence.[22] Senators then decided whether the events narrated should indeed be considered as omens sent by the gods, that is, as prodigies.[23] The usual course may have been the prudent acknowledgement of them all, so as not to run the risk of ignoring a divine sign. However, it is obvious that such acknowledgement was not automatic, as demonstrated by the fact that in 169 some alleged prodigies were rejected.[24] Nevertheless, this is the only documented case of such senatorial rejection.

---

[18] Cato (Beck and Walter, *FRH* 1 F 4.1 = Peter 77; Gel. 2.28.4) notes that explicit mentions of prodigies were included in the *Annales Maximi*. Cf. Beard, North, and Price 1998: 1 38.

[19] Engels 2007: 189–90.

[20] About the *procuratio prodigiorum* see Mommsen 1887–8: III 1059–62; Luterbacher 1904: 33–5; Händel 1959: 2290–5; Bloch 1963: 120–3; Beard 1990: 31; Beard, North, and Price 1998: 1 37–9.

[21] Cf. Bloch 1963: 86.   [22] Liv. 22.1.14.

[23] The prodigies are a good example of the collaboration in the religious sphere between the senate, magistrates, and priests. They are clear evidence of the leading role played by the senate, which had the last word on the subject. Cf. Orlin 2007: 59–60.

[24] Liv. 43.13.6.

Once the deliberations were over, the senate issued the corresponding decree. Only then did the presumed divine signs officially become prodigies. The *senatus consultum* also included the answer to be given to the gods by the community. If the prodigies were already known or were frequent and not too important, senators would order expiatory ceremonies immediately, entrusted to the consuls who could then decide on the specific form in which to celebrate the rituals. In the year 200 the senate resolved that the recently appointed consuls had to carry out sacrifices of higher victims, praying for the success of the war recently started against King Philip, in honour of whichever gods they themselves might decide,[25] and in 199, Livy states that the senate's decree included the obligation to carry out sacrifices of animals to the gods that the consuls deemed appropriate ('quibus diis videretur').[26] However, if the prodigies were unknown or they were considered particularly serious, the senate consulted the experts: pontiffs, augurs, decemvirs in charge of the Sibylline Books, or haruspices, turning either to only one of these priestly colleges or to two of them jointly. Upon receiving an answer, given after an undetermined period – although presumably it was as short as possible – the senate met again to deal with the question and then commissioned the expiatory ceremonies that had been recommended. As in the previous case, the consuls were in charge of the sacrifices.[27]

In the expiation of prodigies there was, therefore, a clear division of roles: any citizen could report or give a warning; only the senate could decide if

---

[25] Liv. 31.5.3.   [26] Liv. 32.1.13–14.

[27] In 213, the consuls conducted the rites requested by the pontiffs (Liv. 24.44.9), and in 203 the pontiffs again determined the gods in whose honour the sacrifices should be celebrated (Liv. 30.2.13; cf. 41.16.6: year 176). On other occasions, the decemvirs were required to consult the Sibylline Books (cf. Orlin 1997: 76–96; Scheid 1998a: 101–3). In the year 200, they determined the necessary rites for the expiation (Liv. 31.12.10); in 187, they decided a *supplicatio* was necessary (Liv. 38.44.7. On *supplicationes* see Halkin 1953. Cf. Hickson Hahn 2007: 247: 'The Romans used the same word (*supplicatio*) to identify public days of prayer and offering for propitiation, expiation, and thanksgiving'); in 173, they designated which animals should be sacrificed, which gods should receive the sacrifices, and the need to celebrate a supplication (Liv. 42.2.6–7); and in 169, they decided which victims had to be sacrificed by the consuls (Liv. 43.13.7–8). In 193, the prodigies became extremely serious. Reports of earthquakes were so frequent that it was decided to stop all public activities, to the point that not even the senate could meet since the consuls, as Livy says, 'were occupied with sacrifices and expiations'. When the decemvirs were eventually requested to examine the Books, a supplication of three days was prescribed as an answer, under the consuls' continuous supervision (Liv. 34.55). Occasionally, it was the haruspices who gave the instructions for the expiation of prodigies (Liv. 24.10.13, year 214). In 199, the senate itself made the decision regarding most prodigies. But the portent reported by the proconsul from Macedonia, P. Sulpicius, was deemed exceptional and caused a consultation of the haruspices, who recommended one day of supplication and sacrifices at all the shrines (Liv. 32.1.14).

it was in fact a case of divine omens worth taking into consideration, and the possible counter-action was determined by the senate; and only the consuls could execute the appropriate answer that should be given to the divinity to achieve the restoration of the relationship between gods and Romans.[28]

As we have already seen, according to Livy the expiation of prodigies took place at the beginning of the consular year, and the expiation ceremonies were celebrated before the consuls left Rome for their provinces. Elizabeth Rawson questioned the information provided by Livy in this respect – as well as being generally sceptical about the data derived from the *Annales* – claiming that, if that were the case, many prodigies would have been waiting for months before they could be presented by the new consuls to the senate.[29] In her opinion, this would have meant an unnecessary danger to the *civitas*, considering that any possible prodigy meant a breach of the *pax deorum*. According to Rawson, Roman religious logic would have demanded expiation as quickly as possible and would not have accepted a delay of several months. The report on portents at the beginning of the consular year would then be the product of a literary arrangement made by Livy, the result of compositional technique rather than historical fact.

There is, nevertheless, a plausible explanation for the chronological positioning of the expiation of prodigies at the beginning of the year, closely linked to the essential presence and involvement of the consuls in the process.[30] Until Sulla's dictatorship, the consuls spent most of their year of office away from Rome, leading their legions. Except in particular cases, they stayed in the *Urbs* only for the first weeks of their office, apart from the usual short stay of one consul to conduct the elections at the end of the consular year. Since it was the consuls – or at any rate, one of them – who had to present the prodigies to the senate and preside over the prescribed acts of expiation, it was necessary to wait until the new consuls took office in order to proceed. At this point the appeasement of the gods was carried out as soon as possible. For other tasks that were the responsibility of the consuls while they were in Rome, the urban praetor could act as a delegate in their absence.[31] It is clear, however, that this was not the case for the expiation of prodigies, which was apparently the exclusive religious responsibility of the

---

[28] Liv. 22.2.1: 'dum consul placandis Romae dis . . .' Cf. Liv. 32.9.4.   [29] Rawson 1971.

[30] Cf. Mommsen 1887–8: III 1059.

[31] Cf. Brennan 2000: 601; 607–8 and (in particular on the religious duties of the urban praetor) 123–5.

consuls.[32] For this reason, the task had to be attended to at the beginning of the consular year, before the consuls left for war.

In this respect, the events of 292 are significant.[33] A plague was having devastating effects on the population of Rome. Given the extremely serious situation of the city, which was obviously seen as a divine punishment, the Sibylline Books were consulted to find a solution that might restore the peace of the gods. However, nothing could be done immediately since the consuls were engaged in the war.[34] Such behaviour in a situation of great urgency would seem to indicate that it was standard practice to wait for the new consuls to jointly expiate all prodigies at the beginning of the consular year. In the same way, in 208, at the height of the Second Punic War, when the praetors had already left for their respective provinces, the new consuls were detained in Rome longer than would have been advisable, in order to complete the sacrifices required for the expiation of prodigies. In that context Livy states that the safety of the Republic depended on the consuls and that this took precedence over emergencies arising from the Hannibalic War in Italy and Hispania.[35] There was a similar occurrence in 186 when the consuls were engaged in the repression of the Bacchanalia: they had not recruited new troops despite having been in office for some time but had not neglected the sacrifices of expiation.[36]

Wissowa considered the expiation of prodigies in Rome above all to be a ceremony of lustration, which would involve a procession under the presidency of the consuls in which the animals to be sacrificed were led.[37] Livy's account does not include details on the specific form in which the expiatory ceremonies were performed. He usually refers to sacrifices of animals but does not mention that the ritual involved a procession through the city. However, the concept of lustration does appear occasionally in his

---

[32] The fact that the urban praetor could be in charge of religious ceremonies intended to recover the peace of the gods in different contexts apart from the strict expiation of prodigies can clearly be seen in what happened in 217, in extraordinary circumstances which imperilled the very survival of Rome (Liv. 22.8–9). One of the consuls, C. Flaminius, had died at the battle of Trasimene, while the other, Cn. Servilius, was not in Rome. Given the emergency situation, a dictator was appointed. The dictator ought to have been designated by the surviving consul, but given that this would have delayed the process, for the first time the dictator Q. Fabius Maximus was appointed by the people. Fabius, considering that the impious behaviour of Flaminius had caused the previous disasters, suggested that the gods be consulted. The consultation was made through the reading of the Sibylline Books by the decemvirs, who advised on a series of measures to be taken to satisfy the gods. Since the dictator was busy with preparations for the war, the senate decided that the urban praetor M. Aemilius should undertake the expiations. Cf. Brennan 2000: 124.

[33] Liv. 10.47.6–7.   [34] An embassy to Epidaurus was also sent later (Liv. *per.* 11).
[35] Liv. 27.23.1; 27.23.4.   [36] Liv. 39.22.4.
[37] Wissowa 1912: 391–2. Rosenberger (1998: 140) sees the rituals having an apotropaic function as a means to lustrate the boundaries of the *Urbs*. Cf. Lucan 1.592–604.

description of the events. The consuls of 186 conducted the sacrifices of expiation and with them 'lustrated the city' ('consules urbem lustraverunt'), according to Livy.[38] This is another reason that would account for the fact that the expiation of prodigies was placed at the beginning of the year, as a rite of purification involving the renewal of the community.

The religious rituals conducted by the consuls varied depending on the prodigies and on the decisions previously taken by the senate or, in exceptional circumstances, by one of the priestly colleges. The most usual response from the senate was the simple celebration of sacrifices. In fact, in Livy's account, the mention of the consular report of prodigies, the senate's decision to carry out sacrifices as a means of expiation, and the subsequent implementation of the senatorial decree by the consuls, practically becomes a repeated formula, although the involvement of the consuls is not always specifically mentioned.[39] But the expiation could require further and more complex rituals. In 191, within the context of the beginning of the war against Antiochus, a senatorial decree established that the consuls should celebrate sacrifices in all the shrines where a banquet for the gods (*lectisternium*) was celebrated throughout the year.[40] In 364 the consuls celebrated a *lectisternium* as a means to restore the peace of the gods.[41] However, sacrificial banquets offered to the gods were very seldom used.[42] It was more frequent for the senate to decree the celebration of supplications for several days.[43] In exceptional cases, sacrifices were also accompanied by the

---

[38] Liv. 39.22.4.

[39] Liv. 24.10.6–13 (year 214); 28.11.5–7 (206); 30.2.13 (203); 31.12.10 (200); 32.1.13–14 (199); 32.9.4 (198); 40.45.4–5 (179); 41.9.4–8 (177); 41.16.6 (176); 42.2 (173); 42.20 (172).

[40] Liv. 36.1.1–3. On *lectisternia* see Rüpke 2007b: 144.

[41] Liv. 7.2.2. Cf. Liv. 5.13.5–6. Cf. Rosenberger 1998: 146–7.

[42] Händel (1959: 2292–3) thinks that *lectisternia* were not related to the expiation of prodigies.

[43] This happened in 217, when the consul Cn. Servilius was asked to deal with the appropriate supplications along with the usual sacrifices (Liv. 22.1.14–15), as well as in 198 (Liv. 32.9.4); 193 (Liv. 34.55); 192 (Liv. 35.21.2); 191 (Liv. 36.2.2–5); 187, at the suggestion of the decemvirs (Liv. 38.44.7); 184 (Liv. 39.38.5); 181 (Liv. 40.19.4–5: three days of 'supplicatio et feriae' should be celebrated in the whole of Italy); Mouritsen (1998: 47–8) thinks that the *supplicatio* and *feriae* were to take place only in the *ager Romanus* near Rome, but Briscoe (2008: 460) rightly points out that 'the plague was not likely to have respected the boundaries of the *ager Romanus*, and it is indeed clear that Latin and Italian communities were affected. Knowledge of this may well have prompted the *decemviri* to include the whole of Italy in their recommendation'). On supplications as a means for the expiation of prodigies see Rosenberger 1998: 143–5. The supplications could derive from other reasons than the expiation of prodigies. In the year 200, within the context of the declaration of war against Macedonia, the consuls decreed three days of supplication 'ex senatus consulto', while consulting the *fetiales* on the way in which the war ought to be declared (Liv. 31.8.2–4). In 190, the senate prescribed *supplicationes* for naval victory and asked the consul Laelius to have twenty victims sacrificed on each day of thanksgiving (Liv. 37.47.4–5). The same happened in 176, when the senate decreed the celebration of prayers of gratitude for the victory of Gracchus in Sardinia and at the same time ordered the consuls to sacrifice forty victims (Liv. 41.17.4). When news of a military victory reached Rome, it was usual

organization of games, such as those commissioned in honour of Apollo in 209.[44]

In most of Livy's references to the expiation of prodigies, he mentions the consuls in the plural as executors of the rites. Only exceptionally does he specify that one of the consuls was in charge of performing them individually. This was the case in 217 for Cn. Servilius, who had to deal on his own with all the religious tasks since his colleague Flaminius had left Rome in a hurry, presumably without even taking the auspices.[45] Something similar happened in 191, when the consul Scipio Nasica conducted the expiatory rituals when his colleague Acilius had already left for the war.[46] On both occasions the participation of only one of the consuls was justified by the other's absence. However, in the year 200 Aurelius seems to have been the person in charge of the sacrifices to placate the gods according to the recommendation of the decemvirs, although his colleague P. Sulpicius Galba was also in Rome.[47] In conclusion, although it seems that the custom was that both consuls participate in the appeasement of the gods, the requirement for joint action may not have been of such a compulsory nature as to invalidate the process if the rituals were not carried out in that manner.

Livy does not usually provide precise information on how long it would take for consuls to perform the rites commissioned by the senate. In 212, he says, they dedicated nine days to sacred matters.[48] In 207 the expiation rituals took an extraordinarily long time. At the beginning of the year, a rain of stones was expiated by means of religious rites for nine days (*novendiale sacrum*). But then other portents followed which also needed immediate expiation. For this purpose, it was necessary to conduct a procession in Rome, a supplication, and another *novendiale sacrum*. These rituals of expiation took a total of twenty days, to which must be added the days that the consulted priests needed to give their instructions on the actions to be taken. This task of the consuls was, nevertheless, considered a priority, and it must have been carried out even before the levy, in spite of the fact that all of this took place in a year in which the Second Punic War was at a decisive stage.[49] In any event, the consuls acted as quickly as possible for two reasons: firstly because of public interest, since the pacification of the gods eradicated all danger to the community and made it possible to restore

---

that neither of the two consuls were in the *Urbs*. If the senate prescribed a prayer of thanksgiving, it was logical that the urban praetor be in charge of its fulfilment, as happened in 191 (Liv. 36.21.9). On *supplicationes* as prayers of thanksgiving for military success, see Hickson Hahn 2004.

[44] Liv. 27.11.1; 27.11.6. The games were held in 208 under the presidency of the urban praetor.
[45] Liv. 22.1. On the abundance of prodigies in 218 and their expiation in 217 see Engels 2005.
[46] Liv. 36.37.2–6.   [47] Liv. 31.12.10.   [48] Liv. 25.7.7–9.
[49] Liv. 27.37. Cf. Liv. 36.37.5. See a detailed account in Rosenberger 2007: 296–7.

normal life in the *civitas*; and secondly because of personal interest, since the consuls could not leave Rome for their provinces without having performed the required rituals, so the longer it took them to carry out the prescribed sacrifices, the longer their stay in the *Urbs* would be.[50]

THE *FERIAE LATINAE*

The second compulsory religious task that was performed by the consuls every year was the celebration of the *feriae Latinae*.[51] It was an annual festival whose date of celebration varied, so upon taking office consuls had to designate the starting day of the celebration that year.[52] The number of days of celebration of the festival appears to have increased since its origin until it reached a duration of four days.[53] The *feriae Latinae*, attended by members of the ancient Latin League, were celebrated in honour of Jupiter Latiaris on the Mons Albanus,[54] and their origin, according to Dionysius of Halicarnassus, went back to the monarchical period, their creator supposedly having been Tarquinius Superbus. The event was a yearly acknowledgment of the kinship between Latin peoples.[55]

The organization and presidency over the festival, which was formally like a lustration and consisted mainly of a sacrifice, belonged to the Roman state. In fact, the Roman *civitas* was represented at the festival by all its magistrates, with the consuls at the head. That is why in their absence from the *Urbs* a prefect of the city (*praefectus urbi feriarum Latinarum causa*) was appointed to take over the government of Rome.[56] According to the Capitoline Fasti, Q. Ogulnius Gallus was exceptionally named *dictator feriarum Latinarum causa* in 257.[57] It is the only example of which we know. The loss of the corresponding book of Livy prevents us from knowing why that year a dictator was in charge of presiding over the *feriae*

---

[50] In his account, Livy sometimes establishes a direct link between the end of the acts of expiation and the departure of the consuls for their provinces: 'consules rebus divinis operam dederunt placatisque diis in provincias profecti sunt' (Liv. 32.9.4). Cf. Liv. 36.37.6; 41.9.8.

[51] On the *feriae Latinae* see Werner 1888; Wissowa 1912: 124–5; Scullard 1981: 111–15; Sabbatucci 1988: 305–8; Liou-Gille 1996: esp. 85–97; Baudy 1998; Marco Simón, forthcoming.

[52] The *fasti feriarum Latinarum* are very fragmentary, and very seldom do they provide the date of celebration of the festival for a given year. Cf. *CIL* I² 1, pp. 57–8.

[53] Dion. Hal. 4.49; 6.95; Plut. *Cam.* 42.5; Str. 5.3.2. Cf. Wissowa 1912: 125.   [54] Liv. 41.27.6 (year 174).

[55] Scullard 1981: 113.

[56] *CIL* VI 1421; Cass. Dio 49.42.1; 53.33.3. See a list of *praefecti feriarum Latinarum* in Werner 1888: 41 ff. Cf. Brennan 2000: 34–8.

[57] Broughton 1951–86: I 207.

Latinae instead of the consuls.[58] The most plausible explanation is the absence from Rome of both consuls, who must have been commanding the Roman legions involved in the First Punic War.[59] Nonetheless, this is not a totally convincing explanation on its own for this exceptional situation, since neither during the Hannibalic War nor during other armed conflicts later on did the consuls neglect the ritual of the presidency of the Latin festival on the Mons Albanus prior to their departure from Rome.

The importance granted by the Roman state to the *feriae Latinae* is demonstrated not only by the fact that all the magistrates of that year had to attend the celebrations on the Mons Albanus, but primarily because the consuls were not entitled to leave Rome to take control of their provinces until the festival had been suitably celebrated under their presidency.[60] Just as in the case of the expiation of prodigies, the consuls' fulfilment of their ancestral religious duties had priority over their military duties. With the apparent exception of the appointment of a dictator in 257, this rule was always observed, even at times of special emergency for Rome, such as during the Second Punic War. Such a prohibition existed throughout the Republican period, and continued to be in force in the first century.[61]

The requirement that the consuls should not take command of the troops in their provinces until the *feriae Latinae* had been celebrated allows us to draw some conclusions concerning the period of time in the consular year during which they stayed in Rome. However, this is only possible in the cases where ancient sources provide a definite date of celebration, which they rarely do, and only from the Hannibalic War onwards. In 212, the consuls and praetors were detained in Rome until the *feriae Latinae* were celebrated on 27 April, and only once the rites at the Mons Albanus were completed could they leave for their provinces.[62] Less than a month and a half had elapsed since the consuls had assumed their office, a period in which they had dealt with different matters with the senate, dedicated several days to the expiation of the terrible prodigies that had occurred in

---

[58] It is not likely that the *dictator feriarum Latinarum causa* was appointed with the sole purpose of being in charge of the government in Rome during the absence of the other magistrates instead of the usual *praefectus urbi feriarum Latinarum causa*. The fact that he is mentioned in the Capitoline Fasti indicates in my opinion that his role was to replace the consuls in one of their annual tasks, just as in other cases a dictator was appointed to preside over the elections in the absence of the consul who should have presided.

[59] Kaplan 1973–4: 174.

[60] Livy provides various instances indicating that only when the consuls were 'liberated' from their obligation of presiding over the Latin festival were they authorized to go to their provinces. Livy expressly states this in 187: 'quibus religionibus liberati consules et dilectu perfecto . . . in provinciam profecti sunt . . .' (Liv. 38.44.8). Cf. Liv. 43.15.3; 44.22.16.

[61] On the celebration of the Latin festival in 91 cf. Flor. 2.6.8–9; *De vir. ill.* 66.12.   [62] Liv. 25.12.1.

Italy, and recruited new soldiers, although they encountered difficulties in completing the levy.[63] This is an example of promptness which can undoubtedly be explained within the context of the urgency provoked by the Second Punic War.

The armed conflict against Macedonia between 171 and 168 caused the festival to be celebrated as early as possible. In 171, the *feriae Latinae* were celebrated on the Calends of June.[64] Livy implies that an earlier date than usual was appointed so that the consuls could go to their provinces as soon as possible, especially to Macedonia, since the war against King Perseus had just begun. However, this is not a particularly short period of time, since two and a half months had elapsed since the consuls assumed their office on 15 March. Rather, we should understand that the earliest possible date was appointed once the people had voted the declaration of war in the comitia,[65] a reform of the legislation on the election of the military tribunes had been passed,[66] the provinces had been allotted to the consuls[67] – this formality was carried out that year later than usual due to the particular circumstances of the time – and the recruitment had finally been completed, once again not without difficulties.[68] Undoubtedly these formalities prolonged the stay of the consuls in Rome and explain why the celebration of the Latin festival on 1 June that year was considered sufficiently early.

Livy does not provide any account for 170 regarding the *feriae Latinae*, although he does so for 169. Given the situation in Macedonia, the whole electoral process, the beginning of the term of office of the new magistrates, and their departure for their provinces had been hastened. The senate commissioned the consul A. Atilius to hold the consular elections in January,[69] and they were indeed held on the 26th of that month.[70] The new consuls raised the issue of Macedonia before the senators as soon as they assumed their office.[71] The consuls conducted the expiation of prodigies as usual,[72] drew lots for their provinces,[73] and exceptionally the levy of the troops was conducted by the praetors because of complaints made by the consuls due to their difficulties in recruiting.[74] Once these tasks were completed, the *feriae Latinae* were celebrated and the consul Q. Marcius Philippus left immediately for Macedonia.[75] According to Livy, the consul left Rome for Brundisium at the beginning of spring.[76] This statement is imprecise, but it appears to place the celebration of the festival at the Mons

---

[63] Liv. 25.4–5; 25.7.   [64] Liv. 42.35.3.   [65] Liv. 42.30.10–11.   [66] Liv. 42.31.5.   [67] Liv. 42.32.4.
[68] Liv. 42.32–3.   [69] Liv. 43.11.3.   [70] Liv. 43.11.6.   [71] Liv. 43.11.12–12.1.   [72] Liv. 43.13.
[73] Liv. 43.15.2.   [74] Liv. 43.14.3–4.   [75] Liv. 43.15.3: 'Latinisque actis Marcius extemplo est profectus.'
[76] Liv. 44.1.1.

Albanus a few days or maybe a few weeks after the Ides of March, unless the consuls assumed their office before that date, which seems improbable, since Livy would almost certainly have mentioned it as it would have been exceptional.

In 168, the senate once again decided to hasten the compulsory formalities in Rome to allow the consuls to go to Macedonia as soon as possible, and for this reason they expressly urged that the *feriae Latinae* be celebrated as early as possible.[77] The appointed date was 12 April,[78] but it appears that they were celebrated even earlier, on 31 March.[79] As planned, the consul L. Aemilius Paulus and the praetor in charge of the fleet, Cn. Octavius, left for Macedonia immediately afterwards. This means that Aemilius Paulus was in Rome for just two weeks after taking office on the Ides of March, an extraordinarily short period of time – probably the shortest on record, along with that of the year 169. During that period the issue of the war appears to have been dealt with repeatedly in the senate, and there had been a hearing in the Curia for the Roman legates sent to Macedonia upon the initiative of the consul-elect Aemilius Paulus.[80] The legates returned from Macedonia around 23 March and took part in the session of the senate that was held the following day.[81] It was decided that the people and the consuls should share the election of the military tribunes, but it seems that the recruitment was conducted only by the colleague of Aemilius Paulus, C. Licinius, a circumstance which undoubtedly lightened the workload of the former.[82]

In general, we must presume that the consuls fixed the earliest possible date for the celebration of the Latin festival, always taking into consideration their other duties in Rome, as well as recruitment, since this would permit them to go to their provinces as soon as possible.[83] Nevertheless, many internal political issues influenced the decision, as is shown by the diversity of known dates. On the other hand, we must take into account that the dates for the *feriae Latinae* in 212 and between 171 and 168 were determined by the ongoing wars, which is the reason Livy highlights them

---

[77] Liv. 44.17.7–8.   [78] Liv. 44.19.4.   [79] Liv. 44.22.16.
[80] The legates had been appointed by the consul of 169, Cn. Servilius, by order of the senate (Liv. 44.18.5; 44.20–1).
[81] Liv. 44.20.1–2.   [82] Liv. 44.21.1–2; 44.21.5.
[83] Livy (42.10.15) states that for 172 the consuls appointed the first available date in the calendar: 'consules ob ea irati senatui, Latinis feriis in primam quamque diem indictis . . .'. It is understood that it was a particularly early date, and Livy presents this as a reprisal of the consuls, who were confronting the senate. Their objective was to leave for the provinces as early as possible, and they claimed that they would not deal with any public issues during their stay in Rome except for matters regarding the administration of their provinces. However, their departure for Liguria was delayed, and they spent a good part of the year in Rome (Liv. 42.21).

in his account. It is reasonable to presume that the common procedure was to act with less haste, and therefore the festival would usually have taken place later, perhaps preferably in May. In fact, this is supported by the data provided by the *fasti feriarum Latinarum*, even for 217–12 during the Hannibalic War.[84] Although it is not possible to establish the exact date of celebration due to the degree of fragmentation, it is plausible to assert that the festival took place around the Nones of May in 214, around the Calends of the same month in 213 and 212 (the latter, as we have already seen, is supported by Livy's report, which gives as the exact date the fifth day before the Calends of May), and some time in May or a little earlier in 217 and 216, and finally in June or a little earlier in 215.

Naturally this presumption applies only to the period of time between the Hannibalic War and 153, when we know that the consuls took office on the Ides of March and therefore the *feriae Latinae* were celebrated in spring. From 153 onwards, the Latin festival must obviously have been celebrated at an earlier date in the year, closer to the Calends of January, when the consuls and the other magistrates took office, except for the tribunes of the plebs, who took office on 10 December. From that time onward they were probably a winter festival. It would not make sense to continue to celebrate them in spring if the intended purpose of an earlier consular takeover was to facilitate the consuls' setting out for their provinces as soon as possible, because they would have had to stay in Rome until then. On the contrary, before the Second Punic War the festival would have taken place later in the year, since the consuls seem to have taken office in May or even later in the cases where we have exact details. In that case it would have been a summer or later festival.[85]

Information available for the year 176 indicates that the month of May could in fact be the time when the *feriae Latinae* usually took place between the Hannibalic War and 153. That year the festival was originally celebrated on the third day before the Nones of May. However, it had to be repeated because there had been a mistake in the completion of the rites: during the sacrifice of an animal, the magistrate of Lanuvium had forgotten to pray for the Roman citizens.[86] The situation became more complicated because one of the consuls, Cn. Cornelius, died in an accident on his return from the Mons Albanus.[87] The senate then commissioned his colleague Q. Petilius to

---

[84] *CIL* I² 1, p. 57.
[85] At the beginning of the fourth century, the *fasti feriarum Latinarum* support the date of celebration of the festival in 396 and 395 in the months of November and September respectively. Cf. *CIL* I² 1, p. 57.
[86] Liv. 41.16.1–2. Cf. Scullard 1981: 114.   [87] Liv. 41.16.3.

organize the elections to appoint a new consul and afterwards to celebrate the *feriae Latinae* for the second time that year, which seems to indicate that the festival could not take place under the presidency of only one consul and that both of them had to attend. Petilius fixed the date for the elections for the third day before the Nones of August and the festival for the third day before the Ides of the same month, three months after the first celebration.[88] All of this meant an extraordinary delay compared to the usual calendar of the consular year.

It was not the first time that Roman religious scruples demanded a repetition of the *feriae Latinae*. This had already occurred in 199, 190, and 179. In 199 and 190, the reason for the repetition was identical, since the traditional distribution of meat to each city, after the sacrifice of the animals, had been carried out inappropriately. In 199 the representatives from Ardea complained for this reason, and the pontiffs decided that the ceremony should be repeated,[89] whereas in 190 the inhabitants of Lavinium complained.[90] Livy does not provide any account of the later date on which the festival was celebrated again, but he states that the consul L. Cornelius Scipio left for his province during the *ludi Apollinares*, therefore in July, almost four months after taking office.[91] It must be presumed that the *feriae Latinae* had been celebrated very recently for the second time. In 179, the pontiffs decided that the festival should be repeated due to the violent storm that broke out at the Mons Albanus during the first celebration.[92] In this case, Livy does not provide any indication of the time of year when the repetition of the festival took place.[93]

CLAVUS ANNALIS

In the year 365 a terrible pestilence struck Rome, causing a great number of deaths, one of the victims being the five-times dictator M. Furius Camillus. In order to placate the gods, stage plays (*ludi scaenici*) were imported from Etruria the following year. This measure did not have the expected effect, since the river Tiber burst its banks and flooded the Circus, which was perceived as another indication of the gods' wrath. In this context, the senate decided that L. Manlius Capitolinus Imperiosus should be appointed as dictator for 363. He held the title of *dictator clavi figendi causa*, and his

---

[88] Liv. 41.16.5–7.   [89] Liv. 32.1.9. Cf. Briscoe 1989: 167.   [90] Liv. 37.3.4. Cf. Briscoe 1981: 294.
[91] Liv. 37.4.4.   [92] Liv. 40.45.2.
[93] The consul Q. Fulvius left for Liguria having not only fulfilled the usual consular tasks in Rome, but also having been in charge of the ten-day celebration of the games he had promised during his war against the Celtiberians (Liv. 40.44.8–12; 40.45; 40.53.1).

task was to drive a nail as a means of fixing the misfortunes endured by Rome in the two previous years and making them disappear following a ritual which had previously been used.[94]

Livy takes this opportunity to produce an excursus on the existence of an ancient tradition in Rome. Livy claims that there was an 'ancient law' ('lex vetusta') written in archaic characters, placed on the right-hand side wall of the temple of Capitoline Jupiter adjacent to the chamber or *cella* dedicated to Minerva. This law prescribed that the *praetor maximus* should drive a nail every year on the Ides of September, that is, on 13 September. It has traditionally been understood from Livy's text that this nail had to be driven into the same wall of the temple of Capitoline Jupiter where the *lex vetusta* was displayed, although Livy does not state so specifically. Livy interprets these annual nails as a form of counting the years.[95] He next cites Cincius the antiquarian as an authority[96] when claiming that nails were also driven into the temple of the goddess Nortia in the Etruscan city of Volsinii to keep count of the years. In Rome, this custom may have been introduced by the consul Horatius when dedicating the temple to Jupiter the year after the expulsion of Tarquinius. Later on, the custom of fixing nails may have passed from the consuls to the dictators. The ritual seems to have fallen into disuse, but in 363 it was considered necessary to revive it with the appointment of Manlius as dictator.[97]

Along with this text in Livy, a passage of Festus also refers to the annual nail: 'The annual nail used to be hammered into the walls of sacred buildings every year, thus serving as a form of counting the years.'[98] This passage, like Livy's, probably comes from Cincius.[99] These two texts, in particular Livy's, have led to significant controversies regarding the existence of the ceremony of the so-called *clavus annalis* and its possible meaning and interpretation.[100] As regards this latter question, despite the fact that both Livy and Festus only see it as a form of counting the years, it seems probable that the ceremony involved, above all, a magic apotropaic ritual,

---

[94] Liv. 7.3.3–4. [95] Liv. 7.3.5–6.

[96] Oakley 1998: II 73. It is difficult to establish the date when Cincius wrote his work, very probably in the first century. He may have been a contemporary of Varro; he seems, in any case, to have been chronologically close to him. Cf. Heurgon 1964.

[97] Liv. 7.3.8.

[98] Fest. p. 49 L: 'clavus annalis appellabatur, qui figebatur in parietibus sacrarum aedium per annos singulos, ut per eos numerus colligeretur annorum.' In all probability, Cic. *Att.* 5.15.1 ('Laodiceam veni pridie Kal. Sext. ex hoc die clavum anni movebis') does not allude to the ritual of the *clavus annalis*, but to a movable nail on a calendar (Oakley 1998: II 75).

[99] Oakley 1998: II 75.

[100] Unger 1873; Leuze 1909: 159–63; Premerstein 1901; Toutain 1915–18; Favaro 1929; Momigliano 1930; Pena 1976; Poma 1978; Aigner Foresti 1979.

well known both in Antiquity and in different cultures even up to the present day.[101] Fixing a nail which implicitly had magical-religious powers was intended to resolve any misfortune or disease that may have affected or that could affect an individual or, as in this case, the Roman community.[102] According to Livy, in Rome this ceremony was held every year on the Ides of September, coinciding with the anniversary of the dedication of the temple to Capitoline Jupiter. This annual regularity may have caused the nails of the Capitolium to become a posteriori a simple system of keeping count of the years, although this may not have been the original purpose of the ritual, but a later consequence.[103]

The ritual of the *clavus annalis* therefore entailed a direct relationship between the Roman community and the gods, meant for the preservation of the *pax deorum*. For this reason, it is logical that those in charge of duly conducting the ritual were the magistrates of the community invested with the highest authority, as we have seen in other ceremonies that were likewise aimed at keeping peace with the gods. When referring to the *lex vetusta*, which presumably made this rite compulsory, Livy alludes to the *praetor maximus* as the person who was responsible for its performance. It is not appropriate here to delve into the debate about the exact meaning of the term, which forms part of the context of the development of the magistracies in the first few decades of the Republican period. Nevertheless it is obvious that Livy understands that the ancient law to which he alludes refers to the supreme magistrate of Rome at the time. The magistrates with the highest *imperium* in the *civitas* had always been in charge of performing the ritual, who were, according to Livy, the *praetor maximus*, the consuls, and later on the dictators. During the early Republic, there was no fixed date for the supreme magistrates to take office. Indeed, we know of quite varied dates. For this reason, it is impossible to establish with certainty whether the ceremony of the *clavus annalis* was originally a purifying ritual linked to the beginning of the consular year, although it is possible that this may have been the case.[104]

In any event, apart from these much-discussed passages, we do not find any ancient source that specifically mentions the performance of the

---

[101] Cf. Plin. *Nat.* 28.63, who claims that epilepsy could be cured by driving a nail into the place where the patient had suffered the fit. Cf. Aigner Foresti 1979: 147–8.

[102] See a thorough study, with copious supplementary bibliography, on the use of nails with a ritualistic or magical end in Alfayé 2009. See also Dungworth 1998.

[103] Oakley 1998: II 75.

[104] Pinsent 1975: 24: 'The date must be connected with those notices which show the consuls taking office on the Kalends of September, and it could be inferred that the fixing of a *clavus annalis* was one of the first acts of the consul who had been first elected and who held the *fasces* for the first month.'

ceremony of the *clavus annalis*. In particular, Livy makes no reference to it in his account of what happened from year to year in his surviving books, although the ceremony undoubtedly existed. At least in the first phase of the Republican period, it must have been one of the tasks of the supreme magistrates, whether they were officially designated *praetores maximi*, consuls, or in any other form. What we do not know is whether this custom ceased rapidly or whether it survived for centuries. When Livy refers to the appointment of a *dictator clavi figendi causa* in 363, he claims that the tradition had been discontinued ('intermisso more') and that it was resumed due to the persistent troubles afflicting Rome. No other source confirms or refutes this assertion. The wars in which Rome was involved were increasingly remote from the *Urbs* as the Republic expanded. Undoubtedly this forced the consuls to spend more time away from the city. If the ritual always had to be performed on 13 September, could the absence of the supreme magistrate have had an influence on the gradual decline of the ceremony? Is there any link between the disappearance of the ritual of the *clavus annalis* and the beginning of a systematic compilation of prodigies, both in Rome and in the whole of Italy, and the subsequent expiation and purification rites?

In any case, it is also obvious that the belief in the magic ritual of fixing a nail in the wall as a means of protection lingered on in the Roman mentality for a long time. In 331 a *dictator clavi figendi causa* was again appointed, according to Livy, with the purpose of placating the gods, since the poisoning of a large number of significant Roman citizens had been perceived as a portent. Livy also states that formerly the habit of fixing a nail had served as a means of stopping the secessions of the plebs, obviously implicitly seen as a sort of disease or disorder of the minds ('alienatas mentes') of certain plebeians, which had to be purified.[105] According to Livy, in 313 a *dictator clavi figendi causa* was once more appointed, which is not confirmed in the *fasti* even though they are preserved for these years. Again, the reason was the plague (*pestilentia*) that was ravaging Rome.[106] Finally, the *fasti* allude for the year 263 to Cn. Fulvius Maximus Centumalus as *dictator clavi figendi causa*, without, however, making any reference to the reason for such an appointment.[107]

---

[105] Liv. 8.18.12. Cf. Poma 1978: 49. On the dictators appointed to perform a religious task, see Kaplan 1973–4: 172–5.

[106] Liv. 9.28.6.

[107] The fact that *dictatores clavi figendi causa* were appointed in both 363 and 263 made Mommsen (1859: 175) wrongly believe in the possibility that they were purifying rituals performed every century. Other preserved data in ancient sources do not back up this theory. Cf. Pinsent 1975: 25. See the detailed argument against Mommsen's theory in Unger 1873.

The *clavus annalis* and the fixing of a nail by a designated dictator are not two distinct traditions. On the contrary, it is basically the same ritual apotropaic concerning the future and expiatory against the past, similar in form although possibly performed at different cultic sites.[108] Livy understood that it was an attempt at recovering a lost rite. Perhaps this was indeed the case and maybe the *clavus annalis* had ceased to exist, at least from the beginning of the fourth century onwards. However, it could well be a case of incorrect interpretation on the part of Livy, who may have understood that the appointment of a dictator specifically for fixing the nail meant that the annual ritual had ceased to exist.[109] This is not necessarily the case. The *clavus annalis* was a ceremony which annually renewed the magic ritual of protection of the community. The *dictator clavi figendi causa* was appointed in extraordinary circumstances to confront an emergency that was causing harm to the community. The two ceremonies are not necessarily incompatible: the annual apotropaic ritual and the extraordinary expiatory ritual could co-exist. In that case, the *dictator clavi figendi causa* could perform the ritual not because he had a superior *imperium* to that of the consuls, as Livy states, but as a surrogate for the consuls in their absence, if they were commanding the army away from Rome, just as in the case when a dictator was appointed to preside over the elections in the absence of the consul who was responsible for this task, or when in 257 a *dictator feriarum Latinarum causa* was appointed exceptionally.[110] The novelty in the fourth century may have been the occasional and extraordinary appointment of a dictator responsible for performing the ceremony in specific circumstances which were considered by the senate to be particularly dangerous.

The scarcity of data and the difficulty in interpreting the preserved texts make it very hard to draw definite conclusions about this matter. Since there are no sound reasons to question Livy's credibility in this respect, it seems undeniable that the ceremony of the *clavus annalis* existed in Rome and that it was performed by one of the consuls, or in any case by the supreme magistrate by whatever name in the first phase of the Republic. The ceremony must have been in use during the fifth century. It may have fallen into disuse from the first quarter of the fourth century onwards, in which

---

[108] Cf. Pena 1976: 256; Poma 1978: 44.

[109] Werner (1963: 30–2) interpreted the expression 'intermisso more' in Livy's text not as a total interruption of the ceremony but as an interruption of the driving of the nail by a dictator. This would mean that the ceremony continued to be celebrated, presumably presided over by the consuls. However, this explanation seems to assume that the dictatorship was a regular and annual magistracy, whereas in fact it was an extraordinary magistracy and only as such can the dictators' occasional participation in the ritual of fixing the nail be understood.

[110] Momigliano 1930: 280.

case perhaps the consuls were not responsible for fixing the nail after 367, the starting point of this monograph. But this is not at all certain. The ceremony may have continued to exist, although if the date of the Ides of September was always upheld, this would pose the problem of the possible absence of the consuls, as the command over the legions caused them to be away from Rome for long periods. Nevertheless, the notion that fixing the nail by a magistrate with *imperium* on behalf of the community had an apotropaic and expiatory effect continued to be present amongst Romans with some continuity at least until the third century, and it remained until a much later time, as is shown by a text of Cassius Dio regarding Augustus, although undoubtedly with important formal distinctions from the archaic ritual.[111]

THE *SACRA* OF LAVINIUM

Two late texts indicate that Roman supreme magistrates had to perform annual sacrifices in the city of Lavinium in joint honour of Vesta and the Penates.[112] In his commentary on Virgil's *Aeneid*, Servius states the following: 'Thus, the question here is whether Vesta is also part of the Penates or is considered as their companion, for when the consuls, the praetors, or a dictator leave their magistracies, they worship the Penates of Lavinium and Vesta at the same time.'[113] On the other hand, Macrobius writes: 'He [Virgil] also used the same name to refer to Vesta, who, in all probability as part of the Penates is clearly their companion, so that when the consuls, praetors, and dictators take over their magistracies, they worship the Penates of Lavinium and Vesta at the same time.'[114]

Clearly, both texts are very similar but there is one significant difference that causes uncertainty as to when exactly the ceremony took place.

---

[111] Cass. Dio (55.10.4) reports that the censors had to drive a nail at the end of their term of office in honour of Augustus. Momigliano (1930: 281–2) thought that the ritual survived until the third century and it was then lost, taking into account that the dictatorship *clavi figendi causa* of 263 is the last time when the ceremony is mentioned. Favaro (1929: 223–9) argued, however, that the *clavus annalis* existed until the time of Augustus, on the grounds of the aforementioned text in Cassius Dio. According to Ogilvie 1978: 95, the ritual may have disappeared in the first century, but the nails were still visible: 'sight-seers in Sulla's day could still see and count the rows of rusty nails'.

[112] See De Ruggiero 1892: 745; Wissowa 1904; Alföldi 1965: esp. 258–65; Radke 1975c: 611; Dubourdieu 1989: esp. 355–61.

[113] Serv. *ad Aen.* 2.296: 'hic ergo quaeritur, utrum Vesta etiam de numero Penatium sit, an comes eorum accipiatur, quod cum consules et praetores sive dictator abeunt magistratu, Lavini sacra Penatibus simul et Vestae faciunt.'

[114] Macrob. 3.4.11: 'eodem nomine appellavit [Vergilius] et Vestam, quam de numero Penatium certe comitem eorum esse manifestum est adeo, ut et consules et praetores seu dictatores, cum adeunt magistratum, Lavini rem divinam faciant Penatibus pariter et Vestae.'

According to Servius, the sacrifices celebrated by Roman magistrates in Lavinium were carried out at the end of their term in office ('cum . . . abeunt magistratu'), whereas, on the other hand, it can be deduced from Macrobius' text that the ceremony was celebrated when the magistrates assumed office ('cum adeunt magistratum').

To resolve the question raised by the divergence of these texts, several propositions have been put forward. Latte, implicitly basing his theory on the fact that Servius' work (fourth century AD) was earlier than Macrobius' (fifth century AD), suggested that 'abeunt magistratu' was the correct version and considered Macrobius' text to be a copyist's mistake.[115] Weinstock, on the other hand, was inclined to consider both readings acceptable, which led him to believe that the sacrifices were celebrated at both the beginning and the end of the magistrates' term in office.[116] Alföldi, however, believed Macrobius' text to be the correct one, holding that Servius' reading was the result of the mistake of a later copyist. Macrobius would have had access to Servius' correct version, from which he gathered the information, but subsequently a copyist would have misspelled 'adeunt' and written 'abeunt' in the transcription of Servius' text.[117] This theory is further supported by another passage in Servius in which the grammarian explicitly states that the sacrifice in Lavinium was carried out when the *imperatores* were on their way to their provinces.[118]

From what is known about consular activities throughout the year, it can be concluded that Alföldi was right, and therefore it is much more likely that the sacrifices in Lavinium were celebrated at the beginning of the consular year, at least in the period prior to Sulla. Once the consuls had departed for their provinces, one of them would usually return to Rome at the end of the year, if possible, to preside over the elections. The other consul would return to the *Urbs* only once his term in office had ended. As consuls, they did not jointly carry out any further civilian tasks or celebrate any other religious ceremonies after leaving Rome. On the contrary, the religious duties involved in the consulship were fulfilled at the beginning of the consular year. Included amongst them could be the annual sacrifices celebrated at Lavinium, where, apparently, the consuls were assisted by

---

[115] Latte 1960: 295 n. 5.
[116] Weinstock 1937a: 428. Cf. Radke 1975c: 611: 'Die römische Beamten mit *imperium* opfern seit alters her in Lavinium beim Amtsantritt bzw. *in provincias ituri* den Penates und der Vesta.'
[117] Alföldi 1965: 261. Dubourdieu (1989: 357) shares the same opinion.
[118] Serv. *ad Aen.* 3.12: 'quos (*Penates) inter cetera ideo magnos appellant, quod de Lavinio translati Romam bis in locum suum redierint: quod imperatores in provincias ituri apud eos primum immolarint.'

priests from Rome, possibly pontiffs, according to another text by Servius that seems to refer to the sacrifice to the Penates.[119]

A possible reference to the sacrifices to Vesta and the Penates can be found in Cato's *Origines*. According to the preserved text, the oxen that ought to have been sacrificed in Lavinium escaped into the forest.[120] If this passage refers to the annual sacrifices in Lavinium, it would be the oldest documented reference to the ceremony, dating it back to the beginning of the second century.[121] The most direct reference is found in a passage from Valerius Maximus in which he claims that the consul C. Hostilius Mancinus, on his way to Hispania, wanted to celebrate a sacrifice in Lavinium, but could not perform it because the chickens that were to be sacrificed had escaped into a nearby forest and could not be found, a circumstance reminiscent of Cato's text.[122] What happened was perceived as a portent. Hostilius Mancinus was consul in 137, and his allotted province was Hispania Citerior, where he was defeated by the Celtiberians. If, as is likely, Valerius Maximus refers not to a private sacrifice but to the state sacrifice that the higher Roman magistrates had to perform in Lavinium, it must have taken place at the beginning of the consular year. According to Valerius Maximus, the events occurred when the consul was preparing to set off for his province. It was the portents which occurred on both occasions that drew the attention of Cato and of Valerius Maximus to the ceremony of the *sacra* in Lavinium.

A final question makes the solution to this issue even more complicated. Livy reports that since 338 the treaty (*foedus*) between Rome and Lavinium was renewed every year and that this happened 'on the tenth day after the Latin festival' ('post diem decimum (*feriarum) Latinarum').[123] Did the ceremony of renewal of the treaty coincide with the sacrifice to the Penates in Lavinium? No ancient text, including Livy, our main source of information, seems to connect the two events. However, Wissowa and Alföldi assumed that it was the same ceremony, and they were probably right.[124] It is unreasonable to presume that the Roman magistrates went to Lavinium twice every year, once to renew the *foedus* between the cities and again to celebrate the sacrifices. On the contrary, it is more logical that both

---

[119] Serv. *ad Aen.* 1.239: 'Aeneae Indigeti templum dicavit, ad quod pontifices quotannis cum consulibus ire solent sacrificaturi.' Cf. Scheid 1981: 169–71; Dubourdieu 1989: 357–9.

[120] Cato, Beck and Walter *FRH* I 188 = fr.55 Peter. Cf. Engels 2007: 719–20: 'Die Annahme Alföldis, es handele sich hier um ein jährliches Staatsopfer an Vesta und die Penaten in Lavinium, muß daher ebenso hypothetisch bleiben.'

[121] Cf. Alföldi 1965: 262 n. 2.   [122] V. Max. 1.6.7. Cf. Liv. *per.* 55. Engels 2007: 540–1.

[123] Liv. 8.11.15.

[124] Wissowa 1912: 518; Alföldi 1965: 262–3. Dubourdieu 1989: 360–1 is sceptical on this question.

ceremonies were conducted simultaneously, since, in fact, the worship of the Penates had historically linked the two communities. Should this be the case, the sacrifices to Vesta and the Penates ought to be located at the beginning of the consular year, immediately after the celebration of the *feriae Latinae*.

However, the greatest difficulty is that the ceremony in honour of the *sacra* in Lavinium is never mentioned by Livy in any historical period, which makes confirmation of these theories impossible. Only once does Livy make a vague reference to the sacrifices in Lavinium in the time of Romulus, also reported by Dionysius of Halicarnassus and Plutarch.[125] Although it is obvious that this information is not credible in itself, it is true that it indirectly confirms the existence of such a tradition. However, the fact that Livy does not mention it once again prevents us from knowing any further details about the ritual. In the preserved books Livy makes no reference to the sacrifices either before or after the *feriae Latinae*, and the celebration of the festival on the Mons Albanus is presented on various occasions as the final event of the civilian activities conducted by the consuls prior to their departure for their provinces.[126] Obviously, Livy does not always report all the events that took place every year, but it seems strange that, in this case, he never refers to a possibly annual solemn ceremony at which the highest Roman magistrates had to act on behalf of the state.

There is no reason to presume that the antiquarian information collected by Servius and Macrobius is false; the sacrifices must have existed. But the lack of references in Livy's preserved work makes it dubious that the ceremony was habitually attended by the consuls.[127] After the compulsory journey to the Mons Albanus, situated about thirty kilometres from Rome, the act of attending the sacrifices in Lavinium, located at a similar distance from the *Urbs*, would have further delayed the journey of the consuls to their provinces. In this regard, it must be recalled that, according to Servius and Macrobius, the ceremony had to be conducted by a magistrate with *imperium*, which means that it could also be celebrated by the praetors or by a dictator. Although there is no certain information regarding the matter, it is possible that the consuls normally entrusted this task to one of the praetors, the urban or the peregrine, and that only on exceptional occasions

---

[125] Liv. 1.14.2; Dion. Hal. 2.52.3; Plut. *Rom.* 23.

[126] Liv. 43.15.3: 'Latinisque actis Marcius extemplo est profectus'. Cf. Liv. 44.22.16.

[127] However, cf. Alföldi 1965: 32: 'The consuls had to provide for the welfare of the Roman state by the three religious acts just mentioned: the *votorum nuncupatio* on the Capitol, the performance of the *Latiar* on the Alban Mountain, and the state sacrifices in Lavinium.'

did one of the consuls go to Lavinium, as Hostilius Mancinus may have done in 137.[128]

The games always retained their original religious nature within Roman society. Since 366, the curule aediles were in charge of the games. These magistrates were also responsible for the organization of the *ludi Megalenses* from 199 onwards, whereas the plebeian aediles were in charge of the *ludi Florales* from 218, the *ludi Ceriales* from 164 and the *ludi plebeii* from 162. In the year 22, according to Cassius Dio,[129] Augustus transferred the care of the games, the *cura ludorum*, to the praetors.[130] Therefore, throughout the Republican period the *cura ludorum* was one of the functions officially assigned to the aediles in Rome, and their names are linked to the celebration of the corresponding games in historical accounts.

However, the presidency over the *ludi Romani* that the aediles had organized was reserved for the higher magistrates since they were invested with *imperium*.[131] This conclusion can be drawn from a text of Livy, in which he claims that the presidency over the chariot racing at the *ludi Romani* was a duty of magistrates with *imperium* ('imperii ministerium').[132] Dionysius of Halicarnassus records a text from the work of Fabius Pictor.[133] The picture would presumably correspond to the games celebrated in 490, but the account of Dionysius of Halicarnassus seems to imply that

---

[128] We could add a passage in Asconius of disputed interpretation: 'crimini dabat sacra publica populi Romani deum Penatium quae Lavini fierent opera eius minus recte casteque fieri' (Asc. 21.7–8 C.). Asconius alludes to the accusation made by Cn. Domitius Ahenobarbus, while tribune of the plebs, against M. Aemilius Scaurus. The latter was accused of having inadequately performed some sacred rituals. Asconius mentions the *sacra publica* of *Lavinium*. The problem consists in determining how Scaurus came to make the ritual error, that is, whether he was acting as a priest or as a magistrate. If he was acting as a priest, it remains an unresolved question whether Scaurus belonged to the college of the pontiffs or to the college of the augurs. The pontiffs were certainly involved in the cult of the Penates in Lavinium, but then we should ask why the accusation of bad practice was directed at Scaurus and not at the *pontifex maximus*. If the ritual error was made by Scaurus as a magistrate, the most likely date would be 115, when he was a consul. Should this be the correct answer, the text of Asconius would be a further reference to the participation of consuls in the public rituals of Lavinium. On the passage of Asconius, see Marshall 1985: 129–33.

[129] Cass. Dio 54.2.3–4.   [130] See Bernstein 1998: 54 and 74–7.

[131] Salomonson 1956: 58–61; Bernstein 1998: 58–63. Bernstein (61–2) argues that the exclusive responsibility for the taking of public auspices belonging to the higher magistrates is the reason why the *ludi Romani* had to be presided over by one of them, since the games were dedicated to Jupiter Optimus Maximus, the supreme divinity of the Roman pantheon. Cf. Mommsen 1887–8: I 245; II 136; II 518; Kunkel and Wittmann 1995: 504 n. 120.

[132] Liv. 8.40.3. Cf. Mommsen 1887–8: I 413 n. 3; Bernstein 1998: 59.

[133] Dion. Hal. 7.71.1–73.4. Cf. Beck and Walter, *FRH* I F 20, 110–17.

Fabius Pictor was providing a description of the ceremonies from his own time.[134] Before the beginning of the games, the traditional procession (*pompa circensis*) took place. The procession went through the Forum from the Capitolium to the Circus Maximus. According to Dionysius, at the head of the *pompa circensis* were 'those who had the supreme power' in the community, while at the end of the parade were statues of the gods carried on men's shoulders.[135] Obviously, this statement cannot refer to the aediles organizing the games, and it must be understood that it was the supreme magistrates, that is, the consuls, who presided over the civic procession and that it was they who would, therefore, preside over the games.[136]

A passage from Ennius recorded by Cicero in his *De divinatione* should be understood in this sense.[137] Ennius describes poetically the sense of anticipation that existed amongst Romans as to which of the two brothers, Romulus or Remus, should govern and after which one of them the new city would be named. The same sense of anticipation, says Ennius, exists amongst the crowd surrounding the consul when he is at the Circus about to give the signal for the beginning of the chariot racing.[138] Ennius uses the past tense ('exspectabat populus') to refer to the time of the mythical founders of Rome, whereas he uses the present tense ('exspectant') with reference to the consul giving the signal, which would seem to indicate that he refers to an action taking place in his own time, at the beginning of the second century. From this passage it can be clearly deduced that the consul is the person in charge of giving the starting order to the participants in the race, which means, once again, that it was the consul who was presiding over the games.

Finally, a passage from Livy confirms beyond doubt the consular presidency over the *ludi Romani*.[139] On 16 September 168, when the second day of the *ludi Romani* was being celebrated, a courier arrived in Rome with news of the victory of the Roman army at Pydna. The courier delivered the dispatches to the consul C. Licinius Crassus, just as he was about to give the signal for the start of the quadriga race in the Circus. The consul then showed the letter to the crowd, who, as a result of the importance of the

---

[134] Dion. Hal. 7.71.1. Cf. Beck and Walter, *FRH* I 116.
[135] Dion. Hal. 7.72.1. Cf. Beck 2006: esp. 144–51.
[136] Beck 2006: 147. Cf. Hölkeskamp 2008: 108: 'Die *pompa* wurde grundsätzlich vom Spielgeber und -leiter angeführt – und das war immer ein Magistrat, zumindest ursprünglich vermutlich ein Imperiumsträger.'
[137] Cic. *Div.* 1.107–8: 'exspectant veluti consul cum mittere signum / volt, omnes avidi spectant ad carceris oras, / quam mox emittat pictis e faucibus currus: / sic exspectabat populus atque ore timebat / rebus utri magni victoria sit data regni.'
[138] Cf. Humphrey 1986: 153–7; Skutsch 1985: 228.   [139] Liv. 45.1.6–7.

news, immediately forgot the games. After that, Licinius Crassus summoned the senate, read the message, and finally announced the victory in Macedonia officially to the people.

Both from Livy's text and from the texts of Fabius Pictor and Ennius, recorded respectively by Dionysius of Halicarnassus and by Cicero, we can deduce that one consul played the role of president of the games (*praeses ludorum*).[140] Dionysius uses the plural form to refer to the magistrates leading the *pompa circensis*. But from the text of Ennius and especially from that of Livy, it may be inferred that the effective presidency of the games belonged only to one of the two consuls. In the case of 168, it is obvious that Licinius Crassus was the only consul then present in Rome. He had been assigned Italy as his province, and he had to deal in particular with the recruiting and provisioning of the soldiers intended for Macedonia.[141] It was his colleague L. Aemilius Paulus who conducted the war in Macedonia.

However, throughout the Republican period prior to Sulla's dictatorship, it was usual for the consuls to spend most of the time away from Rome in their provinces. In particular, when the *ludi Romani* were celebrated, in September, both consuls would usually be away from Rome, which made it impossible for them to preside over the games. As was the case for many other civil functions, the consuls had to preside over the games as supreme magistrates, but when they were not in Rome, the urban praetor would probably act as their representative. Since the games had to be presided over by a magistrate invested with *imperium*, a dictator was appointed to exercise this duty only when the consuls and the praetor were away or unable to attend, as can clearly be deduced from Livy's text regarding the dictatorship of A. Cornelius Cossus Arvina in 322. While according to some sources Cornelius achieved a remarkable victory and obtained a triumph, according to other sources he was exclusively appointed to give the mandatory starting signal for the chariot races in the games, after which he abdicated.[142] In fact, unlike other tasks belonging to the consuls (expiation of prodigies, celebration of the *feriae Latinae*, etc.), whose fulfilment is systematically attributed to the annual consuls by ancient sources, in the case of the presidency over the *ludi Romani* the consuls are rarely mentioned, no doubt because their presence must have been exceptional.[143]

---

[140] According to Dionysius of Halicarnassus (5.57.5), the consul M. Tullius Longus died in the year 500 when he fell off a chariot during the celebration of the *ludi Romani*. This episode would also indirectly show the leading role played by the consuls in the games.

[141] Liv. 44.17.10; 44.19.5; 44.21.11; 44.22.5.   [142] Liv. 8.40.2–3. Cf. Broughton 1951–86: I 150.

[143] Cf. Mommsen 1887–8: I 416; II 136.

Other ancient records confirm the consuls' presidency over the *ludi magni*, extraordinary votive games celebrated in honour of Jupiter in case of a crisis in Rome.[144] In 203, after the consuls assumed their office, the provinces were allotted as usual, and the troops were recruited. The senate then ordered the praetors to go to their assigned provinces but instructed the consuls before leaving Rome to preside over the *ludi magni* that had been vowed by the dictator Manlius Torquatus in 208.[145] Livy then informs us that the consuls carried out the usual sacrifices for the expiation of prodigies reported that year, after which they left for their provinces. However, he does not specifically report that the games took place.[146] The same episode was repeated the following year. Once again the senate commissioned the consuls to celebrate the games vowed by Manlius Torquatus. Although in this case Livy does not give any information on the development of the games, he does state that within the context of the vow pronounced by the dictator in 208 some victims were sacrificed to the gods.[147]

What happened in 208 indirectly highlights the consular responsibility in the celebration of the *ludi magni*, as well as the compulsory presidency over them by a magistrate with *imperium*. In that year, the consul Marcellus died in a battle fought against the Carthaginian army, and his colleague T. Quinctius Crispinus was mortally wounded.[148] Due to these circumstances, the senate decided that, if Crispinus could not return to Rome to preside over the elections, he should appoint a dictator for the purpose. Crispinus, before dying, appointed T. Manlius Torquatus as a dictator, not only to celebrate the elections but also to carry out the *ludi magni* promised by the praetor M. Aemilius in 217.[149] It can be presumed that in normal circumstances the senate would have assigned the presidency over the games to one of the consuls and that only because both consuls had died was the dictator appointed to preside over them.[150] In 322, A. Cornelius Cossus Arvina had been appointed as dictator, and he was expressly entrusted with the celebration of the games,[151] due to the praetor's ill-health and the absence of the consuls, who were leading the army against the Samnites.

---

[144] Cf. Bernstein 1998: 142–57. Liv. 34.44.6 refers to *ludi magni* as *ludi Romani votivi*. Livy never calls the games celebrated following a vow *ludi Romani*. Quinn-Schofield 1967: 102: 'The position appears to be that the *ludi magni* or *ludi maximi* were always games vowed or decreed for a special purpose . . .'
[145] Liv. 30.2.8.   [146] Liv. 30.2.13; 30.3.1.   [147] Liv. 30.27.11.
[148] Liv. 27.26–7; Polyb. 10.32; Plut. *Marc.* 29; App. *Hann.* 50; V. Max. 1.6.9.
[149] Liv. 27.33.6: '. . . comitiorum ludorumque faciendorum causa'. Broughton 1951–86: I 290. Cf. Naevius in Var. *L.* 5.153 or Naev. vv. 28–29 p. 148 Warmington = Nr. 36 fr. 2 p. 226 Marmorale².
[150] See Bernstein 1998: 150–2. Cf. Jahn 1970: 151: 'Die Spiele sind als Prokuration eines Prodigiums, nämlich des Todes beider Konsuln, aufzufassen.'
[151] Liv. 8.40.2–3: 'qui ludis Romanis . . . signum mittendis quadrigis daret'. Broughton 1951–86: I 150.

In all probability the celebration of the *ludi magni* can also be attributed
to the consuls in 194. Once the consuls of that year had taken office, the
provinces had been assigned to them (both received Italy as their province),
and the recruitment had taken place,[152] the senate decreed that the *ver
sacrum* vowed by the praetor A. Cornelius Mammula in 217[153] was to be
celebrated again, along with the *ludi magni* which had been vowed at the
same time.[154] In fact, by senatorial order, the *ver sacrum* had apparently
already been celebrated in 195 under the presidency of the consuls of that
year.[155] But one year later, the pontiff P. Licinius informed the senate
that the ritual had not been properly conducted. The senate demanded
therefore that it be repeated under the supervision of the pontiffs. Livy does
not expressly say that the consuls had to preside over the *ver sacrum* and that
one of them had to preside over the *ludi magni*, but since they were in
charge of that rite in 195 and since the senatorial decree of 194 links both
events, it seems likely that they did so. Livy later confirms that both the *ver
sacrum* and the *ludi magni* were celebrated in 194.[156] However, he states that
the games had been vowed by the consul Servius Sulpicius Galba. There was
no consul by that name until 144. This is undoubtedly a mistake. Livy
confuses him with P. Sulpicius Galba Maximus, who was consul in the year
200 with Macedonia as his province.[157] Indeed, before setting off for Greece
to lead the war against Philip, Sulpicius Galba was requested by the senate
to carry out the vow of games in honour of Jupiter, which he eventually did
despite the opposition of the *pontifex maximus*.[158] Those were the *ludi magni*
that had to be celebrated in 194, since those promised in 217, along with the
ver sacrum, had already been conducted in 208.[159]

In 191, once the war against Antiochus had been declared, the senate
decreed that the consuls should call for a period of supplication to plead for
the success of the Roman army. At the same time, the senators ordered the
consul Manius Acilius Glabrio to vow the celebration of *ludi magni* dedicated to Jupiter.[160] By means of an edict, the consuls proclaimed two days of
supplications,[161] while Acilius fulfilled the vow – before setting off to Greece
on 3 May[162] – according to a formula dictated by the *pontifex maximus*
P. Licinius, recorded verbatim by Livy.[163] The vow makes no mention of

---

[152] Liv. 34.43.3–9.   [153] Liv. 22.9.10–10.6.   [154] Liv. 34.44.1–6.   [155] Liv. 33.44.1–2.
[156] Liv. 34.44.6.   [157] Cf. Münzer 1900: 805.   [158] Liv. 31.9.10.   [159] See Bernstein 1998: 156 n. 208.
[160] Liv. 36.2.2.   [161] Liv. 36.2.5.   [162] Liv. 36.3.14.
[163] Liv. 36.2.3–5: 'si duellum, quod cum rege Antiocho sumi populus iussit, id ex sententia senatus
populique Romani confectum erit, tum tibi, Iuppiter, populus Romanus ludos magnos dies decem
continuos faciet, donaque ad omnia pulvinaria dabuntur de pecunia, quantam senatus decreverit.
quisquis magistratus eos ludos quando ubique faxit, hi ludi recte facti donaque data recte sunto.'

the magistrate or the date and place of celebration of the games, if the promise were to be fulfilled, but in any event the formula leaves the decision in the hands of the senate.[164] However, it is clear from the text that the vow must be fulfilled by a magistrate, as is logical for a public vow pronounced on behalf of the Roman people. Livy does not subsequently inform us whether the vow was actually fulfilled and the games celebrated.

Also in 191, Acilius Glabrio's colleague as consul, P. Cornelius Scipio Nasica, was the protagonist in a different episode that was also connected with the celebration of the games. Two years earlier, as governor of Hispania Ulterior, he made the promise to celebrate games dedicated to Jupiter if the Roman army defeated the Lusitanians.[165] As victory was achieved, Nasica wished to fulfil his vow and celebrate the games before setting off to his province to fight the Boii. For this purpose he requested money from the senate, but the senators refused to provide it, stating that, as he had vowed the games without prior consultation, he therefore had to organize the games with the military spoils obtained or with his own money.[166] Either way, the games were finally celebrated for ten days, presumably while Nasica was still in Rome, and Livy expressly attributes their organization to the consul.[167] Thus, it can be deduced that they were presided over by him as a means of achieving the further renown and popularity attached to their celebration.

In 179, the consul Q. Fulvius, upon entering office, and even before dealing with any matters that concerned him as supreme magistrate, decided to fulfil the vow pronounced in Hispania the previous year on the day of his last battle against the Celtiberians. His vow had consisted of building a temple dedicated to Fortuna Equestris and celebrating games in honour of Jupiter Optimus Maximus, for which purpose he had obtained plunder following his victory in Hispania.[168] Duumvirs were appointed for the construction of the temple. The senate also issued a decree authorizing the celebration of the games while setting a strict limit for the costs, which should not exceed those previously granted to Fulvius Nobilior for the celebration of the games after the war in Aetolia. Consul Q. Fulvius' games were celebrated for ten days with great splendour, despite the limitations.[169]

In 172, the *decemviri sacris faciundis* proclaimed that the city had to be purified due to a series of prodigies that had taken place. They recommended carrying out supplications, offering sacrifices of higher victims both in

---

[164] Briscoe 1981: 220: '*quisquis magistratus* is to be taken as excluding magistrates without *imperium*.'
[165] Liv. 35.1.8.   [166] Liv. 36.36.1. Cf. Bernstein 1998: 272–3.   [167] Liv. 36.36.2.   [168] Liv. 40.44.8–12.
[169] Liv. 40.45.6. Cf. Briscoe 2008: 528.

Rome and in Campania, and, when possible, celebrating games in honour of Jupiter Optimus Maximus for ten days.[170] According to Livy, all the ceremonies were meticulously performed. Livy obviously refers to the sacrifices and public prayers. With regard to the games, the vow was delayed because of the absence of the consuls and because of conflict with the senate regarding the unjust actions of M. Popillius Laenas, consul for 173, against the Ligures Statiellates, with the support of his brother Gaius. Almost at the end of the consular year,[171] the consul C. Popillius returned from Liguria, which had been his province, to preside over the elections. The consular elections took place on 18 February 171, and the praetorian elections were held the following day.[172] It was then that the senate resolved to offer the games to Jupiter following the recommendations of the decemvirs. C. Popillius, still consul at the time, was entrusted with fulfilling the vow in the Capitolium, following words dictated by the *pontifex maximus* M. Aemilius Lepidus.[173] The games had to be celebrated at some point for ten days. The senatorial decree was issued at the same time as the appointed consuls were ordered to carry out sacrifices on the day they took office, praying for success in the war that the Romans were about to begin against Perseus.[174] As in the case of 191, there is no confirmation from the sources that the pledged games were in fact celebrated.

Finally, a passage of Suetonius in his biography of Terence suggests the celebration of games under the presidency of the consul C. Sulpicius Galus in 166.[175] According to Suetonius, in these consular games, for which he does not offer further details, Terence presented his first comedy. We know from Donatus' *didascalia* that Terence's first comedy was the *Andria* and that it was offered at the *ludi Megalenses* organized by M'. Acilius Glabrio and M. Fulvius (Nobilior), both of them curule aediles in 166.[176] From these two known records it seems that the games were organized as usual by the aediles, but the presidency belonged to the consul Sulpicius Galus, which would account for the designation as 'ludi consulares' that Suetonius uses to refer to them.[177] The *ludi Megalenses* used to take place every year

---

[170] Liv. 42.20.3.   [171] Liv. 42.28.1.   [172] Liv. 42.28.4.   [173] Liv. 42.28.8–9.

[174] In Bernstein's opinion (1998: 155), the *ludi votivi* vowed by Popillius must also be understood within the context of the declaration of war as a petition to Jupiter to secure victory in the conflict.

[175] Suet. *vit. Ter.* 4: 'Santra Terentium existimat, si modo in scribendo adiutoribus indiguerit, non tam Scipione et Laelio uti potuisse, qui tunc adulescentuli fuerunt, quam C. Sulpicio Gallo, homine docto et cuius consularibus ludis initium fabularum dandarum fecerit . . .' Cf. Bernstein 1998: 60. Mommsen (1887–8: II 136–7 n. 4) had already drawn attention to the problem.

[176] Donat. *Didasc. Ter. An.* p. 36 Wessner I. Cf. Broughton 1951–86: I 437.

[177] Cf. Bernstein 1998: 60.

between 4 and 10 April.[178] Since at that time the consuls assumed their office
on the Ides of March and they had to carry out their usual duties in Rome
before departing for their provinces – Sulpicius Galus was assigned
Liguria[179] – it is reasonable to presume that the consul was still in the
Urbs when the games were celebrated. The loss of the relevant part of Livy's
work prevents us from knowing any details of Sulpicius Galus' activities in
Rome.

From the preserved testimonies of ancient sources it can be deduced that
the consuls played a double role regarding the celebration of the *ludi*, as
presidents over the games and as promoters of *ludi votivi*. In fact, both
duties were closely linked. The vow taken on behalf of the community
always had to be formulated by a magistrate with *imperium*. The fulfilment
of the vow was likewise assigned to a magistrate invested with *imperium*. In
both cases, this right belonged in the first place to the consuls, as supreme
magistrates, and they could be replaced by the praetors or, exceptionally, by
a dictator.[180] There is definitive testimony to the consular presidency in the
case of the *ludi Romani*, in particular that the consuls gave the starting signal
in the chariot races. Suetonius' text also seems to refer to the consular
presidency over the *ludi Megalenses* in 166, for which there is no further
information in this respect. It may be concluded that the responsibility of
presiding over all the public games was officially assigned to the consuls but
that their presence at them must have been exceptional, since both consuls
would normally be absent when most of the games were celebrated throughout the year. This would usually leave the presidency in the hands of the
urban praetor or, exceptionally, those of a dictator appointed for the
purpose, which means that, in any case, the presidency over the games
was exclusive to magistrates with *imperium*.

As magistrates with *imperium* the consuls had a special role concerning
the *ludi magni votivi*. It was one of the consuls who had to carry out the vow
of the games, always following the senatorial decrees and according to the
instructions of the *pontifex maximus* concerning the suitable ritual. For this
reason, although the decemvirs had prompted the vow of games in 172, it
was necessary to wait for a few months for the consul Popillius to return
from his province to celebrate the elections, in order for him to pronounce
the vow. The *votum* was pronounced on behalf of the *civitas*, and for that

---

[178] Bernstein 1998: 355–7.   [179] Liv. *per.* 46.

[180] Cf. Eisenhut 1974; Bernstein 1998: 148–9. In 360, the senate ordered the dictator to perform the vow
of *ludi magni* dedicated to Jupiter before leaving Rome to lead the army (Liv. 7.11.5). In 208, the
urban praetor was ordered by the senate to present a law by which the *ludi Apollinares* would become
an annual event, and he carried out the vow under those terms (Liv. 27.23.7).

reason the senate was responsible for its fulfilment, as can be seen clearly in the fact that the senators specified the amount of money that could be spent on the organization of the games, as happened in 200, 191, and 172.[181] The state, through the senate, must therefore have been the source of funding for the games. Just as the consul acted as the state's representative in the formulation of the *votum*, so it was also the responsibility of a consul to put the vow into practice, undoubtedly by presiding over the games. Nevertheless, according to the available information, it can be deduced that the designated consul also played an active role in the organization of the games. This seems to be the case for the *ludi* celebrated by the consul Q. Fulvius in 179 and probably those celebrated in 194 as well. On both occasions, the *ludi magni* were celebrated at the beginning of the consular year, in order to facilitate the participation of the consuls appointed by the senate before leaving the *Urbs* for their provinces.

The participation of the consuls in the public games is easily explained by the close relationship that existed between Rome's public religion and the celebration of games that were, above all, a religious act in honour of Jupiter Optimus Maximus, and later, from the Hannibalic War onwards, in honour of other divinities. The consuls acted, therefore, as supreme magistrates of the community, on its behalf and under the orders of the senate, as keepers of the *pax deorum* and promoters of the safety of the *res publica*, the specific purpose of the *ludi magni votivi*.

VER SACRUM

There is only one record in historical times of the celebration of the ritual known as 'sacred spring' (*ver sacrum*) in Rome.[182] Livy mentions it in some detail, within the context of the defeats suffered by the Roman state at the beginning of the Hannibalic War. In 217, after the debacle of the Roman legions at Trasimene, the newly appointed dictator Q. Fabius Maximus summoned the senate on the same day he took office. In the senate, he blamed the consul C. Flaminius – who had died at Trasimene – for the military disasters, not so much because of his lack of skill as commander,

---

[181] Orlin 1997: 41–3.
[182] The only ancient definition of *ver sacrum* is due to Festus p. 519 L. = 379 M.: 'ver sacrum vovendi mos fuit Italis. Magnis enim periculis adducti vovebant, quaecunque proximo vere nata essent apud se, animalia immolaturos. sed quum crudele videretur pueros ac puellas innocentes interficere, perductos in adultam aetatem velabant atque ita extra fines suos exigebant.' About the *ver sacrum* as institution, see Eisenhut 1955; Heurgon 1957 (in particular about the Roman *ver sacrum* 36–51); Eisenhut 1975f; Radke 1980: esp. 110–16; Aigner Foresti 1995; Scheid 1998b; De Cazanove 2000; Hermon 2001: esp. 84–6.

but because he had not fulfilled the duties to the gods that his position as a higher magistrate required and was thus guilty of impiety.[183] His behaviour thus earned the wrath of the gods, according to the dictator, resulting in the punishment of the Roman *civitas* by military defeat. Fabius suggested addressing the gods directly, and the senate agreed that the decemvirs should consult the Sibylline Books to that end. After doing so, the priests advised carrying out a series of expiatory actions to restore the peace of the gods. Among these was the renewal of the vow to Mars, the celebration of *ludi magni* in honour of Jupiter, the construction of various temples, the celebration of a sacrificial banquet for the gods and of supplications, as well as the vow of a *ver sacrum* to Jupiter.[184] All these actions had to be performed if the wars against Carthage and the Gauls were to result in success for the Roman *res publica*.

The urban praetor M. Aemilius was entrusted with the fulfilment of the sacerdotal recommendations, due to the absence of the other consul, Cn. Servilius Geminus, and the need for Fabius to dedicate all his efforts to the war. As a result, the *ludi magni* and the temples that the decemvirs had recommended were vowed by different magistrates.[185] With regard to the *ver sacrum*, its exceptional nature made the praetor consult the pontiffs on the process he should follow to carry out his vow. The *pontifex maximus* L. Cornelius Lentulus decided that the vow of the *ver sacrum* could not be performed without the consent of the people.[186] The performance of the *ver sacrum* would involve the sacrifice of livestock born in the next spring and would therefore result in losses to the many citizens who owned those animals. It was logical therefore that the people be consulted first in order to give consent.[187] For this reason, the praetor presented to the popular assembly a bill, undoubtedly inspired by the *pontifex maximus*, which specified in great detail the procedure to be followed for the sacrifice of the animals affected by the vow in order to avoid mistakes during the rite that might invalidate it.[188] In fact, the bill listed a series of irregularities that

---

[183] Liv. 22.9.10. On the doubtful value of the sources about Flaminius see above, note 11.

[184] Liv. 22.9.11. Heurgon (1957: 39) points out the fact that the vow for the *ver sacrum* was addressed to Jupiter and not to Mars, as was common among the Sabines, or to Apollo, as was usual for the Mamertines. Heurgon believes that this could be explained not only by the nature of Jupiter Optimus Maximus as a national Roman god, but also by the Latins' habit of keeping for this god the first fruits of each year. Cf. Beck 2000: 85–6: the unusual accumulation of religious rites was intended to calm the urban plebs and restore confidence in the future of Rome. See also Beck 2005: 286–7.

[185] Liv. 22.10.9–10.   [186] Liv. 22.10.1.   [187] Scheid 1998b: 420–1.

[188] Liv. 22.10.2–6. Cf. Plut. *Fab.* 4.4: according to Plutarch, the vow was pronounced by the dictator Fabius, who included in it everything that nature offered in the following year, 216, not only animals, but also mountains, plains, and rivers in Italy. About the bill, see Elster 2003: 195–7.

could occur during the sacrifice, not for the purpose of disqualifying the entire process in case they happened, but in order to validate them instead.[189] The text of the bill makes clear that the vowed *ver sacrum* referred only to animals and did not involve the consecration of human beings or the subsequent ritual emigration of Roman young men, as had happened in 'sacred springs' promoted by other Italian peoples.[190] The purpose was to consecrate to Jupiter the livestock produced in one year, specifically pigs, sheep, cattle, and goats. Once the bill was approved by the people, the vow of the *ver sacrum* was carried out by the praetor of Sardinia, A. Cornelius Mammula.[191]

The vow referred to the following *quinquennium* and therefore expired in 212. However, the wars against the Carthaginians and the Gauls to which the vow referred went on much longer. Only in 195 did the senate commission the consuls L. Valerius Flaccus and M. Porcius Cato to celebrate the previously vowed *ver sacrum* before setting off for their provinces. Eisenhut argued that the long wait to execute the vow had been due to the fact that, traditionally, the young men born during the *ver sacrum* had to leave their community when they reached a suitable age and that is why, in his opinion, the rite was celebrated over twenty years later.[192] Incidentally, in 194 the senate also resolved to found eight colonies of Roman citizens, which involved a few thousand individuals leaving Rome, but neither Livy nor any other source makes a connection between that year's colonization and the performance of the *ver sacrum*.[193] On the other hand, as we have already seen, the vow of the *ver sacrum* as pronounced in 217 seemed to involve only animals, not the consecration of human beings. The choice of that particular year was probably due to the fact that at that time the senators considered the survival of the *res publica* to be guaranteed according to the terms of the contract pronounced in the *votum* of 217. It is likely that, as Heurgon pointed out,[194] the final senatorial decision was a direct result of the recent celebration of a triumph *de Galleis Insubribus* by the consul of 196, M. Claudius Marcellus, which would have been considered as the end of the war against the Gauls.

---

[189] Cf. Heurgon 1957: 40–1.

[190] Heurgon 1957: 39; Radke 1980: 115; Briscoe 1989: 332: 'In this case the human element is lacking entirely'; Scheid 1998b: 421 n. 26; De Cazanove 2000: 257 and 260.

[191] Liv. 33.44.1–2. About Mammula, Briscoe 1989: 332.   [192] Eisenhut 1975f: 1182.

[193] Heurgon (1957: 39) considered it a coincidence without political meaning. Cf. Hermon 2001: 85: 'Ce débat pose le problème de savoir si le *ver sacrum* n'est pas une sorte de colonisation militaire de l'époque.' On the colonization see Pina Polo 2006a: esp. 171–8.

[194] Heurgon 1957: 42. Cf. Scheid 1998b: 424.

After reporting the senatorial decree on the fulfilment of the vow, Livy goes on to describe the debate that arose from the proposal to abrogate the *lex Oppia*, which was vehemently opposed by the consul Cato before he left for Hispania.[195] But he does not mention the completion of the *ver sacrum* again until a year later, within the context of the beginning of the consulship of Scipio Africanus and Ti. Sempronius Longus in 194. Once it was decided that Italy would be the province for both consuls, and after carrying out the levy, the *pontifex maximus* P. Licinius Crassus Dives explained, first to the pontiffs' college and then to the senate, that the *ver sacrum* had not been properly conducted the previous year ('non esse recte factum'). The senators decided consequently that it had to be celebrated again under the supervision of the pontiffs ('arbitratu pontificum').[196]

Livy informs us in this passage that the *ver sacrum* was inappropriately conducted in 195, yet he does not provide any details on what the irregularities may have involved. As Heurgon states, the text of the vow taken in 217 contemplated and accepted such a quantity of possible errors during the rite that in practice the only possible irregularity would be that the *ver sacrum* had not been conducted or had not been fully conducted.[197] The new decree from the senate in 194 did not specify who should be in charge of the celebration of the *ver sacrum*, but it can be presumed that, as in the previous year, it had to be conducted by the consuls. However, the *senatus consultum* did expressly mention what livestock ought to be consecrated and, therefore, sacrificed within the context of the *ver sacrum*, which confirms once again that only animals were involved in the ritual. This was livestock born between the Calends of March and the last day of April, during the consulship of Scipio Africanus and Sempronius Longus. In fact, given that until 153 the consuls took over their office on the Ides of March, only from that moment on could we refer properly to the consulship of Scipio Africanus and Sempronius Longus. Therefore, the dates appointed by the senate actually corresponded to two consular years, the end of 195/4 and the beginning of 194/3.[198]

Heurgon explained that 1 March was chosen, though it did not mark the official beginning of spring in the Roman calendar, because that was the day

---

[195] Liv. 34.1–8. Briscoe 1981: 65–6: Cato would have arrived in Hispania in the late summer of 195.

[196] Liv. 34.44.1–3. On the celebration of the *ver sacrum* in 195/4, see Briscoe 1981: 22–3.

[197] Heurgon 1957: 43; Radke 1980: 114–15.

[198] Heurgon (1957: 45 n. 5) believes that the reference to the consular year of Scipio and Sempronius would have been added later on, when the consuls took over on 1 January, so a mistake would have been made in attributing the dates for the *ver sacrum* to only one consulship. On the other hand, Briscoe (1981: 22) argues that the mistake may be that the date appointed by the senate commenced instead on the Ides of March and not on the Calends.

the festival of Mars was celebrated, and it was Mars to whom the *ver sacrum* had originally been dedicated in the Italian world.[199] This argument has a weak point in the fact that the Roman *ver sacrum* was expressly dedicated to Jupiter.[200] Concerning 29 April, which cannot be accounted for according to the details of the calendar, Heurgon saw it as a concession to Roman farmers, to reduce the number of animals that would be sacrificed by lessening the duration of the 'sacred spring' to two months. In fact, since the astronomical calendar did not match the official calendar, the months of March and April that the *pontifex maximus* had appointed were in practice winter months,[201] during which the number of animals born was much smaller than during the spring. In Heurgon's opinion, Licinius Crassus was perfectly aware of this fact, and he appointed these two months to reduce the damage caused to Roman livestock. Thus, the period of time appointed for the *ver sacrum* officially corresponded to the spring, so that the validity of the ritual was ensured without running the risk of awakening the wrath of Jupiter as the final recipient, and at the same time it considerably reduced the resulting damage.[202]

Perhaps the detailed description of the animals to be sacrificed explains why the *ver sacrum* had to be repeated. It is possible that the consuls of the year 195 did not take sufficient care over the proper celebration of the ritual. But it is also possible, alternatively or complementarily, that there was not enough information on the exact livestock that had to be sacrificed. This uncertainty may have prevented the owners of the livestock from sacrificing their animals – it is reasonable to presume that they were reluctant to do so in view of their economic loss – and this would have resulted in the invalidation of the *ver sacrum*. The senatorial decree of 194 removed all doubts on the subject and facilitated the celebration of the *ver sacrum* and its supervision. Nevertheless, Livy does not provide any further information on its celebration in 194, and he simply indicates that it was conducted as well as the *ludi magni*.[203] Nor does he refer to the role that may have been played in the process by the consuls, who, like those of 195 – Cato fighting in Hispania

---

[199] Heurgon 1957: 46–9.   [200] Liv. 22.10.3. Cf. Briscoe 1981: 22.

[201] Briscoe 1981: 22: the dates appointed by the *senatus consultum* corresponded in the astronomical calendar to a period between 31 October or 22 November 195 and 1 or 23 January 194. On the mismatches between the civil calendar and the astronomical calendar at the beginning of the second century, see Mommsen 1859: 67 n. 94; Derow 1976.

[202] Radke 1980: 115–16 is sceptical about this explanation. Cf. Scheid 1998b: 422–3. Marchetti (1973: 495–6) suggests that the omission of the intercalary month from 203 may have been for the purpose of adapting the calendar to the celebration of the *ver sacrum*, in order to avoid economic hardship. But Briscoe (1981: 23) considers this very unlikely.

[203] Liv. 34.44.6.

and Valerius Flaccus fighting against the Gauls – spent most of their year of office fighting against the Boii and the Ligures. In any case, the *ver sacrum* celebrated in 194 seems to have been considered correct, because there are no further references to it or to any other 'sacred spring' in the following years and decades.

To summarize: among the civil functions that the consuls must or could carry out, religious tasks had enormous qualitative significance, not only from the point of view of the exercise of the magistracy but also as an important aspect of the Roman community. The consuls had to take public vows on the first day of their office, praying to the gods for the welfare of the community during their consular year. It was the consuls who had to perform the prescribed rites to expiate the prodigies reported in the previous months. The consuls also had to select the date for the celebration of the *feriae Latinae* as well as to preside over the festival at the Mons Albanus. No other magistrate could replace the consuls at such ceremonies. At the same time, no consul could leave Rome to take command over the army in his province without having properly completed all these rituals. The consuls may also have been responsible for the ceremony of the *clavus annalis*. Likewise, it is possible that, at least occasionally, the consuls presided over the ceremonies for the *sacra* of Lavinium in this Latin city itself. Besides this, the consuls had to preside *ex officio* over the games, although they could only preside over the games if the celebration took place while they were still in Rome. Exceptionally, in the only case in which sources mention the celebration of a *ver sacrum* in Rome, the consuls were responsible for ensuring that the ritual was properly performed. All of these tasks were obviously of a religious nature, although they should not be considered as sacerdotal tasks but as political functions, because the consuls, as the supreme magistrates, acted on behalf of the state with the ultimate purpose of preserving the *res publica*, thus adopting the role of guardians of the *pax deorum*.

CHAPTER 3

Consuls, the agents of diplomacy in the Roman state

In Republican Rome permanent diplomatic representation between states did not exist.[1] Relations were occasional and temporary, depending on changing political circumstances. As a result, there were no 'diplomats' in the modern sense, nor experts in diplomacy. In Rome, it was understood that anyone wanting a political career, and therefore any senator, ought to have a sufficient knowledge of external affairs and should have an understanding of treaties, alliances, and international law in general.[2]

The diplomatic relations of the Roman state were thus in the hands of the magistrates and the senate. In the list of civil functions assigned to consuls in Rome before they took command of their armies, Polybius alludes to the bringing of foreign embassies before the senate.[3] According to the Greek author, the senate was in charge of sending legates to non-Italic states as well as deciding on the response to be given to foreign ambassadors and the treatment they ought to receive in each particular case.[4] Consequently, it is clear that the senate had total control over diplomacy in the city of Rome and that only senators could receive embassies and appoint official legates,[5] but also that when dealing with representatives of other states, the consuls acted as the agents in the diplomatic process.

Indeed, ancient sources frequently refer to the consuls acting on behalf of the Roman state in negotiations with representatives of other states, both in Rome and during the wars in which they were involved. In a military campaign, the magistrate with *imperium* in command of the Roman army – whether a consul, a dictator, or a promagistrate – was the supreme entity representing Rome whom adversaries ought to address. In this context,

---

[1] In general, on diplomacy in Rome during the monarchic period and in the early Republic, see now Canali de Rossi 2005; 2007; Auliard 2006. In particular on foreign embassies in Rome, Mommsen 1864: esp. 343–54; 1887: III 2 1148–57; Willems 1883: II 485–90; Bonnefond-Coudry 1989: esp. 139–43; Linderski 1995; Canali de Rossi 1997; Coudry 2004. See also Zecchini 2006; Ferrary 2007. On the diplomatic relations between Rome and its Italian allies in the second century, Jehne 2009.
[2] Cf. Cic. *Leg.* 3.41.   [3] Polyb. 6.12.2.   [4] Polyb. 6.13.6–7.   [5] Auliard 2006: 20.

there are numerous mentions of embassies sent to consuls to put forward petitions, negotiate, or surrender.[6] Most of the legations received by consuls – and other magistrates with *imperium* – during war had the purpose of surrendering to Rome, asking for peace, or appealing for a treaty.[7]

Two cases illustrate the diplomatic prominence of consuls during a campaign. In 190 King Antiochus informed the praetor L. Aemilius Regillus, who was in command of the fleet in the Aegean Sea and had achieved a great victory at Myonnesus, of his intention to negotiate peace with him. The answer that Antiochus received was that peace could not be discussed without the presence of the consul.[8] In 182, two thousand Ligures presented themselves before the proconsul M. Claudius Marcellus in order to surrender. Marcellus consulted the senate on what procedure to follow. The senatorial answer was that the Ligures ought to be referred to the new consuls, who were to take the appropriate decisions.[9] When legates from the Ligures arrived in Rome the following year to ask for permanent peace, the senate ordered the praetor to answer that they ought to present themselves before the consuls and follow their orders. The senate would only accept that the request for peace was genuine once it was confirmed by the consuls.[10]

Away from the battlefield, ancient sources indicate clearly that, as Polybius claimed, when the consuls were in Rome they were always the persons in charge of introducing to the senate foreign ambassadors who wished to make a request, put forward a claim, or propose a pact with the Roman state. The first example of this given by Livy corresponds to the beginning of the war against the Samnites in 343. The Samnites had

---

[6] Polyb. 1.16.5 (year 263): Hiero of Syracuse sent ambassadors to the consuls to sign a peace treaty, which was signed and sent to Rome for ratification; Polyb. 2.34.1 (222): the Gauls sent legates to the new consuls to ask for peace, and they refused; Liv. 23.5.1 (216): Campanian citizens visited the consul in Venusia; Liv. 24.31.7 (214): the praetors of Syracuse sent a letter to the consul Marcellus; Liv. 25.13.8 (212): the inhabitants of Beneventum sent ten legates to the consuls in their camp in Bovianum; Liv. 31.2.11 (201): the consul P. Aelius Paetus signed a treaty with the Ligures Ingauni; Liv. 32.10.2 (198): the consul Flamininus met Philip in Macedonia to negotiate peace; Liv. 32.19.5 (198): the consul Flamininus sent legates to the Achaeans to make them abandon their support for the king; Liv. 34.11 (195): ambassadors of the Ilergetes went to Cato in his camp near Emporiae; Liv. 36.27.2–3 (191): the Aetolians sent ambassadors to ask the consul Acilius for peace, and he granted them an armistice; Liv. 37.7.6–7 (190): the consul L. Cornelius Scipio gave a truce to the Aetolians, who had sent ambassadors; Liv. 37.44.7–45.1 (190): the citizens of Sardis and other cities sent legates to the consul in order to surrender; Liv. 37.45.19 (190): the consul L. Scipio authorized ambassadors to be sent to Rome; Liv. 38.8–9 (189): Aetolian, Athenian, and Rhodian legates visited the consul Fulvius Nobilior to negotiate peace; Liv. 38.25.1; 38.27.8 (189): in Asia, legates of the Tectosagi and of the Gauls went to the consul Cn. Manlius Vulso to ask for peace. On the decision-making process in foreign relations and the collaboration or competition between senate and commanders in the field see Eckstein 1987.

[7] Auliard 2006: 269–72: fifty per cent of the embassies received by magistrates during a war in the fourth century were surrenders.

[8] Liv. 37.19.2–3.   [9] Liv. 40.16.5–6. Cf. Briscoe 2008: 453.   [10] Liv. 40.34.10–11.

attacked the Campanians, who were forced to appeal to Rome for help. The senate agreed to hold a hearing at which the Campanian ambassadors delivered a speech.[11] On this occasion, Livy does not expressly state that the consuls came with the legates to the Curia and introduced them to the senators, but from the following context their leading role can be deduced. As was to be expected, the Campanian ambassadors requested an alliance with Rome and its help in the war against the Samnites. After the legates had left the Curia, the senate held a debate on what decision to take, undoubtedly in the presence of both consuls. Once the senators had made a resolution, one of the consuls communicated the answer to the Campanian legates, who were waiting outside the senate house.[12]

Having learnt that the senate was not prepared to use force of arms against the Samnites, the leader of the Campanians answered that the city of Capua offered to surrender to Rome (*deditio in dicionem*), so that Rome might defend it as its own. Apparently, the speech of the legate was addressed to the senators.[13] However, from the rest of the account it can be deduced that this episode did not take place inside the Curia but in the vestibule, and that not all the senators were present, but both consuls were, before whom the ambassadors prostrated themselves holding out their imploring hands, as well perhaps as a group of senators.[14] The Campanians' offer must have been transmitted immediately by the consuls to the senators inside the Curia. They resumed deliberations and decided to send legates to the Samnites in order to demand that they refrain from attacking the Campanians, whose territory already belonged to Rome by virtue of a *deditio*. The aggressive response of the Samnites caused the declaration of war. All these events took place at the beginning of the consular year of M. Valerius Corvus and A. Cornelius Cossus Arvina, which is why they were both still in Rome.

Livy's account provides a prime example of the procedure that was commonly used in cases where ambassadors from a foreign state went to Rome to engage in negotiations.[15] If the consuls were in the *Urbs*, they were responsible for managing the diplomatic process. They had to identify the ambassadors by inspecting the official presentation documents issued by their states of origin, inquire into the reason for their presence in Rome, bring the legates to the senate, be present at the Curia during their speeches,

---

[11] Liv. 7.30.1.   [12] Liv. 7.31.1.

[13] Liv. 7.31.4: 'itaque populum Campanum urbemque Capuam, agros, delubra deum, divina humanaque omnia in vestram, patres conscripti, populique Romani dicionem dedimus ...'

[14] Liv. 7.31.5.   [15] Coudry 2004: 530–8.

attend the senatorial debate – undoubtedly taking an active part in it – and finally act as spokesmen for the senate's final decision before the ambassadors. There is no doubt that the decisions were taken by the senators, since they were responsible for Rome's foreign policy, but it is also clear that the consuls, as the supreme magistrates, were in charge of handling the diplomatic process in their role as intermediaries between the Roman state and other communities.

This pattern was subsequently repeated on numerous occasions, as reported by Livy. In 219, Saguntum sent legates to Rome to appeal for military help. Once the legates were in the city, the consuls brought them to the senate to explain their request.[16] The senators decided to send legates to Hispania to investigate the facts reported by the Saguntines. The news then arrived that the siege of Saguntum by Hannibal had already started. The question was resumed, and it was finally decided that, nevertheless, legates should be sent to Hispania. Although the consuls are only mentioned in relation to their introduction of the Saguntine ambassadors before the senate, it ought to be presumed that they were present at the various debates and that they took part in the decision-making process. Livy attributes this episode to the consuls of 218, Scipio and Sempronius Longus, but he is aware that this poses serious chronological problems,[17] since, if the siege of Saguntum lasted seven months, it must have begun in 219 and not in 218, therefore with different consuls. In any event, the arrival of the Saguntine legates must have taken place at the beginning of the consular year, which would explain why the consuls, either those of the year 219 or those of 218, were in Rome. It is possible that the chronological mismatch apparent in Livy's text is somehow connected with the change in the calendar that made the consuls take office earlier than in the past, on the Ides of March, a change that Beck has recently placed within the context of the events that led to the beginning of the Hannibalic war.[18]

In 210, the consul M. Valerius Laevinus played a decisive part in the conflict between the Campanians and the Syracusans. Laevinus, who had been in Greece in the years before 210, had been elected consul in his absence. Illness delayed him on his way to Rome, and for this reason he entered office later than his colleague Marcellus.[19] On his journey to Rome, Laevinus ordered the Campanians to accompany him in order to have their requests dealt with in the senate. A group of Sicilians also arrived in Rome with him.[20] Following the most common course of events, the senate's

---

[16] Liv. 21.6.3. [17] Liv. 21.15.3–4. [18] Beck 2005: 409–11. [19] Liv. 26.26.5–9.
[20] Liv. 26.27.15–17.

annual debate on the *res publica* took place first, in which Laevinus
explained the situation that he had left in Greece, and the question of the
division of provinces between the consuls was also discussed.[21] Command
of Sicily was given to Marcellus and Italy to Laevinus, but the allocation
was changed in view of the complaints expressed by Sicilians against
Marcellus.[22]

Only then were the Sicilian ambassadors received by the senate, where
they delivered a speech.[23] The consul Laevinus then ordered them to leave
the senate chamber in order for the senators to deliberate.[24] But the other
consul, Marcellus, requested that they be allowed to stay to listen to his
speech defending himself against the accusations levelled by the Syracusans.
The legates went back into the Curia and Marcellus made his plea.[25] When
he had finished his speech, both the consul and the legates left the Curia.[26]
The consul Laevinus was then in charge of chairing the debate in the senate
on the petitions made by the Sicilians.[27] Once the senators had made a
decision, both Marcellus and the ambassadors went back into the Curia to
listen to the reading of the *senatus consultum*, and the Sicilian issue was thus
considered settled.[28] The question of the Campanians was then dealt with,
following a similar process to that just described: the introduction of the
Campanians to the senate, a speech by the legates before the senators, the
exit of the Campanians, the deliberation of the senators, and the communication of the decision taken.[29] Both consuls must have been present
during the entire process, although Livy does not explicitly mention this.
As in previous instances, these episodes took place at the beginning of the
consular year, at the time when both consuls were in Rome after Laevinus'
delayed entry into office.

In 209, also at the beginning of the consular year before the consuls left
Rome to go to their provinces, a serious problem arose in connection with
recruitment in twelve Latin colonies, which refused to provide soldiers and
money to continue the war against the Carthaginians. In the sequel, the
consuls Q. Fabius Maximus and Q. Fulvius Flaccus at all times played
leading roles in the attempt to resolve the problem through diplomacy. In
fact, the ambassadors of the twelve colonies addressed the consuls in Rome
to inform them of their decision.[30] The consuls strove to change the legates'
minds with threats and by trying to convince them that their position
amounted to treason against the Roman people. For days, Livy claims,

---

[21] Liv. 26.28–9.   [22] Rosenstein 1995: 54; Beck 2005: 317–19; Vervaet 2006: 628.
[23] Liv. 26.30.1–10.   [24] Liv. 26.30.11.   [25] Liv. 26.31.1.   [26] Liv. 26.31.11.   [27] Liv. 26.32.1.
[28] Liv. 26.32.7.   [29] Liv. 26.33–4.   [30] Liv. 27.9.7.

both consuls alternated in giving speeches before the ambassadors, who would not give in.[31] Only at this point did the consuls take the question to the senate.[32] Once again, the consuls played the leading role in the debate that took place, encouraging and reassuring the senate and affirming that the rest of the colonies would honour their pacts.[33] In fact, the senate left the solution in the hands of the consuls.[34] The consuls then summoned the legates of the other colonies, who showed complete willingness to provide the soldiers that were demanded according to their pacts. So that they might be honoured by the senate for their goodwill, the consuls took them to the Curia and later at the order of the senators before the people.[35] By contrast, the senate decided to punish the traitor colonies with silence, and their legates were neither summoned nor bidden farewell by the consuls; they were simply ignored.[36]

The question was resumed five years later, at the beginning of the consular year 204/3. The contempt towards the Latin colonies that had refused to provide soldiers and money meant that they were excluded from their military obligations during those years. In 204 some senators considered that this grievance should not apply to those colonies that had fulfilled their obligations.[37] The senate ordered the consuls to summon to Rome magistrates and legates from all the recalcitrant colonies before dealing with any other issue.[38] Once in the city, the consuls, following senatorial decisions, demanded as compensation both an extraordinary recruitment of soldiers and an annual tax. According to Livy, the representatives of the colonies refused to accept these conditions, professing that they did not have the means to comply with Roman demands, and repeatedly requested to be allowed to speak to the senate. From this account it appears that they expected to sway the senators, although the consuls had appeared to be inflexible.[39] Finally, the colonies yielded, and the levy was carried out without further problems. In this case, the consuls were leading players throughout the entire negotiation process, although they obviously always acted on behalf of the senate, adhering strictly to its instructions.

In the final years of the Second Punic War, the problems caused by the continuous recruitment of a great number of men for over a decade were felt again. In 207, the consuls declared exceptionally that the so-called *coloniae maritimae*, colonies settled on coasts which had traditionally been exempt from the military service, should provide soldiers.[40] Since the colonies refused to comply with this demand, the consuls summoned their representatives on

---

[31] Liv. 27.9.13.   [32] Liv. 27.9.14.   [33] Liv. 27.10.1.   [34] Liv. 27.10.2.   [35] Liv. 27.10.5–6.
[36] Liv. 27.10.10.   [37] Liv. 29.15.   [38] Liv. 29.15.5.   [39] Liv. 29.15.14.   [40] Liv. 27.38.3–5.

a specific day to speak to the senate. The legates read the decrees of exemption before the senators but, given the circumstances of war, the exemption was upheld only for Antium and Ostia. This episode obviously happened at the beginning of the consular year, in the context of the recruitment, before both consuls set off for their provinces.

In 201 there was a debate on who ought to lead the negotiations with the Carthaginian state to reach a peace treaty after the victory of Scipio at Zama, which to all intents and purposes meant the end of the war. Carthaginian legates went to Rome at the beginning of 201 to participate in the negotiations. Their arrival coincided with the arrival of the ambassadors of King Philip of Macedonia, and they all requested a hearing before the senate. The answer given by the dictator C. Servilius, following orders from the senate, was that they had to wait until the new consuls were elected and that the consuls would grant them a hearing once they had taken office.[41] This procedure was repeated in other cases, and it confirms that, on the one hand, it was usually the consuls who had to deal with diplomacy and, on the other hand, if the consular year was about to end, it was preferable to wait until the new consuls took over their consulship so that any possible previous agreement would not bias their behaviour. The new consuls had their whole year of office ahead of them, which made it easier for them to take more considered decisions, and the decision that was finally taken could also have an influence on the distribution of the consular provinces, depending on whether or not there was an ongoing war and where it was.

The elections did eventually take place, and it was decided to postpone the assignment of provinces to the new consuls until the Carthaginian and Macedonian legates were heard. The consul Cn. Cornelius Lentulus wished to take command of Africa as the successor of Scipio in order to gain the glory of being the final victor over Carthage, but he failed to accomplish his aim, since Scipio's *imperium* was prorogued. The question of whether the Roman people wished to continue the war or to sign a peace agreement with the Carthaginians was connected with this incident. If peace was the desired option, the senators ordered that the tribunes of the plebs ask the people whether peace ought to be negotiated by one of the consuls or by the proconsul Scipio.[42] From the context as narrated by Livy it is understood that the normal course of events would have been that one of the new consuls would lead the diplomatic process. But, as in many other cases, Roman constitutional processes proved to be flexible. Scipio was the great victor of the Hannibalic War, and therefore he deserved the honour of going down

---

[41] Liv. 30.40.4. Cf. Canali de Rossi 1997: 429–30.   [42] Liv. 30.40.14.

in history as the *triumphator* if the conflict was to continue, but also as the negotiator of peace with Carthage if such was the people's decision.

Once this decision was taken, the Macedonian and Carthaginian ambassadors were received by the senate.[43] Livy does not state which magistrate was in charge of bringing them before the senators, but the presence of both consuls in Rome allows no doubt that they presided over the sessions in the senate when the legates spoke. The Macedonians spoke first, and the answer they received from the senators clearly announced the beginning of a new war. The Carthaginians were then received. Their conciliatory speech made the senators incline towards negotiating peace with Carthage, but the consul Lentulus vetoed a *senatus consultum* in this sense. This caused two tribunes of the plebs to ask the people if they wished the senate to issue a *senatus consultum* in favour of peace, and in that case, who ought to negotiate it. The people voted in favour of peace and for Scipio to be the negotiator. The senate acted accordingly and ordered Scipio, along with the usual ten legates, to negotiate a peace agreement with Carthage under whatever terms he considered appropriate.[44] It was only then that the Carthaginian ambassadors returned to their own city. The negotiations were successfully completed, during which Scipio acted as a plenipotentiary. But once an agreement was reached, the proconsul asked the Carthaginians to send ambassadors to Rome in order for it to be confirmed by the senate and the people ('patrum auctoritate populique iussu').[45]

Once the armed conflict against Carthage was over, the war against Philip of Macedonia started immediately. Some time during the year 201 ambassadors from Pergamum and Rhodes arrived in Rome to report aggression suffered at the hands of the Macedonian king.[46] The senators responded by showing their concern about the situation in Asia. But the question of whether a war against Macedonia ought to be started was not dealt with by the senators at this stage; it was referred to the consuls, who were at the time in their respective provinces.[47] The senatorial decision again illustrates consular primacy in the diplomatic field.

Since the question would not be dealt with until the consuls returned to the *Urbs*, the senate decided to send three legates to inform King Ptolemy of Egypt of the defeat of Carthage and to thank him for his loyalty.[48] Although this was the official purpose of their mission, it is probable that it also contained the order to gather first-hand information about what was happening in the eastern Mediterranean region with a view to the imminent

---

[43] Liv. 30.42.   [44] Liv. 30.43.4.   [45] Liv. 30.44.13.   [46] Canali de Rossi 1997: 192–4.
[47] Liv. 31.2.2.   [48] Liv. 31.2.3–4; 31.18.1. Cf. Polyb. 16.27.

outbreak of war.[49] By the end of the consular year, therefore in 200, the consul P. Aelius Paetus returned to Rome to carry out the elections. It was then that the question of Macedonia was openly discussed, in the first session held by the senate after his return.[50] At this stage the senate did not yet resolve to declare war against the Macedonian king, but a legate was sent to monitor the area and to report in writing to the consuls and senators.[51] The declaration of war had to wait until the new consuls had taken office on the Ides of March. After successfully completing the propitiatory sacrifices and drawing lots for their provinces, the consul who was allotted Macedonia, P. Sulpicius Galba, presented a motion to the *comitia centuriata* to declare war against Philip, and in the second session the motion was finally approved.[52] By decree of the senate the consuls ordered three days of supplications, and Sulpicius asked the priests representing Rome in diplomatic dealings, the Fetiales, about the most appropriate way to declare war on the Macedonian king. When they answered that any method would be suitable, the senate authorized the consul to choose the person he deemed appropriate, provided it was not a senator, to proceed with the declaration of war.

Diplomatic questions could also be used in internal political struggles. In 187 the arrival of a foreign embassy at the beginning of the consular year was used by one of the consuls to politically discredit an adversary. The consul M. Aemilius Lepidus brought to the senate the legates from Ambracia, who wished to report the abuses inflicted by the proconsul M. Fulvius Nobilior.[53] He did so to foment hatred against the *triumphator* in Greece even before he returned to Rome. According to Livy, Aemilius alone introduced the ambassadors to the senators instead of both consuls, as was the common practice. In fact, the other consul, C. Flaminius, gave his support to the absent Fulvius during the debate that followed the legates' report. The dispute between the consuls in the senate went on for two days until Flaminius's timely illness allowed Aemilius to put forward a motion in favour of the Ambracians which was approved by the senate.[54]

From all the instances seen so far it can be deduced that it was at the beginning of the consular year that the senate usually received embassies from other states, so as to coincide with the presence of the new consuls in Rome. As we have already seen, when consuls took office, they had to deal with a series of civil functions that were repeated every year. Diplomatic matters constituted a part of these functions.

---

[49] Broughton 1951–86: I 322–3. McDonald and Walbank 1937: 189–90.   [50] Liv. 31.3.1.
[51] Liv. 31.3.6.   [52] Liv. 31.6–8.   [53] Liv. 38.43.1. Cf. Canali de Rossi 1997: 41–2.   [54] Liv. 38.44.3–4.

When dealing with the events of 182, Livy begins with the three main issues that were part of the activities of consuls and senators at the beginning of each consular year, in an order that could vary depending on the greater or lesser degree of urgency given to each of them. Livy refers successively to the allocation of the provinces and the number of soldiers assigned to each of the active fronts of war, the prodigies that had been reported and their expiation, and the reception of foreign embassies. During the decade of the eighties in the second century, Rome's increasing involvement in the internal affairs of the Hellenistic states resulted in a growing presence every year of legates from these territories in the *Urbs*.[55] In particular, in the year 182 embassies sent by Eumenes, Pharnaces and Rhodes were received in the senate, as well as ambassadors from Philip, the Achaeans and the Lacedemonians.[56] They were all in Rome simultaneously at the beginning of the consular year.[57] The Bobbio scholiast provides a valuable text that illustrates the manner in which the embassies were received by the senate.[58] When several legations were in Rome at the same time, the consuls had to establish in what order they ought to be heard by the senators. In general, the most influential and powerful were given priority, although the scholiast also claims that occasionally bribes received by the magistrates decided the order. The *lex de provinciis praetoriis* of the year 100 – or 99 according to Giovannini[59] – indirectly confirms that there was in fact an established order whereby foreign ambassadors were received by the senate and that this order was directly determined by the consuls. In one of its sections, the law

---

[55] In his account of the most relevant events that took place during the consulship of P. Claudius Pulcher and L. Porcius Licinus in 184/3, Livy alludes in the first place, before dealing with any other matter, to the Roman embassy to Greece (Liv. 39.33–5). This embassy was the consequence of a previous embassy sent to Rome by Kings Philip and Eumenes and by the cities of Thessaly (Polyb. 22.11.2–4). All these legates were brought by the consuls – undoubtedly immediately after taking office – to the senate, where they defended their positions before the senators took the decision to send a new legation (Liv. 39.33.1–2). The Achaean ambassadors were also received (Polyb. 22.11.5). The year 183 was exceptional, according to Livy, because of the great number of embassies from the eastern Mediterranean that went to Rome to be received by the senate (Liv. 39.46.6–9). They were *civitates* and *gentes* from Macedonia who wanted to complain about the actions of King Philip, as well as an embassy of King Eumenes, led by Athenaeus, the brother of the monarch. All these embassies were brought to the senate by the consuls before going to their provinces, therefore during the first few weeks of their consulship (Liv. 39.46.6: 'priusquam consules in provincias proficiscerentur, legationes transmarinas in senatum introduxerunt'). Cf. Briscoe 2008: 375.

[56] Liv. 40.2.5–8. Cf. Polyb. 23.9. See Briscoe 2008: 416.   [57] Canali de Rossi 1997: 469–70.

[58] Schol. Bob. ad Cic. *Planc.* 33. (p. 158 St.): 'legationes ab externis populis missae ad senatum solebant ordinari pro voluntate consulum, quae plerumque gratia, nonnumquam et accepta pecunia consules ordinabant, ut introduci ad senatum possent.' Cf. Coudry 2004: 535.

[59] On the contents of the law and its probable dating to February 100, see Ferrary 1977. Cf. Hassal, Crawford, and Reynolds 1974; Crawford 1996: 231–70. Recently Giovannini (2008: 93–100) has argued that the law should be dated to the beginning of 99. Cf. Giovannini and Grzybek 1978.

dictated that the relevant consul had to make sure that any Rhodian embassy arriving in Rome in future was received by the senate outside the normal order (*extra ordinem*).[60] This was a privilege for the Rhodians – attested for the first time –, given their especially friendly relations with Rome, and it involved giving priority to its ambassadors so that they could gain access to the senate ahead of any other envoys who might have arrived in the *Urbs* before them.[61]

The course of events described by Livy for the beginning of the consular year 182/1 may have been the norm. But the Roman state always adapted to the circumstances and urgency of each case, so, as we have already seen, the gravity of reported prodigies may make their expiation a priority. Likewise, on some occasions, diplomatic affairs had precedence, and it could be considered crucial to receive foreign embassies in the senate immediately after the consuls took office.

According to Livy, in 198 the senate dealt with the allocation of provinces in its first meeting at the Capitol after the consuls took office.[62] After drawing lots for the provinces and determining the number of soldiers that ought to be recruited, both consuls brought to the senate a legation sent by King Attalus to complain about the aggression that his kingdom had suffered at the hands of Antiochus.[63] As was usual in these circumstances, the official response of the senate to the ambassadors from Pergamum must have been transmitted by the consuls.[64]

Legates from the tyrant Nabis arrived in Rome in 194 to request the ratification of the treaty that Sparta had signed with Flamininus. The hearing by the senate took place in the temple of Apollo at the beginning of the consular year, just after the new consuls took office, even before the distribution of provinces was discussed.[65] In fact, Livy places the ratification of the treaty as the first political action of the consular year. Consequently, it is clear that in this case the consuls, being present in Rome, must have brought the legates before the senate and later communicated to them the senators' response.

Livy does not provide precise details on the specific time in the year 177 when the foreign embassies were received in the senate. The new consuls took office on the Ides of March. In the customary senate session held on that

---

[60] Crawford 1996: 254 and 263. Cf. Bonnefond 1984: 67–72. See the remarks of Jehne 2009: 157–8.

[61] Ferrary 2009: 140: 'the privilege that is granted to them [the Rhodians] by the law raises the question whether they did not play an important part in the Roman decision to place a magistrate in charge of the fight against piracy again'.

[62] Liv. 32.8.1.   [63] Liv. 32.8.9. Cf. Canali de Rossi 1997: 434–5.   [64] Liv. 32.8.12.

[65] Liv. 34.43.1–2. It is the only instance where the temple of Apollo is mentioned as the place for hearing foreign ambassadors. Cf. Briscoe 1981: 116; Canali de Rossi 1997: 21–2.

day, when the state of the *res publica* was reported and debated, the situation in Sardinia and Histria was dealt with only briefly. The following day the legates from Sardinia were brought to the senate; they had been in Rome for some time but had been told that they would be received only when the new consuls had taken office.[66] The same day, L. Minucius Thermus was also received; he was legate of the consul A. Manlius Vulso in Histria. Ambassadors of the Latin cities also spoke before the senators, complaining about the growing emigration of their citizens to Rome, which was leaving their cities deserted. Once they were all heard, the senate took measures to stop Latin emigration and decided that Sardinia and Histria would be assigned as provinces to the consuls. The need to hear the legates before taking fundamental decisions, such as the yearly allocation of provinces and troops to the magistrates, made the senate give priority to diplomacy in 177.

Since, in general, the consuls spent most of the year away from the *Urbs*, there could be occasions on which they were not in Rome when a foreign embassy arrived. In this case, as we have already seen, the senate sometimes opted to postpone the hearing until the new consuls took office, thus showing a preference for dealing with diplomatic questions at the beginning of the consular year.

This is what happened in the case of the Aetolian legates in the year 190. During the military campaign in Greece, the Aetolians had, following the recommendation of Flamininus, obtained from the consul Acilius Glabrio an armistice which was to last until the outcome of an embassy sent to Rome to negotiate with the senate was known.[67] The Aetolian legates must have arrived in the *Urbs* well into the consular year, in the first months of 190. In any event, when the new consuls of that year took office on 15 March, the Aetolian embassy was in the city and exerted pressure for the question to be addressed as soon as possible, since the agreed period for the armistice was about to elapse.[68] Obviously, the senate had waited until the beginning of the new consular year to confront the Aetolian issue, which then became a priority. Senators debated this question for days once the new consuls had fulfilled their compulsory religious duties – taking the auspices– and even before dealing with the allocation of provinces. Given the failure to reach an agreement, the senate ordered the ambassadors to leave Rome that very day, and to leave Italy within a maximum period of fifteen days.[69]

---

[66] Liv. 41.8.5–6.   [67] Liv. 36.35.1–6.

[68] Liv. 37.1.1. Cf. Polyb. 21.2.3–6. Cf. Briscoe 1981: 289–90; Canali de Rossi 1997: 27–8.

[69] Liv. 37.1.6. It is not the only case in which foreign ambassadors were ordered by the senate to leave Rome and Italy within a given period of time: Liv. 37.49.7–8; Polyb. 29.6.3–4; 31.20.3; 33.11.5; App. *Hann.* 31; Cass. Dio fr.99.2; Sal. *Jug.* 28.2. Cf. Coudry 2004: 544–5. In that same year, 190, also

This also happened at the end of the consular year 209/8 when the arrival of legates from Tarentum, who went to Rome to ask for peace, coincided with the holding of the elections presided over by the consul Fulvius Flaccus, which was therefore already well into 208.[70] The senate asked them to return to deal with the question when the consul Fabius Maximus, who had conquered Tarentum, was in the city. The debate on this question did take place once Fabius had returned to Rome, and he played an active part in it.[71] But by then Fabius was neither a consul nor did he hold any magistracy. Livy refers to this debate after the new consuls had taken office and after mentioning the expiation of prodigies. In this particular case, therefore, it was not the need for a consul to be present at the senate meeting that caused the postponement of the debate, but the fact that it was considered appropriate that the person who had taken Tarentum should express his opinion. Nevertheless, the debate must have also been attended by the consuls of 208, Marcellus and T. Quinctius Crispinus, since they had both been delayed in Rome because of their religious duties, and Livy mentions their departure from the city only once a decision was reached on the question of Tarentum.

In 172, Rhodian legates arrived in the *Urbs* to attempt to respond to accusations made against Rhodes. The senate informed them that they had to wait for the new consuls in order to be received.[72] Livy places these events before the consular elections, which were held on 18 February.[73] Consequently, the Rhodian ambassadors must have stayed in Rome for at least a month before they were received by the senate. Although it is likely that the hearing was held, Livy does not mention it.

In contrast, on other occasions circumstances made it advisable for the legates to be received immediately, without waiting for the new consuls to take office. In those cases, as in other areas of civil affairs, the natural substitute for the absent consuls was the urban praetor. He took the role, usually played by consuls, of mediation between the senate and the ambassadors.

We know of some cases in which the urban praetor is specifically mentioned in relation to this function.[74] This was the case in 341, when during his military campaign, Samnite legates addressed a request for peace to the consul L. Aemilius Mamercus.[75] The consul referred them to the senate in Rome.[76]

---

before the consuls set off for their provinces, legates of Ptolemy and Cleopatra arrived in the city to congratulate the Roman state because Acilius had expelled Antiochus from Greece and to urge the senate to send soldiers to Asia (Liv. 37.3.9–11).

[70] Liv. 27.21.8.   [71] Liv. 27.25.1–5.   [72] Liv. 42.26.9. Cf. Canali de Rossi 1997: 219.

[73] Liv. 42.28.4.

[74] Brennan 2000: 115: 'In these Senate sessions, the *praetor urbanus* was responsible for introducing . . . embassies from (exclusively) friendly or allied communities or peoples.'

[75] Broughton 1951–86: I 134: Mamercinus.   [76] Liv. 8.1.7.

According to Livy, the ambassadors explained their position to the urban praetor T. Aemilius, who then communicated this to the senators, who decided to renew the peace agreement. The senatorial answer was delivered to the Samnites by the same praetor.[77] In 293, both consuls were engaged in the fighting in Samnium, where they had just achieved an important victory. At the same time, the Etruscans rebelled against Rome, causing damage to the territories of some of the Roman allies. As a result, embassies from the allied states arrived in the *Urbs* to complain about what had happened and to ask the Roman state for military help. The praetor M. Atilius immediately brought the ambassadors to the senate, and the senators dealt with the issue, with ensuing declaration of war against the Faliscans.[78] It was unquestionably the proximity of the Etruscan danger to Rome itself, and the fact that the Roman army was momentarily winning on the Samnite front, that made the senate decide not to wait for the consuls to deal with the question but to take the appropriate decision themselves.[79]

However, there are two cases reported by Livy where a peregrine praetor is mentioned. In 183, thousands of Transalpine Gauls had attempted to settle near Aquileia.[80] The consul M. Claudius Marcellus was sent by the senate to prevent the settlement. On the consul's arrival the Gauls surrendered but sent legates to Rome to complain and explain their situation.[81] The Gallic envoys were introduced to the senate by the peregrine praetor, C. Valerius Flaccus,[82] who was also *flamen Dialis* and was therefore obliged to remain in Rome.[83] As we have previously seen, in 181 Ligurian legates went to Rome to ask for peace. The senate told them that they must speak with the consuls for them to certify that their attitude had really changed and that only in that case would a permanent peace treaty be signed. The answer from the senate was reported to the ambassadors by the praetor Q. Fabius Maximus.[84] Fabius held the office of peregrine praetor, as stated

---

[77] Liv. 8.2.1–3.   [78] Liv. 10.45.4.

[79] There are other examples of the urban praetor playing a leading role. In 203 ambassadors of Masinissa and from Saguntum were brought to the senate by the urban praetor P. Aelius Paetus (Liv. 30.17.7; 21.3–5). In 193 the praetor C. Scribonius introduced legates of Antiochus, who was seeking friendship with Rome (Liv. 34.57.2–3). In the year 190, the urban praetor L. Aurunculeius brought to the senate the legates of Placentia and Cremona, who complained about the scarcity of men in both colonies (Liv. 37.46.9). The senate immediately resolved that six thousand families be distributed amongst the two colonies. One year later, in 189, both King Eumenes, Rhodian ambassadors, ambassadors of Antiochus, and other embassies from Asia were heard successively in the senate. They were all brought by the urban praetor (Liv. 37.52–55). Cf. Ferrary 2007:114; Jehne 2009: 155–6.

[80] Liv. 39.45.3.   [81] Liv. 39.54.1–4. Briscoe 2008: 403–4.   [82] Liv. 39.54.5.

[83] Liv. 39.45.4.   [84] Liv. 40.34.10.

by Livy.[85] As in the aforementioned case there is no reason to believe that the urban praetor was away from the city.[86]

Livy gives no explanation for the quite exceptional fact that, on both occasions, the peregrine praetor and not the urban praetor acted as the intermediary between the senate and the foreign legates. Brennan points out that in both cases a defeated people was asking for special treatment from the Romans. In his opinion the peregrine praetor might sometimes be sent to hear the claims of legates of peoples who did not have Roman friendship (*amicitia*), which might explain his role in introducing such embassies instead of the urban praetor.[87] Brennan's statement may be accurate, but the information available in the ancient sources is too scarce to determine whether there were any fixed rules. There may be other explanations for these two exceptions, but the causes remain unclear. In 181 the urban praetor was Q. Petilius Spurinus, who was very active during his term of office, firstly in the recruitment of emergency troops with Fabius, and later in examining and finally ordering the supposed books of Numa to be burnt.[88] Perhaps the decision on the books of Numa preoccupied the attention and time of Petilius to such an extent that the senate discharged him temporarily from other tasks, such as diplomatic affairs, which would normally have fallen under his remit in the absence of the consuls.

Occasionally, epigraphy also illustrates how the debate took place and how decisions regarding a foreign embassy arriving in Rome were taken by the senate. An example is the so-called *senatus consultum de agro Pergameno*, probably dating to 129.[89] The document alludes to the controversy which had arisen between Pergamum and the publicans regarding the boundaries of the Pergamene territory and the levy of taxes. Pergamum sent envoys to Rome to set out their arguments before the senate, which were undoubtedly contested by the publicans. The final outcome was the decree included in the inscription. The first part contains the *senatus consultum*. It acknowledges the ambassadors as allies of Rome and orders a Roman magistrate to conduct an investigation on the controversial issue (lines 7–8). Later on the *senatus consultum* makes it clear that the decision taken after the investigation was carried out must be communicated to the senate, either by the consuls or through the urban praetor (ll. 10–12). The name or position of the magistrate

---

[85] Liv. 40.18.3. Cf. Broughton 1951–86: I 384.

[86] Briscoe 2008: 495: 'There is no need to assume, as Walsh does, that the *praetor urbanus* was not available.'

[87] Brennan 2000: 115–16.   [88] Liv. 40.26.7; 40.29.9–14. Cf. Brennan 2000: 123; Briscoe 2008: 480–5.

[89] *IGRR* IV 262. Sherk 1969: 63–73; 1984: 47–8. Mattingly (1972) points out that Manius Aquillius was the consul of 101 and dates the document to that year. Sherk (1969: 68) dates the decree to 129.

who was to conduct the investigation along with an advisory council (*consilium*) is not preserved. It could have been the urban praetor, who undoubtedly had the ability to carry out this task as the natural substitute for the consuls. However, bearing in mind that the reception of foreign ambassadors usually took place at the beginning of the consular year, when the consuls were in Rome, and that the consuls of 129 are specifically mentioned in the document as being directly in charge of accommodating the envoys, it is more likely that one of the consuls was appointed by the senate to conduct the investigation.

Another interesting epigraphic document, dating from the year 112, is the so-called *epistula L. Calpurni Pisonis et senatus consultum de Itanorum et Hierapytniorum litibus*, which clearly demonstrates the prominence of the consul in resolving conflicts referred to the senate by cities or foreign states.[90] It alludes to a dispute between two Cretan cities over the illegal construction of buildings on land whose ownership was disputed. It was an ancient quarrel, since back in 140 the Roman senate had appointed the city of Magnesia as an arbitrator in the dispute. However, the conflict had recently intensified, causing an armed confrontation between the cities. Rome was resolved to settle the dispute once and for all. For this purpose, the senate decreed that one of the consuls of 112, L. Calpurnius Piso, ought to be in charge of appointing an arbitration tribunal to examine the case and come to a decision. The consul was also to see to the destruction of all the buildings which had been built on the land of the sanctuary of Zeus Dictaeus. The Magnesians were appointed for the second time as arbitrators. They were given one year to make a decision, which must therefore have been communicated to the Roman senate in 111. The preserved inscription refers exclusively to the events occurring in 112 when Calpurnius Piso was consul. It contains a speech delivered by the envoys of Hierapytnia in the senate (ll. 1–55); the subsequent senatorial decree including the tasks which were to be carried out by the consul Piso (ll. 55–74); the decree of the consul authorizing Magnesia to create an arbitration tribunal (ll. 75–88); and finally a letter from the consul to the Hierapytnians ordering them to destroy the buildings which had been built on the disputed land (ll. 89–97).

The solution to the question, as can be deduced from the epigraphic document, followed the usual procedure repeatedly narrated by Livy: the introduction of foreign legates to the senate by a consul or the consuls; a debate in the senate under the presidency of a consul; a senatorial decision in the form of a *senatus consultum* which contained either a final decision or the instructions necessary for reaching one; the charge to the consul to

---

[90] Sherk 1969: 78–85.

execute the senatorial decision and act as the intermediary between the senate and the foreign community or communities which had sought the arbitration of Rome; and the charge to the consul to see to the correct filing of the question and the accommodation of the foreign envoys in accordance with their status.

Likewise, the *lex de provinciis praetoriis* of the year 100 set forth that the consul first elected (*consul prior factus*) ought to write and send to the Hellenistic kings letters whereby they were informed of the main resolutions included in the law, in particular the decision to fight piracy vigorously in the Mediterranean.[91] As pointed out by Ferrary, this was a political decision, since the consul first elected for the year 100 was Marius. The fact that Marius had to act as intermediary between the senate of Rome and the rulers of the Hellenistic states afforded him special importance.[92] In any case, this task was left, as was usual, in the hands of a consul.

Livy and some epigraphical sources provide valuable information regarding the way in which foreign ambassadors were accommodated during their stay in Rome, as well as the procedure followed when they were received by the consuls and the senate. As is shown by the aforementioned *senatus consultum de agro Pergameno* (ll. 17–19), the senate left the consul Manius Aquillius in charge of providing the appropriate accommodation for the Pergamene envoys, according to their status as friends of Rome. Following his orders, the quaestor was to carry out any necessary arrangements.[93] Likewise, the *senatus consultum et foedus cum Astypalaeensibus* of 105 mentions that the consul P. Rutilius Rufus was in charge of ensuring that a copy of the treaty in bronze was deposited at the Capitolium (ll. 6–8).[94] Furthermore, the consul was to order the quaestor to be in charge of providing adequate accommodation and the usual gifts for the legate of Astypalaia (ll. 10–11). As a special honour, the ambassador was allowed to conduct a sacrifice on the Capitolium, if he so wished.

In 204 ten legates from the Sicilian city of Locri arrived in Rome. They arrived at the beginning of the consular year, since Livy narrates the episode immediately after that of the senate taking the measures previously described against the rebel Latin colonies. The legates were received by the consuls, who were sitting in the Comitium ('in comitio sedentibus').[95] The Locrians,

---

[91] Crawford 1996: 254 and 261: 'The senior consul is to send letters to the peoples and states to whom he may think fit . . .' (translation by Crawford).

[92] Ferrary 1977: 647–51. The interpretation will be quite different if one accepts the dating of the law to 99, as proposed by Giovannini 2008: 105–7. See also Ferrary 2009: 138–9.

[93] Sherk 1969: 68; 1984: 45.   [94] *IG* xii 3,173; *IGRR* iv 1028. Sherk 1969: 94–9; 1984: 56–8.

[95] Liv. 29.16.6.

bearing olive branches in the Greek tradition, prostrated themselves 'ante tribunal' and burst into lamentations. The term *tribunal* is used on various occasions, applied to different architectural structures and public places in the centre of Rome. The *tribunalia* were the seats of the praetors in the Forum, and the word *tribunal* is occasionally used in ancient sources to refer to the speakers' platform or rostra, located throughout the Republican period between the Comitium and the forum, until Caesar ordered its transfer to the western end of the forum. In this particular case, *tribunal* must refer to a platform placed in the Comitium, where the consuls were sitting. It could be the rostra, but a passage of Varro makes it clear that Livy refers to the so-called Graecostasis: 'In front of this [the Curia] is the rostra ... To the right of the rostra in the direction of the Comitium is a lower platform, where the legates of the peoples who had been sent to the senate were to wait; this, like many other things, was named after an aspect of its use, being called Graecostasis.'[96] The Graecostasis, literally 'the place of the Greek', was therefore a raised platform where the consuls received foreign embassies – the Greeks being the archetypal foreigners – which was an initial step prior to a possible hearing in the senate, and apparently where, as Livy claims, the consuls were seated.

On the architectural design of the Graecostasis we have no information. According to Coarelli, it must have been located on one of the sides of the Comitium, to the right of the rostra looking towards the forum, that is, in the south-western part of the Comitium, opposite the Curia and near the area where the temple of Concordia and the Basilica Opimia were located from the end of the second century.[97] Recently, Welch has suggested considering the Graecostasis as an independent building near the Comitium, which would place it in the area of what was to be later the temple of Concordia.[98] This would situate it to the west of the speakers' platform, next to the senaculum, a building mentioned by Varro ('above the Graecostasis was the senaculum')[99] where the senators would meet informally before a session of the senate. To the east of the Comitium there would be the Atrium Regium, which, according to Welch, must be considered the first basilica in Rome, the place where the ambassadors of the Hellenistic kings or the kings themselves were entertained when visiting Rome. The Basilica Porcia, built by Marcus

---

[96] Var. *L.* 5.155: 'ante hanc rostra ... sub dextra huius a Comitio locus substructus, ubi nationum subsisterent legati qui ad senatum essent missi; is Graecostasis appellatus a parte, ut multa.'

[97] Coarelli 1995b: 373: the Graecostasis would be the 'suggesto E' in the excavations of Boni, re-examined later on by Gjerstad, which would mean that the platform existed, as the first speakers' platform, since the beginning of the Republican period. Cf. Cic. *Q.fr.* 2.1.3; Plin. *Nat.* 7.212; 33.19. Cf. Connor 1904; Platner and Ashby 1929: 248–9.

[98] Welch 2003: 27–30.   [99] Var. *L.* 5.156: 'senaculum supra Graecostasim'.

Porcius Cato in 184, may have been a response to the necessity of accommodating a larger number of embassies from the eastern Mediterranean as the
influence of the Roman state grew in that region.

To return to the embassy of the Locrians: the consuls enquired as to the
reason for their visit, and the legates replied with complaints about the actions
of Q. Pleminius in their city. They requested a hearing before the senate, and
the consuls acquiesced.[100] Livy next reproduces a long speech of complaint
given before the senators.[101] After this, the leader of the senate (*princeps
senatus*) Q. Fabius asked them about Scipio's behaviour with respect to this
issue. When the ambassadors had replied, they were told to leave the Curia.[102]
A vigorous debate then followed between the senators. The decision reached
was embodied in a *senatus consultum*, whereby the consuls had to appoint
ten senators as legates to accompany the praetor M. Pomponius, along with
two tribunes of the plebs and one aedile, in order to investigate the events
in situ.[103] The enquiry led to the conviction of Pleminius.

Once again, it was the responsibility of the consuls, apparently acting
jointly, to direct the entire process. The consuls were in charge of receiving
the ambassadors from Locri. They authorized the ambassadors to speak
before the senate after weighing the importance of the reported facts.
The consuls listened to the speech of the legates and attended the ensuing
debate. Finally, they appointed the Roman legates who were to be part of
an investigating commission.

The Comitium is mentioned by Livy in connection with the arrival in
Rome of Rhodian legates in 167 as the place where the foreign embassies
waited to be received by the senate and later awaited the answer of the
senators. King Attalus of Pergamon had spoken in the senate, where he had
been welcomed as an ally and friend.[104] But the senate refused to welcome
the Rhodians or to give them a hearing, due to the suspicion that their
performance in the recent conflict had not been that of an ally of the Roman
people.[105] The senatorial decision was in answer to the question posed
by the consul M. Iunius. This same consul was in charge of informing the
Rhodians of the senate's will. He did so when he left the senate session
that was taking place in the Curia, while the Rhodians stood awaiting
him in the Comitium ('stantibus in comitio legatis'). The ambassadors
may have waited for the consul either in the open square formed by the
Comitium opposite the Curia, or rather in the Graecostasis placed on one of
the sides.

[100] Liv. 29.16.7. Cf. Canali de Rossi 1997: 648–51.   [101] Liv. 29.17–18.   [102] Liv. 29.19.3.
[103] Liv. 29.20.4.   [104] Liv. 45.20.1–3.   [105] Liv. 45.20.4–10.

We do not have specific information on the way in which the senate and the magistrates who were in Rome received the news of the imminent arrival of a foreign embassy in the city. However, the reconstruction by Servius in connection with a passage of Virgil, although undoubtedly not factual, may perhaps give an idea of the normal process.[106] According to Servius, the unexpected arrival of legates involved sending scouts to ascertain the purpose of their trip, followed by a consultation with the minor magistrates. Only then did the senate meet them outside the *Urbs*, or were they granted access to the city. As we have seen, the cases reported by Livy indicate that it was not minor magistrates, but the consuls, the urban praetor, or the peregrine praetor who received foreign ambassadors: that is, the superior magistrate who was in Rome and who was entitled to summon and consult the senate, the quaestor being in charge of specific logistical questions regarding the accommodation of the legates during their stay in the city.[107] In any event, this reception was mandatory. In 172, when Illyrian ambassadors arrived in Rome with the purpose of defending their King Genthius from accusations that he was prepared to support Perseus, they were convened before the senators. When they were asked why they had not presented themselves before the magistrate as was the norm ('ut ex instituto') – Livy does not specify which magistrate – in order to introduce themselves and communicate the reason for their visit, and also to be appropriately accommodated, the legates did not know how to answer. The senators decided to expel them from the Curia for not having requested the hearing in accordance with the required procedure.[108]

Visits from foreign ambassadors were therefore attended to in accordance with rules created by the Roman state dependent on the current or previous attitude of the countries in question. Those who were friends or allies of Rome had full freedom to travel to the *Urbs* whenever they deemed it convenient, without prior permission, and possibly even without prior notice.[109] In contrast, those who were considered enemies, and in particular those who were at war with Rome, seemingly needed previous authorization

---

[106] Serv. *ad Aen.* 7.168.   [107] Coudry 2004: 532; Ferrary 2007: 117.
[108] Liv. 42.26.4–6. Cf. Ferrary 2007: 116–17.
[109] Mommsen 1887–8: III 1 597; Linderski 1995: 466; Coudry 2004: 548. Occasionally, the senators could decide to escort an embassy to Rome as a means of showing their good will. Thus, the son of Masinissa was accompanied after disembarking in Puteoli by the quaestor L. Manlius (Liv. 45.13.12). Likewise, King Prusias was escorted by the quaestor L. Cornelius Scipio throughout his entire stay in Italy, from Capua to Rome, in the *Urbs*, and later on his return trip to Brundisium (Liv. 45.44.17). It could be deduced that there was a certain control at the main ports of entry and exit of Italy, which would allow the senate to gain knowledge of the eventual arrival of foreign ambassadors. Cf. Coudry 2004: 546–7.

or the order of a Roman magistrate on campaign. If a Roman general signed a treaty with an enemy state, the next step was its ratification by the senate, for which the ambassadors of that state had to travel to Rome and present themselves before the senators. They could travel in the company of the same commander when the wars took place in Italy, or, more frequently, they were accompanied by legates.[110]

In 190, the Aetolian legates had been forced to leave Rome and Italy. A similar situation occurred the following year.[111] Immediately after the new consuls took office, the senate received the Aetolian ambassadors. The bitter debate did not result in a peace agreement. On the contrary, the ambassadors were, as in the previous year, forced to leave the city and abandon Italy within fifteen days. The senate appointed A. Terentius Varro to oversee them during their return trip and warned the Aetolians that they would only accept a new embassy with the previous authorization of a Roman commander ('permissu imperatoris'), and one which was accompanied by a Roman legate ('si ... cum legato Romano venisset Romam').[112] The imposition of these conditions, clearly exceptional, implies that they were not normally compulsory.

Consequently, the senate, as Polybius claims, decided in each case what treatment ought to be given to the particular embassy. Once again the consuls were in charge of reporting the decisions of the senate. In 171, the envoys of Perseus were requested to abandon Rome immediately, and Italy within thirty days. That is all the information Livy provides.[113] Greek sources add that the expulsion of the ambassadors was accompanied by the expulsion of all Macedonians resident in Italy.[114] The consuls communicated the order to the legates and proclaimed before the popular assembly, undoubtedly through an edict, the expulsion of the Macedonians.

Livy's account in connection with the visit of Carthaginian ambassadors to Rome in 203 provides another specific detail about the reception of foreign envoys. The legates from Carthage were accommodated in the so-called *villa publica* and received by the senate in a session held outside the sacred boundary of the city, the *pomerium*, in the temple of Bellona, where

---

[110] Mommsen 1887–8: III 1150–1; Linderski 1995: 468–9; Coudry 2004: 547–8.

[111] See Linderski 1995: 466–70.

[112] Liv. 37.49.8. Cf. Canali de Rossi 1997: 31–3. When the Aetolians sent their next embassy (Liv. 38.3.7; Polyb. 21.25.10–11), the sources do not report that they had requested the consul's previous permission. Cf. Briscoe 1981: 368: 'It may be that Fulvius' permission was in fact obtained, or the senate may just have ignored its previous decision.' Linderski (1996: 384–5) based on the more detailed text in Polybius (21.26.7–19) rejects Briscoe's suggestion.

[113] Liv. 42.48.4.   [114] Polyb. 27.6.3; Diodor. 30.1; App. *Mac.* 11.9. Cf. Coudry 2004: 546.

1. The Villa Publica as represented on a coin of the *triumvir monetalis* P. Fonteius
Capito (55 BC)

they were brought by the praetor.[115] The same situation was repeated in 197. When the Macedonian ambassadors arrived in Rome to communicate that Philip would accept the conditions imposed by the senators after his defeat at Cynoscephalae, they were accommodated in the *villa publica*. As in the case of the Carthaginians, the legates were received by the senate in a session held in the temple of Bellona.[116]

These buildings, the *villa publica* and the temple of Bellona, were situated very close to each other in the Campus Martius. The *villa publica* was built towards the middle of the fifth century, in the context of the creation of the censors' office, and was expanded in 194.[117] Nothing has been preserved of the building, but according to a representation on a coin of the *triumvir monetalis* P. Fonteius Capito, of the year 55, it is usually thought that it had two floors and that the lower floor had arcades (Fig. 1).[118] The coin, which has the inscription T(itus) Didi(us) / imp(erator) / vil(lam) pub

---

[115] Liv. 30.21.12.
[116] Liv. 33.24.5. In 152, legates of the Celtiberians went to Rome. Those who were considered friends were received as guests in the city; those who had rebelled against Rome were accommodated outside the *Urbs* as was customary. When the moment came, the praetor introduced them in the senate separately (Polyb. 35.2.3–4; App. *Iber.* 49). In 137, the envoys from Numantia were also forced to stay outside of Rome so they would not think that the pact that had been reached with Mancinus was in force, as might have happened had they been accommodated within the city. However, hospitality gifts were sent to them in order to keep alive their hopes of reaching an agreement (Cass. Dio fr.79).
[117] Liv. 4.22.7; 34.44.5.
[118] Platner and Ashby 1929: 581; Coarelli 1981: 268 and 278; Agache 1987: 211–34; 2000: 202–5. Cf. Hamilton 1955; Crawford 1974: I 88.

(licam) [refecit], may have commemorated a renovation of the building commissioned by T. Didius, consul for the year 98 and twice proclaimed *triumphator* in the first decade of the first century. In a letter sent to Atticus in July 54, Cicero indicates that the *villa publica* was included in the renovation plans that Caesar wished to undertake in the area of the *Saepta*.[119] After this, sources do not allude to its existence again. Possibly *imperatores* also stayed in the *villa publica* while they waited to learn whether they were to be granted a triumph,[120] and there, according to Varro, recruitment was carried out and the censors undertook the tasks involved in carrying out the census of the Roman people.[121]

The cases of the Carthaginian legates in 203 and of the Macedonians in 197 exemplify a common practice in Rome, which has already been noted by Mommsen and Willems. Both legates represented states which at that time were at war with Rome and could not be received as guests into the city.[122] Because of this they were banned from entering the *Urbs* and therefore had to stay outside the *pomerium*. Even the meeting of the senate had to be held outside the sacred boundaries of the city to enable the ambassadors to be present.[123]

Nevertheless, it was always left to the senate to establish the official position with regard to any particular embassy. In 111, the senate had already resolved to send a consul to Numidia to commence the war against Jugurtha, and the corresponding army had already been recruited.[124]

---

[119] Cic. *Att.* 4.16.8.   [120] Joseph. *BJ* 7.5,4 (year AD 71).   [121] Var. *R.* 3.2.4.

[122] Mommsen 1887–8: III 1152. Cf. Linderski 1995: 477: 'All others [embassies] were constitutionally divided into two categories: those that were admitted into the city, and those that had to stay outside the walls, or more precisely outside the sacred boundary of the city of Rome, the *pomerium* . . . Only friends of Rome or neutrals or subjects could be received *domi*; the envoys from the foes of Rome had to stay in the sphere of war'; Ferrary 2007: 120: 'On peut admettre, me semble-t-il, que les ambassades sont reçues *extra pomerium* seulement pendant la période qui va de la décision d'entrer en guerre prise par le Sénat et par le peuple jusqu'à la conclusion d'un traité de paix ou jusqu'à une *deditio* formelle, qui mettait fin aux hostilités.' See a typology of embassies received *extra pomerium* and *intra pomerium* in Bonnefond-Coudry 1989: 139–41.

[123] Bonnefond-Coudry (1989: 141–3) questions whether the practice of receiving the legates of enemy states outside the city and of friendly states within the city was unchangeable. On the contrary, she believes that the senate acted in each case as a way of symbolically showing its attitude towards each state. She claims to find support for this theory in the fact that the Campanians and Syracusans were received in 210 inside the *Urbs* as well as supposedly the Aetolians in 190. Linderski (1995: 477 n. 55) objects to the theory of Bonnefond-Coudry, claiming that there is no evidence that the Aetolian legates were accommodated and heard within the *pomerium* and that the Campanian and Syracusan ambassadors represented states which had already made their surrender to Rome and had therefore stopped being enemies (*hostes*) and could not be considered at war any more, as opposed to what happened with a state that had only agreed to a truce. Linderski's conclusion is that there are no 'clear and certain exceptions to the rule established by Mommsen and Willems'.

[124] Sal. *Jug.* 27.

They then received news that an embassy sent by the Numidian king was approaching Rome, and that one of its members was the son of the king. The consul Bestia asked the senate whether it would be appropriate to receive the ambassadors within the *pomerium*. Since the measures that had just been taken meant that Numidia had become an enemy state, the senators determined not to receive the legates unless they had come to surrender and to deliver the monarch, and they also resolved that the ambassadors had to abandon Italy within ten days. Bestia was in charge of informing the Numidian ambassadors of the senatorial decision.[125]

In conclusion, in the field of diplomacy, the consuls, as the highest representatives of the Roman state, acted as spokesmen for the senate, an institution which was invested with the highest authority in conducting foreign policy. The consuls were intermediaries between Rome and foreign states, within Italy and beyond. The consuls played that role equally in the city of Rome and outside it, during their military campaigns. The main difference was that, while they were on the battlefield, their distance from the *Urbs* meant that the consuls had a certain autonomy when taking decisions, although these were always to be confirmed by the senate, whereas in Rome the magistrates always acted in close collaboration with the senate, taking part in its deliberations and scrupulously complying with its instructions.

In the *Urbs*, diplomatic activity tended to be concentrated at the beginning of the consular year, and was therefore one of the civil functions assigned to the new consuls in the first few weeks of their office. It was undoubtedly an important function that demanded considerable time and effort, since in the two hundred years between the end of the third century and the last years of the first century, there were up to eight hundred known embassies from the Greek world alone.[126] At the beginning of the consular year, before setting off for their provinces, both consuls were in Rome, which enabled them to attend the debates on foreign policy held in the senate. The decisions taken as a result of such debates determined the immediate future of the Roman state and, in tandem, that of the provinces and the specific tasks that the new consuls had to undertake during their consulship. These practical reasons account for the fact that senatorial decisions within the context of the policy of alliances or declarations of war were usually taken in the first days or weeks of the consular year.

---

[125] Sal. *Jug.* 28.1–2. See also the senate's refusal to receive Eumenes in 167, narrated by Polybius (30.19). Cf. Coudry 2004: 542.

[126] See the documentation gathered by Canali de Rossi 1997.

They also account for the fact that, at times, the senate made foreign embassies that were already in Rome wait for as long as was necessary until the new consuls took office, so that they could present them before the senate, take part in the ensuing debate, and officially communicate to the legates the senatorial response. It was the senate's function to establish the guidelines for Rome's external affairs, and the permanent nature of its membership meant the continuity of such policy. But its most direct executors changed every year, which was one of the reasons why, in order to avoid possible discrepancies in practical application, it was preferred in the final part of a consular year not to take important decisions which might have compromised the new supreme magistrates' freedom of action.

CHAPTER 4

Communication between the consuls and the people: edicts and contiones

As has been seen in previous chapters, when carrying out their duties the consuls acted chiefly as the transmission system for decisions previously taken by the senate, fulfilling the instructions of the senators. In their role as intermediaries between *senatus* and *populus* they were in charge of making senatorial resolutions known to the people when they were in Rome, according to the formula specifically mentioned by Livy: 'senatus censuit et consules edixerunt' ('the senate resolved and the consuls published an edict').[1] In their absence, one of the praetors, usually the urban praetor, would fulfil this duty.[2] Communication between the consuls and the people took two different forms: in writing through edicts and orally through their personal appearance in a *contio*.

CONSULAR EDICTS

In fact, the two forms of communication complemented each other. As the word *edicere* indicates, an *edictum* should first be proclaimed, that is, announced orally in public.[3] This would take place in a *contio*, the official assembly at which the Roman people received all sorts of information, summoned and presided over by the magistrate who produced the edict.[4] This action was called *edicere pro contione* or *in contione*, and was simultaneously accompanied by the display of the edict in the most frequented public place possible, usually the forum, both means being used in order to inform the maximum number of people.

Livy specifically reports on various occasions the enactment of consular edicts in *contiones*. In 210, several fires started simultaneously in the forum area, causing serious damage to various buildings. It was apparent that they

---

[1] For instance Liv. 40.19.5. [2] On praetorian edicts see Brennan 2000: 132–3.
[3] Cf. Mommsen 1887–8: I 205; Kunkel and Wittmann 1995: 177–81.
[4] Pina Polo 1989: 143–6; 1995: 210.

were caused by arsonists. For this reason, the senate ordered the consul
M. Claudius Marcellus – his colleague was away from Rome at the time – to
issue an edict offering a reward to anybody providing reliable information
on those who had caused the fires. The consul proceeded immediately.[5] In
173, the consul Postumius Albinus issued an edict before the assembly
('pro contione') according to which all Latins had to register in the census
of their towns of origin and not in Rome.[6] Postumius' order was itself the
result of a previous edict, issued in 177 by the consul C. Claudius Pulcher,
intended to restrain the emigration of Latins to Rome.[7]

Consular edicts could refer to many aspects of life in the community. In
the military field, this was usually the method used by consuls to announce
the summons for recruitment (*dilectus*), in accordance with the number of
soldiers assigned to them by the senate. The levying of soldiers was the
exclusive responsibility of the consuls, as Livy states repeatedly, and logically
took place at the beginning of the consular year, before the consuls set off
for their provinces.[8] Only in exceptional circumstances was the recruitment
carried out by praetors instead of consuls. That happened in 186. The
suppression of the Bacchanalia became the top priority for the consuls
to the point where the responsibility for the levy that year fell to the
urban praetor T. Maenius.[9] In 169, the consuls were having difficulties
with enrolment because many citizens were reluctant to join the legions. In
order to solve the problem, the senate, exceptionally, decided that the
praetors C. Sulpicius Galus and M. Claudius Marcellus should be in charge
of the levy.[10] It could also happen that the consuls needed help to complete
the recruitment. In 212, amidst the Hannibalic War, it was difficult to find
available men. Because of this, the senate appointed two commissions of
triumvirs to collaborate in recruitment under the management of the
consuls. One of them was to inspect towns within a fifty-mile radius of
Rome, the other was to operate beyond that limit.[11]

According to Polybius, the consuls proclaimed in a *contio*, by means of an
edict, the day on which people ought to be present in Rome. The new

---

[5] Liv. 26.27.6: 'itaque consul ex auctoritate senatus pro contione edixit.'   [6] Liv. 42.10.3.
[7] Liv. 41.9.9.
[8] Liv. 7.25.7 (year 348); 10.25.1 (295); 22.2.1 (217); 24.11.5–6 (214); 24.44.7 (213); 27.8.11 (209); 27.38.1
   (207); 29.13 (204); 30.2.8 (203); 31.9.6 (200); 32.1.3 (199); 32.9.1 (198); 35.41.3–4 (192); 38.44.8 (187);
   39.29.10 (185); 40.1.2 (182); 40.36.8 (180); 40.44.5 (179); 41.21.1 (174); 42.32.6–8 (171); 44.21.5 (168).
[9] Liv. 39.20.4. Cf. Kunkel and Wittmann 1995: 331.
[10] Liv. 43.14.3–4. In 181, the consuls completed the levy and went to Liguria, but afterwards the senate
   ordered the urban and peregrine praetor to conduct an exceptional levy of troops to face the Ligurian
   danger (Liv. 40.26.7). Cf. Brunt 1971: 630.
[11] Liv. 25.5.5–9.

recruits assembled on the Capitol.[12] The recruitment edict also contained the indications given to the authorities of the Italian allies regarding the number of soldiers to be sent, as well as the day on which the soldiers had to report and the place where they had to assemble.[13] On the appointed day, the magistrates who had issued the edict for the levy had the names of the citizen-soldiers read out in public, and they were to respond upon hearing their name or else be punished for non-attendance.[14] Those who were cited could then plead reasons to be exempt from military service. The magistrates in charge of recruitment, generally the consuls, had to listen and decide whether there were sufficient grounds to accept the requested exemption (*vacatio*).[15]

Consuls also used an edict to call up the troops that were to be under their command. Its purpose was to concentrate them in a given place and march from there to the province that had been allotted to each consul. This edict was also read out in a *contio*. Such was the procedure followed by the consul Q. Minucius Thermus in 193. When news reached Rome that the Ligures had taken up arms, the consul, following instructions from the senate, issued an edict from the rostra ordering the two urban legions, which had been raised the previous year, to go to Arretium within ten days. The edict included the order to recruit two new legions as well as a summons to the Capitol for the magistrates and legates of the Italian allies and the Latins.[16] L. Cornelius Scipio acted similarly in 190. Once he had fulfilled all his civil functions in Rome, he issued an edict in a *contio* whereby both the men that he had recruited and those who were already in Bruttium under the command of the propraetor A. Cornelius Mammula were to meet in

---

[12] Polyb. 6.19.5–7. Cf. Liv. 26.31.11. Brunt (1971: 627) considers Polybius' account 'too unrealistic to be based on personal observation'. In his opinion, Polybius would be following the antiquarian description of an annalist. 'As the extent of Rome's territory and the number of her citizens increased, it must have become inconvenient and unnecessary to bring all *iuniores* to Rome' (631). Cf. Nicolet 1976: 133–40; Kunkel and Wittmann 1995: 332–3; De Ligt 2007: 115–17.

[13] Polyb. 6.21.4–5. Brunt 1971: 626: at least some of the troops were recruited by the municipal authorities. Their representatives were summoned to Rome to meet the consuls, who were to set with them the total number of contingents to be levied. That happened in 193. According to Liv. 34.56.5, the consul Q. Minucius gathered on the Capitol both magistrates and representatives of Latins and allies who were to provide men for the Roman army and were ordered to recruit 15.000 infantry soldiers and 500 cavalry. According to Brunt, 'the Capitol was no doubt chosen because it had once been the place where the *dilectus* was held'. In Polybius' time the Capitol may have continued 'to have been the place where soldiers resident in the city itself or its immediate environs were called up'.

[14] Var. *ap*. Non. 28 L.; V. Max. 6.3.4. According to Valerius Maximus, the consul Curius Dentatus ordered the sale of the properties of a citizen and made him a slave because he did not accept his recruitment. This may have happened in 275.

[15] Brunt 1971: 628–9.   [16] Liv. 34.56.3.

Brundisium on the Ides of the month Quintilis to serve under his command.[17] From there they were to march to Greece. Brundisium was also
the meeting place of the troops ordered through an edict issued by the
consul Acilius in 191. It was the meeting place for the soldiers who had
already served under the consul Quinctius Flamininus and those who
had been levied for the new consul by the Italian allies and the Latins.[18]
On this occasion, Livy does not specifically report that the edict was
made public in a *contio*, but in all probability this would have been the
procedure.[19]

The promulgation of a consular edict was also the chosen form in 214 to
take urgent steps regarding the lack of crewmen for the fleet. Following
orders from the senate, the consuls issued an edict ('consules ex senatus
consulto edixerunt') which ordered the senators and the richest citizens
according to the latest census, completed six years earlier, to supply crewmen and to contribute, in proportion to their wealth, to the expenses that
would be incurred by their service in the fleet for a number of months.
According to Livy, this was the first time that the Roman fleet (*classis
Romana*) had been paid for with private money.[20] Only four years later a
similar consular edict was issued whereby the private citizens were to fund
the expenses of the fleet, given the lack of resources in the public treasury.
This measure elicited strong opposition but the consuls managed to reach a
compromise that was finally accepted.[21] In both cases, the edicts were issued
during the preparations for war at the beginning of each consular year.

In the religious sphere, consular edicts were used to inform citizens of
their obligations towards the gods in response to a recent event. Always
following orders from the senate, the consuls, for example, appointed in an
edict the days of supplication that had been decreed to ask the gods for
help in a military conflict or to thank them for a victory. In 191, once it had
been decided to declare war on King Antiochus, the senate commanded the
consuls to make a promise to celebrate *ludi magni* in honour of Jupiter
should they be triumphant, and to proclaim several days of supplications to
ask the gods for victory. While the consul Acilius Glabrio, who had been
given command of the war against Antiochus, performed the vow in person,
both consuls issued a joint edict proclaiming a supplication of two days.[22]

---

[17] Liv. 37.4.1.   [18] Liv. 36.3.13.
[19] In 294, the consul L. Postumius summoned all his soldiers to Sora by means of an edict (Liv. 10.33.8).
In 181 the assembly point for the soldiers who had been recruited by the consuls was Pisa, since Liguria
was the province that had been allotted to the two consuls (Liv. 40.26.5). Pisa was also the assembly
point for the troops in 180 (Liv. 40.41.9).
[20] Liv. 24.11.7–9.   [21] Liv. 26.35–6.   [22] Liv. 36.2.5.

The essential keeping of the peace of the gods was logically accompanied by the required military preparations. In this context of national emergency, the other consul, Scipio Nasica, issued an edict banning senators, both those who were entitled to speak in the senate and lower magistrates, from leaving the *Urbs* to go to any place that was further than one day's march from Rome. The edict also prohibited more than five senators from being away from Rome at any one time.[23]

In 168, as a result of the great victory achieved by L. Aemilius Paullus over Perseus at Pydna, the senate decreed the celebration of prayers of thanksgiving when the news reached Rome.[24] The decree was implemented as was customary by the consul – obviously the colleague of Aemilius Paullus, C. Licinius Crassus – who issued an edict ordering all the temples in the city to stay open and asking the people to go there to give thanks to the gods.[25] The senate decreed five days of supplications and sacrifices. As a result, an edict was proclaimed before the assembly, undoubtedly again by the consul, appointing the day of the beginning of the period of thanksgiving.[26] Soon afterwards, when news reached Rome that the Roman army had also won in Illyria, a further three days of thanksgiving were decreed. Once again it was the consul who appointed the exact days for the people to perform the corresponding supplications.[27]

In 181, the supplication was occasioned by the great number and significance of prodigies reported that year, as well as by the plague that had spread throughout vast areas. In response, the senate commanded that the consuls should initially celebrate sacrifices but that the sacred books should also be consulted.[28] The decemvirs answered that it was necessary to conduct a supplication in Rome, as well as to decree three days of supplication and *feriae* throughout the whole of Italy. Following the resolution of the priests, the senate passed a corresponding decree, and the consuls issued the edict that implemented this senatorial decision.[29]

The consular edict enacted in 193 in connection with the repeated reports reaching Rome of earthquakes may also be considered in a religious context. The fact that they were, logically, seen as portents that had to be expiated was paralysing public life. It was not feasible to hold a meeting of the senate, and the consuls could not fulfil their duties at the beginning of the consular year since they were permanently in charge of expiating the prodigies. In these circumstances, the consuls issued an edict – as always, following orders from the senate, 'ex auctoritate senatus' – banning the reporting of an

---

[23] Liv. 36.3.2–3.   [24] Liv. 45.2.1.   [25] Liv. 45.2.6.   [26] Liv. 45.2.12.   [27] Liv. 45.3.1–2.
[28] Liv. 40.19.4.   [29] Liv. 40.19.5.

earthquake on any day when public events had already been cancelled in response to another earthquake previously reported.[30]

In all the aforementioned cases, the consuls issued the corresponding edicts while they were in Rome, preferably at the beginning of the consular year. On some occasions, consular edicts could nevertheless be dictated from outside Rome, while the consul was on his way to the city, with the purpose of accelerating the process relating to the question at hand. The text of the edict was sent to Rome as quickly as possible, and it was read out and publicly displayed to make it official according to the normal procedure. At the end of the consular year 207/6, the two consuls who had defeated the army of Hasdrubal at Metaurus were recalled by the senate to Rome, where both of them were to receive the award of a triumph. The consuls came from different parts of Italy, but they were in contact via letter and thus agreed to enter the *Urbs* together.[31] For this purpose they decided that the first of them to arrive in Praeneste should wait for his colleague there, which is what happened. Once they were both in Praeneste, they issued an edict summoning the senators to meet three days later at the temple of Bellona, outside the *pomerium*.[32] Similarly, in the final part of the consular year 192/1, the senators decided that elections should be held as soon as possible. For this purpose, they summoned in writing, through the urban praetor, the consul in charge of presiding over the elections, L. Quinctius Flamininus. The senatorial instructions were very specific: the consul was temporarily to give up command of his troops and return to Rome, and on his way to the city he was to dispatch his edict calling for the elections. The consul acted as the senate requested.[33]

The consuls also issued edicts dealing with socio-economic questions, always by order of the senate. In 206, the progress of the war in Italy permitted the area surrounding Rome, and in general all of Latium, to be regarded as safe. The senate considered it necessary for the farmers to return to normal work in their fields and urged the consuls to deal with this before going to war. The problem did not have an easy solution, since, as Livy claims, many farmers were engaged in the armed conflict, there was a scarcity of slaves, the livestock had been taken, and the houses had been looted. However, a large part of the population, compelled by the consuls,

---

[30] Liv. 34.55.4.   [31] Liv. 28.9.4.

[32] Liv. 28.9.5: 'forte ita evenit ut eodem die ambo Praeneste venirent. Inde praemisso edicto ut triduo post frequens senatus ad aedem Bellonae adesset ...' In 215, at the beginning of the consular year, both consuls had issued an edict in Rome ordering that all the sessions of the senate take place at the Porta Capena (Liv. 23.32.3).

[33] Liv. 35.24.1–2.

returned to the fields.[34] The measure was most probably implemented by means of a consular edict. In this context, the consuls issued another edict for the inhabitants of the colonies of Placentia and Cremona to return to these cities by a specific date.[35] This was in answer to the complaint lodged by legates of both colonies, which were virtually deserted due to the destruction caused by the invasion of the neighbouring Gauls.

Finally, within the context of the repression of the so-called conspiracy of the Bacchanalia in 186, the consuls issued an edict to prevent the flight of those who were involved. The edict expressly banned the conveyance of properties by those who wished to flee, and it also prohibited giving shelter or help in any form to the fugitives.[36]

CONSULAR *CONTIONES*

contiones were the only type of popular assembly in Rome at which speeches could be delivered before the people.[37] They were always officially summoned by a magistrate who presided over the assembly and could allow whomever he deemed appropriate to speak (*contionem dare*). Throughout the year, *contiones* were frequent and dealt with varied issues: assemblies in preparation for judicial business or legislative comitia for informative or political purposes etc. The speeches were mostly delivered from the speakers' platform or rostra, situated between the Comitium and the forum, or from some other place that was symbolically elevated, such as the podium of a temple.[38] In the pre-Sullan period, the consuls summoned and presided over *contiones*, where they displayed their eloquence before the people, but obviously their contribution was curtailed in practice due to their limited presence in Rome. Nevertheless, ancient sources report almost forty assemblies in which consuls took part in the pre-Sullan era.

The vote of a bill (*rogatio*) in the comitia had to be preceded by a debate for the period of a *trinundinum*, the interval between the first and third of three successive market days.[39] This debate had to take place before the people in *contiones*, at which the speakers included not only the person who

---

[34] Liv. 28.11.8.

[35] Liv. 28.11.11: 'consules ex senatus consulto edixerunt ut qui cives Cremonenses atque Placentini essent ante certam diem in colonias reverterentur.'

[36] Liv. 39.17.4.

[37] On the *contiones*, see Millar 1984; 1986; 1989; 1998; Pina Polo 1989; 1995; 1996; Hölkeskamp 1995; Laser 1997; Mouritsen 2001; Morstein-Marx 2004.

[38] Pina Polo 2005a.

[39] On the meaning and duration of the *trinundinum*, Lintott 1965; 1968; Michels 1967: 42, 87, and 191–206; Brind'Amour 1983: 87–96; Pina Polo 1989: 96–105.

proposed the law and others who concurred with him but, according to custom, also those who were not in favour.[40] As we shall see in the chapter on legislation, the fact that the consuls had to be away from Rome during most of the consular year resulted in relatively few laws being proposed by consuls in the pre-Sullan age. In all these cases, the consuls who proposed them obviously spoke in *contiones* defending the appropriateness of their projects, although it is rare for ancient sources to mention their speeches specifically.[41] In other instances, some consuls intervened in the discussion of bills presented by other politicians. We know of at least two examples of such interventions. In 195, the consul Cato, before setting off to Hispania spoke in a *contio* against a tribunician *rogatio* aimed at abolishing the *lex Oppia*.[42] In fact, he had such a great interest in the matter that he delayed his journey to his province until the vote on the bill had taken place. In 122, the consul C. Fannius delivered a speech against the proposal of Gaius Gracchus to grant the allies Roman citizenship.[43]

One of the purposes of the *contiones* was to inform the people on all matters of public interest.[44] In particularly important cases, the role of informants could belong to the consuls, provided that they were in Rome. This happened in 186, once the scope and the gravity of the conspiracy of the Bacchanalia became apparent. After the report produced by the consul Postumius before the senate, the senators decided to ask both consuls to carry out an inquiry (*quaestio*) to find those who were guilty.[45] The consuls then summoned a *contio*, stood on the rostra, and one of them, quite probably Postumius, who had uncovered the matter, gave a speech before the people.[46] The consul reported in general on the character of the cults that were to be banned and on the danger they posed to the community, asking all citizens to be alert to act against them while reassuring them that the senate had already taken the appropriate measures and that the consuls would be responsible for the protection of the state.[47]

In Rome there was not an electoral campaign as such, where candidates delivered speeches in popular assemblies to present their proposals to voters.[48] In the pre-Sullan period the president of the elections, usually one of the consuls, travelled to Rome from his province, appointed a day for holding the elections, and presided over them. Generally, the president of the elections does not seem to have had great influence on the outcome.

[40] Pina Polo 1989: 92–103.
[41] Liv. 31.7.1–15 alludes to the speech delivered by the consul P. Sulpicius Galba in the year 200 during the discussion of his bill to declare war on Philip of Macedonia. Cf. Pina Polo 1989: 268–9.
[42] Liv. 34.1–4; Zonar. 9.17. Cf. Pina Polo 1989: 269.　[43] Iul.Vict. 6.4.　[44] Pina Polo 1989: 139–42.
[45] Liv. 39.14.　[46] Liv. 39.15.1.　[47] Liv. 39.15–17.　[48] Pina Polo 1989: 115–18.

However, in exceptional cases, he could sway the vote of the people in advance, or problems could arise in the electoral process whose resolution had to be dealt with by the president. In the consular year 296/5, the consul Volumnius was called to Rome to hold the elections. Before presiding over the comitia, he convened a *contio* where he explained the difficult situation of the *res publica*, which was simultaneously being challenged by various peoples in Italy. Volumnius openly suggested that it would be advisable to elect as consul Q. Fabius Maximus, the most prestigious general at the time.[49] The first century to vote (*centuria praerogativa*) and the voters of the first class did lean towards Fabius and Volumnius as consuls, but then Fabius requested a halt to the voting and delivered a speech asking for his colleague to be P. Decius Mus, with whom he had a close relationship. Volumnius also spoke in the *contio*, which went on until the end of the day, in support of Fabius. The next day Fabius and Decius Mus were elected.[50] The election was followed by a disagreement between the two consuls, although Livy questions the reliability of this information.[51] Apparently both consuls wished to take command of the war against the Etruscans, with the support of different groups within the senate, which caused verbal confrontations both in the senate and in *contiones* before the people, where the consuls defended their positions.[52] Initially, the command in Etruria was given to Fabius, without drawing lots for the provinces, but finally Decius marched with him when Fabius had demonstrated, once again in a *contio*, that he was prepared to accept the collaboration of his colleague.[53]

A different Q. Fabius Maximus (Verrucosus) was the protagonist of a similar incident in the comitia over which he presided regarding the election of consuls for 214. The first voting century elected T. Otacilius and M. Aemilius Regillus. Fabius interrupted the voting process and delivered a speech in which he pointed out the seriousness of the situation, the significance of the Carthaginian enemy, and therefore the need to appoint as consuls the best-prepared and most militarily experienced persons.[54] When the centuries were called again to vote, Fabius himself was elected consul along with M. Claudius Marcellus.

In the elections for the consular year 206/5 there was an electoral recommendation by the triumphant consuls of 207/6. The day after the joint celebration of their triumph both consuls delivered a speech in the

---

[49] Liv. 10.21.13–22.   [50] Liv. 10.22.

[51] Liv. 10.26.5–7, claims that in some of his sources there are no reports of the dispute between the consuls, but, on the contrary, they presumably went together to Etruria upon taking office. Cf. Broughton 1951–86: I 179.

[52] Liv. 10.24.4–18.   [53] Liv. 10.26.1.   [54] Liv. 24.7.12–18.

usual *contio*, where they praised their legates L. Veturius Philo and Q. Caecilius Metellus for their courage and loyalty.[55] The consular *auctoritas* was a decisive contribution to the later election of Veturius and Metellus as consuls.

At the beginning of the consular year 184/3, a problem arose in replacing the urban praetor C. Decimius Flavus, who had died soon after taking office. Q. Fulvius Flaccus, who was already an aedile, was amongst the candidates to take over the vacant position.[56] Some tribunes of the plebs opposed his candidacy, claiming that nobody could hold two magistracies simultaneously, particularly if they were both curule offices. The senate asked the consul L. Porcius Licinus to persuade the aedile to give up his candidacy, but due to Fulvius' persistence, the senators decided to take the question before the people. The consul summoned a *contio*, in which he explained the problem and the senate's viewpoint, and then Fulvius Flaccus gave his opinion.[57] Given his determination not to withdraw his candidacy and the high probability that, due to his popularity, the people would elect him as a praetor, the senate decided not to fill the vacancy caused by the deceased praetor and exceptionally ordered the peregrine praetor to take over the functions of the urban praetor as well.

After the triumphal parade through the centre of Rome, which was the main act in the celebration of a triumph, the victorious general would attend a *contio* to give details of the military campaign to the people and thus receive the final public acclamation.[58] Although *triumphatores* were mostly promagistrates, some consuls celebrated their triumph when still in office ('in magistratu'). For this reason, we also have some examples of this kind of consular *contio* in ancient sources. In the consular year 191/0, the consul P. Cornelius Scipio Nasica celebrated a triumph over the Boii, although its appropriateness was contested by one of the tribunes of the plebs. The day after the triumphal parade, as usual, the consul spoke in a *contio* about his victory, criticized the tribune for being obstructive, and finally freed his soldiers from their oath and discharged them.[59] Although we do not have explicit testimony to confirm it, undoubtedly

---

[55] Liv. 28.9.20. Cf. Pina Polo 1989: 267.   [56] Liv. 39.39.1. Cf. Brennan 2000: 656.

[57] Liv. 39.39.10–11.

[58] Liv. 45.40.9. Cf. Pina Polo 1989: 147–50. On the triumph, see Künzl 1988; Itgenshorst 2005; Beard 2007.

[59] Liv. 36.40.14. Cf. Pina Polo 1989: 149; 270. The *contio* in which the consul M'. Curius Dentatus intervened may also have taken place after the celebration of his triumph in 290. His speech became an *exemplum* when Dentatus refused to accept more land than was offered as a reward to his soldiers, claiming that a citizen who did not have enough with seven *iugera* was a danger to the community (Plin. *Nat.* 18.18; Cass. Dio fr.37.1; Fron. *Str.* 4.3.12). Cf. Pina Polo 1989: 123–4; 263.

all consuls who celebrated their triumph before leaving their consulship also pronounced *contiones* as *triumphatores*; such is the case of C. Cornelius Cethegus in 196 and M. Claudius Marcellus in 195.[60]

Granting a triumph to an *imperator* occasionally caused heated confrontations between those who were in favour and those who were against. In 294, the consul L. Postumius Megellus demanded that the senate grant him a triumph, but most of the senators opposed it. With the help of three tribunes of the plebs, the consul brought the question before the people. Postumius delivered a speech in a *contio* at which he expounded on why he deserved to celebrate a triumph after defeating the Etruscans and the Samnites and reminded the audience of the precedents for a triumph being granted by the people even without senatorial approval. The consul received full popular support and, according to Livy, celebrated the triumphal ceremony the day after his speech in the assembly.[61]

Funeral eulogies of members of the Roman aristocracy took place in a *contio* convened for the purpose. The speech was usually delivered by a son of the deceased or by a member of his family, mainly because the funeral eulogy (*laudatio funebris*) was not only an act of piety towards the dead person but also, above all, an act of propaganda for the family, for the aristocracy as a whole, and ultimately for the Republican political system.[62] In the pre-Sullan period, only twice are consuls mentioned as the orators pronouncing a *laudatio funebris*, and both instances are somewhat exceptional. In 295, the consul Q. Fabius Maximus pronounced a funeral eulogy for his colleague P. Decius Mus, killed in combat, although he was not a member of his family, in an act that resembled a state funeral.[63] And in 102, the consul Q. Lutatius Catulus delivered the *laudatio* of his mother Popilia. According to Cicero, this was the first time in Roman history that a woman had received such an honour at the rostra.[64]

During their stay in Rome, consuls occasionally convened and presided over or attended *contiones* for many different reasons: assemblies which were celebrated within the framework of elections, informational assemblies, legislative assemblies, assemblies for the purpose of issuing edicts, and post-triumphal or funeral assemblies. Nevertheless the most common and frequent *contiones* in the Republican period were political, that is, those at which the speakers debated current public issues, defended their political

[60] Liv. 33.23.4; 33.37.10.   [61] Liv. 10.37.10–11. Cf. Pina Polo 1989: 149–50; 262.
[62] On the *pompa funebris*, see Flaig 1995; 2003: esp. 49–98; Arce 2000; Pina Polo 2004; Sumi 2005: 41–6; Bücher 2006: 110–15. Especially on the funeral eulogies see Vollmer 1892; Durry 1950; Kierdorf 1980; Pina Polo 1989; 165–8; Flower 1996: 128–58.
[63] *De vir. ill.* 27.5. Cf. Pina Polo 1989: 262.   [64] Cic. *de Orat.* 2.44. Cf. Pina Polo 1989: 167; 282.

allies, or discredited their adversaries etc.[65] The presence of consuls was also more frequent in these types of political *contiones*, either on their own initiative or by invitation of the president of the assembly. The words of a consul, inasmuch as he was the supreme magistrate of the Roman state, had a particular *auctoritas*, and consequently it is logical that the consuls' active participation as orators before the people was appreciated.

Consuls spoke about quite varied topics in the political *contiones* that are attested. The first recorded assembly of this kind that was led by a consul took place in 359, and the decisive element in it was precisely the consular *auctoritas*. According to information provided by Cicero, a popular sedition was about to start. Having heard about this, the consul M. Popillius Laenas, who was at the time performing a public sacrifice as priest of Carmentis (*flamen Carmentalis*), summoned a *contio*. With his speech, of which Cicero provides no details, he managed immediately to silence the riot.[66] The weight of consular *auctoritas* can also be noted in the episode narrated by Valerius Maximus.[67] In 138, due to a rise in the price of corn, the tribune of the plebs C. Curiatius brought the consuls Brutus and Scipio Nasica to a *contio*. His purpose was to obtain from them a commitment for the senate to agree to the purchase of a certain amount of corn in order to bring down the price. However, the consuls opposed this measure. Specifically, Nasica began a speech against the tribune's suggestion which was interrupted by the jeering crowd. Nasica's reaction was to motion them to be silent arguing that he knew better what the interest of the *res publica* was. According to Valerius Maximus, upon hearing these words all those present immediately kept a respectful silence, since they gave more importance to the *auctoritas* of the orator than to the question of the price of corn. In this context, the consul C. Marius may be seen in the same role of pacifying the plebs in December of the year 100. Amidst the crisis caused by the measures promoted by the tribune Saturninus, C. Memmius, a candidate for the consulship for the following year, was murdered. In the face of the social unrest in Rome caused by this action, Marius calmed the people with a speech.[68] This was followed by the episodes that were to lead to the issuance of the *senatus consultum ultimum* and to the murder of Saturninus and his main political allies.

The *contiones* were the appropriate place to defend one's own ideas and to generate a particular personal image, as well as to promote a campaign against a political adversary with the purpose of creating unfavourable

---

[65] Pina Polo 1989: 119–38.   [66] Cic. *Brut.* 56. Cf. Pina Polo 1989: 123; 260.
[67] V. Max. 3.7.3. Cf. Pina Polo 1989: 124; 276.   [68] Oros. 5.17.6. Cf. Pina Polo 1989: 282.

public opinion. The fact that the consuls were usually in Rome for short periods, during which they were engaged in many civil tasks, made it difficult for them to take part in these types of *contiones*. In the year 91, the consul L. Marcius Philippus was one of the most embittered opponents of the legislative measures proposed by the tribune of the plebs M. Livius Drusus. His confrontation with part of the senate, in particular with the great orator L. Licinius Crassus, must be understood within this context. From the scattered information available it appears that the consul used his position as a supreme magistrate to deliver speeches before the people, even stating that the *res publica* was in need of a different senate for its better management.[69]

Due to the main function of consuls as military leaders in the pre-Sullan period, some of their appearances as orators before the people were closely connected with their taking command of the army in a specific war, with self-glorification after achieving victory or with their defence from political attacks after having been defeated. The disastrous beginning of the Second Punic War brought about a debate in Rome on the strategy to be followed in order to defeat the Carthaginian army. This discussion, which obviously took place mainly within the senate, was brought before the people by the consuls of 216. According to Livy, before leaving the city both of them delivered speeches on this question in *contiones*. C. Terentius Varro attacked the prudent and dilatory strategy of the dictator Q. Fabius Maximus in various assemblies, since he considered that it amounted to the prolongation of the war on Italian land for too long a period. He, in contrast, supported an immediate confrontation and even recklessly announced that he would put an end to the war on the first day he faced the enemy.[70] His colleague L. Aemilius Paullus gave only one speech in a *contio* held the day before his departure from Rome. In it, he indirectly defended the strategy of Fabius Maximus and showed himself surprised at the audacity of Terentius Varro, who dared even before taking command of his troops to predict how he would act and what his achievements would be.[71] The debate provoked by both consuls before the people did not, of course, entitle the people to decide on the war strategy; it was only intended to keep them informed and at the same time win over their opinion in favour of one or other course of action. As can be gathered from Livy's text, Terentius Varro's speech was more to the liking of the people, but it was also loaded with demagogical remarks, whereas the speech of his colleague was

[69] V. Max. 6.2.2; Cic. *de Orat.* 3.2. Cf. Pina Polo 1989: 283–4.
[70] Liv. 22.38.6–7 (cf. Plut. *Fab.* 14.2). Cf. Pina Polo 1989: 264.   [71] Liv. 22.38.8–12.

much more realistic and predicted a long war, which later proved to be the case.

In 178, Gaul was allotted to the consul A. Manlius Vulso as his province. From there he invaded Histria, where he was initially defeated. His colleague M. Iunius Brutus then joined him and both armies managed to put an end to the resistance of the Histrians.[72] However, Manlius' failure provoked a reaction in Rome against what some considered to be an inappropriate action. Two tribunes of the plebs of 177, A. Licinius Nerva and C. Papirius Turdus, started a campaign against him, with the ultimate aim of ensuring that his command would not be extended and that he could be prosecuted at the end of his consulship once he had lost his immunity as a magistrate.[73] When the consul Iunius Brutus arrived in Rome to preside over the elections, both tribunes took advantage of the situation to question him on the position in Histria, first in the senate and later on bringing him before the people in a *contio*. The tribunes claimed that it ought to have been Manlius Vulso who returned to Rome to explain why he had left his province to start a war in Histria that did not have the approval of the Roman people.[74]

Still, the senate extended the command of both consuls of 178 in Histria, where they managed to subdue a great number of the indigenous population.[75] This created unease in C. Claudius Pulcher, one of the consuls of 177, who had been allotted the province of Histria. Claudius feared that the success of the proconsuls would leave him no scope to attain a military triumph for himself. Because of this, as soon as news of the success reached Rome, he set off for Histria without performing the mandatory rituals that every consul had to carry out when leaving the *Urbs*.[76] Upon his arrival in Histria, he attacked the proconsuls in a military *contio*, but his authority was not acknowledged by the troops since he had left Rome contrary to tradition.[77] Claudius was forced to return to Rome to perform the prescribed rituals. He stayed in the *Urbs* for just three days, and during his stay he had time to deliver a speech in a *contio*, where he attacked both proconsuls.[78] In view of the discredit caused by his performance until that moment, it was essential for him to communicate to the people his own version of the facts in order to gain the support of public opinion.

In 168 L. Aemilius Paullus was given command of the war against Perseus in Macedonia. When this became known and the senate had taken the corresponding decisions on the number of soldiers to be recruited and on

---

[72] Liv. 41.5.   [73] Liv. 41.6.1–3.   [74] Liv. 41.7.4–10. Cf. Pina Polo 1989: 271–2.   [75] Liv. 41.10.1–5.
[76] Liv. 41.10.5.   [77] Liv. 41.10.7–8.   [78] Liv. 41.10.13. Cf. Pina Polo 1989: 125; 272; Vishnia 1996: 185.

their distribution, the consul summoned an assembly, where he delivered a speech. In his discourse, Aemilius Paullus echoed the enthusiasm of the people for his appointment as head of the troops in Macedonia and showed his resolve to put an end to the war once and for all.[79] After pronouncing this self-laudatory speech, a means of increasing his popularity in preparation for the glory of a future triumph in case he attained victory, as in fact did happen at Pydna, the consul presided over the *feriae Latinae* on Mons Albanus on 31 March and then set off for Macedonia.[80]

The speech (or speeches)[81] delivered by C. Marius after being elected consul for the first time for the year 107 brings to mind that of Aemilius Paullus in that he thanked the people for the trust placed in him to definitively defeat Jugurtha and demonstrated his total confidence that he would triumph in Numidia.[82] As in the case of Aemilius Paullus, Marius spoke in the *contio* that he had summoned and presided over once the senate had decided on the organization of the military operations and especially after it had accepted the request of the consul to recruit more troops. His initial purpose was to galvanize the people, to rouse their patriotism, and thus to have as great a number of people as possible volunteer to join his army. Along with this, the text provided by Sallust allows us to see some of the main principles of Marius' policy, as well as the claims of a 'new man' (*homo novus*) as opposed to the traditional *nobilitas*.[83]

At various times throughout the second century there were difficulties in recruiting soldiers in the context of continual war that was prolonged for years. This happened in 171, when veterans and centurions started to be recruited for the war in Macedonia against Perseus, whose command belonged to the consul P. Licinius Crassus. In view of the protests and the complaints made before the tribunes of the plebs, the consul suggested discussing the question before the people.[84] To this end, he summoned and presided over a *contio*, in which in the first place M. Popillius Laenas, who had been consul two years earlier, spoke in favour of the centurions. Afterwards Crassus intervened, and he ordered the reading out of the decrees on recruitment that had been issued by the senate and encouraged compliance with them. Exceptionally, a centurion, Sp. Ligustinus, was allowed to speak, and he exhorted his colleagues to put themselves at

---

[79] Liv. 44.22.1–15. Cf. Liv. *per.* 44; Polyb. 29.1. Cf. Pina Polo 1989: 125; 274. [80] Liv. 44.22.16.
[81] Plut. *Mar.* 9.2–4. [82] Sal. *Jug.* 84.5–85. Cf. Pina Polo 1989: 281.
[83] On Marius' speech see Skard 1941; Carney 1959; Paul 1984: 207–15; Evans 1994: 71–3: 'Even if the Sallustian oration contains a kernel of truth, it is obviously nothing more than an elaborate invention and bears no strict relation to what might have been said by Marius.'
[84] Liv. 42.33.2.

the service of the senate and the consul. Satisfied with this, the consul concluded the assembly.

Consuls acted as intermediaries between the senate and the people during their stay in Rome, mainly at the beginning of the consular year. In practice, this function meant issuing edicts whereby the people were informed of the provisions that had been approved by the senate. Given the nature of the tasks performed by the consuls in Rome, most of the attested consular edicts refer either to questions regarding the recruitment of troops and, in general, the preparation for military campaigns, or to prescriptions aimed at preserving or recovering the peace of the gods. The consuls were likewise responsible for announcing the elections by means of edicts, as they were the presidents of the electoral process, as well as the sessions of the senate that they were due to preside over. In both cases there are instances of consular edicts issued *ex itinere*, when consuls were on their way to Rome. Finally, the consuls also enacted edicts regarding social and economic questions, such as the order to farmers to return to their fields during the Hannibalic War once Latium was finally considered free from military conflict.

During the whole of the Republican period *contiones* were held in Rome very frequently. Due to the fact that consuls spent most of their time in office outside the city, their participation in this type of assembly in the pre-Sullan age was quite unusual, and consequently consular speeches before the people were also infrequent. Nevertheless, the obvious *auctoritas* of the consuls as supreme magistrates of the *res publica* made their intervention in popular assemblies in different political contexts highly desirable, at times as a means to appease the unrest or the open revolt of the plebs, or simply to provide information to the population on any given matter of public interest. As in the case of the edicts, some of their interventions before the people were directly connected with their main role as military leaders: disputes on the allocation of provinces, patriotic speeches prior to the beginning of a war, recruitment for the army, narration of feats after the celebration of a triumph etc. Occasionally the consuls used their prestige to try to influence citizens when acting as presidents of the electoral process, swaying their vote towards certain candidates. Apart from their compulsory intervention in the *contiones* before the motions that they promoted were put to a vote, on very few occasions did they speak in favour of or against the bills put forward by other politicians. Even though consular oratory before the people was important in the pre-Sullan era, undoubtedly their periods of absence from Rome caused them to be present less often than other magistrates, in particular the tribunes of the plebs.

CHAPTER 5

Consuls as legislators

It is indisputable that the higher magistrates, the consuls amongst them, had the capacity of legislative initiative. In fact, this is one of the functions that Polybius attributes to consuls: to present proposals before the popular assembly while in Rome before setting off for their provinces,[1] a function which is unanimously accepted by all those who have worked on the lawmaking process of the Roman Republic.[2]

An episode that occurred in 210 illustrates this fact.[3] When the moment to hold consular elections arrived, the senate summoned the consul M. Valerius Laevinus to Rome by means of a letter written by the urban praetor.[4] Valerius informed the senate of the latest events in Sicily. Not long before his arrival, the ambassadors of King Syphax had reported on the situation in Africa to the senators, who were alarmed by the news and considered it necessary for the consul to return immediately to his province without waiting for the elections over which he was to preside. The senate requested that before leaving the consul appoint a dictator to be in charge of the elections, a request which brought about a dispute between the consul and the senators. Valerius claimed that he wished to appoint as dictator M. Valerius Messalla, who was the head of the fleet at the time, and that he would make this appointment upon his arrival in Sicily. The senators opposed this, declaring that nobody who was outside of the *ager Romanus* could legally be appointed as dictator.[5] A tribune of the plebs supported the senatorial viewpoint, and finally the senate decreed that the consul, before leaving, was to present a bill before the popular assembly in order for the people to decide who ought to be the dictator, while requesting that the consul appoint the person who was eventually elected. The senatorial decree established that, should the

---

[1] Polyb. 6.12.4.

[2] Mommsen 1887–8: II 127; Bleicken 1975: 103–4; Lintott 1999b: 105. Lawmaking by praetors: Brennan, 2000: 119–20. In general on the legislative process in the Republican period, see Crawford 1996: 1–38; Williamson 2005: esp. 62–128.

[3] Cf. Rotondi 1912: 258; Elster 2003: 237–9.   [4] Liv. 27.4.1–4.   [5] Liv. 27.5.14–15.

consul refuse to comply, the bill would be brought before the people by the praetor – that is, the urban praetor –, and should he also refuse to proceed accordingly, the tribunes of the plebs would ultimately be in charge. Indeed, the consul refused to present the bill and forbade the praetor to do so; therefore the tribunes of the plebs were eventually in charge of the election of the dictator.[6] The episode did not end there, since the consul left Rome before the popular assembly was held because he considered that the appointment of a dictator was his exclusive function. By order of the senate the other consul, M. Claudius Marcellus, appointed the dictator who had been elected.[7]

The events of 210 leave no doubt that consuls, praetors, and tribunes of the plebs were equally entitled to present a *rogatio* before the people ('populum rogare'), that is, to promote a bill.[8] The fact that legally they all had legislative capacity does not mean that all of them put it into practice similarly. From a simple reading of Livy it is apparent that during the pre-Sullan Republican period the tribunes of the plebs were the main legislators, overwhelmingly so in comparison to the higher magistrates.[9]

Sandberg has in recent years published a series of works analysing legislative practice in the Roman Republic.[10] Sandberg exclusively uses for the study of the pre-Sullan political system the existing sources that derive from that period, and not the testimonies of the first century BC, which, when applied to a previous time, distort the reality.[11] Once the risk of late-Republican 'contamination' is eliminated, the author reaches a series of partly novel conclusions. In his opinion, there were not two different tribal assemblies, *concilium plebis* and *comitia tributa*, but only one assembly, exclusively plebeian, which in normal circumstances could only be summoned by the tribunes of the plebs. When the curiate assembly that existed in the first phase of the history of Rome fell into disuse, all the civil legislation, which had until that moment been proposed by the consuls, was concentrated in the hands of the tribal assembly and consequently became the responsibility of the tribunes of the plebs. The power of a legislative assembly was linked to its meeting place. As a result, an assembly such as the *comitia centuriata*, which was convened outside the sacred boundaries of the city (*extra pomerium*), could only decide on military issues and external affairs, whereas civil matters were dealt with exclusively in assemblies summoned within the city (*intra pomerium*), that is, by the tribal assembly.[12]

---

[6] Liv. 27.5.16–17.   [7] Liv. 27.5.18–19. Cf. Vishnia 1996: 59–60; Brennan 2000: 113–14.
[8] Williamson 2005: 16.   [9] Bleicken 1955: 43–73; Thommen 1989: 41–147; Williamson 2005: 16–17.
[10] Sandberg 1993; 2000; 2001; 2004; 2007.   [11] Sandberg 2001: 20–2.
[12] Sandberg 2001: 105–13; 119–31. On the *comitia tributa* see Taylor 1966; Develin 1975; 1977; Farrell 1986.

From all of this, according to Sandberg, the following can be concluded: there is no evidence that the *comitia centuriata* was used to legislate in the pre-Sullan era, except for the declaration of war (*leges de bello indicendo*); laws linked to consuls and, in general, to curule magistrates are very rare and of very questionable historical value, and are only attested with certainty in connection with military and external affairs;[13] and civil legislation was left exclusively in the hands of the tribunes of the plebs before Sulla's reforms. Sandberg even states that in the pre-Sullan period the tribunes of the plebs and not the consuls were the 'leading magistrates' of the Roman Republic in the civil sphere.[14]

Sandberg is absolutely right when he claims that most of the abundant laws that were attributed to consuls by Rotondi have no grounds in ancient sources, but are hypothetical attributions or mere speculation, and in most cases the very existence of some laws is but a supposition.[15] He is also unquestionably correct when arguing that the main promoters of civil laws in the pre-Sullan age were the tribunes of the plebs, who were responsible for the vast majority of them.[16] However, his statement that the expression *legem* or *rogationem ferre ad populum* did not necessarily imply that the magistrates who were the subjects of this action were the *promulgatores* and *rogatores* of the corresponding law is mistaken: the expression *rogationem ferre* must identify the *rogator*, the proposer of a law.[17] Sandberg's thesis suggests that the participation in civil legislative practice of curule magistrates in general and consuls in particular was almost non-existent.[18] As we shall see later on, consular legislation in the pre-Sullan period was certainly rare, yet was significant.

---

[13] In fact, Sandberg only accepts as a certain testimony of a consul being in charge of the *promulgatio* or of the *rogatio* of a law the episode narrated by Livy (31.6.1–2) in connection with the declaration of war on the Macedonian king in the year 200. He also adds the aforementioned episode of Valerius Laevinus in 210 (Liv. 27.5.16–17), as well as the possible attribution to consul M'. Acilius Glabrio of the *lex Acilia de intercalatione* in 191, which he finally dismisses as untenable (Macrob. 1.13.21). Cf. Sandberg 2000: 128 n. 26; 2001: 58–61 and 147–50. Sandberg (2001: 76–9) adds to his list of possible consular laws those which are mentioned by the consuls' names in ancient sources.

[14] Sandberg 2001: 116: 'As a matter of fact, focusing on internal affairs we have to conclude that it was not the consuls, but the tribunes, who were the leading magistrates of the pre-Sullan Republic ... there were two spheres of public life in this period, each one with a separate administration: on one hand a civil sphere under the tribunes and, on the other, a military sphere under consular control.'

[15] Sandberg 2000: 123–6: 'In fact, Rotondi's work can be considered something of a codification of nineteenth-century, particularly German, scholarship' (125). Cf. Sandberg 2001: 63–6.

[16] Sandberg 2001: 96. Cf. Williamson 2005: 16–17.

[17] Sandberg 2001: 100–1. See the review of Crawford 2004. Cf. Williamson 2005: 22 n. 35.

[18] Sandberg 2000: 126: 'The participation of curule magistrates in the legislation of our period is as good as non-existent'; 2001: 97: 'there is no evidence for curule magistrates performing the *promulgatio* or the *rogatio* of other than military laws'.

It is indisputable that the consuls had a leading role in the legislative process of approval of the declaration of war against an enemy state,[19] which took place in the *comitia centuriata*.[20] An example illustrative of the usual procedure is narrated by Livy for the year 200.[21] After signing peace with the Carthaginians, Rome could focus all its attention on the eastern Mediterranean. There, the actions of Philip of Macedonia were generating growing concern amongst Roman senators. From Livy's text it can be gathered that in the final months of 201 there was already a determination in the senate to declare war on Philip as soon as possible.[22] In fact, the decision to start the war seems already to have been taken when the new consuls took office on the Ides of March of the year 200, since, following a senatorial decree, they performed a sacrifice that same day accompanied by a prayer asking the gods for success in the new war that was about to start.[23] The consuls informed the senate that the sacrifices had been carried out adequately and that, according to the haruspices, the gods had heard their prayer, since the victims of the sacrifice had provided favourable omens announcing a victory and the expansion of Roman boundaries.[24] Consequently, the senate resolved that the consul who was allotted Macedonia as his province should bring the question of the declaration of war against Philip before the people.[25]

Macedonia was allotted to P. Sulpicius Galba, who immediately presented a bill to this end before the assembly, therefore just at the beginning of the consular year.[26] Yet the consul's proposal was rejected in the comitia by almost all of the centuries.[27] The senate urged the consul to present the proposal again before the *comitia centuriata*, probably within a relatively short period of time.[28] Before the ballot, Sulpicius Galba addressed the

---

[19] Rich 1976: esp. 13–27. Cf. Walbank 1949.

[20] This is the conclusion derived from ancient sources, almost unanimously accepted: Mommsen 1887–8: III 343; Berger 1940; Rotondi 1912: 57–8; Rich 1976: 13. Paananen's affirmation (1993: 35–6) that declarations of war were usually approved by the tribal assembly on the proposal of the tribunes of the plebs totally contradicts the preserved ancient sources and has no grounds whatsoever. Cf. Paananen 1990: 180–6; Elster 2003: 279 n. 193.

[21] Warrior 1996 (see especially her chronological reconstruction, pp. 37–89). Cf. Rich 1976: 75–87; Harris 1979: 212–18; Gruen 1984: II 382–98; Elster 2003: 278–81.

[22] Liv. 31.1–3.   [23] Liv. 31.5.2–4.   [24] Liv. 31.5.7.   [25] Liv. 31.5.9.

[26] Liv. 31.6.1: 'P. Sulpicio provincia Macedonia sorti evenit isque rogationem promulgavit . . .'

[27] Liv. 31.6.3. Cf. Warrior 1996: 65–6.

[28] The lapse of time between the two *rogationes* has been debated at length: for some it was short, for others it was several months. The state of the question and the debate can be seen in Rich 1976: 76–9, who concludes that only a brief interval elapsed between the refusal of the first bill and the acceptance of the second: 'the assembly voted for war within a month or so of the start of the consular year'. Cf. Warrior 1996: 47: 'The vote for war against Philip could have been passed by the end of Roman April at the very latest.' More sceptical Gruen 1984: II 395: 'How much time elapsed between these two votes simply cannot be established and it is useless to guess.'

people in a *contio*, warning of the negative consequences of not starting a war against Philip at that time.[29] When he had finished his speech the ballot was conducted. On this occasion, the vote was in favour of the bill presented by the consul and, therefore, of the declaration of war.[30] The consuls, in accordance with the senate, decreed three days of supplication and prayers asking for success in the war.

The same pattern was reproduced in 191.[31] When the consular year began, the senate had already resolved to start a war against Antiochus. For this reason, the first task of the new consuls, before drawing lots for their provinces, was to perform sacrifices and say prayers specifically requesting divine help in the development of the new war. The sacrifices were performed adequately, the omens were favourable, and the haruspices asserted that everything indicated a victory and triumph and that the boundaries of Rome would expand as a result, repeating practically the same words that had been used after the propitiatory sacrifices prior to the war against Philip in the year 200.[32] Only then did the senators decide that a bill to declare war on Antiochus should be presented before the people.[33] The person in charge was the consul P. Cornelius Scipio.[34] The bill was passed by the *comitia centuriata*. After drawing lots for the provinces, the senate issued a *senatus consultum* ordering a supplication by both consuls and, in particular ordering the consul M'. Acilius, who had been allotted command over the war, to vow *ludi magni* in honour of Jupiter. The consuls proclaimed a supplication for two days, and the vow was carried out following the formula established by the *pontifex maximus*.[35]

Once again, in 171 the process of declaring war on King Perseus followed similar steps.[36] The need for war was fully accepted by the senate. The senators had already taken important measures in the military field which clearly announced that the conflict was inevitable.[37] In fact, as in previous cases, the senate ordered the consuls-elect for 171, immediately after being elected and before taking office, to perform sacrifices asking for success in the war that the Roman state was about to start.[38] One of the consuls of the

---

[29] Liv. 31.7. Cf. Harris 1979: 214: 'This oration has no claim whatsoever to authenticity, though it may of course accidentally happen to reproduce the arguments Sulpicus really used.'

[30] Liv. 31.8.1.   [31] Harris 1979: 219–23.   [32] Liv. 36.1.1–4.   [33] Rich 1976: 87–8; Elster 2003: 318–19.

[34] Liv. 36.1.5: 'haec cum renuntiata essent, solutis religione animis patres rogationem ad populum ferri iusserunt . . . P. Cornelius eam rogationem pertulit.'

[35] Liv. 36.2.5. When the time to declare war came, the consul Acilius, with the authorization of the senate, consulted the Fetiales on the appropriate way of declaring war on Antiochus and whether it was necessary to declare war on the Aetolians separately (Liv. 36.3.7).

[36] Rich 1976: 88–99; Harris 1979: 227–33; Gruen 1984: II 408–19; Elster 2003: 368–71.   [37] Liv. 42.27.

[38] Liv. 42.28.7.

consular year 172/1, still in office, was requested by the senate to vow games in honour of Jupiter.[39] When the new consuls P. Licinius Crassus and C. Cassius Longinus took office, they carried out sacrifices and prayers following the orders from the senate. The sacrifices were performed suitably and accepted by the gods. The haruspices declared, according to the usual formula, that the good omens indicated that victory, triumph, and the expansion of the boundaries of Rome would be achieved.[40] Only then did the senators order the consuls to bring the question of the declaration of war before the people assembled in the *comitia centuriata*. The bill was proposed before the people and the declaration of war was passed.[41] Once the war had officially been decided upon, the consuls were allotted both their provinces and their troops. In this context the senate decided exceptionally that the military tribunes for the Macedonian war were not to be elected by the people as usual, but directly appointed by the consuls and praetors. To this end, the senate instructed the consuls to make that proposal before the popular assembly.[42]

As can be seen, the procedure was in all three cases basically the same: the decision of the senate to start a war against an external enemy; favourable propitiatory sacrifices; a bill to the people presented and defended by order of the senate by one of the two consuls in 200 and 191, and apparently by both of them jointly in 171; a popular vote in the *comitia centuriata*; and supplications and offerings at all the *pulvinaria* carried out by senatorial decree. The only relevant difference is that in the year 200 the distribution of provinces amongst the consuls was completed before the popular vote, whereas in 191 and 171 it happened afterwards.[43]

It is clear that in all three cases one or both of the consuls acted as *rogator* or *rogatores legis*, as promoter or promoters of the law, as can be deduced both from the absolute similarity between the three procedures, and from the fact that Livy specifically attributes the initiative of bringing the

---

[39] Liv. 42.28.8.   [40] Liv. 42.30.8–9.

[41] Liv. 42.30.10–11: 'patres ... centuriatis comitiis primo <quoque> die ferre ad populum consules iusserunt ... haec rogatio ad populum lata est.' When later on some legates of Perseus arrived in Rome, they were not allowed to enter the city because the war had already been decided by the senate and the people (Liv. 42.36.1). App. *Mac.* 11.9 only alludes to a decision of the senate and does not mention the popular ballot.

[42] Liv. 42.31.5. Cf. Rotondi 1912: 282; Elster 2003: 367–8.

[43] Sumner (1966: 17–18) pointed out this fact, which he considered the ultimate reason why the popular assembly in the first place rejected the *rogatio de bello indicendo* in 200, namely that the people disapproved that a consul had been appointed for a war that was yet to be authorized. This thesis was discarded by Rich (1976: 21 n. 7), who nevertheless believes it probable that the opponents of the war used the problematic procedure as their argument and that this may have been the reason why in 191 and 171 the allocation of the provinces was carried out after the popular vote.

proposal before the people to Sulpicius Galba, to Scipio, and to the consuls of 171 respectively. In the year 200, Livy uses the formula 'rogationem promulgavit', in 191 'rogationem pertulit', in 171 '(rogationem) ferre ad populum' and 'rogatio lata est'. The same expression is used by Livy to refer to the bill regarding the appointment of the military tribunes: 'consules ad populum tulerunt'. Sandberg admits that in the proclamation of war against Philip in 200 the consul Galba acted as *promulgator* and *rogator*, given Livy's explicit account.[44] However, this is the only law of declaration of war for which Sandberg allows that its author was a consul. In his opinion, only the verbs *rogare* and *promulgare* are unequivocal indicators of the identity of the law-proposer, whereas the verb *ferre* does not necessarily indicate such a person. Consequently, the expression 'P. Cornelius eam rogationem pertulit' used by Livy does not, according to Sandberg, necessarily signify that Scipio was the *rogator*.

Sandberg claims that the phrase *consul legem tulit* in general indicates without a doubt that the consul was actually the proposer of the law, but that this does not mean that he brought the proposal before the assembly. Sandberg believes that the consul may have delegated a tribune of the plebs to bring the bill to the assembly, on the assumption that, in his opinion, all Republican legislation in the pre-Sullan period was tribunician.[45] There are indeed known cases where the consuls requested the tribunes of the plebs to bring a certain issue before the plebs. For example, this happened in the same year, 200, when two persons who had been elected curule aediles could not take office immediately, one of them because he was not in Rome as he was acting as proconsul in Hispania, the other, C. Valerius Flaccus, because he was the *flamen Dialis*, a priestly position that prevented him from taking the mandatory oath.[46] Upon Flaccus' request, the senate ordered that, provided the consuls agreed, another person should take the oath in his place. But the question had to be transferred by the consuls, if they considered it appropriate, to the tribunes of the plebs, in order for them to propose the bill to the plebs.[47] The tribunes brought the proposal to the assembly ('tribuni ad plebem tulerunt'), which approved the plebiscite. Something similar happened in 186, within the context of the scandal of the Bacchanalia and their repression. Following the request of the consul Postumius, the senate decided to reward the informers who had revealed the facts. For this purpose, the senate ordered the consul to ask

[44] Sandberg 2000: 128 n. 26.   [45] Sandberg 2000: 127; 2001: 97–104.   [46] Liv. 31.50.6–8.
[47] Liv. 31.50.9. Cf. Elster 2003: 284–6.

the tribunes of the plebs to bring a bill before the people, which they duly did.[48]

Both cases, like the other two instances recorded by Livy in which consuls are explicitly mentioned,[49] demonstrate the institutional collaboration between senate, consuls, and tribunes of the plebs. The consuls acted as the spokesmen of the senate, as was habitual during their stay in Rome, and at the same time as intermediaries between the senate and the tribunes.[50] But in no way can it be concluded from these examples that every time the consuls wanted to propose a bill they had to ask the tribunes of the plebs to be in charge of the lawmaking process in the popular assembly.[51]

Sandberg's excessively restrictive interpretation is untenable. On the three above-mentioned occasions the leading role played by the consuls in the passage of the declaration of war can be deduced categorically from the context. In contrast, there is no mention of a tribune of the plebs making any intervention in the process. To assume that a tribune intervened in it is mere speculation. On the other hand, as we have previously

---

[48] Liv. 39.19.3–7. Rotondi 1912: 276; Watson 1974: 7–8; Elster 2003: 335–7. On the privileges granted to Hispala, see Briscoe 2008: 287–90.

[49] Liv. 30.27.3; 30.41.4. Sandberg (2001: 98) cites six other passages in Livy that could refer to the senatorial practice of asking the consuls or a praetor to address the tribunes of the plebs in order to legislate. Other tribunician laws may actually have had the same origin, although details of the process involved are unknown. On this question, see Kunkel and Wittmann 1995: 611–25.

[50] It was also possible for the senate to make a request to the urban praetor to present a bill before the assembly. This happened in 208, when the praetor P. Licinius Varus brought before the people, by order of the senate, a proposal for the *ludi Apollinares* to be celebrated on the same day every year (Liv. 27.23.7). The fact that the praetor was the instrument of the senate on this occasion can be explained by the special circumstances of the Hannibalic War. The consuls had been retained in Rome because of religious duties, but once these were completed they had to take command of their troops as soon as possible, without waiting for the approval of the proposed law. On the other hand, the praetor was directly involved in the question, since he presided over the *ludi Apollinares* that year. Cf. Rotondi 1912: 260; Brennan 2000: 103–4; Elster 2003: 246–8.

[51] The fact that it was not the consuls who personally transferred the senatorial decision to the assembly may sometimes have been due to their being engaged in other duties that were considered more important at the time. For example, in 186 it was probably more urgent for the consul to handle the repression of the seditious Bacchanalia (Elster 2003: 336). But neither the possible incompatibility with other functions attached to the magistracy, nor the pressure to leave Rome to go to a province, are applicable to all cases where the senate asked a curule magistrate to request a tribune of the plebs to promote a law. This could hardly explain what happened in 167, when the senate ordered the urban praetor Q. Cassius to ask the tribunes of the plebs to produce a bill for the three *triumphatores*, Anicius, Octavius, and Aemilius Paullus, to enable them to keep their *imperium* until the day of celebration of the triumph (Liv. 45.35.4; we find a similar procedure regarding the *ovatio* awarded to the proconsul M. Claudius Marcellus in 211). It is obvious that the urban praetor, forced to stay in Rome during his entire term of office, could in theory have promoted the bill himself, but it was considered more appropriate for the tribunes to be in charge. This suggests that for reasons which are not very clearly explained, some legislative matters were considered inappropriate for the curule magistrates to enact, and it was preferred that the tribunes of the plebs had the initiative for these. Cf. Kunkel and Wittmann 1995: 617–20.

seen, diplomatic activity and foreign affairs were mainly in the hands of the consuls, especially if they were in Rome, as happened in 200, 191, and 171, since the events occurred at the beginning of the consular year. In practice it was common that, as happened in diplomacy, a war that already had senatorial consensus was nevertheless postponed until the new consuls took office so that they could be in charge of all the procedures leading to the official declaration of war and also deal with the recruitment of the troops that would be under their command.[52] In fact, the beginning of the consular year was placed on 1 January in 153 in order for the consul Q. Fulvius Nobilior to take over the campaign against the Segedians in Hispania, against whom Rome had declared war, from the beginning of his term of office.[53] Finally, if we take into account the fact that the popular decision had to be taken in the *comitia centuriata*, the presidency over the assembly by one of the consuls is fully justified. In conclusion, there appears to be no doubt that in all the known cases a consul acted as *rogator* of the laws passed by the people to declare war on an external enemy.

Valerius Maximus' sentence stating that P. Cornelius Scipio Nasica declared war on Jugurtha while a consul in 111 probably ought to be interpreted in this sense.[54] Valerius Maximus' statement must not be taken in its strictly literal sense and ought to be connected with a passage of Orosius, undoubtedly derived from Livy.[55] Orosius' passage must be understood in the sense that the war against Jugurtha was approved by the senate and voted by the people, following the usual procedure.[56] Valerius Maximus' sentence fits perfectly into this pattern and should be understood in the sense that the consul Scipio Nasica was responsible for putting forward and supporting the bill of declaration of war in the comitia.[57]

A more complicated question is whether this was always the procedure for a declaration of war in the pre-Sullan period. Livy's account is in general much more succinct than that described in the aforementioned cases, but there is no doubt that the initiative belonged to the senate while the final decision lay with the vote of the citizens in comitia, in agreement with the

---

[52] Rich 1976: 20–7. Cf. Walbank 1941: 91.   [53] Liv. *per.* 47.

[54] V. Max. 7.5.2: 'P. autem Scipio Nasica togatae potentiae clarissimum lumen, qui consul Iugurthae bellum indixit'.

[55] Oros. 5.15.1: 'Iugurthae Numidarum regi bellum consensu populi Romani senatus indixit.' Cf. Liv. *per.* 64: 'bellum Iugurthae indictum.'

[56] Cf. Rich 1976: 50.

[57] Rich (1976: 102) does not support the thesis that Nasica was the *rogator legis*. In his opinion, Valerius Maximus 'may have meant no more than that Nasica was consul at the time that war was declared, or alternatively that Nasica as consul helped to perform that part of the formal preliminaries of war which fell to the consuls'.

common pattern 'the senate recommends, the people orders' (*senatus censet, populus iubet*).[58] In fact, during the wars fought in Italy in the fourth century and the beginning of the third century, Livy specifically states on numerous occasions that the people had decided on the war.[59] But he does not provide any details of the process; neither does he mention the magistrate in charge of presenting the bill to the people.[60] Yet there is one revealing fact. The declaration of war always occurs at the beginning of the consular year, when the consuls are still in Rome.[61] Livy links the debate on the suitability of starting a war with the taking of office of the new consuls on various occasions: for example, in 325 the consuls posed the question of the war against the Vestini in the senate before it was brought before the people.[62] This points to continuity throughout the pre-Sullan age in the practice of postponing the beginning of a war so as to be the responsibility of the new consuls.

Given these circumstances, it is totally improbable that a magistrate other than one of the consuls, much less a tribune of the plebs, was in charge of bringing the corresponding bill on the declaration of war to the assembly. As long as they were present in Rome, it was in general the consuls who acted as the link between the senate and the people by issuing edicts that reflected the senatorial will. In the event of a declaration of war previously agreed by the senators, it is reasonable to suppose that it would have been the consuls who were to turn the *senatus consultum* into a *rogatio* before the *comitia centuriata* and that they would defend the viability of an external policy that they were to put into practice in the immediate future.

Nevertheless, it is noteworthy that, of the numerous armed conflicts undertaken by the Roman state between 218 and 167, a period for which we have the books of Livy, it is indicated in only a few cases by the Latin author – or any other ancient source – that they were started by popular vote.[63] This suggests the possibility that the procedure was only used in

---

[58] Elster 2003: 370.

[59] Liv. 7.6.7 (year 362); 7.12.6 (358); 8.22.8 (327); 8.25.2 (cf. Dion. Hal. 15.10.2) (326); 8.29.6 (325); 9.45.8 (300); 10.12.3 (298).

[60] Except for 7.12.6, where Livy claims that the new consuls Fabius and Plautius declared the war 'iussu populi'. Probably this may mean that they proposed the question to the assembly, as I believe Nasica's action in 111 ought to be understood (see above, p. 107). The same interpretation could apply to Liv. 7.19.10, in this case in connection with the dictator T. Manlius in 353.

[61] Rich 1976: 22: 'As for war votes, there is no reason to suppose that the senate ever had a *rogatio* for war presented to the assembly other than at the beginning of a consular year, except perhaps for the war vote which led to the acquisition of Sardinia' (cf. ibid. p. 65 n. 23).

[62] Liv. 8.29.2.

[63] Apart from the aforementioned instances, Livy also claims that the declaration of war against Carthage in 218 was voted in the comitia, but he does not allude to the magistrate who presented

certain cases. Rich proposed the following: that the people would be consulted only on wars that had to be fought against enemies located in areas where a permanent province had not yet been created.[64] This was because this type of war usually involved sending a consul, at times both of them, to the region. On the other hand, in the north of Italy or in the permanent provinces, war had become chronic, and it did not need popular approval to be continued. In practice, in the consolidated provinces there was generally a permanent army that could immediately tackle any military problem that might arise there.[65]

The exceptional nature of confrontations against such powerful enemies as Carthage, Philip, Antiochus, or Perseus, which could pose serious trouble, may have made it advisable to have popular support and would account for the vote in the comitia. In these cases the leading role of the consuls is logical, in view of the predictable repercussions of such a decision in the life of the community and the fact that at least one of the consuls would have to take command of the Roman troops immediately. Besides, Carthage and the Seleucid and Macedonian kingdoms were perceived as 'civilized' interlocutors, as states that had a complex internal organization. However, in Hispania, for example, the indigenous peoples were seen from Rome as 'barbarians' with poor culture and lacking a state organization comparable to Rome's or to that of the great Mediterranean powers. This fact may have had an influence on the need to justify and ratify certain wars through popular decision, whereas other wars, for example those fought in Hispania, were perceived as a continuous process of conquest that did not require that legislative effort.

Finally, a consular law closely linked with the military sphere could also be included in this section. In the context of the war against the Celtiberians, the consul C. Hostilius Mancinus was defeated by the Numantines in 137. In order to save his army he was forced to surrender and accept a peace treaty under unfavourable terms. On his return to Rome, the senate refused to ratify this treaty because the stipulations were considered unacceptable and because they deemed Mancinus' performance dishonourable. The senators resolved instead to deliver Mancinus to the

---

the bill before the assembly (Liv. 21.17.4). Rich (1976: 14) also includes amongst the wars fought by Rome that may have been voted by the people the Third Punic War in 149 and the First Mithridatic War (p. 102: presumably at the beginning of the year), as well as the war declared against Carthage in 237 which was avoided by the Carthaginians by paying the Roman state 1200 talents and by giving up their claims to Sardinia. However, Greek sources regarding the beginning of these conflicts (mainly Polybius and Appian) simply allude generically to the declaration of war in each case without specifically stating that it was preceded by popular vote.

[64] Rich 1976: 15.   [65] Rich 1976: 20.

Numantines and commissioned the consuls of 136, L. Furius Philus and Sex. Atilius Serranus, to present before the people a bill to this end.[66] The proposal apparently initially included the handing over of all Mancinus' general staff, but the bill which was finally passed limited the punishment exclusively to the ex-consul. The consul Furius took Mancinus to the gates of Numantia and delivered him to its inhabitants.

Whereas the involvement of consuls in the process of declaring war on an enemy state is obvious from the aforementioned facts, their intervention in civil legislation during the pre-Sullan period is more questionable. In fact, as Sandberg rightly states, there is no certainty of their participation in many laws that Rotondi attributed to consuls. On the contrary, in many cases consular participation is only a hypothesis, if not mere speculation, formulated by modern scholarship. The use of Rotondi's compilation and the lack of alternative general studies have for decades resulted in the mechanical repetition of these hypotheses without consideration of the need for further verification. The reality is that ancient sources only attribute to consuls the promulgation of a few laws during this whole period and that, even in those cases, the circumstances are not always clear.

Actually, difficulties appear the first time Livy mentions a consul as the promoter of a particular law. In 357, the consul Cn. Manlius Capitolinus may have proposed a law ('legem ... tulit') to create a tax on manumissions. What makes this fact extraordinary is that it occurred outside Rome, while he was in the camp at Sutrium with his troops. He may have made citizens under his command vote there after ordering them to organize by tribes (*tributim*) for the ballot, as in normal comitia.[67] The consular bill was passed by the soldier-citizens and, even more surprisingly, the law was also approved as such by the senate, despite the evident irregularity of the process (Livy talks about 'a new example'). However, the tribunes of the plebs thought it a bad example that a law should be passed in a military camp. Although they did not question the approved law, they had another bill passed whereby the maximum penalty was to be applied to those who, from that moment on, gathered the people in an assembly outside the habitual meeting places of Rome. The danger they saw in such action was that the soldiers, linked to a commander through their oath of obedience, might approve measures that would be detrimental to the Roman people as a whole.[68]

---

[66] Cic. *Off.* 3.109. Cf. Cic. *Rep.* 3.28; *de Orat.* 1.181; Eutrop. 4.17; Oros. 5.5.10; App. *Iber.* 83; Liv. *per.* 56; Vell. 2.1.5; Flor. 1.34; Plut. *Ti. Gr.* 7.3. Cf. Broughton 1951–86: 1 486; Rotondi 1912: 297–8; Sandberg 2001: 92; Elster 2003: 447–9.

[67] Liv. 7.16.7. Cf. Elster 2003: 16–18.   [68] Liv. 7.16.8.

This episode is extremely surprising in all its details, and because of this its historical value appears quite dubious at first glance: a consul in the exercise of his military duties convened his soldiers to consider a proposed bill with civil contents; he himself chose the form of the vote, actually turning the assembly into comitia by tribes; the law was ratified later on by the senate despite the procedure, which suggests that the senators did not consider the procedure invalid. The reaction of the tribunes of the plebs could be understood as a way of preventing the lawmaking process being transferred from the civil sphere in the *Urbs*, where they had an important leading role, to the military sphere outside Rome, where at the time only consuls and occasionally dictators had *imperium*. As some scholars have pointed out, Livy's narration is so bizarre and apparently so far removed from constitutional practice that it is hard to believe that it was simply invented.[69]

According to Livy, in the year 300 the consul M. Valerius Corvus promoted ('legem tulit') a *lex de provocatione*, presumably the third on this topic to have been sponsored by members of the gens Valeria since the beginning of the Republic.[70] The purpose of the law seems to have been to improve the protection of citizens in comparison with the previous laws, the first of them presumably approved in 509, the same year in which the monarchy was abolished, the second in 449.[71] The right of appeal (*provocatio*) is a greatly debated question regarding its establishment and enforcement but, in general, scholarship considers this Valerian law of 300 to be genuine.[72] There is therefore no reason to doubt that the consul Valerius was the *rogator* of this law, which is thus the first consular civil law attested in the history of Rome that was passed in the *Urbs*.

In 215 a consular law was enacted with the purpose of electing duumvirs for the dedication of a temple in an unusual context. Q. Fabius Maximus made a request to the senate that he be appointed duumvir in charge of the consecration of the temple of Venus Erycina that he had vowed as dictator

---

[69] Oakley 1998: II 181–2, considers the episode so peculiar that he thinks it must be true, that it cannot be a mere invention. In the same sense, Elster 2003: 18. The episode is discussed in detail by Di Porto 1981.

[70] Liv. 10.9.3. Cf. Rotondi 1912: 235; Sandberg 2001: 76–7; Elster 2003: 98–103. Surprisingly, Livy's epitomist attributes this *lex de provocatione* to a consul called Murena totally unknown in the *fasti* and other written sources: 'lex de provocatione ad populum a Murena consule tertio tunc lata est' (Liv. *per.* 10). Mitchell (1990: 169) does not consider this measure in connection with the *provocatio* a genuine law.

[71] Cf. Rotondi 1912: 190 and 204; Flach 1994: 59–62 and 216–18.

[72] Martin 1970: esp. 74–6; Lintott 1972: 227; Bauman 1973: 34; Develin 1978: esp. 46–55; Hölkeskamp 1987: 200.

some years before. The senate ordered the consul-elect Ti. Sempronius
Gracchus to bring the bill before the people upon taking over his consulship, which he did.[73] Sandberg surmises that it could rather be seen as a
plebiscite promoted by the tribunes of the plebs, although there is nothing
in Livy's text to indicate this.[74]

When referring to the introduction of intercalary months in the Roman
calendar, Macrobius mentions the various attributions made by several
ancient authors. Whereas Licinius Macer, Valerius Antias, and Iunius
attributed the introduction of the intercalary month to Romulus, Numa
Pompilius, and Servius Tullius respectively, other authors placed the beginning of this measure at various times in the Republican period. Sempronius
Tuditanus and Cassius Hemina attributed it to the decemvirs, and Varro to
the consuls of 472. On the other hand, Fulvius Nobilior attributes a law on
intercalation to the consul of 191, M'. Acilius Glabrio.[75] Macrobius does not
give details of this law, which must have governed specific aspects of the
process of introduction of the intercalary months, but which did not
result in their introduction into the calendar. The existence of intercalary
months undoubtedly goes back to a previous age, since the *fasti triumphales*
indicate that the consuls C. Duilius and P. Cornelius Lentulus celebrated
their triumphs respectively in the intercalary months of 260 and 236.[76]

One of the first known laws dealing with bribery (*lex de ambitu*) was
introduced, according to Livy, in 181 by the consuls P. Cornelius Cethegus
and M. Baebius Tamphilus.[77] Livy simply reports this without providing
any details on the process of passage of the law or its contents. But from his
account the interesting fact that the approval of the law must have happened
at the beginning of the consular year can be deduced. Following his usual
order, after providing the names of the new consuls, Livy reports the
allocation of provinces to consuls and praetors as well as the distribution
of the necessary troops. He then describes the prodigies and their expiation.
At this point Livy inserts his sentence about the passage of the *lex de ambitu*,
and then goes on to talk about the foreign embassies brought to the senate.
After that, Livy narrates the events in Macedonia and only later does he
state that the consuls left Rome after completing the recruitment of the

---

[73] Liv. 23.30.13–14. Cf. Rotondi 1912: 253; Orlin 1997: 175–6; Elster 2003: 212–13.

[74] Sandberg 2001: 98–9. See the critical remarks of Crawford 2004: 171–2.   [75] Macrob. 1.13.20–21.

[76] *CIL* I².1 p. 47. Cf. Mommsen 1859: 40; Rotondi 1912: 273; Michels 1967: 101–3; Brind'Amour 1983:
156–7; Elster 2003: 315–18. Sandberg 2001: 60–1: there is no evidence that Acilius Glabrio promoted
any kind of law on the *intercalatio* during his consulship.

[77] Liv. 40.19.11. Cf. Berger 1925; Rotondi 1912: 277; Elster 2003: 339–40. Briscoe 2008: 461: 'It is likely
that this is the law which made electoral bribery a capital offence.'

troops.[78] Therefore, the law was probably sponsored by the consuls, on the authority of the senate ('ex auctoritate senatus'), in the weeks that elapsed from their taking office on the Ides of March to their departure from Rome to take command of their troops.

The *lex Fannia cibaria* was passed in 161. Its promoter was the consul C. Fannius Strabo, as stated by Macrobius and Pliny.[79] Citing Sammonicus Serenus, a grammarian and antiquarian active at the end of the second and beginning of the third century AD, Macrobius adds that, in order to give more authority to the law, it was preferred that the bill be brought before the people by one of the consuls instead of a praetor or the tribunes of the plebs. Implicitly, the antiquarian bestows a somewhat exceptional character on the fact that the law was promoted by a consul.[80] The *lex Fannia* aimed to restrict expenses on banquets and specified the number of guests and even the food that could be served. In this sense it was conceived as a step beyond the *lex Orchia*, since it was stricter.[81] A new sumptuary law was proposed by the consul M. Aemilius Scaurus in 115, also intended to regulate expenses on banquets.[82] The same consul may have also enacted a law on freedmen's suffrage.[83]

Plutarch is the only source that provides the information that C. Laelius wanted to promote an agrarian law, but finally he sensibly backed down when faced with great opposition in the senate.[84] Little is known about the political career of Laelius. He was a praetor in 145 and a consul in 140. We should not necessarily presume that he had previously been a tribune of the

---

[78] Liv. 40.26. This course of events makes it improbable that a different *lex Baebia*, whereby the election of four or six praetors in alternate years was prescribed and whose enforcement is referred to by Livy in 180 (Liv. 40.44.2), may be attributed to the consul Baebius Tamphilus, as suggested by Rotondi 1912: 277–8 (cf. Broughton 1951–86: I 384). Elster (2003: 341) points out that this law was probably promoted by an unknown tribune of the plebs called Baebius in 180 and was immediately enforced in the elections of praetors for the following year. However, Brennan (2000: 169–70, following Mommsen 1887–8: II 198) argues that the *lex Cornelia Baebia de ambitu* included another provision requiring that four and six praetors respectively be elected in alternate years. Consequently there would be only one consular *lex Baebia* connecting the *ambitus* measure and the provision on the number of praetors. Kunkel and Wittmann (1995: 82 n. 96) also imply the existence of only one law, whereas Nadig (1997: 26–8) argues for two different laws. Recently Briscoe (2008: 523) has suggested 'that while the *ambitus* law was carried by both consuls, Baebius alone was responsible for the law on the number of praetors'.

[79] Macrob. 3.17.3–5; Plin. *Nat.* 10.139. Cf. Ath. 6.274 c; Gel. 2.24.3–6.   [80] Sandberg 2001: 102.

[81] Rotondi 1912: 287–8; Elster 2003: 394–400.

[82] Gel. 2.24.12. Mitchell (1990: 197) rejects the historical value both of *lex Fannia* and of *lex Aemilia*, since he considers the attribution to the respective consuls a mistake by the sources. See Sandberg 2001: 101.

[83] *De vir. ill.* 72.5: 'consul [M. Aemilius Scaurus] legem de sumptibus et libertinorum suffragiis tulit'. Cf. Broughton 1951–86: I 531; Rotondi 1912: 320–1; Sandberg 2001: 78 and 93. Williamson (2005: 461) considers it 'uncertain or conjectural.'

[84] Plut. *Ti.Gr.* 8.3–4.

plebs and that it was at that time that he presented his bill. It is therefore probable that this happened during his consulship, chronologically closer to the tribunate of Tiberius Gracchus.[85] In fact, Plutarch mentions Laelius' attempt as a close antecedent of the Gracchan reform.

In the year 106, the consul Q. Servilius Caepio forced through a *lex iudicaria* which eliminated the equestrian monopoly in the courts and re-introduced senators as jurors.[86] It was a compromise law because in the following years juries had to comprise both senators and equestrians.

In the last decade of the second century, two laws regarding the military world were probably passed. This is understandable in a historical context full of dangerous confrontations in the years when the Roman legions were engaged against Jugurtha in the north of Africa and against the Cimbri and the Teutons in different theatres in Italy, Gaul, and even Hispania. Allowing for the recruitment of a higher number of men was presumably the reason why the consul M. Iunius Silanus promoted a bill in 109 abrogating the laws passed some years before that had reduced the period of time for military service.[87] It is not known which specific laws were repealed in 109, although they are commonly ascribed to the Gracchan period.[88] It is possibly one of the consuls of the year 105, P. Rutilius Rufus, to whom should be attributed the law which established the existence of military tribunes directly appointed by the consul, besides those who were usually elected by the people.[89] Festus explains that *Rufuli* was the name given to these military tribunes who were appointed by the consuls and that the law introducing this regulation was promoted by Rutilius Rufus, but he does not specify which magistracy he was holding when he promoted the law.[90] However, it is very likely that this happened during his consulship. We know that Rome and Italy constituted the province of Rutilius Rufus in 105 and that he took important decisions in the military field. He recruited a new army that Marius was to use later on against the Cimbri, and after the defeat at Arausio he issued an edict banning men under thirty-five from leaving Italy.[91]

---

[85] Broughton 1951–86: I 479; Williamson 2005: 458.
[86] Cic. *Inv.* 1.92; *Brut.* 161; 164; 296; *de Orat.* 2.223; *Clu.* 140; Tac. *Ann.* 12.60. Cf. Broughton 1951–86: I 553; Rotondi 1912: 325; Gruen 1968: 158–9; Eder 1969: 140,2; Sandberg 2001: 78. Griffin (1973b) considers the *lex Servilia* an extortion law and not a judiciary law applicable to all the existing tribunals.
[87] Asc. 68 C. Broughton 1951–86: I 545; Rotondi 1912: 324; Williamson 2005: 461.
[88] Brunt 1971: 401 n. 4; 407; Marshall 1985: 242.
[89] Broughton 1951–86: I 555; Rotondi 1912: 478–9; Williamson 2005: 461.
[90] Fest. s. v. Rufuli p. 261 M. = 316 L.: 'Rufuli tribuni mil<itum appellabantur, quos> consul faciebat, n<on populus; de quorum iure quod> Rutilius Rufus leg<em tulerit>.'
[91] Gran. Licin. 21 B. Cf. Marshall 1985: 242.

The process of approval of a bill demanded a debate before the people in *contiones* prior to the presentation of the *rogatio* by the promoter for its passage in the comitia. Until the year 98 we do not know whether there was a standard or legal period of time for completing the public discussion of the bill. In 98, a law was passed establishing the *trinundinum* as the period that had to elapse between the promulgation of a bill and its vote in the comitia, that is, a period that had to include three market days. The bill was put forward by the consuls Q. Caecilius Metellus Nepos and T. Didius.[92]

In various instances in the second century and, in particular, at the beginning of the first, the sources attribute to certain consuls laws regarding one of the greatest problems for the Roman state: the legal integration of the Latins and Italians within the Roman *civitas* or their direct physical integration into the city of Rome proper. Thus, at the beginning of the consular year 177/6, ambassadors from Latin towns arrived in Rome to complain about the growing emigration of their inhabitants to the *Urbs* and to request that those emigrants be forced to return to their towns.[93] The senate admitted that their petitions were fair and took a series of measures intended to resolve the issue. Amongst them was the passage of a law ordering the Latins to leave Rome. In compliance with the orders of the senate, the person in charge of its promulgation was the consul C. Claudius Pulcher.[94]

Some decades later, Valerius Maximus attributes to the consul M. Fulvius Flaccus in 125 an attempt at promulgating a general law to grant Roman citizenship and the right of appeal to the Italian allies.[95] Senatorial opposition prevented his attempt from succeeding, despite the confrontation of the consul and the senate narrated by the Latin author. In order to avoid further deterioration of the situation and to temper the conflict, Flaccus was sent to fight the Salluvii and Vocontii in Gaul. Flaccus' failure to convince the majority of senators of the need for the law that he proposed caused the problem to fester and grow in the ensuing decades. It appears that an important number of Italians had obtained citizenship irregularly in the first years of the first century, and they managed to be included in the lists

---

[92] Cic. *Phil.* 5.8. Cf. Cic. *Sest.* 135; *Dom.* 41; 53; Schol. Bob. 140 St. Rotondi 1912: 335; Sandberg 2001: 78. On the *trinundinum*, see Mommsen 1887–8: III 376–7, who defends its existence already in the early Republic; Lintott 1965: 281–5; Michels 1967: 191–206; Staveley (1972: 144) believed that it could have become conventional already towards the end of the third century.

[93] Liv. 41.8. Cf. Jehne 2009: 149–51.

[94] Liv. 41.9.9. Cf. Rotondi 1912: 280; Elster 2003: 357–9; Williamson 2005: 262.

[95] V. Max. 9.5.1. Cf. Broughton 1951–86: I 510; Rotondi 1912: 306; Sandberg 2001: 92. Regarding the historical context in which the attempt by Fulvius Flaccus was made see Wulff 1991: 218–23; 2002: 60–3.

of citizens without holding the appropriate legal title. In order to stop this process, the consuls of 95, L. Licinius Crassus and Q. Mucius Scaevola, enacted a law, with the support of the majority of the senate, whereby all those Italians who had been included illegally in the lists of the census were to be excluded from them, and a special court was created to punish those who had acted irregularly.[96]

Once the Social War started some years later, Rome decided to use the system of legal enfranchisement to try to end the conflict. The consul L. Iulius Caesar had a law passed at the end of 90 whereby Roman citizenship was granted to all Latins and Italians who had remained loyal and whose original communities declared their desire to obtain this right.[97] Apparently, the law may have included a stipulation that allowed generals to grant citizenship to troops who had distinguished themselves by their loyalty to Rome, as can be deduced from the grant given to the *turma Salluitana* recorded in the so-called Bronze of Asculum.[98] This *lex Iulia de civitate*, an unprecedented concession from the perspective of the Roman state, succeeded in preventing the spread of the conflict, since the Etruscans and Umbrians maintained their loyalty.[99] Actually, the offer was accepted by the vast majority. Naples in Campania and Heraclea in Lucania hesitated to accept Roman citizenship, but they eventually did so. The following year, the consul Cn. Pompeius Strabo sponsored a law that confirmed the forced liberalization of the Roman state, granting the Latin right (*ius Latii*) to the inhabitants of Cisalpine Gaul.[100] This was an initial step towards full Roman citizenship in this region, which was only to be granted in general in the year 49.

During the turbulent decade of the eighties we find some consular laws in the context of the conflict that would eventually lead to open civil war. In 88, after the entry into Rome of the consul L. Cornelius Sulla with his troops, he and his colleague in the consulship, Q. Pompeius Rufus, passed a law to exile the followers of C. Marius[101] and introduced, according to Appian, a series of institutional reforms which anticipated those that were to

---

[96] Cic. *Off.* 3.47; *Balb.* 48; 54; *Brut.* 63. Cf. Broughton 1951–86: II 11; Rotondi 1912: 335; Sandberg 2001: 78–9. Regarding the effects of the law on the conflict between the Roman state and the Italians, see Wulff 1991: 299–304; 2002: 65. On the relationship between the Italians and Rome in the first century, see now Bispham 2007.

[97] Cic. *Balb.* 21; App. *B.Civ.* 1.48; Gel. 4.4.3. Cf. Rotondi 1912: 338–9; Sandberg 2001: 79; Williamson 2005: 326–8.

[98] *CIL* I² 709 = *ILS* 8888.　[99] Wulff 2002: 69; 118–19.

[100] Plin. *Nat.* 3.138; Asc. 3 C. Cf. Cass. Dio 37.9.3. Rotondi 1912: 342; Sandberg 2001: 79. On the contents of the law and its enforcement, Ewins 1955; Wulff 2002: 69–70.

[101] Vell. 2.19.1.

be implemented by Sulla during his dictatorship.[102] Above all, they were intended to restrict the powers, and consequently the political influence, of the tribunes of the plebs and the popular assemblies and thus strengthen the senate. They set forth the compulsory approval by the senate of all bills before they were put to a popular vote. The comitia by tribes were stripped of lawmaking capacity, which remained exclusively for the *comitia centuriata*, whereas the only duty of the plebeian assembly was the election of the tribunes of the plebs. In practice, these two laws left the legislative initiative exclusively in the hands of the senate and granted the members of the first census classes the decision on their approval. A complementary stipulation restricted the capacities of the tribunes of the plebs, although its precise contents are unknown. It was probably a very similar law to that enacted by the dictator Sulla regarding the tribunes in 81. Another law increased the number of senators to six hundred. The new members of the Curia were to be recruited in particular amongst the equites. It is improbable that the consuls had time to put this measure into practice, a measure which was also taken by Sulla later during his dictatorship. Finally, another law established the foundation of twelve colonies, which in all probability never happened.

The last consular regulations of the year 88 did not affect the institutional order but were dictated by the difficult economic situation at the time, which was becoming more acute due to the loss of income from Asia caused by the recent invasion of Mithridates. The immediate result was the excessive debt of many citizens. Due to this, a maximum interest rate for loans was established by law while one-tenth of all existing debts were cancelled.[103] The problem was not solved, since the suffect consul L. Valerius Flaccus carried in 86 a law cancelling three-quarters of all debts.[104]

These are all the consular laws prior to Sulla's dictatorship attested in ancient sources whose existence is certain or probable.[105] Although there may have been other consular laws for which there is no clear evidence,[106] in

---

[102] App. *B.Civ.* 1.59; cf. Liv. *per.* 77. Cf. Rotondi 1912: 343–4. On the authenticity of the laws passed during Sulla's consulship in 88, Keaveney 1982: 67–9. Cf. Williamson 2005: 331–2: 'Never before had Roman consuls turned to public lawmaking on such a scale, under such circumstances, as a deliberate corrective to a prior public and legitimate expression of community-wide wishes.'

[103] Fest. p. 375 M. = p. 516 L. Cf. Rotondi 1912: 344.

[104] Vell. 2.23.2 defines the so-called *lex Valeria de aere alieno* as 'a most shameful law' ('turpissima lex'). Cf. Williamson 2005: 464.

[105] See Williamson 2005: Appendix C, 451–73, containing a list of all reliable laws and proposals between 350 and 25.

[106] Rotondi's catalogue contains other possible consular laws, in all cases very doubtful or mere conjectures: in 338 the *lex Maenia de die instauraticio*, presumably attributed to the consul C. Maenius, but which may have also been promoted by the tribune of the plebs of the same

any event it is a small number, especially if we compare it with the abundant legislative activities of the tribunes of the plebs for the same period.[107] Consuls obviously had legislative capacity, but it is evident that they used it only occasionally, usually following orders from the senate.

The explanation does not lie in any presumed legal restriction on their legislative duties or in any strict regulation of the functions of the consuls and tribunes of the plebs whereby only the latter had the power of civil legislation. The main reason for the lack of consular legislation was the absence of consuls from Rome during most of their time in office, which made it very difficult for them to promote bills. In practice, this could only happen in the first weeks of the consular year, before they departed for their provinces. In fact, all the known laws about the declaration of war were passed at the beginning of the respective consular years, and the same happened in the civil sphere, at least with the *lex Sempronia* that promoted the election of duumvirs for the dedication of a temple in 215, the *lex de ambitu* of the consuls Cornelius and Baebius in 181, and the *lex Claudia* on the Latins in 177. For the other known consular laws there are insufficient details to determine the moment at which they were approved, although they too were probably passed at the beginning of the consular year. Nevertheless, the consular agenda in those first weeks of the year was full of other duties that would have left them very little time for legislative activity: expiation of prodigies, celebration of the *feriae Latinae*, diplomatic matters, recruitment of troops.[108] Although not impossible, it

---

name in 279 (Macrob. 1.11.3–5. Broughton 1951–86: I 193; Rotondi 1912: 228; Elster 2003: 50–1); in 326 the so-called *lex Poetelia Papiria de nexis*, promoted according to Livy by the consuls C. Poetelius Libo and L. Papirius Cursor, but more probably by the dictator C. Poetelius Libo Visolus in 313 (Liv. 8.28; Var. *L.* 7.105; Dion. Hal. 16.5. Mommsen 1962: II 242–3; Rotondi 1912: 230–1; Watson 1974: 9–12; Sandberg 2001: 87 and 99; Elster 2003: 63–71); in 295 the *lex de provincia extra sortem danda*, supposedly promoted by the consul P. Decius Mus, although even Livy questions its authenticity (Liv. 10.24.3–4; 10.26.5; Rotondi 1912: 237; Sandberg 2001: 87; Elster 2003: 112–14); in 269 the so-called *lex Fabia Ogulnia*, whereby the minting of silver coins was introduced in Rome, probably through senatorial decision rather than through a consular law, though the date is, in any event, correct (Liv. *per.* 15; Plin. *Nat.* 33.44; Fest. p. 347 M. = 468–70 L.; Rotondi 1912: 243–4; Sandberg 2001: 88; Elster 2003: 139–40); in 217 the *lex <Fla>minia minus solvendi* attributed to the consul C. Flaminius, who could hardly promote the law, since he was apparently only in Rome for a few days during his term of office (Fest. p. 347 M. = p. 470 L.; Plin. *Nat.* 33.45. Willems 1883: II 438 n. 3; Rotondi 1912: 250; Crawford 1974: II 614; Paananen 1993: 61; Sandberg 2001: 88–9; Elster 2003: 193–4); in 159 a *lex de ambitu* was passed (Liv. *per.* 47: 'lex de ambitu lata'), which is usually attributed to the consuls of that year, probably because of the consular law of 181, but without any supporting arguments to justify this attribution (Rotondi 1912: 288; Sandberg 2001: 42; Elster 2003: 400–1). However, Williamson (2005: 458) includes it in the list of reliable laws and proposals.

[107] Sandberg 2001: 46–54; 67–73.

[108] The *lex Caecilia Didia* of 98 introduced the need for a bill to be debated in *contiones* for a *trinundinum* before it was put to vote (see above, p. 115). It is not certain whether this period of time was also conventionally respected before this date, but there is no doubt that the debate of the

would therefore be difficult for consuls to combine their civil duties in Rome with the enactment and defence of their own bills, and this would account for the scarcity of consular laws. Obviously, this does not exclude other reasons such as, for example, the aforementioned fact that it was preferred that some questions be taken before the people by the tribunes of the plebs rather than by curule magistrates.

From a chronological point of view, in the fourth century only the *lex Valeria de provocatione* is known besides the law that was allegedly promoted by Manlius Capitolinus in 357 in the military camp. The loss of Livy's work may explain the apparent lack of consular laws in the third century. However, when we recover Livy as our main source of information, the situation does not change radically. Apart from the laws of declaration of war, between 218 and 167 the known consular laws are the *lex Sempronia* in 215, the law on intercalary months in 191, the first law dealing with bribery in 181, the *lex Claudia* in 177, and the law of 171 on appointment of military tribunes. Soon after that, in 161, the *lex Fannia cibaria* was passed. The active involvement of consuls in civil legislation increased proportionally in the decades before Sulla's dictatorship. In contrast to the six consular laws attested in more than half a century between 215 and 161, we also know of six between 115 and 89, apart from the package of reforms attributed to the consuls of the year 88, Sulla and Pompeius Rufus, which presaged those carried out by Sulla some years later.

The reason for the increase in consular legislative activity at the end of the second century and the beginning of the first may be found in the increased amount of time the consuls stayed in Rome in comparison with their predecessors, although this is difficult to ascertain if we take into account the absolute paucity of our sources of information for this period. Sandberg, moreover, attributes the change to the tensions between *optimates* and *populares*, which had hindered the traditional cooperation between the tribunes of the plebs and the consuls, forcing the latter to present the bills themselves if they were faced with hostile tribunes in their year of office.[109]

appropriateness of a *rogatio* must always have taken place before the people in one or several *contiones*, which meant for the promoters of a law the obligation to take part in such assemblies and in the subsequent debates. An example of this is the debate on the abolition of the *lex Oppia*, which took place in 195 (Liv. 34.1–8). The consul M. Porcius Cato took part in the discussion, delivering a speech before the people; only after the vote did he set off for Hispania. It is questionable whether there was a specific period of time for the discussion of the *rogationes de bello indicendo* (Rich 1976: 30: 'war motions may have been exempted'), whose urgency may have made it advisable to act promptly. In any event, the speech given in a *contio* by the consul Sulpicius Galba in 200 defending the need to declare war on Philip (see above, p. 103) indicates that at least an assembly to inform the people and request their vote may have been required prior to the vote in the comitia.

[109] Sandberg 2001: 102.

But since, contrary to Sandberg's opinion, it is not demonstrably the case that the consuls usually needed the tribunes to get their legislative initiatives off the ground, this is not an appropriate explanation. However, it is probable that the radicalization of political life in the post-Gracchan period made the senate seek consuls more frequently than before as the promoters of laws regarding questions that were particularly important within the context of the political confrontation at the time. Thus, it seems logical that a consul like Servilius Caepio enacted a new *lex iudiciaria* in 106, which partially returned control over the courts to senators. This law unquestionably had the support of the majority of the senate, and the consul acted as its spokesman.

The senate could issue decrees, but it could not legislate. As supreme magistrates, the consuls had, above all, to be persons whom the senate found trustworthy. It is logical, then, that consular laws had senatorial consensus or were even usually the product of a previous senatorial decision.[110] Sources specifically report that some consular laws were promoted *ex senatus consulto*, following instructions from the senate, amongst them the *lex de ambitu* of 181 or the law that in 177 reflected the senatorial will to return the Latins who lived in Rome to their towns of origin. Most consular laws enacted in the decades before Sulla's dictatorship referred to the sensitive question in those years of the policy of granting citizenship to the allies. It is obvious that such a decisive issue for the internal organization of the Roman state had to remain under the control of the senate, and that explains why it was the consuls of the year 95 who set strict limits on access to citizenship, why one of the consuls of 90, L. Caesar, granted citizenship to loyal allies, and why a consul of 89, Pompeius Strabo, granted Latin rights to the inhabitants of the Cisalpine Gaul. The inclusion or not of the population of Italy en masse within Roman citizenship – or the granting of access to Latin rights – was a question of external affairs and was therefore directly in the sphere of the partnership between the senate and the consuls; hence the predominantly consular legislation on this topic.[111] In contrast, the consul Fulvius Flaccus in 125 did not have senatorial support for his intended policy of granting citizenship, and because of this his attempt subsequently failed. It is relevant to emphasize that Fulvius Flaccus is the only known consul in the pre-Sullan age to attempt to legislate without the senate's approval.

[110] On the involvement of the senate in the lawmaking process cf. Williamson 2005: 14–16.

[111] Which, however, does not mean that the tribunes of the plebs were excluded, since in 89 the tribunes C. Papirius Carbo and M. Plautius Silvanus were the promoters of the *lex Plautia Papiria*, which complemented the *lex Iulia* of the previous year and set forth the rules for the granting of citizenship to the Italians.

Nevertheless, the idea of close dependence of the consuls on the senate in the legislative field extends throughout the entire pre-Sullan period. Consular civil laws were certainly rare, mainly because of the limitations derived from the fact that consuls spent most of the year away from Rome, but in general they did not deal with routine politics. On the contrary, almost all known consular laws referred to enormously important issues in political and official life: the right of appeal; the fight against corruption; the limitation on luxury expenses; the organization of the courts of justice; the policy of granting Roman citizenship; the calendar; and the periods of time that determined the very process of debate of bills. Obviously, many of the tribunician laws had great importance for the community, and some dealt with similar problems to consular laws, but it is clear that the majority of the senate was behind all the laws of the consuls who promoted them and a certain 'official' nature was behind the measures adopted. Since they acted on behalf of the senate, the laws promoted by the consuls had greater *auctoritas*, and that would explain why they were entrusted with the enactment of certain measures of particular importance, as is implied by Macrobius when he refers to the *lex Fannia cibaria* of 161, claiming that it was preferred that a consul propose it rather than the praetors or the tribunes of the plebs. In this sense, we can say that consular laws in the pre-Sullan age were not only rare for practical reasons but they were also, to a certain extent, exceptional laws. It is not necessary to presume that consuls only legislated in times of crisis.[112] They simply did so when the senate considered it necessary to have consular support for a legislative measure of particular importance to the Roman state.

---

[112] Sandberg 2001: 104: 'Consuls, and especially dictators, would legislate themselves only in periods of crisis when the normal political machinery was not at work.'

CHAPTER 6

The jurisdiction of the consuls

Once the praetorship was created, jurisdiction was mainly the responsibility of praetors in Rome throughout the Republican period.[1] In theory, the consuls could preside over formal proceedings on private law, such as adoption, manumission and emancipation.[2] It is possible that they did actually perform such duties and it is reasonable that ancient sources did not see them as important enough to mention, unless something extraordinary happened in the process. However, the usual absence of the consuls from Rome allows us to presume that throughout the pre-Sullan period their intervention in such proceedings would usually be an exception. Nonetheless, it is unlikely, as De Martino claimed,[3] that the consuls did not have civil jurisdiction in the *Urbs*. The consuls would have had no legal restrictions in this respect, given that such jurisdiction derived, after all, from their *imperium*, but their habitual absence from Rome would have made this responsibility, as a matter of custom, fall to the praetors.[4]

However, in exceptional cases the senate entrusted consuls with the task of conducting extraordinary criminal investigations (*quaestiones*) and seeing to the punishments that followed the outcome of their inquiries.[5] The assignment of consuls to perform criminal inquiries and to oversee their consequences had legal grounds in the *ius coercitionis* that resulted from the *imperium* with which they were invested.[6]

Undoubtedly, the best-known of all the attested *quaestiones* is that conducted in 186 regarding the so-called conspiracy of the Bacchanalia.[7]

---

[1] Mommsen 1887–8: II 101; Kunkel and Wittmann 1995: 326–8; Brennan 2000: 125–35.
[2] Cf. Lintott 1999b: 105.   [3] De Martino 1990: I 420–2.
[4] See Leifer 1914: 206–24; Brennan 2000: 63.
[5] Most of the extraordinary *quaestiones* were, nevertheless, the responsibility of the praetors, both the urban praetor and, more often, the peregrine praetor. Cf. Brennan 2000: 127–30.
[6] De Ruggiero 1892: 771; 856–7; Mommsen 1899: 142; 152–4; Lintott 1999b: 105.
[7] On the Bacchanalia, the main work continues to be Pailler 1988 (especially regarding Livy's account and its authenticity, pp. 158–9). Pailler also undertook a vast survey of the bibliography regarding this episode (pp. 61–122). See also, amongst other publications, North 1979; Scheid 1981: 157–9; Gruen 1990; Bauman 1990; Näsström 1992; Nippel 1997; Flower 2002: Takács 2008: 90–8.

Livy's account clearly illustrates the role played by the consuls during the entire investigative process and later suppression, with Sp. Postumius Albinus as the protagonist.[8] The consuls' leading role is also confirmed by the inscription from Tiriolo.[9] According to Livy, the consul Postumius was informed in private of the existence of Bacchic rites of initiation in Rome.[10] His informers were P. Aebutius, who had refused to carry out such rituals, and Hispala Faecenia, a freedwoman. When Postumius decided that he had sufficient details, he went to the Curia to inform the senators.[11] They concluded that such 'conspiracies and nocturnal gatherings' were a danger to the community, so immediate action should be taken to put an end to these acts. The senate then issued a *senatus consultum* whereby, to begin with, the consul Postumius was thanked for having conducted the preliminary inquiries in such an accurate and discreet manner.[12] Afterwards, both consuls were entrusted with the investigation into the actions that were considered illegal, both in Rome and throughout Italy. Edicts were issued for this purpose banning the celebration of the reported rites.[13] Likewise, the consuls were made responsible for the safety of Aebutius and Hispala Faecenia, and they were to endeavour to have other informers report such incidents. Livy describes the commission assigned by the senate to the consuls as a *quaestio extra ordinem*, that is, an extraordinary inquiry.[14]

The consuls did indeed take the measures they deemed appropriate to fulfil the senatorial mandate: they ordered the curule aediles to arrest the priests who performed these rituals; the plebeian aediles to ensure that the rites were not performed in daylight; and the *triumviri capitales* to prevent nocturnal meetings as well as suppress any fires in the city, with the assistance of *quinqueviri*.[15] Once these tasks were assigned, the consuls convened a *contio* with the purpose of informing the people of what had happened.[16] The speech was delivered from the rostra by one of the

---

[8] Liv. 39.8–19. See Briscoe 2008: 230–91.

[9] *CIL* I 196 = I² 581, x 104 = *ILS* 18 = *ILLRP* 511: '(Q.) Marcius L.f. S. Postumius L.f. cos. senatum consoluerunt n(onis) Octob. apud aedem Duelonai.' Cf. Pailler 1988: 57–60; Flower 2002: 93–6.

[10] As pointed out by Flower (2002: 81–2), Bacchic cults already had a long tradition in Italy, so it is difficult to accept that their existence was suddenly discovered in 186. Cf. Scheid 1986: esp. 275–90.

[11] Liv. 39.14.3.　　[12] Liv. 39.14.5.

[13] Livy never claims, regarding the *quaestio de Bacchanalibus* or any other investigation, that a law was passed by the people to create the *quaestio*. However, Mackay (1994: 81, cited by Brennan 2000: 127 n. 250) thinks that the people must have approved, through their vote, all the special inquiries.

[14] Liv. 39.14.6. In the ensuing speech delivered by Postumius before the people, Livy attributes to him the same definition of the tasks given to the consuls by the senate: 'senatus quaestionem extra ordinem de ea re mihi collegaeque meo mandavit' (39.16.12).

[15] Liv. 39.14.9–10.　　[16] Liv. 39.15.1.

consuls,[17] presumably Postumius, given his special prominence until then and in general throughout the entire process, although Livy does not specifically state this.[18] After the speech, the consuls ordered the reading of the senate's decree and offered a reward to anyone reporting a culprit to them.[19] When the assembly ended, the city was seething with unrest. According to Livy, up to 7,000 people of both sexes were said to be involved in the conspiracy. Many committed suicide, others were arrested. Amongst the latter were the founders and supreme priests of the Bacchic cult, who were taken before the consuls and were forced to confess.[20]

Livy goes on to say that there was such a great number of individuals involved that the praetors had to wait for a month, upon the senate's request, before being able to preside over the corresponding trials. That was the period of time needed by the consuls to complete their inquiry.[21] Apart from the large number of the accused, the investigation was hindered by the fact that many people who had been denounced fled the *Urbs*, and the consuls had to find and judge them wherever they were.[22] The outcome of these trials was the imprisonment of a great number of men and women, many of whom were executed.[23] The final task accomplished by the consuls consisted of the destruction of all the cult places dedicated to Bacchic rites, both in Rome and throughout Italy, with the exception of ancient places and those containing a consecrated image.[24] The suppression ended with the senate expressly prohibiting the celebration of the Bacchanalia in future, and only in exceptional cases could it be authorized by a minimum of a hundred senators following a previous formal request from interested parties – not more than five – to the urban praetor.[25]

Finally, the consul Q. Marcius Philippus put before the senate the question of what ought to be done with those who had been used by the

---

[17] Liv. 39.15–16. See Briscoe 2008: 271–6.

[18] Pailler (1988: 597–8) considers that the version transmitted by Livy may be seen as Postumius', which would be the starting point of the tradition. In his opinion, the annalist A. Postumius Albinus may have reflected at length in his work on the question of the Bacchanalia, which was later taken up by Polybius and finally preserved by Livy in the terms that we finally received (pp. 611–12). In the same sense, see Flower 2000: 30–1. But Adam (1994: xli–xlii) is sceptical about the possible use Polybius made of the work of Postumius.

[19] Liv. 39.17.1. Briscoe 2008: 280.

[20] Liv. 39.17.7.

[21] Liv. 39.18.1. According to the first lines of the inscription from Tiriolo, the *senatus consultum* (or rather, the letter addressed to the *foideratei*) was issued as a result of a meeting of the senate held in the temple of Bellona under the presidency of both consuls on the Nones of October, which means that on that date both magistrates were still in Rome. Cf. Flower 2002: 83.

[22] Liv. 39.18.2.   [23] Liv. 39.18.3–6.   [24] Liv. 39.18.7.

[25] Liv. 39.18.8–9. These terms are specifically confirmed in the inscription from Tiriolo (cf. Pailler 1988: 57–60).

consuls as informers to uncover the conspiracy. It was decided to wait until
the consul Postumius returned to Rome after finishing his inquiry.[26] When
this happened – in the meantime Marcius Philippus may have already set
off for Liguria, his province – Postumius proposed a series of economic and
legal rewards both for Aebutius and for Hispala. The senate decided that
the urban praetor was to pay each of them one hundred thousand *asses*
from the public treasury, and that the consul was to agree with the tribunes
of the plebs for them put forward a bill before the people including all
these privileges, which is what happened.[27] Consuls and praetors, both
present and future, were made responsible for the safety of both informers,
and in particular Postumius and Marcius Philippus were to ensure the
impunity of the rest of the informers and decide on what their rewards
ought to be.[28]

Livy thus gave great emphasis to what he undoubtedly considered to be
the most important event to have occurred in the consular year 186/5. In
fact, at the beginning of his narration of the year he had already stressed the
main consular task for that year: the suppression of the domestic conspiracy.[29] Marcius Philippus was the first of the two consuls to complete
his inquiry in the region with which he had been entrusted – probably the
centre and north of Italy, whereas the southern zone was left to
Postumius[30] – and only then did he leave for the province which he had
been allotted to fight the Ligures Apuani.[31] He did so with the troops that
had been recruited, exceptionally, by the urban praetor T. Maenius while
the consuls were engaged in the suppression of the Bacchanalia.[32] In
principle, Postumius had also been allotted Liguria as his province, but
everything seems to indicate that he never went there.[33] While he was
conducting his inquiry in the south of Italy, he had fortuitously discovered
that the recently founded colonies of Sipontum and Buxentum had been
abandoned, which he reported to the senate so that new settlers could be
sent there. This happened at the end of the consular year.[34] Also at the end
of the consular year, when Postumius had completed his inquiry, which
according to Livy was conducted in an impartial and thorough manner, and
had consequently returned to Rome, he was in charge of presiding over the
elections.[35] Therefore, in an exceptional manner, during the consular year
186/5 one of the consuls, Marcius Philippus, dedicated most of his term
of office to an inquiry before going to his province, while the other,

---

[26] Liv. 39.19.1.   [27] Liv. 39.19.3–6.   [28] Liv. 39.19.7.   [29] Liv. 39.8.1–3.   [30] Pailler 1988: 314–24.
[31] Liv. 39.20.1; 39.20.5.   [32] Liv. 39.20.4. Cf. Brennan 2000: 118; 122.   [33] Briscoe 2008: 248.
[34] Liv. 39.23.3.   [35] Liv. 39.23.1.

Postumius, seemingly dedicated nearly all his term as a supreme magistrate to that same *quaestio*.[36]

The thorough report provided by Livy informs us in detail of the tasks given to the consuls and their specific actions within that framework.[37] The procedure ought to be understood within the context of the habitual institutional relations between senate and consuls.[38] The question of the Bacchanalia had a dual political and religious nature which concerned the senate in its double-faceted role as guardian of the civic religion and as the main political institution. Once the significance and danger of the plot became known, the senate logically delegated the highest magistrates, the consuls, to its suppression so that the appropriate measures could be taken by them. In his speech before the *contio*, Postumius puts forward the procedure with total clarity: 'the senate has entrusted my colleague and myself with extraordinary powers for conducting an inquiry . . . and we have charged the subordinate magistrates with the care of the night-watches throughout the city'.[39] The assignment of this task to the consuls was undoubtedly influenced by the fact that the first news on the Bacchic rites was heard by the consul Postumius at the very beginning of the consular year, when both consuls were still in Rome before going to their provinces.[40] Should the consuls have left for Liguria by that time, perhaps the senate might have assigned such a duty to the urban praetor. This is what happened in 198, when news reached Rome about the conspiracy of slaves at Setia. Since the consuls were away (the consul Flamininus was occupied with the war against Philip in Greece, while his colleague Sex. Aelius Paetus was in Gaul), the urban praetor was in charge of suppressing it, following a similar pattern to that of 186: the urban praetor convened the senate to report the facts he had become aware of; the senators ordered the praetor to conduct an investigation; the praetor, along with five legates, recruited 2,000 men, and with them he crushed the revolt; and the informers were rewarded.[41]

---

[36] Broughton 1951–86: I 370–1.
[37] Both Walsh (1996) and Wiseman (1998) have suggested the existence of a theatre play on the events of the year 186 regarding the suppression of the Bacchanalia, in which the main characters may have been Aebutius and Hispala. In contrast, Flower (2000: 30–1) considers the existence both of such a play or of any other play of historic content where Postumius was the protagonist very improbable. Nevertheless, Flower thinks that Livy's account demonstrates that Aebutius and Hispala were actual historical characters.
[38] Pailler 1988: 254–5.   [39] Liv. 39.16.12.   [40] Cf. Liv. 32.26; Pailler 1988: 325–9.
[41] Liv. 32.26. Cf. Zonar. 9.16.6. Cf. Capozza 1966: 140, who sees certain Carthaginian inspiration in the origin of the revolt; Harris 1971: 142: 'the rebels were clearly members of the local serf class'. See also Brennan 2000: 108.

Livy, as we have already seen, considers the consular commission in 186 as a *quaestio extra ordinem*. Pailler, following Mommsen, is undoubtedly right when he rejects the notion that this term might have involved the de facto abolition of the right of appeal (*provocatio*), an abolition which is never referred to by Livy,[42] yet it is true that it is unclear whether those who were prosecuted could actually have appealed after their conviction, given the speed and brutality of the process of suppression. The term *quaestio extra ordinem* simply describes the extraordinary nature, beyond the norm, of the task entrusted to the consuls, who, instead of going to Liguria with their armies, had in exceptional circumstances to deal with the investigation and suppression of the Bacchic rites, not only in Rome but throughout all of Italy.[43] In practice, the consuls effectively led the entire process. They gave the appropriate instructions to the lower magistrates; they informed the people of the events; it was before them that the ringleaders of the conspiracy in Rome were taken; the consuls themselves travelled around Italy breaking up the Bacchic cult, arresting and prosecuting the culprits; they were responsible for the safety of the informers; and finally Postumius suggested what rewards ought to be given to them.

The suppression of the Bacchanalia was therefore an extraordinary consular task, although it is not the only known case in the pre-Sullan period in which the consuls were in charge of an inquiry following orders from the senate. In the period of time covered by this work, the first case goes back to the year 331, according to Livy, who claims to reproduce the astonishing events just as they had been narrated by his sources.[44] In that year many notable persons of the city suspiciously contracted the same disease, which caused the deaths of significant numbers of them. A slave declared before the aedile Q. Fabius Maximus Rullianus that she knew the cause of the epidemic and that she would reveal it if her personal safety were guaranteed. The aedile passed the information on to the consuls, who consulted with the senate.[45] Once the senators agreed to protect the informer, she accused certain women of preparing poisons which were the cause of the death of so many men. The accusation was proved

---

[42] Pailler 1988: 256–7. Cf. Mommsen 1899: 152 n. 1: '. . . wo das ausserordentliche Einschreiten nicht auf die Erweiterung der Competenz, sondern auf die Erledigung dieser Geschäfte ausser der Reihe und vor den übrigen zu beziehen ist'.

[43] Cf. Brennan 2000: 204 n. 149: '. . . the phrase simply means that the consuls received the *quaestio* by decree of the Senate, and not through sortition or *comparatio* of *provinciae* – in a word, "extra sortem"'.

[44] Liv. 8.18.4–11. Cf. V. Max. 2.5.3; Oros. 3.10.1–3; August. *C.D.* 3.17. Cf. Oakley 1998: II 594–602, who considers the episode generally true, although some of the details provided by Livy may be fictitious. Brennan (2000: 127) is more sceptical in general about the *quaestiones* narrated by Livy in the fifth and fourth centuries. See also Kunkel 1962: 57 n. 216.

[45] Liv. 8.18.5.

correct, and up to 170 matrons were convicted. The matter was perceived as a portent, and it was decided to respond, as they had some decades before, by fixing a nail in order to expiate the prodigy.[46] Yet that task was not given to one of the consuls, but to a dictator who was appointed exclusively to fulfil it.

According to Livy, this was the first inquiry into poisoning conducted in the history of Rome.[47] The words 'quaesitum sit' suggest that the Latin author thought that the episode was resolved by means of an extraordinary *quaestio*, which is plausible despite the fact that such instances are rare in that period of the history of Rome.[48] Prior to this date we only know of the consuls being responsible for an inquest in 413 into the murder of P. Postumius Regillensis, consular tribune of 414.[49] This information is questionable, like most data pertaining to archaic Rome.[50] However, it is significant that Livy attributes that inquiry to the consuls of the year.

Livy does not, however, give any details of the manner in which the investigation and the subsequent trials were conducted in 331. Mommsen believed that the inquiry may have been directed by a consul, whereas Bauman thought it was overseen by the aedile Q. Fabius.[51] This latter option is highly improbable, since no aedile is attested ever to have presided over a criminal *quaestio*.[52] On the contrary, from the known instances it can be deduced that such investigations were entrusted to magistrates invested with *imperium*: consuls, praetors or dictators.[53] Bauman claims that in the other three attested cases of investigations into poisoning, in 184, 180, and 152, there is no mention of a consul directing them and that it was the praetors who conducted them.[54] This is true, but these cases do not provide any argument in favour of an aedilician intervention in such extraordinary inquiries. On the contrary, they seem only to reaffirm the idea that such inquiries ought to be in the hands of magistrates with *imperium*. Certainly, the slave who apparently acted as informer in the episode of 331 contacted the aedile initially, but the aedile immediately passed the information on to the consul for him to communicate to the senate. The senatorial answer, in the form of a *senatus*

---

[46] Liv. 8.18.12–13. Cf. Liv. 7.3.5.   [47] Liv. 8.18.11.   [48] Oakley 1998: II 595–6.
[49] Liv. 4.50.4–51.4.   [50] Cf. Kunkel 1962: 57 n. 216; Ogilvie 1978: 611–12.
[51] Mommsen 1899: 143 n. 2; Bauman 1974: 255–8.   [52] Oakley 1998: II 597.
[53] Apart from the investigations where consular participation is attested and the aforementioned inquiry conducted by the urban praetor in 198, two other investigations where dictators were the protagonists are known: in 314, C. Maenius was appointed dictator to investigate *coniurationes* amongst the Campanians (Liv. 9.26.6–22); in 207, the dictator M. Livius Salinator investigated defections in Etruria and Umbria (Liv. 28.10.4–5). In 172, the senate commissioned the urban praetor C. Licinius Crassus to undertake an investigation to determine which Ligures Statiellates had been unjustly enslaved by the consul of 173, M. Popillius Laenas, and should therefore be freed (Liv. 42.21.8). Cf. Vishnia 1996: 132–3; Oakley 1998: II 596; Brennan 2000: 114–15.
[54] Liv. 39.41.5; 40.37.4; 40.43.2–3; *per*. 48. Cf. Bauman 1974: 256.

consultum, was in all probability communicated to the consuls, who were as a rule the direct interlocutors of the senate. Consequently, it may be presumed that following the senate's orders, the two consuls – or only one of them – were in charge of the investigation into the poisoning in 331.

In 314 the trial of the dictator C. Maenius and of his *magister equitum* M. Folius was allegedly held, an episode whose historicity has been vigorously contested.[55] According to Livy, Maenius was appointed as dictator to investigate the existence of conspiracies in Campania,[56] but on his return to Rome, instead of resigning from his office, he used his dictatorship to investigate some supposed plots by renowned Romans to attain magistracies fraudulently. Complaints from many aristocrats finally forced the resignation of Maenius and Folius. The dictator, before resigning, spoke vehemently in his own defence. Directly addressing the consuls at the end of his speech, he requested that they, if the senate were to ask them to conduct an investigation – which indicates that they were the main candidates to be in charge of this type of *quaestio* – start by investigating Folius and himself, so that their innocence could be proven.[57] Once their resignation was effective, Maenius and Folius were, according to Livy, tried before the consuls by order of the senate but were absolved.[58] Beyond the truth or falsehood of this annalistic account, it can be deduced that the management of these types of special inquiries could sometimes be in the hands of the consuls.

Also in the fourth century, in 303, the consuls were asked to conduct a new investigation. The inhabitants of Frusino, a town situated in Latium on the Via Latina, were punished by the Roman state with the loss of one third of their territory, as it was considered that they had been the instigators of the recent revolt of the Hernici. The leaders of the plot were also punished once the consuls had, following orders from the senate, conducted the corresponding inquiry.[59] In his brief account, Livy stresses the fact that

---

[55] Liv. 9.26.5–22. See the statement on the question with supplementary bibliography in Oakley 2005a: III 304–6: 'Livy's account is replete with the anachronistic language and motifs of later politics; and it would explain why scholars have struggled to find a satisfactory interpretation of the episode: it is difficult to interpret because most of the events described by Livy never happened.' Cf. Mommsen 1899: 668 n. 3.

[56] Bauman 1973: 39: 'The *Quaestio Maeniana* is a special commission instigated by the senate, and as such the ancestor of the Bacchanalian and subsequent commissions, except that it is the only instance of such a commission being conducted by a dictator rather than by the consuls.'

[57] Liv. 9.26.19.

[58] Liv. 9.26.20. Bauman (1973: 42–3) believes these consular trials to be fictitious considering that the year 314 was particularly complicated for Rome with regard to its external affairs, so it is quite improbable that the consuls had the time to perform judicial tasks.

[59] Liv. 10.1.3. Cf. Diodor. 20.80.4. The ethnic ascription of the Frusinates, whether to the Volsci or to the Hernici, is not clear. Cf. Salmon 1967: 248 n. 3, who thinks it is a Hernician community; Humbert (1978: 220) believes it is a Volscian town; cf. Oakley 2005b: IV 40–1.

that year was particularly peaceful with regard to external wars, so the consuls only had to carry out a short military skirmish ('parva expeditio') in Umbria.[60] In contrast, he mentions the foundation of the colonies of Sora and Alba.[61] The consuls must therefore have spent a good deal of the year in Rome, and their investigation in nearby Frusino may have been one of their most noteworthy duties.

The loss of Livy's work means that we do not know of other possible consular investigations in the third century. The consuls' intervention in such tasks reappears within the context of the end of the Second Punic War, indirectly in 204 and with direct consular participation in the following year. The accusations lodged by the inhabitants of the Sicilian city of Locri against Scipio Africanus and his legate Q. Pleminius, regarding robbery in the temple of Proserpina, resulted in a vigorous debate in the senate in 204.[62] The discussion ended with the decision to send a legation to the island led by the praetor of Sicily, M. Pomponius Matho, in order to investigate the events. The legation also had to include two tribunes of the plebs, an aedile, and ten other legates, who were to be appointed at the consuls' discretion ('quos iis videretur') from amongst all the senators.[63] As was usual, as part of their diplomatic duties at the beginning of the consular year, the consuls had met the Locrian ambassadors in Rome and had taken them to the senate to lodge their complaints. The matter was undoubtedly considered of great political importance, especially because Scipio Africanus was involved. This importance is demonstrated by the size and standing of the committee of inquiry: four magistrates and ten senators. We cannot know whether in different circumstances the senate would have considered the need for the committee to be led by a consul, but the war had not yet ended and both consuls were engaged for the rest of the year in commanding their troops, Cornelius Cethegus in Etruria and Sempronius Tuditanus in the south of Italy. It is noteworthy, however, that it was not the praetor who was to lead the committee but the consuls who had to appoint the ten legates. This indicates that the ultimate responsibility in this inquiry belonged to the consuls and that the praetor was in fact their natural substitute.[64]

---

[60] Liv. 10.1.4–6.   [61] Liv. 10.1.1–2.   [62] Liv. 29.17–20.

[63] Liv. 29.20.4. Of the ten legates only the name of Q. Caecilius Metellus is known. He had been consul in 206. Cf. Broughton 1951–86: I 309.

[64] As a result of the inquiry, Pleminius was punished for his action, and the praetor strove to take decisions that would please the Locrians and placate the gods (Liv. 29.21). Yet the troubles in Locri did not end there, since in the year 200 the temple of Proserpina was looted again. The senate ordered the consul C. Aurelius to write to the praetor of Bruttium and instruct him to investigate the latest plunder.

In 203, the consul C. Servilius Geminus could not preside over the elections at the end of the consular year, as would have been his duty, because, as had been ordered by the senate, he was engaged in Etruria directing inquiries into conspiracies.[65] A dictator was appointed instead of Servilius to deal with the elections.[66] Etruria was the province allotted to Servilius at the beginning of his term of office, as the year before it had been assigned to the consul Cethegus. It is obvious that it was a highly unstable region, and it was particularly worrying within the context of the Hannibalic War. In fact, between 212 and 200 a Roman army, usually made up of two legions, was permanently positioned in Etruria, and there are indications that at least some element of the Etruscans more or less openly supported the Carthaginians. In the particular case of 203, the suppression was specifically aimed at leading citizens (*principes*) of some unmentioned Etruscan cities.[67]

In the consular year 187/6, the praetor M. Furius Crassipes illegally disarmed the Cenomani, who immediately sent ambassadors to Rome to protest against this action. The senate did not take any decision on the matter, but asked the Gauls to go to meet the consul M. Aemilius Lepidus, who was in the north of Italy, while the senators urged the consul to investigate the events.[68] According to Livy, there was a great debate between the praetor and the ambassadors from Gaul, obviously in the presence of the consul. The resolution taken by the consul was that the arms were to be returned to the Cenomani and that the praetor was to leave the province.[69] Consequently, the consul acted as both the examining magistrate and the judge in the lawsuit, always following orders from the senate.

The consul of 179, Q. Fulvius Flaccus, also received instructions from the senate to conduct an inquiry while he was in his province in command of his troops. Individuals numbering 3,000 had crossed the Alps and entered Italy from Transalpine Gaul. They did so peacefully and asked the Roman state – the senate and the consuls, as Livy says – to be given land on which to settle under Roman sovereignty. The senate did not accept the petition and, on the contrary, ordered them to leave Italy. Additionally, the senate asked the consul Fulvius Flaccus to investigate which of the Gauls had been the instigators of the crossing of the Alps and to punish them for it.[70]

---

[65] Liv. 30.26.12.   [66] Broughton 1951–86: I 311.   [67] Van Son 1963; Harris 1971: 135–41.

[68] Liv. 39.3.2–3. Vishnia 1996: 182–3; Briscoe 2008: 215–16.

[69] According to Diodor. 29.14, the consul also fined the praetor. For a consul fining a praetor in Rome see Liv. 42.9.4. Cf. Brennan 2000: 201.

[70] Liv. 40.53.5–6. Briscoe 2008: 554.

Cicero mentions briefly another internal investigation conducted by a consul in 141. The previous year, the praetor L. Hostilius Tubulus had been appointed as president of the recently created tribunal for murderers (*de sicariis*).[71] During his year of office he allegedly accepted bribes, which in 141 caused the tribune of the plebs P. Mucius Scaevola to take a proposal before the people to investigate Tubulus. When the assembly passed the bill, the senate ordered the start of an inquiry, which was given over to the consul Cn. Servilius Caepio.[72] According to Cicero, Tubulus did not dare to defend himself and preferred to go into exile, which was evidence of his guilt. Yet Asconius, in his commentary on Cicero's *Pro Scauro*, claims that he returned from exile and died of poisoning in prison.[73]

Cicero also alludes to a consular investigation conducted in 138. After news that some renowned persons had been murdered in the woodlands of Sila in Bruttium, the senate commissioned both consuls, P. Cornelius Scipio Nasica and D. Iunius Brutus, to investigate the facts.[74] Cicero narrates various details of the development of the trial against the alleged culprits, a process in which the intervention of the two consuls becomes apparent.[75] In addition, Nasica and Brutus had serious problems with recruitment during their consulship, to the point that they were even imprisoned for a short while by order of some of the tribunes of the plebs, and we know of a confrontation between Nasica and the tribune C. Curiatus regarding corn supplies to the city.[76] These events, like the inquiry into the murders in Bruttium, occurred at the beginning of the consular year, before Brutus set off for his province, Hispania Ulterior. There he achieved important victories over the Lusitanians, which allowed him to reach as far as the river Duero, and for his conquest of a local tribe, the Callaici, upon his return to Rome, he was nicknamed Callaicus.

The last known committee of inquiry in the pre-Sullan period belongs to the Gracchan age. The death of Tiberius Sempronius Gracchus was followed by the repression of a great number of his followers. From the information provided by Cicero and Valerius Maximus, it can be deduced that the presidency over the *quaestio* to investigate and punish them was given by the senate to the consuls of 132, P. Popillius Laenas and P. Rupilius.[77]

---

[71] Broughton 1951–86: I 475. Cf. Brennan 2000: 236.
[72] Cic. *Fin.* 2.54. Cf. Cic. *Fin.* 4.77; *N.D.* 3.74. Cf. Mommsen 1899: 197; 203 n. 1; Münzer 1912a; Broughton 1951–86: I 477.
[73] Asc. 20 C. Cf. Münzer 1912b: 167–8.   [74] Cic. *Brut.* 85.   [75] Cic. *Brut.* 86–8.
[76] Cic. *Leg.* 3.20; V. Max. 3.7.3.
[77] V. Max. 4.7.1. Cf. Cic. *Amic.* 37; Vell. 2.7.3; Plut. *Ti. Gr.* 20. Cf. Broughton 1951–86: I 498; Stockton 1979: 90–1; 119–20.

For such purposes, the consuls gathered together a council to advise them, one member of which was, according to Cicero, C. Laelius. Rupilius dedicated most of the year to finally crushing the slaves' revolt in Sicily and to re-organizing the island. It is likely therefore that his colleague Popillius did all or most of the work of the inquiry, which would explain why later on Gaius Gracchus attacked him on several occasions during his tribunate, within the context of his own law regarding the right of appeal, until he managed to force Popillius into exile in Nuceria, from where he returned only after the death of Gracchus.[78]

In conclusion, the performance of consular jurisdiction is very seldom alluded to by the sources.[79] In the pre-Sullan period there are only eleven *quaestiones* in which consuls are said to have participated as investigators (*quaesitores*). These inquiries are scattered erratically between the second half of the fourth century and the Gracchan period, and our knowledge of them is practically non-existent throughout the second century due to the loss of Livy's work. Undoubtedly the consular *imperium* included the prerogative of presiding over such investigations, but it is equally obvious that these were not part of the habitual duties of the consuls every year.[80] On the contrary, they were always extraordinary *quaestiones*, in the sense that they were commissions given to one of the consuls or to both of them jointly – or to other magistrates – because it was considered that the matter to be investigated was of particular importance or seriousness for the community. The inquiries were always decided by the senate, and their membership and presidency were made up exclusively by the senators.

From the known cases it can be deduced that only magistrates with *imperium* could deal with these extraordinary investigations. Their assignment by the senate to one magistrate or another probably depended on their availability and on the circumstances at each given moment. It may be presumed that the consuls were the first option as long as they were available, something which depended on the international situation and on whether they were in Rome or in their provinces. Otherwise, the inquiry

---

[78] Gel. 1.7.7; 11.13. Stockton 1979: 220.

[79] To the aforementioned cases we should add the punishment inflicted by the consul Curius Dentatus in 275 on a man who did not attend the recruitment when he was summoned, which consisted of the confiscation and sale of his goods (Liv. *per.* 14), and the fine assessed in 172 by the consul M. Popillius Laenas upon his return to Rome on the urban praetor for having prompted the senate to pass a resolution against him regarding the abusive enslavement of the Ligures Statiellates (Liv. 42.9.4; cf. Brennan 2000: 113).

[80] Kunkel 1962: 140: 'Inhaber auch der kriminalrechtlichen Jurisdiktion war von Anbeginn der Prätor. Die Konsuln, die ohne Zweifel allezeit potentielle Jurisdiktionsmagistrate geblieben sind, übten ihre Gerichtsgewalt in Rom nur auf besondere Anordnung des Senats in ausserordentlichen Quästionen aus.'

was entrusted to a dictator or a praetor. In circumstances considered by the
senate to be exceptional, such as those surrounding the Bacchanalia, it was
preferred to adjourn the allocation of provinces that had already taken place
between the consuls and to entrust both of them with the investigation.
This change explains the term *quaestio extra ordinem* used by Livy.

Consuls were entrusted with inquiries regarding wide-ranging matters,
both in internal and external affairs; the inappropriate religious rituals of
the Bacchanalia; murders; external conspiracies; illegal actions of Roman
magistrates, such as Furius Crassipes' actions against the Cenomani; expulsion of foreigners after their unauthorized settlement in Italy; corruption, as
in the case of Hostilius Tubulus; and internal seditions like the Gracchan.
The variety of issues under investigation also determined the scope and period
of action of the consuls in each particular case. In general, the inquiries must
have taken up a small part of the consular year, yet there is one remarkable
exception. The consuls of 186 had to eradicate the Bacchanalia both in the city
of Rome and throughout Italy. Marcius Philippus devoted most of his time in
office to this task, and Postumius virtually the entire year. Investigations
regarding the plots in Etruria or the inhabitants of Frusino were obviously
carried out in those places, whereas the investigations regarding the poison-
ings in 331, Tubulus' presumed corruption, and the Gracchans were conducted exclusively in the *Urbs*. Generally, the senate entrusted the consuls
with presidency over the inquiries while they were still in Rome, even though
the investigation had to be conducted outside the city. But there are also two
known instances where the investigation was assigned to consuls who were
already in command of troops in their respective provinces: Aemilius Lepidus
in 187/6 and Fulvius Flaccus in 179. Finally, the measures taken by consuls
varied in each case within the framework of the different inquiries, although
they always enjoyed great autonomy: executions; rewards to informers; the
return of arms to the Cenomani; the expulsion of the praetor Furius Crassipes
from his province and so forth.

CHAPTER 7

Consuls as promoters of public works

Throughout the Republican period, public works were mostly at the initiative and under the control of the censors from the time when the censorship was established, and to a lesser extent in the hands of the aediles, who were in charge of the care of the city (*cura urbis*).[1] To this end, the censors received from the quaestors the sums of money that the senate had allocated to the planned public works, and they were responsible for letting the corresponding contract (*locatio*).[2] In fact, most of the known public works of the Republican period (aqueducts, buildings for public shows, basilicas, etc.) were promoted by the censors. However, the consuls – and other magistrates – were also involved in the promotion of public works, particularly with regard to the construction of temples and roads, as well as, to a lesser degree, commemorative buildings or other works which were promoted personally by certain consuls.[3] One of the reasons why the consuls undertook public works was that the censors were elected every five years and had a term of office of eighteen months, which meant that, should this have been the exclusive authority of censors, it would have been impossible for a period of three and a half years to start any public works through the necessary *locatio*. Consequently, as in the case of the censors, the consuls also had the authority to let the contract and therefore to avail themselves of public money to finance the corresponding works.[4]

Apart from literary sources, some inscriptions – dating from the first century BC and the Augustan period – also testify to the leading legal role of the consuls in the process of construction of public buildings and their

---

[1] De Ruggiero 1892: 835; 1925: 47–9 (censors); 57–61 (aediles); Gast 1965; Strong 1968; Kolb 1993: 13–14. See a summary of the building works in Rome between 200 and 78 in Coarelli 1977: 20–3, particularly regarding the censors at 4–6.

[2] Liv. 40.46.16; 44.16.9. Cf. Cancelli 1957; García Morcillo 2005.

[3] De Ruggiero 1892: 834–5; 1925: 49–55; Strong 1968: 99. Occasionally, praetors were also in charge of the construction of certain public works, for instance Q. Marcius Rex in 144, who undertook the construction of the Aqua Marcia by order of the senate (Fron. *Aq.* 7).

[4] Trisciuoglio 1998: 100–4; Mateo 1999: 36–8.

further *probatio*, that is, the final approval of the finished works.[5] In any event, almost all the available information on Rome's building activity – and that of Italy in general – comes from Livy, which in fact means that details regarding the construction of significant buildings are scarce from 167 onwards, in comparison to the previous period.[6]

PUBLIC ROADS

For a long time it was believed that the censors had promoted many public roads built in Italy, although, according to Mommsen, the consuls and praetors gradually took on that task too, at least in the late Republic and in territories that were distant from Rome.[7] However, opinion on this matter changed radically due to the works published in the 1960s by Radke and Pekáry,[8] which constituted a turning point on the ever-difficult question of when the roads were built and who their promoters were. Their theories attracted harsh criticism but also prompted wide debate and opened up new perspectives. According to Pekáry, public roads[9] were built by the consuls or praetors, not by the censors.[10] Information regarding roads built before the year 200 is highly dubious, and the idea that the Via Appia is to be attributed, as has traditionally been the case on the basis of ancient sources, to the censor Appius Claudius in 312, should be seriously questioned.[11] Only from the beginning of the second century was there a proper

---

[5] *CIL* VI 1313–14 (78); VI 1384 (AD 10); VI 1385 (AD 2).   [6] Coarelli 1977: 3.

[7] Mommsen 1887–8: II 454.

[8] Radke 1964a; 1964b; 1967; 1973; 1975e; Pekáry 1968. See also the criticism regarding both Radke's and Pekáry's thesis in Wiseman 1970a. Cf. Bodei Giglioni 1974: 79–85; Quilici 1991; Laurence 1999: 11–26.

[9] See a definition of *via publica* in Pekáry 1968: 6. Cf. Laurence 1999: 59–62.

[10] Pekáry 1968: 46–53, esp. 51–3: 'Wir kennen keine einzige Straße, die mit voller Sicherheit als das Werk eines Censors angesehen werden darf; auf keinem Meilenstein bezeichnet sich ein römischer Beamter als Censor; Straßenbauinschriften, auf welchen dieser Rang angeblich vorkommt, sind entweder falsch gelesen oder unrichtig ergänzt; die juristische Literatur der Antike kennt consularische oder prätorische, jedoch keine censorischen Straßen . . .; und schließlich ist die Termination der *via publica* außerhalb der *Urbs* offenbar Aufgabe der Consuln und Prätoren, eventuell auch der Aedilen. Damit scheiden die Censoren als Straßenbauer aus.' Pekáry (86–7) not only questioned the reliability of the sources which state that Appius Claudius built the Via Appia while he was a censor, but he also categorically denied the censorial nature of the Flaminia, Aurelia and Aemilia. On the contrary, he presumed that in earliest times the aediles were occasionally in charge of the public roads (p. 87).

[11] Yet the sources are unanimous in this respect: Liv. 9.29.5; *De vir. ill.* 34.6; *elogium* of Claudius Caecus: '. . . in censura viam Appiam stravit et aquam in urbem adduxit . . .' (*Inscr.It.* XIII 3.12 and 79 = *CIL* I².1 p. 192 × = *ILS* 54). Cf. Fron. *Aq.* 1.4; Liv. 9.29.5; *De vir. ill.* 34.6; Diodor. 20.36.2. Cf. Pekáry 1968: 37–46; Radke (1975e: 1244) argues that the Via Appia may have been built over the *ager publicus* until it reached Formiae by Ap. Claudius Caecus as censor in 312–310, but that its continuation up to Capua can only have been undertaken by him as a consul in 307. In favour of placing the construction of the Via Appia during the censorship of Ap. Claudius, cf. Laurence 1999: 15; Linke 2000: 73; Humm 2005: 8; 41; 134–9; Beck 2005: 171–3.

systematization of the road network in Italy, based on previously existing roads. Radke, however, considered that the only road that in all certainty was built by a censor in the Republican times was the Via Appia. All other roads were promoted by consuls or praetors, as is demonstrated by the fact that, while the term *via censoria* is unknown in ancient sources, the expressions *via consularis* and *via praetoria* are documented.[12]

Epigraphic documentation plays a crucial role in this question, since a large number of milestones from the Republican period expressly mention consuls and, to a lesser degree, other magistrates with *imperium*, yet there are no known cases of milestones that mention censors.[13] It is assumed that the mention of a magistrate on a milestone – like that of an emperor later on – means that he was in charge of the construction of that public road.[14] The legal reason explaining the absence of censors would be the need for a public road (*via publica*) to be built on public land.[15] At times this would obviously involve the implementation of the *ius publicandi*: that is, the power to expropriate private land, which was essential for the planning of a public road that had to cross various territories for tens or even hundreds of kilometres. This *ius publicandi* was the exclusive authority of magistrates who were invested with *imperium*, that is, consuls, praetors, and proconsuls, but censors purportedly did not have such authority.[16] Obviously, the construction of public roads was always subject to final authorization from the senate.

Nevertheless, the available literary and epigraphic sources very seldom permit the definite identification of the builder of a road or the date of its construction. In the following paragraphs I will provide a brief list of all the public roads that may have been built by consuls, mentioning in each case alternative suggestions in historiography, but without going into details of the surrounding debates, which in most cases are very complex and difficult to resolve.[17]

---

[12] Plin. *Nat.* 18.111. A passage in Ulpian is of particular interest in this context: 'viarum quaedam publicae sunt, quaedam privatae, quaedam vicinales. publicas vias dicimus . . . nostri praetorias et consulares vias appellant' (Ulpian, *Dig.* 43.8.2.22).

[13] In fact, the mention of a praetor on a milestone is exceptional (Pekáry 1968: 7). The only known example is that of the praetor of 131, T. Annius Rufus, in Lucania: *ILLRP* 454a. Pekáry (1968: 54) argues that, since it was a road within Italy, Annius may have acted 'als Stellvertreter oder Beauftragter der Consuln'. The role of praetors may have actually been the building of roads in the provinces, and this is what *viae praetoriae* in Ulpian may be referring to (p. 55).

[14] Cf. Siculus Flaccus 146 L.

[15] Ulpian, *Dig.* 43.8.2.21: 'viam publicam eam dicimus, cuius etiam solum publicum est.' Cf. Pekáry 1968: 6, 14, 36.

[16] Radke 1967: 225; 1973: 1434; Pekáry 1968: 14–15. However, Kunkel and Wittmann (1995: 458) are totally against the thesis of Pekáry and Radke, since they believe that there are no reasons to presume that the censors did not have the *ius publicandi* in the Republican period.

[17] Should we accept the thesis of Radke, the number of roads promoted by consuls would be greatly increased. Based mainly on his theory that the fora were created as middle points on a newly built road

The first consular roads that we know of were built in 187.[18] In that year, the consul C. Flaminius defeated the Ligures Apuani and achieved temporary peace in the region. Livy claims that as his province was free from war and he did not want his soldiers to be idle, he undertook the construction of the road between Bononia and Arretium.[19] Livy's account leaves no doubt regarding the role played by the army, at least on occasion, in the construction of roads.[20] On the other hand, his colleague M. Aemilius Lepidus built the so-called Via Aemilia that year, which is attested in both literary and epigraphic sources.[21] It became the main road of the Po Valley, from Placentia to Ariminum, where it was linked to the Via Flaminia, as Livy states.[22] The same Aemilius Lepidus consul of 187 may have been the builder of a road in Samnium, a branch of the Via Appia between Beneventum and Herdonia.[23] This possibility was cautiously pointed out by Degrassi and by Pekáry, taking into consideration that there are other

and that they were given the name of their builder (against this theory see Ruoff-Väänänen 1978: 70–3), Radke proposed in various works the existence of a great number of consular roads. To those mentioned in the following lines we ought to add: a road built in 316 by Popilius in the territory of the Falerni; a road of Ap. Claudius Caecus in Campania in 307; the Via Claudia between 310 and 241; the Via Flaminia, usually considered to have been built by Flaminius as censor in 220, which for Radke may actually have been promoted during his consulship in 223; the Via Minucia in 221; a Via Valeria in Sicily in 210; a road built by Livius in the valley of the river Po in 188; a *via* of Cornelius in the valley of the river Po in 181; a *via* of Sempronius through Umbria and the *ager Gallicus* in 177; a presumed road built by Fulvius Nobilior in 159 from Placentia; and a Via Valeria of unknown chronology. See a summary in Radke 1973: 1432–3. The theses of Radke and their specific application to the chronology and authorship of the Republican public roads were criticized in detail by Wiseman 1970a.

[18] Wiseman (1970a: 137) suggests the consuls of 287 and 285, M. Claudius Marcellus and C. Claudius Canina respectively, were the promoters of the Via Clodia. Bodei Giglioni 1974: 81 n. 58: the Via Appia from Capua to Venusia may have been built by the consul M. Aemilius Lepidus in 285, the Via Caecilia by the consul L. Caecilius Metellus in 283. Toynbee 1965: II 661: the consul of 200, C. Aurelius Cotta, could have been the builder of the Via Aurelia.

[19] Liv. 39.2.6. Strabo (5.1.11) confuses this Via Flaminia (*minor*) with the great Via Flaminia, the main road from Rome to the *ager Gallicus* built by the father of the consul of 187. Cf. Pekáry 1968: 47; Radke 1973: 1433. Sceptical about the reason given by Livy, Briscoe 2008: 214: 'as if a Roman consul would embark on a major road-building programme for no other reason than to give his soldiers something to do'. Barigazzi (1991: 62) suggests that the purpose of C. Flaminius was to control the eastern boundary of the area occupied by Apuani and Friniati in the Apennines.

[20] The role played by the legions in building was not limited to the construction of roads. In 195, after defeating the Boii, the consul L. Valerius Flaccus remained with his army in Placentia and Cremona for the rest of the summer, with the purpose of rebuilding the parts of both cities that had been damaged (Liv. 34.22.3).

[21] Liv. 39.2.10; Str. 5.1.11; *CIL* I² 617 = *ILRRP* 450; *CIL* I² 618–19. Cf. Briscoe 2008: 214–15.

[22] Pekáry 1968: 47; Wiseman 1970a: 126–8. In his works, Radke (1973: 1432) does not question that Aemilius Lepidus was the first promoter, but he thinks that the road was built in various phases by different magistrates, which would be proven by the diverse fora found along this road: Forum Lepidi, Forum Livii, Forum Cornelii, and Forum Gallorum (Radke 1964b: 301–4; 1967: 227–9; 1975a; 1975b). In fact, Radke thinks that the milestone at *CIL* I² 619 dates from a reconstruction of the road carried out by the same Aemilius Lepidus in 175, during his second consulship (Radke 1973: 1432).

[23] *CIL* I² 822 = *ILLRP* 460.

consuls of the same name who could also have been responsible for its construction.[24] Radke, on the other hand, is inclined to think it may have been either the consul of 232 or 221.[25] In fact, there is not enough additional information to favour either of these magistrates with any certainty. In any event, there is no doubt that it was a consular road, as is attested by the preserved milestone. During his second consulship in 175, Aemilius Lepidus may have been the builder of the road between Bononia and Aquileia.[26]

A milestone from the Via Appia, with the name of the consul Cn. Domitius, suggests that the construction of a section of this road was carried out on his initiative.[27] The problem lies in giving a specific date to this construction, since there were consuls of the same name – and with the cognomen Ahenobarbus – in 192, 162, 122, 96, and 32. The consuls of 192, 122, and 32 were engaged in wars during their consulships. We know very little of the consular activity of the other two. Wiseman is inclined to attribute the road to the consul of 162 – actually a suffect consul –, adducing as his reason the fact that the consul's cognomen is not mentioned in the inscription.[28]

A milestone found in Corleone mentions a consul named Aurelius Cotta (the praenomen is not preserved).[29] The road referred to in the inscription linked Agrigentum and Panormus in Sicily. The publisher of the inscription, Di Vita, identified C. Aurelius Cotta as the promoter of the road, which may have been built during one of his consulships, in 252 or 248; on both occasions Sicily was his province.[30] Radke was inclined to opt for the consul of 252.[31] However, Degrassi convincingly argued in support of a much later date than that of the inscription and put forward L. Aurelius Cotta, consul in 144, as the builder of the road.[32] Nevertheless, this identification is not devoid of difficulties, since there is no information linking L. Cotta to Sicily during his consulship. All we know about him is the report provided by Valerius Maximus, according to which the two consuls of that year wished to receive command over the war in Hispania against the Lusitanians. The intervention of Scipio Aemilianus settled the issue, and neither of them received Hispania as his province.[33] No sources report on what tasks were then given to the consuls, but perhaps Cotta took on the construction of the aforementioned road.

---

[24] Pekáry 1968: 48.   [25] Radke 1973: 1432.
[26] Radke 1973: 1433; Quilici 1991: 19. Wiseman 1970a: 136, attributes this road to T. Annius Luscus, consul in 153. Of the same opinion, Bandelli 1988: 32–3.
[27] *CIL* I² 822 = *ILLRP* 460.   [28] Wiseman 1970a: 131 n. 66.   [29] *ILLRP* 1277.
[30] Di Vita 1955; 1963.   [31] Radke 1973: 1432.   [32] Degrassi 1962: 503–8. See also Pekáry 1968: 48.
[33] V. Max. 6.4.2. Cf. Broughton 1951–86: I 470.

A milestone found in Vulci called into question the usual attribution of the Via Aurelia to Aurelius Cotta as a censor in 241,[34] since the inscription mentions a consul Aurelius Cotta.[35] Degrassi suggested the aforementioned L. Aurelius Cotta, consul in 144, or the consul of the same name in 119, as the builder of the road that followed the northern Tyrrhenian coastline. This proposal was accepted as probable by Pekáry,[36] but Wiseman supported the existence of two Viae Aureliae, one old and one new. In his opinion, the old one could indeed have been built by the aforementioned censor in 241, and one of his descendants could have built the new Via Aurelia, perhaps the consul of 119.[37] In any event, one of the consuls Aurelius Cotta of the second century ought to be seen either as the builder of the original Via Aurelia or as the promoter of its reconstruction or renovation.

In contrast, there are no doubts about the attribution to the consul of 148, Sp. Postumius Albinus, of the road from Genua to Cremona.[38] It is also unquestionable that one of the consuls of 132, P. Popillius Laenas, dedicated an important part of his mandate to the construction of public roads in various parts of Italy. A milestone found near Atria attests to his intervention in the construction of a road in the valley of the river Po.[39] The well-known inscription of Polla also indicates his intervention in the southwest of Italy, in Lucania.[40]

Just as the consular authority to build public roads was applicable to Sicily, as we have previously seen, so it also applied to other provinces of the Empire. In 129, the consul M'. Aquillius, along with a senatorial legation, was sent to Asia with the task of re-organizing the province. Aquillius stayed in Asia as a proconsul until 126. Re-organization must have involved the construction of new communication routes. Clear proof of this is the milestone inscription, engraved in both Latin and Greek, in which Aquillius is mentioned as a consul.[41] The fact that Aquillius appears as a

---

[34] See, for example, Nissen 1902: II 299. Cf. Broughton 1951–86: I 219.

[35] *ILLRP* 1288. On the Via Aurelia, see De Rossi 1968.   [36] Pekáry 1968: 48.

[37] Wiseman 1970a: 133–4. Cf. Radke 1973: 1434; Bodei Giglioni 1974: 81 n. 58. On the other hand, Toynbee (II 1965: 660–1) suggests that the Via Aurelia could have been built by C. Aurelius Cotta, consul in 200.

[38] *CIL* I² 624 = *ILLRP* 452. Cf. Broughton 1951–86: I 461; Wiseman 1970a: 140; Radke 1973: 1432.

[39] *CIL* I² 637 = *ILLRP* 453. Cf. Broughton 1951–86: I 497–8; Pekáry 1968: 48; Radke 1973: 1432. See criticisms of Radke's thesis in Wiseman 1970a: 128–30.

[40] *CIL* I² 638 = *ILLRP* 454. Cf. Toynbee 1965: II 671–2; Hinrichs 1967; Burckhardt 1989. All the publishers of the *elogium* of Polla have followed the thesis of Mommsen, who identified P. Popillius Laenas as the builder of the road mentioned in the inscription, except for Verbrugghe 1973, who believes that it was Ap. Claudius Pulcher, consul for 143. In the same sense, Gordon 1983: 87–9.

[41] *CIL* I² 647 = *ILLRP* 455; *CIL* I² 651 = *ILLRP* 456. Cf. Pekáry 1968: 139; Radke 1973: 1432.

consul and not as a proconsul raises the possibility that the planning of the road where the milestone is located was carried out in 129. Yet, significantly, on two milestones in Hispania dating from the last quarter of the second century, both Q. Fabius Labeo and M. Sergius are referred to as proconsuls.[42]

In this sense, the milestone found in the south of France which mentions Cn. Domitius Ahenobarbus *imperator* leaves no doubt as to his identity, but poses the difficult question of whether to attribute the construction of the road to him as a consul or as a proconsul.[43] Ahenobarbus was consul in 122 and was later proconsul in 121 and 120. Throughout this time he was in Gaul, and he eventually obtained a triumph over the Arverni. He was also in charge of organizing the province, including the construction of the Via Domitia named in his honour.[44] Whereas Ahenobarbus may have started construction of the road back in 122, after his resounding victory over the Salluvii, the form of address used in the inscription, *imperator*, is rather an indication of his status as a proconsul.[45]

In 127, the consul L. Cornelius Cinna built the so-called new Latin road.[46] The construction of a road in the valley of the river Arno towards Pisa could possibly be attributed to the consulship of T. Quinctius Flamininus in 123.[47] However, the consul of the same name in 150 cannot be totally discarded, an option which Wiseman is more inclined to opt for.[48] The consul of 117, L. Caecilius Metellus Diadematus, was possibly the builder of the Via Caecilia.[49]

While we must allow for the possibility that new inscriptions may bring to light information to resolve these doubts, the lack of evidence in most cases makes it difficult, if not impossible, to determine who the builder of a road was or whether various parts of a road were built by different magistrates. In any event, from the data currently known it can be deduced that the construction of public roads in Italy was, in the Republican period, mainly in the hands of the consuls,[50] at least during the second century, the time of the greatest activity in the construction of roads, and only exceptionally in the hands of the praetors. In the provinces of the Empire, both

---

[42] *ILLRP* 461–462.   [43] *ILLRP* 460a. Duval 1949.   [44] Wiseman 1970a: 137–8; Radke 1973: 1432.

[45] Duval 1949: 212–14; Pekáry 1968: 68.

[46] *CIL* I² 654 = *ILLRP* 457. Cf. Wiseman 1970a: 139; Radke 1973: 1432.

[47] *CIL* I² 657 = *ILLRP* 458. Cf. Broughton 1951–86: I 512; Radke 1973: 1432.

[48] Wiseman 1970a: 137. Cf. Bodei Giglioni 1974: 81 n. 58.

[49] *CIL* I² 661 = *ILLRP* 459. Cf. Pekáry 1968: 68; Radke 1973: 1432. On the other hand, Wiseman (1970a: 134–6) tends to place the construction in 283, perhaps a rather early date if we take into account the later date of all the other known roads.

[50] Pekáry 1968: 54: 'Die Consuln sind die Strassenbauer par excellence.'

consuls and proconsuls were in charge of this task. The question of whether before the year 200 some of the roads may have been built by the censors, as stated by literary sources, remains open.

VOWS AND THE CONSTRUCTION OF TEMPLES

According to Livy, there were three different phases in the process of construction of new temples and sanctuaries in Rome: the vow (*votum*), the contract (*locatio*), and the consecration or dedication (*dedicatio*).[51] Consuls could take part in all three phases – as well as dictators, praetors, aediles, duumvirs, and promagistrates – although they did so especially in the first phase, in the *votum*, so in fact they became the main promoters of the building of temples throughout the Republic (Table 1).[52]

The first recorded case in ancient sources of a consul vowing the construction of a temple, something which until that point had been in the hands of the dictators, is that of C. Iunius Bubulcus Brutus.[53] Livy reports that while he was a censor in 306 Bubulcus Brutus was in charge of the *locatio* of the temple of Salus, which he had vowed during the war against the Samnites in 311, when he was consul for the third time.[54] The temple of Salus was built on the Quirinal and was dedicated by the same Bubulcus Brutus as dictator in 302.[55] As can be noted, on this occasion the same person was in charge of the three key phases of the construction, the vow, the contract, and the consecration, during his successive magistracies as consul, censor, and dictator.

C. Cornelius Cethegus was also in charge of the whole process of the construction of the temple of Juno in the Forum Holitorium. As a consul, he had vowed a temple to Juno Sospita during his war against the Gauls in 197.[56] From Livy's text it appears that he was personally in charge of the *locatio* during his consulship, and he also dedicated the temple, which was

---

[51] On the construction of temples during the Roman Republic, from various points of view and drawing different conclusions, see, amongst others, the works of Bardon 1955; Stambaugh 1978; Ziolkowski 1992; Aberson 1994; Orlin 1997.

[52] A list of temples together with their vowers and dedicators is to be found in De Ruggiero 1925: 51–5 and Orlin 1997: 199–202. Cf. Aberson 1994: 229–36; Rüpke 2006: 219–20. I consider the *locatio*, as commonly seen, as the process of letting out the contract for the work, in this case the construction of a temple and not, as Ziolkowski (1992: 203–8) argued, as the process of choosing a location for the temple to be built. Against Ziolkowski's theory, see the convincing arguments of Orlin 1997: 139 n. 94. Cf. Robinson 1992: 48–9.

[53] Ziolkowski 1992: 242; Clark 2007: 50–3. [54] Liv. 9.43.25. [55] Liv. 10.1.9. Coarelli 1999c.

[56] Liv. 32.30.10. On Juno Sospita, Fears 1975. On the temple, Coarelli 1996a.

Table 1 *Intervention of consuls in the construction of temples in the pre-Sullan period*

TEMPLUM	VOTUM	LOCATIO	DEDICATIO
QUIRINUS	L. Papirius Cursor Dictator 325 or 310	?	L. Papirius Cursor (son) Consul 293
SALUS	C. Iunius Bubulcus Brutus Consul 311	C. Iunius Bubulcus Brutus Censor 306	C. Iunius Bubulcus Brutus Dictator 302
VICTORIA	L. Postumius Megellus Aedilis curulis? Consul 305?	L. Postumius Megellus? Aedilis curulis 303 or 301?	L. Postumius Megellus Consul 294
BELLONA	Ap. Claudius Caecus Consul 296	?	?
JUPITER VICTOR	Q. Fabius Maximus Rullianus Consul 295	?	?
JUPITER STATOR	M. Atilius Regulus Consul 294	?	?
FORS FORTUNA	Sp. Carvilius Maximus Consul 293	Sp. Carvilius Maximus Consul 293	?
CONSUS	L. Papirius Cursor Consul II 272	?	?
TELLUS	P. Sempronius Sophus Consul 268	?	?
PALES	M. Atilius Regulus Consul 267	?	?
VORTUMNUS	M. Fulvius Flaccus Consul 264	?	?
JANUS	C. Duilius Consul 260	?	?
TEMPESTATES	L. Cornelius Scipio Consul 259	?	?
SPES	A. Atilius Calatinus Consul 258	?	?
OPS OPIFERA	L. Caecilius Metellus? Consul 251	L. Caecilius Metellus? Consul 251	L. Caecilius Metellus? Consul 247
HONOS	Q. Fabius Maximus Verrucosus Consul 233	?	?
HONOS ET VIRTUS	M. Claudius Marcellus Consul 222 / Proconsul 212	?	M. Claudius Marcellus (son) Privatus? Duumvir? 205

Table 1 (*cont.*)

TEMPLUM	VOTUM	LOCATIO	DEDICATIO
IUVENTAS	M. Livius Salinator Consul 207	M. Livius Salinator Censor 204	C. Licinius Lucullus Duumvir 191
FORTUNA PRIMIGENIA	P. Sempronius Tuditanus Consul 204	?	Q. Marcius Ralla Duumvir 194
JUPITER "IN INSULA"	L. Furius Purpurio Praetor 200	L. Furius Purpurio Consul 196	C. Servilius (Geminus) Duumvir 194
JUNO SOSPITA	C. Cornelius Cethegus Consul 197	C. Cornelius Cethegus Consul 197?	C. Cornelius Cethegus Censor 194
VICTORIA VIRGO	M. Porcius Cato Consul 195	?	M. Porcius Cato Privatus? Duumvir? 193
PIETAS	M'. Acilius Glabrio Consul 191	M'. Acilius Glabrio Consul?	M'. Acilius Glabrio (son) Duumvir 181
HERCULES MUSARUM	M. Fulvius Nobilior Consul 189	?	?
JUNO REGINA + DIANA	M. Aemilius Lepidus Consul 187	?	M. Aemilius Lepidus Censor 179
VENUS ERYCINA	L. Porcius Licinus Consul 184	?	L. Porcius Licinus (son) Duumvir 181
FELICITAS	L. Licinius Lucullus Consul 151	?	?
HERCULES VICTOR	L. Mummius Consul 146	?	?
MARS	D. Iunius Brutus Callaicus Consul 138?	?	?
HONOS ET VIRTUS	C. Marius Consul before 101	?	?

consecrated, according to Livy, while he was a censor in 194.[57] Cicero provides some interesting information regarding the worship of Juno Sospita, for which, however, he does not provide any explanation. According to Cicero, each year the consuls had to celebrate a sacrifice in

---

[57] Liv. 34.53.3: 'una (aedes) Iunonis Matutae in foro holitorio, vota locataque quadriennio ante a C. Cornelio consule Gallico bello: censor idem dedicavit.' As can be noted, Livy refers to a temple to Juno Matuta. The change from Juno Sospita in the *votum* to Juno Matuta in the *dedicatio* is probably due to a mistake by Livy or by a copyist. The mistake may derive from confusion with the

honour of Juno Sospita.[58] In the opinion of Coarelli, the temple was restored in the year 90 by the consul L. Iulius Caesar after an act of desecration. The preserved structures would correspond to this reconstruction carried out at the beginning of the first century.[59] In that same year, 194, a duumvir had consecrated a temple to Jupiter 'in insula' which had been vowed six years earlier by the praetor L. Furius Purpurio during the war against the Gauls, and for whose *locatio* he had provided while a consul in 196.[60]

In 294, the consul L. Postumius Megellus consecrated a temple to Victoria on the Palatine, next to the so-called *clivus Victoriae*.[61] He took the vow for the temple while he was a curule aedile some years before, and he had it built with the money obtained from the fines levied during his aedileship.[62] However, Ziolkowski is convinced that it was not an aedilician endeavour. If that was the case, Megellus' office as aedile ought to be dated after 304, since in that year Cn. Flavius became the first aedile to promote a temple in Rome. In his opinion, Megellus vowed the temple during his first consulship in 305 and dedicated it during his second consulship in 294. He would also have been in charge of the *locatio*, probably while he was an aedile in 303 or 301, a magistracy that he would have held after defeating the Samnites as consul.[63]

In 207, the consul M. Livius Salinator vowed a temple to Iuventas during his campaign against Hasdrubal. As a censor in 204 he was in charge of the *locatio* of the temple, eventually dedicated next to the Circus Maximus in 191 by the duumvir C. Licinius Lucullus.[64] In 193, M. Porcius Cato, a private citizen at the time, dedicated the *aediculum* built in honour of

---

temple of Mater Matuta. Cf. Briscoe 1989: 227: '[Matuta] must be wrong, since Matuta is not known as an epithet for Juno, whilst Sospita is known, and is indeed extremely suitable for the present occasion'; Ziolkowski 1992: 77–8; Aberson 1994: 105; Orlin 1997: 63 n. 99.

[58] Cic. *Mur.* 90.   [59] Coarelli 1996a. Cf. Cic. *Div.* 1.99; Obseq. 55.

[60] Liv. 34.53.7. In another passage, Livy (35.41.8) refers to the *dedicatio* of two temples to Jupiter presumably vowed by Furius Purpurio, one of them while he was a praetor in 200 and the other while he was a consul in 196. This is questionable and could be a case of duplication. Cf. Briscoe 1989: 112–14; 1981: 133: the Servilius mentioned would be C. Servilius Geminus. Cf. Broughton 1951–86: I 326 n. 1.

[61] Liv. 10.33.9. Pensabene 2000a.

[62] Broughton (1951–86: I 165) suggests the year 307 for his aedileship. Wachsmuth 1975: the vow would have been taken about 306 or after 304.

[63] Ziolkowski 1992: 172–6; 240. See now Clark 2007: 56–8.

[64] Liv. 36.36.5–6. Cf. Briscoe 1981: 276: 'The true date of the dedication of the temple of Iuventas cannot be determined: the fact that a Cornelius was consul in both 197 and 191 could have led to an error in either direction.' The fact that the person dedicating the temple is a duumvir who is not a member of the vower's family may be explained as follows: the vower had probably died, and his son was at that time in the Eastern Mediterranean commanding the Roman fleet. Cf. Aberson 1994: 131; Coarelli 1996d.

Victoria Virgo that he had vowed two years earlier during his stay in Hispania as consul.[65] The temples of Juno Regina and Diana were vowed by the consul M. Aemilius Lepidus in 187 during his campaign against the Ligures,[66] and in 179, as censor, he dedicated both temples built at the Circus Flaminius.[67] The consecration of both sanctuaries was enhanced by the celebration of stage plays (*ludi scaenici*) for the occasion, funded by the senate.

The case of the temple of Ops Opifera in the Capitolium is debatable. We know that it was dedicated before 186, since in that year it was damaged by lightning, but we have no certain reports on the identity of its promoter.[68] Pliny's mention of a 'Metellus pontifex' as the person dedicating a sanctuary to Ops Opifera has commonly been interpreted in the sense that the temple was rebuilt by L. Caecilius Metellus Delmaticus, consul in 119.[69] However, Morgan and Ziolkowski have defended the theory that Pliny referred to the promoter of the temple, the pontiff L. Caecilius Metellus, consul in 251.[70] According to Morgan and Ziolkowski, Metellus vowed the temple of Ops as a consul in 251/0, during his battle against the Carthaginians in Panormus, and dedicated it in 247, during his second consulship. If this were the case, he would have been personally in charge of the *locatio* of the temple before the end of his first consulship; thus all the responsibility for the construction would have remained his.

On other occasions, it was a son of the vower who eventually dedicated the temple. This is the case for the consul L. Papirius Cursor in 293, who conducted the consecration of the temple of Quirinus that his father, with the same name, had vowed as a dictator during the last quarter of the fourth century, although Livy does not appear to know this particular fact, and he only provides the certain date of the *dedicatio* of the temple.[71] According to Livy, the dedicator of the temple made use of the spoils of war taken from the enemy to decorate the building at the time of the consecration, once the temple had been built. Papirius was dictator, according to Livy, in 325 and

---

[65] Liv. 35.9.6. On the real date of the *dedicatio* see Briscoe 1981: 157. Cf. Pensabene 2000b.

[66] Liv. 39.2.11.   [67] Liv. 40.52.1–3. Cf. Viscogliosi 1995: 1996b; Briscoe 2008: 549–50.

[68] Liv. 39.22.4. On the temple see Aronen 1996.

[69] Plin. *Nat.* 11.174. Cf. De Ruggiero 1925: 54–5. This idea was reasserted by Pouthier 1981: esp. 173–200. According to Pouthier, 'la mention "Metellus pontifex" . . . il ne peut s'agir que de L. Caecilius Metellus Delmaticus' (p. 190). Metellus Delmaticus would have restored and rededicated the temple to Ops on the Capitolium, which had been built by A. Atilius Calatinus in the middle of the third century.

[70] Morgan 1973; Ziolkowski 1992: 122–5: there is no trace of a rededication of the temple, since Pliny only mentions its dedication. More recently Clark (2007: 300–5) has pointed to the possibility that the original foundation was made by L. Caecilius Metellus in the First Punic War and that the temple was refounded by Metellus Delmaticus.

[71] Liv. 10.46.7. Cf. Plin. *Nat.* 7.213. Coarelli 1999b.

310; however, the *fasti consulares* and the *fasti triumphales* give 324 and 309 as the dates of his dictatorships.[72] On both occasions he obtained triumphs, so it is possible that he pronounced the vow during either of his two dictatorships. According to Ziolkowski, the vow of the dictator L. Papirius Cursor represented a turning point. The temple of Quirinus had been built with the spoils of war obtained by Papirius during his different magistracies, and that would account for the long period of time needed for its construction.[73] It is in fact one of the longest periods of time between the vow and the consecration of a temple, thirty-three years if we place the vow in Papirius' first dictatorship, or at least sixteen years if we place it in the second. Significantly, the senate did not appoint duumvirs to carry out the dedication of the temple, which would have hastened the fulfilment of the vow. On the contrary, the senators waited until the son of the vower held the consulship to entrust him with that task.[74]

In 222 the consul M. Claudius Marcellus vowed a temple to Virtus during the battle of Clastidium, in the war against the Gauls.[75] Marcellus repeated the vow in 212 as proconsul on the occasion of the seizure of Syracuse, promising a temple dedicated to Honos and Virtus.[76] When Marcellus became a consul again in 208, in spite of the fact that the Hannibalic War was at its height, he was retained in Rome because of the religious scruples imposed by the pontiffs. The priests considered that one sanctuary could not be dedicated to two different divinities, in this case to Honos and Virtus, and that, therefore, two temples had to be built.[77] Eventually, the solution seems to have been to renovate the temple of Honos that Fabius Maximus had promoted and to build as an annex a chamber dedicated to Virtus.[78] The new temple of Honos and Virtus, situated next to the Porta Capena, was dedicated in 205 by Marcellus' son. He had the same name as his father, who died in 208, and it is not recorded that he held any position as a magistrate in the year of the dedication (until then he had only been a military tribune),[79] or that he was appointed as duumvir for that purpose, although this should not be ruled out.[80] In any case, the dedicator certainly had the senate's authorization.

---

[72] Broughton 1951–86: I 147–8; 162–3.
[73] Ziolkowski 1992: 240–2: the temple would have been vowed in 325; the fact that the temple was dedicated more than thirty years after it was vowed 'is the best proof that the *aerarium* did not participate in its construction'. On the distinction between *praeda* and *manubiae* see Churchill 1999.
[74] The fact is emphasized by Orlin 1997: 180.   [75] Liv. 27.25.6; 29.11.13. Cf. Beck 2005: 307–8.
[76] V. Max. 1.1.8.   [77] Liv. 27.25.6–10; V. Max. 1.1.8.
[78] Cf. Eisenhut 1975c; Palombi 1996b; Beck 2005: 323–4; Clark 2007: 67–8.
[79] Broughton 1951–86: I 292.
[80] Liv. 29.11.13. Cf. Cic. *Ver.* 4.121; *Rep.* 1.21; Liv. 25.40.1–2. Orlin (1997: 170–1 and n. 25) holds categorically that Marcellus' son dedicated the temple in 205 as a *privatus* and rules out the possibility

The second temple, built in honour of Venus Erycina next to the Porta Collina, was dedicated in 181 by the duumvir L. Porcius Licinus, who was the son of the consul of the same name who had pronounced his vow in 184 during the war against the Ligures.[81] In 181 the temple of Pietas in the Forum Holitorium was dedicated by the duumvir Manius Acilius Glabrio.[82] He too was the son of the vower, the consul of the same name in 191. He had made his vow on the day of his victorious battle at Thermopylae against Antiochus. Furthermore, at an undetermined date, probably while still consul, Acilius Glabrio may also have let the contract for the temple following instructions from the senate, so that the entire process of construction remained in the hands of the same family.[83] Livy only mentions that the vower of the temple took charge of the contract with the senate's authorization, but he does not disclose which office Acilius Glabrio held at the time. After acting as consul in Greece in 191, he did not hold another political position and was never elected censor, a magistracy in which he could have been in charge of the *locatio*. It therefore seems reasonable to presume that he commissioned the construction of the new temple on his return from Greece, once his vow was accepted by the senate.[84] The 'family' nature of the temple is emphasized by the fact that the duumvir – who thus began a political career that would eventually see him become a suffect consul in 154 – had a golden statue of his father placed in the temple, the first of its kind in Italy, as Livy claims.[85]

However, it was normal for a different person from the one who had made the vow to be in charge of the *locatio* or the *dedicatio* or both. The senate sometimes appointed extraordinary magistrates to be in charge of the building of a temple once it had been vowed. They were known as *duumviri aedi locandae* or *duumviri aedi dedicandae*, and they were responsible for the *locatio* and the *dedicatio* of the temple respectively.[86] From the available information, it appears that the senators took the initiative in appointing

---

that Livy omitted his appointment as *duumvir aedi dedicandae*. This contradicts the opinion put forward by Mommsen (1887–8: II 618–20) and supported by the scholarship (see Ziolkowski 1992: 222–3; 308) that only magistrates could dedicate temples.

[81] Liv. 40.34.4. Cf. Briscoe 2008: 493–4. Coarelli 2000b: it is possible that there were two temples dedicated to Venus Erycina *extra portam Collinam*, one built after 211 by Marcellus and the other built between 184 and 181 by L. Porcius Licinus.

[82] Ciancio Rossetto 1999; Clark 2007: 70–1.

[83] Liv. 40.34.5. Cf. V. Max. 2.5.1. Briscoe 2008: 494–5.

[84] Cf. Orlin 1997: 48. However, Aberson (1994: 106–7) sees the expression 'ex senatus consulto' as a sign of the appointment of Acilius Glabrio as *duumvir aedi locandae*.

[85] Papi 1995.

[86] Mommsen 1887–8: II 618–19; Liebenam 1905; Siber 1952: 112; Waldstein 1975. See a list of duumvirs in Orlin 1997: 211.

the duumvirs and that their appointment was made through one of the consuls or the urban praetor. In 217 the urban praetor M. Aemilius appointed C. Pupius and Caeso Quinctius Flaminius as duumvirs for letting the contract for the temple of Concordia that the praetor L. Manlius Vulso had vowed in Gaul two years earlier.[87] The following year, two new duumvirs were appointed, the brothers M. Atilius and C. Atilius, to take charge of the dedication of the aforementioned temple of Concordia.[88] This process shows how different persons could be the protagonists of the three phases of the construction of a temple. In 215, a different situation occurred, since the appointment of the duumvirs was done by the people. Q. Fabius Maximus made a request to the senate that he be appointed as the duumvir for the consecration of the temple of Venus Erycina that he had vowed as dictator.[89] The senate decreed that the elected consul Ti. Sempronius Gracchus should put this question to the people upon entering office.[90] Fabius was indeed appointed as a duumvir, along with T. Otacilius Crassus, who had to carry out the consecration of the temple of Mens, which he had vowed as a praetor.[91]

The first record of the existence of duumvirs goes back to the middle of the fourth century, when duumvirs were in charge of the construction of the temple of Juno Moneta that had been vowed by the dictator L. Furius Camillus in 345.[92] In 294, the consul M. Atilius Regulus vowed a temple to Jupiter Stator during the Samnite War.[93] He did so in the middle of battle: raising his hands to heaven and with a voice loud enough to be heard, he pledged the construction of the temple if the god halted the flight of the Roman army and they defeated the Samnites.[94] Later on, Livy provides Fabius Pictor's version of this event, according to which the temple was vowed during the battle of Luceria. But since many centuries earlier Romulus had already taken the same vow of building a temple to Jupiter Stator and only a sanctuary (*fanum*) existed, the senate ordered the new temple to be built immediately to avoid the harm that the lack of fulfilment could cause to the *res publica*.[95] Livy does not describe the procedure followed, but Orlin presumes that the senate would have appointed duumvirs for the construction of the temple.[96]

In most cases, the information provided by the sources does not allow us to discern the protagonists of each of the phases of the construction of a specific

[87] Liv. 22.33.7–8.   [88] Liv. 23.21.7.   [89] Holleman 1989.
[90] Liv. 23.30.14. On the chronology of the events, see Broughton 1951–86: I 258 n. 10.
[91] Liv. 22.10.10 (*votum*); 23.31.9 (*dedicatio*).   [92] Liv. 7.28.4–6.
[93] Cf. Ziolkowski 1992: 245; Coarelli 1996b.   [94] Liv. 10.36.11.   [95] Liv. 10.37.15.
[96] Orlin 1997: 158.

temple. Usually, only the name of the promoter is known through the formulation of the corresponding vow – either because it is expressly mentioned or because it can be deduced from the available sources – but we do not have additional data on the subsequent building process or, in particular, on the person who was finally in charge of its consecration once it had been built.

This is the case for a good number of temples built in the first half of the third century, such as the temple dedicated to Bellona, which was vowed in 296 by the consul Ap. Claudius Caecus during the war against the Etruscans.[97] The temple was built outside the *pomerium* and dedicated on 3 June, but we do not know the year of the *dedicatio*, the identity of the person who carried it out, or who was in charge of the *locatio*. The same can be said about the temple of Jupiter Victor, which the consul Q. Fabius Maximus Rullianus vowed in 295 during the war against the Samnites.[98] The temple was probably built on the Quirinal and its 'birthday' (*dies natalis*) was 13 April according to Ovid.[99] In 293, the consul Sp. Carvilius Maximus contracted for the construction of a temple to Fors Fortuna with the spoils obtained in the war in which he defeated the Etruscans and the Samnites.[100] In all probability, he vowed the temple as well, although Livy does not record it. In 272, the consul L. Papirius Cursor, who during his first consulship in 293 had dedicated the temple to Quirinus vowed by his father, pledged during his second consulship, after the surrender of Tarentum, that a temple to the god Consus would be built on the Aventine.[101] In 268 it was the consul P. Sempronius Sophus who vowed a temple to Tellus, as a way of placating the gods after the earthquake that happened at the height of the battle against the Picentes.[102] The temple was built on the Esquiline, in the Carinae.[103] The following year the consul M. Atilius Regulus vowed a temple to Pales after his victory against the Sallentini.[104] In 264, 260, 259, and 258 the consuls M. Fulvius Flaccus, C. Duilius, L. Cornelius Scipio, and A. Atilius Calatinus vowed temples respectively to Vortumnus,[105] Janus,[106] the Tempestates,[107] and Spes.[108]

---

[97] Liv. 10.19.17. Cf. *Inscr. It.* XIII.3 79 = *CIL* I² p. 192, IX–X. Viscogliosi 1993.   [98] Liv. 10.29.14.

[99] Ov. *Fast.* 4.621. Cf. Eisenhut 1975d. Coarelli 1996c: the temple may have been dedicated in 289 by the son of the person who vowed it, Q. Fabius Maximus Gurges.

[100] Liv. 10.46.14. Cf. Ziolkowski 1992: 38–9; Orlin 1997: 31. Clark 2007: 235 n. 101: 'Carvilius' temple is most reasonably identified with that at the sixth milestone [of the Via Portuensis].'

[101] Fest. p. 228 L. Cf. Eisenhut 1975a; Ziolkowski 1992: 24; Andreussi 1993; Orlin 1997: 200: *votum* in 273.

[102] Flor. 1.14.2; V. Max. 6.3.1b. Sempronius Sophus was censor in 252.   [103] Coarelli 2000a.

[104] Flor. 1.15.   [105] Fest. p. 228 L.   [106] Tac. *Ann.* 2.49.

[107] *CIL* VI 1287 = I 32 = I² 9. Cf. Ovid *Fast.* 6.193–194.

[108] Cic. *Leg.* 2.28; Tac. *Ann.* 2.49. Cicero (*N.D.* 2.61) attributes to Calatinus the temple of Fides on the Capitolium, but he does not specify whether he promoted its construction during one of his consulships in 258 or, preferably, 254 (so De Ruggiero 1925: 53) or while dictator in 249 (so Orlin 1997: 200). The temple to Spes was built in the Forum Holitorium. Cf. Clark 2007: 59–60.

In the second half of the third century, various occasions are known of consuls vowing temples.[109] In 233 Q. Fabius Maximus Verrucosus pledged – Cicero in fact uses the verb *dedicare* – a temple to Honos during the war against the Ligures.[110] This temple to Honos was situated outside the *porta Capena*, near the temple of Mars.[111] Towards the end of the Second Punic War, in 204, the consul P. Sempronius Tuditanus vowed a temple to Fortuna Primigenia during his campaign in Bruttium.[112] The temple was built on the Quirinal and dedicated in 194 by a duumvir appointed for that purpose.[113]

In the second century, the consul M. Fulvius Nobilior must have taken the vow for a temple dedicated to Hercules Musarum, perhaps in 189, during the war against the Aetolians.[114] The temple of Felicitas on the Velabrum was promoted by L. Licinius Lucullus, apparently with the spoils obtained in his military campaigns in Hispania as consul in 151.[115] The destroyer of Corinth, L. Mummius, promoted the construction of a temple dedicated to Hercules Victor on the Caelian as a result of his victory in Greece, and it was built with the spoils of war.[116] We do not know much about the temple built in honour of Mars promoted by D. Iunius Brutus

---

[109] As well as the temples cited later on, it must be noted that a Lutatius Catulus promoted the construction of a temple to Iuturna in the Campus Martius (Serv. *ad Aen.* 12.139). It may have been the consul of 242, C. Lutatius Catulus, or Q. Lutatius Catulus, consul in 102. De Ruggiero (1925: 53) favours the option of the consul of 242 (although he places him in 241); cf. Eisenhut 1975e. On the other hand, Cicero (*N.D.* 3.52) attributes to the consul of 231, C. Papirius Maso, the construction of a 'delubrum Fontis'.

[110] Cic. *N.D.* 2.61. On the military campaign cf. Plut. *Fab.* 2.1.

[111] Palombi 1996b; Clark 2007: 67.   [112] Liv. 29.36.8. Coarelli 1995a.

[113] Liv. 34.53.6. Livy confuses the name of the vower, whom he calls P. Sempronius Sophus. However, there is no consul of that name during the Second Punic War. He clearly refers to Sempronius Tuditanus. Furthermore, Livy claims that Sempronius himself had conducted the *locatio* of the temple when he was a censor. This cannot be true, since Sempronius Tuditanus was a censor in 209, whereas the vow for the temple took place in 204. Seguin (1974: 19 n. 55) suggests that the contract for the construction of the temple was let by Scipio Africanus as a censor in 199, '. . . afin d'accélérer l'édification du temple, soit par amitié pour les Sempronii, soit parce qu'il attachait un prix personel à honorer la Fortune'. This seems highly improbable, not only because the sources do not provide any indication of it, but also because it would be exceptional since the norm was the personal or family continuity in the process of construction of a temple. On the text of Livy, see Briscoe 1981: 132–3.

[114] Cic. *Arch.* 27. Cf. *CIL* vi 1307 = *CIL* i 615 = *ILS* 16 = *ILLRP* 124; *CIL* xiv 2601 = *CIL* i² 616 = *ILS* 17 = *ILLRP* 322. Cf. Eisenhut 1975b; A. Viscogliosi (1996a) surveys the various dates proposed for the dedication of the temple: 189 he finds too early; 187, the year of the triumph of Nobilior; and 179, which he finds more likely.

[115] Cass. Dio 22 fr.76.2; cf. Cic. *Ver.* 4.2.4; Strab. 8.6.23; Plin. *Nat.* 34.69. Cf. De Ruggiero 1925: 54; Orlin 1997: 131. Pietilä-Castrén (1987: 126 n. 15) interprets Cassius Dio's sentence in the sense that Lucullus built the temple after the war in Hispania and not with the riches obtained during that war. See also Palombi 1995: the temple must have been dedicated after 146, or perhaps even after 142.

[116] *CIL* i² 626 = *VI* 331 = *ILLRP* 122 = *ILS* 20: 'hanc aedem et signu(m) Herculis Victoris imperator dedicat.' Cf. De Ruggiero 1925: 54; Ziolkowski 1988; Orlin 1997: 193–4. Pietilä-Castrén (1987: 142–3) thinks that the temple was dedicated before Mummius' triumph in 145, when the *imperator* was still outside the city walls awaiting the award of his triumph. That would mean that the temple, a rather

Callaicus. The temple may have been vowed in 138, while Brutus was consul, within the context of his victorious campaigns in Hispania Ulterior against the Lusitanians, for which he was awarded a triumph upon his return to Rome. The temple was apparently built with the spoils obtained in Hispania.[117] C. Marius promoted a temple to Honos and Virtus with the spoils from the war against the Cimbri and Teutones in 102 or 101.[118] The temple must have been dedicated after 101.[119]

As can be seen, Rome was progressively filled with temples dedicated to many different divinities as its domain expanded, first in Italy and later in the Mediterranean. From the details provided by the ancient sources we can deduce that the most common procedure for promoting the construction of a new temple in Rome was that a magistrate with *imperium* pronounced a vow for a temple during a military campaign under his leadership, offering a pledge to a certain divinity should the Roman army achieve victory.[120] Obviously, this kind of vow was exceptional,[121] but there are no fixed patterns that explain why one general decided to pronounce it but another commander in similar circumstances did not, and personal factors probably played an important role in the decision. The sources mention the dictators A. Postumius Albus, in 496, and M. Furius Camillus, in 396, vowing to construct temples before leaving Rome to start their military campaigns.[122] In both cases the dictators acted *ex officio* following orders from the senate, 'ex senatus consulto'. However, these are exceptional cases. Whereas in the first two centuries of the Republic the dictators had been the vowers of temples, from the end of the fourth century onwards the consuls became the principal but not exclusive promoters, since other magistrates continued to vow new temples. There is no known case of a consul taking a vow to construct a temple 'ex senatus consulto' before leaving for his province. On the contrary, all the known consular vows for temples took place away from Rome, before, during, or after a battle and on the personal initiative of the

small private *aedicula* in opinion of Pietilä-Castrén, would have been built in approximately one year. Eisenhut (1975b) believes it is not clear that it was a public building and thinks that it may have simply been a private *aedicula*. See also Palombi 1996a.

[117] Plin. *Nat.* 36.26; Prisc. *Gramm.* 8.17.4 = Nep. fr. 26 Peter; V. Max. 8.14.2. Cf. Ziolkowski 1992: 101–3; Zevi 1996; Orlin 1997: 131; 194.

[118] *CIL* XI 1831 = *ILS* 59: 'de manubiis Cimbris et Teuton. aedem Honori et Virtuti victor fecit'. Clark 2007: 124–6.

[119] Cf. De Ruggiero 1925: 55; Eisenhut 1975c; Orlin 1997: 131; 194. Palombi 1996c: the temple may have been vowed during the battle against the Teutons at Aquae Sextiae in 102, and it was built after the victory against the Cimbri near Vercelli in 101.

[120] Liv. 10.42.7 claims that it was usual to pronounce vows for temples to the gods at times of danger in battle.

[121] Orlin 1997: 31: 'approximately nine out of ten generals did not vow a new temple while on campaign'.

[122] Dion. Hal. 6.17.3; Liv. 5.19.6.

respective consuls, apparently without any previous order or authorization from or by the senate.[123] A different case is that of the temple of Concordia, whose construction was entrusted by the senate to the consul L. Opimius in 121, after the repression of the followers of C. Gracchus.[124] Opimius fulfilled the senate's order and let the contract for the temple, certainly before the end of the consular year, once a lustration to purify the *Urbs* had taken place after the bloody confrontation that had occurred.

Between 367 and Sulla's dictatorship, there is evidence that almost thirty temples were promoted by consuls, and the figure may in fact have been higher since some of the temples whose vower is unknown may also have been vowed by consuls. This means that, at the very least, almost 50 per cent of all the temples built in Rome during that period – for two-thirds of which there is certain or probable information about their vowers – were promoted by consuls through a vow taken during a military campaign, acting therefore as chief commanders of the Roman legions. The vow had a contractual nature, so that only in the case of a Roman victory would the temple be built as fair payment for the services provided by the divinity that had intervened.[125]

It seems apparent, therefore, that the magistrate who pronounced the vow for a temple, even if he did so on his own initiative, carried it out under the powers bestowed upon him by his office. As we have already seen, a consul – or another magistrate with *imperium* – sometimes made vows for the cele-bration of games following orders from the senate. In this context it is obvious that his vow was not personal and that he acted *ex officio*. However, in the case of the vow of a magistrate pronounced without the senate's previous order, the question is whether its fulfilment depended exclusively on the person who had taken it and whether it was binding for the Roman state. Did the magistrate at the time of pronouncing his vow act individually, or did he act implicitly on behalf of the community? Was the vower personally obliged to fulfil his vow, or was his promise binding for the community?

Mommsen defended the theory that the fulfilment of the vow was the exclusive concern of the magistrate who had pronounced it and not of the state.[126] However, most scholars have adopted the opposite viewpoint,

---

[123] Weigel (1982–3 188 n. 40) mentions the possibility that the vower of a temple may have previously received a recommendation from the *pontifices* or *decemviri sacris faciundis* on 'the appropriate deities who needed special recognition'. The sources do not support such a suggestion at all. Cf. Orlin 1997: 45 n. 36.

[124] Plut. *C.Gr.* 17.6; App. *B.Civ.* 1.26; August. *C.D.* 3.25. Cf. Gasparri 1979; Pina Polo 2006b: 94–5. See also Ferroni 1993b.

[125] Hickson 1993: 92–3; Orlin 1997: 35. See a list of formulae and expressions used when making vows in Hickson 1993: 91–105.

[126] Mommsen 1887–8: III 1062.

considering that a magistrate with *imperium* always acted as representative
of the *civitas* and that his promise was therefore binding for the state. This
idea has been backed more recently by Ziolkowski, who believes that all the
vows taken by magistrates with *imperium* for the benefit of the community
ought to be considered as *vota nuncupata* and therefore had to be assumed
by the state, because they were taken on its behalf.[127] The sources are not
clear in this respect, so it seems that Orlin's viewpoint is more appropriate
considering the pragmatic flexibility that was typical of the institutions of
the Roman Republic.[128] Certainly, it cannot be concluded from the sources
that there was at some point a general rule on whether the vows made by the
generals during a military campaign were binding for the state. Rather, it
seems that the senate, once the magistrate's report on his return to Rome
had been heard, decided in each case if it was appropriate to assume the vow
and, therefore, to give authorization for the construction of the corresponding temple. In any case, this must not be seen as something exceptional, but
as the usual course of events in the relationship between the senate and a
magistrate with *imperium* acting away from Rome. Exactly the same happened, for example, when a governor, using his powers, decided to sign an
alliance or any other agreement with a foreign state. The pact had to be
subsequently ratified or rejected by the senate. In the same manner, the
vow, which should be seen as a pact between the magistrate and a divinity,
had to be approved by the senate in Rome.[129] Nevertheless, if the Roman
army had achieved victory, which meant that the divinity had fulfilled its
part of the pact appropriately, it would be difficult not to assume the vow as
a binding obligation for all the community, since not doing so would
involve putting the peace of the gods at risk.[130] We can therefore presume
that a *votum* followed by military success for its vower must have been
binding for the state in practice.

If the senate gave its authorization, the construction of the temple then
began, financed in some cases by spoils from the war and on other occasions
by the state itself. Nevertheless, even if the state assumed the magistrate's

---

[127] Fest. 176.3 L.: 'vota nuncupata dicuntur quae consules, praetores, cum in provinciam proficiscuntur, faciunt.' Ziolkowski 1992: 195–8.

[128] Orlin 1997: 45–75, esp. 45–9 and 74–5.

[129] Bardon 1955: 173; Orlin 1997: 160. *Contra* Ziolkowski 1992: 308: 'Thus a magistrate's vow to build a temple to a deity, native or foreign, whether or not recognized by the state, did not require a confirmation by another party and could not be ruled invalid.'

[130] Cf. Magdelain 1943: 115: '*votum* désigne non un don immédiat, mais un don futur, que ne sera accompli que si la divinité exauce la prière qui lui est adressée'; Scheid 1998b: 424: 'Les Romains n'acquittaient un voeu que si la divinité invoquée avait accompli la prestation demandée . . . un voeu n'est exécutoire que si la condition est remplie'.

vow, the vower of a temple clearly retained a certain responsibility regarding the fulfilment of his *votum*, which never ceased to have a highly personal component. The formula used by Appius Claudius Caecus on the battle-field in 296 is specific: 'Bellona, if you grant us victory today, I, in return, vow a temple to you.'[131] It is a personal call by the consul upon Bellona and, therefore, he is responsible for the fulfilment of his vow, although it was assumed by the community later on.

Undeniably that is one of the reasons – another very important reason being the search for renown and prestige – why the vower was actively involved in the construction of the promised sanctuary and was personally in charge of the *locatio* and/or the *dedicatio*.[132] Concerning the contract, it is evident that a good part of the building activity in Rome belonged to the censors[133] and, to a lesser extent, to the aediles. However, only in exceptional circumstances did a censor carry out the *locatio* of new temples. In the two known cases, the temples of Salus and Iuventas, the censors Iunius Bubulcus and Livius Salinator contracted the respective works in 306 and 204, not so much because they were censors, but because they had person-ally vowed the temples as consuls.[134] Conversely, consuls also assumed responsibility for contracts of public buildings, including temples, although to a lesser extent than the censors. It is commonly assumed that the contract for the work took place immediately after a consul returned to Rome after taking his vow.[135] Aberson believes that, at least at the stage when the military campaigns took place relatively near Rome, allowing for a rapid return of the military commanders to the *Urbs*, the consuls would have time to conduct the *locatio* of the temples they had vowed prior to leaving office.[136] It seems reasonable that this was the case, as long as the senate did not see any obstacles for the construction of the promised temple, and this might be the reason why the ancient sources do not generally report who was in charge of the contract, presuming that the vower would carry out such a task.[137] However, Orlin is sceptical in view of the lack of

---

[131] Liv. 10.19.17: 'Bellona, si hodie nobis victoriam duis, ast ego tibi templum voveo.'

[132] Trisciuoglio 1998: 132: 'la condizione di *voti damnatus*, acquisita dal magistrato con l'esaudimento del voto da parte della divinità, implicava un vincolo personale di natura religiosa che doveva inevita-bilmente fissare la titolarità dell'appalto in capo allo stesso *imperator* votante'.

[133] Polyb. 6.13.3.

[134] A third, and very peculiar, case is that of the temple of the Magna Mater, where the censors expressly acted upon receiving the order from the senate. Cf. Orlin 1997: 142–3.

[135] Mommsen 1887–8: III 1049–51; Bardon 1955: 166–74; Stambaugh 1978: 557–65; Robinson 1992: 48.

[136] Aberson 1994: 105 and 114.

[137] Morgan 1971: 500 n. 2: 'it is to be doubted that a consul or other magistrate would willingly surrender to other men the letting of a contract, when there was any chance that those men would have different views on the building-contractors to be patronized'.

confirmation by the sources. In his opinion, the only rule that can be deduced from ancient sources is that when an individual had vowed a temple, he used his next magistrature, whether as a consul or as a censor, to conduct the *locatio* in the event that it had not already been carried out.[138]

What is certain is that the contracting out of work by the consul who had made the promise immediately after his vow is only confirmed with certainty in the case of Sp. Carvilius in 293, who after his return from his victorious campaign against the Etruscans carried out the contract of the temple to Fors Fortuna while he was still consul, since Livy describes these events before referring to the elections for the following year.[139] The temple of Juno Sospita in the Forum Holitorium may possibly also be included here. This temple, according to Livy, was vowed and contracted by C. Cornelius Cethegus within the context of the Gallic War in 197.[140] The close link established by Livy may logically demonstrate that the *locatio* followed the *votum* of the consul more or less immediately, but the text does not expressly state this.[141] The same applies to the temple of Pietas, vowed and contracted by Acilius Glabrio, perhaps as a consul in both cases.[142]

On the other hand, we have some testimonies for the *locatio* occasionally being carried out years after the temple was vowed, although in every case the magistrate in charge of the contract is the same person who had previously taken the vow. This, in any event, demonstrates again that there appears in general to have been a close relationship between the person who took the vow and the person who conducted the *locatio*. This is the case for Bubulcus, who as a censor in 306 let the contract for the temple of Salus which he had vowed as consul in 311; for L. Furius Purpurio in 196, who as consul conducted the *locatio* of a temple to Jupiter that he had promoted in the year 200 while he was a praetor;[143] and for Livius Salinator, who as consul vowed a temple to Iuventas in 207 and let its contract in 204 as a censor. The deciding factor in these politicians' being entrusted with the *locatio* was not their magistracies as such, but the common fact of seeking personal or family continuity in the process of building the temple.

It is therefore clear that Roman politicians who had vowed the construction of a temple during one of their military campaigns used their

---

[138] Orlin 1997: 144–7. [139] Liv. 10.46. [140] Liv. 34.53.3.
[141] Cf. Aberson 1994: 105. Orlin (1997: 145 n. 120) has doubts about it, since the text by Livy contains some errors.
[142] Liv. 40.34.5.
[143] Orlin 1997: 146: 'This incident confirms that it was the personal connection, not the specific magistracy of the censorship, that lay behind the previous temple contracts for Salus, Iuventus, and Fortuna Primigenia let by Bubulcus, Salinator, and Tuditanus.'

subsequent magistracies to promote the building process, as emerges from the testimony given by Livy on Q. Fulvius Flaccus. As propraetor in Hispania he had vowed in 180, in the case of victory over the Celtiberians, the celebration of games and the construction of a temple to Fortuna Equestris, for which he had reserved part of the spoils. Once he was elected consul in 179, his first objective was to clear himself and the Roman state of the vows he had taken.[144] The state's direct involvement in the fulfilment of the vows made by the general can be deduced from Livy's text. The consul managed to get the senate to appoint duumvirs to contract the building work on the temple. The fact that Fulvius did not personally conduct the *locatio* is probably explained by his wish to leave as quickly as possible for the war against the Ligures.[145] Should this not have been the case, we can reasonably presume that he would have personally contracted the work as a consul. Nevertheless, this did not mean that Fulvius renounced control over the construction of the temple that he finally dedicated as censor in 173.[146]

Some politicians managed to complete the circle of obtaining glory and renown attached to the construction of a temple by also performing the dedication while they held a magistracy.[147] As dictator, Bubulcus dedicated the temple to Salus in 302. Bubulcus himself had vowed it as a consul in 311 and had contracted the work in 306 as a censor. L. Postumius Megellus, as consul in 294, dedicated the temple of Victoria that he had vowed some years before. Cornelius Cethegus carried out the consecration of the temple of Juno Sospita as censor in 194. He had vowed the temple himself as consul. The temples of Juno Regina and Diana were dedicated in 179 by Aemilius Lepidus as censor. The vow had taken place during his consulship in 187. Cato's case is a peculiar one. During his campaign in Hispania he vowed a shrine to Victoria Virgo. The fact that it was a small sanctuary facilitated its prompt construction, so the shrine was dedicated by Cato two years later, in 193, when he did not hold a magistracy. It appears therefore that Cato carried out the consecration as a private citizen unless the senate appointed him duumvir for the purpose, a fact that is not documented.[148] The other possible case of a private citizen being in charge of the

---

[144] Liv. 40.44.8–12: '... liberare et se et rem publicam religione votis solvendis dixit velle'.

[145] Cf. Pietilä-Castrén 1987: 113–14; Aberson 1994: 110–12.   [146] Liv. 42.10.5.

[147] Cf. Orlin 1997: 162: 'This tendency for the same man to vow and dedicate the temple offers further confirmation that from a religious viewpoint the temple vows were considered personal vows, *vota privata* in the sense that they were to be fulfilled by the same man who undertook them.'

[148] Cf. Orlin 1997: 170–1 and n. 25. This contradicts the generally accepted theory that the *dedicatio* of a temple by *privati* was banned. Cf. Wissowa 1901.

consecration of a temple is that of M. Claudius Marcellus' son, regarding the temple of Honos and Virtus in 205.

It can be seen in Table 1, which contains the details of the consuls' intervention in the construction of temples, that although they were frequently vowers of temples and possibly also generally in charge of letting their contracts, it was unusual for a consul to be in charge of the dedication. In fact, in the period of time studied here, there is only sure evidence of two cases, which incidentally occurred in two consecutive years.[149] One of them is the aforementioned temple of Victoria dedicated by L. Postumius Megellus in 294. Livy provides detailed information on the time of the consular year when the sanctuary was dedicated.[150] Illness forced Postumius to stay in Rome while his colleague went to Samnium. The adverse development of the war against the Samnites meant that Postumius had to take command of his army even before he had completely recovered, but before leaving Rome he dedicated the temple. The dedication took place, therefore, in the first months of the consular year.

The other instance is the temple of Quirinus dedicated by L. Papirius Cursor in 293. The temple had been vowed by his father, and this family link unquestionably accounts for the fact that the consul was in charge of the dedication. As in other cases, it can be presumed that the act of consecration was delayed specifically so that the vower or a relative, preferably a son, could be in charge, so that the prestige attached to the construction of a new temple in Rome would remain from beginning to end within the family. Livy's text in this case also allows us to determine quite precisely the moment when the consecration took place.[151] Papirius, along with his fellow consul, fought against the Samnites during most of the year of his office and won a resounding victory. While his colleague went to Etruria to continue the military operations, Papirius went to Rome to celebrate the triumph,

---

[149] A possible third case is questionable. The Anatolian goddess Cybele, known in Rome as Magna Mater or Mater Deum, was taken to the *Urbs* from her original sanctuary in Pessinus following the instructions of the *decemviri sacris faciundis*. The statue of the goddess was transported by ship to the port of Ostia in 204 and from there on to Rome. The senate decided that it should be welcomed by a virtuous young man, P. Cornelius Scipio Nasica (Liv. 29.14.9). According to the *periochae*, Scipio Nasica himself, while consul in 191, was the person in charge of carrying out the dedication of the temple that had been built for the goddess on the Palatine: 'P. Cornelius Scipio Nasica cos. aedem matris deum, quam ipse in Palatium intulerat, vir optimus a senatu iudicatus, dedicavit'(Liv. *per.* 36). This is probably a mistake, since this report from the *periochae* contradicts the text of Livy, who attributes the dedication of the temple to the *praetor urbanus et peregrinus* in 191, M. Iunius Brutus (Liv. 36.36.4). Briscoe (1981: 274–5) considers the choice of Brutus as the dedicator of the temple as a political compromise to avoid a possible confrontation between the two consuls of that year, Nasica and Glabrio, both of whom had expressed their wish to conduct the dedication. Brennan (2000: 124) sees practical motives in the selection of the urban praetor as dedicator.

[150] Liv. 10.33.9.   [151] Liv. 10.46.

apparently in winter, since Livy reports that all of Samnium was covered in snow when Papirius set off for Rome. After celebrating his triumph, while still a consul, says Livy, Papirius dedicated the temple to Quirinus and left Rome again to go into Samnite territory, where he spent the rest of the winter. Therefore, the dedication of the temple took place in the middle of winter, in the second half of the consular year.[152]

This poses another interesting question regarding the construction of temples in Rome. The personal responsibility for the new temple implicitly assumed by the vower was somehow also extended to his descendants, so it is not unusual that one of his sons assumed the consecration, thus emphasizing the continuity, usually when the promoter of the temple had already died. It was obviously a case of seeking glory, political renown, and family promotion. Promoting a new temple was a sign of prestige and a means of perpetuating one's name. As far as possible, the vower would certainly wish for that honour to remain within his family, and for the whole process of the construction of the temple, from the *votum* to the *dedicatio*, including the *locatio* if possible, to be under his responsibility or that of one of his sons. In fact, nearly three-quarters of the temples on the dedication of which there are available data were dedicated by the vower or by his son.[153] The consecrations of the temples of Pietas and Venus Erycina in 181, conducted by duumvirs appointed by the senate for this purpose, who were the sons of the respective vowers, as well as the aforementioned dedication of the temple of Quirinus in 293 by the consul Papirius Cursor, constitute further proof of this fact.

Notably, this had to involve co-operation between the senate and the promoter of a temple, or rather, between the senate and the family, since it was the senators who ultimately had to authorize and approve the entire process of constructing the temple.[154] A new temple was obviously the

---

[152] The festival of the *Quirinalia* was celebrated on 17 February (Ov. *Fast.* 2.475–7).

[153] Aberson 1994: 181: 'On constate qu'aux époques pour lesquelles notre documentation historique apparaît comme suffisemment fiable, la continuité au niveau personnel ou, à défaut, gentilice, était la plupart du temps assurée tout au long du processus d'acquittement des voeux dimicatoires de temples.' Cf. Orlin 1997: 188.

[154] Cf. Orlin 1997: 180–2. After the attempt of the curule aedile Cn. Flavius in 304 to dedicate a sanctuary to Concordia, the senate issued a decree, approved by the people as law, by which nobody could dedicate a sacred building or shrine without the authorization of the senate or a majority of the tribunes of the plebs (Liv. 9.46.7). Previously, the *pontifex maximus* Cornelius Barbatus had opposed Flavius' intention, arguing that only consuls or *imperatores*, according to the *mos maiorum*, could carry out the dedication of a temple (Liv. 9.46.6). In practice, it appears that only the senate supervised the process of the dedication of the temples by appointing or authorizing the dedicators, since we do not have any testimony of the tribunes of the plebs carrying it out at any stage (Mommsen 1887–8: iii 1050). On the law passed in 304 about the right of dedication see Ziolkowski 1992: 220–34; Orlin 1997: 163–6.

property of the *civitas*, but the community allowed its promoter and his family to have principal significance. Not only did the senate have to assume the vow, approve the contract, and expressly authorize the dedication, the latter since 304, but it is also clear that the pace of construction of a temple was adapted to the *cursus honorum* of the vower, when possible, so that he could personally be in charge of the subsequent stages in the building process instead of appointing duumvirs who might accelerate the construction. The case of Bubulcus is an exception because he consecutively held the magistracies of consul, censor, and dictator within a period of nine years, which was the time it took to build the temple. In other cases the period of construction was much longer, no doubt so that the vower might be able to conduct the dedication. In other cases, the death of the vower or other circumstances made it impossible for him to assume the *locatio* and/or the *dedicatio* and required either one of his sons or duumvirs appointed for this purpose to complete it.

It is clear, therefore, that those vowing temples had a personal interest in either themselves or one of their sons taking charge of the construction and dedication, and the senate tended to accept this. Nevertheless, this was not always the case. There are also temples that were dedicated by duumvirs who had no family relationship with the vower, although usually it is not possible to give an explanation for this procedure. It might be that there was no descendant who could complete this task or that the vowers had enemies within the senate who prevented him or his family from acquiring additional prestige.[155] In any case, it is complicated to draw conclusions based on general behaviour patterns because the dedicators of most of the temples built during the Roman Republic are unknown.

PUBLIC BUILDINGS AND MONUMENTS IN ROME

Besides the temples already mentioned, the consuls also contributed, although in a small way, to the monumentalization of the city of Rome, by promoting the construction of buildings and monuments, such as porticos, columns, statues etc.[156] From a chronological point of view, the first event of this kind known through ancient sources had as its protagonist

---

[155] See the relevant considerations adduced by Orlin (1997: 182–7), who highlights the fact that the consecration of four temples by persons who were not related to the vower is concentrated between 194 and 191, perhaps because the senate wanted to have greater control over the construction of temples or to limit the excessive influence of certain generals detrimental to the senate's own power.

[156] *CIL* 1² 635 = *ILS* 22: 'Ser. Folvius Q.f. Flaccus cos muru locavit de manubeis.' Servius Fulvius Flaccus was consul in 135. Nothing is known about the location of the wall mentioned in the inscription.

the consul C. Maenius in 338. Maenius attached several beaks (*rostra*) from enemy ships to the speakers' platform in the Forum after Rome's first major naval victory against Antium during the Latin War.[157] From that time on the speaker's platform was called the rostra. As far as we know, this was the first self-glorifying monument in Rome's history.[158]

In 293 Sp. Carvilius Maximus, after his victorious return from the military campaigns in which he defeated the Etruscans and the Samnites, undertook the contract of the temple of Fors Fortuna, which in all probability he had previously vowed. But he also, with the abundant metal obtained from the weapons seized from the defeated enemy, ordered the construction of a statue of Jupiter. It was a colossal statue, no doubt several metres high, since Pliny claims that it could be seen from the sanctuary dedicated to Jupiter Latiaris on the Mons Albanus.[159] With the rest of the metal, Carvilius also ordered a statue of himself to be built at the foot of the statue of Jupiter. The use of the present tense by Pliny suggests that both statues still existed in his time.

M. Fulvius Flaccus, consul in 264, is mentioned in two identical and fragmentary inscriptions from the bases of statues erected in the Forum Boarium after his capture of the Etruscan town of Volsinii. They read 'M. Folvius, son of Quintus, consul, dedicated (it) after Volsinii had been captured.'[160] According to Coarelli, the inscriptions show the reorganization by the consul of the whole sacred area of Sant'Omobono.[161] As Millar emphasizes, Fulvius is in fact the earliest consul in the history of Rome who is recorded as such in contemporary documentary evidence.[162]

The consul C. Duilius defeated the Carthaginians in a naval battle in the year 260. As a result of his victory, he was the first to celebrate a naval triumph in Rome.[163] To commemorate his success, a victory column adorned with the beaks of ships (*columna rostrata*) was erected in the forum.[164] An inscription containing a eulogy of Duilius[165] belonged to this column, on which a statue of Duilius himself was possibly placed.[166]

---

[157] Liv. 8.14.12; Plin. *Nat.* 34.20; Flor. 1.5.10.   [158] Welch 2006: 500.

[159] Plin. *Nat.* 34.43. Cf. Sehlmeyer 1999: 113–15.

[160] 'M. Folvio Q(uinti) f(ilius) cosol d(edet) Volsinio capto.' See Torelli 1968.

[161] Coarelli 1989: 213–16.   [162] Millar 1989: 144.

[163] Liv. *per.* 17; V. Max. 3.6.4; Plin. *Nat.* 34.20; Tac. *Ann.* 2.49; Flor. 1.18.9–10. Beck 2005: 218–21.

[164] Quint. 1.7.12. Cf. Plin. *Nat.* 34.20; Sil. Ital. 6.663–6. From the texts of Pliny and Quintilian it is clear that the column was in the forum, and the possibility that there was another column dedicated to Duilius, as could be deduced from the location provided by Servius (*ad Georg.* 3.29: 'ante circum a parte ianuarum') must be discarded. It must be a simple mistake by Servius. Cf. Chioffi 1993; Welch 2006: 500. However, Platner and Ashby (1929: 134) accepted the existence of two columns.

[165] *Inscr. It.* XIII, 3 69 = *CIL* VI 1300 = I² 25 = *ILS* 65 = *ILLRP* 319.

[166] This is the opinion of Sehlmeyer 1999: 117–19.

From the texts that mention this column it is clear that the monument was erected in honour of Duilius, undoubtedly by order of the senate, but they do not specify who was in charge of its construction. In a passage of Quintilian there is a reference to a 'columna ... posita', and in the eulogy of Duilius in the Forum of Augustus can be read 'statua ... posita'. If it had been a work promoted personally by Duilius it would rather be 'statuam ... posuit', but 'posita' does not mean that he ought to be ruled out as its promoter.[167] The hypothesis that Duilius himself was in charge of the *locatio* of the column once this honour had been granted by the senate is perfectly possible. He may have contracted for the work in the same year (260) as a consul, before finishing his term of office, or in 258, when he was censor. However, the fact that the construction of the column was closely related to his successes as a consul, as well as the fact that this honour was in all probability linked to the granting and celebration of a triumph, makes the construction of the monument more likely to have been started immediately after the triumph, still in 260. In that case, and in the absence of censors, it seems plausible that the senate gave to Duilius, while still a consul, the task of being in charge of the construction of the column in his honour and memory once he had returned to Rome.

Just five years later, in 255, another *columna rostrata* was built in honour of M. Aemilius Paullus, as a result of the naval triumph achieved during his consulship. This time the column was placed in the Capitol. Its existence is known indirectly through information provided by Livy for the year 172, when the monument was destroyed by lightning.[168] As in the case of the column of Duilius, in all probability it must have been an honour granted by the senate, but the problem lies in establishing who was in charge of its construction.[169] Similar considerations to those pertaining to the column of Duilius may apply. The senatorial authorization to build the monument must be linked to the granting and the celebration of the triumph, and it is probable that the contract for the column was issued immediately. In this context, and also taking into account the absence of censors, since the new ones did not take office until 253, it is possible that the consul Aemilius Paullus himself was in charge of its construction.

---

[167] Sehlmeyer 1999: 119.

[168] Liv. 42.20.1: 'in suspensa civitate ad expectationem novi belli, nocturna tempestate columna rostrata in Capitolio bello Punico <priore posita ob victoriam M. Aemili> consulis, cui collega Ser. Fulvius fuit, tota ad imum fulmine discussa est.'

[169] Sehlmeyer 1999: 120: 'Das passiv *posita* läßt den Auftraggeber zwar offen, doch suggeriert es die Zustimmung des Senates.' Palombi (1993) claims that M. Aemilius Paullus obtained the triumph 'ed evidentemente la facoltà di erigire la colonna rostrata'.

Two of the known porticos in the *Urbs* from the Republican period may have been promoted at different times by consuls, in direct connection with the celebration of military triumphs, as in the case of the columns. The older is known as the Porticus Octavia. Pliny and Festus report on its existence.[170] From both sources it can be concluded without a doubt that the portico was built by Cn. Octavius, and it can be indirectly deduced – in particular from Pliny's text – that its construction must have followed his naval triumph over King Perseus, the greatest success in his political and military career. Octavius celebrated his triumph on 1 December 167, upon his return from Macedonia. In 163/2 he was part of a senatorial legation sent to the eastern Mediterranean, and he died during this embassy. Consequently, the construction of the portico must presumably have started at some point between December 167 and the spring of 163, when the legation must have set off for the Orient.[171]

It is possible that the *locatio* was carried out immediately after the return of the propraetor to Rome, within the context of the celebration of the triumph. However, unlike the columns of Duilius and Aemilius Paullus, the Porticus of Octavius was not a monument granted by the senate as an honour to the *triumphator*, but a building for public use whose construction should probably be linked to the spoils supplied to the public funds. For this reason, in contrast with both columns, its construction may not necessarily be linked to the celebration of the triumph of its promoter, who may have promoted the building at a later time with the authorization of the senate. Cn. Octavius was consul in 165, and given this background, it is a significant fact – pointed out by Cicero – that Octavius was the first member of this plebeian family to achieve the consulship, something which Cicero relates to the construction of a house on the Palatine, which he himself did after his consulship in 63.[172] It is more probable that it was during his consulship that Octavius started the construction of the portico,[173] a building which, as eventually happened, was to serve as a monument to preserve his memory and allow him a role in posterity. On the other hand, as consul, Octavius could legally carry out the contract for the works, presumably during his stay in Rome at the beginning of his term of office. Certainly, the possibility that this portico was promoted by Octavius before his consulship as a means of becoming popular amongst

[170] Plin. *Nat.* 34.13; Fest. 188 L.
[171] Olinder 1974: 121; Richardson Jr 1976: 60–1; Pietilä-Castrén 1987: 120: the construction of the portico must have started soon after Octavius' return from Macedonia 'in 166 at the latest'; Viscogliosi 1999b.
[172] Cic. *Off.* 1.138.
[173] This was already pointed out, without any argumentation in this respect, by De Ruggiero 1925: 50.

voters must also be borne in mind. In any event, the information is insufficient to establish the claims of either option.

A similar problem is posed by the Porticus Metelli as regards the date of the beginning of its construction. The portico was built by Q. Caecilius Metellus Macedonicus. It was in fact one of a group of porticos which surrounded two temples, dedicated to Juno Regina and to Jupiter Stator.[174] As can be deduced from the text of Velleius Paterculus, Metellus promoted it after celebrating his triumph over Macedonia. However, its construction has traditionally been placed in 147 or 146,[175] which is impossible if we take into account that Metellus was fighting in Macedonia between 148 and possibly the last months of 146.[176] The portico must, rather, have been started some time after the return of Metellus to Rome. The question becomes complicated if we concede that the temple to Jupiter Stator was also vowed by Metellus during his campaign in Macedonia, which would probably have meant that the construction of the portico was linked to the temple.[177] If Metellus Macedonicus was indeed the promoter of the temple, and we presume that he himself may have contracted for the work, the *locatio* could have been completed during his consulship in 143, as maintained by Morgan, but it could have also been conducted immediately after his return to the *Urbs*.[178] In any event, whether or not Metellus was the vower and promoter of the temple of Jupiter Stator, it is possible that he carried out the contract of his portico as a consul in 143, although this, as in the previous case of Octavius, is only a hypothesis.[179]

The construction of the Porticus Minucia presumably also followed the celebration of a triumph, on this occasion the victory of M. Minucius Rufus over the Scordisci in 106.[180] Minucius was consul in 110 and later proconsul between 109 and 106. It was probably after this date when the work on the portico began.[181] Hence, in this case it does not seem to have been a consular work.

---

[174] Vell. 1.11.3. Cf. Viscogliosi 1999a. [175] Platner and Ashby 1929: 424.

[176] Olinder 1974: 94–5. Cf. Boyd 1953: 155: 'The date at which Metellus enclosed the temples of Juppiter Stator and Juno Regina in his Porticus is uncertain. It was almost certainly after his triumph in 146 BC, but presumably not long after, since one of the probable reasons for the building of the Porticus was to provide a site for the twenty-five equestrian statues of the *turma Alexandri*, which Metellus brought to Rome after the reduction of Macedonia'; Pietilä-Castrén 1987: 130–1.

[177] Morgan 1971: 504 n. 2. *Contra* Boyd 1953: 154. Cf. Richardson Jr 1976: 61.

[178] Morgan (1971: 499–504) argues in favour of 143 as the date of the *locatio* of both temples (in his opinion, the temple of Juno Regina could have also been vowed by Metellus). Implicitly, Orlin (1997: 193 n. 6) assumes that the construction of the temple of Jupiter Stator may have been started by Metellus before 143.

[179] The construction of the portico was placed in the consulship of Metellus by Cressedi 1954: 143.

[180] Vell. 2.8.3. [181] Coarelli 1999a.

In 121 the construction of the so-called Fornix Fabianus started. It was in fact a triumphal arch erected in the easternmost part of the forum on or near the Via Sacra by one of the consuls of that year, Q. Fabius Maximus Allobrogicus, to commemorate his victory over the Allobroges.[182] It was the first triumphal arch built in the forum, a great honour granted by the senate to the victor over the Gauls.

The colleague of Fabius during the consulship, L. Opimius, was also considered by the senate as a victor to a certain extent, although not over an external enemy but over the plebs led by C. Gracchus, against whom the *senatus consultum ultimum* had been ruthlessly implemented. Obviously, for this reason Opimius could not receive the honour of the triumph, but instead as a reward the senate granted him the task of building a temple dedicated to Concordia towering above the Forum.[183] Ancient sources record the existence of a Basilica Opimia located near the temple of Concordia, in all probability built by the same Opimius.[184] Although it is not explicitly stated, the basilica was very probably built at the same time as the temple, and its contract must have been let by Opimius himself at the end of his consulship.[185] In fact, there is no other possibility, since after his consulship, Opimius only held the office of legate; thus only in 121 could he contract for both the temple and the basilica.

WATERWORKS

Expansion throughout Italy meant at times that the Roman state had to undertake great waterworks with the purpose of increasing the amount of farmland. From the information provided by ancient sources it can be deduced that at least three of these works were, with certainty or probability, dealt with by consuls in the pre-Sullan period.

As a censor, M'. Curius Dentatus started the construction of the so-called Anio Vetus in 272.[186] But earlier, as a consul, he must have tackled the task of draining the plains of Reate with the purpose of gaining farmland in a vast and fertile zone. This conclusion may be reached from the two reports provided by Varro and Cicero. According to Varro, as cited by Servius, a consul whose name is not mentioned promoted the diversion of the water

---

[182] Cic. *Planc.* 17; *Ver.* 1.19; *de Orat.* 2.267; Sen. *Dial.* 2.1.3. The arch was restored later by his grandson in the year 56 (*CIL* I² 762 = VI 1303). Cf. Platner and Ashby 1929: 211–12; Chioffi 1995; Welch 2006: 506; Hölkeskamp 2006b: 486.

[183] Plut. *C.Gr.* 17.6; App. *B.Civ.* 1.26; August. *C.D.* 3.25.   [184] Cic. *Sest.* 140. Cf. Var. *L.* 5.156.

[185] Platner and Ashby 1929: 138–9; Ferroni 1993a. Cf. Hafner 1984.

[186] Fron. *Aq.* 1.6; *De vir. ill.* 33.8–9.

coming from lake Velinus in order to drain the area.[187] Cicero, on the other hand, attributes this work to a M'. Curius.[188] Throughout the history of the Republic there is only one Curius who reached the consulship.[189] It is M'. Curius Dentatus, who was consul on three occasions, in 290, 275, and 274. Therefore, this public work should in all probability be attributed to him.[190]

The work must have consisted of the construction of an artificial drainage canal in order to make agricultural exploitation possible on the plain of Rosea, located between Reate and Interamna Nahars, a famously fertile area in antiquity.[191] Dentatus probably completed it or at least started it during his first consulship, in 290, in direct connection with the distribution of lands that he carried out in the territory of the Sabines after his victory over them.[192] Hermon, as already pointed out by Montero, argues that the drainage works of the plains of Reate and the distribution of the resulting farmland could have been complemented simultaneously by the construction of a road, the Via Curia, that would facilitate communications between Reate and Rome.[193] All of this involved considerable planning on the part of the Roman state and, in particular, of the consul Curius Dentatus.

Livy's *periochae* provide succinct information regarding the waterworks carried out by the consul M. Cornelius Cethegus in 160.[194] According to the text, the senate gave the consul as his *provincia* the task of draining the marshlands of the *ager Pomptinus*, and turning them into farmland. The so-called *paludes Pomptinae* were a vast area situated to the southwest of the Alban hills, between these and the Tyrrhenian Sea. They were famous in antiquity for being dangerous lands to cross and for causing diseases such as malaria.[195] The Roman state built canals through the marshes, to facilitate crossing and also to acquire farmland.[196] The task entrusted to Cethegus was to renovate these canals or to build further canals to increase the habitable land. Unquestionably, his was only one of the actions carried out over time in this region to make it suitable for human habitation, although it is, nevertheless, the first attested action.

---

[187] Serv. *ad Aen.* 7.712.   [188] Cic. *Att.* 4.15.5.   [189] Broughton 1951–86: I 183.

[190] Forni 1953: esp. 224–7. Cf. Münzer 1901; Nissen 1902: I 313.

[191] Var. *R.* 1.7.10. On the characteristics of the drainage works undertaken by Dentatus, see White 1970: 160; 169. Cf. Hermon 2001: 185.

[192] *De vir. ill.* 33.5–6; Col. 1.praef.14; V. Max. 4.3.5; 1.3.10; Plin. *Nat.* 18.18; Fron. *Str.* 4.3.12; Flor. 1.10.2–3; Plut. *Apophth. M'.Curi* 1.

[193] Montero Herrero 1980; Hermon 2001: 186–7. However, Forni (1953: 228) attributes the construction of the road to the censorship of Curius Dentatus in 272.

[194] Liv. *per.* 46.   [195] Radke 1975d; Sonnabend 1996.

[196] On the canal or canals of the *paludes Pomptinae*, Vitr. 1.4.12; Lucan 3.85; Hor. *S.* 1.5.11–23. Cf. White 1970: 169–70.

Due to the loss of Livy's books, we do not know of any further activity by Cethegus during his consulship. No ancient source mentions that the waterworks in the *ager Pomptinus* were followed by distributions of land, but it should not be ruled out that the two actions were linked, as seems to have happened in the case of Reate and Curius Dentatus.[197]

It is likely that a work of a similar nature to those undertaken by Curius Dentatus and Cornelius Cethegus may be attributed to another consul. Strabo reports that M. Aemilius Scaurus, the same one, he says, who built the Via Aemilia which crossed Pisa and Luna, drained the swamps that had traditionally existed in Cisalpine Gaul, and built waterways from the river Po to Parma.[198] Scaurus was consul in 115 and censor in 109. His censorship has traditionally been linked to the construction of that road, but it is more probable that he promoted it as a consul. It is also likely that this engineering work, which undoubtedly demanded the expropriation of private lands for the construction of the waterways, was promoted in 115 by the consul Aemilius Scaurus. In this respect, we should bear in mind that during his consulship Scaurus fought and defeated various Gallic and Ligurian peoples in Cisalpine Gaul and obtained a triumph *de Galleis Karneis*.[199] Given this background, and making use of his knowledge of the land, he may have resolved to undertake these works which, like those carried out by Curius Dentatus and Cethegus, must have entailed the extension of farmland in the region.

Finally, amongst the known consular waterworks, we should include the so-called *fossae Marianae*.[200] The canal was built by C. Marius, perhaps during his fourth consulship in 102.[201] According to the explanation given by Plutarch, Marius tried to solve the problem of navigation in the delta of the Rhone, where the great amount of silt deposited by the river made the navigation of ships supplying the Roman army difficult. For this purpose he took his soldiers to this area, since they were idle at that time, and had them build a great canal which served to divert part of the Rhone towards another section of the coast, thus creating a wide bay where, sheltered from the wind and the waves, ships could land without problems. Marius later gave control of the canal to the Massaliotes, who profited greatly from it thanks to the fees paid by the ships that used it.[202]

[197] Cf. Hermon 2001: 185.   [198] Str. 5.1.11.   [199] *De vir. ill.* 7.
[200] Plut. *Mar.* 15.2–3; Str. 4.1.8; Mela 2.5; Plin. *Nat.* 3.34.
[201] Ooteghem (1964: 190–5), however, thinks that the construction of the canal took place in 103.
[202] Weynand 1935: 1385; White 1970: 170.

In summary, in the pre-Sullan period the consuls were, to a certain extent, active promoters of the monumentalization of Rome. Throughout the third and second centuries, the consuls were the promoters of many of the temples, dedicated to a great variety of deities, that were built in the city. The process usually started with a vow pledged by a consul while leading the legions as commander-in-chief of the Roman army. The consular promise was subsequently endorsed by the senate, and the works for the temple could then begin. Although the temples thus promoted were of course always public, the process of construction and consecration was linked as closely as possible to the person who had made the vow and to his family, which essentially turned each of the temples into a monument to the prestige and glory of its promoter and his descendants. In fact, this private link remained for decades and even centuries: some temples, and likewise various other public buildings, were periodically renovated or restored by members of the same family, in what could be considered an act of remembrance by the whole of Roman society for the role played by that family in the history of Rome.

The consuls were also the promoters of monuments which were to play prominent roles for centuries on the urban landscape of the capital of the Empire. Such is the case for columns, porticoes, arches, statues etc., which several consuls had built with the senate's consent, generally after the celebration of a triumph following an important military victory achieved by them in the process of expanding the Roman Empire. Although clearly of a different nature from the temples built after a consular vow, these buildings were also lasting monuments erected to the glory of those who had contributed to Rome's grandeur. As such, they were essentially monuments which reasserted in an exemplary way the history of Rome itself and that of the Republican system of government, of which Roman aristocrats acted as the undisputed leaders and protectors.

Outside Rome, some consuls set in motion, always with the authorization of the senate or following the senate's orders, sizeable public works which were to contribute considerably to the socio-economic development of Italy. Consuls were the promoters of some of the works which involved the draining of what had until then been insalubrious marshlands, making them fertile regions for farming. Moreover, most of the roads built in Italy, in particular during the second century, were promoted by consuls who lent them their name, once again as a means of securing for themselves a place in history. The overland communications network in Italy, and also part of the fluvial network created in certain areas as a result of the aforementioned drainages, was consequently, to a great extent, the product of consular activity in the pre-Sullan period.

CHAPTER 8

Colonization and distribution of land

In the pre-Sullan period the consuls, always under orders from the senate and depending on the circumstances, played a more or less leading role in the control of public land (*ager publicus*) and its possible distribution amongst colonists, either individually or for the foundation of Roman or Latin colonies. Since they were the supreme magistrates, supervision of the use of the land owned by the Roman state also justified consular intervention in the creation of fora on the roads the consuls promoted in Italy.

CONTROL OF THE *AGER PUBLICUS* AND DISTRIBUTION OF LAND

On several occasions and in different contexts, ancient sources mention that the consuls were responsible for controlling the use and limits of the *ager publicus* or of carrying out the distribution of public land. In the first case, we have information from Livy regarding the problems of misappropriation of public land in Campania in the first quarter of the second century. In 173, the two consuls were allotted Liguria as their province. However, the senate decided that one of them, L. Postumius, should travel to Campania to establish the precise boundary between the public and private land.[1] Livy adds that it was common knowledge that some persons had unlawfully appropriated public land by the simple process of moving the borders of their plots and invading the *ager publicus*. Postumius' mission was to recover for the Roman state the land thus lost. It was clearly a considerable problem which affected the Roman economy enough to justify the dedication of a consul to trying to solve it. In fact, Postumius did not even set foot in his province, Liguria, and stayed in Campania for the entire year, attending to the question of the *ager publicus* until he eventually returned to Rome to hold the elections.[2]

---

[1] Liv. 42.1.5. Cf. Pina Polo 1987: 165–6; Gargola 1995: 124–5. [2] Liv. 42.9.7–8.

Postumius was relatively successful in his task, since Livy informs us that a great part of the misappropriated land was recovered by the Roman state.[3] But the problem was structural rather than incidental, and for this reason it was not completely resolved.[4] The failure of Postumius' action was to a great extent due to the fact that he did not try to compile a new register of property, the only real way to rearrange the land and to legally fix the limits between public and private land.[5] Some years later, in 165, the senate sent the urban praetor P. Cornelius Lentulus to Campania, according to Granius Licinianus, to purchase from landowners the public lands which were being used illicitly.[6] According to this version, it was an attempt at buying with public money some land which in fact already belonged to the state. The reasoning behind it was to try to compensate the users of the land for the investments and improvements made on it. Cicero's version is significantly different, since he specifies that the land that was to be purchased was private and not public. At any rate, it is interesting from an institutional point of view that, while a consul was commissioned in 173, it was the urban praetor who was entrusted with the task in 165. It is further testimony indicating that the urban praetor usually acted as the natural substitute for the consuls in many of their civil functions, mainly within the city of Rome but also for other tasks that had to be performed within Italy.

As regards distribution of public land, the oldest testimony for this kind of action goes back to the year 290. The consul M'. Curius Dentatus managed to defeat first the Samnites and later on the Sabines. At the end of his term of office he celebrated the corresponding triumphs over both peoples. According to Velleius Paterculus, the Sabines received that year the rights of citizenship without the franchise (*civitas sine suffragio*).[7] At the same time, part of their territory became public land and was distributed individually amongst Roman citizens.[8] Sources do not provide details as to the form in which the land was distributed, but they speak in general of a senatorial decision to set a limit of seven *iugera* – fourteen according to *De viris illustribus* – as the standard size of the plots to be given to the citizens.[9]

---

[3] Liv. 42.19.1.
[4] Despite the fact that the tribune M. Lucretius passed a bill in 172 whereby the censors were to rent out this land (Liv. 42.19.2).
[5] Levi 1922: 243.
[6] Cic. *Leg. agr.* 2.82; Gran. Licin. 9 Flemisch. Broughton 1951–86: 1 438; Gargola 1995: 125–6; Brennan 2000: 108.
[7] Vell. 1.14.6. [8] *De vir. ill.* 33.5–6.
[9] V. Max. 4.3.5; 1.3.10; Plin. *Nat.* 18.18; Fron. *Str.* 4.3.12; Flor. 1.10.2–3; Plut. *Apophth. M'. Curi* 1. Col. 1. praef.14: apart from the distribution of Curius Dentatus, a second distribution of land is mentioned which could also have taken place in the first quarter of the third century, promoted by C. Fabricius,

It seems clear that the colonization of the Sabine territory was promoted by Curius Dentatus, and the sources unanimously ascribe the project to him.[10] However, it is not so evident that the process of distribution of the land was also managed in practice by the consul, although it is a plausible possibility.[11] Nevertheless, the sources do not mention the existence of a commission elected by the people. The distribution of land must have been linked to the drainage works in the region near lake Velinus, on the plain of Reate, which Dentatus promoted as a consul.[12] In the environs of the lake there are indications of divisions of land that took place in a very ancient period, which perhaps ought to be connected with his consulship in 290. In particular, Hinrichs identified some signs of land distribution on the plain of Reate which could correspond to that period.[13] It is therefore probable that Dentatus distributed land on the plain between Reate and Interamna Nahars.[14] Both projects, the waterworks and the apportioning of individual plots of land, could have been planned after the conquest by the consul Dentatus, who could thus have given Roman citizens the land after having added agricultural value to it, whereas the bulk of the Sabine territory must have remained in the hands of its former inhabitants.

In the year 200, the distribution of land known as *trientabula* took place. When public funds were exhausted in 210 due to the strain of the war that Rome was fighting against Carthage, some wealthy Roman citizens lent money to the state in order to continue the war.[15] Six years later, M. Valerius Laevinus, who was one of the consuls when the loan was given, raised in the senate the question of its refund. Prompted by the consuls, the senators agreed to reimburse the loan to those citizens gradually, in three biennial

---

consul in 282 and 278: '... itemque C. Fabricius et Curius Dentatus, alter Pyrrho finibus Italiae pulso, domitis alter Sabinis, accepta, quae viritim dividebantur, captivi agri septem iugera non minus industrie coluerit, quam fortiter armis quaesierat.'

[10] Münzer 1901: 1841; Forni 1953: 235; Gargola 1995: 105.

[11] Frank (1911: esp. 367–73) does not give any credence to ancient sources regarding the distribution of Sabine land and argues that in that period a consul would not have had the power to carry out such a distribution of the *ager publicus*. Càssola 1962: 92 n. 8: 'è chiaro che il Dentato non agí in quanto console, sibbene in quanto portavoce dei contadini, che imposero la propria volontà al senato ricorrendo anche alla violenza'. See also Beck 2005: 193–4.

[12] Serv. *ad Aen.* 7.712; Cic. *Att.* 4.15.5. Cf. Brunt 1969: 123–4; Hermon 1997; 1998.

[13] Hinrichs 1974: 41–2. Cf. Gargola 1995: 108 n. 29.

[14] Hermon 1997: 39: 'Les opérations agraires en 290 semblent bien avoir eu lieu encore sous l'emprise de l'*imperium militum* de M'. Curius Dentatus'; Hermon 2001: 185 and 189. Hermon (1998: 61) argues that the beneficiaries of the allocation of land carried out by Dentatus would have been his own soldiers. This is certainly suggested by the text in Frontinus (*Strat.* 4.3.12). However, it rather seems to be a retrojection of what happened in the first century onto an era in which the determining social factors were quite different.

[15] Liv. 26.36.8.

payments.[16] The consuls of 204 were designated to make the first payment; those of 202 and 200 were to pay the next instalments on behalf of the Roman state.[17]

However, when the time to make the last payment came in the year 200, the Roman state did not have funds available to meet the debt, since once the war against Carthage was over it had to face a war against Macedonia. This situation gave rise to complaints from those who had lent their money.[18] The senate then decided to give the creditors land instead of money.[19] In proportion to the money they were owed, they were to receive public land within a fifty-mile radius of the city of Rome, fertile and well-populated land with good access to markets. The consuls of that year, P. Sulpicius Galba and C. Aurelius Cotta, were given the task of making a correct assessment of the land that was to be given, apportioning it to the creditors, and fixing an annual rent for it of one *as* per *iugerum*. It was merely a symbolic sum whose main purpose was to preserve its condition as public land. The distributed lands were called *trientabula* because they corresponded to the payment of one third of the debt.[20] That same year, in 200, both decemvirs and triumvirs were elected. The former were to complete the delivery of the land to the veterans of the wars in Hispania and Africa, whereas the latter were in charge of taking the new colonists to Venusia.[21] However, the question of the *trientabula* was apparently left exclusively in the hands of the consuls of that year.

FOUNDATION OF COLONIES

Livy's description of the process of repopulating the colonies of Cremona and Placentia in the consular year 190/89 illustrates the procedure usually followed for the approval of new colonies, as well as how the colonists who were to become their inhabitants were enlisted. In the allocation of provinces, Greece was given to L. Cornelius Scipio, whereas his colleague, C. Laelius, was allotted Italy.[22] After narrating extensively the events that had taken place in the Eastern Mediterranean, Livy relates the arrival in Rome of envoys from the colonies of Placentia and Cremona.[23] This may have happened in the final part of the consular year since Livy mentions that the elections over which Laelius was to preside were held soon afterwards.

---

[16] Liv. 29.16.1–3.   [17] Liv. 29.16.3.   [18] Liv. 31.13.2–4.   [19] Liv. 31.13.5–9.

[20] Lintott 1992: 38: 236–7. It is possible that not all the creditors accepted the exchange of money for land, since in 196 there was still a final payment of the debt of the Hannibalic War (Liv. 33.42.2). Cf. Vishnia 1996: 164.

[21] Liv. 31.49.5–6.   [22] Liv. 37.1.10.   [23] Liv. 37.46.10–11.

Placentia and Cremona had been founded as Latin colonies in 218.[24] Their ambassadors were introduced in the senate by the urban praetor, L. Aurunculeius. They complained before the senators about the considerable decrease in the number of colonists, partly due to the war and to disease and partly because many had fled in fear of the danger posed by the Gauls.

In answer to their complaints the senate ordered that the consul Laelius, if he approved ('si ei videretur'), should enrol six thousand families ('sex milia familiarum conscriberet') to be distributed between both colonies. The appointment of Laelius was due to the fact that the consul was in Cisalpine Gaul and that he must therefore have had a good knowledge of the region and its troubles. The urban praetor, in his turn, was to see to the election of the triumvirs who were to be in charge of the actual settlement of the new colonists.[25] As is shown by the fact that the envoys of the Latin colonies were taken to the senate by the urban praetor, both consuls were away from Rome at the time, Scipio in Greece and Laelius in Cisalpine Gaul. Laelius returned soon afterwards to preside over the elections.[26] It was at this point that the consul executed the senatorial decree and enlisted the new colonists. Furthermore, he suggested the foundation of two new colonies on the land that had belonged to the Boii. The proposal was accepted by the senators.[27] In fact, however, of the two agreed colonies, only Bononia was founded in 189.[28]

From Livy's narration we can deduce that roles were shared in the process of colonization. The approval for the creation of a new colony or, as in this case, for the granting of a supplement to pre-existing colonies, was logically the responsibility of the senate, and the senators issued a *senatus consultum* to this end. Likewise, the senators decided on the number of colonists, the location of the colony, and the characteristics that ought to be met by the new settlements (size of the plots to be allotted etc.). In this particular case, the urban praetor was in charge of the election (*creatio*) of the *triumviri coloniis deducendis* who were to distribute the land amongst the new colonists. Triumvirs were frequently appointed for the foundation of colonies, mainly in the last quarter of the third century and the first third of the second, a period for which Livy's text provides information on the extensive colonization promoted by the Roman state. Although it was not a regular magistracy, it must have been a prestigious position, of great responsibility,

---

[24] Salmon 1969: 66–9; Bandelli 1988: 6–11; Gargola 1995: 57. On the colonization in Italy during the second century, see Pina Polo 1988; 2006a.
[25] On the commissions *agris dandis adsignandis*, see Mommsen 1887–8: II 625–39.
[26] Liv. 37.47.1.   [27] Liv. 37.47.2.   [28] Salmon 1969: 101.

as is shown by the fact that many of the appointees were ex-consuls or ex-praetors.[29]

The task of selecting the colonists in 189 was left to the consul. When describing the process, Livy uses the verbs *conscribere* and *scribere*, both of which were terms frequently used regarding the enrolment of troops.[30] These terms unquestionably refer to the crucial act of writing down the names of the colonists, which symbolized their designation for the new colony.[31] It can plausibly be presumed that the process followed for the conscription of colonists consisted of the candidates going to Rome – probably to some spacious public place[32] – and reporting to the officials who worked for the consul in order to show their disposition to join one of the colonies; and finally the magistrate produced a list of the chosen colonists. Nevertheless, Livy provides no information on the procedure or on the origin of the new colonists.[33] The fact that only one of two Latin colonies proposed by Laelius could be founded indicates that at the time there was insufficient demand to provide colonists for Placentia and Cremona as well as for new settlements. The task of the consul and of the triumvirs must, nevertheless, have been a difficult one, since Laelius was appointed proconsul for 189 and his *imperium* in Cisalpine Gaul was prorogued.[34]

Are the events of 190/89 a reflection of the usual process of the foundation of colonies? Unfortunately, very seldom does Livy provide specific details on the process of colonization other than a mere mention of the name of the new colonies and, on occasion, the number of expected colonists. In 313, Latin colonies were founded in Suessa and Pontiae. In addition, the senate issued a decree ordering the foundation of the Latin colony of Interamna Sucasina.[35] It set the number of colonists at four thousand, but left the consuls of the consular year 312/11, M. Valerius Maximus and P. Decius Mus, the task of choosing (*creavere*) the triumvirs who had to conduct the distribution of land and of sending (*misere*) the colonists to the new town.[36] As in the previous case, the consuls – or, more probably, only one of them[37] – must have been in charge of enlisting the

---

[29] Gargola 1995: 60–3; Vishnia 1996: 144–7.

[30] *conscribere*: Caes. *Gall.* 1.10; 1.24, Sal. *Cat.* 59.5 etc. *scribere*: Liv. 8.8 and 21.40, Sal. *Jug.* 43.3 etc. See the use of *scribere* for the colonizing process in Liv. 8.16.14; 39.23.4.

[31] Cf. Gargola 1995: 64–7.

[32] Moatti (1993: 14–15) suggests as likely locations the Campus Martius or the Villa Publica.

[33] Salmon 1969: 101: 'It may be suspected that many, and perhaps even a majority, of the recruits which the Romans did manage to enlist for their colonies in these years were non-Romans.'

[34] Liv. 37.50.13.   [35] Salmon 1969: 58–9.   [36] Liv. 9.28.8.

[37] Decius had to stay in Rome due to a serious illness, and a dictator had to be appointed to be in charge of the war in Etruria, while Valerius defeated the Samnites (Liv. 9.29.3).

colonists to be sent to the new foundations, and this is what Livy might be referring to when using the verb *mittere*.

However, while in 189 the election of the triumvirs was the responsibility of the urban praetor, in this case the consuls, according to the text in Livy, were also to be in charge. The explanation is probably as follows. In 189, neither of the two consuls was in Rome. In particular, Laelius, who was to direct the colonization process, was away. Consequently, as in many other tasks pertaining to the consuls, Laelius was naturally replaced by the urban praetor.[38] The decision to found Interamna Sucasina was unquestionably taken at the end of the consular year 313/12. For that reason, the senate preferred the new consuls, who were taking office shortly thereafter, to be in charge rather than to leave the task in the hands of those who were about to vacate office. The new consuls may have dealt with the enrolment of colonists and the election of triumvirs in the first few weeks of their term of office, before leaving Rome. Thus, the praetor's intervention was unnecessary.

This may indicate indirectly that when at least one of the consuls was in Rome, it was generally – but not always, as we shall see – his responsibility to deal with the process of the foundation of colonies, although in the text of Livy the urban praetor more frequently has this function, because both consuls were usually commanding the army. The events of 199 confirm this theory. In that year, the senate ordered the consul L. Cornelius Lentulus to see to the appointment of the triumvirs who were to recruit supplementary colonists for Narnia.[39] The senatorial decree was the answer to the complaints made by the envoys from Narnia, who lamented the decrease in the number of inhabitants. In his account of the year 199, Livy refers successively to the allocation of provinces, the expiation of prodigies, the celebration of the *feriae Latinae*, which had to be repeated, and finally the various embassies arriving in Rome from Carthage, Gades, Narnia, and Cosa.[40] Immediately after mentioning the foreign embassies, Livy states that the consuls, once all their duties had been resolved in Rome, departed for their provinces.[41] According to Livy, the decision to recruit colonists for Narnia was taken, consequently, at the beginning of the consular year. Both consuls were present in the city and, in fact, it should have been they who introduced the ambassadors of Narnia to the Curia. As a logical consequence, one of them, before leaving, was in charge of the election of the colonization commission. Livy does not say anything about whether

---

[38] Brennan 2000: 120: 'When no superior magistrate was present, the *praetor urbanus* had full competence to hold elections for minor magistrates and members of special commissions.'
[39] Liv. 32.2.7.   [40] Liv. 32.1–2.   [41] Liv. 32.3.1.

the new colonists had to be recruited by the consul, the praetor, or the triumvirs.

In 334, the new consuls Sp. Postumius Albinus and T. Veturius Calvinus proposed the foundation of a colony in Cales. The senate accepted the proposal and decided to create the colony with 2,500 colonists. Triumvirs were appointed to this end.[42] Although Livy's account on this occasion is much briefer, it is obvious that the events took place at the beginning of the consular year, before the consuls had left for their provinces. It is reasonable to think that the consuls – or one of them – were in charge of the election of the commission.

As regards the colony of Cales, there is an epigraphic testimony that must be taken into account. The colony received a supplement in the first quarter of the second century, about which Livy does not provide any information. However, it is mentioned in the eulogy of P. Claudius Pulcher: '[P. Claudius Ap. f. P. n. Pulcher | colono]s adscripsit Cales co(n)s(ul) cum | [L. Porcio III vi]r coloniam deduxit Graviscam.'[43] We know through Livy that P. Claudius Pulcher was indeed one of the triumvirs who founded the colony of Gravisca in 181, as indicated in the inscription.[44] According to the eulogy, Claudius Pulcher was also in charge of assigning an undetermined number of new colonists to the colony of Cales. In that case it is not mentioned that he did it as a member of a colonization commission or while holding another office, mention of which would seem reasonable, as in the case of the foundation of Gravisca.[45] The inscription may be plausibly interpreted in the sense that P. Claudius Pulcher had to recruit and send the supplement to Cales when he was a consul in 184, the year when his colleague in the consulship was L. Porcius Licinus, that is, the inscription should be read as follows: 'P. Claudius Pulcher assigned colonists to Cales while a consul along with L. Porcius and founded the colony of Gravisca as a triumvir.'

To return to the question of the appointment of colonization commissions, it is not clear that there was a fixed rule according to which a consul must always be in charge of their election if one of them was in Rome. The decision was clearly in the hands of the senate and was taken according to the political circumstances at the time, which are not always known. In 186, the consul Postumius Albinus informed the senate that the colonies of Sipontum and Buxentum were deserted. He did so at the end of the

---

[42] Liv. 8.16.14. Cf. Vell. 1.14.3. Rotondi 1912: 228.   [43] *CIL* I² XXXII = *ILS* 45.

[44] Liv. 40.29.2. Broughton 1951–86: I 386.

[45] Broughton 1951–86: I 373, places this action in 185 and speculates that P. Claudius Pulcher might have acted as a member of a special unspecified commission for which there is no further notice in ancient sources.

consular year during which Postumius had had to investigate and punish Bacchic cult practices in various regions of Italy. It was on this tour of Italy that he accidentally discovered the depopulation of the two colonies. A senatorial decree was immediately issued for the urban praetor T. Maenius to see to the appointment of triumvirs.[46] Maenius was put in charge of this task by the senate despite the fact that the consul Postumius was in Rome at the time, having returned to preside over the elections.[47] The simple fact that the consul was busy with the elections as well as with the final decisions resulting from the inquiry into the Bacchanalia[48] may have led the senators to relieve him of the colonial task and appoint the urban praetor to deal with it instead.

The process is also applicable to *viritim* colonization. In 201, the urban praetor M. Iunius Pennus was ordered by the senate to elect the decemvirs who were to distribute land in Samnium and in Apulia individually amongst the veterans of the Hannibalic War.[49] This occurred at the end of the consular year, when the consul P. Aelius Paetus had already returned to Rome from his province to preside over the elections.[50] As in Postumius' case, the reason why the senate preferred to appoint the praetor and not the consul, who was present in the city, to be in charge of the appointment of a colonization commission may have been their desire not to overload the agenda of Aelius Paetus. The consul not only had to supervise the electoral process, but he was simultaneously busy attending to the requests of the senate in response to the moves made in the Eastern Mediterranean by Philip and the resulting complaints from Rome's allies.[51] This was presumably a priority for the senate, which is understandable since it was eventually to lead to the declaration of war against the Macedonian king.

But in all the other known instances, it was the urban praetor who was in charge of the election of the colonization commission. In 295, a plebiscite ordered the urban praetor P. Sempronius Sophus to deal with the election of the triumvirs for the foundation of Minturnae and Sinuessa.[52] Both consuls were fighting away from Rome. In 194, the election of the triumvirs for the foundation of two colonies was presided over by the urban praetor Cn. Domitius Ahenobarbus, also in the absence of both consuls.[53] Finally, in 173 the urban praetor also appointed the decemvirs who were to carry out the individual distribution of land in Liguria and Gaul.[54]

---

[46] Liv. 39.23.4.   [47] Liv. 39.23.1. Cf. Brennan 2000: 120 n. 182.   [48] Liv. 39.19.   [49] Liv. 31.4.1–3.
[50] Liv. 31.3.1–2; 31.4.4.   [51] Liv. 31.2.1; 31.3.1–2.   [52] Liv. 10.21.4; 10.21.7–10.
[53] Liv. 34.53.2. Cf. Brennan 2000: 119: 'The consul P. Cornelius Scipio Africanus was probably not yet in the city, which explains why the *praetor urbanus* was taking responsibility for the task.'
[54] Liv. 42.4.4.

How were the triumvirs or decemvirs elected for the foundation of colonies or for the *viritim* distribution of land? The most common opinion is that they were always elected by the people in the assembly of tribes.[55] It can be deduced from Livy that it was a magistrate with *imperium*, a consul or an urban praetor, who was personally responsible for their election, always prompted by a *senatus consultum*.[56] The consul or the praetor could convene and preside over the comitia where the triumvirs or decemvirs were elected. This can be clearly construed from the events of the year 194. The tribune of the plebs Q. Aelius Tubero, following orders from the senate, took before the people a bill to found two Latin colonies in the south of Italy.[57] Once the law had been passed, two commissions were appointed for three years to complete the foundation. Both groups of triumvirs were elected in comitia held on the Capitol under the presidency of the urban praetor Cn. Domitius Ahenobarbus.[58]

The exercise of the consulship – or of any other magistracy – was not incompatible with belonging to a colonization commission. In two instances we know of a consul taking part in a commission for the foundation of colonies during his consulship. In 197, upon the proposal of the tribune of the plebs C. Atinius,[59] the creation of five colonies of Roman citizens was passed. To implement the foundation, triumvirs were appointed for three years.[60] Amongst them were Ti. Sempronius Longus and Q. Minucius Thermus, who were elected praetors for 196, respectively receiving Sardinia and Hispania Citerior as provinces. Thermus remained in Hispania for a good part of 195 and Longus' *imperium* in Sardinia was prorogued for the same year. He was also elected consul for 194.[61]

---

[55] Cic. *Leg.agr.* 2.17 claims that the *comitia tributa* had always been in charge of electing the commissions. Mommsen 1887–8: II 629: the common process was to submit the election to the *comitia tributa*, but the competent comitia were determined in each particular case; De Ruggiero 1892: 837: the election of those who were to found the colony and distribute the land was made in the *comitia centuriata* and possibly also in the *tributa*; Hinrichs 1974: 22: from the third century onwards the elections were always held in *comitia tributa*; Gargola 1995: 58: the election was carried out in *comitia tributa*; Hermon 2001: 218: probably in *comitia tributa*.

[56] Liv. 9.28.8: 'triumviros creavere ac misere colonorum quattuor milia insequentes consules'; 32.2.7: 'tresviros creare L. Cornelius consul iussus'; 10.21.8: 'praetor triumviros in ea loca colonis deducendis creare' (in this case, after the approval by a plebiscite passed by the tribunes of the plebs); 31.4.1: 'decreverunt patres ut M. Iunius praetor urbanus, si ei videretur, decemviros … crearet'; 37.46.10: 'decrevit senatus … ut L. Aurunculeius praetor triumviros crearet ad eos colonos deducendos'; 39.23.4: 'triumviri ad colonos eo scribendos ex senatus consulto ab T. Maenio praetore urbano creati sunt'; 42.4.3: 'decemviros in eam <rem> ex senatus consulto creavit A. Atilius praetor urbanus.'

[57] Liv. 34.53.1.   [58] Liv. 34.53.2.

[59] Cf. Broughton 1951–86: I 336: Atinius was a tribune of the plebs in 196.   [60] Liv. 32.29.3–4.

[61] See the reconstruction of the facts in Gargola 1995: 67–8.

The five colonies (Puteoli, Volturnum, Liternum, Salernum and Buxentum), with 300 colonists each, were actually founded in 194. In that context, Livy repeats the names of the triumvirs and emphasizes the fact that Sempronius Longus was also one of the consuls for that year,[62] which means that the commission was operative in 196, 195, and 194. In practice it seems that only one of the triumvirs, M. Servilius Geminus, could actually deal with the enlisting of colonists during his three-year term of office. As regards Sempronius Longus, his collaboration in the project could only have happened, at any rate, during his consulship. The order of events narrated by Livy for the year 194 is as follows: diplomatic matters, allocation of provinces, election of censors, celebration of *ver sacrum* and games, foundation of colonies, expiation of prodigies, departure of consuls for their provinces, and the war events for the year.[63] It is evident that Livy structured the events of the year to facilitate their understanding, although this does not necessarily imply that that order corresponds to a precise chronological series of events. Nevertheless, it is possible that Sempronius Longus carried out his functions as a triumvir at the same time as he was acting as a consul at the beginning of his term of office, during his stay in Rome before leaving for his province in the north of Italy. The simultaneous presence of the three members of the commission for a few months in the *Urbs* probably made it possible to produce an official and final list of colonists and the specific terms for the foundation. But the fact that all the colonies were founded in the south and that Sempronius Longus was leading the war against the Ligures and Boii in the north of Italy seems to rule out his participation as a triumvir in leading the expedition of colonists to the new colonies.

Something similar may have happened in 183, when the colony of Saturnia was founded. One member of the commission which founded it was Q. Fabius Labeo, who was consul that year.[64] Labeo already had some experience in these tasks, since the previous year he had been part of a different commission for the foundation of Potentia and Pisaurum.[65] As in Sempronius Longus' case, it seems apparent that he had to combine both positions. Liguria was allotted to Labeo as his province, but Livy claims that he did nothing remarkable,[66] perhaps because a substantial part of his time was dedicated to his colonizing task.

---

[62] Liv. 34.45.1–2. Different triumvirs dealt with the foundation of other colonies that same year (Liv. 34.45.3–5).
[63] Liv. 34.43–6.   [64] Liv. 39.55.9. Cf. Broughton 1951–86: I 380.
[65] Liv. 39.44.10. Cf. Broughton 1951–86: I 377.   [66] Liv. 39.56.3.

The manner previously described in which, according to Livy, the recruitment of colonists for repopulating Placentia and Cremona took place, as well as the senatorial resolutions regarding the foundation of Interamna Sucasina, are the plainest testimonies in ancient sources for the part played by consuls in the colonization process. In both cases, there is no doubt about their leading role. A different question is whether the consuls on each and every occasion were totally or partially in charge of managing the colonization. De Ruggiero categorically asserted that the enlistment of colonists could only be carried out by the consuls, and the same opinion was held by Mommsen.[67] Hinrichs, however, considered that the case of Placentia and Cremona was an exception and that it was mentioned by Livy for this very reason. In his opinion, the commission was usually in charge of the recruitment of colonists.[68] More recently, Hermon has also vehemently rejected the intervention of the consuls in the process of colonial foundations.[69] However, Hermon disregards Livy's text concerning the supplement for Placentia and Cremona, where the participation of the consul Laelius is unquestionable. As regards the text on Interamna, Hermon considers that Livy differentiates between the *senatus consultum* and its enactment, but she denies that the senate gave the consuls the task of convening the assembly of tribes to elect the triumvirs and presumably any other function regarding the colonization.[70] Nevertheless, Hermon argues that all the tasks regarding the colonization process were the responsibility of the commission: the selection of colonists or beneficiaries of individual distributions, the definition of the territory, and the internal organization of the colony.[71] Gargola also believes that the commission was in charge of recruiting the colonists.[72]

The data from ancient sources only allow us to conclude that the consuls were at least on some occasions entrusted by the senate with the management or the commencement of a specific process of colonization, recruiting colonists – certainly at least in 190/89, the supplement of Placentia and Cremona, probably in 312/11 for Interamna Sucasina, possibly in the case of the supplement of Cales in 184 – and dealing with the election of the colonization commission – at least in 312/11, in 199, and probably in 334. Perhaps this latter task was more frequently carried out by the urban

---

[67] Mommsen 1887–8: II 344; De Ruggiero 1892: 837.   [68] Hinrichs 1974: 15.

[69] Hermon 2001: 218: 'Aucune prérogative n'est reconnue aux consuls pour définir une procédure de fondations coloniales.'

[70] Hermon 2001: 215 n. 52. Cf. Hermon 1989: 172–3.   [71] Hermon 2001: 215.

[72] Gargola 1995: 64: 'The first major official responsibility of the commissioners probably was the enlistment of the colonists.'

praetor, given the usual absence of the consuls from Rome. The presence or absence of the consuls was the determining factor in whether a consul or the urban praetor was to be given this task by the senate. The specific mission of distributing land amongst the new colonists once they had been recruited was, without a doubt, the task of the commissioners.[73] But known data do not allow us to conclude with certainty whether the magistrates with *imperium*, the consuls or the urban praetor, had necessarily to be responsible for the selection of colonists, or whether this task could also be performed by the commissioners, something which probably depended on each particular case.[74]

A final episode must be cited in this context, which is the alleged colonization sponsored by C. Marius at the end of the second century. The unsuccessful agrarian legislation of L. Appuleius Saturninus was an attempt at establishing an exceptional procedure within the context of the mutually convenient political alliance among the tribune of the plebs, the praetor C. Servilius Glaucia, and the consul C. Marius. In the year 100, Saturninus passed a bill according to which colonies should be founded in Sicily, Achaea, and Macedonia.[75] The colonies were destined for the veterans of Marius' army, and he, as a consul, apparently had personally to be in charge of their foundation. Furthermore, the bill entitled Marius to grant Roman citizenship to three non-Romans in each colony. The issuance of the *senatus consultum ultimum* and the subsequent murder of Saturninus thwarted the enactment of the law, although it is possible that some veterans actually received land in Africa.[76]

THE CONSTITUTION OF FORA IN ITALY

Due to the scant attention paid by ancient sources, the creation of fora in Italy in the Republican period is a debated question, regarding both the dates of their constitution and the identities of their possible founders. As

---

[73] Apparently, the *triumviri* enjoyed *imperium* in the exercise of their functions (Liv. 34.53.1). Cf. Hinrichs 1974: 14–17. However, Mommsen (1887–8: II 631) denied that triumvirs had *imperium*.

[74] Liv. 39.23.4 ('triumviri ad colonos eo scribendos ... creati sunt') suggests that the enrolment of colonists could be done by the triumvirs. Moatti (1993: 16) leans towards the option that regular magistrates had to be in charge of enlisting colonists, but she doubts that there were fixed rules on this matter, since there are also known instances where the triumvirs were in charge of recruiting them. On the practicalities of the foundation of a colony, see Moatti 1993: 23–30; Gargola 1995: 64–70.

[75] Cic. *Balb.* 48; *De vir. ill.* 73.5; Plut. *Mar.* 29. By 103 Saturninus had already proposed a law to grant one hundred *iugera* of land in Africa to the veterans of Marius (*De vir. ill.* 73.1). Cf. De Ruggiero 1892: 837.

[76] Gargola 1995: 176: 'some settlers, at least, were to be installed in colonies'. Salmon 1969: 129: 'Marius himself seems to have been responsible for practically no formal colonization.'

can be inferred from a text in Festus, the fora were created to serve as sites where trials and *contiones* could be held, that is, assemblies of the people without legislative power, while they could also function as marketplaces.[77] There is no information in ancient sources either on the manner in which any of the known fora was created or on whether the settlements were founded *ab initio* or were pre-existing. Known archaeological data about some fora indicate that they were settlements that already existed in the pre-Roman period and which continued under Roman dominion.[78] Obviously, available data are not sufficient to establish a general rule, but it can be gathered clearly that a forum did not necessarily have to be a population centre founded in a place which had not been inhabited before.[79]

However, this does not mean that there was no procedure for the creation of fora as new communities. In fact, the phrase used by Festus is *fora constituere*, and the same terminology is used in the *lex Mamilia Roscia Paeducea Alliena Fabia*.[80] The text of the law differentiates between the *deductio* of a *colonia* and the *constitutio* of a *municipium*, a *praefectura*, a *forum*, or a *conciliabulum*.[81] The *deductio* of a colony involved the foundation of a new town and a supply of population for it, even if the colony overlapped with a pre-existing settlement. On the other hand, the creation of a *municipium* meant a change in the legal status of an already existing community without involving a supply of new population. In practice, an urban centre received the status of a *municipium* by decision of the Roman state. In the *lex Mamilia*, the *constitutio* of a forum is linked to that of a *municipium*, which clearly means that the process was similar from a legal point of view. That is, the creation of a forum did not actually mean the foundation or *deductio* of a new settlement, but a 'founding' act from the legal point of view, since the Roman state may have granted that status to a pre-existing population centre.[82] Beyond this, it is hard to establish which may have been the specific measures and consequences that resulted from

---

[77] Fest. p. 74 L.: 'alio, in quo iudicia fieri, cum populo agi, contiones haberi solent ...' Cf. Schubert 1996: 97.

[78] See on this matter the data provided by Ruoff-Väänänen 1978: 16–19.

[79] From these data, Ruoff-Väänänen (1978: 19) concludes: 'Considering these facts it does not seem justified to speak about the Romans as founders of the fora.'

[80] *FIRA* I p. 139, KL. V: 'qui hac lege coloniam deduxerit, municipium praefecturam forum conciliabulum constituerit, in eo agro, qui ager intra fines eius coloniae municipii fori conciliabuli praefecturae erit, limites decumanique ut fiant terminique statuantur curato ...' Cf. Crawford 1989; Schubert 1996: 98.

[81] Crawford 1989: 184: 'Our text, in fact, appears to be part of a statute intended to establish colonies and to constitute *municipia*, *praefecturae*, *fora* and *conciliabula*; to distribute land and to establish *limites* and *decumani*.'

[82] Schubert 1996: 98: 'Die Konstituierung der *fora* war ganz offensichtlich ein Gründungsakt.'

the constitution of a forum: a legal gathering of a rural population around the new forum? A change of the legal status of its inhabitants?[83]

If there was an official act of *constitutio* of a forum, it is obvious that the senate had the final word on its approval. But its actual application on-site must have been the responsibility of a magistrate.[84] As we have seen previously, the consuls at times undertook tasks regarding the distribution of land and the setting of limits in the use of public land.[85] Many of the fora known in Italy that were founded in the Republican period have a *gentilicium* which identifies them: Forum Cornelii, Forum Lepidi, Forum Popilii, etc. Does this *gentilicium* correspond to the name of the person who had been in charge at the time of the *constitutio* of the forum, as Festus points out?[86]

In this sense, it has been accepted unanimously for decades that the constitution of fora may have been directly linked to the construction of roads undertaken by Rome throughout Italy.[87] A Forum Popilii would imply the existence of a Via Popilia, and, vice versa, at some point on a given road there must have been a forum constituted by the builder of the road. This hypothesis was complicated by the thesis proposed by Radke, for whom the fora may have been created systematically at the central point of a road. Radke's thesis has many weak points and has been criticized extensively and convincingly by various scholars.[88]

Ruoff-Väänänen, in her monograph on the Italian fora, not only rejected Radke's thesis but also the theory that links the constitution of fora to the construction of roads, because in her opinion there is no ancient evidence to support it. One of the bases for the theory is the well-known *elogium* from

---

[83] Toynbee 1965: II 662: 'A forum named after a member of a Roman noble gens is likely (unlike a forum named after some non-Roman nation) to have been a settlement of Roman citizens who retained their citizenship.'

[84] *Contra* Ruoff-Väänänen 1978: 23.

[85] Ruoff-Väänänen (1978: 20–1) does not take into consideration data which attest to the intervention of consuls in the process of colonization, which leads her to conclude, in my opinion wrongly, the following: 'The fact that the consuls cannot have apportioned land or marked frontiers on the strength of their magistracies is attested to by ancient authors. In the cases when the consuls or a proconsul participated in such measures they were assisted by five, or ten, senatorial commissioners respectively. In the light of these facts it does not seem possible that the consuls could on the strength of their magistracies have constituted fora either.'

[86] Fest. p. 74 L.: 'primo negotiationis locus, ut forum Flaminium, forum Iulium, ab eorum nominibus, qui ea fora constituenda curarunt; quod etiam locis privatis et in viis et agris fieri solet.'

[87] That is, in fact, the starting point of Radke's thesis on the central location of the fora on Roman roads (see bibliography in the section regarding the construction of roads). Before him, other authors argued the connection between roads and fora, for example Rudolph 1935: 164. Cf. Toynbee 1965: II 660; 663; 667; 671; Hinrichs 1967: 254.

[88] Wiseman 1970a; Ruoff-Väänänen 1978: 70–3.

Polla in Lucania.[89] Ruoff-Väänänen rejects the usual interpretation of
the final sentence of the eulogy ('forum aedisque poplicas heic fecei'), in
the sense that the builder of the road between Rhegium and Capua had
also founded a forum, understood as a settlement, in Polla or nearby. In her
opinion, the most logical interpretation of the sentence is that the person to
whom the eulogy is addressed had a forum built, meaning a public square,
as well as public buildings.[90]

As regards the link between the *gentilicia* of a great number of fora and
the roads upon which they were located, Ruoff-Väänänen considers it
possible, although in her opinion there is no evidence for it.[91] She thinks
that the *gentilicia* were additional Roman names that were given to the local
names of the fora, which would actually have been different. However, the
author does see a correlation between the Roman names of certain fora and
the names of Roman commanders who were active in the area.[92] But she
does not consider this hypothesis plausible either, since we only know a
small proportion of the Roman magistrates, and in many cases we do not
even know precisely where their provinces were, so attribution to a consul,
praetor, or any other magistrate would always be uncertain, because other
magistrates of the same *nomen* for whom we have no available information
may have been active in the region of each forum. She believes it is more
likely that those magistrates had gained a local *clientela* in the areas where
they had promoted the construction of a road or performed their administrative duties, and that it was those clients who later on had asked their
patron for the constitution of a forum, or perhaps the senate had ordered a
member of that family to create a forum in the area where his ancestor had
formed his *clientela*.[93] In practice, Ruoff-Väänänen's criticism of the theory
of the close link between the construction of a road and the creation upon it
of one or more fora does not offer an alternative that can account for the
constitution of the fora or their *gentilicia*.

It is probable that not all fora had the same origin, and it certainly seems
that Radke was incorrect in claiming that each and every one of them
had been created as a midpoint of a new section of a road built in Italy.
However, it is reasonable to link at least a number of fora to the construction
of the road on which they are located. And it is likewise reasonable to link

---

[89] *CIL* I² 638 = *ILLRP* 454.   [90] Ruoff-Väänänen 1978: 11–12.   [91] Ruoff-Väänänen 1978: 34–5.
[92] Ruoff-Väänänen 1978: 35–6: 'When we study the geographical distribution of the Italian fora we may
notice that there is a certain correlation between the Roman names that appear in the nomenclature
of the fora and the names of the Roman officials who had been active in the respective areas.'
[93] Ruoff-Väänänen 1978: 36 n. 226: '. . . road building was a way to gain new clients. This might explain
the homonymy of certain roads and fora.'

their name to the name of the person who was in charge of the constitution of the forum, who may have been the constructor of the road or a magistrate who had been active in the region, militarily or otherwise. This is an easier solution than that proposed by Ruoff-Väänänen, who suggested that descendants of that magistrate or his local clients may subsequently have given the magistrate's name to the forum, which is mere speculation. However, there are relatively abundant instances of Roman generals giving their name to indigenous settlements, as may have been the case for the fora.

At least some of the fora may therefore have been constituted by Roman magistrates, following orders or with authorization from the senate. It is possible that their constitution may have been directly linked to the construction of the roads where the fora were located or in connection with the activities of magistrates in the region, which were mainly of a military nature. The *gentilicia* of the fora and the names of the corresponding roads could therefore help to identify those who were in charge of the creation of the fora. However, the task is far from simple, since, as we have seen elsewhere in this monograph, for a good number of the roads in Italy doubts remain about the names of their builders and the dates of their construction. In any case, it seems clear that the consuls and, to a lesser extent, the praetors and perhaps the censors were ultimately responsible for the construction of roads, particularly in the second century. Following this reasoning, it is plausible that the consuls were also in charge of the constitution of at least some of the known fora. The problem is in identifying them.

Radke has suggested the following identifications, some of them already supported by other authors:[94] P. Cornelius Cethegus, consul in 181, may have given his name to Forum Cornelii, now Imola;[95] M. Fulvius Nobilior, consul in 159, could be the creator of Forum Fulvii in Liguria (Villa di Foro, near Alessandria);[96] M. Aemilius Lepidus, consul in 187, could have been in charge of the constitution of Forum Lepidi, also known as Regium Lepidum (Reggio), located on the Via Aemilia which was built by the same consul;[97] Forum Livii (Forlì), perhaps named after C. Livius Salinator, consul in 188, was also located on the Via Aemilia;[98] P. Popillius Laenas, consul in 132, could be the creator of two fora, one named Forum

---

[94] Radke 1967: 229–30; 1975b. See the criticism of Ruoff-Väänänen 1978: 16.
[95] Toynbee 1965: II 667.
[96] Toynbee (1965: II 672–3) attributes the creation of Forum Fulvii, as well as the construction of the Via Fulvia, to the consul of 125, Q. Fulvius Flaccus.
[97] Radke (1964b: 301–4) takes as a starting point that the Via Aemilia was promoted by Aemilius Lepidus but was built in different phases by various magistrates. An indication of this would be the existence of fora named after those magistrates.
[98] Toynbee 1965: II 663.

Popilii, now Polla, in Lucania,[99] the other, now Forlimpopoli, on the Via Aemilia;[100] Ti. Sempronius Gracchus, consul in 177 – former governor in Hispania Citerior and founder of Gracchurris (Alfaro, La Rioja), an indigenous town named after him – could have been in charge of the constitution of Forum Sempronii (Fossombrone). Other authors have suggested the foundation in Cisalpine Gaul of Forum Licinii by C. Licinius Crassus, consul in 168,[101] and of Forum Clodii (Fórnovo di Taro) by M. Claudius Marcellus, consul for the second time in 155.[102]

As can be noted, these are all consuls of the first two-thirds of the second century. At any rate, while these identifications are widely accepted, they are in fact only hypotheses, since neither do ancient sources confirm them nor is there a definite chronology for the constitution of the fora. Certainly, as Ruoff-Väänänen pointed out, in some of these cases other magistrates of the same *nomen* as those proposed, holding different offices (consul, proconsul, etc.), were also active in these areas, and it cannot be ruled out that they may have promoted fora which were named after them.[103]

The use and distribution of public land in Rome was the responsibility of the senate. Both the founding of new colonies and the settlement of individual peasants on public land were ultimately the decision of the senators. Obviously, consuls played a role in the control of public land as supreme magistrates and the executive arm of the senate. One example of this, although in extraordinary circumstances due to the importance given to Campania, was the task entrusted by the senate to the consul Postumius in 173 to retrieve the public land which had been seized by private owners in the previous few years.

More commonly, the consuls were in charge of organizing the individual apportionment of land in recently conquered territories or, in an exceptional case, of the allocation of public land to private creditors as repayment of the debt incurred by the Roman state after the Second Punic War. Ancient sources also show that the consuls took an active part in the policy

---

[99] As I have previously mentioned, Ruoff-Väänänen (1978: 11–12 and 69) interprets the word *forum* in the *elogium* from Polla as public square, which in her opinion invalidates the alleged identification of Polla as Forum Popilii. Mommsen identified P. Popillius Laenas as the builder of the road mentioned in the so-called *elogium* from Polla, whose first line is missing. All the later editors of the inscription have followed Mommsen's thesis, except for Verbrugghe 1973, who believes it was Ap. Claudius Pulcher, consul in 143. Cf. Gordon 1983: 87–9.

[100] *CIL* I² 637 = *ILLRP* 453. Cf. Toynbee 1965: II 670–1.   [101] Ewins 1952: 65; Toynbee 1965: II 669.

[102] Ewins 1952: 64; Toynbee 1965: II 669.

[103] For example, Q. Fulvius Flaccus fought as consul in Liguria in 179; M. Fulvius Nobilior was in Liguria as consul in 159 and as proconsul in 158; M. Fulvius Flaccus was proconsul in Liguria in 123 (Broughton 1951–86: I 391–2; 445–6; 514–15). Cf. Ruoff-Väänänen 1978: 36 n. 223.

of colonization that led to the foundation of a large number of Roman and Latin colonies throughout Italy in the pre-Sullan age. At times, a consul put forward a motion in the senate for the foundation of new colonies or, as in the year 186, the consul Postumius Albinus urged the senators to send supplementary settlers to the uninhabited lands of Buxentum and Sipontum. In general, the consuls were, by order of the senate, in charge of some of the steps in the process of creating a new colony, amongst them the voluntary recruitment of new settlers or the election of the commission of three or ten men who were to deal with the practicalities of the founding of the colonies and the distribution of land. Nevertheless, these tasks were not exclusive to the consuls. The urban praetor was occasionally in charge in their place. Whether they were entrusted to one of the consuls depended on their presence in Rome at the time when the colonization process was set in motion, but it also depended on the consuls' availability in relation to the rest of their civil functions and, above all, their military duties. One particular case is that of the fora which were created along many of the roads built in Italy in the Republican period, which bore the name of their creator, probably very often a consul who had also been the promoter of the road.

CHAPTER 9

Appointment of a dictator

Until the end of the third century it was common to appoint a dictator as an extraordinary magistrate, either as commander-in-chief of the Roman army in the case of an emergency or to perform a specific task for a certain period of time, such as presiding over elections.[1] The designation of a dictator was always decided by the senate, although his official appointment had to be made by a consul, who was entrusted with the task by the senators, except in exceptional circumstances.[2] The appointment had to follow a series of traditional rules: it had to be made at night, in silence, and in a place located within the limits of Roman soil (*ager Romanus*).[3]

Livy makes it clear in a few cases during the Second Punic War that the appointment of a dictator was the exclusive right of the consuls. In 217, after the defeat at Trasimene, where consul C. Flaminius died, the senate decided to appoint a dictator. The practical problem was that the living consul, Cn. Servilius Geminus, the only person who could make the appointment, was away from Rome, and the military situation made it very difficult to contact him in order to demand his return. Due to this, Livy says, for the first time in the history of Rome the people elected a dictator by voting in comitia.[4]

Seven years later, the delicate military situation forced the senate to take the decision to make the consul M. Valerius Laevinus, who was to preside over the elections, go to his province immediately without waiting for the elections to be held. In his place, a dictator for holding elections (*comitiorum*

---

[1] It is obviously not appropriate here to give an in-depth analysis of the characteristics of the Roman dictatorship. On this subject, see Bandel 1910; Hartfield 1982; Hurlet 1993; as well as Kunkel and Wittmann 1995: 665–719 and the pages on the dictatorship in Lintott 1999b: 109–13.

[2] Kunkel and Wittmann 1995: 196; Lintott 1999b: 110.

[3] Hinard 2008: 49: 'On n'a pas, en effet, suffisamment insisté sur le fait qu'un dictateur ne pouvait être 'dit' que par un consul et que cette règle était bien plus qu'un simple rituel: la dictature, magistrature d'exception et qui soumettait les autres magistratures pendant la durée de son exercice, n'était véritablement légitime que si elle s'insérait dans le dispositif institutionnel en place, ce dont témoigne la *dictio* consulaire, de nuit, dans un silence absolu ...'

[4] Liv. 22.8.5–6. Cf. Polyb. 3.87–88. Cf. Beck 2000: 85: the election took place in May.

habendorum causa) had to be appointed.[5] The consul agreed to this solution and proposed designating M. Valerius Messalla, who was in Sicily acting as fleet commander (*praefectus classis*), as a dictator. His proposal was to make the appointment effective upon his arrival in Sicily. However, the senate refused to accept this procedure, claiming that nobody who was outside the *ager Romanus* could be appointed as dictator. Instead, the senate decreed that the consul was to put the question to a vote in order for the people to decide whom they wished to have designated as dictator. The consul was to limit himself to appointing the person elected. In anticipation of the apprehension that such a measure could cause the consul, the senate added that, should Valerius Laevinus refuse, the urban praetor was to call for elections and, should he also refuse, the tribunes of the plebs were to carry out this duty.

Indeed the consul did refuse to put before the people something which he considered to be within his exclusive sphere of action ('quod suae potestatis esset') and forbade the urban praetor to act in his place. The motion was brought by the tribunes to the comitia, where Q. Fulvius Flaccus was elected. But the consul also refused to appoint him officially as dictator and left Rome to return to Sicily. The senate then wrote urgently to the other consul, M. Claudius Marcellus, to ask him to take charge of appointing the dictator elected by the people, which is what eventually happened.[6] From Livy's text it is not clear whether the consul Marcellus had to return to Rome or whether the appointment was made in the field.[7]

What happened in 217 demonstrates the general constitutional flexibility of Republican Rome and also represents an absolutely exceptional case. The appointment of a dictator had to be made by a consul – this is unquestionable – but circumstances forced a change in this process, and the dictator was simply elected directly by the people. In 210, the people once again elected the dictator due to the refusal of the consul Laevinus to comply with the orders of the senate. However, the intervention of the consul continued to be considered essential in the appointment of the dictator, to the extent that the other consul was taken away from the battlefield despite the military emergency at the time, even though the sole task of the appointed dictator was to hold the elections. Both episodes make it plain that the appointment of a dictator was an exclusive prerogative of one of the consuls

[5] Liv. 27.5.14–19. [6] Liv. 27.5.19. Cf. Beck 2005: 320.
[7] Brennan (2000: 114 n. 127) rejects the examples provided by Livy of dictators in the fourth century being appointed *in castris* (Liv. 7.21.9; Liv. 9.38.13–14), and he considers that either Marcellus in 210 or else T. Quinctius Crispinus in 208 were the first to appoint a dictator 'in the field'.

unless a situation of absolute emergency arose, such as that of 217. Unlike other consular tasks, it seems that it was not possible for the designation of a dictator to be handled by the urban praetor.[8]

Livy provides various testimonies to the process of the appointment of a dictator by a consul. In 216, the senate decided to appoint a dictator to carry out the revision of the list of senators. The person chosen for this task was M. Fabius Buteo. In order to appoint him officially, the consul C. Terentius Varro was summoned to Rome. He thus had to leave the command of his troops in Apulia, rush to the *Urbs*, and appoint the new dictator the night after his arrival, following the orders from the senate.[9] The consul returned to Apulia the following night, again in haste, without letting the senate know of his plans, so that he would not be forced to stay in Rome as the electoral president.[10]

Between 208 and 205 dictators were also appointed for various reasons. In 208, one of the consuls died in a military operation, and the other, T. Quinctius Crispinus, was mortally wounded. Crispinus died at the end of the consular year, but not without having appointed within the *ager Romanus* a dictator in charge of presiding over the elections and the *ludi magni*.[11] The following year, the consul Claudius Nero appointed his colleague Livius Salinator as dictator entrusted with the task of presiding over the elections.[12] And in the consular year 205/4, the consul P. Licinius Crassus, who had to preside over the elections, sent a dispatch to the senators informing them that disease was decimating his troops and that, given the circumstances, he did not consider it appropriate for him to go to Rome. He requested the authorization of the senate to appoint a dictator as

---

[8] Sulla and Caesar were appointed dictators in the first century. In neither of the two cases was it possible for a consul to appoint them. Sulla was designated dictator in 82 by an interrex, L. Valerius Flaccus, since the two consuls had died. Caesar, in his turn, was appointed by the praetor M. Aemilius Lepidus. The two consuls of 49, avowed anticaesareans, were away from Rome, since they had gone to Greece with Pompey within the context of the recently started civil war. In all probability, if at least one of the consuls had been available in 82 and 49, he would have been in charge of the actual appointment of Sulla and Caesar as dictators, as long as he was willing. Their respective death and absence made it impossible to keep the tradition and fostered innovation, in accordance with the typical flexibility of the Roman constitutional order, whereby traditional customs were observed whenever possible, but when the context did not allow for such observance, there was no problem in changing the traditions. Nevertheless, the question was debated, as is shown by the letter sent by Cicero to Atticus on 25 March 49 (Cic. *Att.* 9.15.2). The topic had already been dealt with in Cic. *Att.* 9.9.3, a letter of 17 March. From these two Ciceronian letters we can deduce that there was a need for the respective decrees of the senate and of the augurs (which involved Cicero, as an augur) to entitle a praetor to appoint a dictator, something which in principle was illegal. But Cicero believes that it would be done, just as Sulla had already been appointed dictator by an interrex, which in theory was also illegal. Hurlet 1993: 48–9: 'Le décret des augures semble donc être le moyen de permettre à un magistrat autre que le consul de nommer le dictateur.' See also Hinard 1988: 89 n. 15; 2008: 45–9; Vervaet 2004.

[9] Liv. 23.22.10–11.   [10] Liv. 23.23.9.   [11] Liv. 27.33.6.   [12] Liv. 28.10.1–5.

the electoral president. The senators gave him their consent, and the consul appointed Q. Caecilius Metellus as dictator.[13]

Besides the aforementioned cases, all of which occurred at the end of the third century during the Hannibalic War, Livy specifically mentions two more appointments of dictators made by consuls in the final years of the fourth century. In 312, the consul P. Decius Mus was detained in Rome because of illness. Since he could not take command of his troops, Decius designated C. Iunius Bubulcus, following orders from the senate.[14] Two years later, setbacks suffered by the Roman army made the senate decide that the solution was, once more, to appoint a dictator. It was apparent that L. Papirius Cursor, the great *imperator* at the time, was to be the one chosen. He had to be appointed by the consul Q. Fabius Maximus Rullianus, with whom he had a well-known feud. For this reason, the senate sent a delegation to deal directly with the consul, who, 'at night and in silence, as is the custom' ('nocte deinde silentio, ut mos est'), appointed Papirius, complying with the senate's order quite reluctantly.[15]

---

[13] Liv. 29.10.1–3; 29.11.9. [14] Liv. 9.29.3. [15] Liv. 9.38.13

CHAPTER 10

Consuls presiding over elections

One of the tasks performed by consuls during their term in office was to preside over the annual elections.[1] This was not a function exclusive to consuls, as it could also be carried out by a dictator or an *interrex*.[2] In fact, in the fourth century, the sources do not explicitly allude to any consul ever acting as president over electoral comitia – which obviously does not mean that they did not perform such a task – yet we know of the intervention of *interreges*, as well as of the appointment of dictators, solely to conduct the election process in various years throughout that century.[3] Between 367 and 298, the presidency over elections belonged to a dictator or an *interrex* on sixteen occasions, or at least this was the intention, since at times the appointment of a dictator was challenged for a variety of reasons. For the remaining years one of the consuls must have presided over the elections.

In the consular year 297/6 Q. Fabius Maximus Rullianus was the first attested consul to act as president over elections.[4] From then on, the presidency of dictators and *interreges* became exceptional,[5] and it was more commonly the consuls who were in charge.[6] We know the name of the presiding consul for some of the years at the beginning of the third century and for almost every

---

[1] Lintott 1999b: 105.   [2] Mommsen 1887–8: I 215; II 80–1.

[3] *Interreges*: year 355 (Broughton 1951–86: I 124); 352 (I 126); 351 (I 127); 340 (I 136); 332 (I 142); 326 (I 146); 320 (I 153); 298 (I 174). Dictators: 351 (Broughton 1951–86: I 127); 350 (I 128); 349 (I 129); 335 (I 140); 327 (I 145); 321 (I 151); 320? (I 153); 306 (I 166). On the generally sparse information for this period see p. 14.

[4] Liv. 10.15.7.

[5] Electoral presidency of an *interrex* is known for 291 (Broughton 1951–86: I 183) 222 (I 233), and 216 (I 250), and of a dictator for 280 (Broughton 1951–86: I 191), 231 (I 226), 224 (I 231), 216 (I 248), 213 (I 263), 208 (I 290–291), 207 (I 295), 205 (I 301), 203 (I 311), and 202 (I 316).

[6] What happened in 207/6 is extraordinary. When the time for the elections came, it was decided to appoint a dictator. One of the consuls, C. Claudius Nero, appointed the other consul, M. Livius Salinator, as dictator to preside over the elections, and immediately afterwards he resigned in order to resume his office as a consul. As such, he carried out a mission at the end of his term following the orders of the senate (Liv. 28.10.1–5). The fact that an active consul was appointed dictator was rare, although there was a precedent in 339 (Liv. 8.12. Cf. Mommsen 1887–8: I 514 n. 1; Broughton 1951–86: I 137). Nevertheless it is surprising that he was appointed *dictator comitiorum habendorum causa*, in spite of the fact that both consuls were in Rome at that time and nothing seemed to prevent Livius

year between the beginning of the Second Punic War – during which, due to the military situation, dictators were mainly in charge of the electoral process – and 167. The lack of Livy's books leaves us without further information regarding the rest of the pre-Sullan period, although it is to be presumed that the same practice applied to those years for which details are not available.

In the pre-Sullan age there was no fixed date for the elections, which were held at the end of the consular year. Since it was common for both consuls to spend most of their year of office away from Rome, one of them had to return to the *Urbs* for the sole purpose of presiding over the elections. The question of whether there was any rule for appointing one of the consuls to this task was studied by Taylor and Broughton, linking it directly to the order in which the consuls appear in the official lists of the Republican period.[7] Both authors assumed that the order in which the consuls are mentioned, both in the Capitoline Fasti and by Livy and subsequent sources deriving from his work, is the same in most cases, which cannot be merely coincidental.[8] In the post-Sullan period, there is evidence on various occasions that the consul who appeared in the first place was the *consul prior factus*, that is, the one who had reached the necessary electoral majority first and had therefore been the earlier of the two to be elected. According to Taylor and Broughton, this would be the criterion used to establish the order of the consuls in the *fasti*, and not their age, as had been suggested before their article was published.[9] The consul first elected would also have the honour of holding the fasces in the first month of the year, and he would then alternate their tenure with his colleague.[10] Taking into account the fact that in the post-Sullan period both consuls generally stayed in Rome during their entire term of office, or for most of it, this would mean that the first consul held the fasces, and therefore the government of Rome, in the odd months. Since in the first century elections were usually held in July, the seventh month, the first consul mentioned in the official list ought

---

Salinator himself from presiding over the elections as a consul without the need to be appointed dictator. Livy does not provide any explanation for this extraordinary fact. Broughton (1951–86: 1 298 n. 1) suggests that perhaps Nero, who appears in the *fasti* in the first place, wanted to give priority to his colleague by appointing him as dictator. However, this idea is based on the theory that the consul first elected was the one who had to preside over the elections, something that, as will be seen, cannot be deduced from an analysis of the sources.

7 Taylor and Broughton: 1949; 1968. Cf. Linderski 1965; Drummond 1978.

8 Taylor and Broughton 1949: 3: the order is identical in over seventy per cent of the years.

9 Taylor and Broughton 1949: 9: 'the consul elected first had priority in holding the fasces, and the privilege of having his name appear first in the official lists'.

10 See the critical remarks on this subject by Drummond 1978: 82: 'It is important to keep firmly distinct priority of election, priority in the consular list and priority of tenure of the *fasces*. There is no necessary connection between any or all of these, nor is there any ancient text which clearly demonstrates such a relationship.'

to be the president of the elections.[11] Less conclusively, Taylor and Broughton assumed that in the pre-Sullan period one consul had priority over the other, and that the fasces were held alternately between both consuls when they were in Rome at the same time.[12]

The two authors published an article on the same question two decades later which basically maintained the same viewpoint although it qualified their conclusions. In their opinion, in the pre-Sullan age, when both consuls were usually away from Rome, presidency over the electoral comitia was not the responsibility of the consul first elected, but was decided by drawing lots (*sortitio*) or through an agreement between the consuls (*comparatio*). Generally, the consul who was closer to Rome or less engaged from a military point of view was chosen to preside over the elections.[13] In contrast to their previous article, Taylor and Broughton suggested that the presidency over the elections in the post-Sullan period could also be resolved by an agreement between the consuls or, more frequently, by means of drawing lots between them and that it did not depend on the order of their election.[14]

Some years later, Rilinger published an important work in which he dealt in great detail with the question of the presidency over the elections in Republican Rome and its presumed influence over the elections.[15] In contrast to the thesis defended by prosopographers since Münzer, Rilinger reached the main conclusion that the president of the elections – whether a consul, an *interrex* or a dictator – certainly had the means to influence the election of one or other candidate during the process, but he did not habitually do so except on certain special occasions and under unusual circumstances. With regard to our question, Rilinger fully accepted the 'old thesis' of Taylor and Broughton and maintained that, although there are too many gaps in ancient sources to provide reliable statistical data, in both pre-Sullan and post-Sullan times being elected first was of great significance for the appointment of the presidents of the elections.[16]

From these premises, we can analyse available ancient sources – which consist almost exclusively of Livy – to see what specific information they may provide on the process for determining which of the consuls was put in charge of the presidency of the elections. Table 2 lists the names of all the

---

[11] Taylor and Broughton 1949: 5.   [12] Taylor and Broughton 1949: 7–9.
[13] Taylor and Broughton 1968: 167. Cf. Kunkel and Wittmann 1995: 196–8.
[14] Taylor and Broughton 1968: 171.   [15] Rilinger 1976.
[16] Rilinger 1976: 40–59 (54: 'Auch die Betrachtung dieses Zeitraums [207–168] unter statistischen Gesichtspunkten deutet darauf hin, dass eine Verbindung zwischen der Stellung in den Fasten und der Wahlleitung besteht'; 58: 'Solange allerdings keine neuen Fakten auftauchen, ist es m.E. auf Grund der Untersuchungsergebnisse sinnvoll anzunehmen, dass bei der Regelung der Wahlleiterbestellung die Tatsache, dass jemand *primus renuntiatus* war, hervorragende Bedeutung hatte').

Table 2. *Consuls as presidents over elections in the pre-Sullan period*

CONSULS PRESIDING OVER ELECTIONS (Livy)	ORDER IN FASTI	ORDER IN LIVY	PROVINCIA
297/6 Q. Fabius Maximus Rullianus (10.15.7–12)	I	I	Samnium
296/5 L. Volumnius Flamma Violens (10.21.13)	2	2	Samnium-Campania
294/3 M. Atilius Regulus (10.36.18)	2	2	Samnium-Apulia
293/2 L. Papirius Cursor (10.47.5)	I	–	Samnium
218/17 Ti. Sempronius Longus (21.57.4)	2	2	North Italy
215/14 Q. Fabius Maximus Verrucosus (24.7.11)	Cos. suffectus	Cos. suffectus	Campania
214/13 Q. Fabius Maximus Verrucosus (24.43.5)	–	I	Campania
212/11 Ap. Claudius Pulcher (25.41.10)	–	2	Campania
211/10 Cn Fulvius Centumalus (26.18.4)	–	I	Apulia
210/9 M. Valerius Laevinus (27.4.3-4)	–	2	Sicily
209/8 Q. Fulvius Flaccus (27.20.13)	–	2	Lucania-Campania
206/5 L. Veturius Philo (28.38.6)	2	I	Lucania-Bruttium
204/3 M. Cornelius Cethegus (29.38.2)	I	I	Etruria
201/200 P. Aelius Paetus (31.4.4)	2	2	Gaul (North Italy)
200/199 C. Aurelius Cotta (31.49.12)	2	2	Gaul (North Italy)
199/8 L. Cornelius Lentulus (32.7.8)	I	I	Gaul (North Italy)
198/7 Sex. Aelius Paetus Catus (32.27.5)	2	I	Gaul (North Italy)
196/5 M. Claudius Marcellus (33.42.7)	2	2	Gaul (North Italy)
195/4 L. Valerius Flaccus (34.42.3)	2	I	Gaul (North Italy)
194/3 P. Cornelius Scipio Africanus (34.54.1)	I	I	Gaul (North Italy)
193/2 L. Cornelius Merula (35.6.7)	I	I	Gaul (North Italy)

Table 2. (*cont.*)

CONSULS PRESIDING OVER ELECTIONS (Livy)	ORDER IN FASTI	ORDER IN LIVY	PROVINCIA
192/1 L. Quinctius Flamininus (35.24.2-3)	1	1	Liguria
190/89 C. Laelius (37.47.1)	2	2	Gaul (North Italy)
189/8 M. Fulvius Nobilior (38.35.1–3)	2	1	Aetolia
188/7 M. Valerius Messala (38.42.1)	2	1	Liguria
187/6 C. Flaminius (39.6.1)	2	2	Liguria
186/5 Sp. Postumius Albinus (39.23.1)	1	1	South Italy (Bacchanalia)
185/4 Ap. Claudius Pulcher (39.32.5)	1	1	Liguria
183/2 M. Claudius Marcellus (39.56.3)	2	1	Liguria-Histria
182/1 Cn. Baebius Tamphilus (40.17.8)	2	1	Liguria
181/80 M. Baebius Tamphilus (40.35.1)	2	1	Liguria
179/8 Q. Fulvius Flaccus (40.59.4)	2	1	Liguria
178/7 M. Iunius Brutus (41.7.4)	1	1	Liguria-Histria
177/6 C. Claudius Pulcher (41.14.3)	1	1	Histria-Liguria
176 Q. Petilius Spurinus (extra election) (41.16.5)	2	(only consul alive)	Present in Rome
176/5 C. Valerius Laevinus? (41.18.16)	Cos. suffectus	Cos. suffectus	Liguria
173/2 L. Postumius Albinus (42.9.7)	1	1	Campania
172/1 C. Popillius Laenas (42.28.1)	1	1	Liguria
170/9 A. Atilius Serranus (43.11.3–6)	2	–	Liguria-Gaul
169/8 Cn. Servilius Caepio (44.17.2–3)	2	2	Italy-Gaul

consuls who we can be absolutely certain presided over elections in the pre-Sullan period. The order in which the consuls are mentioned, in the first or the second place, both in the *fasti consulares* and by Livy, is also included, along with the territory of the province from which they had to travel to

Rome to hold the elections. Of the forty known consuls, thirteen are mentioned in the first place in the *fasti*, twenty in the second place, two of them are suffect consuls, and there are no data available for five of them since the *fasti* for those years are not preserved. In Livy the numbers are different: twenty-three are mentioned by the Latin author in the first place when he refers to the outcome of the vote in each election, twelve in the second place, two of them are suffect consuls, and he does not provide any details for three of them. Consequently, according to the *fasti*, most of the known consuls presiding over elections had been elected in the second place. According to Livy, in contrast, most of them were the first elected.

Taylor and Broughton gave more credence to Livy than to the *fasti*.[17] However, there is a striking fact that may help to explain the discrepancy between the *fasti* and Livy and which would tilt the weight of credibility towards the *fasti*. It may be noted in Table 2 how all the consuls who appear in the first place in the *fasti* are also mentioned in the first place by Livy. In contrast, up to nine consuls mentioned in the second place in the *fasti* become first consuls for Livy. This could be a mere coincidence, but it could also be due to a change made by Livy on account of the time in which he lived. If it is true that from Sulla onwards the consul first elected usually presided over the elections, Livy could have presumed that this may have been the norm throughout the Republican period, and he may have thought that the consuls whom his sources claimed had presided over the comitia must consequently have been the ones elected first. This might have led him erroneously to modify the order that appears in the *fasti*, which, however, would be the correct order.

Whether this hypothesis is correct or not, one thing that can certainly be deduced from the preserved data is that in the pre-Sullan period there was no set rule according to which the consul elected first ought to preside over the elections. It could be he, but it could also be his colleague. As in other institutional aspects of the Roman Republic, we should view the process rather in the light of procedural flexibility, and not as a rigid course of action, which would not have accorded with the Roman mentality.[18] Unquestionably, the decision about the presidency of the elections was influenced by the historical circumstances at each time, in view of the needs of the Roman state and its external policies, and according to the availability of each of the consuls, regardless of who had been elected first. As already

---

[17] Taylor and Broughton 1949: 9; 1968: 166. However, Drummond (1978: 97–9) argues that there are no reasons to believe that Livy is more reliable.
[18] Cf. Drummond 1978: 82–3.

pointed out by Taylor and Broughton,[19] the decisive factors in each case must have been the remoteness or proximity of the consuls to the *Urbs*, as well as their military activity. It is logical to presume that the consul who was nearer and/or could leave the command of the troops with less jeopardy was favoured. In this respect, from the details shown in Table 2 it can be deduced that all the consuls who are known to have acted as presidents of the elections went to Rome from somewhere in the Italian peninsula – except for Sicily in 210/9 and especially Aetolia in 189/8 – Histria being the remotest region. As regards the appointment process, we may picture direct appointment by the senate, drawing of lots, or a mutual agreement between both consuls. In the known instances there are testimonies to all three procedures.

As already mentioned, in the pre-Sullan period elections to fill annual magistracies usually took place at the end of the consular year. In this sense, there are various generic time references of the kind 'in exitu anni' ('at the end of the year'),[20] when Livy says in his account that the time to hold the elections had come. Obviously that does not mean that in the Republican period there was a specific period of time for the elections. This would change as the date for the consuls to take up their office changed. Until the third century the date of the elections could be extraordinarily changeable. Throughout the third century, if it is true that the consuls took office on 1 May, as Mommsen believed, the elections could have been held in spring; since the Hannibalic War they were held in winter, probably in January or February; and from 153 they took place in autumn.

In the first quarter of the second century, data provided by Livy are at times so precise that they allow us to establish with certainty the date of the elections in a given year. In 170, the elections were held on 26 January.[21] In 187, the consul M. Valerius Messala returned to Rome 'almost at the close of the year' ('exitu prope anni'). Elections were held twelve days before the Calends of March, on 18 February.[22] In 171, the consul C. Popillius Laenas also returned for the elections, again at the end of the consular year. Consular elections took place on 18 February, and elections for praetors were held the following day.[23] In these last two cases, the elections were therefore held just under a month before the new magistrates took office. But there are some known cases of elections taking place even later. In 178,

[19] Taylor and Broughton 1968: 167.
[20] Liv. 25.41.8; 38.35.1; 31.4.1–4; 31.23.1. However, for 210 Livy places the time when the senate considers holding the elections at the end of the summer (Liv. 27.4.1). See also Liv. 29.38.2.
[21] Liv. 43.11.6.   [22] Liv. 38.42.1–2. Briscoe 2008: 148.   [23] Liv. 42.28.1; 42.28.4.

elections were held only a few days before the Ides of March, which means that the new consuls took office immediately after the voting.

Since both consuls were usually away from Rome during their term of office, one of them had to return specifically to preside over the elections.[24] It is possible that the name of the consul who had to preside over the elections was already fixed at the beginning of the year, when the consular provinces were allotted. There is evidence to suggest that this may have been the common practice. Livy states it expressly on some occasions, as for example for 176, when exceptional circumstances occurred. At the beginning of the year Pisa and Liguria were decreed as consular provinces. The consul who was allotted Pisa was to return in due course to Rome to preside over the elections.[25] Thus, no importance is given to who may have been the consul elected first. Pisa, and therefore the elections, was allotted to Cn. Cornelius Scipio Hispallus, but he died after an accident on his return from the *feriae Latinae*.[26] His colleague, Q. Petillius, presided over the extraordinary elections held on 3 August, where C. Valerius Laevinus was elected suffect consul.[27] In principle, he was to preside over the elections to be held at the end of the year. However, there were legal doubts as to whether a suffect consul could be in charge of this task, also in view of the fact that his colleague Petillius had died in battle in Liguria.[28] The gap that follows in Livy's text prevents us from knowing the final decision, perhaps the appointment of an *interrex*. In this case it was the senators who indirectly decided who was to be the consul in charge of the elections when they assigned the provinces at the beginning of the consular year.

A similar case occurred in 192. Italy was allotted in principle as a province to both consuls. The senatorial decree included the obligation for them to decide, either by mutual agreement or through drawing lots, which of them was to be in charge of the elections. It was also added that whoever was given that task could not leave Italy with his legions.[29] This proviso was due to the fact that the outbreak of war against Antiochus was perceived as imminent. It is clear therefore that, as was customary, the criterion of proximity to Rome was decisive in the assignment of the electoral presidency. L. Quinctius Flamininus was eventually allotted Gaul and the

---

[24] For the consular year 167/6 Livy claims that the two consuls returned to Rome for the elections, and he seems to imply that both of them presided over the vote (Liv. 45.44.1). Livy probably did not know the name of the president of the elections and thus preferred to use the plural form. There are no other data that could lead us to think that, on any occasion, both consuls were ever presidents of the elections. However Kunkel and Wittmann (1995: 196) assume as certain the information of Livy.

[25] Liv. 41.14.8–9. [26] Liv. 41.16.3. [27] Liv. 41.17.5–6. [28] Liv. 41.18.16. [29] Liv. 35.20.2–3.

elections.[30] When the time came, the senate ordered Flamininus to return to Rome to preside over the vote and on his way to the *Urbs* he was to send to the city the edict calling for the elections.[31]

The same probably happened in 198. At the beginning of the year the senate decided that the consular provinces should be Macedonia and Italy, and it was resolved that they should be assigned by agreement between both consuls or by lot.[32] Macedonia fell to Flamininus, Italy to Aelius Paetus. The latter was, ultimately, the electoral president, and returned to Rome from Gaul.[33] Livy does not mention this, but it can logically be presumed that when establishing the consular provinces, it was also determined that the consul who was to remain in Italy would be in charge of the elections as well, for it would have been absurd to make Flamininus return from Greece.

A peculiar situation came about when the senate decided that the consular provinces should be Asia and Aetolia. They were both remote territories, involving a very long journey for each of the consuls. However, the custom of the electoral president being a consul prevailed, and it was arranged that the consul who was allotted Aetolia, the nearer of the two to Rome, was to be in charge of the elections, both for consuls and for censors. In any event, the possibility of changing this was left open, should it be necessary, since the senatorial decree included the proviso that this ought to be so only if it was in the interest of the state ('si per commodum rei publicae facere posset'), and should anything occur, the consul in Aetolia was to inform the senate of his inability to be present in Rome during the elections.[34] When the end of the consular year approached, the consul M. Fulvius Nobilior temporarily left his command of the army in Aetolia and, once he had presided over the consular elections in Rome, immediately returned to his province, where his *imperium* was extended for one year.[35]

Nevertheless, even though the decision was taken at the beginning of the year, it was subject to change, mainly due to military circumstances. It can be inferred from Livy's text that in 210 the person in charge of presiding over the elections was the consul M. Claudius Marcellus and that this commission had already been given to him at the beginning of the year. He had probably been appointed because his province was the war against Hannibal in the south of Italy, whereas the province of his colleague M. Valerius Laevinus was Sicily, and he was in charge of the fleet. When the moment came, Claudius informed the senate that it was not advisable

[30] Liv. 35.20.7.   [31] Liv. 35.24.2.   [32] Liv. 32.8.1.   [33] Liv. 32.27.5.   [34] Liv. 37.50.6–7.
[35] Liv. 38.35.1.

for him to leave his army due to the danger posed by Hannibal. The senate accepted his argument and bade the urban praetor send a message to Valerius – along with the letter from Claudius – informing him that he was to return to Rome.[36] Valerius Laevinus was the electoral president that year even though, as Livy says, he was away from Italy, which demonstrates that an attempt was always made for the consul who was in charge of the elections to be on the Italian peninsula.[37]

Well into the consular year 193/2, a letter was received by the senate from the consul Q. Minucius Thermus. He was in Pisa at the time, engaged in a seemingly endless war against the Ligures, and claimed he could not leave his command at that moment without putting the *res publica* at risk. Minucius had been allotted the presidency over the elections after drawing lots ('comitia suae sortis esse'), but he asked the senate to exempt him from this task given the military situation in his province. He also requested that, should the senators consider it appropriate, they ask his colleague L. Cornelius Merula to replace him, since he had already finished his campaign against the Boii in the north of Italy, and, should he refuse, to appoint *interreges*. The senate ordered the urban praetor to appoint two legates to go in person to discuss this question with Merula, who accepted the task.[38]

In exceptional cases we find that there were political motives to account for the change. In the consular year 185/4 the presidency was held by M. Sempronius Tuditanus, but his colleague Ap. Claudius Pulcher rushed back to Rome in order to arrive before him so that he could preside over the elections in his place. The reason was that one of the candidates was his brother P. Claudius Pulcher, whom he wanted to support against his rivals. The senate apparently acquiesced in the forced change of president, and eventually P. Claudius managed to be elected as consul for the following year.[39] This is no doubt a good example of how the electoral president could lobby to have a favoured candidate elected. Just three years later, the consuls, who were both in Liguria, reached an agreement to appoint one of them, Cn. Baebius Tamphilus, as the electoral president.[40] This was not a question of overturning a decision taken previously, but of an agreement

---

[36] On the role of the urban praetor as intermediary between the senate and military commanders during a campaign, see Brennan 2000: 116–17.

[37] Liv. 27.4.1–4.

[38] Liv. 35.6.1–7. On other occasions, Livy does not explain the reasons for the change, although we ought to suppose that they were probably military reasons. For example, in 187/6 by drawing lots the presidency was assigned to M. Aemilius Lepidus, but he could not go to Rome, so he was replaced by his colleague C. Flaminius (Liv. 39.6.1). Cf. Brennan 2000: 117.

[39] Liv. 39.32.5–13. Cf. Vishnia 1996: 183.   [40] Liv. 40.17.8. Cf. Vishnia 1996: 183–4.

reached by consensus. However, as in the previous case, his reason for undertaking this task was of a personal nature, given that his brother was a candidate. As in the previous instance of the Claudii, he too was eventually elected.

Thus there are records indicating that presidency over the elections was fixed at the beginning of the consular year. However, there are also testimonies which show that the appointment of the electoral president was occasionally decided just before the elections on the basis of the political or military circumstances of the time. Initiative in this respect always came from the senate, although the final decision was left in the hands of the consuls.[41]

During the Second Punic War, in different circumstances, the senate asked the consuls to decide who ought to preside over the elections. In the consular year 217/6, the urban praetor, following orders from the senate, wrote to the consuls asking one of them to come to Rome for the consular elections, adding that the day of the elections was to be appointed by the consul. The consuls replied that leaving command of the army at that moment would pose a serious risk and that it would be better to appoint an *interrex*. The senators accepted the reasonable refusal of the consuls, but they resolved to appoint a dictator to preside over the elections.[42] Likewise, at the end of the consular year 212/11, the senate instructed the urban and peregrine praetor P. Cornelius Sulla to send a letter to the consuls, who were in Capua. The senators asked one of the consuls to return to Rome to preside over the elections, precisely because at that time Hannibal was far away and there were no great military operations in progress near Capua. In the letter, the senate did not indicate which of the two consuls should be in charge of the task, a decision that was left up to the magistrates. They were both in the same place and in the same military situation, so in principle there were no reasons to prefer either of them.[43] According to Livy, the consuls agreed ('inter se consules compararunt') that Fulvius Flaccus should stay in Capua, while Claudius Pulcher went to the *Urbs*.[44] In this case it is clear that the senate decided the appropriate time to hold the elections, but it was the consuls who then agreed on who was to be in charge of the assignment. Who was first elected consul does not seem to have had any

---

[41] Kunkel and Wittmann 1995: 322–3.   [42] Liv. 22.33.9–11. Cf. Brennan 2000: 121.

[43] The previous year, when the moment for the elections came, it was noted that the situation of the war did not permit either of the consuls to go to Rome. For this reason, it was decided to appoint a dictator for this purpose. The consul Ti. Sempronius Gracchus appointed C. Claudius Centho as dictator. Cf. Liv. 25.2.3.

[44] Liv. 25.41.8–10.

relevance. In 204, when the time arrived, the senate decided to call upon the consul M. Cornelius Cethegus to preside over the elections. The reason given by Livy is that at that time there was no war in his province, Etruria, whereas the situation was more unsettled in the south of Italy where his colleague was.[45] After holding the elections, Cethegus returned to Etruria to resume command of his troops.

In the consular year 178/7, once the danger in Histria seemed to have been overcome, the senate passed a decree requesting the consuls to agree which one of them was to go to Rome to hold the elections.[46] They were both in Histria at the time and it was finally M. Iunius Brutus who presided over the elections.[47] A similar situation occurred in the consular year 172/1, when the senate decided to send letters to the consuls, who were both in Liguria, requesting that 'whichever of the two of them could' should go to Rome to preside over the elections.[48] C. Popillius Laenas was eventually in charge, but Livy does not explain whether they reached this decision by casting lots or through an agreement.

In all the cases mentioned, the appointment of the consul in charge of the elections took place either through agreement of the consuls or by drawing of lots. However, there are some examples in which the imperative language used by Livy would lead us to think that the senate may have directly designated one of the consuls for this task, well into the consular year. On various occasions Livy uses the phrase 'comitiorum causa Romam revocatus' to refer to a consul who was summoned by the senate to go to Rome in order to preside over the elections.[49] In other instances, instructions given by means of a senatorial decree were very specific. Thus, in 177/6, the senate ordered the consul C. Claudius Pulcher to hold the elections as soon as possible and then to return to his province.[50] And in 170/69, the senate asked the consul A. Atilius Serranus to return to Rome as soon as possible to issue his electoral edict in order to hold the elections at the end of January, as did indeed happen.[51] The following year the request for the elections to be held as soon as possible was repeated to the consul Cn. Servilius Caepio, who complied by immediately appointing the date for the elections and stating that he would return to Rome by that time.[52]

From Livy's evidence we cannot clearly deduce whether those consuls had already been appointed before the beginning of the consular year, and the senate simply indicated to them the appropriate moment to hold the

[45] Liv. 29.38.2–5. [46] Liv. 41.6.1. [47] Liv. 41.7.4. [48] Liv. 42.25.14.
[49] Liv. 10.21.13; 39.56.3; 40.35.1. Cf. Liv. 26.22.2. [50] Liv. 41.14.3. [51] Liv. 43.11.3.
[52] Liv. 44.17.2–3.

elections, or whether the appointment was made directly by the senate at that time. In my opinion, the first option is more likely,[53] for example in the case of Servilius Caepio, whose province was Italy and who travelled throughout Gaul during his time in office, whereas his colleague was stationed in Macedonia. From the cases previously seen, in all probability the assignment of the province of Italy to Servilius must have been linked to the electoral tasks, since it would have been absurd for the consul who was in Greece to be in charge. The same would apply to C. Claudius, who was in Liguria while his colleague was in Sardinia, and to Atilius, who spent the year in Liguria and Gaul while his colleague was in Greece.

Consuls presided over the elections of higher magistrates,[54] both consuls and praetors, which were apparently held on consecutive days.[55] They also dealt with the election of new censors. The consul in charge of the election of censors was also in charge of the consular elections, and being appointed president for one also implied presidency over the other.[56] But the date of each was different. Consular elections took place, as we have seen, at the end or, in any event, in the second half of the consular year, whereas the censorial elections were usually held at the beginning of the consular year. In 214, on the very day when consuls took office, the senate decreed that it had to be decided, either by drawing lots or by consensus, which of the two was to be in charge of the election of censors, which ought to be held before they left the city to take command of the army.[57] This task was assigned to the consul Q. Fabius Maximus, who presided over the censorial elections once he had expiated the prodigies and recruited new soldiers.[58] The election of consuls took place at the end of the consular year, also under the presidency of Fabius Maximus.[59] This pattern was repeated in 209: the consul Q. Fulvius Flaccus called for the elections of new censors at the beginning of the consular year, after placating the gods and carrying out military arrangements,[60] and he returned to Rome for the consular elections at the end of the year.[61] The same happened in 199, when the consul L. Cornelius Lentulus was in charge of the consular elections after returning

[53] To the aforementioned instances the case of Cornelius Lentulus in 199/8 could be added. The consul was summoned by the senate to preside over the consular elections (Liv. 32.7.8), but he had already presided over the elections of new censors at the beginning of the year, which indicates that his appointment as an electoral president had taken place at the beginning of the consular year.

[54] Livy does not provide any information for the pre-Sullan period that might prove that consuls presided over the *comitia tributa* where curule aediles and quaestors were elected. Cf. Kunkel and Wittmann 1995: 473; 514.

[55] Liv. 38.42.3; 39.23.2; 41.8.1; 42.28.1; 42.28.4; 43.11.7 (two days later); 45.44.1–2.   [56] Liv. 37.50.7.

[57] Liv. 24.10.1–2.   [58] Liv. 24.11.6.   [59] Liv. 24.43.5. Cf. Beck 2005: 297.   [60] Liv. 27.11.7.

[61] Liv. 27.20.13.

from his province[62] and of the censorial elections before he had gone there. In his narrative, Livy writes of the election of censors after describing the events in Macedonia, and he claims that Lentulus had stayed in Rome.[63] Only then did he go to Gaul, whence he returned to the *Urbs* for the consular elections. In 184 hard-fought censorial elections took place. Livy does not provide the name of the president for that year, but he does say specifically that the consuls, as well as the praetors, set off for their provinces only after the new censors had been elected.[64]

Regarding the electoral process, the consul was responsible for a number of specific tasks.[65] Amongst them, in the first place, was to set a date for the elections by means of an edict.[66] The electoral president had scope to do so within the time limits fixed by the senate, which was, as we have seen, in charge of deciding the electoral period based on public interest.[67] The senate indirectly marked this period when summoning the consul to Rome to preside over the elections by virtue of a decree ordering the magistrate to start the process as soon as possible.

For the post-Sullan period there are sufficient data to determine the electoral process in some detail, from the formal declaration of the candidates' desire to compete (*professio*) to the official announcement of the candidates elected (*renuntiatio*), continuing through the taking of auspices,[68] the *contio* which was held before the comitia,[69] and the date for the *trinundinum*, which was compulsory after the enactment of the *lex Caecilia Didia* in 98. All these steps were presided over by the magistrate in charge of the elections. However, for the pre-Sullan age information is scarce and at times contradictory, which makes it difficult to reconstruct the process. For example, it is difficult to know whether or not there was a *professio* and, if there was, how it was performed, apart from the necessary approval of the names of the candidates by the president.[70] In any event, an essential difference must be taken into account: the fact that after Sulla the consuls stayed in Rome, whereas before his dictatorship they had spent most of the year away from the *Urbs*. As we have already seen, the consul who was the electoral president went to Rome from his province, temporarily leaving his troops.

---

[62] Liv. 32.7.8. [63] Liv. 32.7.1. [64] Liv. 39.41.5. [65] See Rilinger 1976: 60–112.
[66] Liv. 31.49.12. Cf. Liv. 43.11.3. [67] Rilinger 1976: 92–3. [68] Rilinger 1976: 94–105.
[69] Rilinger 1976: 105–12.
[70] Astin (1962) argued that the *professio* was compulsory at least from the beginning of the second century. In contrast, Earl (1965) considered that at the end of the second century the *professio* was not yet legally set, although it may have existed as an administrative practice, and that it was possibly Sulla who made it legally compulsory. This opinion is shared by Hall 1972: esp. 15–17. Also Staveley (1972: 146–8) believes that strict regulations regarding the *professio* only existed in the first century. Cf. Rilinger 1976: 63–91.

Generally he did so for the sole purpose of presiding over the comitia. After the elections were held, sources do not always provide specific information on the activity of the consul, but he probably returned to his province to resume his command until the end of his time in office, as we know with certainty happened in some cases.[71]

Therefore the electoral process had to be completed promptly. In some cases the urgency of the procedure is made clear. In order to speed up the process, the edict calling for the elections could be issued by the consul either from the place where he was in command of his troops, or while he was on his way to Rome, so that the elections could take place immediately after his arrival. This was possible once the custom of issuing the edicts in writing had begun, at least by the end of the third century.[72] In 169/8, Servilius Caepio received instructions from the senate stating that elections had to be held as soon as possible. His reaction was to send a written dispatch to Rome including his edict announcing the elections, which was read out to the senate by the urban praetor.[73] The edict could also be issued during the consul's journey to Rome. This was done, for instance, by Q. Fabius Maximus in 215/14, so when he arrived in Rome he went directly to the Campus Martius to hold the elections.[74] In 192/1 Flamininus followed suit, complying with the decree of the senate which had been sent to him via the urban praetor, ordering him to issue an edict announcing the elections on the road to Rome ('ex itinere').[75] The promptness in the electoral process leads us to believe that some of the deadlines and formalities which existed in the first century probably did not apply in the pre-Sullan period, simply for practical reasons.

In conclusion, we cannot deduce from ancient sources that in the pre-Sullan age electoral presidency belonged to the consul who was elected first. The president at the yearly elections of higher magistrates, as well as at the censorial elections every five years, was designated by drawing lots,

---

[71] In the consular year 207/6, the consul M. Livius Salinator presided over the elections as dictator appointed for this purpose. After the elections, he went to Etruria and Umbria to conduct an inquiry by order of the senate (Liv. 28.10.4–5). In 204/3, Cornelius Cethegus returned to Etruria after the elections (Liv. 29.38.5). In 195/4, Valerius Flaccus returned to the north of Italy (Liv. 34.42.4). In 188 Fulvius Nobilior went to Rome from Aetolia to preside over the elections, and he returned to his province, where his *imperium* was extended (Liv. 38.35.3). In 177/6, Claudius Pulcher was ordered to return to his province in the north of Italy once the elections had been held (Liv. 41.14.3).

[72] Rilinger (1976: 90–1) following Mommsen (1887–8: I 205–6), supposed that the introduction of edicts calling for elections in writing instead of simply announcing them orally should be dated to the beginning of the second century. However, the report regarding Q. Fabius Maximus in 215/14 indicates an earlier date.

[73] Liv. 44.17.3.   [74] Liv. 24.7.11.   [75] Liv. 35.2.2.

by mutual agreement of the two consuls, or indirectly by the senate when setting the allocation of provinces at the beginning of the consular year. Proximity to Rome and availability depending on the military situation of each consular province were key factors in the appointment of one consul or the other. Nevertheless, the appointment was not fixed by strict preset rules, but was rather governed by flexibility and versatility depending on the circumstances of each particular time. In the electoral process the senate and the consuls clearly complemented each other. Senators had to initiate the process and decide the time of year when the elections were to be held, by issuing an order for the appointed consul to return to the *Urbs*. The consul, for his part, was entitled to set the date for the elections by means of an edict and was in charge of all the practicalities involved in the elections, as well as presiding over them and proclaiming the winners.

CHAPTER II

The consular year in the pre-Sullan age

As we have seen in the previous chapters, once the consuls took office, they stayed on in Rome for a number of weeks before setting off for their provinces to take command of their armies. During this time they were required to attend to a series of civil functions, the multiplicity of which explains Polybius' assertion that during their presence in Rome, the consuls were the supreme magistrates of the administration of the Roman state, always subordinate to the senate.[1] When the consuls left the *Urbs* to command their armies, supreme political responsibility in the city was transferred to the urban praetor,[2] who dealt with most of the duties that would have fallen to the consuls had they been present in Rome.[3]

On the very day they took office, after visiting the Capitol together, the two consuls attended a meeting with the senate at which all the topical political questions, and above all the military situation, were discussed. It was a genuine debate on the 'state of the community', which preceded the allocation of the annual provinces amongst the higher magistrates and the fixing by the senators of the number of soldiers to be levied, as well as their distribution amongst the magistrates with *imperium*.

In the religious field, it was compulsory for the consuls to pronounce the public vows (*vota publica*) on the Capitol on their first day as magistrates, and they also had to assign the date for the celebration of the *feriae Latinae*, see to the expiation of the prodigies that had occurred in the previous months both in Rome and in Italy, and preside over the Latin festival on the Mons Albanus. The presence of the consuls was essential in all these

---

[1] Polyb. 6.12.1.   [2] Cf. Liv. 24.9.5.

[3] Brennan 2000: 601; 607–8. Actually, that could have been the reason for the creation of the praetor-ship in the fourth century, and not exclusively to deal with the administration of justice as is misinterpreted by Livy, following what was indeed the main function of the urban praetor in his own time (Brennan 2000: 61–2). Brennan (pp. 98–135) extensively analyses the functions of the urban praetor, in particular from the Hannibalic War onwards and throughout the second century. On the relationship between consulship and praetorship in the fourth and third centuries see Bergk, forthcoming.

religious acts. It possibly also fell to them to preside over the annual ceremony in honour of the *sacra* in Lavinium, although it is likely that the consuls may have delegated this task to another magistrate with *imperium*. Exceptionally, the supervision of the *ver sacrum* that took place in Rome in 195, which had to be repeated the following year due to a technicality, also pertained to the consuls. Another consular task was to preside over the *ludi Romani* if the consuls – or at least one of them – were in Rome during their celebration, as well as to take the vow and the presidency over *ludi magni* celebrated by order of the senate.

A second task that had to be completed by the consuls during the first few weeks of their term of office encompassed diplomatic matters. The consuls were in charge of receiving the numerous embassies arriving in Rome from Italy and the whole Mediterranean area; the greater the Roman expansion, the more frequent the embassies were. The consuls had to introduce foreign ambassadors to the senators, attend the ensuing debates, and report to the envoys the decisions taken by the senate. Therefore, the consuls acted as heads of diplomacy for the Roman state, always in agreement with the guidelines laid down by the senate.

Subordination of the consuls to the senate was constant throughout the Republican period. The function of the consuls was mainly to act as the executors of the general policy and of the specific decisions taken by the senators. An illustration of this is the role played by the consuls in the appointment of a dictator. The senators always had to decide whether the appropriate conditions existed for appointing a dictator, who was assigned certain tasks. But, apart from exceptional circumstances, the appointment of a dictator had to be made by a consul. In their role as supreme magistrates, the consuls also acted as intermediaries between the senate and the people during their stay in Rome, both by issuing edicts and through their active participation in *contiones*. In this respect, the consuls acted, like the other magistrates, as orators before the people in those assemblies, although usually with limitations because of their brief stay in the *Urbs*.

Occasionally, the consuls also dealt with other tasks in very different areas of the civil administration of the state. At times they were in charge of controlling the public land owned by Rome, as in the case of the consul Postumius in 173 in Campania; they directed the distribution of public land and may also have had an active part in the process of colonization, either in the enrolment of new colonists or in the election of the commission in charge of the actual foundation of colonies and the settlement of colonists. Some consuls may also have been in charge of the foundation of fora located in various territories in Italy; these fora would have been named after the consuls and could have been created as links in the construction of the road network.

The consuls' intervention in the legislative process was limited in comparison with that of other Republican magistrates, particularly the tribunes of the plebs. Only exceptionally did the consuls promote new laws, and they almost always did so following the instructions of the senate, usually promoting bills regarding significant issues for Roman society as a whole. Their limited contribution in the legislative sphere was not the result of a legal inability to promote new laws, but was due mainly to their short stay in Rome, where the legislative process took place.

The exercise of consular jurisdiction was also exceptional. In extraordinary circumstances the senate could order one or both of the consuls to conduct an investigation. The inquiry could refer to widely differing crimes and offences and could be conducted either in Rome or in Italy. In general, it must have taken up a small portion of the consular year, although in particularly serious cases it may have become the consuls' main task for a given year, as was the case in 186 with the Bacchanalia.

With regard to public works, the consuls certainly played a decisive part in the construction of the communications infrastructure throughout the Italian peninsula. Many of the roads built in Italy in the Republican period, particularly during the second century, were promoted by consuls. It was also the consuls' task to direct some of the large-scale waterworks aimed at draining vast areas of Italy to make them arable. In Rome, the consuls also made a contribution to the development of the urban landscape by promoting the construction of a great number of temples which were erected in the city over the course of the centuries, as well as, to a lesser extent, other memorial buildings and monuments, such as columns, arches, and porticoes.

Most of the civil functions fulfilled by the consuls – at any rate, their religious duties – were carried out at the beginning of the consular year, at the same time as the levying of new troops that were to be under the command of the consuls in their provinces. To all these activities we must also add the presidency over the elections of censors, when required. The fulfilment of their religious duties, in particular the celebration of the *feriae Latinae*, marked the end of their obligatory presence in Rome, and only then were the consuls allowed to depart for their provinces.[4]

---

[4] Livy usually puts it similarly, although with a slight variation in the phrasing: Liv. 23.32.13: 'et Romae consules transactis rebus quae in urbe agendae erant movebant iam sese ad bellum'; 32.3.1: 'rebus quae Romae agendae erant perfectis consules in provincias profecti'. Cf. Liv. 31.22.3; 32.29.5; 42.36.8.

In the pre-Sullan period, it was exceptional for a consul to remain in Rome for all or most of his term of office. The norm was always that the consul devoted most of the consular year to war, commanding the armies that had been assigned to him. As Polybius states, when referring to magistracies during the pre-Sullan age, the consuls were mainly the supreme commanders of the Roman army. The reasons why a consul very occasionally stayed in Rome during all or most of his term of office vary in each case: illness, religious reasons, or a direct order from the senate for strategic purposes.

Illness was the reason why, according to Livy, in the consular year 312/11 the consul P. Decius Mus could not leave the city and was forced to appoint a dictator following a senatorial resolution on account of the critical military situation.[5] In 294, the consul L. Postumius Megellus had to delay his departure from Rome due to illness, but eventually, although he had not fully recovered, he took command over his troops because of alarming news received about the war against the Samnites.[6] When, later on, the consul asked for a triumph to be awarded to him after his victories, it was initially denied. One of the reasons given, according to Livy, was his delay in leaving Rome to take command of his army.[7]

A consul could be forced to stay in Rome for religious reasons. This happened in the case of the consul A. Postumius Albinus in 242, who was banned by the *pontifex maximus* from leaving the city to take over his military command because he simultaneously held the office of priest of Mars (*flamen Martialis*). The *pontifex* argued that, should he leave, he would not be able to meet his religious duties.[8] To provide for this contingency, the praetor Q. Valerius Falto was sent in his place to accompany the other consul as commander of the fleet.[9]

The consular year 186/5 was exceptional for the two consuls, since the senate entrusted them with the extraordinary inquiry that was to suppress the Bacchanalia, a task that took up most of their year, both in Rome and in

---

[5] Liv. 9.29.3. However, in *De vir. ill.* 27 an alleged triumph obtained by Decius over the Samnites is mentioned, although no other ancient source attests to it. Cf. Broughton 1951–86: I 159.

[6] Liv. 10.32.1; 10.33.8.   [7] Liv. 10.37.6.

[8] Liv. *per.* 19. Cf. Liv. 37.51.1–2; V. Max. 1.1.2; Tac. *Ann.* 3.71. In the year 205, the fact that P. Licinius Crassus was *pontifex maximus* influenced his consulship, so he was allotted Bruttium as province because he could not leave Italy due to his religious duties (Liv. 28.38.12).

[9] Cf. Broughton 1951–86: I 218. However, there was no conflict between the simultaneous office of the consulship and the position of *princeps senatus*. In the year 209, the censors appointed Q. Fabius Maximus to this position, despite the fact that, as consul, he was to leave Rome soon afterwards (Liv. 27.11.12), and he would therefore temporarily be unable to hold his position as head of the senate. Cf. Beck 2000: 89.

Italy. In fact, the first lines of the inscription from Tiriolo refer to the meeting of the senate held at the temple of Bellona, which is where the text included in the inscription must have been agreed before it was then distributed throughout the Italian peninsula. The senate session took place under the presidency of the two consuls, Q. Marcius and Sp. Postumius, on the Nones of October of 186, which means that both of them were in Rome on that date.[10]

A special case occurred in 168. L. Aemilius Paullus was assigned to the war against Perseus in Macedonia, whereas his colleague C. Licinius Crassus was ordered to guarantee the supply of troops and material to Macedonia, for which purpose he received Italy as his province.[11] For this reason, he was, unusually, in Rome in the month of September presiding over the *ludi Romani* when news arrived of the victory in Pydna.[12] Something similar had already happened in 202. Etruria was the province of the consul M. Servilius Pulex, but he had to stay on in Rome by order of the senate until the senators knew exactly what the situation was in Africa.[13] He could only set off for his province after a long delay, having appointed a dictator to preside over the elections so that he would not have to return to deal with that task, as would normally have been the case.[14] In 199, the consul P. Villius Tappulus went to Macedonia, while his colleague L. Cornelius Lentulus, who had been allotted Italy as his province, stayed in Rome to preside over the elections for censor, amongst other reasons. Only after the great defeat of Cn. Baebius Tamphilus against the Insubres did he leave the *Urbs* to take command of his troops in Gaul.[15]

A completely different situation occurred in the first consulship of Ap. Claudius Caecus in 307. The senate had extended the term of office of Q. Fabius Maximus Rullianus in Samnium, this time as a proconsul, because of his military success the previous year. On the other hand, his colleague in the consulship, L. Volumnius Flamma, had been given the command of the campaign against the Sallentini. Having been thus prevented from attaining military glory, Claudius Caecus remained in Rome during his consulship, according to Livy, dealing with 'city matters' ('urbanae artes') with the purpose of consolidating his sphere of influence.[16] Livy's assertion sounds rather like an accusation against the consul, who is depicted as having personally taken the decision to remain in Rome

---

[10] *CIL* I 196 = I² 581, x 104 = *ILS* 18 = *ILLRP* 511. As a matter of fact, the date corresponded to 11 June in the astronomical calendar (Derow 1973: 350).
[11] Liv. 44.17.10; 44.19.5; 44.21.11; 44.22.5.   [12] Liv. 45.1.6–7.   [13] Liv. 30.38.6.   [14] Liv. 30.39.4.
[15] Liv. 32.7.1; 32.7.7.   [16] Liv. 9.42.4. Cf. Beck 2005: 178.

exclusively with a view to his own interest. This must be seen within the context of the creation of an image of Claudius Caecus in ancient histor-iography as a demagogue who had built his power base among the urban plebs.[17] However, it is highly improbable that the consul took the decision without consulting the senate, which was ultimately in charge of the allocation of the provinces. Once the provinces which required military command had been allotted, the senate must have, exceptionally, ordered Claudius Caecus to remain in Rome. Livy provides no further information on the specific activities of the consul in the *Urbs*, which must have been of a civil rather than military nature. His assertion that he dealt with 'city matters' does not give sufficient clarification of the question. It is possible that Claudius Caecus could have spent his consulship in 307 promoting or continuing some of the civil works that are attributed to him as a censor in 312–311, a position which was actually extended in 310, an unusual but in fact unsurprising situation if we bear in mind the scale of works such as the Via Appia or the first great aqueduct in the city.[18] Perhaps it was precisely their continuation or culmination that made the senate decide or authorize that the consul should remain in Rome.

In some cases we have the exact date when the consuls left Rome. Thus, in 212, both they and the praetors departed for their provinces immediately after the celebration of the *feriae Latinae*, on the fifth day before the Calends of May.[19] Just under a month and a half had elapsed since they had taken office. In 206, Livy simply says that the consuls left Rome at the beginning of the spring, without giving a precise date.[20] The same information is provided for the year 169, when the departure of the consuls was accelerated in view of the situation in Macedonia.[21] In 191, the consul Acilius left Rome on the fifth day before the Nones of May to take command of his soldiers, whom he had ordered to assemble in Brundisium on the Ides of May.[22] The praetors also left Rome around the same time. Acilius may have gone to war while his colleague, Scipio Nasica, may have been forced to stay on in the *Urbs* for a longer period in order to deal with the expiation of prodigies.[23] A year later, the consul Scipio Asiaticus joined his army in

---

[17] Humm 2005: 101–2.

[18] Linke 2000: 72–3; Humm 2005: 8; 257; Beck 2005: 171–3; 177–8. Radke (1975e: 1244) argues that the Via Appia up to Capua could only have been completed by Claudius Caecus during his consulship in the year 307. On the other hand, it is unlikely that Livy refers to Claudius Caecus' eloquence when he mentions his *artes urbanae*, a possibility which is suggested by Humm 2005: 140; 508.

[19] Liv. 25.12.1.   [20] Liv. 28.11.8.

[21] Liv. 44.1.1. L. Aemilius Paullus also arrived in Macedonia in the year 168 at the beginning of the spring (Liv. 44.30.1).

[22] Liv. 36.3.14.   [23] Liv. 36.37.2–6.

Brundisium during the *ludi Apollinares*, in July, about four months after taking office.

As may be observed, the moment when the consuls left Rome varied considerably according to the circumstances of each year. It could happen just a few weeks after they took office, or they may have had to remain in Rome for several months. Very different reasons could account for an alteration of the planned consular agenda and could result in a delay, sometimes quite substantial, in the departure of the consuls for their provinces.

In 198, Flamininus, despite his eagerness to go to Greece to lead the military operations there, was forced to stay in Rome for a good part of the year to attend to his religious duties. Besides the usual expiation of the prodigies which had occurred in the months prior to his taking office, the fact that other prodigies happened during the consular year prevented him from leaving the *Urbs*.[24] As always, the restitution of the peace of the gods had priority for the consuls over military matters. In fact, Livy says that had he been able to go to his province earlier, Flamininus would no doubt have achieved a final victory in Greece.

In 176 a series of events considerably delayed the departure of the consuls from Rome. The *feriae Latinae* were celebrated on the third day before the Nones of May, but they had to be repeated because of an error in the ritual. Upon his return from the celebration on the Mons Albanus, the consul Scipio Hispallus died in an accident, and as a result a suffect consul had to be elected.[25] The Latin festival was celebrated again on the third day before the Ides of August.[26] Only then could the consuls set off for their provinces, six months after taking office.[27]

In 210, apart from dealing with the usual religious and diplomatic matters, the consuls had been involved in the resolution of the economic difficulties that were troubling the Roman state in the midst of the conflict against the Carthaginians. They had issued an edict whereby the citizens were to lend money in order to pursue the war under the best possible conditions.[28] Only once they had obtained this financial backing did they take over their military command. By the time the consul Laevinus reached

---

[24] Liv. 32.9.1; 32.28.6.   [25] Liv. 41.16.1.   [26] Liv. 41.16.3.

[27] Liv. 41.17.6 claims that the senate ordered the suffect consul, C. Valerius Laevinus, to take command of his province in Etruria as soon as he was elected. His departure from Rome took place, according to Livy, on the Nones of August. Should this be the case, it would mean that he did not attend the repetition of the *feriae Latinae* that were to be celebrated just a few days later. Is this a mistake by Livy, in view of the fact that the formality of the two consuls presiding over the Latin festival was always fulfilled? Was the suffect consul not under the obligation to attend the Mons Albanus?

[28] Liv. 26.35–6.

Sicily, Livy states that a good part of the consular year had already elapsed, but does not provide a precise date.[29]

In other instances, difficulties in the recruitment of troops could account for the delayed departure of the consuls for their provinces. This situation is described by Livy for 185, although he gives no further details on the specific problems in the levy.[30] In the year 180, besides the recruitment there was a series of exceptional events that forced the consuls to remain in Rome longer than usual. One of the consuls died in suspect circumstances, and the same happened to one of the praetors and to other distinguished members of society. All of this was perceived as a portent which had to be expiated. New elections were held to replace the deceased consul. This accumulation of events resulted in a considerable delay in all public affairs.[31]

Generally, the consuls left Rome as soon as possible after having appropriately completed their religious duties. However, if we look at the events of 195, they seem to have had a certain freedom of action when taking this decision. That year, Cato stayed on in the city until the comitia had voted the abrogation of the *lex Oppia*, whose continuation he had vehemently defended at the *contiones* prior to the voting.[32] Only then did he leave for Hispania, thus delaying his departure longer than would have been necessary. Perhaps this delay was helped by the fact that there was a discrepancy at the time between the official calendar and the real calendar, which meant that taking office on the Ides of March actually corresponded in the astronomical calendar to November or December.[33] Therefore Cato must actually have left for his province at the beginning of spring, a suitable date to start military actions for the suppression of the revolt of the Iberian peoples, which were eventually a success.

Disputes between the consuls and the senate could also alter the course of events in the consular year. In 172 there was a bitter conflict regarding both the crimes perpetrated by M. Popillius Laenas the previous year and the provinces that were to be allotted to the consuls in 172.[34] As a result of this confrontation, the consuls left for their provinces very late in the year, perhaps in July or August, although Livy does not provide the precise dates.[35]

The consuls' departure from the *Urbs* for their provinces (*profectio consularis*) was a civic-military display with the religious ingredients that typically surrounded any public act in Rome. Livy gives an account of such departures for the first time in the early second century. However, it is quite

[29] Liv. 26.40.1.   [30] Liv. 39.29.10.   [31] Liv. 40.37.8.   [32] Liv. 34.1–4; 34.8.4.
[33] Holzapfel 1885: 344; Marchetti 1973: 477; Derow 1976: 272.   [34] Liv. 42.10; 42.21.   [35] Liv. 42.22.1.

probable that this was not a novelty, but a procession that had traditionally been conducted from the Capitol to one of the gates of the city on the way to the province.[36] On the day of his departure, the consul abandoned his *toga praetexta*, the white garment with a purple border stripe which was one of the insignia of the consuls, and left Rome *paludatus*, that is, wearing the military uniform, the *paludamentum*,[37] and accompanied by the lictors, who were the symbol of the consul's authority and also wore the *paludamentum*. The procession also included the friends of the consul, prominent citizens, and military tribunes and other officers who were part of the *consilium* of the consul. As in all public acts, the higher the number of persons in the procession and the more conspicuous their social standing, the larger the celebrity and renown for the consul who was leaving for war and the greater the impact of the event. Without a doubt, the consul must have done everything in his power to make his departure from Rome an act of self-glorification. Thus, it was recalled that Aemilius Paullus had been accompanied upon his departure to Macedonia in April 168 by an unusual crowd in anticipation of what was to be his great victory in Pydna.[38]

Three years earlier, the mention of the departure from Rome of the consul P. Licinius Crassus to take command in the war against Perseus was used by Livy to reflect on the *profectio consularis*.[39] It was, as Livy says, an act which 'was always carried out with dignity and grandeur' ('semper . . . cum magna dignitate ac maiestate geritur'). Those who escorted the consul did so in order to honour the man upon whom the safety of the Republic rested, but also to witness the spectacle ('studium spectaculi'), as they wondered whether he would be able to defeat a rival of such magnitude as the Macedonian king and whether they would later witness another procession led by him in the form of a triumph moving towards the Capitol. Just as the description of the departure of Aemilius Paullus anticipates his victory, in the hesitation shown in Livy's account about Licinius Crassus the reader can see a veiled anticipation that the consul's action was not to be fully successful.

---

[36] See Sumi 2005: 35–41; Hölkeskamp 2006a: esp. 53–4; Hölkeskamp, forthcoming. Also, Rüpke 1990: 135–6. Feldherr (1998: 9–10) has a perfect grasp of the symbolism attached to the act: 'The spectacle of the consul's *profectio* provides a representation of the Republic in microcosm; the consul's progress takes him from the physical and religious center of the city, the Capitolium, where he has just attempted through his prayers to engage the power of the gods on the state's behalf, to its periphery and the distant battlefield, where, if he has been successful, that power will manifest itself in Roman victory . . . The citizens' glimpse of the consul provides their link to the totality of the state, the *summa res publica*, that he is entrusted to defend.'

[37] Var. *L.* 7.37. Cf. Liv. 36.3.14; 37.4.2; 41.17.6.   [38] Liv. 44.22.17.

[39] Liv. 42.49.1–10. Cf. Sumi 2005: 35.

There was a symbolic significance to the location of the beginning of the procession. It started at the point where the parade of the two consuls had finished on the day of their taking office, the temple of Jupiter, the same point to which the consul who was now leaving Rome was expected to return, should he be successful, to celebrate the triumph, which would finally close the circle. The act implicitly recalled the departure from the city of so many consuls who had previously returned triumphantly, and was a reminder for the spectators of Rome's historical grandeur.[40]

Mommsen stated that the *profectio consularis* ended at the *pomerium* of the *Urbs*, the sacred boundary of the city, the point at which, after crossing it, the civil magistrate became a military commander in accordance with the geographic differentiation that Mommsen made between *imperium domi* and *imperium militiae* (see the Introduction).[41] Most scholars agree with Mommsen that the *pomerium* differentiated between the civilian world inside and the military world outside the city.[42] Arguing against this opinion, Giovannini pointed out that the preserved texts never mention the *pomerium* as a relevant point in the transformation of the consul as a civil magistrate into a military commander.[43] In his opinion, the *pomerium* did not have any role in the ceremony. The key point is that the consul would have received the order or authorization from the senate to go to his province and that would be expressed technically as *paludatus exire*, implying in practice the symbolic change from the toga into the military cloak.[44]

Within the context of the debate resulting from the triumph awarded to Aemilius Paullus in 167, Livy describes how both the consuls and the praetors pronounced their vows on the Capitol before leaving Rome, just as when they returned after a victory they immediately went to the Capitol to thank the gods who had helped them achieve their objectives.[45] The solemn pronouncement of vows on the Capitol (*nuncupatio votorum*) was

---

[40] Feldherr 1998: 10 and 12.

[41] Mommsen 1887–8: I 63–4: 'Der zur Übernahme des Comandos aus der Stadt abziehende Magistrat überschreitet diese Grenze unter feierlichen Formen. Nachdem für diesen Act besondere Auspicien auf dem Capitol eingeholt sind und der Feldherr den höchsten besten Gott, dem er hofft dereinst den Siegeslorbeer darzubringen, die üblichen Kriegsgelübde geleistet hat, blasen die Hörner zum Abmarsch; der Feldherr so wie seine Lictoren legen das Kriegskleid (*paludamentum*) an und die Freunde und die Menge geben ihm das Geleit bis über die Stadtgrenze, das Pomerium. Fortan ist der Magistrat Feldherr.'

[42] See for instance Rüpke 1990: 29–41; Liou-Gille 1993. For his part, Drogula (2007: 435–42) thinks that the consuls within the *pomerium* only possessed *potestas*, and they needed to take up *imperium* beyond the *pomerium* to obtain a province and command a military force.

[43] Giovannini 1983: 16–17.   [44] Giovannini 1983: 18–19. Liv. 40.26.6. Cf. Liv. 41.5.6–8; 42.27.6–8.

[45] Liv. 45.39.11. When describing the events of the year 174, Livy highlights once again the fact that the *nuncupatio votorum* was compulsory for the consuls before leaving for their provinces (Liv. 41.27.3).

absolutely essential, like the taking of auspices by the consul on the morning of his departure and other religious rituals already mentioned in which the consuls had to take part as keepers of the peace of the gods. In 177, according to Livy, the consul C. Claudius Pulcher left Rome at night without pronouncing his vows on the Capitol, in order to reach his province as soon as possible.[46] Upon his arrival in Histria, the two promagistrates who were commanding the troops, M. Iunius Brutus and A. Manlius Vulso, refused to accept his authority, arguing that the consul had not departed appropriately. These were clearly sufficiently compelling arguments, since Claudius had to return to Rome and, although he delivered a speech against Iunius and Manlius in a *contio* in the city, he left the *Urbs* again only once he had pronounced the vows on the Capitol.[47]

Usually the two consuls remained in their provinces until the end of their term of office, especially when Roman expansion took place outside Italy and the consuls had to wait for their replacements to take over command. But there were cases when an earlier return to the *Urbs* was possible. In the consular year 293/2, due to the intense cold and the snow that covered Samnium, the consul L. Papirius Cursor decided to leave the region and return to Rome. There, he was awarded a triumph, which he celebrated while still a consul ('in magistratu').[48] In 175/4, the consul M. Aemilius Lepidus was in charge of suppressing a revolt in Patavium. Once the city had been pacified, since he had no other urgent matters to deal with in his province, he returned to Rome, no doubt long before the end of the consular year.[49]

As we have seen, the norm was for one of the consuls to return to Rome by order of the senate at the end of the consular year in order to preside over the elections. In general, the consul in question returned to his province after holding the elections to resume command of his troops. At times, a consul may have been awarded a triumph before the end of his term of office and celebrated the triumphal parade while still a consul, no doubt a glorious ending to the consular year. Besides the aforementioned Papirius Cursor in 292, in 196, 195, and 190, C. Cornelius Cethegus,[50] M. Claudius

---

[46] Liv. 41.10.5: 'C. Claudius consul veritus, ne forte eae res provinciam <et> exercitum sibi adimerent, non votis nuncupatis, non paludatis lictoribus, uno omnium certiore facto collega, nocte profectus, praeceps in provinciam abiit.' Cf. Sumi 2005: 279–80 n. 90.

[47] Liv. 41.10.7; 41.10.12–13. Cf. Drogula 2007: 436: 'Claudius was rebuffed because, having neglected the necessary rituals when leaving the *pomerium*, he lacked *imperium* altogether: he had not possessed it in Rome, and he failed to take it up when leaving the city.' Likewise, Flaminius in the year 217 could not be legally considered as a consul because he had not fulfilled his compulsory religious duties, amongst them the taking of auspices and the *nuncupatio votorum*, before leaving Rome (Liv. 21.63.7–9).

[48] Liv. 10.46.1–2.   [49] Liv. 41.27.4.   [50] Liv. 33.23.4.

Marcellus,[51] and Scipio Nasica[52] respectively celebrated their triumphs before the end of the consular year. In 178, the consul Q. Fulvius Flaccus celebrated his triumph just before presiding over the elections for the higher magistracies, which was the reason why he had returned to Rome, therefore also within his consular year.[53]

All the above serves as a summary of what were, or could have been, the civil functions of consuls which had to be completed in the consular year during the pre-Sullan period. Livy's account allows us to reconstruct the consular functions as a whole, both regular and extraordinary, but very seldom does he provide detailed and comprehensive information for a specific year. However, the consular year 190/89 is something of an exception, because it yields a clearer picture of what the *officium consulare* usually consisted of in the period prior to Sulla's dictatorship.

The consuls L. Cornelius Scipio Asiaticus and C. Laelius took office on 15 March 190, after performing the religious rituals attached to the assumption of the consulship: taking of auspices and vows on the Capitol.[54] Livy does not mention the debate 'on the state of the community' (*de republica et de provinciis*) that would normally mark the beginning of the political year in Rome. That year, what was considered the most urgent question to be dealt with in the first meeting of the senate was the issue of the Aetolians, whose envoys had been in Rome for some time waiting for the new consuls to take office. The debate in the senate, with the participation of the Aetolian envoys, the senators, and, obviously, the new consuls, went on for a number of days. Finally the ambassadors were given an answer, and they were ordered to leave Rome and Italy.[55] As heads of diplomacy for the Roman state, it was the consuls who, no doubt, had to act as intermediaries during the whole process and were ultimately responsible for communicating the final decision to the Aetolians. Afterwards, the generally delicate question of the allocation of provinces was discussed in the senate. The two consuls were both striving to have Greece as their province. The allocation did not come from a mutual agreement or the drawing of lots, but was left in the hands of the senate. After a debate, Greece was allotted to Scipio and Italy to Laelius.[56] As a complement to this decision, the senate decreed the number of soldiers who were to be in each of the consuls' armies.[57]

In Livy's account, the next consular task of the year was the expiation of the prodigies which had occurred in the previous months and been

[51] Liv. 33.37.10.   [52] Liv. 36.40.10.   [53] Liv. 40.59.4.   [54] Liv. 37.1.1.   [55] Liv. 37.2-6.
[56] Liv. 37.1.7–10.   [57] Liv. 37.2.2–4.

acknowledged as such by the senate. The consuls conducted the appropriate sacrifices following the instructions of the pontiffs.[58] The other religious ceremony that had to be presided over by the consuls in the first part of the consular year, the *feriae Latinae*, had unusually to be celebrated twice, because the ritual had not been conducted appropriately the first time.[59]

Forty-three Aetolians guarded by two cohorts arrived in Rome either during the celebration of the Latin festival or afterwards, as well as the ambassadors of the Egyptian sovereigns Ptolemy and Cleopatra. In both cases the consuls must have been responsible for dealing with them. Scipio Asiaticus ordered the cohorts to return to Greece and the Aetolian notable citizens to be taken to Lautumiae, the quarry that was used as a prison.[60] In contrast, the Egyptian envoys were welcomed and entertained at the senate, where they were, without a doubt, introduced by the consuls as was the norm when they were present in the *Urbs*.

Once all these duties had been fulfilled, including the levy of the new troops, Scipio Asiaticus issued an edict, which was announced in a *contio*, whereby he summoned his soldiers to gather on the Ides of July in Brundisium, in order to embark for Greece.[61] He appointed his legates and left Rome wearing the *paludamentum*.[62] This took place while the *ludi Apollinares* were being celebrated, coinciding with a lunar eclipse reported by Livy. We know that the eclipse happened on 14 March of the astronomical year, which corresponded to 11 July 190 in the official calendar. Scipio had therefore needed almost four months to deal with all the civil tasks that he had been entrusted with that year. He set off for his province in the middle of the summer according to the calendar, but it was actually at the beginning of the astronomical spring, with sufficient time to tackle significant military operations in Greece, which he eventually did.

During his stay in his province, Scipio not only directed military operations but also undertook considerable diplomatic activity on behalf of the Roman state. Amongst other actions, Livy narrates how Athenian envoys went to see the consul to plead with him for the Aetolians and they finally obtained an armistice from Scipio.[63] It was pointed out to Antiochus that a peace treaty could not be signed without the express consent of the consul and that therefore the question could not be discussed unless Scipio was present.[64] The consul wrote a letter to Prusias to give him his assurance of the continuity of Roman friendship.[65] King Eumenes met the consul on the Hellespont.[66] Later on, the consul granted a hearing to

---

[58] Liv. 37.3.1–3.   [59] Liv. 37.3.4.   [60] Liv. 37.3.8–11. Cf. Liv. 32.26.17.   [61] Liv. 37.4.1.
[62] Liv. 37.4.2.   [63] Liv. 37.6.4; 37.7.6–7.   [64] Liv. 37.19.2–6.   [65] Liv. 37.25.8.   [66] Liv. 37.26.3.

Heraclides of Byzantium, an ambassador sent by Antiochus to negotiate peace.[67] Envoys from various cities (Tralles, Magnesia, Ephesus, Sardis) came to surrender to Scipio after his victory in Magnesia.[68] The consul was eventually fully responsible for setting the conditions of the peace with Antiochus.[69]

While this was happening in Greece and Asia, the consul Laelius had stayed on in Italy. Since he had not taken part in any significant military actions, Livy obviously pays much less attention to him, and therefore little is known of his activity. Well into the consular year, when neither of the two consuls was in Rome, a delegation from the colonies of Placentia and Cremona arrived in the city to complain about the lack of men in their respective cities. In the absence of the consuls, they were introduced in the senate by the urban praetor Aurunculeius.[70] The senators resolved that the consul Laelius should be in charge of enlisting 6,000 families to live in these colonies. The urban praetor was to appoint the triumvirs who had to conduct the distribution of land.[71] Laelius returned from Gaul to preside over the consular elections.[72] During his stay in the city at the end of the consular year, he not only enlisted new colonists for Placentia and Cremona, but also proposed the foundation of two new colonies on the territory of the Boii, a proposal which was accepted by the senate.[73] When news arrived that the Roman army had won the naval battle of Myonnesus, thanksgivings were ordered, and Laelius received instructions from the senate to sacrifice twenty-two victims per day.[74] Livy finishes the narration of the consular year 190/89 with the confrontation caused by the consular elections which were presided over by Laelius and with the names of the higher magistrates elected.[75]

The consular year 190/89 may be considered as a typical year in terms of the tasks undertaken by the two consuls. As was usual throughout the pre-Sullan period, the consuls spent most of their term of office away from Rome, commanding their respective armies in their provinces. While one of them was dealing with Greece and Asia, the other remained in Italy. This combination was normal during the second century, so that one of the consuls was not too far from Rome and could return in case of an emergency and, in any case, was available to go to the city to preside over the elections at the end of the consular year. The two consuls dealt jointly with religious and diplomatic duties in Rome at the beginning of the year and conducted the levy separately. Scipio was also very active during the

---

[67] Liv. 37.34.8. [68] Liv. 37.44.7–45.1. [69] Liv. 37.45. [70] Liv. 37.46.9. [71] Liv. 37.46.10–11.
[72] Liv. 37.47.1. [73] Liv. 37.47.2. [74] Liv. 37.47.4–5. [75] Liv. 37.47.6–7.

war from a diplomatic point of view. Laelius, acting upon a senatorial decision but also on his own initiative, dealt with matters relating to colonization. The elections for higher magistracies presided over by Laelius were the last of the significant events that took place during that consular year.

PART II

The consular functions in the post-Sullan age (80–50)

CHAPTER 12

The supposed lex Cornelia de provinciis ordinandis *and the presence of consuls in Rome in the post-Sullan period*

The central question in the second and shorter part of this monograph is the same as in the first: to determine exactly what the consuls did during their term of office. In order to try to answer this question we must discuss, as an initial step, the supposed existence of a *lex Cornelia de provinciis ordinandis*, which presumably would have modified, from Sulla's dictatorship onwards, the powers and functions of consuls. It was Mommsen who put forward the doctrine which was accepted for decades and which continues to be the starting point of the analysis carried out by many scholars. According to Mommsen, who took as his starting point the distinction he drew between *imperium domi* as an exclusively civil power within the *Urbs*, and *imperium militiae* as a military power beyond the *pomerium*,[1] Sulla sponsored during his dictatorship a law on the government of provinces whereby the power to govern a province was removed from consuls and praetors and they were forced to remain in Rome. Only once their term of office had expired would they receive military command as proconsuls or propraetors in a province. Therefore, according to Mommsen, from Sulla onwards the consuls lost their military *imperium*, and there was a clear difference between the urban civil power and the extra-urban military power of higher magistrates.[2] This question is essential for the subject of this book, since it could be presumed that both the compulsory presence of the consuls in Rome and the fact that they were deprived of their military command may have meant a significant change in their functions in comparison with the pre-Sullan period.

---

[1] See the remarks of Giovannini 1983: 7–30.
[2] Mommsen's doctrine is expounded in many sections of his *Römisches Staatsrecht* (1887–8): I 57–9; II 94–5; II 214–15; III 1086–7; III 1104; etc. Of course, innumerable authors followed Mommsen, and it is both impossible and unnecessary to list all of them here. Amongst them: Meyer 1975: 118–20; De Martino 1990: I 415–17; Bleicken 1995: 177–8.

Some scholars pointed out the fact that ancient sources never mention the existence of a *lex Cornelia de provinciis ordinandis* as described by Mommsen and by the modern scholarship that follows him.[3] However, this argument is not sufficient to warrant the conclusion that the contents of the supposed law were also non-existent.[4] It was Balsdon who, in an article published in 1939, seriously questioned Mommsen's doctrine for the first time.[5] Balsdon proved that between 79 and 53 a large number of consuls set off for their provinces before the end of their term of office and only some of them remained in Rome throughout their entire consulship.[6] He concluded categorically: 'I do not see how anybody who is not blinded by a preconceived theory could maintain, in face of this evidence, that there was any legal or even conventional restraint on a consul's leaving Rome for his province before the expiry of his consular year.'[7]

But neither the evidence supplied by Balsdon nor the strength of his conclusions was enough for scholarship to rule out Mommsen's thesis. In 1956, Ernesto Valgiglio, beginning with the evidence provided by Balsdon which demonstrated the departure of the consuls for their provinces during their term office, deepened the criticism of Mommsen's view.[8] According to Valgiglio, Mommsen's thesis was a legal absurdity. Given that the Gracchan law of 123, whereby the consular provinces were determined

---

[3] Rotondi 1912: 353.

[4] Cobban (1935) is a good example of the contradiction between accepting the existence of a *lex Cornelia de provinciis ordinandis* while verifying in ancient sources that this supposed law was not usually observed. Cobban conceded that the law existed basically in the same terms as Mommsen: the magistrate exercised his *imperium* in Rome; the promagistrate, in the provinces. Despite being aware of the exceptions in its application, he concluded: 'The many exceptions do not affect the general application of this rule' (72). However, later on he stated: 'Although Sulla established the general rule that the magistrate should go to his province at the end of his year of office at Rome, he did not lay this down as a hard and fast regulation' (75). And he went on to conclude that Mommsen was wrong when claiming that Sulla abolished the military command of consuls and banned them from leaving Rome during their term of office. That is, Cobban started from an acceptance of the existence of the *lex Cornelia*, but in fact his arguments left the law with no content.

[5] Balsdon 1939. But Willems (1883: II 578–9) had already pointed out that some consuls had unquestionably left Rome during their consulship, which would go against the supposed *lex Cornelia*: 'La loi Cornélienne, a-t-elle étendu aux provinces consulaires l'innovation qu'elle introduisit pour les provinces prétoriennes, de telle sorte que désormais les deux consuls étaient obligés de rester à Rome pendant l'année de leur consulat, et qu'ils n'avaient le droit de se rendre dans leurs provinces qu'après leur sortie de charge, comme proconsuls? Nous ne le pensons pas. Dans les vingt années qui suivirent la loi Cornélienne, les exemples de consuls ... s'y rendant eux-mêmes pendant leur consulat, sont trop nombreux pour que nous puissions admettre que ce furent autant de dérogations à la loi.'

[6] Balsdon 1939: 61–3.   [7] Balsdon 1939: 63.

[8] Valgiglio 1956: esp. 132–40. See, however, the criticism expressed by Balsdon (1958: 69–70), who questioned Valgiglio's thesis about the presumed expansion of the *pomerium* throughout Italy and that consuls went to their provinces of their own accord. Balsdon pointed out that a consul always needed the express authorization of the senate, since without it he would not be *ornatus*, that is, he would have neither an army nor funds to pay for the expenses.

before the election of the consuls, was still in force, a consul was legally in control of a province from the moment he took over the magistracy, yet he was allegedly banned from ruling it on account of the *lex Cornelia*.[9] Consuls had always been, above all, the supreme commanders of the army. Depriving them of military command would have been a radical change to the tradition (*mos maiorum*), a drastic innovation that can hardly have been sponsored by a conservative like Sulla.[10] The conclusion reached by Valgiglio was that there was no such thing as a Sullan law separating the civil and military powers of consuls and, consequently, the consuls had military *imperium* from the very moment they took office, and they remained in Rome or went to their provinces depending on the prevailing circumstances of their consulship.[11]

Valgiglio's book had little influence, and, consequently, his arguments against Mommsen's theory fell into oblivion.[12] Over a quarter of a century had to elapse until Adalberto Giovannini published his fundamental monograph *Consulare imperium*, which finally dismantled Mommsen's thesis. Giovannini demonstrated that the supposed *lex Cornelia de provinciis ordinandis* had never existed.[13]

On the one hand, Giovannini studied in detail the relationship between the consuls and their provinces between 80 and 53, restating and extending what Balsdon and, paradoxically, even Mommsen had already expounded: many consuls set off for their provinces during their consulship.[14] Mommsen had opted to see these cases as mere exceptions to the *lex Cornelia*, but Giovannini demonstrated that what actually seems to have been exceptional was a compliance with the supposed law, since there is definite evidence for only a minority of consuls having remained in Rome during the entire consular year. On the other hand, despite the fact that this law had allegedly deprived consuls of their most important prerogative, military command, it is never mentioned by any ancient author. Contemporaries of the law like Cicero or Sallust do not talk about it, and neither do later historians like Appian, who notably mentions all the other institutional reforms carried out by Sulla.[15] However, two laws of great importance for the government of provinces, the *lex Sempronia de provinciis consularibus* and the *lex Pompeia de provinciis*, are

---

[9] Valgiglio 1956: 132.   [10] Valgiglio 1956: 133.   [11] Valgiglio 1956: 135–6.

[12] Very few scholars accepted the thesis that there was not a Sullan law forcing consuls to remain in Rome. Amongst them, we could mention Keaveney 1982: 172.

[13] Giovannini 1983: 73–101.   [14] Giovannini 1983: 83–91.

[15] Giovannini (1983: 77–83) refuted the meaning that Mommsen attributed to the sources that, according to him, demonstrated the existence of the *lex Cornelia* (Cic. *N.D.* 2.3.9; *Div.* 2.76; Vell. 2.31.1; Caes. *Civ.* 1.6), while highlighting two Ciceronian texts (Cic. *Att.* 8.15.3; *Prov.* 36–37) which clearly indicate that a consul had to have a province from the very moment of his taking office.

well known to ancient authors, who mention them in different contexts.[16]
Giovannini reached the logical conclusion: the *lex Cornelia* never existed and is
but a historiographic fiction whose fabrication goes back as far as the sixteenth
century, although it was Mommsen who, considering it as a fact, and therefore
deeming it unnecessary to prove its existence, made it unquestionable due to his
scholarly *auctoritas*.[17]

From these considerations, and bearing in mind what ancient sources do
state, Giovannini infers the following: as in the period before Sulla's dictatorship, the consuls were given a province from the very moment they took
office; the consuls took possession of their province during their consulship
and acting as consuls, once they had fulfilled their duties in Rome, as in the
past; they had to have the authorization of the senate to leave the *Urbs* and go
to their province, but they had authority over it from the beginning of their
term of office.[18] In short, Sulla's dictatorship did not mean a break, but rather
a continuation, of the power the consuls were invested with.

But Mommsen cast a long shadow, and it is difficult to uproot opinions
which have been repeated for decades. In the last twenty years several
scholars have ignored the arguments produced by Giovannini, generally
without even discussing them, and have continued to accept Mommsen's
thesis. In this sense, doubts about the historicity of the *lex Cornelia de
provinciis ordinandis* are accepted, but the idea is also defended that from
Sulla's dictatorship onwards a practice was introduced according to which
the consuls had to remain in Rome to deal exclusively with civil functions,
and that the following year they took on the military *imperium* as promagistrates in a province.[19] Therefore, Mommsen's thesis continues to survive
practically unaltered since its original formulation.

For this reason it is not surprising that another scholar, Klaus Girardet, has
recently felt compelled to resume the arguments presented by Balsdon,
Valgiglio and above all Giovannini, and to argue, once more, the non-
existence of the *lex Cornelia*. In his opinion, until the time of Augustus,
there was no legal change in the consular *imperium*, which included both the
imperium domi and the *summum imperium militiae*. What he calls the
'demilitarization' of the consulship only took place from Augustus onwards.[20]

---

[16] On the *lex Sempronia* Cic. *Prov.* 3; *Fam.* 1.7.10; *Balb.* 61; Sal. *Jug.* 27.3. On the *lex Pompeia* Cass. Dio
40.46.2; 40.56.1–2.
[17] Giovannini 1983: 97–101.   [18] Giovannini 1983: 90.
[19] See, amongst others, Hantos 1988: 89–120, esp. 108–9; 659 n. 381; Diehl 1988: 208; Kunkel and
Wittmann 1995: 18; Schulz 1997: 48–50.
[20] Girardet 2001: 155–61. Girardet (1990: 90) totally agrees with Giovannini's main thesis. See also
Girardet 1992. Girardet's theses have been explored further by Hurlet 2008.

Consequently, practically up to the present day, the debate on the existence of a *lex Cornelia de provinciis ordinandis* seems to persist or, at least, a discussion on the supposed practice according to which the consuls remained in Rome during the entire consular year after the dictatorship of Sulla. For my part, I believe it has been sufficiently proved that Mommsen's thesis is wrong, and it is not worth debating it once again. In this respect I refer readers to the book by Giovannini, whose thesis I substantially agree with.[21] In any event, the essential starting point for my study is to determine, as far as possible, the amount of time that consuls spent in Rome in the post-Sullan period and whether there were any rules regarding their presence in the *Urbs* or their departure for their provinces.

In this respect, the thorough study carried out by Giovannini for the period between 80 and 53 is also essential.[22] He reached the following conclusions. Of the fifty-six consuls between 80 and 53, one of them died at the beginning of his term of office: L. Caecilius Metellus in the year 68.[23] For twenty-one of them we do not know for certain whether they received a province or when they took command over it. Another twenty-one of them left for their provinces during their consulship. Two of them exercised their authority over their provinces through legates (C. Calpurnius Piso in 67 and Pompey in 55). Ten consuls did not govern any province, either during their consulship or afterwards, in most cases because they themselves renounced the task. This means that they remained in Rome during their entire consulship. Finally, only one consul strictly complied with the norm set by Mommsen. This was Caesar, consul in 59 and proconsul from the beginning of 58.[24]

The data supplied by Giovannini can be completed with data for 52–50. The year 52 was completely exceptional, with Pompey as sole consul (*consul sine collega*) and Q. Caecilius Metellus Pius Scipio Nasica as second consul only in the last five months of the year. Pompey combined his consulship

---

[21] To this debate we could add the recent contribution of Drogula 2007, already mentioned in the Introduction. Drogula in his article does not tackle the possible existence of a *lex Cornelia de provinciis ordinandis*, nor does he specifically deal with the consular *imperium* in the first century. But from his thesis it should necessarily be deduced that all those consuls who in the post-Sullan period remained in the city during their entire consulship, without going to a province, never had *imperium*, but exclusively *potestas*, except for those who had exceptionally been granted *imperium* within the *pomerium* to face an extraordinary situation in the context of the enactment of the *senatus consultum ultimum*, as would have been the case of Cicero against the plot of Catiline.

[22] Giovannini 1983: 83–90.

[23] Metellus died at the beginning of the year. Servilius Vatia was elected suffect consul, but he also died, so the other consul, Q. Marcius Rex, was left to govern on his own for the rest of the year (Cass. Dio 36.4.1).

[24] Giovannini 1983: 89–90. See also the conclusions of Balsdon (1939: 63), to a great extent similar to Giovannini's.

with his office as proconsul in the two Iberian provinces, Hispania Citerior and Ulterior, where two legates were respectively in charge of government on his behalf. Metellus remained in Rome and did not go to any province the following year. During 51 and 50 the debate about Caesarian command dominated Rome's politics. The consuls for those two years remained in Rome during their consulship.

As opposed to the homogeneity of previous centuries, it is striking that in the post-Sullan period the consuls' activities are quite varied. Some consuls had to take over military command during their consulship as a matter of urgency. That was the case in the year 63 for C. Antonius. Initially he had been allotted Cisalpine Gaul as his province, but he exchanged it with Cicero, who had been given Macedonia. But in November, amidst the crisis caused by the plot of Catiline, the senate gave Antonius military command against the rebels in Etruria, where he went immediately.[25] In 78, the revolt that broke out in the Etruscan city of Faesulae prompted the senate to send the two consuls commanding their legions to Etruria.[26] On that occasion this also involved a change in the province that had been originally allotted to the consuls, since Lepidus had been given Transalpine Gaul.[27] In 72, the two consuls, L. Gellius Publicola and Cn. Cornelius Lentulus, fought Spartacus and were defeated, first separately, then jointly. For that reason by order of the senate they were relieved of their command, which was given instead to Crassus.[28]

These three examples clearly show that the consuls continued to be the supreme commanders of the Roman army and that the senate would resort to them in the first place in case of a problem that required immediate military intervention. It is particularly remarkable that in 78 Lepidus was sent despite the fact that by then he had already shown his wish to introduce reforms, which had triggered his confrontation with the senate. But Lepidus was consul and therefore the principal individual in charge of keeping public peace in Italy.[29] Military accountability of consuls in situations of

---

[25] Cic. *Mur.* 84.   [26] Sal. *Hist.* 1.66 = 1.58 McGushin (vol. 1 128–9).   [27] App. *B.Civ.* 1.107.

[28] App. *B.Civ.* 1.117; Liv. *per.* 96; Plut. *Crass.* 9.7–10.1. The consuls were relieved of the command of the legions for having been ignominiously defeated by the slaves, but this does not mean that their *imperium* was abrogated or that they were forced to resign. They continued to be consuls, but from then until the end of their term of office they must have remained in Rome. In fact, in November 72, they intervened in the senate and proposed that no provincials could be tried in their absence, clearly in connection with the issue of the Sicilian Sthenius (Cic. *Ver.* 2.2.95). With respect to the military command of the two consuls and their replacement with Crassus see Shatzman 1968: 347–50; Rubinsohn 1970; Marshall 1973: 118–19; 1976a: 26; Ward 1977: 83.

[29] Gruen 1974: 14. However, Labruna (1975: 48) argues that sending the two consuls jointly to Etruria was a compromise solution found by the senators, who did not trust Lepidus to be sent on his own in command of the legions or to be left alone in Rome in charge of the matters of the *res publica*.

emergency was obviously not only limited to Italy, but applied to the entire empire.[30] In 74, L. Licinius Lucullus exchanged the province that had initially been allotted to him for the command in Asia in the war against Mithridates, which had just broken out again, and possibly the same happened to his colleague M. Aurelius Cotta.

Apart from these exceptional cases which were due to the urgency of the situation, we know with certainty, or can consider highly probable, that during their consulship a large number of consuls departed for the provinces that had been assigned to them. It is possible that the consul Metellus Pius went to Hispania in 80, leaving Sulla as the sole consul in Rome for part of that year.[31] In 79, the consuls P. Servilius Vatia and Ap. Claudius Pulcher set off for their respective provinces, Cilicia and Macedonia, before their term of office had expired, although their exact date of departure is unknown.[32] Some years later, the consul C. Scribonius Curio suppressed a riot near Dyrrachium. When discussing this event, Frontinus calls him consul, which means that in all probability the episode took place in 76, while Curio was still a consul.[33] The following year, the consul C. Aurelius Cotta left for Gaul during his consulship, temporarily leaving Hortensius as the only great orator present in Rome, since at the time Cicero was in Sicily as a quaestor.[34] In 74, Lucullus had received Cisalpine Gaul in the allotment of provinces at the beginning of the year.[35] However, Lucullus wanted to be in command of the war against Mithridates, which was considered inevitable

---

[30] Besides the aforementioned, another possible case of an urgent allocation of consular provinces has been discussed. In March 60 the senate, showing concern about the unstable situation in Gaul, urged the two consuls to conduct the sortition of Cisalpine and Transalpine Gaul as soon as possible (Cic. *Att.* 1.19.2). Both Balsdon (1939: 62) and Broughton (1948: 73–6 (also Shackleton Bailey 1965–70: 1 334)) think that there was a special decree of the senate that modified the previously decreed consular provinces following the *lex Sempronia*, given the new situation of emergency. However, Giovannini (1983: 87 n. 37) argues that Cicero does not mention a *senatus consultum* and that it would be the usual drawing of lots that had to be done every year between the two consuls. In his opinion, the situation in Gaul in 61 could already have been alarming enough for Cisalpine and Transalpine Gaul to be designated as the consular provinces. In any event, the emergency situation did not last long. In particular, in June Q. Caecilius Metellus Celer opposed the bill of the tribune Flavius, who threatened to veto his departure for his province. Metellus Celer replied that he did not mind that possible veto, and Cicero hints that the consul lost all interest in his province once he saw that he could not have a glorious triumph, since the territory had already been pacified (Cass. Dio 37.50.4; Cic. *Att.* 1.20.5). At the beginning of 59 Metellus Celer opposed Caesar's agrarian law and died in his house on the Palatine at the beginning of April that year (Cic. *Cael.* 59), which indicates that he never went to his province. We know nothing about the actions of his colleague L. Afranius.

[31] This is how both Cobban (1935: 75) and Giovannini (1983: 83) interpret the text in App. *B.Civ.* 1.97.

[32] Sal. *Hist.* 1.127 M = 1.115 McGushin (vol. 1 181). Cf. Giovannini 1983: 84.

[33] Fron. *Str.* 4.1.43. Cf. Giovannini 1983: 84. *Contra* Balsdon 1939: 61.

[34] Cic. *Brut.* 318. Cotta's departure might have taken place when there were still a few months until the end of the consular year. Cf. Giovannini 1983: 80 and 85.

[35] Plut. *Luc.* 5.2.

in the short term. The death of the proconsul L. Octavius in Cilicia in the first few months of the year gave him the chance to manoeuvre to take command in Cilicia and in Asia.[36] Once he achieved this end, he left for the eastern Mediterranean, while still a consul.[37] His colleague M. Cotta went to Bithynia, also during his consulship, after receiving command of a fleet.[38] In 73, the consul M. Terentius Varro Lucullus was probably already in his province, Macedonia, before his consulship was over.[39]

In the decade of the sixties the situation did not vary substantially. In 69, Q. Hortensius Hortalus renounced the province that had been allotted to him, Crete, and it was then given to his colleague, Q. Caecilius Metellus.[40] The situation in Crete was very tense. In 70 an armed conflict already seemed likely to break out on the island, and it is even possible that Crete was decreed as one of the consular provinces for 69, in compliance with the *lex Sempronia*.[41] The response from the Cretans was to send an embassy to Rome with the purpose of reaffirming their friendly relations with the Roman state. The ambassadors must have been received in the senate at the beginning of the year 69. Initially, the senate voted in favour of confirming the friendship with the Cretans, but P. Cornelius Lentulus Spinther vetoed this.[42] Rome then sent an ultimatum that required the handing over of hostages and the payment of indemnity. The Cretans did not reply, and the senate declared war. Metellus led the legions who fought in Crete, where he remained until 66. Data provided by ancient sources do not specify the moment when Metellus left for his province, which may have been either at the end of 69 or the beginning of 68.[43] We have no further information regarding the actions of Metellus in Rome during his consulship. However, if the Cretan ambassadors were received at the beginning of the year and it was then that Lentulus Spinther vetoed the

---

[36] Plut. *Luc.* 6. Rosenstein 1995: 55; Vervaet 2006: 639–40.

[37] Cf. Cic. *Mur.* 33; *Flac.* 85. See on the debated question of when the Third Mithridatic War started and, consequently, when Lucullus went to the East, Broughton 1951–86: II 106–8; Ooteghem 1959: 55–7; Keaveney 1992: 188–205. All of them agree that Lucullus was already in the East during his consulship. See also Balsdon 1939: 61. However, McGing (1984: 12–18) argued that the war started in the spring of 73, and that Lucullus and Cotta were sent to the East at the end of 74, but only to prepare for war, without starting hostilities. Nevertheless, in this case also the consuls seem to have left Rome before the end of their consular year.

[38] Keaveney 1992: 72.

[39] According to Giovannini (1983: 85) the text in Cic. *Ver.* 2.2.24 ('Lucullus, qui tum in Macedonia fuit') would prove this. Cicero refers to Dio's sentence by Verres, which may have taken place during the consulship of Varro Lucullus. *Contra* Balsdon 1939: 61.

[40] Cic. *Ver.* 2.3.222; Cass. Dio 36.1a; Plut. *Pomp.* 29.2.   [41] Morstein Kallet-Marx 1995: 309.

[42] Morstein Kallet-Marx 1995: 310: Lentulus Spinther was probably a tribune of the plebs in 69.

[43] Giovannini (1983: 86) does not express an opinion in this respect. For his part, Morstein Kallet-Marx (1995: 311) thinks that Metellus started military operations in Crete at the beginning of 68.

decision of the senate, the ultimatum must have been made simultaneously or soon afterwards. The senate no doubt allowed some time for the envoys to return to their homeland and for the Cretans to make a decision before declaring war. The declaration of war sparked by the Cretan silence may plausibly have happened in the second half of the year. If the matter was seen as urgent, and there is no doubt that a declaration of war was a matter of importance, Metellus' departure could have occurred in autumn, while he was still a consul.

In the ensuing two years, the conflict against Mithridates continued to be the key point in Rome's external politics and brought about the appointment of new generals to command the troops. In 68 Q. Marcius Rex, the sole consul in office after the successive deaths of L. Metellus and of the suffect consul, was given command of the war against Mithridates instead of Lucullus. According to Cassius Dio, Marcius Rex left for the East during his consulship.[44] The text of Cassius Dio does not provide a specific date. But the fact that Marcius Rex was the only consul suggests that he must have spent practically the entire year in Rome and that possibly only towards the end of the year could he have left the *Urbs*. The following year, M'. Acilius Glabrio received through a *lex Gabinia* the command in Bithynia and Pontus, also replacing Lucullus. Once more, Cassius Dio states that he took over the government of his provinces during his consulship, without providing a specific date.[45] Throughout 67, the other consul, C. Calpurnius Piso, was extraordinarily conspicuous in Rome's political scene, opposing the proposals of the tribunes Cornelius and Gabinius. Piso was also in charge of presiding over the elections. In all those activities, in particular during the harsh confrontation against Cornelius, the sources speak exclusively about Piso as the protagonist. The conflict between Piso and Cornelius took place around the date when elections had to be held, therefore in the summer. The lack of a mention of Glabrio suggests that perhaps the consul left for the East at a relatively early stage and that he spent a good part of the year away from Rome. In fact, by the beginning of 66 it was known in Rome that Glabrio had not made any substantial advance in his military operations, a circumstance which opened an excellent chance to turn Pompey, once more, into a saviour. In that context, the tribune Manilius sponsored his law to give command of the war against Mithridates to Pompey.[46]

---

[44] Cass. Dio, 36.2.2. Cf. Ooteghem 1959: 140 and 153; Giovannini 1983: 86; Keaveney 1992: 115.
[45] Cass. Dio, 36.14.4. Balsdon 1939: 61–2; Giovannini 1983: 86.
[46] On Glabrio's military incompetence cf. Cic. *Man.* 5. Cf. Keaveney 1992: 120–2.

In the second half of the decade of the sixties, apart from the aforementioned command of Antonius against the Catilinarians in the year 63, we have no definite information about consuls leaving for their provinces during their consulship and practically no information regarding the consular provinces in those years.[47]

With regard to the fifties, in 58 the consuls L. Calpurnius Piso Caesoninus and A. Gabinius respectively received, thanks to a *lex Clodia*, the provinces of Macedonia and Syria. Both of them left for their provinces wearing the military cloak, the *paludamentum*, before the end of their consulship.[48] At the beginning of the following year the consular provinces had already been *ornatae*, that is, they had been given appropriate funding and troops by the senate.[49] The two consuls, Lentulus Spinther and Metellus Nepos, were active throughout the year with regard to the return of Cicero and the passing of the law that put Pompey in charge of the supply of grain to Rome, amongst other matters. In the last few months of the year, a debate arose regarding the appropriateness of delaying the elections until Clodius, a candidate for the aedileship, was tried. In a letter sent to his brother Quintus, Cicero describes the senate session in which this matter was dealt with at the beginning of December.[50] In his letter, Cicero lists the most conspicuous of those present, amongst whom he mentions some consulars, the consuls elect and some praetorians, but not the consuls of 57. This has led to the supposition that they had already left Rome, since it would be unlikely that, had they been present in the city, they would not have attended the session of the senate, or, had they attended, that Cicero would not have mentioned them.[51] According to Plutarch, Metellus Nepos attended the conference at Luca in April 56.[52] If Plutarch is right, did

---

[47] In 61, Cicero boasted of having snatched away the province of Syria from the consul M. Pupius Piso, to whom it had been alloted (Cic. *Att.* 1.16.8). Apparently, Syria had been designated as a consular province according to the *lex Sempronia*, but Cicero had managed to turn it into a praetorian province, a status that continued to apply to this territory until 58. We do not know which other province may have been given in exchange to Pupius Piso. Cf. Giovannini 1983: 87. However, in his comment on the Ciceronian text Shackleton Bailey (1965–70: 1 318) considers it unlikely that Syria was a consular province in 60, since it was ruled by the *praetorius* L. Marcius Philippus. Perhaps there was a proposal, either by a tribune of the plebs, or by the senate, to change the distribution of provinces and give Syria to Pupius Piso, but the proposal was not accepted.

[48] Cic. *Pis.* 13. Cf. Giovannini 1983: 88.   [49] Cic. *Att.* 3.24.2.

[50] Cic. *Q.fr.* 2.1.1: 'senatus fuit frequentior quam putabamus esse posse mense Decembri sub dies festos. consulares nos fuimus et duo consules designati, P. Servilius, M. Lucullus, Lepidus, Volcacius, Glabrio...'

[51] Balsdon 1939: 62; Giovannini 1983: 88. The consuls were certainly in Rome at the beginning of October, since they were in charge of the contract for the work to rebuild the *porticus Catuli*, which took place immediately after the senate decreed on 2 October that Cicero's house on the Palatine be returned to him (Cic. *Att.* 4.2.5).

[52] Plut. *Caes.* 21.2. Gruen 1969b: 97.

Metellus Nepos go to Luca, travelling from his province of Hispania Citerior? This would involve accepting that he temporarily abandoned the province that he was ruling as proconsul. Or did he travel from Rome? This would mean that he had not yet left the *Urbs* and therefore an alternative explanation should be given for his absence from the session of the senate in December. On the other hand, Stein highlighted a text of Fenestella which records the presence of the consul Lentulus Spinther in Rome on 10 December 57, when, as was usual, the new tribunes of the plebs took office.[53] Stein suggested that the absence of the consuls in the aforementioned senate session may have been due to their preparations for setting off for their provinces. For this reason or some other, the fact is that there is cause to doubt that the consuls had actually left for their provinces before the end of 57.

In the year 55, the *lex Trebonia* granted to the consul Pompey the government of Spain for five years and, to Crassus, Syria for the same period of time. But while Pompey preferred to remain in Rome and send his legates to Hispania, Crassus left for Syria before the expiry of his consulship, despite bad omens and the opposition of some tribunes of the plebs.

Finally, in 54, two letters by Cicero written to Atticus and to his brother indicate that the consul Ap. Claudius Pulcher was prepared to leave for his province in Cilicia, even without the support of a *lex curiata*, and to bear the expenses himself.[54] The letters are dated to the second half of October. We know that Ap. Claudius actually served as governor in Cilicia until he was replaced by Cicero in the year 51, but we do not know exactly when he left for his province. If he left during his consulship, it must have been in November or December 54, since in October he must still have been in the *Urbs*. Related to this question is an inscription indicating that Ap. Claudius pronounced a vow to rebuild the propylon of the sanctuary of Eleusis.[55] The inscription states that Ap. Claudius made his vow as consul, and the work presumably started while he was an *imperator* ('co(n)s(ul) vovit [im]perato [r coepit . . .]'). Thus, we may suppose that Claudius made his *votum* when, still a consul, he visited Eleusis on his way to Cilicia. This would place his pledge in November or December 54 and would indirectly prove that Claudius did leave Rome during his consulship.

---

[53] Fenestella *ap*. Non. 615 L (fr. 21 Peter): 'itaque ut magistratum tribuni inierunt, C. Cato . . . contionibus adsiduis invidiam et Ptolemaeo . . . et Publio Lentulo consuli, paranti iam iter, cogitare secundo quidem populi rumore coepit.' Stein 1930: 37 n. 198. Cf. Millar 1998: 159.

[54] Cic. *Att*. 4.18.4; *Q.fr*. 3.2.3. Cf. Cic. *Fam*. 1.9.25. See Giovannini 1983: 89; Rosenstein 1995: 52; Drogula 2007: 436–7. On the *lex curiata* see Brennan 2000: 18–20.

[55] *CIL* I^2 775 = III 547 = *ILS* 4041 = *ILLRP* 401.

In the ensuing years, the strained atmosphere in Rome led to changes in the institutional patterns that had regularly applied until then. The consuls of 53 could only take office in July of that year, and nothing is known about their provinces. In 52 the violent episodes that followed the murder of Clodius took place and led to the appointment of Pompey as sole consul, and in the next two years the debate about Caesar's command dominated the political scene. All the consuls of these years remained in Rome during their consulship.

In most cases it is complicated to establish the exact time in the consular year when the consuls left Rome for their provinces. In the case of an emergency, it is obvious that the departure took place immediately, once the corresponding consuls had been allotted a specific province. In other cases, it depended on the particular circumstances at the time, although it has already been pointed out that the departure of the consuls must have happened towards the final part of the year. Besides all the examples already examined, there are other cases for which a possible or likely date of departure from Rome can be established.

If the Third Mithridatic War did indeed break out in 74, as most scholars accept, it is obvious that the consuls Lucullus and Cotta were already fighting in the eastern Mediterranean by the second half of that year. According to Keaveney, Lucullus may have left Rome towards the middle of the August of 74.[56] Lucullus was still in Rome when the senate issued a *senatus consultum* to investigate the allegations of corruption against the tribunal of Iunius.[57] The decree was also addressed to the consuls-elect for the year 73. That means that the elections had already been held, which places it in July–August.[58] Lucullus disregarded a senatorial order concerning a lesser matter that could only delay his departure and preferred to set off for the East. On the other hand, the decree was addressed exclusively to Lucullus, and not to his colleague Cotta, which means that the latter must have left before Lucullus, probably as soon as he received the command of the fleet in Bithynia. If Lucullus had to wait a little longer, it must have been precisely because he had to preside over the elections and also perhaps because he had to recruit a new legion before going to war.[59] Nevertheless,

---

[56] Keaveney 1992: 74 and 188–9. Ooteghem (1959: 60–1) places the departure of Lucullus possibly in September.

[57] Cic. *Clu.* 137.

[58] Sherwin-White (1984: 165) dated the senatorial decree to November 74, so the arrival of Lucullus in the eastern Mediterranean may not have happened until the first few months of 73. However, Keaveney (1992: 189) dismantled with compelling arguments the thesis of Sherwin-White.

[59] Keaveney 1992: 72.

Lucullus may have reached Ephesus, and from there Phrygia, by the beginning of autumn 74, in time to liberate Cyzicus, which was under siege by Mithridates, and afterwards to go to the aid of the defeated Cotta.[60]

The following year it is probable that Varro Lucullus was already in Macedonia while he was still a consul. If this were the case, the date of his departure must be placed in November or December 73, since both he and his colleague C. Cassius Longinus were in Rome on 16 October, as shown by the *senatus consultum de Oropiis*, by which the consuls declared themselves in favour of the inhabitants of the Boeotian town of Oropus in their litigation against the publicans.[61]

In 58 it is certain that the two consuls, Piso and Gabinius, left for their respective provinces in the second half of the year, at any rate before 10 December. This information is provided by Cicero. In his speech in favour of Sestius, he specifically places the departure of the two consuls wearing the military uniform before the taking of office by the tribunes of the plebs, which happened, as is well known, on 10 December every year.[62] Therefore, the consuls left Rome at some point between the elections and the taking of office by the tribunes, probably in autumn.[63]

The consul Crassus left for Syria, his province, in the first half of November 55, probably around the Ides of that month. We know this because of a letter sent by Cicero to his friend Atticus.[64] The letter was written between 14 and 17 November,[65] and in it Cicero claims that Crassus had left Rome wearing the *paludamentum*. Obviously, the departure of Crassus had taken place just before the letter was written, and Cicero records it as a piece of news that could be of particular interest to Atticus.

As can be observed, available data are not sufficiently conclusive to determine whether there was a pre-established rule on the date or time of the year when the consuls had to leave Rome to go to their provinces. Balsdon, following a suggestion made previously by Stevens, suggested that in the post-Sullan period there may have been two significant dates for provincial government: the Calends of March and the Ides of November.[66] In his opinion, 1 March would be the date when the consular provinces were designated for the following year, once the foreign embassies had been

[60] Broughton 1951–86: II 107; Giovannini 1983: 85. It should be pointed out that this was the first time for the two consuls of one year both to be given command in Asia Minor, which shows a determined movement of strategic interests towards the East. Cf. Sherwin-White 1984: 163.

[61] Cf. Sherk 1969: 133–8; 1984: 85–7.   [62] Cic. *Sest.* 71–2.

[63] Grimal (1967: 156) places the departure of Piso and Gabinius from Rome for their provinces exactly on 24 November 58. Cf. Balsdon 1939: 62; Giovannini 1983: 88.

[64] Cic. *Att.* 4.13.2. Cf. Balsdon 1939: 62; Broughton 1951–86: II 215; Giovannini 1983: 89.

[65] Shackleton Bailey 1965–70: II 104–5.   [66] Stevens 1938: 181–3; 200–2; Balsdon 1939: 65–8.

received by the senate during February and the external political situation had been analysed in depth.[67] November 13 would be the date by which the consuls were free from their civil tasks in Rome and could depart for their provinces.[68] This could be indirectly confirmed by the approximate dates of departure from Rome of the consuls of 58 and 57, as well as that of Crassus in 55. According to Balsdon, leaving Rome before 10 December would have the added benefit for the consuls of avoiding the risk of the new tribunes of the plebs bringing up any obstructive measures against their departure.

Balsdon's suggestion was taken up again by Giovannini, who, in light of the importance that the date of 1 March had in the debates about the end of Caesar's command in Gaul, considered that it was that day when, once religious and diplomatic matters had been dealt with, the debates of the senate properly started.[69] By that time the senate was in a position to decide whether it was necessary to send the consuls to their provinces immediately, whether it was more convenient to change the consular provinces because there was a sudden emergency elsewhere in the empire, or whether it was best for the consuls to remain in Rome. This would explain why the allotment of the consular provinces for each year at times took place in March, as was the case for 60, although it is more probable that the allocation was usually done at the beginning of the year, as had traditionally been the case in previous centuries.[70]

Concerning the date of 13 November, it is possible, as we have already mentioned, that November was frequently the month when the consuls set off for their provinces. But it is not at all certain that there was a pre-established date from which the departure of the consuls was authorized. Rather, everything depended upon the circumstances of the given moment. Just as some consuls remained in Rome all year while others departed for their provinces, we might think that, likewise, the time chosen to leave the *Urbs* must have depended on the demands of internal or external politics each year. Nevertheless, it seems that the most common occurrence was that the consuls left Rome in the autumn or, even closer to the end of the year, in the months

---

[67] Balsdon 1939: 68: 'By the end of February, then, the Senate would be better placed than at any other time in the year to settle the praetorian provinces for the praetors in office and to consider the consular provinces for the consuls of the following year.'

[68] Balsdon 1939: 67: 'The Ides of November may have been in this late post-Sullan period the date after which magistrates were free of routine duties, if they had spent the year in Rome, and could go off to their provinces.'

[69] Giovannini 1983: 142–3.

[70] That is the most probable interpretation of Sal. *Hist.* 2.10 M. for 75 and of Plut. *Luc.* 5.2 for 74. On the other hand, from Cic. *Ver.* 2.3.222, it seems to follow that the sortition of the consular provinces for 69 took place when Hortensius was still a consul-designate. Cf. Giovannini 1983: 85–6. His conclusion is: 'La *sortitio* des provinces consulaires pouvait se faire soit au début du mandat des intéressés soit au moment de leur départ.'

of November or December. It is striking that the journeys of the consuls to the provinces took place at a time of year when the weather conditions were not the most favourable for sailing in the Mediterranean.[71] However, as Balsdon states, the fact is that we do have examples of at least some governors leaving then, in the same way that December and January must have been the months when the envoys from other states throughout the Mediterranean, in particular from the East, set off to arrive in Rome in time to be received in February. This means that, although undoubtedly there must have been difficulties, the winter months were considered fit for sailing in the Mediterranean and, therefore, for the transport of Roman consuls.[72]

As opposed to those who departed for their provinces, a number of consuls of the period between 80 and 50 remained in Rome during their entire consulship. We have certain knowledge of this in at least seventeen cases: Sulla (80), D. Iunius Brutus and M. Aemilius Lepidus (77), Pompey and Crassus (70), Q. Hortensius (69), L. Aurelius Cotta (65), Cicero (63), Q. Caecilius Metellus (60), Caesar and M. Calpurnius Bibulus (59), Pompey and Q. Caecilius Metellus Pius Scipio Nasica (52), Ser. Sulpicius Rufus and M. Claudius Marcellus (51), L. Aemilius Lepidus Paullus and C. Claudius Marcellus (50).[73]

It is initially surprising that, at least in some specific cases, the decision to remain in Rome seems to have been taken by the consuls themselves.[74] Without a doubt it was Sulla, whose power was undisputed at the time, who decided not to leave the *Urbs* during his consulship in 80.[75] In 77, the senate wanted to send the two consuls, D. Iunius Brutus and Mam. Aemilius Lepidus, to Hispania to confront the rebellious Sertorius. Both of them refused to accept this mission, which was finally undertaken by Pompey as proconsul.[76] In the year 70, the two consuls also remained in Rome during

---

[71] Balsdon 1939: 68.

[72] It must be taken into account that before the reform of the calendar carried out by Caesar, the official Roman year did not usually match the astronomical year, because the necessary intercalary months were not always introduced when it was appropriate. This meant that the winter months could at times correspond in fact to other times of the year, which would have different weather conditions. For example, Crassus left for the East in the first half of November 55. In fact, 1 November corresponded to 23 September in the astronomical calendar (Marinone 2004: 398). It is likely that Ap. Claudius Pulcher left for Cilicia in November (or December) 54. In this case also the official year was ahead of the astronomical year, since 1 November was actually 5 October (Marinone 2004: 404). The same happened in 68, when Marcius Rex was able to depart for his province at the end of his term of office, since he had acted in practice as a sole consul during the entire year. In 68, 1 November was the astronomical 13 October (Marinone 2004: 315). This situation is repeated in other instances between 80 and 50.

[73] Giovannini 1983: 89.   [74] Rosenstein 1995: 55.   [75] Cf. App. *B.Civ.* 1.97; 103.

[76] Cic. *Phil.* 11.18. Gruen (1974: 19) thinks that the reason for the refusal of the consuls may simply have been a reluctance to get involved in a venture whose final outcome was uncertain. On the other hand, Sumner (1964: 46) points to a political decision within the faction to which the two consuls presumably belonged. Cf. Giovannini 1983: 84.

their consulship and the following year did not take a province as proconsuls either.[77] But we also know that Pompey publicly renounced a province. According to Velleius Paterculus, Pompey swore while a consul that he would not take on any province 'ex consulatu'.[78] According to Giovannini, the expression *ex consulatu* must not be understood as a synonym of *post consulatum*, 'after the consulship'. Pompey was not renouncing the province that should be allotted to him after his consulship, but the province to which he was entitled due to his consulship.[79] Undoubtedly, in accordance with the *lex Sempronia*, both consular provinces had been assigned beforehand. Velleius Paterculus speaks of his renouncing any province ('se in nullam provinciam … iturum'), not only the allocated consular province but also any other that could be allotted to him in case of a change in the circumstances.

For his part, the consul Cicero exchanged with his colleague Antonius the provinces that had originally been allotted to each of them. In the end, Cicero renounced going to his province, and indeed he did not leave Rome during his consulship or afterwards. The announcement of his renouncing the province was made before the people at a *contio* possibly held in May or June 63.[80] But on 1 January Cicero had already made his intentions clear. That day, the new consuls usually pronounced a speech before the senators in the temple of Capitoline Jupiter at the opening of the consular year. In 63 that speech became a plea against the agrarian bill of Servilius Rullus. In his oration, Cicero solemnly declared that, if circumstances in Rome did not change and if there were no further duties that he could not ignore, he renounced holding a provincial government.[81]

It is clear that a consul could not go to his province without the senate's authorization, largely because the senate had to finance the needs of the consul in the province by providing him with money and troops. Actually, when Cicero renounced his province, it had already been *ornata*, that is, the budget had already been approved as well as the soldiers that he could have.[82] Likewise, it seems unthinkable that a consul could independently take the decision of renouncing his province without having received the senate's authorization. In Cicero's particular case, his speech at the *contio* was no doubt the public announcement of a decision that must have been

---

[77] The fact that the two consuls were in Rome at the end of the year is shown by the information reported by App. *B.Civ.* 1.121 and Plut. *Pomp.* 23.1–2, according to which Crassus and Pompey became reconciled before the people when their consulship was about to expire.
[78] Vell. 2.31.1. [79] Giovannini 1983: 79–80.
[80] Cic. *Att.* 2.1.3; *Pis.* 2; *Fam.* 5.2.3. Cf. Allen Jr 1952: 236–7. [81] Cic. *Leg. agr.* 1.26.
[82] Cic. *Pis.* 2. Cf. Giovannini 1983: 87.

previously discussed and authorized by the senate.[83] All in all, in the post-Sullan period, the consul's will appears to have played a more important role than in previous centuries. Between the fourth and second centuries, almost all the consuls went to their corresponding provinces, in Italy or beyond, and very few of them, always as an exception, remained in Rome during their consulship. They were therefore under the obligation of going to their provinces, and that obligation was not questioned. After Sulla, the consuls maintained their military command, and provinces were assigned to them. But they were not apparently under any pressing obligation to go; they could simply go if they wanted, but in fact a great number of them preferred, in agreement with the senate, to remain in Rome, no doubt arguing that such a decision was in the best general interest of the Republic.

We should also refer briefly to the question of how the *lex Pompeia de provinciis* of 52 would have had an influence on the consular functions in the subsequent years. According to Cassius Dio, in 53 the senate passed a decree ordering an interval of five years to elapse between the magistracies and the government of a province.[84] The *senatus consultum* was ratified in 52 by the consul Pompey, and it became law.[85] Cassius Dio states that the law applied to both praetors and consuls, which in practice would have meant that the consuls had forfeited their capacity as military commanders. The consuls of 51 and 50 certainly remained in Rome during the entire year and did not go to any province afterwards. In their turn, the consulars Cicero and Calpurnius Bibulus were designated governors of Cilicia and Syria respectively in 51, many years after being consuls. This has generally been explained as the consequence of the enforcement of the *lex Pompeia de provinciis*.[86] However, Giovannini argued that this law only applied to the praetorian provinces and not to consular provinces, which continued to exist as they had until then.[87] In fact, as Caelius tells Cicero in a letter

---

[83] Millar 1998: 97: 'This change involved no popular vote to override the Senate's previous arrangements; but it did still require to be enacted publicly before a *contio*.'

[84] Cass. Dio, 40.46.2.   [85] Cass. Dio, 40.56.1.   [86] On this question, see Marshall 1972.

[87] Giovannini (1983: 114–19) argues that only from the year 27 onwards did the consuls cease to be by law the commanders-in-chief of the Roman army and thus solely hold civil power. The thesis that argues that the *lex Pompeia* only applied to praetorian provinces had already been suggested by Cobban 1935: 86 n. 1. Cf. Cic. *Fam.* 8.8.5–8. The thesis of Giovannini was accepted by Nicolet 1992 and Roddaz 1992, as well as by Girardet (1990), who suggested placing this Augustan law in the year 19 or 18. However, more recently Ferrary (2001: 111–13) has argued that there is no evidence whatsoever of a law which deprived consuls of their military *imperium* being passed either in 27 or in 19–18. In the same sense, Hurlet, forthcoming, demonstrates that in practice Augustus, although there was no law regarding this, did in fact deprive the consuls of their military power. See also Hurlet 2008: 232: 'La seule loi à avoir réformé le mode d'attribution des provinces publiques est la *lex Iulia* pour laquelle il n'y a aucune raison de proposer une datation autre que 27, ce qui conduit à faire remonter à cette année la date à partir de laquelle les consuls furent légalement dans l'incapacité de partir en province

written in November 51, the senate had considered the possibility of sending the consuls to Syria, which allegedly would have infringed the *lex Pompeia* had it been applicable to consular provinces. The consuls resisted and finally managed to avoid departing.[88] According to Giovannini, if the consuls of 51 and 50 remained in Rome during their consulship, it was, as in other known cases of the previous three decades, because they decided to remain and the senate did not object to their decision.[89] The reason behind this may be found in the internal situation in Rome and in the struggle for power involved in resolving the crucial Caesarian issue, in which the consuls played a very active part.

In conclusion, there is no evidence of the existence of the *lex Cornelia de provinciis ordinandis*. Mommsen's thesis was not only that the consuls did not go to their provinces during their consulship, but that they could not do so, that they were banned from going. This is not true, as already pointed out by Balsdon, Valgiglio, and, above all, by Giovannini. In the post-Sullan age, the consuls were able to go to their provinces during their consulship but they did not always do so. The conclusions that can be drawn from the data given here are, as could only be expected, similar to those reached by Giovannini. Between 80 and 50, at least twenty-two consuls left Rome to go to their provinces before their year as consul had expired and subsequently remained there as proconsuls for variable periods of time. This makes up over one-third of the total. Perhaps there were more, since we have no information on the provinces for approximately one-third of the consuls in the post-Sullan period. On the other hand, at least seventeen consuls remained in Rome during their entire consulship, which is over one-quarter of the total. Logically, and for the reason already stated, in this case it may well have been more. It is not easy to determine the reason why consuls behaved differently. The decision seems to have been based on internal and international political circumstances, mainly senatorial decisions, but the will of those involved also seems to have been a determining factor.

Nevertheless, from the available data incontrovertible evidence arises: whereas in the pre-Sullan period the consuls barely remained in Rome for

l'année de leur magistrature. Les fastes confirment qu'aucun des consuls postérieurs à l'année 27 n'est parti en province pendant l'année de leur consulat, pas plus que la quasi-totalité des consuls des années antérieures.'

[88] Cic. *Fam.* 8.10.2.

[89] Hurlet 2008: 222–3, categorically rejects the thesis of Giovannini and Girardet: 'Mon interprétation est simple: la *lex Pompeia* définissait également le mode de collation de toutes les provinces, prétoriennes et consulaires, abrogeant ainsi la *lex Sempronia* . . . Il faut plutôt retenir que les consuls furent privés très provisoirement, de 52 à 49, de la possibilité de partir en campagne l'année même de leur consulat en raison du délai quinquennal qui fut alors instauré.' Ferrary (2001: 105–7) has also shown his opposition.

more than a few weeks before setting off for their provinces, in the post-Sullan age the consuls who left the *Urbs* did so much later in the year than the consuls of previous centuries and remained in Rome for most of their term of office. In this sense, the behaviour of the consuls in this period was quite homogeneous. It seems obvious that this fact cannot be attributed to a *lex de provinciis* enacted by Sulla, but was there a regulation or a senatorial recommendation in this respect? Was there a specific chronological point when the consuls began to invert their functions and to spend most or all of the consular year in Rome instead of in their provinces, or was it a gradual process that was eventually accepted in practice?

The longer presence in Rome of the consuls in the post-Sullan period is connected with a change in the role of the consulship as a magistracy in this period: although still invested with the highest military authority, the part played by the consulship became much more relevant in the day-to-day government of Rome itself. In this sense, it is likely that the presence of the consuls in the city was the result of a process that made it obvious that this was more convenient. However, it is difficult to confirm this, on the one hand because available information from ancient sources for the end of the second century and the first two decades of the first century is generally meagre, and on the other hand because during most of this period Rome lived through exceptional circumstances. In the last few years of the second century, Rome had to confront Jugurtha in the north of Africa and the invasion of the Cimbri and the Teutones in Gaul, Hispania, and Italy. The consuls, in particular Marius, were the chief commanders of the Roman army and led the military operations in these conflicts. The role of consuls mainly as *imperatores* does not seem to have changed substantially in comparison to previous periods.

The first decade of the first century is particularly obscure. It is practically impossible to reconstruct the activities of the consuls in those years. We know absolutely nothing about some of them, either their actions in Rome or in the provinces that were given to them. Just a few details are known, one of which is of particular interest. According to Asconius, Q. Mucius Scaevola, consul in 95, renounced his province.[90] There is no doubt of the meaning of the phrase, since the expression used by Asconius, *deponere provinciam*, is exactly the same as that used by Cicero on several occasions to

---

[90] Asc. 15 C.: 'L. autem Crasso collega fuit Q. Scaevola pontifex qui, cum animadverteret Crasso propter summam eius in re publica potentiam ac dignitatem senatum in decernendo triumpho gratificari, non dubitavit rei publicae magis quam collegae habere rationem ac ne fieret s.c. intercessit. *idem provinciam*, cuius cupiditate plerique etiam boni viri deliquerant, *deposuerat* ne sumptui esset oratio.'

refer to the voluntary renunciation of his consular province in 63.[91] Consequently, Scaevola voluntarily renounced the government of the province that had been allotted to him.

However, we know that Scaevola was, at some stage, governor in Asia, where his fight against the abuses of the publicans earned him an excellent reputation amongst the population of his province, to the point that an annual festival was established in his honour.[92] All of this was despite the fact that he was in Asia for only nine months before he left the province in the hands of his legate P. Rutilius Rufus. Scaevola may have been the governor of Asia as a result of his praetorship in 98 or as a consequence of his consulship in 95. Therefore, the renunciation of his province could have taken place either during his praetorship or during his consulship. Broughton maintained that Scaevola had been governor in Asia in 97, after his praetorship.[93] In contrast, Badian argued that his command in Asia had been held in 94, after his consulship.[94] Badian's main argument is that Rutilius Rufus served under the orders of Scaevola as a legate in Asia and that in his opinion it is unlikely that such a prestigious consular would have agreed to be the legate of a governor whose rank was only praetorian. But a consular being a member of a praetorian governor's team was neither impossible nor illegal and, as Broughton pointed out in his response to Badian's thesis, the friendship between the two politicians may have overridden the question of hierarchy.[95] Broughton is probably right that the renunciation of the province happened during the consulship. That is also the most logical reading of the text in Asconius, who mentions first the conflict starting between the two consuls, Crassus and Scaevola, because of the celebration of the triumph by the former, and then mentions the renunciation of the province. Thus, the context clearly points towards the year 95.

That means that Scaevola, renouncing his consular province, must have remained in Rome during his term of office as consul and set a precedent for later politicians such as Pompey and Cicero, who, as we have seen, publicly renounced their consular provinces and remained in the *Urbs* all year. We also know that Scaevola, along with his colleague Crassus, sponsored a law that forced the Italians who had been illegally included in the census to

---

[91] Cic. *Phil.* 11.23; *Pis.* 5; *Att.* 2.1.3. Balsdon (1937: 8–10) demonstrated that *deponere provinciam* cannot mean that Scaevola had left one province where he had been acting as a governor, but that he had refused to go to the province that had been allotted to him. See the commentary of Lewis 2006: 210–12.

[92] Cic. *Att.* 5.17.4–5; *Att.* 6.1.15; *Ver.* 2.2.51; Liv. *per.* 70; Diodor. 37.5.1–4.   [93] Broughton 1951–86: II 7.

[94] Badian 1956. In favour of the thesis of Badian, Schiavone 1987: 209 n. 115.

[95] Broughton 1951–86: III 145–6. In total agreement with Broughton, Marshall 1985: 110–11. See also Marshall 1976b; Ferrary 2000: 163–5.

return to their places of origin. This must have happened at the beginning of the consular year. Crassus did go to his province, and he achieved military victories in Cisalpine Gaul. On his return to Rome he asked the senate to award him a triumph. But Scaevola opposed this and vetoed the *senatus consultum*. When discussing this in the aforementioned passage, Asconius refers to Scaevola as Crassus' colleague; hence this episode presumably happened at the end of the consular year.[96] What we know about the consulship of Scaevola is actually very similar to what we know of the activities of a good number of consuls in the post-Sullan period.

The decade of the eighties was characterized by successive wars and civil strife. It started with the Social War, in which the consuls of each year led, as was usual, the troops that had to confront the rebellious allies. It continued in 88 with the march on Rome of the consul Sulla and the taking of the city and the subsequent repression.[97] Sulla only departed Rome for the eastern Mediterranean to take command of the war against Mithridates once he had presided over the elections, probably at the end of the year. In the absence of Sulla, L. Cornelius Cinna took power and held the consulship between 87 and 84. Episodes of violence and the expectation of the return of Sulla continued throughout the so-called *dominatio Cinnana*: Cinna himself was removed from office by the senate in the year 87 but regained power by force as Sulla had done, the consul Cn. Octavius was murdered, and a bloody repression of Cinna's adversaries ensued.[98] The decade ended with the civil war that finally led to the Sullan dictatorship.

Once more, available sources on the decade of the eighties are scarce and difficult to use, because in general they tend to be biased against Cinna. Little is known with certainty about the specific actions of the consuls in 87–84, other than information emphasizing the presumed Cinnan tyranny. The year 87 witnessed episodes of violence and a new civil war that ended with the taking of Rome by the Cinnans. Cicero states that the consul Octavius pronounced many speeches in *contiones* in Rome, showing an eloquence until then unknown.[99] But in 86 and 85 the inhabitants of the *Urbs* sensed a return of stability. The consuls for 86 were Cinna and Marius, the latter being replaced after his death by L. Valerius Flaccus. In 85 Cinna was consul again, along with Cn. Papirius Carbo, and the same pair also held the consulship in 84, when Cinna was murdered while he was busy with the military preparations in the face of the imminent return of Sulla

---

[96] Asc. 15 C. Cic. (*Inv.* 2.111) classifies Crassus as a consul. Cf. V. Max. 3.7.6. Cf. Marshall 1985: 111–12; Broughton 1951–86: iii 145.
[97] See now Hinard 2008: 27–41.   [98] Lovano 2002: 25–51.   [99] Cic. *Brut.* 176.

and his troops.[100] Having regained power in Rome at the end of 87, Cinna seems not to have left the city at any stage to control a consular province. Everything seems to indicate that Cinna remained in Rome during the entire year in 86 and 85, although towards the end of 85 the consuls had already begun some military moves with Sulla in mind. It is possible that Carbo also spent the year 85 in Rome; at any rate, there is no information regarding his leaving for a province.

As can be seen, the evidence is very scarce and corresponds to an historical moment when, to some extent, institutional normality was replaced by exceptional circumstances caused by violence and civil wars. What we do know is that a consul voluntarily renounced his province in the year 95 and decided, presumably with the senate's agreement, to remain in Rome. It must be pointed out that Scaevola had a great reputation in Roman society of his time and was considered an excellent jurist,[101] while as pontiff he systematized the Roman civic religion.[102] His decision, which had few precedents in the history of Rome, must therefore have been based on his own *auctoritas*. On the other hand, everything seems to indicate that during the eighties it was not unusual for one or both consuls to remain in Rome during their entire term of office. When in 80 Sulla became consul after having been dictator, he did not leave the city either. Obviously, he had also remained in Rome the whole time or most of the time as dictator. In other words, after Sulla's dictatorship it was no longer extraordinary for some of the supreme magistrates of Rome to spend their term of office in the city, without taking over military command, in order to deal with political matters. In this sense, it could be added that in the final years of the second century, and at the beginning of the first century, the number of consular laws that were passed had increased compared to previous centuries, which may perhaps point to a longer presence of the consuls in Rome. In fact in 88, for instance, if the information that we have is correct, the consuls Sulla and Pompeius Rufus sponsored an unprecedented number of laws.

In more than fifty years between the tribunate of Ti. Sempronius Gracchus and Sulla's dictatorship, Rome and Italy had lived through several episodes of violence that had been seen by the senate majority as a danger to the status quo: the tribunates of the Gracchi brothers in 133 and 123–122; the tribunates of Saturninus in the last years of the second century; the tribunate of M. Livius

---

[100] Lovano 2002: 53–77.
[101] On the crucial importance of Scaevola in the development of Roman law, see Schiavone 1987: 25–108. Cf. Alexander 2006: 247.
[102] Aug. *C.D.* 4.27. Cf. Rüpke 2007a: 168, with supplementary bibliography.

Drusus in 91, a prelude to the outbreak of the Social War; the tribunate of
P. Sulpicius Rufus in 88; the taking of Rome by Sulla in that same year and the
repression that followed; the taking of Rome by Cinna; and the civil war. In
that period, there were repeated political murders in the *Urbs*, and on two
occasions the so-called *senatus consultum ultimum* had been issued, expressly
calling on the consuls for a restoration of order, as was accomplished by the
consuls Opimius and Marius respectively in 121 and 100. In this context, it is
probable that an opinion gradually grew within the senate in favour of a longer
presence of the consuls in Rome. The presence of the consuls in the *Urbs*
guaranteed an immediate response in case of the outbreak of a crisis. At the
same time, their political leadership could serve as a balance against possible
seditious actions by the tribunes of the plebs, as was shown by the confrontation of the consul Piso against the tribunes Cornelius and Gabinius in 67 or of
the consul Cicero against the tribune Rullus in 63.[103]

The longer presence of the consuls in Rome in the post-Sullan period
may therefore have been the consequence of a process that over the previous
years of the Sullan dictatorship had gradually made it clear that it was
convenient for the consuls to spend more time dealing with political matters
in the city than commanding the army in a province, without losing their
military *imperium* at any stage. But we do not know whether at some point,
perhaps during Sulla's dictatorship, the senate issued a decree recommend-
ing that consuls remain in Rome during most of their term of office from
that time on. It certainly fits well with the spirit of the Sullan reforms, in the
sense of limiting the leadership of tribunes of the plebs in the political arena,
that the consuls remained in Rome as an instrument of control against
possibly seditious tribunes, but we do not know if within the whole of the
Sullan legislation there might have been a specific rule in this respect.
Ancient sources certainly do not mention either a senatorial decree or a
law that regulated the presence or absence from Rome of consuls. As we
have seen, in the post-Sullan period consuls generally left Rome, when they
did leave, in the autumn. By then the annual elections had been held, so the
consuls designated for the following year had been proclaimed.[104] In this

---

[103] In general on the oratorial confrontation of consuls against seditious tribunes, see Cic. *Mur.* 24.

[104] Giovannini (1983: 90 n. 38) suggested as an explanation for the presence of the consuls in Rome their
obligation to be present at the elections. In the previous centuries, one of the consuls would return to
Rome from his province to preside over the elections, but in the first century it would not have been
practical to make him interrupt his activities in such remote places as Hispania or Syria. For that
reason they may have preferred to bring forward the annual elections, so that the consuls could set off
for their provinces afterwards. Indeed, there is every indication that, except perhaps in situations of
great emergency, no consul left Rome in the first half of the year. The two of them, both the consul
who had to preside over the elections and his colleague, left after the elections had been held, usually

context, it must be taken into account that during the first century the designated consuls were given priority in speaking in debates in the senate,[105] and that they had a much more prominent role to play in political life than in previous periods. The designated consuls seem to have been in close contact with the consuls on active service in the second half of the year, and in some cases they played a significant political role at the end of the year when the consuls were absent.[106] In the presence of the consuls in Rome, and in the greater political significance of the designated consuls, it can perhaps be sensed that there was a convention or rule in the post-Sullan period for the consulship to be, in practice, the magistracy that was always in charge of the community, in close relation with the senate.

In short, in the years between the dictatorship of Sulla and the beginning of the civil war between the Pompeians and Caesarians, the consuls who eventually left for their provinces during their consulship had remained in Rome for most of the year, in particular until the autumn in the cases for which we have precise or approximate data. Other consuls preferred to remain in the *Urbs* throughout the entire year. This is a decisive difference in comparison to consuls of the pre-Sullan period, because their continuous and prolonged presence in Rome must necessarily have had an influence on their actions, their functions, and their capacity to participate in Roman politics. With this point established, the following pages will be dedicated to analysing how the *officium consulis* was modified or remained unchanged from the Sullan dictatorship onwards.

in the summer. However, it does not seem to have been common for the consuls to leave immediately after the elections, but some months later. In other words, the consuls were present at the elections in the post-Sullan period, but that was not the only reason for their longer presence in Rome.

[105] Mommsen 1887–8: III 973; Meier 1997: 259.

[106] In December 61 the designated consul Metellus Celer, confronting a tribune of the plebs, managed to prevent the banned *ludi Compitalicii* from being celebrated: Cic. *Pis.* 8.

CHAPTER 13

Consular functions from the year 80 to 50

In the post-Sullan period, the civil functions the consuls carried out in practice were very similar to those performed by them in previous centuries. Some of the tasks, in particular the religious duties and those regarding international relations of the Roman state, remained virtually unchanged and continued to be completed mainly at the beginning of the year. Understandably, the form of communication of the consuls with the rest of the Roman citizenship continued to be through official edicts as well as their words as orators before the people in *contiones*. The fact that after Sulla's dictatorship the consuls remained in Rome for a much longer period than in previous centuries resulted in an increase in the number of consular edicts and speeches delivered by the consuls at popular assemblies. The main consequence of the consuls' presence in Rome during the entire year (or most of it) was their conspicuousness on Rome's political scene, their participation in day-to-day politics, in the senate or public debates, in the making of big or small decisions: in short, in the daily management of the community. Without a doubt, one of the most significant changes from the pre-Sullan period was the greater importance that the consuls began to have in the legislative field. The number of consular laws increased considerably, and in some cases we can see genuine legislative programmes aimed at introducing important reforms in the administration of justice, the use of land, the struggle against violence or corruption etc., all of which were crucial questions in the late Republican period.

Next we shall analyse, always based on available sources, the civil functions which the consuls are known to have performed in the period between 80 and 50. As in the first part of the book, I have striven, wherever it is feasible and as much as possible, to organize the different sections following the order in which those functions were completed by the consuls throughout the year. Hence, the first two sections deal respectively with religious and diplomatic matters, while the subsequent sections are devoted to public works promoted by the consuls, much fewer and of lesser relevance than in the pre-Sullan period, and to the communication with the people by means of edicts and speeches in *contiones*. A brief section is devoted to the few extraordinary investigations in which some consuls were involved. Obviously, both the promotion of public works and the issuing of edicts or participation in popular assemblies were actions that consuls could perform at any time during the year. Next follows a section dealing with the presidency of the consuls over the annual elections, generally held in the summer, perhaps preferably in July, although there is evidence of elections taking place much later, always in the second half of the year. As I mentioned earlier, legislative work was one of the consular duties which was greatly expanded in the post-Sullan age. The abundant consular laws which were passed in this period, put forward at any time during the year according to preserved evidence, are analysed next. Finally, the last section is devoted to the participation of the consuls in all manner of issues and debates that would arise in the day-to-day politics of Rome and which forced consuls to assume greater prominence in the public life of the city, always, of course, depending on the specific circumstances at each given time and on the personality of each consul.

RELIGIOUS MATTERS

As in previous centuries, the consuls, as the supreme magistrates, continued in the post-Sullan period to be the main intermediaries between the *civitas* and the gods of the Roman civic religion. As such they remained in charge of performing certain rituals which, as we have seen, were aimed at securing the peace of the gods. These are basically the same rituals as in the pre-Sullan period. However, we have very few details on the performance of these rituals in the preserved sources because of the lack of Livy's systematic narrative.

The ceremonies carried out on 1 January on the occasion of the consuls' taking of office must have remained almost unchanged. These ceremonies included fundamental religious aspects. The consuls had to take the necessary auspices of investiture at the beginning of the day and later perform the obligatory sacrifice of an ox in honour of Jupiter.[1] The appropriate performance of the sacrifices was followed by the 'vows for the safety of the state' (*vota pro salute rei publicae*) taken by the incoming consuls, after which the first session of the senate in the new year was held. Nothing seems to have changed in comparison to the pre-Sullan period, although our main source of information in this respect is the aforementioned text of Ovid, which was written later.[2]

---

[1] Cf. Tert. *Ad nat.* 1.10.18.   [2] Ovid, *Pont.* 4.4.27–42. See above, p. 18 and nn. 40–1.

As we have seen in the chapter regarding the religious tasks of consuls in the pre-Sullan era, there is sufficient evidence to conclude that the consuls were entrusted with the presidency over the public games celebrated in the *Urbs*. However, their absence from Rome for most of the year must generally have made it impossible in practice for the consuls to act as presidents over the games, in particular from the time when the wars in which they intervened were increasingly remote from Rome. But between 80 and 50 most of the consuls stayed in the *Urbs* until the autumn or even for the entire year, a circumstance which did enable them to preside over the public games. Particularly since we have reports, exceptionally, of a consul presiding over the *ludi Romani* in the pre-Sullan period,[3] it is logical to presume that the same must have happened in the first century, since the games were celebrated in September, generally when the two consuls were present in Rome. As opposed to the pre-Sullan era, the presidency over the *ludi Romani* must have become one of the normal religious tasks of the consuls in the first century.

The other two religious duties that can be attributed to consuls in this period are the expiation of prodigies and the presidency over the *feriae Latinae*. As regards the expiation of prodigies, the practically unanimous opinion is that throughout the first century both the compilation of prodigies occurring in Rome and Italy and their ensuing expiation progressively fell into disuse. This theory seems to have firm support from a brief passage of Livy, where the Latin author somewhat longingly laments the fact that in his time there was no longer the custom of publicly announcing the prodigies that had happened and recording them in the *annales*.[4]

The supposed progressive disappearance of the expiation of prodigies in the first century has had different explanations.[5] Bloch linked this fact to the ascent of charismatic *imperatores* in this period and to the appearance of prodigies and omens related to certain persons, both favourable and unfavourable, which did not require expiation.[6] According to Liebeschuetz, the expiation of prodigies was closely linked to the Republican system. Once this crumbled within the context of the successive civil wars throughout the first century, traditional methods to keep the peace of the gods were no longer applicable.[7] MacBain placed the end of the Roman tradition of expiation of prodigies in the Social War. From then on, the public portent

---

[3] Liv. 45.1.6–7.   [4] Liv. 43.13.1.
[5] See a review of the various theories in Rosenberger 1998: 210–14.   [6] Bloch 1963: 138–46.
[7] Liebeschuetz 1979: 58. In the same sense, Sacchetti 1996: 240–1: ' . . . la religione entra in crisi quando entra in crisi questo orizzonte politico, ed i prodigi come segno di vita comunitaria non hanno più senso quando la vita comunitaria non c'è più'; 'Il passaggio dal *prodigium* tradizionale . . . all'*omen* personale è anch'esso un sintomo del cambiamento storico in atto fra II e I secolo a.C.'

may have given way to the private omen related to the great *imperatores* of the first century and later on to the emperors. Until the Social War, the expiation of prodigies that had taken place in different places in Italy had served to emphasize the close connection between the Italian cities and Rome and to create a feeling of belonging to the same community. After the granting of Roman citizenship to all Italian peoples, the expiation of prodigies may have ceased to be necessary as an expression of the unity of Italy, and that may have been an important reason for its gradual disappearance.[8] Rosenberger also placed the decline of the expiation of prodigies at the beginning of the first century, when they lost their meaning against the background of the civil wars, the usurpation of power by the great generals of this period, and the declining value that divine signs had for the Roman people.[9]

It is evident that the first century brought about substantial changes in Roman society and that these must have had an influence on the religious beliefs and practices of the Romans, although nowadays scholarship seems to have completely ruled out the old theory of a gradual decline in belief that would have run parallel to the crumbling of the Republic. It is possible that, at least to a certain extent, the scrupulous compilation of prodigies and their expiation until then were the victims of that process of change and that they lost significance within the civic religion. However, we must also consider that the loss of Livy's work may have distorted our view of the period. Between the beginning of the Second Punic War and 167 we frequently have a detailed description of the known prodigies and their expiation. Livy does not include them at the beginning of his account for every year, but he does so for many years. Unfortunately, we cannot know whether Livy continued to include a list of prodigies in the books on the late Republican age, and therefore we cannot properly compare their relevance in the two periods, because we have no annalistic account of the first century.

However, for the first century we do have the compilation made by Obsequens, who is indebted to Livy. Other authors complete the picture, mainly Cassius Dio and Pliny, as well as, exceptionally, Cicero.[10] It is obvious that the number of portents mentioned by the sources for this period is lower than in previous centuries. Between 190 and 150, Obsequens

---

[8] MacBain 1982: 80–1. On Rome's territorial competence in the expiation of prodigies in Italy, see Ruoff-Väänänen 1972.
[9] Rosenberger 1998: 244.
[10] See the compilation of prodigies in the first century in MacBain 1982: 100–4, also in Rasmussen 2003: 106–9.

reports the existence of prodigies in nineteen years, nearly half of the total; between 150 and 120 in eighteen years, a little more than half of the total; and finally, between 120 and 80 he mentions prodigies in twenty-seven years, two-thirds of the total. In all Obsequens, following Livy, describes portents in almost 60 per cent of the years between 190 and Sulla's dictatorship, whereby a gradual increase of prodigies during this time can be noted. However, between 80 and 50, ancient sources mention portents in only eleven years, just over one-third of the total.[11] It is clear, then, that proportionally, from Sulla's dictatorship onwards, the sources refer to fewer years with prodigies than in the pre-Sullan period.

All in all, the number of portents continued to be relatively important and some of them had an unquestionable social impact. As in previous periods, the prodigies described included earthquakes, showers of stones, talking animals, sudden rises of the Tiber, and so forth. Special importance was given to lightning that struck the statues of deities, an event which was thought to have negative consequences for the maintenance of the peace of the gods. This happened in the year 65, when a flash of lightning hit the Capitol and struck the statue of the Capitoline wolf and of Jupiter; in 56, when lightning struck the statue of Jupiter on the Mons Albanus; and in 53, when lightning swept through the city and killed several people and destroyed various statues of the gods. Although the sources generally provide few details, we know for certain that, at least on some occasions, the haruspices or the Sybilline Books were consulted to find the appropriate response to the prodigies. In fact, it was following the response of the haruspices that the statue of Jupiter destroyed in 65 was rebuilt and taken to the Forum, and games were celebrated for ten days. In the year 53 a lustration of the *Urbs* was carried out.

In short, it is possible that in the post-Sullan period less importance was given to prodigies compared to previous decades. But it is unquestionable that different kinds of events which were perceived as portents continued to be reported to the senate and that, as in previous centuries, depending on the senatorial decision, they did or did not officially become public prodigies. The procedure that followed will not have differed much from that traditionally applied to the expiation of prodigies. Either the senate

---

[11] That is, the years 78 (Plin. *Nat.* 10.50); 76 (Obseq. 59; Plin. *Nat.* 2.100); 65 (Obseq. 61; Cic. *Cat.* 3.19–20; *Div.* 1.19–20; Cass. Dio, 37.9.2); 63 (Obseq. 61; Plin. *Nat.* 2.137; Cass. Dio, 37.25.1–2); 60 (Obseq. 62); 56 (Cass. Dio, 39.15–16; 39.20.1–2; Cic. *Har.*); 54 (Cass. Dio, 39.60–1; Plin. *Nat.* 2.147; Obseq. 64); 53 (Obseq. 63; Cass. Dio, 40.17.1); 52 (Cass. Dio, 40.47.1–2); 50 (Obseq. 65; Plin. *Nat.* 2.147; 7.243). Prodigies are also known for most years of the decade of the forties.

took a decision directly regarding the response to be given to the reported portents, or it was preferred to consult one of the priestly colleges. Although it is unusual for the sources regarding this period to mention it, there is no doubt that the answer must have involved some kind of public expiation. In other words, regardless of whether there were few or many prodigies acknowledged as such in the post-Sullan age, it is clear that the community could not ignore them, since they endangered proper relations with the gods. All prodigies required an adequate response in the form of ceremonies of expiation, and those ceremonies always had to be presided over by the consuls. Although we do not have express confirmation in ancient sources, it seems reasonable to suppose that the process of acknowledgement and expiation of the public prodigies continued to take place at the beginning of the year, probably in January, and that it was therefore one of the first tasks of the new consuls, as it had been in previous centuries. According to Aulus Gellius, M. Terentius Varro wrote an opuscule for Pompey in 71 with which he wanted to brief his friend, recently elected consul for the first time, on the functioning of the senate, of which he had not been a member until then. One of the many observations contained in his text stated that divine matters had to be dealt with and resolved in the senate before human matters.[12] No doubt the expiation of prodigies was one such divine matter that had to be tackled in the senate at the beginning of the year.

There is no doubt that the *feriae Latinae* continued to be celebrated on the Mons Albanus as usual, both in the late Republican period and throughout the entire Principate. There are sufficient data to certify this: amongst others, the partial preservation of the *fasti feriarum Latinarum*. However, explicit references to this ritual in ancient sources dealing with the post-Sullan period are very scarce.

As in previous centuries, two specific tasks concerned the consuls: assigning the date for the celebration of the Latin festival and presiding over the ceremonies. Directly linked to these actions was the appointment of a prefect of the city (*praefectus urbis*), who had to deal with the government in Rome in the absence of the consuls and the other magistrates. This appointment sparked one of the first arguments between the consuls of 78, M. Aemilius Lepidus and Q. Lutatius Catulus. The two consuls had a confrontation over the public funeral in honour of Sulla, which Lepidus opposed, nor could they reach an agreement on who was to be made

---

[12] Gel. 14.7.9: 'de rebusque divinis prius quam humanis ad senatum referendum esse'. Cf. Giovannini 1983: 142.

praefectus urbis.[13] The brief Sallustian reference does not give any names of the possible candidates to hold this office, but it indirectly indicates that it was the consuls who appointed the prefect, or at least proposed such an appointment, and that apparently it was usual to seek a consensus between the two colleagues.[14]

Setting the date for the celebration of the *feriae Latinae* depended on the proposal made and presumably previously agreed upon by the consuls. The proposal was made in the senate and once it had been approved it became a *senatus consultum*. It must be taken into account that the date had to be set sufficiently in advance, since the ceremony had to be attended not only by Roman magistrates and senators but also by the authorities of the Latin cities. For this reason, the consuls must have put forward their proposal in the first few days of the year, when, as we have seen, religious matters were given priority in the senatorial debates. This adds further acrimony to the criticism expressed by Caelius about the consuls of the year 50. In a letter addressed to Cicero, who was in Cilicia at the time, Caelius sarcastically emphasized that the consuls had done nothing significant till then and that the only thing they had achieved was to pass the decree on the celebration of the Latin festival.[15] The letter was written at the end of February, and the date of the festival had probably been set at the beginning of the year. Caelius was thus highlighting the incompetence of the consuls, who after two months in office had only managed to solve a matter which was but a mere formality.

As we have seen, the *feriae Latinae* were celebrated on very varied dates in the pre-Sullan period, but at any rate in the first few weeks of the consular year, if possible, in order to advance the departure of the consuls for their provinces. In the post-Sullan period, this urgency no longer applied, since the consuls remained in Rome for all or most of the year. However, the practice was maintained, and the festival continued to be celebrated in the

---

[13] Sal. *Hist.* I 54 M. = I 47 McGushin (vol. I, 113): 'de praefecto urbis quasi possessione rei publicae magna utrimque vi contendebatur.' Cf. Criniti 1969: 375–6; Gruen 1974: 14; Funari 1996: I 129. On the consulship of Lepidus, see Hayne 1972; Labruna 1975; Bauman 1978; Weigel 1992: 14–19; Allély 2004: 26–9; Arena, forthcoming.

[14] Cassius Dio supplies two exceptional pieces of information on the figure of the *praefectus urbis*, which must be understood within the context of the institutional chaos following Caesar's murder. In 42, the Greek author claims that the prefect of the city presided over the *feriae Latinae*, although this task did not belong to him (Cass. Dio, 47.40.6). Cassius Dio includes this fact after a list of portents that had occurred that year. In 36 no *praefectus urbis* was appointed during the celebration of the Latin festival. Some praetors were in charge of his duties. Aediles were not appointed for that year either, and their tasks were carried out instead by praetors and tribunes of the plebs (Cass. Dio, 49.16.2).

[15] Cic. *Fam.* 8.6.3.

first few months of the year. It is more complicated to establish whether a specific time was preferred for its celebration.

The aforementioned letter from Caelius seems to indicate that the festival had not yet taken place at the end of February, simply that the date had been set for its celebration, perhaps in March. A more specific detail is provided by a letter sent by Cicero to his brother Quintus towards the middle of March 56. In this, Cicero says that the *feriae Latinae* had just been celebrated, that is, in the first few days of March.[16] The year 56 was an exception, since the festival had to be repeated again a few months later due to an error in the performance of the ritual in the first ceremony.[17] This had already happened on several occasions in the pre-Sullan age. Furthermore, in 56 there was another extraordinary event, when many senators refused to attend the second festival on the Mons Albanus as a protest against the joint candidacy of Pompey and Crassus for the consulship of 55.

In the poem about his consulship, partially preserved in *De divinatione*, Cicero alludes to the Mons Albanus being under snow during the celebration of the Latin festival.[18] Without a doubt he refers to the *feriae Latinae* over which he presided during his consulship in 63. The presence of snow clearly indicates that it was wintertime. An intercalary month was introduced in 63, so the official year lasted one month longer. January 1 was in fact 14 December 64 in the astronomical calendar, and the official 29 February was in fact 11 January.[19] That may have been the moment of the celebration of the festival, in the middle of winter. But it could also have been celebrated during the intercalary month, which astronomically corresponded to the period between 5 February and 3 March, during which the Mons Albanus could also have been covered in snow. In fact, in view of the fact that the month of January must have been partially taken up by the discussions regarding the agrarian bill presented by the tribune Servilius Rullus, in which Cicero was very actively involved, and that February was reserved for diplomatic questions, it is possible that it was preferred to fix in advance the celebration of the *feriae Latinae* during the intercalary month.

Therefore, the few known instances we have seem to point towards a tendency to celebrate the Latin festival in March, or as the case may be, in the intercalary month, although the data are certainly not sufficient to allow us to draw definite conclusions. February was probably discarded because it

---

[16] Cic. *Q.fr.* 2.4.2.   [17] Cass. Dio, 39.30.4.

[18] Cic. *Div.* 1.18: '. . . cum tumulos Albano in monte nivalis / lustrasti et laeto mactasti lacte Latinas . . . '. Cf. Pease 1920: 104.

[19] Marinone 2004: 342–8.

was then that the senate received foreign embassies, and, logically, the consuls and other magistrates must have attended the debates that may have been raised. However, we must not rule out the possibility that the festival could have been celebrated in January, perhaps towards the end of the month. In the narration of the events occurring in Rome in the year 44, Suetonius claims that Caesar entered the city after having presided over the *feriae Latinae*. He then goes on to describe the offering of a crown made by Antonius to Caesar during the *Lupercalia*, that is, in the middle of February.[20] Hence, the Latin festival had been celebrated before, probably at the end of January. The years when Caesar governed Rome as consul or dictator were exceptional for many reasons, but perhaps the celebration of the *feriae Latinae* in January was not extraordinary. Nevertheless, as in previous centuries, there was obvious flexibility in the date of the festival, which undoubtedly depended on internal political factors which in most cases are not within our grasp.[21]

A text of Cassius Dio regarding the year 43 indicates that in the first century it was nevertheless compulsory for a consul to preside over the *feriae Latinae* before leaving Rome to take command of his army. In the context of the situation of enormous tension that Rome and Italy were experiencing at the time, the consuls left the *Urbs* without the festival having been celebrated. Cassius Dio claims that there was no example of other cases when this had happened without such a breach of the tradition resulting in misfortunes for the community.[22] In this manner, the Greek author anticipates the death of many people in the conflicts that ensued, including the death of the two consuls.

Besides the traditional responsibility of the consuls in the expiation of the prodigies and the celebration of the *feriae Latinae*, in the post-Sullan age the consuls occasionally dealt with other religious issues. In fact, the decisions taken by the senate in connection with Roman civic religion had to be put into practice by the consuls as the executors of the senatorial decrees. Thus, for example, in the speech given by Cicero in 56 to the senators on the response of the haruspices, he mentions a *senatus consultum* setting forth the obligation to make a registry of the consecrated sites in Rome.[23] The senatorial decree was the product of a suggestion included specifically in the response of the haruspices. The consuls for the year 56, Cn. Cornelius

---

[20] Suet. *Jul.* 79.2–3.
[21] The *fasti feriarum Latinarum* corresponding to 27–23 are preserved (*CIL* 1² 1, p. 58). In those years the festival was celebrated well into the year: in 27 in May, in 26 in April, in 25 and 24 in June, and in 23 possibly in July.
[22] Cass. Dio, 46.33.4–5.   [23] Cic. *Har.* 11.

Lentulus and L. Marcius Philippus, were in charge of making the registry and the list of consecrated sites that had to be delivered to the senate.

We find another example of the consuls' superior authority in the religious sphere in the reconstruction of the lost Sibylline Books. In 83, the books were destroyed by the fire that razed the temple of Jupiter on the Capitol, where they were housed.[24] In 76, the senate ordered the consuls Cn. Octavius and C. Scribonius Curio, or perhaps only the latter,[25] to see to the reconstruction of the Books. To this end, a senatorial commission was created and was sent to various colonies in Italy, to Greece, and to other cities where there was a sibyl, in particular Ionian cities of Eretrian origin in Asia Minor.[26] The commission managed to gather about one thousand sibylline verses, which served to partially reconstruct the former books. The consuls were in charge of replacing them on the Capitol, which was being rebuilt at the time under the direction of Q. Catulus.[27]

In 58, the consuls were the protagonists in two episodes in the religious sphere, which have questionable elements and have been the subject of debate. The first of them involved the consular action against the Egyptian cults in Rome, known only through late Christian sources. Tertullian refers to this action in two passages. In his *Apologeticum* he ascribes to the two consuls, L. Calpurnius Piso Caesoninus and A. Gabinius, the banning of the worship of the gods Serapis, Isis, Harpocrates, and Anubis on the Capitol, as well as the destruction of the shrines that were dedicated to them.[28] In a passage of his work *Ad nationes*, for which he mentions Varro as a source, he expands this information and gives more specific details. The shrines dedicated to the Egyptian deities on the Capitol were destroyed by order of the senate but rebuilt in the wake of violent popular protests. But then on 1 January 58 the consul Gabinius supported the order of the senate and upheld the prohibition on rebuilding the shrines despite popular pressure. Gabinius' intervention took place while he was publicly examining the suitability of the animals that were to be solemnly sacrificed within the context of pronouncing the customary vows at the beginning of each year.[29] Tertullian's texts are complemented by a passage of Arnobius, who attributes the measure to the two consuls but adds no further information.[30]

---

[24] Dion. Hal. 4.62.5–6. Cf. Tac. *Hist.* 3.71; 4.54. See Flower 2008.
[25] Lactantius mentions on one occasion the two consuls being in charge of this task, though on another occasion he only alludes to Curio.
[26] Lactant. *Div. inst.* 1.6.14; *Ira Dei* 22.6. Cf. Dion. Hal. 4.62.6.
[27] Scheid 1998a: 102. On the Sibylline Books see the study by Monaca 2005.　　[28] Tert. *Apol.* 6.8.
[29] Tert. *Ad nat.* 1.10.17–18. Cf. Schneider 1968: 218–19; Vanderbroeck 1987: 239–40.
[30] Arn. *Adv. nat.* 2.73.1.

To these data it could be added that Seeck defended an emendation to a letter from Cicero to Atticus, according to which it should read 'ut prae hoc Isis Curiana stare videatur'. The letter was written in May 59, and from the emended text Seeck concluded that a statue of Isis might have been destroyed in Rome in the first half of 59, before Gabinius' intervention.[31] Conversely, Takács demonstrated that the conjecture 'Isis Curiana' is not acceptable because the text of the letter has nothing to do with Isis and therefore there is no reference in the Ciceronian letter to the destruction of a presumed statue of Isis belonging to a Curio.[32]

All in all, there is no need to accept the Ciceronian emendation anyway, since the interpretation that by the year 59 actions had probably already been undertaken against the worship of Egyptian gods can easily be deduced from the passage of Tertullian *Ad nationes*. The sequence of events must have been as follows: a senatorial decree ordering the destruction of shrines to Isis, Serapis, Harpocrates, and Anubis; the actual destruction of the altars; the reconstruction carried out by force by a part of the plebs; and the destruction of the new shrines by order of the consul Gabinius, or of the two consuls, at the beginning of 58.[33] Gabinius had to face the protests of the followers of Egyptian cults when he was about to perform the traditional sacrifices on the Calends of January, just before the usual first annual session of the senate. It is probable that Gabinius reaffirmed his will to uphold and enforce the *senatus consultum* in that senate session and perhaps also in the usual speech of presentation before the people that the consuls would deliver at the beginning of their term of office. The measure must have been carried out in the following days, in any case at the beginning of 58. It is clear that, as with anything concerning Rome's official religion, the decision about accepting foreign cults belonged to the senate. But also, as was usual, the enforcement of the senatorial decision was left in the hands of the consuls.

These texts have brought about speculation on the possibility of the existence by that date of a temple or sanctuary dedicated to Isis on the Capitol. In this context, Versluys recently argued convincingly that there is nothing in the episodes that took place in 59/8 that refers to the existence of such a sanctuary.[34] They simply demonstrate that, in the first half of the first century, the main Egyptian gods were worshipped on the Capitoline Hill and that this worship resulted in the raising of altars in their honour.

---

[31] Cic. *Att.* 2.17.2. Seeck 1908: 642–3. The emendation had been suggested before by Ziehen (1898: 341). The commonly accepted reading is: 'iacet enim ille sic ut <phocis> Curiana stare videatur'.
[32] Takács 1995: 60–2.   [33] See Tschudin 1962: 16; Turcan 1989: 88; Takács 1995: 63.
[34] Versluys 2004: 427–8.

What happened also shows that there was already by then a substantial group of worshippers of Egyptian cults in Rome. In fact, in the following years there were repeated actions against them.[35] In 53, the senate ordered the demolition of the private sanctuaries that had been erected in honour of Isis and Serapis.[36] In all probability, the responsibility for enforcing the senatorial order belonged to the consuls. An event narrated by Valerius Maximus could possibly be placed in the year 50.[37] According to the Latin author, when the senate decreed that the sanctuaries of Isis and Serapis had to be destroyed, no worker dared do it. Then, the consul L. Aemilius Paullus removed his *toga praetexta*, took an axe with his own hands, and broke the doors to the temple. Coarelli suggested identifying the Aemilius Paullus mentioned by Valerius Maximus either as the consul of 182 or as the consul of 168, actually the same person.[38] Against this identification, there is the usually short stay of the consuls in Rome in the second century. Both in 182 and 168 Aemilius Paullus fought in his province, and in particular, in 168 he had to face the severe challenge of leading the war against Perseus. Naturally, it is not impossible that they had time to tackle the destruction of the sanctuaries of the Egyptian gods before leaving Rome, but it is more plausible to attribute that action to L. Aemilius Lepidus Paullus, consul in 50.[39] The historical context supports this thesis, on the one hand, because in the middle of the first century the Egyptian cults undoubtedly had a larger number of followers than in the first half of the second century and, on the other hand, because in 59–58, 53, and again in 48[40] we know that the senate took steps against those Egyptian cults.[41]

According to a passage of *De haruspicum responso* by Cicero, in 58 the consul Piso Caesoninus was also involved in an action connected with the religious sphere. The consul destroyed a *sacellum* dedicated to Diana situated on the Caelian Hill.[42] Ogilvie proposed to identify this shrine as a Dianium mentioned by Livy 'on the top of the Cyprius Vicus' ('ad summum Cyprium vicum'), and he thought that the destruction might have been much earlier than in 56, when Cicero delivered his speech.[43] However,

---

[35] Nippel (1988: 113) suggests a link between the repeated conflicts with the worshippers of Egyptian cults and the activities of the followers of Clodius.

[36] Cass. Dio, 40.47.3.   [37] V. Max. 1.3.4.   [38] Coarelli 1984: 462–3.

[39] This is the mainstream opinion. See Turcan 1989: 89; Versluys 2004: 432, who highlights the fact that Valerius Maximus organizes his work by topics, not chronologically, and therefore the context where the episode is included is not decisive.

[40] Cass. Dio, 42.26.2.

[41] However, if the text in Valerius Maximus refers to the year 50, it is surprising that the episode is not mentioned by Cassius Dio, who does mention the senatorial decrees passed in 53 and 48.

[42] Cic. *Har.* 32.   [43] Liv. 1.48.4. Ogilvie 1978: 193.

it seems clear that the orator refers to a recent event ('his temporibus') that was well known by his audience. The destruction of a shrine which Cicero describes as 'great and most sacred' ('maximum et sanctissimum') can only be seen as something done officially by order of the senate. The executor of the senatorial decree must therefore have been a consul, which takes us in all probability to the consul of 58, L. Piso. Lenaghan suggested that there may have been a connection between the aforementioned action against the Egyptian cults and the destruction of the sacellum of Diana, 'especially if this cult of Diana were foreign, orgiastic, or in any way unruly'.[44] However, nothing in Cicero's passage suggests that orgiastic or forbidden rites were put into practice. Cicero makes it clear that some of the senators listening to him were neighbours of the shrine and that many of them had carried out sacrifices ('sacrificia gentilicia') in it. The context conveys rather a respectable place instead of a site where actions against the tradition were performed. The *sacellum* of Diana on the Caelius must have been destroyed in 58 by the consul L. Piso Caesoninus, but we do not know the reason for it.

DIPLOMATIC AND INTERNATIONAL MATTERS

In the pre-Sullan period, the consuls, if they were present in the *Urbs*, were in charge of introducing in the senate the foreign ambassadors arriving in Rome. As the supreme magistrates, they presided over the debates that were held in the senate regarding the interventions of foreign envoys and informed the latter of the senatorial decisions that may have resulted from the debates. The consuls were therefore the heads of Roman diplomacy. Because of this, it was preferred to concentrate diplomatic activity in the first few weeks of the consular year so that the consuls could participate before setting off for their provinces.

In the post-Sullan period there were no substantial variations with regard to the practices summarized above. The consuls continued to play the same role in Roman diplomacy, and the ambassadors continued to be received by the senate at the beginning of the year, even though in that period the time frame was broader since the consuls remained in Rome much longer than in previous centuries. The sole variation was a law that was passed fixing the month of February as the time when foreign embassies were received by the senate. It was a *lex Gabinia* sponsored by Aulus Gabinius, who was tribune of the plebs in 67 and consul in 58. Although Gruen proposed that the law

---

[44] Lenaghan 1969: 145.

may have been passed during the consulship of Gabinius,[45] the practically unanimous opinion is that it was a tribunician law of the year 67.[46]

The law basically set forth that the month of February had to be reserved by senators to receive foreign ambassadors. In fact, it was a reflection in the law of what had been the practice for a long time. A passage from the *Verrinae* indicates that back in the year 70, February was usually the month designated for the reception of foreign legates.[47] According to Cicero, at the time there were some legates from Miletus in Rome impatiently waiting to know the names of the consuls-designate and for the month of February to arrive. The two events were obviously closely linked. Elections for the following year had not yet been held, so it was still not known who the new consuls would be who would introduce the Milesians in the senate. The Ciceronian text suggests the importance that the consuls had for the Milesians, since they had to deal with them regarding the issues that had caused them to go to Rome and, unquestionably, their favourable or unfavourable position could have a crucial influence on the senate's decisions. Likewise, it indicates that ambassadors could spend several months in Rome waiting to be received by the senate, as was the case here.

Two letters from Cicero confirm the existence of the *lex Gabinia*. In one of them, written to Lentulus towards the middle of January 56, Cicero states, without alluding to any law, that the entire month of February was reserved for the foreign embassies.[48] In the second letter, addressed to his brother Quintus and written towards the middle of February 54, Cicero says that from the Calends of February until the Calends of March the senate was busy receiving legates 'every day' (*cottidie*).[49] In the passage it is clear that it is not a mere customary practice, but an obligation set forth by the *lex Gabinia*. As Bonnefond proposed, *cottidie* must not be understood strictly in the sense that the senate received foreign embassies every day of the month, but every day on which the senate could legally meet, that is the non-comitial days, which in February were twenty-two days out of a total of twenty-eight.[50]

If the Gabinian law mainly confirmed a normal practice, seemingly without introducing significant changes, it may be asked what the *raison d'être* of the law was. In that respect, the few references of the sources to the

[45] Gruen 1974: 252–3.
[46] See, in particular, Bonnefond 1984. Broughton (1951–86: III 97–8) also considers that the most probable view is that the tribune Gabinius was the author of the law in 67. In the same sense, Balsdon 1939: 68; Griffin 1973a: 209–10; Williamson 2005: 404.
[47] Cic. *Ver.* 2.1.90. Cf. Canali de Rossi 1997: 332.   [48] Cic. *Fam.* 1.4.1.   [49] Cic. *Q.fr.* 2.11.3.
[50] Bonnefond 1984: 62.

law do not provide any explanation. It is clear that, as a great power, Rome dealt with foreign states constantly, and its diplomatic relations had become increasingly complex since it came into direct contact with the Hellenistic world in the second century. It is probable that the embassies arriving every year in the *Urbs* from lands throughout the Mediterranean began by the first century to reach a number that was making it more complicated to attend to them appropriately.[51] Consequently, it is possible that diplomatic tasks in the senate had greatly expanded, thus making it difficult for senators to undertake other issues. The meaning of the Gabinian law would then be to limit to the month of February the time devoted to foreign ambassadors.[52] This, in turn, hampered consular tasks in February, since the consuls had to attend these 'international' sessions of the senate.

Nevertheless, for this period we know of some exceptional actions of the senate in connection with the reception of embassies. In 56, the senators resolved, at the beginning of February, to adjourn the scheduled hearings of foreign envoys until the Ides of that month.[53] In this case it is but a brief postponement, keeping to the rule of designating February for international matters. Something different happened in 61, when the senators decided that they would not deal with any of their usual matters until a bill was brought to the people to approve the creation of a jury that was to try Clodius regarding the question of the Bona Dea. Amongst those matters Cicero mentions the allocation of the praetorian provinces and the hearing of the embassies.[54] Finally, in the year 60 Cicero states in another letter that the obstruction caused in the senate by Cato in the debate on the revision of the contracts of the publicans in Asia would make it necessary to delay the reception of the embassies.[55] In all three cases, there are extraordinary circumstances which indirectly show once again that February was as a rule the exclusive month for dealing with foreign embassies.

However, this does not mean that in other months of the year legates from other states could not be received if it was deemed necessary or urgent, or that international matters could only be dealt with in the senate in February.[56] Rome's institutional legal system was distinguished by its flexibility, and making a prohibition of this kind would have been against

---

[51] Canali de Rossi (1997: 297–369) compiles all the embassies arriving in Rome from the eastern Mediterranean from 81 to 50. To all of these, already a large number in itself, we must obviously add those coming from the north of Africa and from the entire Occident.

[52] Bonnefond (1984: 96–8) places the passing of the law within the political context of 67 and connects it to the fight against corruption. In her opinion, it tried to prevent ambassadors from being tempted to bribe the consuls to appoint a specific time for the reception of embassies, so that they would be received by the senate as soon as possible.

[53] Cic. *Q.fr.* 2.3.1. [54] Cic. *Att.* 1.14.5. [55] Cic. *Att.* 1.18.7. [56] Bonnefond 1984: 66.

its very nature. All the embassies arriving in Rome in the previous months and presenting themselves officially to the consuls would be introduced in the senate following an order pre-determined by the consuls themselves, as shown by the *lex de provinciis praetoriis* of the year 100.[57] Their hearing was concentrated, so far as possible, in the month of February, but without excluding the possibility of extraordinary receptions at other times during the year.[58]

Some types of information in ancient sources, including epigraphic documents, supply evidence of the consuls' direct intervention in diplomatic and international matters in the post-Sullan period. In 78, three Greek navarchs were granted, through a decree of the senate, a series of privileges as a reward for services rendered during the wars in Italy, probably with reference to the Social War. We know of this thanks to the so-called *senatus consultum de Asclepiade.*[59] The three beneficiaries were Asclepiades of Clazomene, Polystratos of Carystos and Meniskos of Miletus. They were pronounced 'friends of the Roman people' ('amici populi Romani') and received, as a great honour, Roman citizenship along with fiscal exemptions. They were also given other honours important from a symbolic point of view, such as being allowed to offer sacrifices on the Capitol or receiving the habitual treatment reserved for ambassadors when in Rome.

According to the first few lines of the inscription, the *senatus consultum* was sponsored by the consul Q. Lutatius Catulus, and the decree was passed eleven days before the Calends of June.[60] Likewise, the senatorial decree included an order to the two consuls of 78 to ensure that a copy in bronze of the so-called *formula amicorum* – a register of friends of the Roman people – was kept in the Capitolium.[61] In all probability the navarchs received at the same time a copy of the senatorial decree. Besides this, the consuls, one or both of them, were responsible for sending official letters to the Roman magistrates in Macedonia and Asia informing them of the senatorial decree and of the privileges granted to the three beneficiaries and their descendants,

---

[57] Bonnefond 1984: 67–72; Crawford 1996: 254 and 263. Cf. Giovannini 2008: 93–100.

[58] Obviously, not all the embassies were received. In some cases the senate, and the consuls on behalf of the senate, refused to hear the legates from certain enemy states, as was the case in 78 with the ambassadors sent by Mithridates, who were denied a hearing on the grounds that Sulla had just died and that the senate was very busy with other questions. This happened at the beginning of the year, perhaps in February. Criniti (1969: 410) places this episode in the spring.

[59] *CIL* I² 588 = *IG* XIV 951 = *IGR* I 118; Sherk 1969: 124–32. See the new edition and translation by Raggi 2001. Cf. Canali de Rossi 1997: 320–4.

[60] 'Q. Lutatius Q.f. Catulus co(n)s(ul) senatum consuluit a.d. XI K. Iun. in comitio … quod Q. Lutatius Q.f. Catulus co(n)s(ul) verba fecit … '

[61] Cf. Valvo 2001.

so that they and their successors would abide by them and respect them. The letters would enable the navarchs to enjoy a privileged position in their cities.[62] Although the two consuls are mentioned in the *senatus consultum* as being in charge of the enforcement of the decree, the mention of only Catulus as the sponsor suggests that the rupture between Catulus and Lepidus, which was to become deeper in the following months, had already taken place.[63]

Also in the year 78, the treaty (*foedus*) which had linked the Spanish town of Gades to Rome for decades was renewed. Cicero mentions the signing of the friendship treaty within the context of his speech in favour of the Gaditan L. Cornelius Balbus in a trial where the issue was whether or not the grant of Roman citizenship to Balbus had been legal. The orator clarifies that the initiative was taken by the Gaditans ('Gaditani . . . postulaverunt'), who presented a request to the senate to renew the *foedus* or to sign a new one in order to consolidate their preferential relation with the Roman state.[64] The request was made during the consulship of Catulus and Lepidus in 78. We do not have further details on the date when the senate discussed the question, but it seems plausible that the Gaditans sent an embassy of notables who were received by the senators at the beginning of the year, as was usual, and it was then when the senate resolved to sign the new treaty. From the Ciceronian text it can also be gathered that it was in particular the consul Catulus who defended the suitability of signing the treaty, which in fact was a new *foedus* rather than a mere renewal of the former one.[65] As in similar cases, the decision was taken by the senate, and the consul acted as its spokesman and legal representative as well as the intermediary between the Roman state and the foreign community.

The same must have happened in 75, when the Roman state signed a *foedus* with Hiempsal, king of Numidia, whereby Rome gave assurance to the monarch regarding the possession of some land on the North African coastline, which actually expanded the territory under his control. According to Cicero, the consul C. Aurelius Cotta was the sponsor of the treaty and he apparently negotiated its terms.[66] We must presume that a similar process to that described in the case of the Gaditans was followed: the Numidian embassy to Rome, its reception in the senate, a debate with the active intervention of the consul, and approval of the treaty.

---

[62] Ferrary 2009: 128–9. [63] That is the opinion of Criniti 1969: 410. [64] Cic. *Balb.* 4–35.
[65] Cic. *Balb.* 39: '. . . et hoc foedere Catuli senatusque auctoritate se nobiscum coniunctissimos esse arbitrati sunt'. Criniti 1969: 410–11.
[66] Cic. *Leg. agr.* 2.58. Cf. Jonkers 1963: 27.

Between 74 and 73 Rome witnessed litigation started by the inhabitants of the Boeotian town of Oropus against the publicans who operated in their region. We know what happened thanks to an epigraphic document which includes a letter addressed to the inhabitants of Oropus by the consuls of the year 73, M. Terentius Varro Lucullus and C. Cassius Longinus, mentioned at the beginning of the inscription (ll. 1–2), as well as the *senatus consultum* containing the decision taken.[67] The question goes back to Sulla's presence in Greece in the decade of the eighties. To fulfil a vow taken by the *imperator*, the temple of Amphiaraus received an important amount of land which was considered inviolable. On Sulla's return to Rome, this concession was confirmed by means of a *senatus consultum*. However, some years later the publicans disregarded this and tried to levy taxes in the area which was supposed to be exempt. The people from Oropus refused to pay and sent an embassy to Rome. This resulted in a *senatus consultum* during the consulship of Lucullus and M. Aurelius Cotta in 74 (ll. 3–4). The senatorial decree must have put those consuls in charge of taking a decision after conducting the mandatory investigation. For unknown reasons, in 74 no decision was taken in this respect. The explanation may lie in the fact that the two consuls left for the East within the framework of the war against Mithridates. For this reason they may not have had time for a question that they might have considered minor.

So the problem was inherited by the consuls of 73. In any case, the litigation must not have been devoid of legal and political issues, as is shown by the fact that it was not resolved until 14 October 73 in the Basilica Porcia (ll. 5–6), ten months after the consuls had taken office. According to the previous senatorial decree, the decision was taken by the consuls with the advice of a council formed by fifteen senators, whose names are listed in the inscription (ll. 7–16).[68] The inquiry unquestionably included interviews with the representatives of Oropus and of the publicans. Finally the consuls resolved in favour of the people of Oropus and against the publicans. The decision was presented and defended before the senate by the consuls two days later, on 16 October. The senators ratified it and turned the sentence into a *senatus consultum* which is reproduced in the inscription (ll. 59–69). The entire responsibility of the consuls of 73 for the solution of the dispute is pointed out on various occasions in the inscription in describing the procedure which was followed: they took the decision (ll. 2–3), they defended it before the senate (ll. 30–1), and only they are mentioned in the senatorial decree as being responsible for the decision taken (ll. 64–5).

[67] *SIG*[3] 747; *FIRA* I 36; Sherk 1969: 133–8; 1984: 85–7. Cf. Cic. *N.D.* 3.49.   [68] Cf. Crook 1955: 4–5.

The document is of great importance not only as an example of consular activity in Rome but also because it shows beyond doubt that the publicans acted in the decade of the seventies in Boeotia as tax collectors.[69] The apparently excessively long period needed to issue a report ought probably to be understood within the context of the numerous conflicts which emerged throughout the first century regarding the roles of the publicans in various territories of the Empire where communities had, at the same time, different legal and political relations with Rome. At stake was the economic profit not only of those private societies but also of the Roman state. But we must also bear in mind that the interests of the publicans were also those of many Roman senators, and that they frequently had to find a difficult balance which affected not only the economy but also politics.

The tension between publicans and the city of Mytilene can also explain the approval of the so-called *senatus consultum de agris Mytilenaeorum* in 55.[70] Mytilene had confronted Rome during the First Mithridatic War. The defeat had resulted in Mytilene's becoming a community obliged to pay tribute to Rome (*civitas stipendiaria*) around the year 80. The loss of independence had led in the economic field to the exploitation of the territorial possessions of Mytilene by the publicans. The city was freed in 62 by Pompey, as a concession to his friend Theophanes, who came from Mytilene.[71] This obviously turned Pompey into a patron and great benefactor of the city, which accorded him multiple honours.[72]

But perhaps the rights of Mytilene were not fully respected by the publicans, which must have prompted its inhabitants to send an embassy to Rome to request that their privileges be confirmed. The year 55 was, without a doubt, the most appropriate for sending a legation since their patron, Pompey, was at the time consul for the second time, which gave the ambassadors crucial support in the senate.[73] Indeed, in the preserved document, Pompey appears as the magistrate who presided over the session where the question was dealt with, and there is no doubt that the consul successfully defended the position of the people of Mytilene.[74] The usual

---

[69] Hill 1946: 38–9.   [70] Sherk 1963; 1969: 143–5; Canali de Rossi 1997: 357–8.
[71] Vell. 2.18.3; Plut. *Pomp.* 42.4.   [72] Cf. Amela Valverde 2001: 102 n. 91.
[73] The *senatus consultum* should be dated to one of the three years when Pompey was consul. Of all of them, the year 55 is the most probable for various reasons, one of them being the mention in line 12 of the document of a censor by the name of Servilius, no doubt P. Servilius Vatia Isauricus, censor in 55. On the other hand, a passage of a Ciceronian letter dating from that year (Cic. *Att.* 4.11.1), where the economic difficulties of the publicans are mentioned, can be set into the context of the senatorial decree on the land of Mytilene. Cf. Sherk 1969: 145.
[74] Pompey may have also been the author of a partially preserved letter accompanying the *senatus consultum*. Cf. Sherk 1969: no. 51; Canali de Rossi 1997: 358.

process must have been followed: an embassy to Rome; its presentation before the consuls to explain the reason for the expedition, in this case preferably to Pompey; the introduction of the legates to the senate and debate with the decisive consular intervention; and the approval of a *senatus consultum*. The senatorial decree reasserted the right of the use of certain land by the inhabitants of Mytilene, and thus excluded the publicans from collecting taxes on it.

Finally, fiscal matters are also the central point of the *lex Gabinia Calpurnia de insula Delo*, a copy of which is preserved in an epigraphic document.[75] Although it is a consular law, it is included in this section because it reflects the consuls' intervention in international matters. The law was passed in 58, and according to its contents it essentially exempted the island of Delos from the payment of taxes to Rome.[76] At the beginning of the inscription the names of the two consuls of 58, Gabinius and Piso Caesoninus, who appear as the joint authors of the law, must be restored (ll. 1–2).[77] The law may have been sponsored following a previous decision of the senate carried out by the consuls, or perhaps, on the contrary, it was the consuls who took the legislative initiative. Should the latter option be correct, everything seems to indicate that Gabinius must have been the main promoter of this measure.[78] This would explain the fact that the document makes a laudatory mention of the Gabinian law of 67, which put an end to the problem of the pirates in the Mediterranean, and that the first voter of the law was a close relative of the consul himself, A. Gabinius Capito (l. 4).[79]

Probably the law was ultimately a response to a request made by the Delians, perhaps through an embassy sent to Rome. The exact date when the motion was voted on by the people is not preserved. We know that the voting took place six days before the Calends of an unknown month, the name missing in the inscription (l. 3).[80] According to the suggested reconstruction, an embassy from Delos may have been received by the Roman senate at the beginning of February. In view of the requests made by the legates, either the senate urged the consuls to sponsor a law to satisfy the wishes of the Delians, or the consuls, perhaps Gabinius in particular,

[75] *CIL* I² 2500; Nicolet 1980a; 1980b; Crawford 1996: 1 345–51.
[76] On the fiscal exemptions granted to Delos by the Roman state, see Nicolet 1980a.
[77] Nicolet 1980a: 15.   [78] Nicolet 1980a: 16–17.
[79] Linderski and Kaminska-Linderski 1973. On the importance of the first voter in legislative comitia see Staveley 1969.
[80] Nicolet 1980a: 31: if an intercalary month was introduced that year, the date of the voting could have been 19 Februrary 58.

suggested that a law be brought before the people.[81] In either case, there is no doubt that the senate and the consuls acted in coordination and by mutual agreement.

In short, in the post-Sullan period, the consuls had basically the same functions in the field of international politics as in the pre-Sullan age. They continued to be the heads of Roman diplomacy, the intermediaries between the senate and foreign states represented by embassies sent to Rome, and the spokesmen of the external policy of the senate. Their role in senatorial debates was often such as to have a decisive influence on the decisions of the senate, as is shown by Pompey's intervention in 55 in favour of Mytilene and, possibly, by Gabinius' intervention in 58 in favour of Delos. Diplomatic tasks continued to be dealt with, as earlier, at the beginning of the year, and from 67 onwards the Gabinian law made it compulsory to reserve the month of February for the reception of foreign envoys. Nevertheless, the fact that the consuls remained in Rome the entire year, or most of it, made it possible for them to intervene directly in diplomatic and international matters beyond the month of February, should it be necessary. We have the examples of the *senatus consultum de Asclepiade*, passed in May 78 and sponsored by the consul Catulus, and the *senatus consultum de Oropiis*, which in October 73 put an end to a long investigation carried out by the consuls of that year.[82]

PUBLIC WORKS

In the pre-Sullan period, in particular during the third and second centuries, consuls promoted and were responsible for a large number of public works carried out both in the city of Rome and in Italy (temples, roads etc.). However, in the first century consular participation in this field was limited.

The most important public works project in this period was the restoration of the temple of Jupiter on the Capitolium, due to the importance of the building. The temple had been destroyed by fire in 83. During the period of Sullan domination, the building apparently received little

---

[81] Nicolet 1980a: 33.

[82] Further information from ancient sources could refer to a consular intervention regarding international politics. Plin. *Nat.* 28.30 reports an incident which occurred when an envoy from Cyprus named Evagon, of the Ophiogenes, arrived in Rome. According to Pliny, the Ophiogenes were immune to the bite of snakes. In order to confirm this, he was put in a *dolium* full of snakes by order of the consuls, and he survived the experiment unharmed. Pliny does not provide any indications to place this episode in a particular period, and it is not reported by any other source. Canali de Rossi (1997: 359) plausibly points out that the event might have occurred in the Republican period, considering the role played by the consuls.

attention.[83] Five years later, the senate appointed one of the consuls of 78, Catulus, to be in charge of the reconstruction work. This is well known, both through various ancient authors who mention Catulus as 'supervisor for the rebuilding of the Capitolium' ('curator restituendi Capitolii') or who refer to the Capitolium as his work,[84] and through two inscriptions which provide further relevant information:

'Q. Lutatius Q.f. Q.[n.] Catulus co(n)s(ul) substructionem et tabularium | de s(enatus) s(ententia) faciundum coeravit [ei]demque prob[avit].'[85]

'[Q. Lu]tatius Q.f. Q.n. C[atulus co(n)s(ul) de s]en(atus) sent(entia) faciundu[m coeravit] eidemque [p]rob[avit].'[86]

As can be noted, Catulus not only rebuilt the temple of Jupiter, but he was also in charge of the construction of a substructure (*substructio*) and of the Tabularium. The *substructio* was a great platform on which the whole Capitoline complex rested, an essential work to connect the Forum with the Capitoline Hill. The Tabularium was a detached building located on the higher part of the complex and the venue where the state's archives were housed.[87] Unquestionably, it was a work on a grand scale which went on for several years. When reporting that the Sibylline Books were placed again on the Capitolium in 76, Lactantius adds that the reconstruction work directed by Catulus was in progress.[88] In the summary of the work of Livy under the year 69, it is claimed that the temple of Jupiter on the Capitolium was dedicated by Catulus that year.[89] But that was not the end of the work or of Catulus' intervention. We know through Suetonius that Caesar, on the first day of his praetorship in 62, quoted Catulus in a speech before the people. His purpose was to question the work carried out by Catulus and enact a bill to entrust another person with the management of the reconstruction of the temple. Caesar was forced to give up after determining that Catulus had great support amongst the *optimates*.[90] Cassius Dio claims that Caesar wanted Pompey to be in charge of the work on the temple of Jupiter Capitolinus so that he would have the glory of finishing the temple and having his name inscribed instead of that of Catulus.[91] As proved by the

---

[83] Flower 2008: 80–4.   [84] Gel. 2.10.2; Cic. *Ver.* 2.4.69.

[85] *CIL* 1² 737 = VI 1314 = *ILS* 35 = *ILLRP* 367.   [86] *CIL* 1² 736 = VI 1313 = *ILS* 35a = *ILLRP* 368.

[87] Mura Sommella 2000; Tucci 2005. Cf. De Ruggiero 1925: 69; Criniti 1969: 378–9; Aberson 1994: 260.

[88] Lact. *Ira Dei* 22.6.   [89] Liv. *per.* 98. Cf. Flower 2008: 78–9.

[90] Suet. *Jul.* 15. Suetonius claims that those *optimates* attended en masse the assembly convened by Caesar, instead of meeting the new consuls, as was usual on the first day of the year, when the consuls paraded from their respective homes to the Capitolium to perform the sacrifices, pronounce the annual vows, and convene the first meeting of the senate of the year.

[91] Cass. Dio, 37.44.1–2. Cf. Flower 2008: 85.

aforementioned inscriptions, Catulus was in charge of the work on the
Capitolium to the end, although we do not know the exact date of
completion. He was in charge of the contract for the work, its supervision,
and the final *probatio*, that is, the verification that the work had been
completed in accordance with the contract.[92]

The other consul of the year 78, M. Aemilius Lepidus, was involved in
the restoration of the Basilica Aemilia.[93] Pliny reports this fact and states
that Lepidus not only decorated the Basilica with shields (*clipei*) containing portraits of his ancestors, but also used that decoration in his own
house.[94] The reverse of a coin shows the Basilica Aemilia, on whose front
the *clipei* stand out with the legend AIMILIA on the top, M LEPIDVS on
the bottom, REF(ecta) on the left side and S(enatus) C(onsulto) on the
right (Fig. 2).[95] The coin was minted in 61 by the son of the consul of
78 and future triumvir. It clearly commemorates the restoration carried
out by his father and suggests that the work went beyond the mere
embellishment of the building with *clipei*, as Pliny says, and that it was
quite extensive.[96] The censor of 179, M. Aemilius Lepidus, had taken
part in the original construction of the Basilica, and throughout the
first century several members of the gens Aemilia were in charge of its
renovation, so the building was always linked to the family. That could
mean that the initiative for the restoration of the Basilica possibly came
from the consul Lepidus himself. The inscription SC on the coin suggests
that a senatorial decree approved the restoration and authorized Lepidus
to carry out the proposed work. This would place the beginning of the
work on the Basilica Aemilia in 78, under the direction of the consul
Lepidus.[97] As is well known, the tension between Lepidus and the senate
grew during the year and ended in a military confrontation and the death
of Lepidus. The authorization for the work must therefore have been
given at the beginning of the year. It is impossible to know whether the
work was finished during 78 or, in view of its large scale, continued for a
longer period.

---

[92] In the state archives copies were kept of the work contracts, so that it could at any time be verified
whether the contractor had complied with the terms of the original contract. Likewise, copies of the
probatio, with the approval of the person who was in charge of the construction work, were also kept.
See Brélaz 2003.

[93] On the archaeological identification of the Basilica Aemilia with the remains of three long parallel
walls found on the eastern end of the forum, to the east of the Temple of Castor, see Steinby 1987.
Cf. Fuchs 1956.

[94] Plin. *Nat.* 35.13.   [95] Crawford 1974: no. 419/3a-b.   [96] Steinby 1993; Wiseman 1993.

[97] Allély (2004: 27) thinks that Lepidus became rich during his stay in Sicily in 80 as propraetor and that
it was after his return that he dealt with the restoration of the Basilica Aemilia.

2. Denarius of Marcus Lepidus depicting the Basilica Aemilia (61 BC)

Some of the great *imperatores* in this period, in particular Pompey and
Caesar, competed in the construction of great buildings for public use in
Rome as a means of gaining popularity. Pompey also sought a way to make
his consulships coincide with the inauguration of buildings promoted by
him, surrounding the occasions with great pomp to turn them into grand
popular ceremonies and to magnify his importance as consul. During his
second consulship in 55, his theatre was inaugurated. It was a work of great
size and significance, since it was the first permanent theatre built of stone in
Rome. The attached portico was inaugurated along with the theatre. The
inauguration was accompanied by great games organized by Pompey himself, for which no expense was spared: the entertainments included combats
between men and animals, athletic games, and musical performances.[98] The
inauguration of the theatre and the subsequent games probably took place
in the month of August.[99]

Pompey's theatre was not an isolated building; on the contrary, it
involved the comprehensive restructuring of a vast area of the Campus
Martius, including the portico already mentioned, a garden, and the

[98] Cass. Dio, 39.38, provides a detailed description of the games. Cf. Ooteghem 1954: 402–11; Seager
2005: 124; Greenhalgh 1981: 54–60. Pompey had already organized great votive games during his first
consulship in 70 in order to gain popularity (Cic. *Ver.* 1.31; Ps.-Asc. 217 St.). Pompey had promised to
organize the games if he defeated Sertorius. Gelzer 2005: 68: the games were celebrated between
16 August and 1 September 70.

[99] This chronology can be deduced from a letter written by Cicero at the end of September (Cic. *Fam.*
15.1), and from the commentary of Asconius about the time when Cicero pronounced his speech
against Piso, a few days before the inauguration of the theatre (Asc. 1 C.). Marshall (1985: 81–2) places
the date of the dedication of Pompey's theatre on 12 August. See also Lewis 2006: 193–4. Cf. Gros
2000b.

so-called Curia Pompeii. The whole complex was probably not fully completed by 55, but Pompey rushed the inauguration of the theatre, the most
spectacular part, to make it coincide with his consulship. Three years later,
Pompey used his third consulship to inaugurate another part of the complex, seeking once more to gain the greatest political benefit and a display of
his prominent role in the community.

We know of a related incident thanks to Aulus Gellius.[100] The Latin
author considers the question of whether it is more appropriate to use the
term *tertium* or *tertio* to refer to someone who was holding a magistracy
for the third time. Gellius quotes Varro as an authority on the matter,
who differentiated between *quarto*, which would mean 'in the fourth
place', and *quartum*, 'for the fourth time'. Thus, Ennius had been correct
in writing 'Quintus pater quartum fit consul' in the sense that Quintus had
been appointed a consul for the fourth time. In this context Gellius, quoting
Cicero's freedman Tiro, recounts how Pompey, when intending to place an
inscription in his theatre, hesitated as to whether it should refer to him in his
third consulship as *tertium* or *tertio consul*. Pompey asked Cicero for his
opinion, and the diplomatic Arpinate, not wanting to fall out with other
philologists who may have had a different point of view from his, suggested
that he should not have either *tertium* or *tertio* inscribed, but the abbrevia-
tion *tert.*, which could be interpreted either way. This must have happened
in 52, during Pompey's third consulship, when he carried out the dedication, according to Gellius, of a temple of Victory (*aedes Victoriae*) located at
the top of his theatre. In all probability it is an error by Gellius. He should,
in fact, have been referring to the dedication of the sanctuary of Venus
Victrix which was at the top of Pompey's theatre, whose grandstand
served as the main access to the temple.[101] The epithet Victrix could refer
to Pompey's victories in the seventies and sixties.

In this area of consular self-representation we could include the possible
intervention of Pompey's colleague in the consulship in the second half
of 52. In a letter from Cicero to Atticus, he mentions the placement
by Metellus Scipio of equestrian statues on the Capitolium in honour
of previous Scipiones, among them Scipio Nasica.[102] In fact, Cicero is

---

[100] Gel. 11.7.

[101] Plin. *Nat.* 8.20; Tert. *Spect.* 10.5. Gros 2000a: the dedication took place on 12 August 52. Cf. Welch
2006: 512.

[102] Cic. *Att.* 6.1.17. Cf. Coarelli 1969: 145–7: in particular the sculpture of Nasica would be homage to
the promoter of the repression of Ti. Sempronius Gracchus, who was murdered very near the area
where the statues of the Scipiones had now been placed. Against this symbolic interpretation,
Landwehr 1985: 41. On the gallery of portraits of Metellus Scipio and its hypothetical relation to the
iconography of tyrannicide in Rome, Pina Polo 2006b: 88–92. See also Sehlmeyer 1999: 189–90.

mocking Metellus Scipio, who had been adopted by Metellus Pius, for not knowing the story of his natural family, since he had confused Scipio Aemilianus with Scipio Nasica in the series of statues. The statues had already been placed on the Capitolium before February 50, when Cicero's letter was written. It is probable, then, that the gallery of portraits may have been made, or at least started, during the consulship of Metellus Scipio.[103] Just like his colleague Pompey, he may thus have wanted to leave an enduring memento of his consulship, linking the grandeur of his family to the symbolism of an emblematic site for Romans.

In 57, the consuls were involved in the issue of Cicero's house. In a letter to Atticus in the middle of September, just a few days after his return to Rome, Cicero informed his friend that he was expecting the decision that the pontiffs had to make regarding the restitution of his house. Cicero considered two options. If the consecration of the site of his house made by Clodius to the goddess Libertas were nullified, he would recover the land to rebuild his dwelling and would also receive compensation for the house that had been demolished in his absence. If, on the contrary, the consecration were kept, he would be paid compensation for both the house and the site. In any case, the consuls had to be in charge of carrying out either decision, always in line with a corresponding senatorial decree.[104]

In another letter written at the beginning of October, Cicero recounts in detail how, once the pontiffs had given their reply, on 2 October after two days of deliberations the senate passed a decree returning to Cicero the site where his house used to be. The question had been put forward for debate by the consuls Lentulus and Metellus Nepos.[105] Immediately afterwards, the consuls saw about putting the *senatus consultum* into practice. On the one hand, the consuls valued Cicero's house at two million sesterces and assessed the value of his other properties which had been damaged. On the other hand, the consuls commissioned the reconstruction of Catulus' portico, situated next to Cicero's house.[106] This portico, originally built by Q. Lutatius Catulus after the victory against the Cimbri in 101, had been extended by Clodius during the exile of Cicero using part of the site of the house of the Arpinate.[107] The extension of the portico was immediately

---

[103] Ooteghem 1967: 306.   [104] Cic. *Att.* 4.1.7.

[105] Cic. *Att.* 4.2.1–5; *Har.* 13. On 29 September, Cicero had pronounced his speech *De domo sua* before the pontiffs, which was crucial for the annulment of the consecration of the site of his house on the Palatine. On the ideological content of the Ciceronian speech see Marco Simón and Pina Polo 2000. Cf. Kumaniecki 1959; Lenagham 1969: 19.

[106] Cic. *Att.* 4.2.5. On the location of the house of Cicero and of the Porticus Catuli, see Cerutti 1997. Cf. Millar 1998: 157.

[107] Cic. *Dom.* 102.

demolished by the contractors who had been commissioned to carry out the work by the consuls.

A third letter written on 23 November shows the progress of the work. Cicero informs his friend Atticus that a Clodian armed gang had ejected the workers who were rebuilding his house on the Palatine and had also knocked down Catulus' portico, which was being restored.[108] The work in progress was supposed to return the portico to its original size, and it is clear that it had started immediately after the consuls had carried out the *locatio*, since Cicero claims that when the building was destroyed by Clodius' men it was nearly roof high.

As can be observed, there were few public works for which there is evidence of the consuls' intervention in the post-Sullan period. Besides Pompey's theatre complex, which is not properly a consular work although the inaugurations of its components were carried out to coincide with the consulships of Pompey, the only known cases are the restorations of existing buildings (the temple of Jupiter on the Capitol, the portico of Catulus, and possibly the Basilica Aemilia) approved by the senate and of which one or both of the consuls of the year were put in charge. The only completely new building built in this period under consular auspices was the Tabularium, the work on which was in fact linked to the restoration of the temple of Jupiter and of the substructure that had to support the entire Capitoline complex.

Outside Rome, we know of the building activity of the consul Ap. Claudius in the Greek sanctuary of Eleusis through an inscription. The preserved inscription on the architrave of the lower propylon is as follows:

'[Ap. Claudi]us Ap.f. Pulche[r] propylum Cere[ri | et Proserpi]nae co(n)sul vovit [im]perato[r coepit | Pulcher Clau]dius et Rex Mar[cius fec]erun[t ex testam (ento)].'[109]

In November or December 54, Ap. Claudius set off from Rome for his province, Cilicia. On his way, he must have stopped in Eleusis, where he made the vow to rebuild the propylon of the sanctuary. He did so, as the inscription states, while still a consul (*consul vovit*). The work presumably started when Claudius was already in Cilicia (*imperator coepit*), where he remained until he was replaced by Cicero in 51. The work went on for several years, but its promoter did not see its completion, since Claudius died in 49 in Euboea. It is possible that his death might have stopped the

---

[108] Cic. *Att.* 4.3.2. These events occurred on 3 November (Marinone 2004: 111). Cf. Vanderbroeck 1987: 251.

[109] *CIL* I² 775 = III 547 = *ILS* 4041 = *ILLRP* 401.

work for a certain period of time. Nevertheless, as stated in the inscription, two of his nephews saw to finishing the propylon in agreement with the will of Ap. Claudius, who had probably assigned a sum of money for this purpose.[110]

Cicero indirectly confirms that the work was in progress at least from the end of 51, although it probably started much earlier. In a letter to Atticus on 20 February 50, he claims to have heard that Ap. Claudius was building a propylon in Eleusis.[111] Next, Cicero shows his disposition to compete with Claudius and asks Atticus if he would find it appropriate for him to promote the construction of a propylon in the Academy of Athens, because he would like to leave a memorial of himself there. In a further letter, Cicero expresses his concern that while Claudius' work was going ahead, his own project in the Academy was halted.[112]

EDICTS, *CONTIONES* AND CONSULAR INVESTIGATIONS

As in previous centuries, the issuance of edicts and the ability to speak at a *contio* were, in the post-Sullan period, the two official ways in which consuls could communicate with the people of Rome. Sources do not mention many consular edicts for this period. Probably one of the greatest producers of consular edicts was M. Calpurnius Bibulus in 59. In protest at the approval of the agrarian law sponsored by his colleague Caesar, Bibulus locked himself in his house from the end of January until the end of the year. From his home, he issued a great many edicts in which he claimed to be constantly watching the sky to find unfavourable omens, thus threatening the possibility of repealing the Caesarian laws as illegal. The edicts of Bibulus were spread throughout Rome and eagerly read by all those who, like Cicero, opposed the measures that were being introduced by Caesar. Bibulus even wrote speeches addressed to the people which were also spread around the city, referred to by Cicero as *contiones*.[113] With this tactic, Bibulus managed to bring about the unpopularity of the three allies, Caesar, Pompey, and Crassus, at least among certain sectors of the population.[114] But Bibulus' edicts were not only the result of an obstructionist tactic, they also had practical effects as consular edicts, despite the special

---

[110] Wiseman (1970b: 211) admits that it is impossible to establish with certainty when the propylon of Eleusis was finished, but he suggests that this could have happened around the year 37. Cf. Clinton 1986: 1505.

[111] Cic. *Att.* 6.1.26.   [112] Cic. *Att.* 6.6.2. See Schneider 1998: 437–8.

[113] Cic. *Att.* 2.20.4. Cf. Cic. *Att.* 2.19.2; 2.21.4.

[114] Meier 1982: 264–5; Gruen 1974: 92; Millar 1998: 130–1.

circumstances in which they were issued. The best evidence for this is the edict that postponed the elections, which had initially been scheduled for the summer, until October.[115]

Valerius Maximus narrates an exceptional event which happened in 77 in which the consul Mamercus Aemilius Lepidus Livianus was involved.[116] A priest of the goddess Cybele named Genucius had inherited some goods. The urban praetor had approved the will in the first place, but the consul opposed it and abrogated the praetorian decision. The consul argued that Genucius had castrated himself voluntarily according to the rituals of the cult of Cybele and could not be considered legally a man or a woman. Valerius Maximus praises the moralizing decree of the consul Mamercus Lepidus, whose conservatism is well known through some of his other actions.[117]

As in previous centuries, edicts were usually announced in *contiones*. In 58, a consular edict forced L. Aelius Lamia, an equestrian who was a friend of Cicero's, to go into exile at least two hundred miles from Rome. The edict of banishment (*relegatio*), attributed to the consul Gabinius by Cicero, was read by the consul himself before the popular assembly.[118] The reason for the banishment was the support for Cicero shown by Lamia and by other equites in the context of the exile of the Arpinate. Although Cicero suggests that it was an illegal edict, he had threatened Catiline in 63 with the same punishment.[119]

In the pre-Sullan period, the participation of the consuls in *contiones* was relatively rare compared to other magistracies, in particular the tribunate of the plebs. The reason was not a reluctance to take part in the assemblies of the people but was due, rather, to the usual absence of the consuls as well as the scanty consular legislative activity. Both factors changed radically in the first century and for this reason, the sources very often mention the consuls as orators before the people in the post-Sullan age.[120]

In particular, the consuls took part in two types of *contiones*: legislative and political.[121] The fact that it was mandatory to publicly debate a *rogatio*

---

[115] Cic. *Att.* 2.20.6. Cf. Cic. *Att.* 2.21.5. Meier 1982: 89; Gruen 1974: 144.   [116] V. Max. 7.7.6.

[117] Sumner 1964: 46–7; Gruen 1974: 123.   [118] Cic. *Sest.* 29. Pina Polo 1989: 298.

[119] Kelly 2006: 65–6.

[120] Pina Polo (1989: 286–307) collects all the known *contiones* for the period between 80 and 50. See also Pina Polo 1996: 186–91: the lists of orators taking part in *contiones* in the late Republican period show that the tribunes of the plebs were always the main orators before the people, before and after Sulla's dictatorship. After the tribunes, the consuls were the magistrates who participated most in *contiones*. But whereas known consular participation before 80 is scarce, from that moment on the instances reported by the sources increase considerably.

[121] Millar 1998: 120–1: 'The other essential feature of this period was the continued presence of the consuls in Rome through all or most of their year of office, which only served to afford more opportunities for direct public confrontations over legislation.'

for a period of three market days before the bill was finally voted by the people required the promoters of the *rogatio* to summon and preside over several assemblies where both they and other orators spoke for and against the bill. We know of some legislative *contiones* with consular intervention, but logically their number must have been much higher, since, as we shall see later, the quantity of consular laws in the post-Sullan period was relatively high. Some of the popular assemblies were recorded by ancient sources because of their far-reaching social effects. At the beginning of 61, the Bona Dea scandal and the subsequent discussion on how Clodius should be brought to trial engulfed the political scene in Rome. A good example of this is the assembly held on the last day or the penultimate day of January. It was the *contio* before the voting of the *rogatio Pupia* on the special court to try Clodius. The consul Pupius Piso, who had convened it, was the first to speak against the proposed law despite being its sponsor upon the senate's request. He was followed by Cato, Hortensius, and Favonius. Finally, the meeting of the comitia, which was supposed to take place after the *contio*, was not held, and the question was returned to the senate.[122]

In January of 59 the debate of the agrarian law sponsored by the consul Caesar also had great social repercussions. The sources refer to the *contiones* prior to the voting in the comitia, where both Caesar and his political allies, Crassus and Pompey, spoke in favour of the bill and the consul Bibulus and Cato spoke against it, which caused the latter to be thrown off the speaker's platform and taken to prison because of his obstructive tactics.[123] It is interesting to note that Caesar forced the presence of Bibulus on the speaker's platform to make him state his opinion about the bill, in the knowledge that it would be difficult for him to give specific arguments against it before the people, as eventually happened, although Bibulus resisted the pressure and claimed that he would not allow revolutionary measures to be introduced during his consulship.[124]

Cicero's return from exile was the prevailing issue in the first half of 57. After several failed attempts, the law authorizing Cicero to return to Rome was eventually passed in August in the *comitia centuriata*. The sponsor of the bill, the consul Lentulus Spinther, Pompey, and other senators defended it in one of the *contiones*.[125]

---

[122] Cic. *Att.* 1.14.5. Moreau 1982: 112; Vanderbroeck 1987: 235; Pina Polo 1989: 295; Gruen 1974: 248; Tatum 1999: 79; Morstein-Marx 2004: 186–8.

[123] Cass. Dio, 38.4–6; App. *B.Civ.* 2.10–12; Plut. *Cat.min.* 33; *Pomp.* 47.4. Vanderbroeck 1987: 236–7; Pina Polo 1989: 296–7.

[124] Morstein-Marx 2004: 166–7.

[125] Cic. *Sest.* 107–8; *Pis.* 34; 80; *Red. Pop.* 26; *Red. Pop.* 16–17. Pina Polo 1989: 301.

The *auctoritas* attached to the consuls due to the fact that they were the supreme magistrates meant that they were asked to give their opinion about major questions in *contiones* summoned by other magistrates. Throughout the decade of the seventies the question of the tribunician power was recurrent.[126] Back in the year 78, the restitution of all their powers to the tribunes of the plebs was considered for the first time. Some of the tribunes for that year questioned the consul Lepidus about this in a *contio*. He replied that the restoration of the tribunician power would have a negative impact on the public interest and, according to Granius Licinianus, he managed to convince most of those present at the assembly with his reasoning. Licinianus claims that the speech of the consul was preserved and that he used it for his historical reconstruction.[127] In 76, the tribune Sicinius again carried out a campaign in favour of the full restoration of the tribunician power and brought the two consuls to a *contio* to state their opinion. Only C. Scribonius Curio spoke before the people, while his colleague Octavius listened to him from the speakers' platform.[128]

Valerius Maximus praises the firm attitude of the consul C. Calpurnius Piso in 67. The praetor of 69, M. Lollius Palicanus, whom Valerius Maximus describes as 'a most seditious man' (*seditiosissimus*), had gained significant popularity. Palicanus was running for the consulship of 66. Since Piso was to preside over the elections, some tribunes of the plebs who supported Palicanus demanded the presence of the consul in a *contio*.[129] There they asked Piso before the people whether he would agree to make the official proclamation (*renuntiatio*) of Palicanus should he be elected by the majority of the popular vote. The consul stated outright that he would not. According to Valerius Maximus, this answer was decisive in Palicanus' defeat.[130]

At the beginning of 58, Clodius increased his accusations against Cicero for having executed the Catilinarian plotters in 63. He then promoted his *lex de capite civis Romani*, which punished any magistrate who had executed a Roman citizen with no prior conviction, a law clearly directed against Cicero. Clodius sought the public support of some of the most prominent people at the time. In the process of discussing his bill, he took Caesar,

---

[126] Millar 1998: 55–67.   [127] Gran. Licin. 33.14 Flemisch. Millar 1998: 58.
[128] Cic. *Brut.* 217; Sal. *Hist.* 3.48.8 = 3.34.8 McGushin (vol. II 89–90). Pina Polo 1989: 286.
[129] Vanderbroeck 1987: 226, suggests that the tribunes of the plebs may have been C. Cornelius and A. Gabinius, who, like Palicanus, were very close to Pompey. It was Palicanus who, while a tribune of the plebs, convened in the autumn of the year 71 the assembly where the designated consul Pompey announced the reforms that he intended to carry out as consul (Cic. *Ver.* 1.45). Pina Polo 1996: 38–9.
[130] V. Max. 3.8.3. Pina Polo 1989: 289; 1996: 50; Meier 1997: 88 n. 147.

Crassus, and the two consuls, Piso and Gabinius, to a *contio* held on 20 February at the Circus Flaminius. All of them spoke openly or implicitly in favour of Clodius' bill, thus clearing the way for Cicero's exile.[131]

Cicero is an excellent example of the use of *contiones* during his consulship. Until the year 63 he had only acted sporadically as an orator before the people. In fact, his first intervention in a *contio* took place when he was a praetor in 66.[132] But throughout his consular year he made use of his power to convene a *contio* (*potestas contionandi*) to deliver numerous speeches before the popular assembly.[133] In January, he spoke on three occasions before the people to reject the agrarian bill of the tribune P. Servilius Rullus. The second and third of the speeches *De lege agraria* are preserved and only references are left of the fourth (the first speech had been delivered before the senate).[134] He announced before the people that he renounced the province that had been allotted to him and that he preferred to stay in Rome during his consulship for the good of the Republic.[135] Also in a *contio*, he invited the people to desist from their hostile actions against L. Roscius Otho.[136] In the context of the trial against C. Rabirius, Cicero delivered his *Pro Rabirio perduellionis reo* in a *contio*.[137] And, of course, on two occasions he spoke before the people denouncing the Catilinarian conspiracy, in the speeches that constitute the second and third of the Catilinarians. His last action as consul was in fact a speech in a *contio*. On the last day of the year he wanted to give the usual farewell speech before the people, where the consul

---

[131] Cic. *Sest.* 33; *Pis.* 14; *Red. Pop.* 13; 17; Plut. *Cic.* 30–1; Cass. Dio, 38.16–17. Cf. Grimal 1967: 38–9; Nippel 1988: 115–16; Pina Polo 1989: 299; Morstein-Marx 2004: 264. In 58 an important factor against Cicero was the easy access to the speakers' platform of some of his most conspicuous detractors as magistrates with the power to summon a *contio*. When a demonstration of members of the equestrian order took place in Rome in favour of Cicero, the answer of the consul Gabinius was to deliver a speech before the people against the equites. According to Cicero, he even threatened them with proscriptions (Cic. *Sest.* 28; *Red. Pop.* 12; 32; *Planc.* 87). The aforementioned consular edict ordering the *relegatio* of Lamia is part of this context of suppression of the support given by the equites to Cicero. The tribune Clodius also summoned a *contio* to attack the equites (Cass. Dio, 38.16.5).

[132] Cic. *Man.* 1–2. Cf. Pina Polo 1996: 18–19; 124.

[133] Pina Polo 1989: 291–3; Millar 1998: 95–7; Marinone 2004: 82–7. On Cicero's attitude regarding the *contiones* and the persons who usually attended, see Pina Polo 1996: 119–26; Morstein-Marx 2004: 121–3; 207–30.

[134] Cic. *Leg. agr.* 2 and 3. Cf. Cic. *Att.* 2.1.3; Plut. *Cic.* 12.2–5. On the Ciceronian speeches and the contents of the law, Ferrary 1988; Morstein-Marx 2004: 191–3; Williamson 2005: 63–77.

[135] Cic. *Att.* 2.1.3; *Pis.* 5; *Fam.* 5.2.3; Cass. Dio, 37.33.3–4. Crawford 1984: 82–4: the speech was delivered in May or June, and it is unknown whether it was published or not.

[136] Cic. *Att.* 2.1.3; Plut. *Cic.* 13.4. Cicero gave this speech in front of the temple of Bellona, in an assembly that he convened after Roscius Otho had been booed during the games for having had a law passed while he was a tribune of the plebs, four years earlier, whereby fourteen rows of seats, just behind the senators, were reserved for the equites (Vanderbroeck 1987: 230; Nippel 1988: 59). Roscius Otho was probably praetor in 63 (Broughton 1951–86: II 167). On the speech, Crawford 1994: 213–18.

[137] Cic. *Att.* 2.1.3; Cass. Dio, 37.27–8.

publicly swore that he had obeyed the laws during his consulship, in a similar manner to the oath that he had taken at the beginning of his term of office. The tribune of the plebs Metellus Nepos tried to stop him, accusing him of having ordered the execution of Roman citizens without a trial. Nevertheless, Cicero went to the speakers' platform to take his oath, which allowed him to make a brief defence of his consular year.[138] Throughout the entire year, Cicero had kept frequent contact with the people by means of his participation in *contiones*.

An agenda of consular speeches before the people like Cicero's would have been impossible in the pre-Sullan period, but it must not have been an exception in the first century. We have more information for 63 than for other years thanks to Cicero's ambition for a glorious place in history. The more or less frequent intervention of consuls in *contiones* could depend on various factors, mainly the nature of the political events for the specific year and the consuls' own wishes. But it is reasonable to suppose that, as supreme magistrates present in Rome, they must have spoken regularly from the speaker's platform.

The *contio* was the appropriate place to promote political programmes which their sponsors knew would meet the opposition of the senatorial majority. In 78, the consul Lepidus delivered a speech in an assembly recorded by Sallust, in which he harshly attacked the Sullan regime and proposed the restitution of civil rights to the proscribed, the return of the exiles etc.[139] According to the Sallustian text, the speech seems to have been given while Sulla was still alive, but this seems unlikely.[140] In 75, the consul C. Aurelius Cotta once again sponsored a law entitling the tribunes of the plebs to hold higher magistracies. Either as part of the process of discussion of the bill or as a means of creating a favourable political atmosphere towards this measure, according to Sallust, the consul delivered a *contio* making an appeal to Roman citizens for concord.[141]

While from his home Bibulus was spreading speeches written by him against Caesar in the form of pamphlets in 59, Caesar always had the option of legally convening a *contio* to counteract the theses of his political adversary, and we know that he did so. When Bibulus issued an edict to

---

[138] Cic. *Fam.* 5.2.7; *Pis.* 6–7; Plut. *Cic.* 23.2–3; Cass. Dio, 37.38.2. Millar 1998: 112–13.

[139] Sal. *Hist.* 1.55 = 1.48 McGushin (vol. I 28–32).

[140] See Hayne 1972: 665; Gruen 1974: 12–13. However, Criniti (1969: 381) believes it possible that the speech was delivered in January or February, when Sulla was still alive. Labruna (1975: 25–31 and 151) agrees with this thesis.

[141] Sal. *Hist.* 2.47 = 2.44 McGushin (vol. I 50–2). Pina Polo 1989: 286–7; Morstein-Marx 2004: 262. On the speech McGushin 1992: I 208–17.

delay the consular elections, around the month of July, Caesar replied by summoning an assembly in which he criticized the obstructive tactics of his colleague.[142] Caesar also tried to gain political profit from an obscure episode that became public in the autumn. There was a supposed plot to murder Pompey and perhaps Caesar as well. He took the question before the people in one or several *contiones*, making Vettius stand on the speakers' platform to confess who had given the orders to commit these crimes.[143] In this manner, Caesar tried to present himself and his allies before the people as the victims of those who were opposed to the reforms that the consul had introduced, in order to counteract the propaganda that those groups had been spreading for months against him. Aware of the importance of direct contact with the people, Bibulus himself tried, after leaving the voluntary seclusion that had taken up virtually his entire consulship, to give his viewpoint on the political situation at a *contio*. On the last day of the year, he convened the usual assembly to swear that he had acted in compliance with the law. Bibulus wanted to go further and give a political speech, but Clodius, who had already taken office as a tribune of the plebs, prevented him from doing so.[144]

Access to the speakers' platform did not guarantee the success of a campaign carried out in *contiones*. At the conference of Luca it was agreed that Pompey and Crassus should run as candidates in the consular elections for 55. The official confirmation of their candidacy roused opposition in some sectors of the Roman aristocracy. One of the consuls of 56, Lentulus Marcellinus, declared himself openly against the candidacy of the two *imperatores*, in at least one *contio*, while he criticized the excessive power of Pompey and the progressive reduction of freedom in Rome.[145] Despite this opposition, their candidacies went ahead, and both Crassus and Pompey were elected.

On the other hand, *contiones* continued in the first century to be one of the most important means of informing the people of community matters. At times, the consuls themselves wished to report the decisions taken by the senate in a popular assembly. This is what happened in September 57, when the consuls convened and presided over a *contio* to read the senatorial decree whereby Pompey was put in charge of the supply of grain to Rome for the next five years. When Cicero's name was mentioned, the persons who were

---

[142] Cic. *Att.* 2.21.5. Pina Polo 1989: 297.
[143] Cic. *Att.* 2.24.3; *Vat.* 24; Suet. *Jul.* 20.8; Cass. Dio, 38.9.4; App. *B.Civ.* 2.12 and 17. Vanderbroeck 1987: 239.
[144] Cass. Dio, 38.12.3. Pina Polo 1989: 298.
[145] V. Max. 6.2.6; Cass. Dio, 39.28.5. Pina Polo 1989: 302–3.

attending gave him an ovation, so he was called upon to speak. Just returned from exile, Cicero was at the time a private citizen, and he took this opportunity to deliver a speech thanking the people, known as *Post reditum ad Quirites*.[146]

As in the pre-Sullan age, in the first century few judicial investigations were extraordinarily entrusted to consuls by means of a *senatus consultum*. In the summer of 74, the senate issued a decree ordering the investigation of the accusations of corruption made against Iunius' tribunal.[147] Oppianicus had been sentenced to exile, but there were rumours that his son-in-law Cluentius, whom Oppianicus had allegedly tried to poison, had bribed the members of the jury. The tribune of the plebs Quinctius, who had been Oppianicus' defence lawyer, used the rumours to create a favourable climate of opinion to have the verdict reversed. The senate then issued a decree ordering the creation of a special inquiry charged with investigating the facts. In his later speech in favour of Cluentius, Cicero praised both the consul Lucullus and the consuls designated for 73 for having ignored the senatorial order, which Cicero considered groundless and merely the product of slander against his client.[148] The *senatus consultum* was therefore issued when the elections for 73 had already been held, probably in July or August,[149] and for that reason the investigation was entrusted to the designated consuls and to Lucullus (the other consul of 74 must have already left Rome by then), who must by then have been making preparations to set off for the East to take over command of the war against Mithridates. It seems that the investigation was never carried out.

In contrast, the investigation resulting from the conflict between the Sabine communities of Interamna and Reate was completed in the year 54. The sources do not explain the nature of the problem, which probably went back to an earlier time and must have been connected with the floods that periodically occurred in the area since a canal had been built in the third century linking the lake Velinus and the river Nar.[150] In all probability, the recurrence of the problem caused the senate to take part in the matter and order an investigation. We know of its existence thanks to Cicero, who spoke before the inquiry commission on behalf of the people of Reate, with whose aristocracy he maintained close ties.[151] In order to gain first-hand

---

[146] Cic. *Att.* 4.1.6; Cass. Dio, 39.9.1. Pina Polo 1989: 301.
[147] Ooteghem 1959: 46; Keaveney 1992: 188–9; Gruen 1974: 33–4.   [148] Cic. *Clu.* 136–7.
[149] Sherwin-White (1984: 165) defers the issuance of the *senatus consultum* until November. Against this, with good arguments, Keaveney 1992: 189.
[150] The problem was not completely solved in 54, since it was raised again in 15 AD (Tac. *Ann.* 1.79).
[151] Meier 1997: 37.

knowledge of the circumstances which created the problem, Cicero was invited by the notables of Reate to go to their town. The Arpinate must have travelled there at the beginning of July, since he claims to have returned to Rome seven days before the Ides of the month of Quintilis.[152] Although Cicero says nothing on this matter, the hearing which was to conclude the investigation must have been held in Rome, on the one hand because, if it had happened during his stay in Reate, he would, no doubt, have informed Atticus of the outcome in the letter, and on the other hand because Cicero claims that the case was resolved before the consuls ('apud hos consules') and ten legates.[153] It is unlikely that the two Roman consuls left Rome to pass sentence in Reate or Interamna. The legates appointed by both cities, amongst them Cicero, must have taken part in the hearing, and afterwards the consuls must have given their verdict.[154]

PRESIDENCY OVER ELECTIONS

Elections, and in particular the elections of new consuls, continued in the first century to be one of the great political events of the year. From Sulla's dictatorship onwards, July seems to have been the month when the elections of the magistrates for the following year were held.[155] There are ancient sources that certify this preference.[156] In 70 and 61, the consular elections were held on 27 July;[157] in 54, the elections were scheduled for 28 July but were eventually held much later;[158] and in 58 they must have taken place before 17 July.[159] However, we also know of elections held at other times of the year. In 78, a revolt in Etruria had caused the two consuls to be sent there to suppress it. These circumstances must have delayed the elections. When the senate ordered Lepidus to return to Rome to preside over the elections, the consul refused and asked for a further consulship to be given

---

[152] Cic. *Att.* 4.15.5–6.

[153] Cic. *Scaur.* 27. One of the consuls of 74 was Ap. Claudius Pulcher. A passage of Varro (Var. *R.* 3.2.3) mentions a visit of Ap. Claudius to Reate regarding the conflict between this city and Interamna. Shackleton Bailey (1965–70: II 209) doubts that Cicero and Varro refer to the same event, as has been traditionally accepted, since there is nothing in Varro's book three to place the dialogue in 54.

[154] Crawford 1994: 178–9.

[155] In this respect, there is unanimous agreement. See, for example, Mommsen 1887–8: I 584, 5; III 973; Nicolet 1976: 324; Meier 1997: 258–9.

[156] Cf. Michels 1967: 58–9.   [157] Ps. Asc. 21 (212 St.); Cic. *Att.* 1.16.13.

[158] Cic. *Att.* 4.15.8. In that letter, written on 27 July on the eve of the elections, Cicero already said that he thought it possible that the elections would be delayed.

[159] Cic. *Att.* 3.12.1 mentions Metellus Nepos as a designated consul. The letter was written on 17 July, which means that the consular elections had been held before that date, in all probability in the first half of July. Cf. Grimal 1967: 152.

to him.[160] The request was illegal and obviously unacceptable to the senate, and eventually the so-called *senatus consultum ultimum* was enacted against Lepidus.[161] In 67, the senate authorized the consul Piso, who was at the time the president of the electoral process, to present a bill once the day for the elections had been appointed, something which was forbidden by law. The discussion of the *lex Calpurnia de ambitu* meant a delay of the elections.[162] In 59, a consular edict by Bibulus deferred the elections until 18 October.[163] In 56, the opposition roused by the candidacy of Pompey and Crassus caused the elections to be deferred until they were eventually held at the beginning of 55. Pompey and Crassus, once elected, took office immediately, and the elections for the other magistrates of the year 55, which had also been postponed, were held.[164] Pompey probably presided over those elections.[165]

From then on, exceptionality became the norm as regards the time when the elections were held, due to the convulsive political circumstances of the second half of the decade of the fifties.[166] As mentioned above, in 54 the elections could not be held when they were due. The delay was caused by the corrupt practices in which the candidates were involved.[167] Two of them, C. Memmius and Cn. Domitius Calvinus, reached a private agreement with the consuls of the year 54 according to which the latter would lobby for them in the electoral campaign. In exchange, should they be elected, Memmius and Domitius Calvinus were to support the consuls' aspiration to obtain proconsular *imperium*. The candidates deposited a large sum of money as a guarantee. The agreement was unexpectedly made public by Memmius in the senate in September.[168] This not only broke the coalition but also resulted in the official accusation of corruption against all the candidates. The obvious consequence was the delay of the elections, which had initially been scheduled for 28 July 54 and were variously postponed.[169] The year ended with no consuls-elect, and the interregnum

---

[160] App. *B.Civ.* 1.107; Plut. *Pomp.* 16.4; Sal. *Hist.* 1.77.15 = 1.67.15 McGushin (vol. 1 142).

[161] Criniti 1969: 421–5; Labruna 1975: 53; 158–9; Gruen 1974: 14–15. In particular on the so-called *senatus consultum ultimum* Ungern-Sternberg 1970: 79–80; Duplá 1990: 113–14.

[162] Gruen 1974: 132.   [163] Cic. *Att.* 2.20.6.

[164] As opposed to the pre-Sullan period, for which we do not have sources specifically indicating the consular presidency over the *comitia tributa*, where the elections for curule aediles and quaestors were held, for the first century some texts confirm this without a doubt: Cic. *Planc.* 49; *Fam.* 7.30.1. Kunkel and Wittmann 1995: 473; 514.

[165] Plut. *Pomp.* 52; Plut. *Cato min.* 42; Cass. Dio, 39.32. Cf. Taylor and Broughton 1949: 11 n. 19; Ward 1977: 272–3; Seager 2005: 122; Meier 1997: 294.

[166] On Roman politics in the decade of the fifties, see Wiseman 1994.

[167] The events are studied in detail by Gruen 1969a. Cf. Seager 2005: 126–7; Meier 1997: 11–12.

[168] Cic. *Att.* 4.15.7; 4.16.6; 4.17.2.   [169] Cic. *Q.fr.* 2.15.3.

went on well into 53. In fact, the elections took place in July. That is, the consuls of 53 were elected and took office in the summer of the same year. Eventually, Domitius Calvinus and M. Valerius Messala were elected.[170]

Moreover, the consuls of 53 were unable to hold elections for the year 52. The candidates for the consulship were T. Annius Milo, Q. Caecilius Metellus Scipio and P. Plautius Hypsaeus. The situation was complicated by Clodius' candidacy for the praetorship.[171] In the senate, Clodius accused Milo of having run up huge debts and of being insolvent. Clodius wanted Milo to be banned from candidacy for the consulship on the grounds that he would try to recoup his losses at the expense of the public treasury or by sacking the province that was allotted to him. Clodius' speech was answered, also in the senate, by a speech delivered by Cicero, who repeatedly accused Clodius of having provoked violence during his tribunate in 58. The consuls even had stones thrown at them, allegedly by the Clodian gangs, and at least Calvinus was injured.[172] All these events must have taken place in the autumn of 53, or at any rate after the month of July, when the consuls took office. We are unaware of the impact that the Ciceronian speech may have had, but it is clear that Milo's candidacy went ahead.

In this context, Cassius Dio attributes to the consuls of 53 the proposal of a decree which was passed by the senate (the only known senatorial decision during their consulship), according to which consuls and praetors were only to take up a provincial government five years after the exercise of their magistracy.[173] The objective of the decree, according to Cassius Dio, was to reduce tension between candidates, since they could no longer have immediate access to a lucrative provincial government. Nevertheless, the elections could not be held, and once again the year 52 began without designated consuls. The spiral of violence culminated in the murder of Clodius at the hands of Milo's gang. His death provoked significant disturbances, which led to the designation of Pompey as sole consul on 24 of the intercalary month of the year 52, after the cancellation of the elections by the senate.[174]

---

[170] Plut. *Pomp.* 54.2–3; Cass. Dio, 40.45.1. Gruen 1974: 149 n. 120: the conflict which caused the enormous delay of the elections for 53 must not be seen as something deliberately provoked by Pompey to create a favourable atmosphere for his candidacy.

[171] On the electoral campaign for the consulship and the praetorship of 52, Tatum 1999: 234–9.

[172] Cass. Dio, 40.46.3; Schol. Bob. 172.16 St.: 'lapidibus duo consules ceciderunt.' The phrase belongs to fragment 13 of *De aere alieno Milonis*, the speech with which Cicero answered Clodius' attack against Milo. The two consuls are Domitius Calvinus and Valerius Messala. Cassius Dio only mentions the injuries suffered by Calvinus. On the Ciceronian speech, see Kumaniecki 1977; Crawford 1994: 282–6; 297.

[173] Cass. Dio, 40.46.2 (cf. 40.30.1). The decree was turned into a law by Pompey in 52.

[174] Asc. 36 C. Cf. Seager 2005: 134–5; Vanderbroeck 1987: 263–5; Nippel 1988: 136–44; Gruen 1974: 152–3.

A few months later, Metellus Pius Scipio Nasica was elected as his colleague for the last five months of the year.[175] Pompey was able to preside as normal over the elections for 51, at which Ser. Sulpicius Rufus and M. Claudius Marcellus were elected.

As can be noted in all the aforementioned cases, the delay of the elections was due to extraordinary circumstances.[176] Everything seems to indicate that the norm was that they were held in the summer, apparently most often in the month of July, although the sources confirming this are scarce. The elections of 63, presided over by Cicero, were also held in the summer, perhaps in July.[177] The consul promoted, on the day before the scheduled date for the elections, a *senatus consultum* with the purpose of delaying them, adducing the situation of emergency created by the ominous threats of Catiline, who was one of the candidates. His purpose was, ultimately, to prevent Catiline from being elected as a consul. When the elections took place, Cicero turned up on the Campus Martius escorted by guards and wearing a protecting cuirass, to preside over the elections in this way.[178]

As in the pre-Sullan period, a consul had to be in charge of the management of the entire electoral process, from the approval of candidacies to the proclamation of the winners, obviously with the obligation of ensuring that the electoral comitia were carried out in compliance with the law. From 80 to 50 we know the names of some of the consuls who certainly or very probably presided over the consular elections: Piso in 67, Volcatius Tullus in 66, Cicero in 63, Caesar in 59,[179] and Metellus Nepos in 57.[180] It has been

---

[175] Ooteghem 1967: 305–6.

[176] To the aforementioned cases we could add the elections of 62, which perhaps were also postponed for political reasons. According to Cassius Dio and Plutarch, Pompey sent his loyal lieutenant M. Pupius Piso to Rome to run for the consulship of the year 61. Pompey asked for the elections to be delayed until Pupius Piso could put forward his candidacy and he could campaign in his favour. Plutarch (*Pomp.* 44.1–2; *Cato min.* 30.1–2) says that his request was refused. Cassius Dio (37.44.3), on the other hand, claims that the elections were deferred. According to Gruen 1974: 85, the contradiction could be resolved as follows: the elections were delayed to allow Pupius Piso to return from the East, but not long enough to allow Pompey to reach Rome to campaign in his favour. In any event, Pupius Piso was elected. Cf. Meier 1997: 19.

[177] Marinone 2004: 82.   [178] Cic. *Mur.* 51–2; Plut. *Cic.* 14.5–8; Sal. *Cat.* 26.5. Cf. Rawson 1975: 70–1.

[179] In 59, an edict issued by Bibulus postponed the elections until October. This suggests that Bibulus was in principle the consul in charge of presiding over the electoral process; hence he was to appoint the date for the elections. But finally they had to be presided over by his colleague Caesar, since Bibulus remained secluded in his home until the last day of the year. See the discussion on the validity of the enforcement of Bibulus' edict in Rilinger 1976: 55–7.

[180] In November 57, Metellus Nepos was trying to delay the elections for aedile that he was to preside over (Cic. *Att.* 4.3.3–4). The idea that the same consul had to preside over all the elections, that is, of the consuls, praetors, aediles, and quaestors, led Taylor and Broughton (1968: 169 n. 15) to suppose that Metellus Nepos had previously presided over the elections of consuls and praetors. Linderski (1965: 432) suggested that in November, Metellus Nepos could be replacing his colleague, Lentulus

debated whether there was a rule that determined by law which of the two consuls ought to be designated to preside over the elections. Lily Ross Taylor and T. R. S. Broughton initially presumed that it was the consul first elected who had to be in charge of the electoral process. Given that priority in being elected would also, in their opinion, determine who was to have the fasces each month, the consul first elected would have the fasces in January and, from then on, in all the odd months.[181] Since the elections were usually held in the seventh month of the year, their presidency would always fall to the consul first elected, who would also be mentioned in the first place in the *fasti consulares*.[182] After the criticism expressed by Linderski,[183] the aforementioned authors changed their thesis and defended the idea that in the first century, as in previous centuries, there was not a pre-established rule to determine which consul was in charge of the elections. In the pre-Sullan age, it was most common for the consul nearer to Rome to return to the *Urbs* to preside over the elections. Since in the first century the two consuls remained in Rome during the entire year or for most of it, this criterion was no longer applicable. For this reason, the appointment would be made, as before Sulla's dictatorship, either by agreement of the consuls (*comparatio*) or, perhaps more commonly, by drawing lots (*sortitio*).[184]

The fact that the consul who was to preside over the elections did not arrive in Rome just a few days before they took place, as happened before Sulla, but was present in the city throughout the entire campaign made it more feasible for him to influence the electoral process. Some consuls even denied candidacy to certain individuals or rejected their eventual election. This latter happened in the case of the aforementioned Piso in 67, who claimed at a *contio* that under no circumstances would he accept Palicanus' election as consul and that, should he win, he would refuse to make his official proclamation.[185] In 66, the consular elections had to be held twice under the presidency of the consul Volcatius Tullus, because those who had

---

Spinther, who had already left Rome and would have actually been the electoral president. However, a text in Fenestella (*ap.* Non. 615 L. = fr. 21 Peter) shows that Lentulus Spinther was present in Rome on 10 December, when the tribunes of the plebs took office, which would mean that in all probability he was also in Rome in November and that Metellus Nepos consequently was not replacing him. Therefore, Metellus must have been the electoral president in 57. Cf. Rilinger 1976: 55.

[181] However, see Drummond 1978: 86: 'priority of election . . . may also have conferred priority in the tenure of the *fasces*, but at present this can be no more than an attractive hypothesis'.

[182] Taylor and Broughton 1949: 4–6; 12 n. 24.   [183] Linderski 1965: 423–42.

[184] Taylor and Broughton 1968: 171. Against this opinion Rilinger (1976: 57–8) for whom the first thesis of Taylor and Broughton would still be correct, that is, the consul first elected had to preside over the elections. Cf. Kunkel and Wittmann 1995: 197 n. 350; Meier 1997: 197 n. 219.

[185] V. Max. 3.8.3.

been elected in the first place were convicted for corruption under the Calpurnian law.[186] But that was not the only major event linked to the consular elections of the year 66. L. Sergius Catilina also wanted to be a candidate. Acting as the electoral president, Volcatius, according to Asconius, convened a public advisory board (*consilium publicum*) and decided not to accept his candidacy.[187]

Occasionally, a consul could use his *auctoritas* to campaign for or against a candidate. Pupius Piso openly supported L. Afranius in the elections for the consulship of the year 60. Both of them had fought in the East as Pompey's legates, and in the ensuing years they continued to be loyal to him.[188] Afranius was indeed elected consul thanks to Pompey's support.[189] The consul Lentulus Marcellinus, on the other hand, was adamantly against the candidacy of Pompey and Crassus for the consulship of 55 and even spoke openly against them both in *contiones* and in the senate.[190] To a lesser extent, his colleague Philippus also criticized the candidacy.[191] Marcellinus managed to have the elections delayed until the beginning of 55, but once he and Philippus ended their term of office he could not prevent the elections or prevent Crassus and Pompey from being elected.[192] Intervention in the electoral process could obviously apply to other magistracies. The only known consular activity of Q. Caecilius Metellus Pius in the year 80 (his colleague was Sulla) is the unconditional public support that he gave to C. Calidius as a candidate to be a praetor. Before the people, he spoke of his and his family's appreciation of the support granted them by Calidius, and that he was particularly indebted to the candidate for having sponsored during his tribunate a law which allowed his father, Metellus Numidicus,

---

[186] Cass. Dio, 36.44.3–5; Asc. 75 C. L. Aurelius Cotta and L. Manlius Torquatus were the defeated candidates in the first place. Cotta and the son of Torquatus (the fact that it was the son of the candidate and not he himself who promoted the accusation is shown at Cic. *Sul.* 49–50; *Fin.* 2.62) accused the winners, P. Cornelius Sulla and P. Autronius Paetus, of corruption. They were condemned, and in the second elections Cotta and Torquatus were the winners. Although other cases of accusations of electoral corruption against candidates-elect are known, the conviction of Sulla and Autronius is an exception. Cf. Marshall 1985: 261–2; Vanderbroeck 1987: 227–8; Gruen 1974: 272; Lewis 2006: 281.

[187] Asc. 89 C. This could be the origin of the so-called first conspiracy of Catiline narrated by Sallust (*Cat.* 18). Catiline and Autronius allegedly planned to murder the new consuls Cotta and Torquatus on 1 January 65. Cf. Cic. *Cat.* 1.6. On the text of Asconius see Marshall 1985: 303; Lewis 2006: 297.

[188] Gruen 1974: 223. Both of them were supposed to act on behalf of Pompey's interests in Rome, but their consulships are obscure, and Gruen (86–7) sees them rather as a burden for Pompey due to their inefficiency. This was also Cicero's opinion of Afranius (*Att.* 1.18–20).

[189] Cass. Dio, 37.49.1.

[190] V. Max. 6.2.6; Cass. Dio, 39.28.5; 39.30,1–3; Plut. *Pomp.* 51.5–6; *Crass.* 15. Millar 1998: 166.

[191] Cass. Dio, 39.27.3 refers to the two consuls; Cic. *Q.fr.* 2.4.4. Gruen 1969b: 98.

[192] Gruen 1969b: 99; Meier 1997: 286.

to return from exile. Cicero was amazed that a *homo nobilissimus* like Metellus Pius, who was also consul at the time, did not hesitate to make this public statement, which, in his opinion, did not demean his dignity but magnified it.[193]

One of the main consequences of the consuls' longer presence in Rome in the post-Sullan period was their greater intervention in the legislative process. Until Sulla's dictatorship, the tribunes of the plebs were clearly the main legislators, much more so than the consuls, praetors, and dictators, the latter only appointed until the Hannibalic War. In the post-Sullan age, the tribunes continued to be the sponsors of most of the laws passed in that period, but the number of consular laws increased considerably.[194] The main reason was the presence of the consuls in Rome. This gave them the time and tranquillity that the legislative process demanded from the point at which a bill was considered, put into writing, and officially turned into a *rogatio*, until it was finally voted on after the debate before the people during the mandatory interval of three market days, the *trinundinum*. In the pre-Sullan period, military preparations, and the fact that the consuls left Rome for their provinces as soon as possible, made it difficult for them to act as legislators. From 80 to 50, in contrast, consular laws are frequent, and some consuls in particular sponsored intense reform work through legislative initiative. In fact, it could be stated that whereas between the fourth and second centuries it was mainly their military deeds as *imperatores* which gave a place in posterity to consuls, during the first century amongst the main achievements of the consuls as politicians were the laws that they sponsored, without detriment to the military exploits they carried out almost always as proconsuls, which led to even greater acclaim.

Pompey, Crassus, and Caesar, three of the greatest commanders of the first century, are also good examples of consuls as legislators. Pompey and Crassus shared the consulship in 70 and 55. On both occasions they were the authors of important laws. In particular Pompey had planned a genuine programme of reforms that he was determined to implement during his first

---

[193] Cic. *Planc.* 69; V. Max. 5.2.7. Cf. Ooteghem 1967: 186.
[194] Williamson 2005: 16–17: from 200 to 134, the percentage of consular laws was 18 per cent of the known total and just 7 per cent in the period from 133 to 91 (although in absolute terms the number of consular laws was higher). From 91 to 44, 44 per cent of the laws passed were sponsored by tribunes of the plebs, while consular laws amounted to 25 per cent. Williamson (pp. 52–4) provides a list of proposers of laws from 91 to 44.

consulship, publicly announcing from the beginning that he intended to spend his entire term of office in Rome without going to any province.[195] In the autumn of 71, while still a consul-elect, he announced his planned reforms in a *contio* convened for him outside the *pomerium* of the city by the tribune Palicanus. According to Cicero, the consul-designate promised, to the cheers of the people who had gathered to listen to him, to return full powers to the tribunes of the plebs, as well as to reform the courts.[196] Pompey kept his promise regarding the restitution of the full tribunician powers at the beginning of his consulship in the year 70. It is questionable whether the *lex de tribunicia potestate* should be attributed exclusively to Pompey or whether it was sponsored jointly with his colleague Crassus.[197] In three different passages, Cicero mentions only Pompey as the author of the law.[198] In contrast, Asconius attributes the law to the two consuls in a comment on a passage of the Ciceronian defence of Cornelius in 65.[199] McDermott explains the mention of Crassus in this context because he was part of the jury in the trial against Cornelius. Cicero simply wished to flatter him in that manner. The other two sources that have occasionally been quoted to back the thesis of a joint law should also be discarded, in his opinion. Sallust mentions the two consuls only as a chronological reference ('when Pompey and Crassus were consuls'), and Livy's *Periochae* contain too many errors to make the attribution to the two consuls believable, which can be explained due to the need to synthesize.[200] In short, according to McDermott, the Ciceronian passages in the *Verrinae* and in *De legibus* decisively demonstrate that the law was exclusively sponsored by Pompey.[201]

   Although the sources probably do not allow for such a definite conclusion as McDermott's, the most probable option is that Pompey was indeed the sole author of the law. As we have already seen, when he was a

---

[195] Vell. 2.31.1.   [196] Cic. *Ver.* 1.45. Millar 1998: 63–5.

[197] Several sources make it clear that there were frequent disagreements between the two consuls during their consulship (Plut. *Pomp.* 22.3; *Crass.* 12.2) and that both competed in seeking maximum popularity. Pompey organized great games, and Crassus offered an enormous public banquet and the free distribution of corn (Cic. *Ver.* 1.31; Plut. *Crass.* 12.3. Cf. Ward 1977: 101; Gruen 1974: 28 n. 68). In fact, both Appian (*B. Civ.* 1.121) and Plutarch (*Pomp.* 23.1–2) report that the reconciliation of the two consuls happened in the forum before the people at the end of the year, probably at a *contio* (Vanderbroeck 1987: 222).

[198] Cic. *Ver.* 1.44; *Leg.* 3.22; 3.26.   [199] Asc. 76 C. Cf. Marshall 1985: 264.

[200] Sal. *Cat.* 38.1; Liv. *per.* 97.

[201] McDermott 1977. *Contra* Seager 2005: 37 n. 91: Cicero does not mention Crassus in connection with the law because he has no reason to do so in that context, yet Asconius clearly states that it is a law of the two consuls. In his turn, Ooteghem (1954: 145) accepted the joint authorship on the basis of Livy's *Periochae* and suggested that the question may have been the result of a previous pact between the consuls-elect. Rotondi (1912: 369) considered it a *lex Pompeia Licinia*.

consul-elect he had already promised before the people to restore the tribunician authority. If, as Cicero claims, it was a question that had great repercussions amongst citizens, there is no reason to believe that Pompey, once he had given his word, willingly gave prominence to his colleague in this matter, for whom there is no evidence that he had made any move in this respect. Pompey must have sponsored the law after receiving the authorization of the senate. Crassus did not object to the *rogatio*, and it is even possible that he openly supported it, but he must not have been the official *rogator* along with his colleague. In any case, there was no reason for Crassus to oppose a law which seems to have had the endorsement of most of the senate.[202] In the previous years, the question had been recurrent due to the demands of various tribunes. In fact, back in 75 the consul C. Aurelius Cotta had sponsored a law entitling the tribunes of the plebs to hold higher magistracies afterwards, thus abrogating the prohibition introduced by Sulla during his dictatorship.[203] The issue was therefore ripe by the year 70, and this explains why the Pompeian law met no opposition.

The other promise made by Pompey as consul-elect was also put into practice during his first consulship, although not by him but by the praetor L. Aurelius Cotta, the author of a law reforming the structure of courts.[204] As in the case of the tribunician restoration, the measure seems to have had the consensus of Rome's ruling class. Possibly both Pompey and Crassus backed the law, although the sources do not mention this specifically.[205]

In 55, Crassus and Pompey were the consuls again. Their personal relationship was then much closer than it had been in the year 70. The political agenda that they had planned to follow was based mainly on the agreement previously concluded in Luca. Securing the proconsular

---

[202] Several scholars accept that it was indeed a joint action involving the two consuls, perhaps the only one in the entire consulship. But most of them speak cautiously about cooperation or collaboration without openly declaring themselves regarding the authorship of the law. Cf. Marshall (1976a: 54), who thinks that there is no reason to doubt that Crassus supported the law; Ward (1977: 103) speaks of cooperation between the two consuls but thinks the law would exclusively have had Pompey's name; Gruen 1974: 28; Millar (1998: 66) attributes the law to the two consuls; Southern (2002: 54–5) considers that the tribunician restoration was the only joint action of the two consuls; Williamson (2005: 356) calls it *lex Pompeia Licinia* ('in association with Crassus, Pompey enacted a measure to revive the tribunate').

[203] Sal. *Hist.* 3.48.8 = 3.34.8 McGushin (vol. II 89–90); Asc. 67 and 78 C. On the Sallustian fragment, Funari 1996: I 362. On the law, Rotondi 1912: 365; Marshall and Beness 1987: 369; Gruen 1974: 26–7.

[204] Cic. *Phil.* 1.20; Liv. *per.* 97; Plut. *Pomp.* 22.3; etc.

[205] Gruen 1974: 34–5. Ward (1977: 106) thinks that the reform of the courts must have meant a conflict between Crassus and Pompey. That would explain why Cotta's law was not sponsored until the autumn. This law would be a compromise solution reflecting, above all, Pompey's wishes. Cf. Marshall 1976a: 56: the two consuls must have supported the *lex Aurelia* to gain popularity amongst the equestrians; Seager 2005: 37–8; Gelzer 2005: 68.

command of the *imperatores* was a fundamental question. A law of the tribune Trebonius gave Crassus the government of Syria for five years, and Pompey was granted the government of the two provinces in Hispania for the same period of time.[206] Once their personal aims had been achieved, the consuls presented to the vote a different law whereby the command of Caesar in Gaul was expanded.[207]

Besides the Trebonian law on the consular provinces and the consular law regarding Caesar, both Crassus and Pompey introduced new laws in an attempt to tackle the recurrent problems in Roman society during the previous years, such as electoral corruption, the use of violence, and the operation of courts.[208] Crassus sponsored the *lex de sodaliciis*, aimed against organized groups who influenced the elections by intimidation and buying of votes.[209] As Linderski proved, the law was probably the enactment of a senatorial decree issued in February 56,[210] wherein the contents of the *lex Licinia* were broadly laid out.[211] Pompey, in his turn, sponsored a *lex iudiciaria*. Although the law is not well known, its aim was apparently to establish a more rational system of selecting jurors by creating an annual list of potential jurors for all the criminal lawsuits. The purpose was to avoid the potential arbitrariness of a system which until then depended on the will of the urban praetor. On the one hand, the law preserved the regulations of the Aurelian law of 70, in the sense that the jurors were to be senators, equites and *tribuni aerarii*. But from that moment onwards, only those with the highest income within those three groups could be selected as members of a jury.[212]

---

[206] Liv. *per.* 105; Cic. *Att.* 4.9.1; Vell. 2.46.2; Cass. Dio, 39.33–6; Plut. *Pomp.* 52; *Crass.* 15. Ooteghem 1954: 398–9; Ward 1977: 274; Seager 2005: 123.

[207] Cass. Dio, 39.36.2; Vell. 2.46.2; Plut. *Pomp.* 52.3; *Crass.* 15.5; *Cat.min.* 43.5–6; Cic. *Att.* 7.9.4. Although Plutarch claims that the law which expanded Caesar's command was also promoted by Trebonius, Cassius Dio, who attributes it to the two consuls, is more credible. Cf. Ooteghem 1954: 399–400; Ward 1977: 276.

[208] Gruen 1974: 233, considers that Crassus and Pompey's legislation was aimed at achieving a strengthening of the Republican institutions. On the contrary, Ward (1977: 272 n. 24) argues that the real purpose was to obtain more personal power for themselves, which was incompatible with the Republican system. Cf. Ooteghem 1954: 401; Rotondi 1912: 405–7; Gelzer 2005: 148.

[209] Cic. *Planc.* 36; Schol. Bob. 152 St. Gruen 1974: 230: the *sodalitates* do not appear to have been dissolved, but some of their activities were declared illegal.

[210] Cic. *Q.fr.* 2.3.5.

[211] Linderski 1961; Ward 1977: 270–2; Riggsby 1999: 22–3. It has been widely debated whether the *lex Licinia* (as well as the previous *senatus consultum*) was expressly directed against Clodius' actions. Tatum (1999: 225–6) thinks that neither the senatorial decree of 56 nor the *lex Licinia* of 55 were aimed at removing the *collegia* which were loyal to Clodius. The law did not ban the traditional methods of canvassing for votes, but it punished the illegal actions carried out by the *sodalitates*, in particular the use of bribery. On Clodius' leadership of the urban plebs see Nippel 1988: 108–28; Will 1991: 47–111.

[212] Cic. *Pis.* 94; *Phil.* 1.20; Asc. 17 C. Cf. Gruen 1974: 232; Lewis 2006: 212.

A *lex Pompeia de parricidiis*, discussed by the imperial jurists, can possibly be attributed to Pompey's second consulship.[213] The crime of parricide, punishable by the capital penalty, had been tried at first by the popular assembly; by the first century it was under the jurisdiction of the permanent courts. Apparently, the Pompeian law specified the blood relations which were included within the crime of parricide. Contemporary sources do not mention the law, for which we do not have any further details, and we do not know why Pompey thought it was necessary. Finally, Cassius Dio reports that the two consuls had planned to sponsor a law to limit the excessive luxury of the highest classes of Roman society. This was merely an idea or, at the most, a bill which was never voted on, since according to Cassius Dio the consuls gave it up after having been persuaded to do so by Hortensius.[214]

Pompey's third consulship took place amidst the exceptional circumstances experienced in Rome in 52. The year started without the elections having been held, in a climate of political tension. The murder of Clodius provoked an outburst of social violence along with a great popular mobilization which demanded Milo be condemned. The disturbances in the city, which included an arson attack on the Curia during Clodius' funeral, made the senate issue the so-called ultimate decree, the *senatus consultum ultimum*.[215] It was in this context that Pompey was appointed sole consul, *consul sine collega*, an ingenious manner of putting one sole ruler at the head of the Roman state without calling him a dictator.[216] The main objective was to pacify Rome and bring back institutional normality to the community. Pompey used the power given to him to promote an ambitious legislative agenda with which he intended to introduce reforms in several areas of Roman society and administration.[217]

In the previous few years, violence and corruption, closely linked to each other, had been two of Rome's greatest problems. The existing legislation had proved to be insufficient, and for this reason Pompey introduced two

---

[213] *Digest.* 48.9; Paul. *Sent.* 5.24. Gruen 1974: 246; Lintott 1999a: 41.

[214] Cass. Dio, 39.37. Rotondi (1912: 405) attributes the bill only to Pompey. Williamson (2005: 468) refers to it as *rogatio Pompeia sumptuaria*. However, Cassius Dio constantly talks about the two consuls as the sponsors. Cf. Ward 1977: 269–70.

[215] On the events which occurred during Clodius' funeral and in the ensuing days, Nippel 1988: 128–36; Sumi 1997; Pina Polo 2009: 97–9. On the enactment of the *senatus consultum ultimum*, Duplá 1990: 137–9.

[216] Asc. 36 C.

[217] Rotondi 1912: 410–11. Gruen (1974: 155) describes the Pompeian legislation of 52 as 'sober, firm, and conservative'. Tac. *Ann.* 3.28.1 claims that Pompey's objective was to reform the customs, but he adds that the methods used did nothing but worsen the situation. Cf. Lintott 1999a: 200–1.

new laws concerning acts of violence (*de vi*) and corruption (*de ambitu*) in the first few days of his consulship, both of which were backed by previous corresponding senatorial decrees.[218] The *lex de vi* was in fact an ad hoc law. It did not abolish the previous laws against violence but introduced specific rules to combat the situation of 52. These regulations allowed for an important number of summary trials to be held by creating a temporary court that was specifically in charge of trying the crimes committed in the previous few months, which made it possible to restore order quickly in Rome.[219]

Another consular law against violence was in force at the time.[220] The only reference to it appears in a text of Cicero. In 56, Cicero delivered a speech in defence of Caelius, who had been accused of making use of violence. The orator expressly claims that the accusation had taken place in accordance with a *lex de vi* of Q. Catulus. He does not specifically identify this individual but says that the law was passed at a time of serious danger for the Republic and amidst armed confrontations between Roman citizens.[221] The problem is that the Ciceronian passage does not provide significant details that allow us to identify with any certainty the moment when the law was passed.

Kelly recently suggested that the law was passed in 102 and that its sponsor was Q. Catulus, consul for that year and also the father of the consul of 78. In his opinion, the episodes of violence that took place in the city of Rome in 103–102 would fit better within the description given by Cicero, whom Kelly believes to be referring to events which occurred in the

---

[218] Asc. 36 C. On the *lex de vi* Cic. *Mil.* 15; 70.

[219] Gruen 1974: 234–6, in particular on the trials of 52 pp. 337–50. Cf. Seager 2005: 137; Nippel 1988: 138; Lintott 1999a: 123; Riggsby 1999: 105–7; Gelzer 2005: 160–1.

[220] The sources mention two laws against violence, a *lex Lutatia* which, as we shall see later, it seems can plausibly be attributed to the consul of 78, and a *lex Plautia* (or *Plotia*), a praetorian or, more probably, tribunician law of unknown author and date. Mommsen identified the *lex Lutatia* with the *lex Plotia de vi*, assuming that Catulus had a tribune of the plebs pass the law in his name. However, Cicero's text is very clear in this respect. The expression 'Catulus ... tulit' unquestionably means that Catulus himself sponsored and defended it before the assembly. Yet the relation between the two laws continues to be debated up to the present day: whether one replaced the other or the two of them were in force simultaneously or they were two separate and interconnected and mutually complementary laws, which seems most likely. In this respect, see Hough 1930; Cousin 1943; Labruna 1975: 98–112; Lintott 1999a: 109–16: the hypothesis of Lintott is 'that the *lex Plautia* only dealt with cases of violence against private citizens which were judged in one way or another to be against the interests of the state' (p. 116); Riggsby 1999: 79–80: 'The best solution to the contradiction seems to be that the *lex Lutatia* was passed originally and specifically to deal with Lepidus' insurrection (in 78), and that a later *lex Plautia* succeeded it'; Harries 2007: 107: 'the Lex Plautia *de vi* was passed between 78 and 63, when a threat of its use was invoked against Catiline'.

[221] Cic. *Cael.* 70: '... quam legem Q. Catulus armata dissensione civium rei publicae paene extremis temporibus tulit ...'.

Urbs.[222] However, mainstream opinion is that the law was passed in 78 by the consul Q. Catulus.[223] The context of civil confrontations briefly described by Cicero can certainly be attributed to 78, when the conflict between Catulus and Lepidus took place. Without a doubt, Kelly is correct in claiming that the situation in 103–102 was serious. But it is also true that in 78, a consul, no less, rebelled against the senate, disobeyed it, and the events finally ended in a civil war. A law against violence is perfectly understandable in this context. The problem is placing it chronologically in the course of the events of that year and the following year, as well as determining its contents. Catulus' law could have created a special court to face Lepidus' insurrection, but the fact that it continued to be in force in 56 suggests that it created a permanent court in charge of trying violent crimes.[224] The Pompeian law of 52 did not abrogate it but simply speeded up the judicial procedure to give a rapid response to the chaotic situation at the time.

The *lex Pompeia de ambitu*, unlike the law against violence, was intended to be permanent. It was actually in force for a long time and was the main tool for fighting corruption in the following years.[225] According to Appian, the law contained a retroactive provision going back to 70, the year of Pompey's first consulship.[226] But two other consular laws against corruption had been passed during the almost two decades between Pompey's first and third consulship. In 67, legislation *de ambitu* was one of the topics which caused political confrontation. The tribune C. Cornelius wanted to introduce a law on this matter, but the senate considered that the penalties proposed in the bill were too strict. Therefore what was being discussed was not whether or not it was advisable to pass a law against corruption, but its contents. The senate then asked the consul Piso to draft an alternative bill. That was the bill which was eventually approved by the people, not without previous disturbances in Rome.[227] All of this happened in the summer of 67. In fact, Piso received extraordinary authorization from the senate to present his law after the date for the elections had been fixed, which was

---

[222] Kelly 2005.

[223] That is the opinion of Hough 1930; Labruna 1975: 83–6; Nippel 1988: 211 n. 62; Cloud 1994: 524; Gruen 1974: 225; Lintott 1999a: 110–22; Harries 2007: 59; 107.

[224] Labruna 1975: 95; Gruen 1974: 226; Lintott 1999a: 121.   [225] Gruen 1974: 236–7.

[226] App. *B.Civ.* 2.23. Cf. Plut. *Cat.min.* 48.3; Cic. *Att.* 13.49.1

[227] See a detailed account of the events in Gruen (1974: 213–15), who sees as the key to the confrontation between Cornelius and Piso not a conflict between reformists and reactionaries, but the enmity between Piso and Pompey, whose political ally Cornelius was. See also McDonald 1929; Griffin 1973a; Vanderbroeck 1987: 226–7.

forbidden by law until the elections had taken place.[228] At any rate, the conflicts caused the elections to be deferred. Although Cassius Dio claims that the law was sponsored by the two consuls, all other ancient sources exclusively mention Piso in the confrontation against Cornelius.[229] Thus, we can in all probability speak of a *lex Calpurnia de ambitu*, as Asconius and Cicero do.[230] According to Cassius Dio, the stipulated penalties must have been quite strict: resignation from the magistracy which had been illegally obtained, expulsion from the senate, and payment of a fine.[231]

In 63, the consul Cicero sponsored a new *lex de ambitu*.[232] Cicero himself mentions it in various passages, where he gives some details of its contents. The law banned the offering of gladiatorial games during the two years prior to the presentation of a candidacy for a magistracy, unless it was a commitment made by testament with a fixed date.[233] The stipulated penalty was exile for the candidate convicted.[234] Another clause punished the false pretexts used by jurors to avoid taking part in the juries for which they had been selected.[235] The Ciceronian law was inspired by the jurist Sulpicius Rufus, but the final result was apparently less radical than Cicero's friend would have wished. Nevertheless, it must have complemented the former *lex Calpurnia* by better defining the concept of *ambitus* while expanding the punishment. In the following years, the Ciceronian law was essential in the fight against corruption.[236]

---

[228] Cass. Dio, 36.39.1. The prohibition is known through schol. Bob. 148 St., where there is mention of some *leges Aelia et Fufia* which may have been passed towards the middle of the second century (Broughton 1951–86: I 452–3; Weinstock 1937b: 216–17; Bleicken 1955: 57–8). Sumner (1963) places the laws around the tribunate of Tiberius Gracchus. In Sumner's opinion, they are two different laws, and the *lex Fufia* in particular is the law that banned the proposal of a law in the period of time between the elections' being called and their completion. This opinion is shared by Marshall 1985: 97–8. See also Astin 1964. Yakobson 1999: 179: since, as a private citizen, a candidate could not sponsor a law, the aim of the law would be to avoid political cooperation between candidates and allied tribunes of the plebs.

[229] Cass. Dio, 36.38.1.

[230] Asc. 69 C.; Cic. *Mur.* 67. Cf. Williamson 2005: 372; Lewis 2006: 277. Rotondi (1912: 374) considers that the law was proposed by the two consuls but that Glabrio did not take part in the defence of the *rogatio* or in the voting in the comitia, but he does not satisfactorily account for Glabrio's total absence in the debate.

[231] Cass. Dio, 36.38.1. Riggsby 1999: 22–6.

[232] Rotondi 1912: 379; Rawson 1975: 70; Gruen 1974: 221–4.

[233] Cic. *Vat.* 37. Cicero also mentions his *lex de ambitu* at *Mur.* 3 and 67.

[234] Cic. *Planc.* 83. A passage in Cassius Dio (37.29.1) regarding Catiline suggests that the exile introduced by Cicero as a penalty for corruption could last up to ten years.

[235] Cic. *Mur.* 47.

[236] See, however, the considerations of Riggsby 1999: 152: 'The fact that further electoral legislation (*lex Licinia de sodaliciis, lex Pompeia de ambitu*) followed so soon afterward suggests that Cicero's legislation was not in fact a compelling practical success.' Cicero tried to pass another law during his consulship (Cic. *Leg.* 3.18). It was an attempt at eliminating the *legationes liberae*, by which senatorial legates travelled anywhere within the empire in a private capacity but with the authorization of the senate,

To return to 52, two further Pompeian laws completed the consul's legislative agenda. The *lex de iure magistratuum* demanded that when a person made his official application for candicacy to a magistracy, he should be present in Rome. According to Cassius Dio, Pompey introduced an amendment to his own law stating that Caesar was exempt and that, when the moment came, he could present his candidacy in his absence.[237] On the other hand, the *lex de provinciis* turned a senatorial decree passed in 53 into a law.[238] It set forth that at least five years had to elapse from the time when a politician held a magistracy in Rome until a province was allotted to him. Cassius Dio supposed that this measure was applicable both to consuls and to praetors.[239] This would have meant the abrogation of the *lex Sempronia*, which had been in force since 123, because it would no longer have been necessary for the senate to fix the consular provinces before the elections, since the consuls were not to receive command of a province until five years later.[240] However, Giovannini argued that the Pompeian law only applied to the praetorian provinces and not to the consular ones, which in his opinion continued to exist as they had until then.[241]

In the second part of 52, Pompey shared the consulship with his colleague Metellus Scipio. Cassius Dio attributes to the latter a law abrogating the measures introduced by Clodius regarding the censorship during his tribunate.[242] The law dealt with the application of the censorial mark (*nota censoria*), which had been limited by Clodius with the purpose of eliminating potential abuses on the part of the censors when expelling senators from the senate. Apparently, the law of 52 restored their full powers to the censors, although the details are unknown.[243]

Caesar's consulship in 59 was characterized by the approval of several laws sponsored by the consul alone.[244] At first Caesar wished to act, as was usual for a consul, in cooperation with the senate. Consular legislation usually started with a motion (*relatio*) made in the senate by the consul or consuls who sponsored the bill. Once it had been given the approval of the senators, the text was drafted and the *rogatio* was officially presented for debate before the people in *contiones*. Caesar soon realized that he would have to face

---

which meant that they were treated by the provincials as the representatives of Rome, causing great expense. Cicero did not accomplish his aim because his bill was vetoed by an unknown tribune of the plebs, but he at least achieved a compromise whereby the *legationes* would have the limited duration of one year. Cf. Rotondi 1912: 379–80; Gruen 1974: 253; Marinone 2004: 82.

[237] Cass. Dio 40.56.1; Suet. *Jul.* 28.3; Caes. *Civ.* 1.32.3. Gruen 1974: 456–7; Gelzer 2005: 164.

[238] Cass. Dio 40.46.2.   [239] Cass. Dio 40.56.1. On the law, see Marshall 1972.

[240] Seager 2005: 138–9; Gruen 1974: 458–60; Gelzer 2005: 164.   [241] Giovannini 1983: 114–19.

[242] Cass. Dio 40.57.1–3.   [243] Rotondi 1912: 412; Ooteghem 1967: 305; Gruen 1974: 257 n. 177.

[244] Williamson 2005: 376–9.

the opposition of the senators and the obstructionism of his colleague Bibulus.[245] In these circumstances, Caesar could not expect to be able to present his bills *ex senatus consulto*, with the authorization of the senate, yet he could not renounce his political and legislative agenda. It was then that he demonstrated in public the support of his allies, Pompey and Crassus, and when he resolved to dispense with the opinion of the senate and present his bills directly to the people.[246] This meant a break with the traditional relationship between consuls and senate in the legislative field.

Caesar was a legislating consul, as were many others in the post-Sullan period, but the decisive difference was that he was at least partly a legislator who would bypass the senate and even confront it if necessary. This exceptional conduct had only one known precedent, the consul M. Fulvius Flaccus in 125, although he did not manage to pass his bill granting citizenship to the Italians due to lack of support. In that sense, Caesar acted more like some tribunes of the plebs than as a consul was expected to act. Normally, the consuls had acted as the driving force of the senate, drafting in the form of a *rogatio* the senatorial decisions which had previously become *senatus consulta*. But Caesar had his own political agenda and his own legislative programme, partly agreed previously with Crassus and Pompey. This is a remarkable novelty, and one which was decisive for the future.

The first law proposed by Caesar was an agrarian law. The bill was discussed during the month of January and was probably voted on and passed at the end of that month, despite the opposition of his colleague Bibulus, who, from then on, secluded himself in his house.[247] The law contained some of the points included in the failed agrarian bills which the tribunes Rullus and Flavius had tried to pass in the previous years. Except for Campania, the Caesarian law declared all public land in Italy available for apportioning amongst those who were not landlords. The operation was to be funded with the spoils obtained by Pompey in the East. In order to distribute the land, a commission of twenty members had to be appointed, from which Caesar was expressly excluded.[248] This law was

[245] Lintott 1999a: 143–5.
[246] Gruen 1974: 91. Gruen (141) describes Caesar's consulship of 59 as 'a memorable and pivotal chief magistracy'.
[247] A detailed chronology of Caesar's consulship can be found in Taylor 1951; Meier 1961. On the agrarian law, see Balsdon 1967: 59–60; Gelzer 1968: 71–3; Meier 1982: 259–64; Gruen 1974: 397–8; Millar 1998: 126–8. In general, on Caesar's laws, Rotondi 1912: 387–91.
[248] Cass. Dio, 38.1–2; App. *B.Civ.* 3.5; 3.24; Plut. *Caes.* 14.2–3; Suet. *Jul.* 20.3; Cic. *Fam.* 13.4.2.

probably complemented and expanded in May by a second agrarian law, which did include the land in Campania.

The rest of Caesar's laws of 59 had a more political and administrative nature[249] and, to a certain extent, were the product of the pact made with Pompey and Crassus.[250] On the one hand, Caesar had the Pompeian acts in the Orient ratified, a question which had frustrated Pompey ever since his return.[251] He confirmed Ptolemy Auletes as the king of Egypt.[252] He sponsored a *lex de publicanis* with which he intended to please Crassus, exempting the publicans of Asia from the payment of one-third of the amount due on contracts which they had signed with the Roman state.[253] He passed a *lex de repetundis* which apparently included a large number of provisions.[254] This suggests a very detailed regulation, a law based on sound knowledge of the problems posed by the relationship between governors and provincials, which was intended to be in force for a long time. In this case, it is probable that the law had the previous approval of the senate and that some distinguished senators even collaborated in drafting it.[255]

As can be noted, the consular laws of the post-Sullan period mentioned so far governed many varied issues, all of them vital to Roman administration, society, and politics: corruption, violence, provincial administration, relations with the provincials, the agrarian issue, tribunician power, the censorship, and the courts. Other questions were also dealt with by consular laws of the time. One of them was the food supply of Rome, a problem which until then had been mainly in the hands of the tribunes of the plebs. In the first century it was also a question dealt with by tribunes such as Clodius, who sponsored a *lex frumentaria* in 58. But the dimensions of the problem in the post-Sullan period, when the population of the *Urbs* was growing rapidly and social disturbances caused by the shortage of food were more frequent, brought it to the attention of some consuls.[256]

The political agenda of Lepidus in 78 included the approval of a *lex frumentaria* concerning the corn supply. This social measure, aimed at the lowest classes, was, like other measures planned by Lepidus, a challenge to the Sullan regime, since Sulla had eliminated the distribution of corn

[249] In the administrative sphere we could include the decision to create a kind of chronicle (*acta diurna*) in which the minutes of the senate and of the popular assemblies were published (Suet. *Jul.* 20.1).

[250] Meier 1982: 265–6.

[251] *B. Alex.* 68; Suet. *Jul.* 19.4; Plut. *Pomp.* 48.3 etc. Cf. Broughton 1951–86: II 188.   [252] Cic. *Att.* 2.16.2.

[253] Cass. Dio, 38.7.4; Cic. *Att.* 2.16.2; *Planc.* 35.

[254] Cic. *Fam.* 8.8.3; *Sest.* 135; *Vat.* 29; etc. Cf. Broughton 1951–86: II 188.

[255] Meier 1982: 274; Gruen 1974: 239–42; Riggsby 1999: 123–4. Canfora (2007: 81) considers the *lex repetundarum* the most important legislation of the first Caesarian consulship.

[256] On the popular mobilizations in Rome caused by the food shortage, see Vanderbroeck 1987: 121–3.

amongst the plebs. It also tried to resolve the growing difficulties posed by piracy in the transport of goods in the Mediterranean, a problem which was not new but which was to become a growing concern in the following years and eventually led to Pompey's intervention. The corn supply to Rome suffered because of this, with entailed shortages and high prices, which obviously largely affected the urban plebs. According to Granius Licinianus, our only source regarding Lepidus' initiative, the frumentary law was passed 'with no opposition' ('nullo resistente').[257] This seems to indicate that the senate did not seriously oppose the law, nor did the other consul, Catulus, veto it, which suggests that there was a basic consensus on the seriousness of the problem. The law may have been voted on in the first few months of the year, before the conflict between Lepidus and the senate broke out. Licinianus claims that the law set forth the delivery of five *modii* of wheat per month to the people. Although the verb *dare* is used, it must not be understood that the distribution was free of charge, something which was only introduced twenty years later by Clodius. However, it is possible that the law stipulated a specific number of beneficiaries. Lepidus' objective must rather have been to regularize the supply of corn and to stabilize the prices at a more affordable level for most of the population of Rome.[258]

Given the political confrontation of the following months in the year 78, which ended in a civil war in which Lepidus died, it is impossible to know whether the frumentary law was actually implemented and was continuously in force or was abolished in 77 to eradicate any trace of the rebellious consul.[259] In any event, the difficulties with the grain supply continued and created a social problem of great magnitude. In 75, the consul C. Aurelius Cotta delivered in a *contio* a rather pessimistic speech regarding the shortage of food in Rome.[260] There were violent riots in the city, and the two consuls and one candidate for the praetorship, Q. Caecilius Metellus, later called Creticus, were even attacked in the forum.[261] The approval that year of a law

---

[257] Gran. Licin. p. 34 ed. Flemisch: '<et> legem frumentariam nullo resistente tutatus est, ut annonae quinque modii populo darentur et alia multa pollicebatur: exules reducere, res gestas a Sulla <rescindere>, in quorum agros milites deduxerat, restituere.'

[258] Allély 2000: 37–40. Regarding the *lex Aemilia frumentaria* see also Berchem 1939: 15–16; Rotondi 1912: 364; Hayne 1972: 664; Labruna 1975: 32–3; Rickman 1980: 166; Virlouvet 1994.

[259] Criniti (1969: 397–9) thinks that the distribution of grain was free, but believes that the law was not enforced and even questions whether it was voted on. Virlouvet (1994: 13) argues that the Aemilian law was not abolished and that the frumentary law of 73 simply complemented Lepidus' law. On the other hand, Allély (2000: 40) thinks that it was abolished and that this would explain why a new frumentary law was passed five years later. See also Rickman 1980: 166.

[260] Sal. *Hist.* 2.47 = 2.44 McGushin (vol. I 50–2). Cf. Perl 1965; Rickman 1980: 167; Vanderbroeck 1987: 131–2; 220–1; Gruen 1974: 35–6.

[261] Sal. *Hist.* 2.45 = 2.42 McGushin (vol. I 50; 209–10).

on the levy of Sicilian tithes sponsored by the two consuls, Cotta[262] and L. Octavius, was probably directly connected with these events. According to Cicero, the consuls, with the authorization of the senate, dealt with the letting of the tithes of wine, oil, and other products in Sicily.[263] Until then, the contracts had been let on the island and had been open to people of various origins, including Sicilians. Although Cicero's text does not clarify the question, the new law mainly benefited the Roman publicans, and possibly the objective was to accelerate the arrival of supplies from Sicily and to lower the price of the products, in order to relieve the lack of supplies in the markets. In a situation considered as urgent by the senate, the consuls thus took on the role that should have been played by the censors. In this context, we must bear in mind that in this period the censorship was filled very irregularly. In fact, the last censors had been those of 86, and no new censors were elected until the year 70.

Either because Lepidus' frumentary law had been abrogated or because it turned out to be insufficient, the consuls M. Terentius Varro Lucullus and C. Cassius Longinus had a new *lex frumentaria* passed in 73.[264] According to Rickman, the *lex Terentia Cassia* stated or re-stated a ration of five *modii* per month, and about forty thousand people benefited from it. This is a low figure in proportion to Rome's total population, which seems to indicate that the number of beneficiaries of the frumentations had been limited by the *lex Terentia Cassia* itself or some time before.[265] From the Ciceronian texts, it can be gathered that the law not only dealt with the apportioning of corn but also included the prices that had to be paid in Sicily for the corn that was regularly produced in the form of taxes, and it also authorized the purchase of additional amounts of Sicilian corn.[266] Possibly along the lines of the consular law of 75, the *lex Terentia Cassia* aimed to bring to Rome the

---

[262] Cotta sponsored another law, which Asconius (67) calls *de iudiciis privatis*. Its content is completely unknown. According to Asconius, the law was abrogated the following year by his own brother, M. Aurelius Cotta, consul in 74. See Rotondi 1912: 365; Marshall 1985: 236; Gruen 1974: 33 n. 92.

[263] Cic. *Ver.* 2.3.18. Carcopino 1914–19: 80–1; Broughton 1951–86: II 96; Rotondi 1912: 365; Rickman 1980: 40; Kunkel and Wittmann 1995: 329 n. 117.

[264] Cic. *Ver.* 2.3.163; 2.5.52 (Cicero calls it *lex frumentaria Terentia Cassia*); 2.3.173 (although in this passage he calls it simply *lex Terentia*).

[265] Rickman 1980: 166–8. Cf. Berchem 1939: 15–6; Rotondi 1912: 366; Nippel 1988: 110–11; Gruen 1974: 36; 385; Lintott 1999a: 87.

[266] Rowland Jr 1965: 81: with the 3 million *modii* which had to be received as taxes, apart from the 3,800,000 *modii* which could be purchased, Rowland maintains that the Sicilian corn alone could have fed about 180,000 persons with portions of 5 *modii* per month. Rickman (1980: 168) accepts the calculations made by Rowland, but he considers that this does not mean that the number of beneficiaries of the frumentations was 180,000 but that it was, in fact, much lower. However, Gruen (1974: 385 n. 108) believes that the figure given by Rowland is excessive.

maximum amount of corn possible at a reasonable price, in order to avoid the lack of basic food in the *Urbs*.

The simple fact that a consul in 78, seemingly with no opposition from his colleague or from the senate, as well as the two consuls in 75 and 73 with support from the senate, had laws passed to secure the supply and to facilitate the distribution of corn and other products to the population of Rome, indicates the enormous magnitude of the problem. Measures which until then had usually been dealt with by the tribunes of the plebs, and which had met with the reluctance of the senate due to the expense they involved for the public treasury, were now sponsored by the highest magistrates of the community. All in all, these laws did not bring about a complete solution of the supply problems, which to a great extent were not incidental but structural.[267] Endemic piracy in the Mediterranean was one of the main reasons for the supply problems. In order to eradicate it, Pompey received in 67 an extraordinary *imperium* as a result of the Gabinian law. In just a few months, Pompey defeated the pirates and presumably put an end to the problem. Ten years later, Pompey himself was granted proconsular *imperium* for five years in order to secure the supply of corn.[268] Once again, the situation in Rome was serious. The scarcity of food in the city caused prices to go up incessantly, and there was a real threat of famine for the plebs. The meeting of the senate where the question was debated took place while the crowd was protesting outside.[269] In these circumstances, Cicero, who had just returned from exile, suggested that Pompey be put in charge of the provisioning of Rome (*cura annonae*).[270] The proposal was approved by the senate, and the two consuls, Lentulus and Metellus Nepos, immediately drafted a bill which was passed in the comitia. All of this happened in September 57.[271]

Other consular laws of the post-Sullan period dealt with questions of institutional procedure. In 62, the consuls D. Iunius Silanus and L. Licinius

---

[267] In the year 70, the consul Crassus boosted his popularity with a free distribution of corn amongst the plebs, to the point that he fed the population of Rome for three months with his own resources (Plut. *Crass.* 12.2). This episode confirms that the situation of scarcity in the city was recurrent during those years and that relieving it was an excellent way of winning the plebs' support.

[268] Rotondi 1912: 402.

[269] Cic. *Dom.* 11 states that the meeting of the senate was held in the temple of Concordia. Cass. Dio, 39.9.2, places the meeting of the senate on the Capitolium and portrays the protesters as so desperate that they threatened to set themselves alight and the temple along with them. Cf. Vanderbroeck 1987: 249–51.

[270] Cic. *Att.* 4.1.6–7; Cass. Dio, 39.9.3. Gruen (1969b: 81) explains the support of the consul Lentulus Spinther for granting the *cura annonae* to Pompey as a means of separating the latter from the task of reinstating Ptolemy Auletes to the Egyptian throne, in which both of them were interested.

[271] Marinone 2004: 111.

Murena sponsored a law making it compulsory to place in the public treasury (*aerarium*) a written copy of all the laws so as to avoid fraudulent alterations of the text.[272] It is practically the only remarkable action known of these two consuls. Mommsen construed the law in the sense that the proposed bills which had not yet been voted on had to be deposited at the *aerarium*.[273] One of the bases to support this conclusion was the passage of Suetonius in which he claims that Pompey changed the text of his *lex de iure magistratuum* to include a section whereby Caesar was expressly excluded from the obligation of being present in Rome to be able to present his candidacy.[274] However, Landucci already demonstrated that Mommsen was mistaken, since Suetonius clearly refers to a law whose text was engraved in bronze and deposited at the *aerarium*.[275] The other text on which Mommsen based his theory, from Cicero's *De legibus*, does not unequivocally prove his thesis either.[276] Cicero does not necessarily talk about reality in his *De legibus* but about ideas, so it could simply be his wish that the texts of the proposed bills also be deposited prior to being voted on.[277]

The *lex Iunia Licinia* would, then, be a good example of how a custom, after a period of time, could become a law which, in all probability, included some new specifications and punishments for those who committed some kind of fraud. The author or authors of a law would be required to deposit the exact text at the public treasury, either immediately after its approval by the comitia or at the end of their magistracy.[278] Nevertheless, we must not confuse the deposit at the *aerarium* with the publication of the law. The text was made public by means of an edict and in *contiones* during the period of discussion of the bill, as the term *promulgare* indicates.[279]

In all probability, a Pupian law mentioned by Cicero must be placed in 61, since M. Pupius Piso is the only member of the *gens Pupia* who held major political offices in the first century, including his consulship in that year.[280] The law banned senate meetings on days on which the comitia

---

[272] Schol. Bob. 140 St. Cicero mentions the law on various occasions, referring to it both as *lex Iunia Licinia* and as *lex Licinia Iunia*: Cic. *Att.* 2.9.1; 4.16.5; *Sest.* 135; *Vat.* 33; *Phil.* 5.8. Cf. Rotondi 1912: 383–4; Gruen 1974: 254; 292.

[273] Mommsen 1887–8: II 546.   [274] Suet. *Jul.* 28.3.   [275] Landucci 1896.   [276] Cic. *Leg.* 3.11.

[277] von Schwind 1940: 29; Dyck 2004: 476–7.

[278] Williamson 2005: 395–6: 'The *lex Licinia Iunia* appears to have regulated the entry of statutes in the public record by instituting some manner of supervision that guaranteed that the statute entered in the record was the same statute approved at the assembly.' Cf. Millar 1998: 115.

[279] Fest. p. 224 L.: 'promulgari leges dicuntur cum primum in vulgus eduntur, quasi provulgari.' On the *lex Iunia Licinia* see in particular von Schwind 1940: 28–32.

[280] Gruen 1974: 252; Williamson 2005: 467.

could meet (*dies comitiales*) and is attested to with certainty at least for the months of January and February, although the prohibition probably applied to the whole year.[281]

The rest of the consular laws in the post-Sullan period referred to very specific questions of various kinds, and we know with certainty that they were mostly sponsored in line with a previously approved senatorial decree. This is the case for the *lex Gellia Cornelia* in 72. The two consuls sponsored in accord with the senate ('ex senatus sententia') a law which legalized the granting of citizenship to provincials of Hispania which Pompey had carried out in accordance with his advisory council ('de consili sententia') during his stay in Hispania in the context of the Sertorian war.[282] Gruen suggested, probably rightly, that although Cicero only refers to Pompey, the law must have also covered the grants of citizenship carried out by Metellus Pius in Hispania.[283] The end of the Sertorian war involved the imposition of penalties and the granting of awards to the people of Hispania who had respectively stood for Sertorius or for the senatorial troops. No doubt the two commanders of the Roman legions, Pompey and Metellus, had been in charge of taking these decisions, which amongst other things involved granting full Roman citizenship in some cases.[284] As regards the chronology of the *lex Gellia Cornelia*, the law must have been passed in close connection with the end of the Sertorian war, either when M. Perperna died or, more probably, when the last rebellious towns of Hispania were taken by the Roman troops.[285]

One of the two consuls of 72, Lentulus Clodianus, promulgated a law whereby all those who had purchased properties from the persons proscribed by Sulla for a very low price were to pay the state certain sums of money.[286] The law was preceded by the approval of a senatorial decree.[287] Finally, in November 72, the two consuls proposed in the senate that no provincial could be accused if he was absent. The senatorial proposal tried to

---

[281] Cic. *Fam.* 1.4.2; *Q.fr.* 2.2.3; *Sest.* 74. Cf. Caes. *Civ.* 1.5.4.

[282] Cic. *Balb.* 19. Cf. *Balb.* 32–3. Rotondi 1912: 367.   [283] Gruen 1974: 37.

[284] In fact, in his speech in favour of Archias, Cicero claims that Metellus Pius granted citizenship to many, a reference which probably alludes to his stay in Hispania: 'qui civitate multos donavit' (*Arch.* 26). In another passage of *Pro Balbo*, Cicero elaborates by saying that Metellus Pius granted citizenship to a Quintus Fabius, from the city of Saguntum (Cic. *Balb.* 50). A further general reference to the granting of citizenship carried out by the Roman *imperatores* can be found at Cic. *Balb.* 37.

[285] The chronology of the Sertorian War is far from certain. The death of Perperna must have occurred in the spring of 72, and the conquest of the last towns of Hispania took place in the ensuing months, very probably before the end of that year, when the senate asked Pompey and Metellus to return to Rome. Spann (1987: 135) suggests that Perperna outlived Sertorius by just a few months; Konrad (1994: 217; 1995: 187) places the taking of Calagurris by Afranius in 71.

[286] Sal. *Hist.* 4.1 = 4.1 McGushin (vol. II 40–1; 139: 'There is no indication that the law was ever promulgated'). Sandberg 2001: 61.

[287] Cic. *Ver.* 2.3.81–82. Cf. Gruen 1974: 36.

avoid abuse such as had occurred in the case of the accusation made by Verres against Sthenius in Sicily.[288] The motion was approved in the senate, but there is no evidence to suggest that it became law.

In the first few weeks of 61, political debate was practically engulfed by the Bona Dea scandal. Clodius' actions were considered an offence to the gods and therefore a danger to the maintenance of the *pax deorum*. The senate decided by a large majority to create a special jury to judge him. The bill to form the jury was presented by the two consuls, Piso and Messala.[289] However, due to his friendship with Clodius, Piso spoke against his own bill in a *contio* during the discussion of the *rogatio*.[290] The fact is interesting because it shows that a consul had the moral obligation to obey, at least formally, an order from the senate even when, as in this case, he disapproved of it. The disturbances caused by the Clodians made voting on the law impossible. After the senate had been summoned again, Piso tried to convince the senators that it was best to abandon the bill. However, the senators not only stood by the need to create an extraordinary jury, but they refused to deal with any other official matter until their *senatus consultum* had been implemented.[291] Eventually, a compromise was reached: the consular *rogatio* was rejected and, in exchange, another one promoted by the tribune of the plebs Q. Fufius Calenus was passed.[292]

In the year 60, Clodius was also involved in another controversial incident, when he decided to carry out the transition from the patrician order to the plebeian (*transitio ad plebem*) so that he could later on compete for the tribunate of the plebs. Clodius reached an agreement with the tribune C. Herennius for the latter to promote a law that would transfer him from the patriciate to the plebs. But the bill had to be voted on by the *comitia centuriata*, which required a higher magistrate to promote it officially. The consul Metellus Celer, Clodius' brother-in law, did so, but the *rogatio* met with a tribunician veto and did not succeed.[293] Metellus Celer was actually against Clodius' plan, but he may have been forced to take responsibility for the bill due to family ties.[294]

---

[288] Cic. *Ver.* 2.2.95. Sthenius had been summoned by Verres to Syracuse on the Calends of December (Cic. *Ver.* 2.2.94–8). This places the motion of the consuls, very probably, in November.

[289] Cic. *Att.* 1.13.3; Asc. 53 C.; Suet. *Jul.* 63.   [290] Cic. *Att.* 1.14.4.   [291] Cic. *Att.* 1.14.5.

[292] On the events, see Moreau 1982: 93–116; Gruen 1974: 248; Millar 1998: 118–20; Tatum 1999: 73–80; Williamson 2005: 380–1.

[293] Cic. *Att.* 1.18.4–5: Cicero reproached Metellus Celer for having taken on the proposal regarding Clodius' *transitio ad plebem*. On the veto of the *rogatio* Cic. *Att.* 1.19.5.

[294] On Metellus Celer's opposition to Clodius' wishes, Cic. *Att.* 2.1.4. Cf. Benner 1987: 42; Tatum 1999: 97.

A final consular law was passed in 57,[295] which, after several failed attempts, authorized Cicero's return from exile.[296] In the month of July the senate, on the initiative of the consul Lentulus, issued a decree asking the consuls to promote a law to this end. Lentulus and Metellus Nepos drafted the law, which was passed by the *comitia centuriata* on 4 August.[297] Cicero returned to Rome immediately and entered the city on 4 September.[298] While Lentulus was at all times a firm defender of Cicero, who mentions him repeatedly as the real sponsor of the law, Metellus Nepos changed his attitude from initial open opposition to eventual reluctant support of the measure.[299]

THE CONSULS IN THE DAY-TO-DAY POLITICS OF THE *URBS*

Along with the considerably increased legislative activity of the consuls in the post-Sullan period compared to previous centuries, the other fundamental change in consular functions was the much greater involvement of the consuls in day-to-day Roman politics. It is what Fergus Millar called the 'late-Republican "politicization" of the consulship'.[300] As with legislative activity, the main reason was not a modification of the consular powers or a change in the functions performed by consuls. It was their continuous presence in Rome which made it possible that their intervention in senatorial debates, their support for or opposition to certain legislative initiatives, their active participation in courts etc. was now constant and often decisive. To analyse in detail all the actions which could be considered political would amount to giving a broad outline of Roman politics in the first century, which is obviously beyond the purpose of this book and is the central topic of many monographs and specialized papers. In this section, I shall simply point out some of the most significant actions that may serve as examples of the purely political activity of consuls during this period.

On several occasions, one or both of the consuls opposed political or legislative initiatives of the tribunes of the plebs. One of the greatest concerns for tribunes in the decade of the seventies was the full restoration of the tribunician power that had been curtailed by Sulla. The restoration

---

[295] To this could be added the *lex Gabinia Calpurnia de insula Delo* passed in 58, which basically exempted the island of Delos from Roman taxes, and whose contents have been set out in the section dealing with the consuls' responsibility in international matters (see p. 268).

[296] Rotondi 1912: 403.   [297] Cic. *Red. Sen.* 27; *Red. Pop.* 17; *Dom.* 75; 87; *Sest.* 109.

[298] Marinone 2004: 110–11.   [299] Cass. Dio, 39.8.2. Cf. Gruen 1969b: 83.

[300] Millar 1998: 124. Cf. Millar 1995: 239.

was unsuccessfully pursued in 76, 74, and 73 respectively by the tribunes Cn. Sicinius,[301] L. Quinctius, and C. Licinius Macer. In all three cases they met the fierce opposition of the consuls. Cicero narrates an incident about Sicinius. When the tribune took the consul Curio and his colleague Cn. Octavius to a *contio* so that they could express their opinion about tribunician power before the people, Octavius remained seated, troubled with some illness, while Curio constantly moved about when giving his speech, as he usually did. In his reply, Sicinius said sarcastically that Octavius should be grateful to his colleague because by moving around he had kept the flies away, which otherwise would have devoured him, for he was totally still.[302] Nevertheless, Curio's viewpoint prevailed and Sicinius' attempt did not succeed.[303] The same happened two years later when the consul Lucullus spoke against Quinctius, probably at the beginning of the year, and at any rate before the consul set off for the East to take command of the war against Mithridates.[304] In 73, it was Licinius Macer who demanded full tribunician power. On this occasion, he probably faced the opposition of the consul Varro Lucullus, and as in the two previous cases, his attempt failed.[305]

Piso in 67 provides a good example of a consul actively involved in all the major political issues and debates of the year. As we have seen, Piso promoted a law against corruption and, as president of the elections, refused to accept the potential election of Palicanus as consul. Besides, he firmly, though unsuccessfully, opposed the *lex Gabinia*, which would give wide powers to Pompey in the fight against piracy. Piso even tried to prevent the levy of troops by Pompey once he had received the extraordinary command and was arrested because of this.[306] He also confronted Cornelius regarding the new law against corruption which the tribune was trying to introduce. The political debate became violent and finally Piso presented his own *lex de ambitu* with senatorial approval.[307] Cornelius also presented a bill whereby any exemption from a law had to have the previous approval of the people.

---

[301] Sallust gives L. as the *praenomen* of Sicinius; Cicero, on the other hand, Cn. Broughton (1951–86: II 93) accepts Cn.

[302] Cic. *Brut.* 217; Quint. *Inst.* 11.3.129. Pina Polo 1989: 286.

[303] Sal. *Hist.* 3.48.10 = 3.34.10 McGushin (vol. II 90–1).

[304] Sal. *Hist.* 3.48.11 = 3.34.11 McGushin (vol. II 92); Plut. *Luc.* 5.4. On the agitation stirred up by Quinctius from the speaker's platform, Cic. *Clu.* 110–12. Cf. Ooteghem 1959: 53–4; Marshall and Beness 1987: 371–2; Vanderbroeck 1987: 100–1; Pina Polo 1989: 287; Keaveney 1992: 59; Gruen 1974: 25. On the reflection of the *res urbanae* in Rome in 74 in the work of Sallust, Perl 1975: 322–4.

[305] Sal. *Hist.* 3.48 = 3.34 McGushin (vol. II 86–98) reproduces the speech of Licinius Macer. Sumner 1964: 43; Pina Polo 1989: 287; McGushin 1994: II 93–4; Gruen 1974: 25.

[306] Cass. Dio 36.24.3; 36.37.2; Plut. *Pomp.* 27.1–2. Vanderbroeck 1987: 225.

[307] Cass. Dio 36.38.1; Asc. 58 C. Gruen 1974: 213–14.

Piso was against this measure too, which caused a new episode of violence, in which the fasces of the consul were broken by the crowd.[308] Cornelius' law was eventually passed, but in a much more moderate version than the original.

Obviously, Cicero also provides an example of political activity during his consulship. Apart from the suppression of the Catilinarian conspiracy, we have already mentioned the approval of the *lex Tullia de ambitu* and his successful opposition to the agrarian law of the tribune Servilius Rullus. Cicero was also against a proposal presented by a tribune of the plebs, whose name is unknown, to restore political rights to the descendants of those who were proscribed by Sulla.[309] The consul delivered a speech which is not preserved, in which, on the one hand, he showed that the tribunician proposal was to his liking but at the same time argued that passing it could revive dangerous ghosts and that it would be wiser to leave things as they were. The law was not passed.[310]

In the year 60, while the Pompeian consul L. Afranius went practically unnoticed, his colleague Metellus Celer was involved in intense political activity.[311] He opposed the approval of the measures taken by Pompey in the East, both as consul and earlier as consul-elect.[312] He refused to accept the demands of the publicans in connection with their contracts in Asia. He confronted the tribune Flavius on account of the agrarian law which the latter wished to enact, probably at the beginning of the year. Flavius threatened to prohibit the consul from going to his province and even had him imprisoned temporarily, but Metellus achieved his purpose in that the tribunician proposal was not passed.[313] Metellus also opposed the attempt of his brother-in-law Clodius to be transferred to the plebs, although, as already stated, he was finally forced to allow the tribune Herennius' bill on the *transitio ad plebem* to be presented to the *comitia centuriata*, a bill which, nevertheless, was never voted on.[314]

The courts were, throughout the late Republican period, one theatre of the political war. Many public men took part in trials as accusers or

---

[308] Cass. Dio 36.39.2–4; Asc. 58 C. See Lewis 2006: 262–3. Cf. Nippel 1988: 62; Gruen 1974: 437; Millar 1998: 82–4.

[309] Cass. Dio 37.25.3.

[310] Quint. *Inst.* 11.1.85; Cic. *Att.* 2.1.3; *Pis.* 4; Plut. *Cic.* 12.1; Plin. *Nat.* 7.117. Cf. Rawson 1975: 66; Crawford 1994: 205–11; Gruen 1974: 415.

[311] Cic. *Att.* 1.20.5 describes Metellus as an 'excellent consul' ('egregius consul'), while claiming that Afranius' consulship was not actually a consulship.

[312] Cass. Dio 37.49.3. Gruen 1974: 130–1; Meier 1997: 272.

[313] Cic. *Att.* 1.18; 2.1.8; Cass. Dio 37.50.4. Ooteghem 1967: 273–5; Gruen 1974: 396.

[314] Cic. *Att.* 2.1.4–5; *Har.* 45; Cass. Dio 37.51.1–2.

defenders. Some consuls also did so during their term of office,[315] Cicero being a good example. During his lifetime, the Arpinate delivered numerous speeches before the courts in defence of his friends and clients. In 63 he did so on three occasions. He defended C. Calpurnius Piso at a trial in which the consul of 67 was accused of extortion (*de repetundis*).[316] Cicero was thus repaying Piso's support during his electoral campaign.[317] The defendant was acquitted. Cicero also defended C. Rabirius, who had been accused of being responsible for the murder of the tribune L. Saturninus almost forty years earlier. His speech, which is preserved, was not only a plea in favour of his client. At least in the written version which has reached us, the *Pro Rabirio perduellionis reo* was also a passionate defence of the *senatus consultum ultimum* as an instrument for the defence of the state and at the same time a justification of his own actions in the suppression of Catiline's supporters.[318]

Finally, Cicero defended L. Licinius Murena, a consul-elect. Murena had been accused of having won the election through corruption. His accusers were Cato and Sulpicius Rufus, one of his rivals, whom Cicero had actively supported during the electoral campaign. However, in the trial he preferred to defend Murena.[319] Cicero was aware of the complicated situation he was in during the trial. Cato and Sulpicius Rufus were publicly renowned for their integrity, which implicitly gave strength and legitimacy to the accusation. The accusation was also legally grounded on the recently passed *lex Tullia de ambitu* which Cicero himself had promoted. In these circumstances, it is not surprising that the Arpinate used the first part of his intervention before the court to justify why he had accepted the defence of Murena against his friends and political allies, seemingly undermining the authority of his own anti-corruption law.[320] The trial took place amidst the crisis caused by the conspiracy of Catiline, who had left Rome to command the rebellious troops in Etruria. In these circumstances, Cicero made an appeal for unity within the Roman ruling class so that a

---

[315] In earlier periods, it is exceptional to find a consul taking part in a trial in favour of a defendant. This happened in 120, when L. Opimius was accused by the tribune of the plebs P. Decius because of the suppression of the Gracchans, which Opimius led while a consul during the previous year. The consul C. Papirius Carbo took part in his defence: Cic. *de Orat.* 2.106; Liv. *per.* 61.

[316] Cic. *Flac.* 98; Sal. *Cat.* 49.1–2. Crawford 1984: 77–8; Marinone 2004: 86.

[317] Cic. *Att.* 1.1.2. Gruen 1974: 266.

[318] Cic. *Att.* 2.1.3; Cass. Dio 37.27; Suet. *Jul.*12. Ungern-Sternberg 1970: 81–5; Rawson 1975: 66–9; Vanderbroeck 1987: 230–1; Nippel 1988: 105–6; Duplá 1990: 115–21; Gruen 1974: 278–9; Millar 1998: 106–8; Marinone 2004: 86; Morstein-Marx 2004: 225–8; Pina Polo 2005b: 144–5. In particular on the strategy followed by Cicero in his speech in defence of Rabirius see Primmer 1985.

[319] Cic. *Flac.* 98; Quint. *Inst.* 6.1.35; Plut. *Cic.* 35.4. Gruen 1974: 273; Marinone 2004: 87.

[320] Rawson 1975: 77: 'Murena was pretty obviously guilty.'

condemnation of Murena could not indirectly legitimize Catiline's actions. We can presume that the arguments used by Cicero were not alien to the judges, who determined that the defendant was innocent, and this allowed him officially to become a consul on 1 January 62.[321]

The intervention of a consul in a trial logically granted extra *auctoritas* to the opinion expressed. However, it is difficult to determine whether Cicero was an exception or whether it was frequent for a consul to act as an orator at a trial, because we have very few available instances.[322] Cicero himself makes a brief reference to the consul Torquatus, who defended Catiline in 65.[323] Other consulars took part in the trial in defence of Catiline, and even Cicero considered the possibility of doing the same, although in the end he was not involved.[324] It is practically Torquatus' only known action during his consulship. Plutarch makes a vague reference to the allegedly frequent interventions of Pompey in court during his first consulship in the year 70, but we do not know of any specific trial in which he took part.[325] In an inscription in Greek, the city of Miletus made a dedication in honour of Lucius Domitius Ahenobarbus, who is called *hupatos* and a patron of the town. Canali de Rossi suggests that while a consul in 54, Ahenobarbus may have acted as an advocate in favour of the Milesians in a trial *de repetundis*, perhaps initiated against T. Ampius Balbus, governor of Asia in 58, and that this could account for the inscription.[326] In the same year 54, the other consul, Ap. Claudius Pulcher, managed to delay the trial that the tribunes of the plebs wanted to start against Gabinius.[327] This happened at the beginning of the year. However, later on the consul himself attacked Gabinius and even accused him of *maiestas*.[328]

Besides consular interventions in the legislative process and in court, we know of many other varied political actions of the consuls from 80 to 50, for example regarding the granting of honours to certain *imperatores*. In 79, P. Servilius Vatia, who was originally against the granting of a triumph to Pompey upon his victorious return from Africa, ended up supporting it.[329] Cicero, in his turn, claims for himself the merit of having managed as consul to enable Lucullus to celebrate his triumph over Mithridates and

[321] Millar 1998: 99–101; Pina Polo 2005b: 125.
[322] Alexander 1990: in his compilation he mentions Cicero as the sole consul taking part in trials during the post-Sullan period.
[323] Cic. *Sul.* 81.   [324] Gruen 1974: 271.   [325] Plut. *Pomp.* 23.3. Cf. Greenhalgh 1980: 69.
[326] Canali de Rossi 1997: 360. According to Gruen (1974: 314) the trial had taken place in 55, perhaps when Ahenobarbus was a consul-designate, but not yet a consul. On the trial, Alexander 1990: 137 (no. 281).
[327] Cic. *Q.fr.* 2.11.3.   [328] Cic. *Q.fr.* 3.2.3. Gruen 1969b: 102; 1974: 324; Seager 2005: 128–9.
[329] Plut. *Pomp.* 14.5.

Tigranes in 63.[330] In 54, the aforementioned Ap. Claudius Pulcher helped
C. Pomptinus to celebrate a triumph. The celebration took place after a
long delay, since Pomptinus was granted the triumph for having defeated
the Allobroges in 62/1. But when on 2 November he intended to enter
Rome as a *triumphator*, he was stopped by two praetors and a tribune of the
plebs, who claimed that the law which granted him the triumph had been
passed irregularly. The intervention of the consul Claudius Pulcher was
decisive in allowing Pomptinus eventually to celebrate the triumph.[331]

News of the Roman legions achieving a victory was obviously received
in Rome with jubilation. The victorious general could expect to obtain a
triumph on his return. But in the meantime he gained immediate popularity,
and all the citizens talked about him. In practice this usually involved the
celebration of some days of thanksgiving to the gods. In 63, when news
reached Rome that Mithridates had died, Cicero delivered a speech in
the senate in which he suggested that ten days of supplications should
be celebrated for Pompey's victories, an unprecedented duration, which
reflected the importance of the event and particularly honoured Pompey.[332]
The Ciceronian speech was not published, but his petition was apparently
successful. However, in the year 50 it was Cicero himself who was eager for
supplications to be ordained because of his achievements in Cilicia. To this
end, he wrote a letter to the consul C. Claudius Marcellus asking him to
help him in the senate.[333] The consul complied with the request, and the
supplications were approved despite Cato's initial opposition. Cicero wrote to
Marcellus later to thank him for his collaboration.[334]

In contrast, we also know of some instances of consuls opposing the
granting of honours, mainly the case of Lepidus in 78, when he unsuccessfully tried to impede the ostentatious funeral of Sulla. It was his first great
confrontation with his colleague Catulus.[335] In 54, the consul Domitius
Ahenobarbus opposed the planned funerary honours of Iulia, Pompey's
wife and Caesar's daughter. A funeral eulogy was pronounced in honour of

---

[330] Cic. *Ac.* 2.3. According to Plutarch, Lucullus' request for a triumph had initially met with the
opposition of the tribune of the plebs Memmius, and only through the intervention of important
persons in Rome's political scene could the people be persuaded of the suitability of the triumph:
Plut. *Luc.* 37.1–2.

[331] Cic. *Att.* 4.18.4; *Q.fr.* 3.4.6; *Fam.* 3.10.3; Cass. Dio 39.65.2. Broughton 1951–86: II 225; Vanderbroeck
1987: 261.

[332] Cic. *Prov.* 27. Rawson 1975: 66; Crawford 1984: 90–1.   [333] Cic. *Fam.* 15.10.

[334] Cic. *Fam.* 8.11.1; 15.11.

[335] Plut. *Pomp.* 15.3; *Sul.* 38.1; App. *B.Civ.* 1.105. Cf. Criniti 1969: 403; Gruen 1974: 12. Hayne (1972:
663–4) thinks that Lepidus opposed the funeral because he thought there was a danger of public
disturbances and because the planned luxury surrounding it would go against the *lex sumptuaria*
which had been recently approved by Sulla himself.

Iulia from the rostra, and she was later buried in the Campus Martius. Ahenobarbus fruitlessly argued that use of that space required a special decree to authorize it.[336]

Throughout the year multiple public issues were brought to the attention of the consuls, who, as supreme magistrates of the *civitas*, had to state their opinion before the people and, above all, in the senate. It is the dynamic of day-to-day politics in which the consuls played a central role in the first century. When the letter that Pompey had written from Hispania asking for further resources to fight Sertorius reached Rome, a debate was raised in the senate on whether meeting his demands was advisable.[337] The two consuls of 74 were in favour of sending Pompey what he had asked for, and their opinion determined the decision of the senate. The Pompeian letter was read out in the senate in January 74, according to Sallust. Pompey had threatened to return to Italy if he was not given what he had asked for. His return was not in the consuls' interest, in the first place because they would lose prominence in Rome, and in the second place because one or both of them could be forced to replace Pompey in Hispania or even confront the Sertorians on Italian soil if the war shifted, a danger which was perceived as real at that moment. All of this occurred while the war against Mithridates was unavoidable, and the two consuls, in particular Lucullus, aspired to obtain command over it. Both patriotism, which demanded the Sertorian rebels be defeated, and personal interests had an influence in the consuls' defence of the requests made by Pompey.[338]

At the end of the decade of the sixties and in the first half of the fifties, first Clodius himself, due to his intrusion into the rituals of the Bona Dea, and later Clodius and his confrontation with Cicero became issues of public interest. The consuls, obviously, could not stay detached from it. In 61, the two consuls held opposing views regarding what ought to be done with Clodius as a result of the Bona Dea scandal. While Piso Frugi actively supported Clodius, his colleague Messala declared himself to be in favour of using severe measures against this sacrilegious act. By order of the senate, the two consuls drafted the bill which set forth the creation of an extra-ordinary court, but Piso later distanced himself from this in public.[339] In contrast, in 58 both Piso Caesoninus and Gabinius openly supported Clodius against Cicero. This lack of support from the consuls was a

---

[336] Cass. Dio 39.64. Broughton 1951–86: II 221; Vanderbroeck 1987: 259; Pina Polo 1989: 304; Millar 1998: 177–8.
[337] Sal. *Hist.* 2.98 = 2.82 McGushin (vol. I 58–60).
[338] Plut. *Pomp.* 20.1–2. Ooteghem 1959: 47–8; Keaveney 1992: 51–3.
[339] Lacey 1974; Tatum 1999: 73–9.

determining factor in Cicero's decision to go into exile, and the Arpinate bitterly complained about this, especially in his speech against Piso. One year later, the consul Lentulus worked incessantly to attain the return of Cicero. His efforts eventually paid off and resulted in the law that authorized the return of the orator, which was also, though reluctantly, endorsed by his colleague Metellus Nepos. But this was no reason for the latter to abandon Clodius, whom he supported that same year in his conflict against Milo, who was to be responsible for the murder of Clodius some years later. In fact, it appears that twice during that year Metellus prevented Milo from starting a prosecution for violence against Clodius.[340]

Lentulus Marcellinus was particularly active in 56. We have previously seen that he openly rejected the candidacy of Crassus and Pompey for the consulship of 55, although he could only manage to delay the elections until that year. But Marcellinus was also very actively involved in the burning question of the reinstatement of Ptolemy Auletes to the throne of Egypt. He denied that this should be accomplished by a general and his army, which set him against the proconsul Lentulus Spinther. But he was also against the proposal of the tribune of the plebs L. Caninius Gallus that Pompey should reinstate Ptolemy without an army, just with two lictors.[341] The Egyptian issue was also, in the first place, an ingredient of internal conflict within Roman politics, and power and influence were at stake; hence the decisive consular intervention. Marcellinus' colleague Philippus criticized the extension of Caesar's command in Gaul and for this reason he confronted Cicero, as can be gathered from his speech *De provinciis consularibus*.[342]

The question of the Caesarian command and of Caesar's aspiration to a second consulship was to become increasingly dominant in the political scene of the ensuing years. This happened particularly in 51 and 50, when the consuls Marcus and Gaius Claudius Marcellus participated constantly in the debate that would finally lead to the civil war: they constantly campaigned against Caesar's provincial government and presented motions to force the *imperator* to return to Rome as soon as possible.[343] In this anti-Caesarian context, Plutarch and Appian narrate the actions of the consul M. Marcellus against a citizen from Novum Comum in 51. Caesar had

---

[340] Cic. *Mil.* 40; *Sest.* 89; *Att.* 4.3.3–4; *Fam.* 5.3.2; Cass. Dio 39.7.4. Ooteghem 1967: 292; Gruen 1974: 295–6.

[341] Cic. *Fam.* 1.1.2; 1.2.1; *Q.fr.* 2.4.5; Plut. *Pomp.* 49.6; Cass. Dio 39.16.1. Gruen 1969b: 82.

[342] Cic. *Prov.* 18; 21.

[343] The events are described in detail by Gelzer 1968: 179–94; Meier 1982: 422–37; Gruen 1974: 460–4 and 475–90; Jehne 1997: 72–9.

recently turned Novum Comum into a colony.[344] Marcellus refused to accept that the Caesarian action was legitimate and did not consider that the inhabitants of Novum Comum were Roman citizens. He probably even presented, albeit unsuccessfully, a motion in the senate for Caesar's decision to be repealed.[345] For this reason, the consul ordered a prominent citizen of Novum Comum to be flogged in public, which was actually a message directed at Caesar and a way of showing contempt towards his decisions.[346] His colleague Ser. Sulpicius Rufus was much more moderate. In a letter written to him by Cicero in 46, he recalls how in the first few months of his consulship, Sulpicius Rufus had prophetically already noted in the senate the risk of an eventual civil war.[347] Sulpicius Rufus himself had vetoed a senatorial decision to conduct an extra levy of men with the purpose of reinforcing Cicero's troops in Cilicia and Bibulus' in Syria. The reason behind the bill was, without a doubt, the supposed danger posed by the Parthians, which gradually subsided in the following months.[348]

These are just some of the political matters reported by ancient sources in which the consuls were actively involved during the period from 80 to 50. Many other matters of greater or lesser significance undoubtedly took up their time, from the moment when, by being present in Rome, consuls became key participants in the permanent political debate surrounding them, obviously with varying intensity depending on the character and personality of each consul.[349]

---

[344] Suet. *Jul.* 28.3. Cf. Wolff 1979. [345] Cic. *Att.* 5.2.3. Shackleton Bailey 1965–70: III 193.
[346] Plut. *Caes.* 29.2; App. *B.Civ.* 2.26. [347] Cic. *Fam.* 4.3.1. [348] Cic. *Fam.* 3.3.1.
[349] Meier (1997: 14) emphasizes the importance of the strong personality of consuls such as Cicero in 63, Metellus Celer in 60, or Caesar in 59 in their decisive influence on the course of events during their consulships.

CHAPTER 14

The consular year in the post-Sullan period

As we have already seen, the list of consular functions from 80 to 50 was long and qualitatively significant: the consuls received foreign embassies and introduced them to the senate; they took an active part in granting honours to individuals who had distinguished themselves by their actions in favour of the Roman state; they concluded or renewed treaties for whose implementation they were ultimately responsible; the consuls' intervention in debates in the senate regarding all sorts of questions was constant, and they promoted a large number of senatorial decrees; they were entrusted with the enactment of the *senatus consulta* once they had been passed, whether they had sponsored them or not; they legislated on very varied aspects of social life and the economy and politics of the Roman *civitas*, such as electoral corruption, distribution of public land, the corn supply, the courts, and the tribunician power; they were the representatives of the community before the gods of the Roman civic religion and had to ensure that relations with them were appropriate by conducting acts of expiation, supplications, and the traditional *feriae Latinae*, over which they had to preside; when necessary, they acted against deities and rituals which were perceived as pernicious, as in the case of the consul Gabinius in 58, who acted against the Egyptian cults; they took part in political debates before the people in *contiones* which were convened by them or by other magistrates and often had to give their opinion on topical public matters; they issued edicts on different subjects; they were occasionally entrusted by the senate with certain exemplary public works, such as the reconstruction of the Capitolium and the erection of the Tabularium, a joint endeavour which was overseen by Catulus; sometimes they acted in court giving testimony in favour of the defendant; exceptionally, they presided by order of the senate over investigations, as in the case of the conflict between the towns of Interamna and Reate in 54; they presided over elections, which were usually held in the summer but due to political circumstances could be deferred for weeks or even months, as happened on several occasions; they positioned themselves in favour of or against all sorts of questions resulting from political debate, such as granting honours to military commanders, the return from exile of public persons such as Cicero, and so forth.

In conclusion, in the central years of the first century the consuls played an essential role in the politics of Rome, and it can be asserted that both internal and external policy was directed by the consuls as the supreme rulers of the Roman state. As Gruen put it, 'the consul could be a pivotal figure. Presiding officer in the senate, initiator of senatorial motions and comitial legislation, holder of elections – the state's chief executive.'[1] The function of the consuls as chief executives of the Roman state was facilitated and encouraged by the fact that in the post-Sullan period the consuls remained in Rome for most of their term of office and a large number of them did not even leave the city to go to the provinces which had been allotted to them.

From this central role given by the Roman constitution to the consulship as an institution, the greater or lesser prominence of a given consul depended on several factors, mainly his personal ability but also the political context of the time. For example, some of the great *imperatores* of this period were also outstanding legislators, in particular Pompey and Caesar. The *auctoritas* which Pompey enjoyed in Rome greatly contributed to making him one of the greatest legislators of the time, promulgating during his consulships laws regarding central issues for Roman politics and society. But this must be seen within the context of the exceptional situation in Rome in 55 and above all in 52, which made it advisable to introduce reforms and drastic measures in order to alleviate the corruption and violence which were feeding off each other, a task that was promoted by the legislative work undertaken by Pompey. Caesar was also an important legislator during his consulship in 59. As opposed to Pompey and to the other consuls of this period, Caesar acted against the will of the majority of the senate while focusing on the agrarian issue, which until then had been dealt with by the tribunes of the plebs. This alteration in the usual conduct of a consul was possible, of course, because of Caesar's strong personality but also thanks to the unbeatable support of his allies, Pompey and Crassus.

In the period from 80 to 50, therefore, there are some general patterns of behaviour that apply to the consulship as an institution, and certain functions which all consuls were expected to perform during their term of office. Starting from this general situation, some consuls became real political leaders in Rome, taking the initiative in policy matters during

---

[1] Gruen 1974: 87.

their term of office, whereas others preferred to adopt a secondary role with regard to the senate or their colleagues, and some even went totally unnoticed to the point that no consular action of theirs is known, as is the case, for example, of the consuls of 71, Lentulus Sura and Aufidius Orestes, the great orator Hortensius, consul in 69, the consuls of 64, L. Iulius Caesar and C. Marcius Figulus, or those of 53, Cn. Domitius Calvinus and Messala Rufus, who took up their office well into the year.

There is one year during the post-Sullan period for which we have a considerable amount of information to establish the main events that occurred: the year 63, which had thirteen months because an intercalary month was introduced between February and March.[2] Cicero in particular made sure to leave a record, both for his contemporaries and for posterity, of the most noteworthy events he was involved in as consul that year. This allows us to reconstruct with some degree of accuracy his consular year, which, in regard to the actions of the two consuls, was in part similar to any other consulship of the period and partly different, due, of course, to the suppression of the Catilinarian conspiracy.[3]

As had been usual from 153 onwards, the two consuls of 63, M. Tullius Cicero and C. Antonius, took office on 1 January. They performed the customary rituals on that day: first the taking of auspices, later the sacrifice of two oxen and the making of the vows on the Capitolium. Once the religious duties had been fulfilled, the two consuls attended the senate's first session of the year in the temple of Jupiter on the Capitolium. As dictated by tradition, this meeting dealt with the most pressing problems of internal and external politics. The senators gave their views on these matters and, in particular, the new consuls established their political position and announced, if necessary, their scheduled actions. On 1 January 63 Cicero's entire speech in the senate, or a substantial part of it, was devoted to criticizing the agrarian bill which had been presented a few days earlier by the tribune of the plebs P. Servilius Rullus. His speech was published later and it is known as the first in the series *De lege agraria*. In it, the consul strove to present an extraordinarily negative vision of Rome, supposedly

---

[2] See the correspondence of dates in the official calendar in 63 with the dates in the astronomical calendar in Marinone 2004: 342–8.

[3] What follows is just a brief synopsis of the events of 63, stressing mainly those where the two consuls were involved. It is evident that there is a vast bibliography on Cicero and, in particular, on his consulship. Without being exhaustive, see in this respect Peterson 1920: 222–85; Gelzer 1969: 71–104; Stockton 1971: 84–142; Shackleton Bailey 1971: 27–34; Rawson 1975: 60–88; Lacey 1978: 30–42; Mitchell 1979: 177–242; Habicht 1990: 16–52; Fuhrmann 1992: 62–70; Jehne 2000; Everitt 2001: 82–107; Pina Polo 2005b: 107–30. The chronology of the Ciceronian consulship has been detailed by Marinone 2004: 82–7.

beleaguered not by external enemies but by internal dangers, by plots which threatened to destroy the established order and to replace it by some form of tyranny.[4] Against this critical situation, Cicero offered himself as a guide willing to put into practice a firm policy to save the Republic. He announced that, should the situation persist, he was determined not to go to his province but to remain in Rome instead to preserve the internal order.

In the ensuing days, Cicero gave three further speeches against the project sponsored by Servilius Rullus. Only some testimonies of the last speech are preserved[5] and the other two, which are preserved, were given in *contiones* before the people. The second speech *De lege agraria* was probably delivered on 2 January. It was not unusual for the consuls to convene a *contio* at the beginning of the year to address the people and to thank the citizens for electing them.[6] Cicero did this, using the *contio* as an opportunity to bring to the attention of those who attended the meeting the exceptional fact that he was a *homo novus*, a 'new man' who had achieved the consulship through his personal effort.[7] But he also turned this presentation before the people after taking office into a plea against Servilius Rullus, by presenting a picture of Rome in danger, as he had done in the senate, and making the crisis seem even more dramatic. In order to face it, he, once again, offered his determination and claimed that the peace and freedom of the Romans had been placed under the patronage of his consulship.[8] The picture given by Cicero seems clearly and suspiciously exaggerated compared to the actual circumstances at the time. But when the speeches were later published, an opportunity which may have been used to modify the texts in order to suit the author's interests, their contents showed the consul as the great protagonist of the year and almost as a visionary who was able to predict, with his immense political skill, the disorder which Catiline was to provoke some months later. Cicero was the leader that Roman society needed to save itself, a role for which he had offered himself before the senate and the people, while he was creating a self-portrait, the image that he wished to offer to his fellow citizens and to posterity.[9]

In his speeches against the agrarian bill, Cicero continuously omitted the heart of the matter: that is, the several decades-long need to implement

---

[4] Cic. *Leg.agr.* 1.26.
[5] Crawford 1984: 79–81: from the letter written by Cicero to Atticus in June 60 (Cic. *Att.* 2.1.3) it can be deduced that Cicero sent the four speeches to his friend to be published, but the last one was either lost or never published.
[6] Pina Polo 1989: 156.　　[7] Cic. *Leg.agr.* 2.1–3.　　[8] Cic. *Leg.agr.* 2.9.
[9] In the first part of his speech against Piso, given in 55, Cicero gave a summary of his consular achievements, all of them, according to him, aimed at avoiding the breakdown of the Republican system (Cic. *Pis.* 4–7).

agrarian reform to enable the great mass of small farmers to survive in the rural areas of Italy, as well as to facilitate the return to farming of all those who had fled the country in large numbers to go to the cities. The consul focused on discrediting the project politically, alluding to the excessive power which would be granted to the decemvirs who were to put it into practice or to the loss of income that the public treasury would suffer, but he did not provide an alternative solution to the obvious socio-economic problems in Italy.

Rullus's proposal was apparently not even voted on, because the tribune withdrew it. Cicero presented this fact as his first great victory as consul. Without a doubt, the Ciceronian arguments, aimed mainly at arousing suspicion and creating fear and confusion around the bill, must have had some influence on the outcome. However the threat of a veto made by another tribune of the plebs, as well as the insufficient support that Rullus possessed, not only within the ruling classes but also within the urban plebs, seems to have been more decisive. All of this happened in the first fortnight of January. We do not know the position of the other consul, Antonius, on the agrarian bill.

The two consular provinces planned for 63 were Macedonia and Cisalpine Gaul. The allotment between the two consuls presumably took place in one of the senate sessions held in the same month of January, perhaps even in the session of 1 January. Cicero was initially given Macedonia, while Cisalpine Gaul was allotted to Antonius. The provinces were assigned funds and troops by the senate in accordance with their needs.[10] But neither of the two consuls was to go to his province during their consulship. In the first place, the consuls exchanged the provinces that had been allotted to them. Antonius apparently preferred the more lucrative Macedonia, and Cicero had no interest in it, so he did not have any objections to taking Cisalpine Gaul. Antonius could only go to Macedonia when he was proconsul in the year 62, once he had finally defeated Catiline. Cicero, as he had already declared in his speech in the senate on 1 January, renounced the government of Cisalpine Gaul. He made his decision public in a *contio*, although in all probability it had been previously discussed and accepted by the senators.[11] In fact, in the same session of the senate where the consul proposed his renunciation he could have given a speech claiming that Cisalpine Gaul, which had by then become a praetorian province,

[10] Cic. *Pis.* 5.
[11] Cic. *Att.* 2.1.3; *Pis.* 5; Cass. Dio, 37.33.4. Crawford 1984: 83: this speech may have been delivered in May or June.

should be given to Metellus Celer with the same endowments as originally provided for it by the senate as a consular province. Cicero says that he also maintained that the province should be given to Metellus in *contiones*. Cisalpine Gaul was indeed allotted to Metelus Celer by means of drawing lots, in which Cicero claims to have had a decisive influence, although he does not specify in what form.[12]

From the year 67, a *lex Gabinia* set forth the obligation to devote the senate sessions of the month of February to the reception of the foreign legates who had arrived in Rome and requested to be heard in the senate. This law actually regularized and set a precise timeframe for what had been a long-standing practice, since it was customary for the senate to receive foreign envoys at the beginning of the consular year, coinciding with the presence of the consuls in Rome. In fact, at the beginning of 63, several foreign legations were in the *Urbs*, and the consuls Cicero and Antonius had to deal with them in order to ascertain the nature of their claims before taking them to the Curia, should the senators find it appropriate. The consuls must also have presided over the senate sessions in February where the ambassadors were received and reported to the latter the decisions taken by the senate.[13]

After the month of February, which was devoted to diplomatic questions, the rest of the year was open to possible consular initiatives in both the senate and the legislative sphere. Nothing is known in this respect of the actions of Antonius, who seems to have spent most of his consulship in the shadow of his much more active colleague. Nevertheless, the two of them, as was mandatory, presided jointly over the *feriae Latinae* celebrated on the Mons Albanus. The sole reference to this is provided by Cicero himself, who claims that the Mons Albanus was covered in snow at the time of the celebration.[14] This piece of information does not allow us to determine with certainty the precise date when the Latin festival took place that year, since there could have been snow at any time during the winter. However, in view of the fact that in the month of January Cicero was deeply involved in fighting the proposal of Servilius Rullus, that February was taken up with diplomatic activities, and that the date for the celebration had to be designated beforehand by the consuls so that not only the magistrates of Rome but also the representatives of the Latin cities could plan for their

---

[12] Cic. *Fam.* 5.2.3–4. Cf. Gelzer 1969: 83; Crawford 1984: 85–7.
[13] Canali de Rossi (1997: 167; 334–5; 586) lists several embassies from the Eastern Mediterranean which were received in Rome in 63.
[14] Cic. *Div.* 1.18.

presence on the Mons Albanus, it seems plausible to place the dates of celebration of the *feriae Latinae* some time during the intercalary month that followed February.

In the ensuing months we know of a great number of actions of a very varied nature undertaken by Cicero, actions whose chronology is generally difficult to establish, although all of them probably occurred before suspicions about Catiline's conspiracy emerged. In the legislative field, the only law promoted by Cicero that was eventually passed was the *lex Tullia de ambitu*. Its purpose was to define more accurately the crime of corruption; it expanded the applicable penalties and was sponsored by the consul on the basis of a previous senatorial decree.[15] However, it was not the only law that Cicero tried to pass. He proposed eliminating the senatorial legations to different parts of the empire, which involved abuses and significant expenses for the provincials, who had to entertain senators visiting their territories.[16] His project did not go forward, given that a tribune of the plebs announced that he would veto it, but he managed to get the senate to set a time limit of one year's duration for these embassies. From the Ciceronian text it can be gathered that his proposal never went beyond the senate, where he claims to have had the support of the majority of senators. The tribune's statement in the session where the matter was discussed, declaring that he would veto the project, doubtless dissuaded Cicero from putting his idea in writing in the form of a text to be officially presented for debate before the people.

On the other hand, Cicero opposed a bill sponsored by a tribune of the plebs which tried to return full civic rights to all the descendants of those who had been proscribed by Sulla.[17] In an attempt at shaping an aristocracy which shared his ideas and destroying any opposition within it, the dictator had perpetrated the murder of hundreds of persons and the exile of many others by proscribing them. To prevent future problems, he had also decreed a prohibition of the sons of any proscribed person from holding any public magistracy. Nearly twenty years later, although political circumstances were different and a substantial part of the Sullan constitution had been modified, the exclusion was still in force. Cicero even delivered a speech on the subject which he sent to his friend Atticus in the year 60 to be published along with the rest of his consular speeches. He called it *De proscriptorum filiis*.[18] On the one hand, the measure was to his liking insofar as it sought concord amongst Roman citizens, but he opposed it because he considered it ill-timed and because he thought that it could put

---

[15] Cic. *Vat.* 37; *Mur.* 3; 47; 67; *Planc.* 83. Cf. Poma 2005.   [16] Cic. *Leg.* 3.18.
[17] Quint. 11.1.85; Cic. *Pis.* 4; Plut. *Cic.* 12.1; Plin. *Nat.* 7.117; Cass. Dio 37.25.3.   [18] Cic. *Att.* 2.1.3.

the internal balance of the Roman-Italian elite at risk. His arguments were successful, and the bill was not passed. Discrimination continued to be in force until 49.

Until his consulship, Cicero had shown little interest in appearing before the people in *contiones*. The senate and the courts had almost exclusively been the arenas in which he had deployed his oratorical skills. But his role as a consul caused him to change his attitude, and he gave several speeches before the people throughout the year 63, some of which have already been mentioned, as in the case of those against Rullus' agrarian reform or the public announcement of his renunciation of his province. He also delivered a speech in a *contio* in favour of L. Roscius Otho, who had been attacked during the celebration of the games because of a law which reserved seats in the theatre for the equites.[19]

At least twice during his consulship Cicero defended in the senate the granting of honours to generals after their victories in the battlefield. On the one hand, he favoured the proposal that, after a long wait, Lucullus be granted a triumph as a result of his campaigns in the East against Mithridates and Tigranes,[20] and he managed to get ten days of supplications celebrated because of the victories obtained by Pompey, also in the East, and in particular because of the death of Mithridates after two decades of armed conflict.[21] The importance of the event is reflected by the unusual duration of the supplications. By defending such an honour, Cicero sought to secure the future support of Pompey, who was soon to return to Rome after his brilliant performance in the East.

Presumably in the first half of 63, Cicero acted twice in court, in defence of his friend C. Calpurnius Piso, who was accused of extortion and finally acquitted,[22] and also in defence of C. Rabirius.[23] The trial of Rabirius was, above all, a political event which must be understood in the context of the controversies existing within the Roman ruling class on the use of force to suppress internal dissent, a debate which would be raised again a few months later regarding Catiline's conspiracy. Rabirius was accused of the murder, thirty-seven years earlier, of the then tribune Lucius Appuleius Saturninus, after the proclamation of the so-called *senatus consultum ultimum*. Bringing back to life events which had occurred almost four decades earlier was mainly a way of questioning the legitimacy of the exceptional

---

[19] Cic. *Att.* 2.1.3; Plut. *Cic.* 13.4.   [20] Cic. *Ac.* 2.3.

[21] Cic. *Prov.* 27. Marinone (2004: 83) places the approval of the supplications in honour of Pompey at the end of summer; Rawson (1975: 66) thinks that the supplications took place in the first part of the year.

[22] Cic. *Flac.* 98; Sal. *Cat.* 49.1–2.   [23] Cic. *Att.* 2.1.3; Cass. Dio 37.27; Suet. *Jul.* 12.

measures taken by the senate, which in practice cancelled the citizens' rights and which attempted to legitimize the murder of individuals who were perceived as dangerous by the majority of the senate. The prosecution aimed to highlight the public condemnation of the abuse inflicted in the name of the 'ultimate decree of the senate' and to defend the right of a fair trial before the courts, and the right of appeal in case of a conviction, as fundamental ingredients of the freedom of all Roman citizens.

The importance of the trial is marked by the eminence of the orators who acted for the defendant: Hortensius and the consul Cicero, whose speech *Pro Rabirio perduellionis reo* is preserved. Aware of the significance of the case, which went beyond the mere accusation of murder, Cicero focused more on the political consequences of a potential conviction than on the strictly legal defence of the defendant, which had already been dealt with by Hortensius. Cicero's intervention was a passionate defence of the *senatus consultum ultimum* as a legitimate tool for the preservation of the established order and ultimately of the role of the senate as the guardian of Rome. For this reason, Cicero started and finished his speech claiming that it was not his friendship with the defendant but rather his position as a consul that had made him consider it one of the duties of his office to undertake the defence of Rabirius, for it was not his innocence that was at stake but the very survival of the Republic.[24] Be that as it may, Ciceronian eloquence was not to be the deciding factor in the outcome of the trial. A loophole in the legal process of holding popular assemblies allowed the comitia which were to determine the guilt or innocence of Rabirius to be suspended, and he was finally set free. Nevertheless, Cicero considered the episode as another great political success in his consular year.

In 63, Cicero presided over the electoral process. The consular elections were held, as usual, in the summer, probably in the month of July. Cicero used his influence to prevent Catiline, who was running for the consulship again, from being elected. On the day of the elections, Cicero presided over them on the Campus Martius, escorted by his personal guard and wearing a protective cuirass.[25] By doing this he was making a statement on the threat of violence, of which he accused Catiline, and personifying as consul the danger that, according to him, was threatening the Republic.

Cicero also succeeded in this battle, and Catiline was not elected, but his defeat made him resort to forming a conspiracy in order to seize power. The conspiracy of Catiline was to be at the centre of Rome's political scene in the last few months of the year, and its suppression was to be the consul Cicero's

---

[24] Cic. *Rab.* 2; 38.   [25] Cic. *Mur.* 51–2; Plut. *Cic.* 14.5–8; Sal. *Cat.* 26.5.

great final victory. The events are well known, and it is not necessary to give a detailed account of them here.[26] Cicero led at each stage, first during the unveiling of the conspiracy and later in its suppression. Cicero's greatest merits in his handling of the crisis were his skills at gathering intelligence to keep him informed of the preparations of the conspirators and his capacity to anticipate events. These, along with his clever oratorial skills and his firm use of the instruments of moral and political authority deriving from his position as consul, made it possible for the revolt to be thwarted while still at an early stage and prevented episodes of violence from breaking out in Rome.

By September, the consul seems to have warned the senate that Catiline was preparing a plot in several regions of Italy, but the senators did not lend credence to his words, which they thought were too alarmist. However, on 21 October, Cicero could finally produce more tangible evidence in the Curia, where he read out some anonymous letters warning of the danger of a revolt in Etruria and about the preparations for the murder of prominent members of the Roman elite.[27] At the consul's insistence, the senate decreed the *senatus consultum ultimum*.[28] On the 27th of that month, the rebellion did break out in Etruria, but there were no openly suspicious moves in the *Urbs*, so Catiline remained free. The situation took a new turn on 7 November. The previous night the core conspirators had gathered to plan their next actions: Catiline was to leave Rome to meet the men who had taken up arms in Etruria, while the rest were to lead the insurrection in Rome, and Cicero was to be murdered. But the consul gained immediate knowledge of their plans. His reaction was to protect his own life and summon the senate to a meeting in the temple of Jupiter Stator. In this senate session, held on 8 November, Cicero delivered the first of his *Catilinarians*, which was followed the next day by a second speech against Catiline given before the people at a *contio* convened by the consul himself.

Catiline's departure for Etruria to command the men who had taken up arms finally made it clear that the conspiracy was real. The senate gave the consul Antonius command over the troops which were to put an end to the insurrection in Etruria. Antonius, who had seemingly not had any political significance during the year, left Rome at once leading his army while Cicero remained in the *Urbs* keeping watch over the security of the city.[29]

---

[26] See for example Nippel 1988: 94–104, as well as the aforementioned bibliography regarding Cicero's consulship.

[27] Cic. *Cat.* 1.4–7; Cass. Dio 37.31.1; Plut. *Cic.* 15.5.

[28] The approval of the *senatus consultum ultimum* could have taken place either in the session of the senate on 21 October or in the session held the following day. Cf. Crawford 1984: 89 n. 5.

[29] Sal. *Cat.* 36.3.

Antonius did not return to Rome again during his consulship. Near Pistoria, at the beginning of 62, he defeated and killed Catiline, and the insurrection thus came to an end. Afterwards, Antonius went to Macedonia, his consular province, as proconsul.

In the second half of November, the trial of Murena, consul-elect for 62, took place. Murena was accused of corruption during the electoral campaign, following the recently passed *lex Tullia de ambitu*. Cicero did not hesitate to defend Murena, and he was not the only one who realized the political importance of the trial, in which other heavyweights of the public scene, Hortensius and Crassus, also took part as defenders.[30] In his speech *Pro Murena*, Cicero explained his decision to be involved on account of his old friendship with the defendant but, once again, mainly because he thought it was a moral obligation of his position as consul.[31] He did not even question whether the accusation was plausible, because what was in danger in the trial was not the status of the defendant, but the Roman state itself. Cicero's thesis was that, while Catiline and his supporters were plotting, the community could not afford to convict one of the consuls-elect. This would have weakened the state and would have spurred Catiline on, who could then try to justify his insurrection by appealing to the presumed corruption which had deprived him of the consulship. Cicero convinced the jurors, and Murena was acquitted.

In the meantime, the plotters had not given up their plans in Rome. Thanks to the collaboration of some envoys from the Allobroges who had arrived in the city, Cicero was finally able to obtain conclusive evidence of the involvement of several Roman politicians in the conspiracy. The consul convened the senate on 3 December in the temple of Concord. The Catilinarian plotters were forced to confess and were arrested.[32] After leaving the senate meeting, Cicero delivered the third of his *Catilinarians* before the people. A final question to be resolved was the fate of the conspirators who were under arrest, some of whom were persons of social and political importance. To this end, Cicero again convened a session of the senate on 5 December. Under the consul's presidency several senators spoke, some of them in favour of the death penalty and others against it. Cicero then gave the fourth of his *Catilinarians*. In his speech he said he was prepared to accept the decision of the senate, whatever it was, and to execute it, although he seemed to lean towards the capital penalty. When the majority of the senators finally voted in favour of the death penalty, the

---

[30] Cic. *Flac.* 98; Quint. *Inst.* 6.1.35; Plut. *Cic.* 35.4.   [31] Cic. *Mur.* 5.
[32] Cic. *Cat.* 3.5; *Pis.* 5; *Dom.* 134; Sal. *Cat.* 46.2–6; Cass. Dio 37.34; Plut. *Cic.* 19.1.

consul did not object at all. On the contrary, he hurried to carry out the senatorial decree immediately. As consul, he was personally in charge of directing the execution of the plotters in the Tullianum on the same day, 5 December.[33]

The year 63 was about to end. From the perspective of Cicero, he had begun his consular year by saving Rome from the ruin that Rullus' agrarian reform would have meant, had continued by supplying political arguments in favour of the *senatus consultum ultimum* as a necessary senatorial tool for the maintenance of the established order, and had ended it by successfully suppressing the Catilinarian conspiracy. In all fairness, he should be proclaimed saviour of Rome, a title with which he obsessively referred to himself in the ensuing years.[34]

However, in the last few weeks of his consulship Cicero was already suffering the pursuit of those who did not consider the execution without a trial of the Catilinarian plotters to have been legal. The tribunes of 62, L. Calpurnius Bestia and, above all, Q. Metellus Nepos, publicly attacked Cicero from the time they took office on 10 December 63, accusing him of having acted illegally. On the last day of the year, 29 December, it was customary for the outgoing consuls, if they were present in Rome, to deliver a speech before the people which was a farewell and a recapitulation of their actions. The tribune Metellus Nepos vetoed Cicero's speech, arguing that one who had ordered the death of fellow-citizens without having heard them in a trial did not deserve to be heard by the citizens. The tribune only allowed him to speak to take the customary oath of an outgoing magistrate, declaring that he had complied with the laws of the Roman state. Nevertheless, when he spoke, Cicero did not use the usual formula for his oath, but he said that he had saved his nation, which was received by the people with enthusiasm.[35] That was Cicero's last action as consul.

In conclusion, the year 63 provides a good example of the consular year in the post-Sullan period. Each consul was given a consular province, but while one of them renounced it, his colleague was forced by circumstances to unexpectedly turn the fight against Catiline into his *provincia*. In this manner, Cicero decided to remain in Rome during the entire year, whereas Antonius was in the city until November, when he set off for Etruria. Since he was totally eclipsed by Cicero, little else is known about the consular performance of Antonius, who at the beginning of the year must have fulfilled the religious and diplomatic duties of the consuls along with his

---

[33] Plut. *Cic.* 22.1–5; Sal. *Cat.* 55. [34] Cic. *Cat.* 4.2.
[35] Cic. *Fam.* 5.2.7; *Pis.* 6–7; Plut. *Cic.* 23.2–3; Cass. Dio 37.38.2.

colleague. In contrast, Cicero's intense activity caused him to become involved in all matters which occupied Rome's political scene throughout the year: he sponsored some laws, opposed others, spoke often before the people, intervened in trials, promoted senatorial decrees, and presided over the elections. As consul, Cicero tried to be the centre of Roman politics during the year 63, and, to a great extent, he succeeded.

CHAPTER 15

Conclusion

Acting in close collaboration with the senate, the consuls were the chief magistrates of the Roman state throughout the Republican period. The distinctive feature of the magistracy was the *imperium* with which consuls were invested. It was a unique *imperium* which granted them supreme command, in both the civil and the military sphere. This supreme command involved specific functions and tasks performed by consuls.

– On the one hand, the consuls were always the supreme commanders of the Roman army, in both the middle Republic and the late Republic, since the consuls did not lose their military *imperium* after Sulla's dictatorship, although from that moment onwards they attained prominence in the military field much less frequently.

– As the right hand of the senate, the consuls were the magistrates the senators relied upon most, those whom they called upon in cases of serious crisis. Thus it is reasonable that the consuls were those referred to initially in most instances in which the so-called 'ultimate decree of the senate' or *senatus consultum ultimum* was proclaimed. This put them in charge of the defence of the state, according to the formula *videant consules ne quid res publica detrimenti capiat* ('let the consuls see to it that the Republic suffer no harm'). By doing this, their prominent position in the *cursus honorum* and their ultimate accountability for the restoration of the internal order of the community were underlined.

– On the other hand, the consuls undertook wide-ranging civil functions in many different fields. The consuls were at all times the guardians of the peace of the gods (*pax deorum*), acting as the supreme representatives of the community in its relations with the gods of Roman civic religion. As such, they presided over sacrifices of expiation, games – if they were present in Rome – and community ceremonies, in particular the *feriae Latinae*.

– They were also always the heads of Roman diplomacy, some of their duties being to deal with all the foreign embassies arriving in Rome on political missions, to introduce the legations to the senate, and to preside over the sessions that discussed the matters that had brought the envoys from other states to the *Urbs*. Likewise, the consuls were in charge of reporting to the ambassadors the decisions taken by the senate and implementing those decisions.

– The consuls used two forms of communication with Roman citizens: edicts, issued on very varied matters, and speeches pronounced before the people in *contiones*, which became more frequent in the first century as a result of the consuls' longer presence in Rome.

– The consuls always had legislative capacity, and they used it in both the middle and late Republic, although the number of consular laws increased considerably during the first century. In the legislative sphere, the consuls always acted in agreement with the decisions previously taken by the senate. In this sense, Caesar is an exception, as he sponsored laws against the will of the majority of the senate.

– The senate, on extraordinary occasions, entrusted the consuls with the investigation of certain matters of particular importance, both within the *Urbs* and outside it.

– The consuls promoted and were in charge of large-scale public works, either on their own initiative or by order of the senate. For instance, they were the main promoters of the temples that were gradually erected in Rome between the fourth and second centuries, as well as many of the roads built in Italy, in particular during the second century and, probably, some of the fora set up along those roads.

– Depending on the circumstances, the consuls variously participated in the process of colonization in Italy between the fourth and second centuries, promoting at times the foundation of colonies or their repopulation or possibly directing the process of recruitment of colonists or the appointment of a commission in charge of the colonization.

– The consuls were in charge of appointing a dictator in cases when the creation of this extraordinary magistracy had been previously decided by the senate. This prerogative was always in force, but in the case of the two dictators of the first century, Sulla and Caesar, political circumstances made it impossible for them to be appointed by a consul.

– Finally, save in exceptional cases, the consuls presided over the elections each year.

All these consular functions, both military and civil, remained essentially the same for centuries. What changed was the larger or smaller share they had in the consuls' activities during their consular year, due partly to changing historic circumstances in Rome (for example, from the

Hannibalic War onwards no dictators were appointed until Sulla) and partly to the fact that certain activities in which the consuls had usually taken a more or less important role disappeared or slowed down (the pace of construction of temples in Rome and roads in Italy was not the same in the mid-Republic as in the first century, and the dynamic process of colonization in Italy in the second century was an impossibility in the first century).

The main transformation in the work of the consuls throughout the Republican period, however, was the difference in the amount of time devoted to military and civil functions in the consular year. Between the fourth and second centuries, the consuls spent most of the consular year leading the legions, first in Italy and later on in different regions of the Mediterranean, as Rome expanded her dominion. The consuls only devoted a small part of the year, of varying duration depending on political circumstances, to civil functions. Most of these civil functions were usually performed in the *Urbs*, where the consuls remained for just a few weeks, or two or three months at the most, before setting off for their provinces. In contrast, in the post-Sullan period only a small proportion of the consuls took command over their legions during their consular year. Those who did usually left Rome well towards the end of the year; therefore they stayed in the city on average for ten or eleven months. The rest of the consuls remained in Rome for their entire term of office.

The consuls' longer stay in Rome in the last century of the Republic significantly modified the nature of the magistracy. Now the consuls were not only able to, but had to become much more actively involved in day-to-day political questions. They continued to carry out the same religious, diplomatic, or electoral functions as had traditionally belonged to consuls, but their intervention in the senate was now constant, and their public appearance in *contiones* was much more frequent than before; likewise, consular legislation in the first century was much more abundant than in previous centuries, although always notably smaller in amount than tribunician legislation. During most of the Republic, Rome's highest magistrates were, therefore, mainly *imperatores*, their main function being to act as commanders-in-chief of the Roman army wherever its presence was needed. In the post-Sullan period, on the other hand, we can speak mainly of consuls as politicians and, although they never ceased to have military command, many did not exert it in practice during their consulship.

Since Mommsen, it had been thought that the stay of the consuls in Rome in the first century was the result of a law passed by the dictator Sulla, whereby the consuls had been deprived of their military command and were forced to remain in the *Urbs* during the entire consular year. First Balsdon, then Valgiglio, and finally above all Giovannini demonstrated that Mommsen's thesis was incorrect: there was never a Sullan law banning consuls from taking over command of their troops in the provinces that had been allotted to them and forcing them to stay in Rome. However, it is an indisputable fact that in the post-Sullan period many consuls remained in the *Urbs* during their entire term of office. The presence of the consuls in Rome brought about a remarkable change in the weight given to their civil and military activities in the post-Sullan age. Throughout the first century there was fundamentally a process of 'politicization' of the consulship, while military responsibility in the provinces of the empire fell mainly to proma-gistrates and occasionally to private citizens (*privati*). Fergus Millar put it perfectly: '. . . the annually elected magistrates, above all the two consuls, who for centuries had been mainly *imperatores* and were now for a few decades primarily "politicians" in Rome . . .'[1]

Until the first century, consuls were expected to be, above all, good commanders-in-chief of the army and, as such, to protect Rome militarily and even to expand her dominion to regions which had not been conquered or were beyond her control. In the first century, however, it was unusual for the consuls to fight in armed conflicts during their year in office. Those who left Rome generally did so at the end of the year, with just enough time to reach their province and make preparations for war, should they be neces-sary, but with no time to tackle sizeable military operations while still consuls. In the first century, the consuls were expected, above all, to be political leaders rather than military chiefs. This does not mean that a consul could not have military ambitions as part of his political career and that his potential successes in the battlefield were not appropriately valued by his fellow citizens. But seeking military glory was, much more so than before, dependent on the will of the politicians themselves. Let us look, for example, at Cicero and Caesar. Both of them remained in Rome during their respective consulships. Both of them strove to show during their year in office their capacity as leaders in the political scene of the *Urbs*, albeit along very different lines. But while Cicero renounced his province and did everything within his power to be excused from taking part in the military world that was alien to him – until he had no alternative but to go to Cilicia twelve years after his consulship – Caesar sought military glory in Gaul immediately after his consulship, just as in the year 61 he had been involved in notable armed conflicts in Hispania Ulterior. The military element played a small part in the consulship during the first century, although

---

[1] Millar 1998: 197.

war continued to be important in Roman society and therefore in the process of gaining renown for many public men.

The change experienced by the consulship in the first century is, without a doubt, a reflection of the changes that were taking place in Roman society and politics in the late Republican period, which was different in so many ways from the Middle Republic. After Rome's great expansion in the Mediterranean in the third and second centuries, there was still room for great military deeds, as attested by the successes achieved by Pompey in the East and Caesar in Gaul. In a competitive society like Rome, it is clear that military glory never ceased to be a source of prestige and popularity for the winners. In this sense, the late Republican period was unquestionably an era of great *imperatores*. Yet the consulship in the first century was no longer a magistracy from which military glory could be attained. The consulship then took on a primarily civil nature; the consul in the first century was, above all, a politician, a manager of the *res publica*. The glory of a consul did not derive from his victories in the battlefield but from the laws he sponsored for the benefit of the community or from his initiatives before the senate: in short, from his leadership skills in Rome.

Despite being the supreme magistrates of the Roman state, for centuries the consuls had been noticed very little by their fellow citizens. After a few weeks in the city they would leave to fight far away from Rome, and only a few of them returned as victors to lead a triumphal parade amongst the crowds of their fellow-citizens. Only occasionally did news from them reach the city, or were their victories or defeats reported to the people in *contiones*. In contrast, in the first century consuls were permanently conspicuous in Rome, and constantly played their part before the people. The consuls attended the sessions of the senate, frequented the forum and other public places in the city, went to popular assemblies, met other politicians on a daily basis, issued edicts, pleaded cases before the courts, and engaged in ceaseless political activity.

Whereas between the fourth and second centuries the consuls were absent magistrates who performed their functions mostly outside Rome, in the first century the key to the consulship was largely the fact that the consuls were ubiquitous in the *Urbs*. This was crucial in the transformation of the magistracy. The consuls progressively became the centre of the political scene in Rome while their prominence as military commanders simultaneously decreased. This new mainly civil role of the magistracy was readily adopted by the consuls of the post-Sullan period. It is particularly noteworthy that, at least in some specific cases, we know that the decision to remain in Rome during the entire year and not to go to a province was taken voluntarily by the consuls themselves, as was the case of Pompey in the year 70 and of Cicero in 63. Caesar himself spent his entire consular year in Rome sponsoring an ambitious legislative programme against the senate and gaining popularity as a politician before seeking military glory in Gaul. While up to the beginning of the first century the consuls' main task was to win wars, from Sulla onwards the function of the consuls was to govern the *res publica* in Rome. What society demanded from the consuls of the first century was, above all, the leadership skill to manage and guide the politics of the community. The presence of the consul-politicians in the city led them to perfect and put into practice skills which had not in previous centuries had the same significance for the consul-generals: their visibility, their powers of persuasion, their eloquence, their determination; in short, the decisive significance of the human factor on the political scene.

Bibliography

JOURNAL ABBREVIATIONS FOLLOW *L'ANNEE
PHILOLOGIQUE.*

Aberson, M. (1994) *Temples votives et butin de guerre dans la Rome républicaine,* Rome

Adam, A.-M. (1994) *Tite-Live, Histoire Romaine, vol. 29, Book 39,* Paris

Agache, S. (1987) 'L'actualité de la Villa Publica en 55–54 av. J.-C.', in *L'Urbs: espace urbain et histoire (Ier siècle av. J.-C. – IIIe siècle ap. J.-C.): Actes du Colloque International organisé par le Centre National de la Recherche Scientifique et l'Ecole Française de Rome (Rome, 8–12 mai 1985),* 211–34. Rome

(2000) s.v. villa publica, *LTUR* v: 202–5

Aigner Foresti, L. (1979) 'Zur Zeremonie der Nagelschlagung in Rom und in Etrurien', *AJAH* 4: 144–9

(1995) 'La tradizione antica sul "ver sacrum"', in *Coercizione e mobilità umana nel mondo antico,* ed. M. Sordi, 141–7 Milan

Alexander, M. C. (1990) *Trials in the late Roman republic: 149 BC to 50 BC,* Toronto

(2006) 'Law in the Roman Republic'. In *A companion to the Roman Republic,* ed. N. Rosenstein and R. Morstein-Marx, 236–55. Oxford

Alfayé, S. (2009) 'Nails for the dead: a polysemic account of an ancient funerary practice'. In *Magical practice in the Latin West: Papers from the international conference held at the University of Zaragoza, 30th Sept. – 1st Oct. 2005,* ed. R. Gordon and F. Marco, 427–56. Leiden

Alföldi, A. (1965) *Early Rome and the Latins,* Ann Arbor, MI

Allély, A. (2000) 'Les Aemilii Lepidi et l'approvisionnement en blé de Rome (IIe-Ie siècles av. J.-C.)', *REA* 102: 27–52

(2004) *Lépide le triumvir,* Bordeaux

Allen Jr, W. (1952) 'Cicero's governorship in 63 BC', *TAPhA* 83: 233–41

Amela Valverde, L. (2001) 'Inscripciones honoríficas dedicadas a Pompeyo Magno', *Faventia* 23: 87–102

Andreussi, M. (1993) s.v. Consus, aedes, *LTUR* I: 321–2

Arce, J. (2000) *Memoria de los antepasados. Puesta en escena y desarrollo del elogio fúnebre romano,* Madrid

Arena, V. (forthcoming) 'The consulship of 78 BC. Catulus versus Lepidus: an *optimates* versus *populares* affair'. In *Consuls and res publica. High office holding in the Roman Republic*, ed. H. Beck, A. Duplá, M. Jehne, and F. Pina Polo. Cambridge

Aronen, J. (1996) s.v. Ops Opifera, aedes, *LTUR* III: 362–4

Astin, A. E. (1962) '"Professio" in the abortive election of 184 BC', *Historia* 11: 252–5

(1964) 'Leges Aelia et Fufia', *Latomus* 23: 421–45

Auliard, C. (2006) *La diplomatie romaine. L'autre instrument de la conquête. De la fondation à la fin des guerres samnites (753–290 av. J.-C.)*, Rennes

Badian, E. (1956) 'Q. Mucius Scaevola and the provinces of Asia', *Athenaeum* 34: 104–23

(1990) 'The consuls, 179–49 BC', *Chiron* 20: 371–413

Balsdon, J. P. V. D. (1958) Review of E. Valgiglio, *Silla e la crisi repubblicana*, Florence 1956, in *Gnomon* 30: 69–70

(1937) 'Q. Mucius Scaevola and *ornatio provinciae*', *CR* 51: 8–10

(1939) 'Consular provinces under the late Republic', *JRS* 29: 57–73

(1967) *Julius Caesar: a political biography*, New York

Bandel, F. (1910) *Die Dictaturen der römischen Republik*, Diss., Breslau

Bandelli, G. (1988) *Ricerche sulla colonizzazione romana della Gallia Cisalpina. Le fasi iniziali e il caso aquileiese*, Rome

Bardon, H. (1955) 'La naissance d'un temple', *REL* 33: 166–82

Barigazzi, A. (1991) 'Liguri Friniati e Apuani in Livio', *Prometheus* 17: 55–74

Baudy, D. (1998) s.v. Feriae Latinae, in *Der Neue Pauly*, 477. Stuttgart

Bauman, R. A. (1973) 'The *lex Valeria de provocatione* of 300 BC', *Historia* 22: 34–47

(1974) 'Criminal prosecutions by the aediles', *Latomus* 33: 245–64

(1978) 'Il "sovversivismo" di Emilio Lepido', *Labeo* 24: 60–74

(1990) 'The suppression of the Bacchanals: five questions', *Historia* 39: 334–48

Beard, M. (1990) 'Priesthood in the Roman Republic'. In *Pagan priests: religion and power in the Ancient World*, ed. M. Beard and J. North, 19–48. London

(2007) *The Roman triumph*, Cambridge, MA

Beard, M., North, J., and Price, S. (1998) *Religions of Rome*, 2 vols., Cambridge

Beck, H. (2000) 'Quintus Fabius Maximus – Musterkarriere ohne Zögern'. In *Von Romulus zu Augustus. Große Gestalten der römischen Republik*, ed. K.-J. Hölkeskamp and E. Stein-Hölkeskamp, 79–91. Munich

(2005) *Karriere und Hierarchie. Die römische Aristokratie und die Anfänge des cursus honorum in der mittleren Republik*, Berlin

(2006) 'Züge in die Ewigkeit. Prozessionen durch das republikanische Rom'. In *Repúblicas y ciudadanos: modelos de participación cívica en el mundo antiguo*, ed. F. Marco Simón, F. Pina Polo and J. Remesal Rodríguez, 131–51. Barcelona

(forthcoming) 'Consular power and the Roman constitution. The case of *imperium* revisited'. In *Consuls and res publica: high office holding in the Roman Republic*, ed. H. Beck, A. Duplá, M. Jehne, and F. Pina Polo. Cambridge

Beck, H. and Walter, U. (2001) *Die frühen römischen Historiker*, Darmstadt

Benner, H. (1987) *Die Politik des P. Clodius Pulcher*, Stuttgart

Berchem, D. van (1939) *Les distributions de blé et d'argent à la plèbe romaine sous l'Empire*, Geneva

Berger, A. (1925) s.v. *lex Cornelia Baebia de ambitu*, *RE* XII.2: 2344

(1940) s.v. *leges de bello indicendo, RE Suppl.* VII: 383

Bergk, A. (forthcoming) 'The development of the praetorship in the third century BC'. In *Consuls and* res publica: *high office holding in the Roman Republic,* ed. H. Beck, A. Duplá, M. Jehne, and F. Pina Polo. Cambridge

Bernstein, F. (1998) *Ludi publici. Untersuchungen zur Entstehung und Entwicklung der öffentlichen Spiele im republikanischen Rom,* Stuttgart

Bispham, E. (2007) *From Asculum to Actium: the municipalization of Italy from the Social War to Augustus,* Oxford

Bleicken, J. (1955) *Das Volkstribunat der klassischen Republik. Studien zu seiner Entwicklung zwischen 287 und 133 v.Chr.,* Munich

(1975) *Lex publica. Gesetz und Recht in der römischen Republik,* Berlin and New York

(1995) *Die Verfassung der Römischen Republik,* 7th edn. Paderborn

Bloch, R. (1963) *Les prodiges dans l'antiquité classique,* Paris

Bodei Giglioni, G. (1974) *Lavori pubblici e occupazione nell'antichità classica,* Bologna

Bonnefond, M. (1984) 'La lex Gabinia sur les ambassades'. In *Des ordres à Rome,* ed. C. Nicolet, 61–99. Paris

Bonnefond-Coudry, M. (1989) *Le sénat de la République romaine de la guerre d'Hannibal à Auguste: pratiques délibératives et prise de décision,* Rome

Bouché-Leclercq, A. (1931) *Manuel des institutions romaines,* Paris

Boyd, M. J. (1953) 'The Porticoes of Metellus and Octavia and their two temples', *PBSR* 21: 152–9

Brélaz, C. (2003) 'Publicité, archives et séquence documentaire du contrat public à Rome'. In *Tâches publiques et entreprise privée dans le monde romain,* ed. J. J. Aubet, 27–56. Geneva

Brennan, T. C. (2000) *The praetorship in the Roman Republic,* Oxford

Brind'Amour, P. (1983) *Le calendrier romain. Recherches chronologiques,* Ottawa

Briscoe, J. (1981) *A commentary on Livy, Books XXXIV–XXXVII,* Oxford

(1989) *A commentary on Livy Books XXXI–XXXIII,* Oxford

(2008) *A commentary on Livy, Books 38–40,* Oxford

Broughton, T. R. S. (1948) 'More notes on Roman magistrates', *TAPhA* 79: 63–78

(1951–86) *The magistrates of the Roman Republic,* 3 vols. Atlanta, GA

Brunt, P. A. (1969) 'The enfranchisement of the Sabines'. In *Hommages à Marcel Renard,* ed. J. Bibauw, II: 121–9. Brussels

(1971) *Italian manpower 225 BC–AD 14,* Oxford

Bücher, F. (2006) *Verargumentierte Geschichte. Exempla Romana im politischen Diskurs der späten römischen Republik,* Stuttgart

Burckhardt, L. A. (1989) 'Gab es in der Gracchenzeit ein optimatisches Siedlungsprogramm? Bemerkungen zum Elogium von Polla und den viasiei vicani aus dem Ackergesetz von 111 v.Chr'. In *Labor omnibus unus. Gerold Walser zum 70. Geburtstag dargebracht von Freunden, Kollegen und Schülern,* ed. H. E. Herzog and R. Frei-Stolba, 3–20. Stuttgart

Canali de Rossi, F. (1997) *Le ambascerie dal mondo greco a Roma in età repubblicana,* Rome

(2005) *Le relazioni diplomatiche di Roma. Vol. I: Dall'età regia alla conquista del primato in Italia (753–265 a.C.) con una apéndice sulla più antica inscrizione greca del Lazio*, Rome

(2007) *Le relazioni diplomatiche di Roma. Vol. II: Dall'intervento in Sicilia fino alla invasione annibalica (264–216 a.C.)*, Rome

Cancelli, F. (1957) *Studi sui censores e sull'arbitratus della lex contractus*, Milan

Canfora, L. (2007) *Julius Caesar, the people's dictator*, Edinburgh (1st edn, Rome and Bari 1999)

Capozza, M. (1966) *Movimenti servili nel mondo romano in età repubblicana*, Rome

Carcopino, J. (1919) *La loi de Hiéron et les Romains*, Paris

Carney, T. F. (1959) 'Once again Marius' speech after election in 108 BC', *SO* 35: 63–70

Càssola, F. (1962) *I gruppi politici romani nel III secolo a.C.*, Trieste

Catalano, P. (1960) *Contributi allo studio del diritto augurale*, Turin

Cerutti, S. M (1997) 'The location of the houses of Cicero and Clodius and the Porticus Catuli on the Palatine Hill in Rome', *AJPh* 118: 417–26

Chioffi, L. (1993) s.v. Columna Rostrata C. Duilii, *LTUR* I: 309

(1995) s.v. Fornix Fabianus, *LTUR* II: 264–6

Churchill, J. B. (1999) 'Ex qua quod vellent facerent: Roman magistrates' authority over *praeda* and *manubiae*', *TAPhA* 129: 85–116

Ciancio Rossetto, P. (1999) s.v. Pietas, aedes in Foro Holitorio / in Circo Flaminio, *LTUR* IV: 86

Clark, A. J. (2007) *Divine qualities: cult and community in Republican Rome*, Oxford

Clinton, K. (1986) 'The Eleusinian mysteries: Roman initiates and benefactors, second century BC to AD 267', *ANRW* II 18.1: 1499–539

Cloud, D. (1994) 'The constitution and public criminal law', in *The last age of the Roman republic, 146–43 BC*, eds. J. A. Crook, A. Lintott, and E. Rawson, *Cambridge Ancient History*, 2nd edn. IX: 491–530. Cambridge

Coarelli, F. (1969) 'Le *tyrannoctone* du Capitole et la mort de Tiberius Gracchus', *MEFRA* 81: 137–60

(1977) 'Public building in Rome between the second Punic war and Sulla', *PBSR* 45: 1–23

(1981) *Roma*, Rome and Bari

(1984) 'Iside Capitolina, Clodio e i mercanti di schiavi', in *Alessandria e il mondo ellenistico-romano. Studi in onore di Achille Adriani*, III: 461–75. Rome

(1989) *Il Foro Boario. Dalle origini alla fine della Repubblica*, Rome

(1995a) s.v. Fortunae tres, aedes, *LTUR* II: 285–7

(1995b) s.v. Graecostasis, *LTUR* II: 373

(1996a) s.v. Iuno Sospita (in Foro Holitorio), aedes, *LTUR* III: 128–9

(1996b) s.v. Iuppiter Stator, aedes, fanum, templum, *LTUR* III: 155–7

(1996c) s.v. Iuppiter Victor, templum, *LTUR* III: 161

(1996d) s.v. Iuventas, aedes, *LTUR* III: 163

(1999a) s.v. Porticus Minucia Vetus, *LTUR* IV: 137–8

(1999b) s.v. Quirinus, aedes, *LTUR* IV: 185–7

(1999c) s.v. Salus, aedes, *LTUR* IV: 229–30

(2000a) s.v. Tellus, aedes, *LTUR* v: 24–5

(2000b) s.v. Venus Erucina, aedes (ad Portam Collinam), *LTUR* v: 114–16

Cobban, J. M. (1935) *Senate and provinces 78–49 BC*, Cambridge

Connor, J. O. (1904) *The Graecostasis of the Roman forum and its vicinity*, Madison, WI

Cornell, T. J. (1995) *The beginnings of Rome: Italy and Rome from the Bronze Age to the Punic Wars (c. 1000–264 BC)*, London

Coudry, M. (2004) 'Contrôle et traitement des ambassadeurs étrangers sous la République romaine', in *La mobilité des personnes en Méditerranée de l'Antiquité à l'époque moderne. Procédures de contrôle et documents d'identification*, ed. C. Moatti, 529–65. Rome

Cousin, J. (1943) 'Lex Lutatia de vi', *RHD* 22: 88–94

Crawford, J. W. (1984) *M. Tullius Cicero: the lost and unpublished orations*, Göttingen

(1994) *M. Tullius Cicero: the fragmentary speeches*, 2nd edn. Atlanta, GA

Crawford, M. H. (1974) *Roman Republican coinage*, 2 vols., Cambridge

(1989) 'The lex Iulia agraria', *Athenaeum* 67: 179–89

(1996) ed. *Roman statutes*, 2 vols., London

(2004) review of K. Sandberg, *Magistrates and assemblies. A study of legislative practice in Republican Rome*, Rome 2001, in *CR* 54: 171–2

Cressedi, G. (1954) 'Le fasi costruttive del Portico di Ottavia', *Palladio* 4: 143–4

Criniti, N. (1969) *M. Aimilius Q.f. M.n. Lepidus 'ut ignis in stipula'*, Milan

Crook, J. (1955) *Consilium principis. Imperial councils and counsellors from Augustus to Diocletian*, Cambridge

De Cazanove, O. (2000) 'Sacrifier les bêtes, consacrer les hommes. Le printemps sacré italique', in *Rites et espaces en pays celte et méditerranéen. Etude comparée à partir du sanctuaire d'Acy-Romance (Ardennes, France)*, ed. S. Verger, 253–77. Rome

Degrassi, A. (1962) 'Nuovi miliari arcaici', in *Hommages à Albert Grenier*, ed. M. Renard, 499–513. Brussels

De Ligt, L. (2007) 'Roman manpower and recruitment during the Middle Republic', in *A companion to the Roman army*, ed. P. Erdkamp, 114–31. Oxford

De Martino, F. (1990) *Storia della costituzione romana*, 2nd edn., 2 vols., Naples

De Rossi, G. M. (ed.) (1968) *La Via Aurelia da Roma a Forum Aureli*, Rome

De Ruggiero, E. (1892) s.v. Consul, in *Dizionario epigrafico di antichità romane*, II: 679–862. Rome

(1925) *Lo stato e le opere pubbliche in Roma antica*, Turin

De Saint-Denis, E. (1942) 'Les énumerations de prodiges dans l'oeuvre de Tite-Live', *R.Phil.* 16: 126–42

Derow, P. S. (1973) 'The Roman calendar, 190–168 BC', *Phoenix* 27: 345–56

(1976) 'The Roman calendar, 218–191 BC', *Phoenix* 30: 265–81

Develin, R. (1975) 'Comitia tributa plebis', *Athenaeum* 53: 302–37

(1977) '*Comitia tributa* again', *Athenaeum* 55: 425–6

(1978) '*Provocatio* and plebiscites: early Roman legislation and the historical tradition', *Mnemosyne* 31: 45–60

Di Porto, A. (1981) 'Il colpo de mano di Sutri e il "plebiscitum de populo non sevocando". A proposito della "lex Manlia de vicensima manumissionum"'. In *Legge e società nella Repubblica romana*, ed. F. Serrao, 1: 307–84. Naples

Di Vita, A. (1955) 'Un milliarium del 252 a.c. e l'antica via Agrigento – Palermo', *Kokalos* 1: 10–21

(1963) 'Una recente nota e la datazione del miliario siciliano del console C. Aurelius Cotta', *Latomus* 22: 478–88

Diehl, H. (1988) *Sulla und seine Zeit im Urteil Ciceros*, Hildesheim

Drogula, F. K. (2007) '*Imperium, potestas*, and the *pomerium* in the Roman Republic', *Historia* 56: 419–52

Drummond, A. (1974) *The history and reliability of the early* fasti consulares: *with special reference to the so-called plebeian consuls*, unpublished D.Phil. thesis, Oxford

(1978) 'Some observations on the order of consuls' names', *Athenaeum* 56: 80–108

Dubourdieu, A. (1989) *Les origines et le développement du culte des Pénates à Rome*, Rome

Dungworth, D. (1998) 'Mystifying Roman nails: *clavus annalis, defixiones* and *minkisi*', in *TRAC 97*, ed. P. Barker, 148–59. Oxford

Duplá, A. (1990) *Videant consules. Las medidas de excepción en la crisis de la República romana*, Saragossa

Durry, M. (1950) *Eloge funèbre d'une matrone romaine (éloge dit de Turia)*, Paris

Duval, P.-M. (1949) 'A propos du milliaire de Cneus Domitius Ahenobarbus trouvé dans l'Aude en 1949', *Gallia* 7: 207–31

Dyck, A. R. (2004) *A commentary on Cicero* De Legibus, Ann Arbor, MI

Earl, D. C. (1965) 'Appian BC 1,14 and "professio"', *Historia* 14: 325–32

Eckstein, A. M. (1987) *Senate and general: individual decision-making and Roman foreign relations, 264–194 BC*, Berkeley, Los Angeles, and London

Eder, W. (1969) *Das vorsullanische Repetundenverfahren*, Munich

Eisenhut, W. (1955) s.v. Ver sacrum, *RE* 1.15: 911–23

(1974) s.v. votum, *RE* Suppl. XIV: 965

(1975a) s.v. Consus, *Der Kleine Pauly*, I: 1295. Munich

(1975b) s.v. Hercules, *Der Kleine Pauly*, II: 1056. Munich

(1975c) s.v. Honos, *Der Kleine Pauly*, II: 1213–14. Munich

(1975d) s.v. Iuppiter, *Der Kleine Pauly*, III: 3–4. Munich

(1975e) s.v. Iuturna, *Der Kleine Pauly*, III: 25. Munich

(1975f) s.v. Ver sacrum, *Der Kleine Pauly*, V: 1181–3. Munich

Elster, M. (2003) *Die Gesetze der mittleren römischen Republik*, Darmstadt

Engels, D. (2005) 'Eo anno multa prodigia facta sunt. Das Jahr 218 als Wendepunkt des römischen Vorzeichenwesens', in *Mantik. Profile prognostischen Wissens in Wissenschaft und Kultur*, ed. W. Hogrebe, 151–66. Würzburg

(2007) *Das römische Vorzeichenwesen (753–27 v.Chr.). Quellen, Terminologie, Kommentar, historische Entwicklung*, Stuttgart

Evans, R. J. (1994) *Gaius Marius: a political biography*, Pretoria

Everitt, A. (2001) *Cicero: a turbulent life*, London

Ewins, U. (1952) 'The early colonisation of Cisalpine Gaul', *PBSR* 20 (n.s.7): 54–71
  (1955) 'The enfranchisement of Cisalpine Gaul', *PBSR* 23: 73–98
Farrell, J. (1986) 'The distinction between *comitia* and *concilium*', *Athenaeum* 74: 407–38
Favaro, G. (1929) 'Il *clavus annalis* e il *dictator clavi figendi causa*', in *Atti I Congresso Nazionale Studi Romani*, II: 223–9. Rome
Fears, J. R. (1975) 'The coinage of Q. Cornificius and augural symbolism on late Republican denarii', *Historia* 24: 595–6
Feeney, D. (2007) *Caesar's calendar: ancient time and the beginnings of history*, Berkeley, Los Angeles, and London
Feldherr, A. (1998) *Spectacle and society in Livy's history*, Berkeley, Los Angeles, and London
Ferrary, J.-L. (1977) 'Recherches sur la législation de Saturninus et de Glaucia', *MEFRA* 89: 619–60
  (1988) 'Rogatio Servilia agraria', *Athenaeum* 66: 141–64
  (2000) 'Les Gouverneurs des provinces romaines d'Asie Mineure (Asie et Cilicie), depuis l'organisation de la province d'Asie jusqu'à la première guerre de Mithridate (126–88 av. J.-C.)', *Chiron* 30: 161–93
  (2001) 'A propos des pouvoirs d'Auguste', *CCGG* 12: 101–54
  (2007) 'Les ambassadeurs grecs au Sénat romain'. In *L'audience. Rituel et cadres spatiaux dans l'Antiquité et le haut Moyen Age*, ed. J.-P. Caillet and M. Sot, 113–22. Paris
  (2009) 'After the embassy to Rome: publication and implementation'. In *Diplomats and Diplomacy in the Roman World*, ed. C. Eilers, 127–42. Leiden and Boston
Ferroni, A. M. (1993a) s.v. Basilica Opimia, *LTUR* I: 183
  (1993b) s.v. Concordia, aedes, *LTUR* I: 316–20
Flach, D. (1994) *Die Gesetze der frühen römischen Republik*, Darmstadt
Flaig, E. (1995) 'Die *Pompa Funebris*. Adlige Konkurrenz und annalistische Erinnerung in der Römischen Republik'. In *Memoria als Kultur*, ed. O. G. Oexle, 115–48. Göttingen
  (2003) *Ritualisierte Politik. Zeichen, Gesten und Herrschaft im Alten Rom*, Göttingen
Flower, H. I. (1996) *Ancestor masks and aristocratic power in Roman culture*, Oxford
  (2000) '*Fabula de Bacchanalibus*: the Bacchanalian cult of the second century BC and Roman drama'. In *Identität und Alterität in der frührömischen Tragödie*, ed. G. Manuwald, 23–35. Würzburg
  (2002) 'Rereading the *senatus consultum de Bacchanalibus* of 186 BC: gender roles in the Roman Middle Republic'. In *Oikistes. Studies in constitutions, colonies and military power in the Ancient World offered in honor of A. J. Graham*, ed. V. B. Gorman and E. W. Robinson, 79–98. Leiden
  (2008) 'Remembering and forgetting temple destruction. The destruction of the temple of Jupiter Optimus Maximus in 83 BC'. In *Antiquity in Antiquity. Jewish and Christian pasts in the Graeco-Roman world*, ed. G. Gardner and K. L. Osterloh, 74–92. Tübingen

Forni, G. (1953) 'Mario Curio Dentato uomo democratico', *Athenaeum* 31: 170–240

Frank, T. (1911) 'On Rome's conquest of Sabinum, Picenum and Etruria', *Klio* 11: 367–81

Fuchs, G. (1956) 'Zur Baugeschichte der Basilica Aemilia in republikanischer Zeit', *MDAI(R)* 63: 14–25

Fuhrmann, M. (1992) *Cicero and the Roman Republic*, Oxford and Cambridge, MA (1st edn, Munich and Zürich 1989)

Funari, R. (1996) *C. Sallusti Crispi Historiarum Fragmenta*, 2 vols., Amsterdam

García Morcillo, M. (2005) *Las ventas por subasta en el mundo romano: la esfera privada*, Barcelona

Gargola, D. J. (1995) *Lands, laws and gods. Magistrates and ceremony in the regulation of public lands in Republican Rome*, Chapel Hill, NC and London

Gasparri, C. (1979) *Aedes Concordiae Augustae*, Rome

Gast, K. (1965) *Die zensorischen Bauberichte bei Livius und die römischen Bauinschriften*, Diss. Göttingen

Gelzer, M. (1968) *Caesar, politician and statesman*, Oxford (1st edn, Munich 1940)

(1969) *Cicero, ein biographischer Versuch*, Wiesbaden

(2005) *Pompeius. Lebensbild eines Römers*, Stuttgart (1st edn, 1959)

Giovannini, A. (1983) *Consulare imperium*, Basle

(2008) 'Date et objectifs de la *lex de provinciis praetoriis* (*Roman Statutes*, n° 12)', *Historia* 57: 92–107

Giovannini, A. and Grzybek, E. (1978) 'La lex de piratis persequendis', *MH* 35: 33–47

Girardet, K. M. (1990) 'Die Entmachtung des Konsulates im Übergang von der Republik zur Monarchie und die Rechtsgrundlagen des augusteischen Prinzipats'. In *Pratum Saraviense. Festschrift für Peter Steinmetz*, ed. W. Görler and S. Koster, 89–126 Stuttgart = K. M. Girardet (2007) *Rom auf dem Weg von der Republik zum Prinzipat*, 385–423. Bonn

(1992) 'Zur Diskussion um das *imperium consulare militiae* im 1. Jh. v.Chr', *CCGG* 3: 213–20 = K. M. Girardet (2007) *Rom auf dem Weg von der Republik zum Prinzipat*, 425–33. Bonn

(2001) '*Imperia* und *provinciae* des Pompeius 82 bis 48 v.Chr.', *Chiron* 31: 153–209 = K. M. Girardet (2007) *Rom auf dem Weg von der Republik zum Prinzipat*, 1–67. Bonn

Göll, H. (1859) 'Über den *processus consularis* der Kaiserzeit', *Philologus* 14: 586–612

Gordon, A. E. (1983) *Illustrated introduction to Latin epigraphy*, Berkeley, Los Angeles, and London

Greenhalgh, P. (1980) *Pompey, the Roman Alexander*, London

(1981) *Pompey, the Republican prince*, London

Griffin, M. T. (1973a) 'The tribune C. Cornelius', *JRS* 63: 196–213

(1973b) 'The "leges iudiciariae" of the pre-Sullan age', *CQ* 23: 108–26

Grimal, P. (1967) *Etudes de chronologie cicéronienne (années 58 et 57 av. J.-C.)*, Paris

Gros, P. (2000a) s.v. Venus Victrix, aedes, *LTUR* v: 120–1

(2000b) s.v. Theatrum Pompei, *LTUR* v: 35–8

Gruen, E. S. (1968) *Roman politics and the criminal courts, 149–78 BC*, Cambridge, MA

(1969a) 'The consular elections for 53 BC'. In *Hommages à Marcel Renard*, ed. J. Bibauw, II: 311–21. Brussels

(1969b) 'Pompey, the Roman aristocracy, and the conference of Luca', *Historia* 18: 71–108

(1974) *The last generation of the Roman Republic*, Berkeley, Los Angeles, and London

(1984) *The Hellenistic world and the coming of Rome*, 2 vols., Berkeley, Los Angeles, and London

(1990) 'The Bacchanalian Affair'. In *Studies in Greek Culture and Roman Policy*, 34–78. Leiden

Habicht, Chr. (1990) *Cicero, the politician*, Baltimore and London

Hafner, G. (1984) 'Aedes Concordiae et Basilica Opimia', *AA*: 591–6

Halkin, L. (1953) *La supplication d'action de grâces chez les Romains*, Paris

Hall, U. (1972) 'Appian, Plutarch, and the tribunician elections of 123 BC', *Athenaeum* 50: 3–35

Hamilton, J. R. (1955) 'T. Didius and the Villa Publica', *NC* 15: 224–8

Händel, P. (1959) s.v. *prodigium*, *RE* XXIII: 2283–96

Hantos, Th. (1988) *Res publica constituta. Die Verfassung des Dictators Sulla*, Stuttgart

Harries, J. (2007) *Law and crime in the Roman world*, Cambridge

Harris, W. V. (1971) *Rome in Etruria and Umbria*, Oxford

(1979) *War and imperialism in Republican Rome, 327–27 BC*, Oxford

Hartfield, M. E. (1982) 'The Roman dictatorship: its character and its evolution', PhD diss., Berkeley, Ann Arbor, MI

Hassal, M., Crawford, M., and Reynolds, J. (1974) 'Rome and the Eastern provinces at the end of the second century BC', *JRS* 64: 195–220

Hayne, L. (1972) 'M. Lepidus (cos. 78): a re-appraisal', *Historia* 21: 661–8

Hermon, E. (1989 (1998)) 'Les *priscae latinae coloniae* et la politique colonisatrice à Rome', *AJAH* 14.2: 144–79

(1997) 'M'. Curius Dentatus et les ventes questoriennes au IIIᵉ siècle av. J.-C.', *Scripta Classica Israelica*, 16: 32–42

(1998) 'Conquête et aménagement du territoire dans la Sabine du IIᵉ siècle avant J.-C.', *Cahiers des études anciennes* 34: 55–64

(2001) *Habiter et partager les terres avant les Gracques*, Rome

Heurgon, J. (1957) *Trois études sur le 'ver sacrum'*, Brussels

(1964) 'L. Cincius et la loi du clavus annalis', *Athenaeum* 42: 432–7

Hickson, F. V. (1993) *Roman prayer language: Livy and the Aeneid of Vergil*, Stuttgart

Hickson Hahn, F. (2004) 'The politics of thanksgiving'. In *Augusto augurio: rerum humanarum et divinarum commentationes in honorem Jerzy Linderski*, ed. Chr. F. Konrad, 31–51. Stuttgart

(2007) 'Performing the sacred: prayers and hymns'. In *A companion to Roman religion*, ed. J. Rüpke, 235–48. Oxford

Hill, H. (1946) 'Roman revenues from Greece after 146 BC', *CPh* 41: 35–42

Hinard, F. (1988) 'De la dictature à la tyrannie. Réflexions sur la dictature de Sylla'. In *Dictatures. Actes de la table ronde réunie à Paris les 27 et 28 février 1984*, ed. F. Hinard, 87–96. Paris

(2008) *Sullana varia. Aux sources de la première guerre civile romaine*, Paris

Hinrichs, F. T. (1967) 'Der römische Strassenbau zur Zeit der Gracchen', *Historia* 16: 162–76

(1974) *Die Geschichte der gromatischen Institutionen. Untersuchungen zu Landverteilung, Landvermessung, Bodenverwaltung und Bodenrecht im römischen Reich*, Wiesbaden

Hölkeskamp, K-J. (1987) *Die Entstehung der Nobilität. Studien zur sozialen und politischen Geschichte der römischen Republik im 4. Jht. v.Chr.*, Stuttgart

(1995) '*Oratoris maxima scaena*. Reden vor dem Volk in der politischen Kultur der Republik'. In *Demokratie in Rom? Die Rolle des Volkes in der Politik der römischen Republik*, ed. M. Jehne, 11–49. Stuttgart

(2006a) 'Pomp und Prozessionen. Rituale und Zeremonien in der politischen Kultur der römischen Republik', *Jahrbuch des Historischen Kollegs*: 35–72

(2006b) 'History and collective memory in the Middle Republic'. In *A companion to the Roman Republic*, ed. N. Rosenstein and R. Morstein-Marx, 478–95. Oxford

(2008) 'Hierarchie und Konsens. *Pompae* in der politischen Kultur der römischen Republik'. In *Machtfragen. Zur kulturellen Repräsentation und Konstruktion von Macht in Antike, Mittelalter und Neuzeit*, ed. A. H. Arweiler and B. M. Gauly, 79–126. Stuttgart

(forthcoming) 'The Roman Republic as theatre of power: the consuls as leading actors', in *Consuls and res publica: high office holding in the Roman Republic*, ed. H. Beck, A. Duplá, M. Jehne, and F. Pina Polo. Cambridge

Holleman, A. W. J. (1989) 'Q. Fabius' vow to Venus Erycina (217 BC) and its background'. In *Punic wars*, ed. H. Devijver and E. Lipinski, 223–8. Leuven

Holzapfel, L. (1885) *Römische Chronologie*, Leipzig

Hough, J. N. (1930) 'The Lex Lutatia and the Lex Plautia de vi', *AJPh* 51: 135–47

Humbert, M. (1978) *Municipium et civitas sine suffragio. L'organisation de la conquête jusqu'à la guerre sociale*, Rome

Humm, M. (2005) *Appius Claudius Caecus. La république accomplie*, Rome

Humphrey, J. H. (1986) *Roman circuses: arenas for chariot racing*, Berkeley, CA

Hurlet, F. (1993) *La dictature de Sylla: monarchie ou magistrature républicaine? Essai d'histoire constitutionnelle*, Rome

(2008) 'Le passage de la République à l'Empire: questions anciennes, nouvelles réponses', *REA* 110: 215–36

(forthcoming) 'Consulship and consuls under Augustus'. In *Consuls and res publica: high office holding in the Roman Republic*, ed. H. Beck, A. Duplá, M. Jehne, and F. Pina Polo. Cambridge

Itgenshorst, T. (2005) *Tota illa pompa: der Triumph in der römischen Republik*, Göttingen

Jahn, J. (1970) *Interregnum und Wahlkandidatur*, Kallmünz

Jehne, M. (1997) *Caesar*, Munich
  (2000) 'Marcus Tullius Cicero – der Neuling, der zu spät kam'. In *Von Romulus zu Augustus. Grosse Gestalten der römischen Republik*, ed. K.-J. Hölkeskamp and E. Stein-Hölkeskamp, 250–67. Munich
  (2009) 'Diplomacy in Italy in the second century BC'. In *Diplomats and diplomacy in the Roman world*, ed. C. Eilers, 143–70. Leiden and Boston
Jonkers, E. J. (1963) *Social and economic commentary on Cicero's* De lege agraria orationes tres, Leiden
Kaplan, A. (1973–4) 'Religious dictators of the Roman Republic', *Classical World*: 172–5.
Keaveney, A. (1982) *Sulla: the last Republican*, London
  (1992) *Lucullus: a life*, London and New York
Kelly, B. (2005) 'The law that Catulus passed'. In *Roman crossings. Theory and practice in the Roman Republic*, ed. K. Welch and T. W. Hillard, 95–118. Swansea
Kelly, G. P. (2006) *A history of exile in the Roman republic*, Cambridge
Kierdorf, W. (1980) *Laudatio funebris. Interpretationen und Untersuchungen zur Entwicklung der römischen Leichenrede*, Meisenheim am Glan
Kolb, A. (1993) *Die kaiserliche Bauverwaltung in der Stadt Rom. Geschichte und Aufbau der cura operum publicorum unter dem Prinzipat*, Stuttgart
Konrad, C. F. (1994) *Plutarch's Sertorius. A historical commentary*, Chapel Hill, NC and London
  (1995) 'A new chronology of the Sertorian war', *Athenaeum* 83: 157–87
Kübler, B. (1900) s.v. Consul, *RE* iv.1: 1112–38
Kumaniecki, K. (1959) 'Ciceros Rede De haruspicum responsis', *Klio* 37: 135–52
  (1977) 'Ciceros Rede De aere alieno Milonis', *Klio* 59: 381–401
Kunkel, W. (1962) *Untersuchungen zur Entwicklung des römischen Kriminalverfahrens in vorsullanischer Zeit*, Munich
Kunkel, W. and Wittmann, R. (1995) *Staatsordnung und Staatspraxis der römischen Republik. Vol. 2, Die Magistratur*, Munich
Künzl, E. (1988) *Der römische Triumph. Siegesfeiern im antiken Rom*, Munich
Labruna, L. (1975) *Il console sovversivo: Marco Emilio Lepido e la sua rivolta*, Naples
Lacey, W. K. (1974) 'Clodius and Cicero: a question of *dignitas*', *Antichthon* 8: 85–92
  (1978) *Cicero and the end of the Roman Republic*, London
Landucci, L. (1896) 'La pubblicazione delle leggi nell'antica Roma', *Atti e Memorie della Reale Accademia di Padova*, 12: 119–49
Landwehr, Ch. (1985) *Die antiken Gipsabgüsse aus Baiae. Griechische Bronzestatuen in Abgüssen römischer Zeit*, Berlin
Laser, G. (1997) *Populo et scaenae serviendum est. Die Bedeutung der städtischen Masse in der späten römischen Republik*, Trier
Latte, K. (1960) *Römische Religionsgeschichte*, Munich
Laurence, R. (1999) *The roads of Roman Italy. Mobility and cultural change*, London and New York
Leifer, F. (1914) *Die Einheit des Gewaltgedankens im römischen Staatsrecht*, Munich

Lenagham, J. O. (1969) *A commentary on Cicero's oration* De haruspicum responso, The Hague and Paris

Leuze, O. (1909) *Die römische Jahrzählung. Ein Versuch, ihre geschichtliche Entwicklung zu ermitteln*, Tübingen

Levi, M. A. (1922) 'Una pagina di storia agraria romana', *Atene e Roma* 3: 239–52

Lewis, R. G. (ed.) (2006) *Asconius. Commentaries on speeches by Cicero*, Oxford

Liebenam (1905) s.v. *duoviri*, *RE* v: 1801–2

Liebeschuetz, J. H. W. G. (1979) *Continuity and change in Roman religion*, Oxford

Linderski, J. (1961) 'Ciceros Rede pro Caelio und die ambitus- und Vereingesetzgebung der ausgehenden Republik', *Hermes* 89: 106–19 = J. Linderski (1995) *Roman questions. Selected papers*, 204–17. Stuttgart

(1965) 'Constitutional aspects of the consular elections in 59 BC', *Historia* 14: 423–42

(1995) 'Ambassadors go to Rome', in *Les relations internationales*, ed. E. Frézouls and A. Jacquemin, 453–78. Paris

(1996) 'Cato Maior in Aetolia'. In *Transitions to empire. Essays in Greco-Roman history, 360–146 BC, in honor of E. Badian*, ed. R. W. Wallace and E. M. Harris, 376–408. Norman, OK

Linderski, J. and Kaminska-Linderski, A. (1973) 'A. Gabinius A. f. Capito and the first vote in the legislative *comitia tributa*', *ZPE* 12: 247–52

Linke, B. (2000) 'Appius Claudius Caecus – ein Leben in Zeiten des Umbruchs'. In *Von Romulus zu Augustus. Große Gestalten der römischen Republik*, ed. K.-J. Hölkeskamp and E. Stein-Hölkeskamp, 69–78. Munich

Lintott, A. (1965) 'Trinundinum', *CQ* 59: 281–5

(1968) 'Nundinae and the chronology of the Late Roman Republic', *CQ* 62: 189–94

(1972) '*Provocatio*. From the struggle of the orders to the Principate', *ANRW* 1.2: 226–67

(1992) *Judicial reform and land reform in the Roman Republic*, Cambridge

(1999a) *Violence in Republican Rome*, Oxford, 2nd edn. (1st edn, 1968)

(1999b) *The constitution of the Roman Republic*, Oxford

Liou-Gille, B. (1993) 'Le *pomerium*', *MH* 50: 94–106

(1996) 'Naissance de la ligue latine. Mythe et culte de fondation', *RBPh* 74: 73–97

Lippold, A. (1963) *Consules: Untersuchungen zur Geschichte des römischen Konsulates von 264 bis 201 v. Chr.*, Bonn

Lovano, M. (2002) *The age of Cinna: crucible of Late Republican Rome*, Stuttgart

LTUR = *Lexicon topographicum urbis Romae*, ed. M. Steinby, 6 vols. Rome 1993–2000

Luce, T. J. (1977) *Livy: the composition of his history*, Princeton, NJ

Luterbacher, F. (1904) *Der Prodigienglaube und Prodigienstil der Römer*, Burgdorf

MacBain, B. (1982) *Prodigy and expiation: a study in religion and politics in Republican Rome*, Brussels

Mackay, C. (1994) 'The judicial legislation of C. Sempronius Gracchus', PhD diss., Harvard. Cambridge, MA

Magdelain, A. (1943) *Essai sur les origines de la sponsio*, Paris

(1968) *Recherches sur l' "imperium", la loi curiate et les auspices d'investiture*, Paris

Marchetti, P. (1973) 'La marche du calendrier romain de 203 à 190 (années Varr. 551–564)', *AC* 42: 473–96

Marco Simón, F. (forthcoming) 'The *feriae Latinae* and the religious task of the consuls' in *Consuls and* res publica*: high office holding in the Roman Republic*, ed. H. Beck, A. Duplá, M. Jehne, and F. Pina Polo. Cambridge

Marco Simón, F. and Pina Polo, F. (2000) '*Concordia* y *libertas* como polos de referencia religiosa en la lucha política de la república tardía', *Gerión* 18: 261–92

Marinone, N. (2004) *Cronologia ciceroniana*, 2nd edn., ed. E. Malaspina. Rome

Marshall, A. J. (1972) 'The Lex Pompeia de provinciis (52 BC) and Cicero's imperium in 51–50 BC: constitutional aspects', *ANRW* I.I: 887–921

Marshall, B. A. (1973) 'Crassus and the command against Spartacus', *Athenaeum* 51: 109–21

(1976a) *Crassus. A political biography*, Amsterdam

(1976b) 'The date of Q. Mucius Scaevola's governorship of Asia', *Athenaeum* 54: 117–30

(1985) *A historical commentary on Asconius*, Columbia, MO

Marshall, B. and Beness, J. L. (1987) 'Tribunician agitation and aristocratic reaction 80–71 BC', *Athenaeum* 65: 361–78

Martin, J. (1970) 'Die Provokation in der klassischen und späten Republik', *Hermes* 98: 72–96

Mateo, A. (1999) *Manceps, redemptor, publicanus. Contribución al estudio de los contratistas públicos en Roma*, Santander

Mattingly, H. B. (1972) 'The date of the SC de agro Pergameno', *AJPh* 93: 412–23

McDermott, W. C. (1977) 'Lex de tribunicia potestate (70 BC)', *CPh* 72: 49–52

McDonald, A. H. (1957) 'The style of Livy', *JRS* 47: 155–72

McDonald, A. H. and Walbank, F. W. (1937) 'The origins of the second Macedonian war', *JRS* 27: 180–207

McDonald, W. (1929) 'The tribunate of Cornelius', *CQ* 23: 196–208

McGing, B. C. (1984) 'The date of the outbreak of the third Mithridatic war', *Phoenix* 38: 12–18

McGushin, P. (1992–94) *Sallust. The Histories. Translated with an introduction and commentary*, 2 vols., Oxford

Meier, Chr. (1961) 'Zur Chronologie und Politik in Caesars erstem Konsulat', *Historia* 10: 68–98

(1982) *Caesar*, Berlin

(1997) *Res publica amissa: Eine Studie zur Verfassung und Geschichte der späten römischen Republik*, 3rd edn., Frankfurt (1st edn, Wiesbaden 1966)

Meißner, B. (2000) 'Gaius Flaminius – oder: wie ein Außenseiter zum Sündenbock wurde'. In *Von Romulus zu Augustus. Große Gestalten der römischen Republik*, ed. K.-J. Hölkeskamp and E. Stein-Hölkeskamp, 92–105. Munich

Meyer, E. (1975) *Römischer Staat und Staatsgedanke*, 4th edn, Zurich

Michels, A. (1967) *The calendar of the Roman Republic*, Princeton

Millar, F. (1984) 'The political character of the Classical Roman Republic, 200–151 BC', *JRS* 74: 1–19
  (1986) 'Politics, persuasion and the people before the Social War (150–90 BC)', *JRS* 76: 1–11
  (1989) 'Political power in mid-Republican Rome: Curia or Comitium?', *JRS* 79: 138–50
  (1995) 'The last century of the Republic: whose history?', *JRS* 85: 236–43
  (1998) *The crowd in Rome in the Late Republic*, Ann Arbor, MI
Mineo, B. (2006) *Tite-Live et l'histoire de Rome*, Paris
Mitchell, R. E. (1990) *Patricians and plebeians: the origin of the Roman state*, Ithaca, NY and London
Mitchell, T. N. (1979) *Cicero: the ascending years*, New Haven, CT and London
Moatti, C. (1993) *Archives et partage de la terre dans le monde romain (IIe siècle avant – Ier après J.-C.)*, Rome
Momigliano, A. (1930) 'Ricerche sulle magistrature romane. I. Il dictator clavi figendi causa', *BCAR* 58: 29–55 = *Quarto contributo alla storia degli studi classici e del mondo antico*, 273–327. Rome 1969
Mommsen, Th. (1859) *Die römische Chronologie bis auf Caesar*, Berlin
  (1864) 'Das römische Gastrecht', *Römische Forschungen*, I: 319–54. Berlin
  (1864–79) *Römische Forschungen*, 2 vols., Berlin
  (1887–8) *Römisches Staatsrecht*, 3 vols. in 5, Leipzig
  (1899) *Römisches Strafrecht*, Leipzig
Monaca, M. (2005) *La Sibilla a Roma: i libri sibillini fra religione e politica*, Cosenza
Montero Herrero, S. (1980) 'M. Curius Dentatus y la vía Curia', *Memorias de Historia Antigua* 4: 61–3
Mora, F. (1999) *Fasti e schemi cronologici: la riorganizzazione annalistica del passato remoto romano*, Stuttgart
Moreau, Ph. (1982) *Clodiana religio. Un procès politique en 61 av. J.C.*, Paris
Morgan, M. Gwyn (1971) 'The Portico of Metellus: a reconsideration', *Hermes* 99: 480–505
  (1973) 'Metellus Pontifex and Ops Opifera; a note on Pliny Naturalis Historia 11.174', *Phoenix* 27: 35–41
  (1977) 'Calendars and chronology in the First Punic War', *Chiron* 7: 89–117
Morstein Kallet-Marx, R. (1995) *Hegemony to Empire: the development of the Roman Imperium in the east from 148 to 62 BC*, Berkeley, Los Angeles, and Oxford
Morstein-Marx, R. (2004) *Mass oratory and political power in the Late Roman Republic*, Cambridge
Mouritsen, H. (1998) *Italian unification*, London
  (2001) *Plebs and politics in the Late Roman Republic*, Cambridge
Münzer, F. (1900) s.v. Sulpicius Galba n° 64, *RE* IVAI: 801–8
  (1901) s.v. Curius no 9, *RE* IV: 1841–2
  (1912a) s.v. Hostilius, *RE* VIII: 2514–15
  (1912b) 'Die Todesstrafe politischer Verbrecher in der späteren römischen Republik', *Hermes* 47: 161–82
Mura Sommella, A. (2000) s.v. Tabularium, *LTUR* V: 17–20

Nadig, P. (1997) *Ardet Ambitus. Untersuchungen zum Phänomen der Wahlbestechungen in der römischen Republik*, Frankfurt

Näsström, B.-M. (1992) 'The Bacchanalia: development and suppression'. In *A conciliation of powers: the force of religion in society*, ed. G. Aijmer, 110–18. Göteborg

Neuendorff, A. (1913) *Die römischen Konsulwahlen von 78–48 v.Chr.*, diss. Breslau

Nicolet, C. (1974) 'Polybe et les institutions romaines'. In *Polybe. Entretiens sur l'antiquité classique*, vol. 20, ed. E. Gabba, 209–58. Geneva

(1976) *Le métier de citoyen dans la Rome républicaine*, Paris

(1980a) ed. *Insula sacra: la loi Gabinia-Calpurnia de Délos (58 av. J.-C.)*, Rome

(1980b) 'La lex Gabinia-Calpurnia de insula Delo et la loi "annonaire" de Clodius (58 av. J.-C.)', *CRAI*: 259–87

(1992) 'Autour de l'imperium', *CCGG* 3: 163–6

Nippel, W. (1988) *Aufruhr und 'Polizei' in der römischen Republik*, Stuttgart

(1997) 'Orgien, Ritualmorde und Verschwörung? Die Bacchanalien-Prozesse des Jahres 186 v.Chr.' In *Große Prozesse der römischen Antike*, ed. U. Manthe and J. von Ungern-Sternberg, 65–73. Munich

Nissen, H. (1902) *Italische Landeskunde*, 2 vols., Berlin

North, J. (1979) 'Religious toleration in Republican Rome', *PCPS* n.s.25: 85–103

(2006) 'The constitution of the Roman Republic', in *A companion to the Roman Republic*, ed. N. Rosenstein and R. Morstein-Marx, 256–77. Oxford

Oakley, S. P. (1998) *A commentary on Livy Books VI–X*, vol. II, Oxford

(2005a) *A commentary on Livy Books VI–X*, vol. III, Oxford

(2005b) *A commentary on Livy Books VI–X*, vol. IV, Oxford

Ogilvie, R. M. (1978) *A commentary on Livy, Books 1–5*, Oxford

Olinder, B. (1974) *Porticus Octavia in Circo Flaminio*, Stockholm

Ooteghem, J. van (1954) *Pompée le Grand, bâtisseur d'empire*, Brussels

(1959) *Lucius Licinius Lucullus*, Brussels

(1964) *Caius Marius*, Brussels

(1967) *Les Caecilii Metelli de la République*, Brussels

Orlin, E. M. (1997) *Temples, religion and politics in the Roman Republic*, Leiden, New York, and Cologne

(2007) 'Urban religion in the Middle and Late Republic', in *A companion to Roman religion*, ed. J. Rüpke, 58–70. Oxford

Paananen, U. (1990) 'Leges de bello indicendo e comizio centuriato', *Athenaeum* 78: 180–6

(1993) 'Legislation in the *comitia centuriata*', in *Senatus populusque Romanus: studies in Roman legislation. Acta Instituti Romani Finlandiae* 13, 9–73. Helsinki

Pailler, J.-M. (1988) *Bacchanalia. La répression de 186 av. J.-C. à Rome et en Italie: vestiges, images, tradition*, Rome

Palombi, D. (1993) s.v. Columna Rostrata M. Aemilii Paulli, *LTUR* I: 307–8

(1995) s.v. Felicitas, aedes, *LTUR* II: 244–5

(1996a) s.v. Hercules Victor, aedes et signum, *LTUR* III: 23–5

(1996b) s.v. Honos et Virtus, aedes, *LTUR* III: 31–3

(1996c) s.v. Honos et virtus, aedes Mariana, *LTUR* III: 33–5

Papi, E. (1995) s.v. Equus: M' Acilius Glabrio, *LTUR* II: 224

Paul, G. M. (1984) *A historical commentary on Sallust's* Bellum Jugurthinum, Liverpool

Pease, A. S. (1920) *M. Tulli Ciceronis De divinatione liber primus*, Urbana, IL

Pekáry, T. (1968) *Untersuchungen zu den römischen Reichsstrassen*, Bonn

Pena, M. J. (1976) 'La lex de clavo pangendo', *Hispania Antiqua* 6: 239–65

Pensabene, P. (2000a) s.v. Victoria, aedes, *LTUR* V: 149–50

   (2000b) s.v. Victoria Virgo, aedicula, *LTUR* V: 150–1

Perl, G. (1965) 'Die Rede Cottas in Sallusts Historien', *Philologus* 109: 75–82

   (1975) 'Das Kompositionsprinzip der Historiae des Sallust (zu Hist. fr. 2,42)', in *Actes de la XIIe Conférence Internationale d'Etudes Classiques 'Eirene'. Cluj-Napoca 2–7 Octobre 1972*, 317–37. Amsterdam

Peterson, T. (1920) *Cicero: a biography*, Berkeley

Pietilä-Castrén, L. (1987) *Magnificentia publica: the victory monuments of the Roman generals in the era of the Punic Wars*, Helsinki

Pina Polo, F. (1987) 'La estructura agraria de la Península Itálica en el siglo II a.C.', *Veleia* 4: 159–70

   (1988) 'La colonización romana en el siglo II a.C.', in *Actas Ier Congreso Peninsular de Historia Antigua*, ed. G. Pereira, III: 107–25. Santiago de Compostela

   (1989) *Las contiones civiles y militares en Roma*, Saragossa

   (1995) 'Procedures and functions of civil and military *contiones* in Rome', *Klio* 77: 203–16

   (1996) *Contra arma verbis. Der Redner vor dem Volk in der späten römischen Republik*, Stuttgart

   (2004) 'La celebración de la muerte como símbolo de poder en la Roma republicana', in *Ceremoniales, ritos y representación del poder*, ed. H.-D. Heimann, S. Knippschild, and V. Mínguez, 143–79. Castellón de la Plana

   (2005a) 'I Rostra come espressione di potere della aristocrazia romana', in *Popolo e potere nel mondo antico*, ed. G. Urso, 141–55. Pisa

   (2005b) *Marco Tulio Cicerón*, Barcelona

   (2006a) 'Deportation, Kolonisation, Migration: Bevölkerungsverschiebungen im republikanischen Italien und Formen der Identitätsbildung'. In *Herrschaft ohne Integration? Rom und Italien in republikanischer Zeit*, ed. M. Jehne and R. Pfeilschifter, 171–206. Frankfurt am Main

   (2006b) 'The tyrant must die: preventive tyrannicide in Roman political thought', in *Repúblicas y ciudadanos: formas de participación cívica en el mundo antiguo*, ed. F. Marco Simón, F. Pina Polo, and J. Remesal Rodríguez, 71–101. Barcelona

   (2009) 'Eminent corpses: Roman aristocracy's passing from life to history'. In *Formae mortis: el tránsito de la vida a la muerte en las sociedades antiguas*, ed. F. Marco Simón, F. Pina Polo, and J. Remesal Rodríguez, 89–100. Barcelona

Pinsent, J. (1975) *Military tribunes and plebeian consuls: the fasti from 444 V to 342 V*, Stuttgart

Platner, S. B. and Ashby, Th. (1929) *A topographical dictionary of ancient Rome*, London,

Poma, G. (1978) 'Le secessioni e il rito dell'infissione del *clavus*', *RSA* 8: 39–50
(2005) 'La *lex Tullia de ambitu* e la difesa ciceroniana di Murena', *Rivista storica dell'antichità* 35: 275–92

Pouthier, P. (1981) *Ops et la conception romaine de l'abondance dans la religion romaine jusqu'à la mort d'Auguste*, Rome

Premerstein, A. von (1901) s.v. *clavus*, *RE* IV: 2–4

Primmer, A. (1985) *Die Überredungsstrategie in Ciceros Rede pro C. Rabirio*, Vienna

Quilici, L. (1991) 'Le strade romane nell'Italia antica'. In *Viae publicae romane*, 17–24. Rome

Quinn-Schofield, W. K. (1967) 'Ludi, Romani magnique varie appellati', *Latomus* 26: 96–103

Radke, G. (1964a) 'Die Erschliessung Italiens durch die römischen Strassen', *Gymnasium* 71: 204–35
(1964b) 'Römische Strassen in der Gallia Cisalpina und der Narbonensis', *Klio* 42: 299–318
(1967) 'Namen und Daten: Beobachtungen zur Geschichte des römischen Strassenbaus', *MH* 24: 221–35
(1973) s.v. Viae publicae Romanae, *RE Suppl.* XIII: 1417–686
(1975a) s.v. Aemilia via, *Der Kleine Pauly*, I: 90. Munich
(1975b) s.v. Forum, *Der Kleine Pauly*, II: 602–3. Munich
(1975c) s.v. Penates, *Der Kleine Pauly*, IV: 611. Munich
(1975d) s.v. Pomptinus ager, *Der Kleine Pauly*, IV: 1041–2. Munich
(1975e) s.v. Viae publicae, *Der Kleine Pauly*, V: 1243–5. Munich
(1980) 'Anmerkungen zu den kultischen Maßnahmen in Rom während des Zweiten Punischen Krieges', *WJA N.F.* 6b: 105–21

Raggi, A. (2001) 'Senatus consultum de Asclepiade Clazomenio sociisque', *ZPE* 135: 73–116

Rasmussen, S. W. (2003) *Public portents in Republican Rome*, Rome

Rawson, E. (1971) 'Prodigy lists and the use of the Annales Maximi', *CQ* 21: 158–69
(1975) *Cicero: a portrait*, London

Rich, J. W. (1976) *Declaring war in the Roman Republic in the period of transmarine expansion*, Brussels
(1997) 'Structuring Roman history: the consular year and the Roman historical tradition', *Histos* (www.dur.ac.uk/Classics/histos/1997/rich1.html)
(2005) 'Valerius Antias and the construction of the Roman past', *BICS* 48: 137–61

Richardson Jr, L. (1976) 'The evolution of the Porticus Octaviae', *AJA* 80: 56–64

Rickman, G. (1980) *The corn supply of Ancient Rome*, Oxford

Riggsby, A. M. (1999) *Crime and community in Ciceronian Rome*, Austin, TX

Rilinger, R. (1976) *Der Einfluß des Wahlleiters bei den römischen Konsulwahlen von 366 bis 50 v. Chr.*, Munich

Robinson, O. F. (1992) *Ancient Rome: city planning and administration*, London

Roddaz, J.-M. (1992) '*Imperium:* nature et compétences à la fin de la République et au début de l'Empire', *CCGG* 3: 189–211

Rosenberger, V. (1998) *Gezähmte Götter. Das Prodigienwesen der römischen Republik*, Stuttgart

  (2007) 'Republican *nobiles:* controlling the *res publica*'. In *A companion to Roman religion*, ed. J. Rüpke, 292–303. Oxford

Rosenstein, N. (1995) 'Sorting out the lot in Republican Rome', *AJPh* 116: 43–75

Rotondi, G. (1912) *Leges publicae populi Romani*, Milan

Rowland Jr, R. J. (1965) 'The number of grain recipients in the late Republic', *Act. Antiq. Scient. Hung.* 13: 81–3

Rubinsohn, Z. (1970) 'A note on Plutarch, Crassus X 1', *Historia* 19: 624–7

Rudolph, H. (1935) *Stadt und Staat im römischen Italien*, Leipzig

Ruoff-Väänänen, E. (1972) 'The Roman public *prodigia* and the *ager Romanus*', *Arctos* 7: 139–62

  (1978) *Studies on the Italian fora*, Wiesbaden

Rüpke, J. (1990) *Domi militiae. Die religiöse Konstruktion des Krieges in Rom*, Stuttgart

  (2006) 'Communicating with the gods', in *A companion to the Roman Republic*, ed. N. Rosenstein and R. Morstein-Marx, 215–35. Oxford

  (2007a) *Römische Priester in der Antike. Ein biographisches Lexikon*, Stuttgart

  (2007b) *Religion of the Romans*, Cambridge (1st edn 2001)

Sabbatucci, D. (1988) *La religione di Roma antica dal calendario festivo all'ordine cosmico*, Milan

Sacchetti, L. (1996) *Prodigi e cronaca religiosa. Uno studio sulla storiografia latina arcaica*, Rome

Salmon, E. T. (1967) *Samnium and the Samnites*, Cambridge

  (1969) *Roman colonization under the Republic*, London

Salomonson, J. W. (1956) 'Chair, sceptre and wreath: historical aspects of their representation on some Roman sepulchral monuments', diss. Groningen

Sandberg, K. (1993) 'The *concilium plebis* as a legislative body during the Republic'. In *Senatus populusque Romanus. Studies in Roman legislation. Acta Instituti Romani Finlandiae*, 13: 74–96. Helsinki

  (2000) 'Tribunician and non-tribunician legislation in mid-Republican Rome'. In *The Roman Middle Republic*, ed. C. Bruun, 121–40. Rome

  (2001) *Magistrates and assemblies: a study of legislative practice in Republican Rome*, Rome

  (2004) 'Consular legislation in pre-Sullan Rome', *Arctos* 38: 133–62

  (2007) 'Polybius of the consuls: an interpretation of *Histories* 6,12,4', *Arctos* 41: 75–88

Scheid, J. (1981) 'Le délit religieux dans la Rome tardo-républicaine'. In *Le délit religieux dans la cité antique (Table ronde, Rome, 6–7 avril 1978)*, 117–71. Rome

  (1985) *Religion et piété à Rome*, Paris

  (1986) *L'association dionysiaque dans les sociétés anciennes*, Rome

  (1998a) *La religion des Romains*, Paris

(1998b) 'Les incertitudes de la voti sponsio. Observations en marge du ver sacrum de 217 av. J.C.'. In *Mélanges de droit romain et d'histoire ancienne. Hommage à la mémoire de André Magdelain*, ed. M. Humbert and Y. Thomas, 417–25. Paris

Schiavone, A. (1987) *Giuristi e nobili nella Roma repubblicana*, Rome and Bari

Schmidt, P. L. (1968) *Iulius Obsequens und das Problem der Livius-Epitome: Ein Beitrag zur Geschichte der lateinischen Prodigienliteratur*, Mainz

Schneider, A. (1968) *Le prémier livre Ad nationes de Tertullien. Introduction, texte, traduction et commentaire*, Rome

Schneider, W. Chr. (1998) *Vom Handeln der Römer: Kommunikation und Interaktion der politischen Führungsschicht vor Ausbruch des Bürgerkriegs im Briefwechsel mit Cicero*, Hildesheim

Schubert, C. (1996) *Land und Raum in der römischen Republik. Die Kunst des Teilens*, Darmstadt

Schulz, R. (1997) *Herrschaft und Regierung. Roms Regiment in den Provinzen in der Zeit der Republik*, Paderborn

von Schwind, F. (1940) *Zur Frage der Publikation im römischen Recht*, Munich

Scullard, H. H. (1981) *Festivals and ceremonies of the Roman Republic*, London

Seager, R. (2002) *Pompey. A political biography*, 2nd edn, Oxford

Seeck, O. (1908) 'Zur Geschichte des Isiskultus in Rom', *Hermes* 43: 642–3

Seguin, R. (1974) 'La religion de Scipion l'Africain', *Latomus* 33: 3–21

Sehlmeyer, M. (1999) *Stadtrömische Ehrenstatuen der republikanischen Zeit*, Stuttgart

Shackleton Bailey, D. R. (1965–70) *Cicero's letters to Atticus*, 7 vols., Cambridge
(1971) *Cicero*, London

Shatzman, I. (1968) 'Four notes on Roman magistrates', *Athenaeum* 46: 345–54

Sherk, R. K. (1963) 'Senatus consultum de agris Mytilenaeorum', *GRBS* 4: 217–30
(1969) *Roman documents from the Greek East*, Baltimore, MD
(1984) *Rome and the Greek East to the death of Augustus*, Cambridge

Sherwin-White, A. N. (1984) *Roman foreign policy in the East, 168 BC to AD 1*, London

Siber, H. (1952) *Römisches Verfassungsrecht in geschichtlicher Entwicklung*, Lahr

Skard, E. (1941) 'Marius' speech in Sallust Jug. Chap. 85', *SO* 21: 98–102

Skutsch, O. (1985) *The Annals of Q. Ennius*, Oxford

Soltau, W. (1888) *Die römischen Amtsjahre auf ihren natürlichen Zeitwerth reducirt*, Freiburg

Sonnabend, H. (1996) s.v. Ager Pomptinus, *Der Neue Pauly* 1: 250–1

Southern, P. (2002) *Pompey the Great*, Stroud

Spann, P. O. (1987) *Quintus Sertorius and the legacy of Sulla*, Fayetteville, AR

Stambaugh, J. E. (1978) 'The function of Roman temples', *ANRW* II 16.1: 554–608

Staveley, E. S. (1969) 'The role of the first voter in Roman legislative assemblies', *Historia* 18: 513–20
(1972) *Greek and Roman voting and elections*, London

Stein, P. (1930) *Die Senatssitzungen der ciceronischen Zeit*, Münster

Steinby, E. M. (1987) 'Il lato orientale del Foro Romano: proposte di lettura', *Arctos* 21: 139–84

(1993) s.v. Basilica Aemilia, *LTUR* 1: 167–8

Stevens, C. E. (1938) 'The terminal date of Caesar's command', *AJPh* 59: 169–208

Stockton, D. (1971) *Cicero: a political biography*, Oxford

(1979) *The Gracchi*, Oxford

Strong, D. E. (1968) 'The administration of public building in Rome during the Late Republic and Early Empire', *BICS* 15: 97–8

Sumi, G. S. (1997) 'Power and ritual: the crowd at Clodius' funeral', *Historia* 46: 80–102

(2005) *Ceremony and power. Performing politics in Rome between Republic and Empire*, Ann Arbor, MI

Sumner, G. V. (1963) 'Lex Aelia, lex Fufia', *AJPh* 84: 340–50

(1964) 'Manius or Mamercus?', *JRS* 54: 41–8

(1966) 'The chronology of the outbreak of the Second Punic War', *PACA* 9: 5–30

Takács, S. A. (1995) *Isis and Sarapis in the Roman world*, Leiden, New York, and Cologne

(2008) *Vestal virgins, sibyls, and matrons: women in Roman religion*, Austin, TX

Tatum, W. J. (1999) *The patrician tribune Publius Clodius Pulcher*, Chapel Hill, NC and London

Taylor, L. R. (1951) 'On the chronology of Caesar's first consulship', *AJPh* 72: 254–68

(1966) *Roman voting assemblies*, Ann Arbor, MI

Taylor, L. R. and Broughton, T. R. S. (1949) 'The order of the two consuls' names in the yearly lists', *MAAR* 19: 3–14

(1968) 'The order of the consuls' names in official Republican lists', *Historia* 17: 166–71

Taylor, L. R. and Holland, L. A. (1952) 'Janus and the *Fasti*', *CPh* 47: 137–42

Thommen, L. (1989) *Das Volkstribunat der späten römischen Republik*, Stuttgart

Torelli, M. (1968) 'Il donario di M. Fulvio Flacco nell'area sacra di S. Omobono', *Quad. Ist. Top. Ant. Univ. Roma* 5: 71–6

Toutain, J. (1915–18) 'Le rite de la plantation du clou', *MSAF* 25: 43–80

Toynbee, A. J. (1965) *Hannibal's legacy. The Hannibalic War's effects on Roman life*, 2 vols., London

Trisciuoglio, A. (1998) *'Sarta tecta, ultrotributa, opus publicum faciendum locare'. Sugli appalti relativi alle opere pubbliche nell'età repubblicana e augustea*, Naples

Tschudin, P. F. (1962) *Isis in Rom*, diss. Aarau

Tucci, P. L. (2005) 'Where high Moneta leads her steps sublime: the Tabularium and the temple of Juno Moneta', *JRA* 18: 6–33

Turcan, R. (1989) *Les cultes orientaux dans le monde romain*, Paris

Unger, G. F. (1873) 'Der römische Jahresnagel', *Philologus* 32: 531–40

Ungern-Sternberg, J. von (1970) *Untersuchungen zum spätrepublikanischen Notstandsrecht. 'Senatus consultum ultimum' und 'hostis'-Erklärung*, Munich

Valgiglio, E. (1957) *Silla e la crisi repubblicana*, Florence

Valvo, A. (2001) 'Formula amicorum, commercium amicitiae, philias koinonia'. In *Linguaggio e terminologia diplomatica dall'antico oriente all'impero bizantino. Atti del Convegno Nazionale, Genova 19 Novembre 1998*, ed. M. G. Angeli Bertinelli and L. Piccirilli, 133–45. Rome

Van Son, D. W. L. (1963) 'The disturbances in Etruria during the Second Punic War', *Mnemosyne* 16: 267–74

Vanderbroeck, P. J. J. (1987) *Popular leadership and collective behavior in the late Roman republic (80–50 BC)*, Amsterdam

Verbrugghe, G. P. (1973) 'The elogium from Polla and the First Slave War', *CPh* 68: 25–35

Versluys, M. J. (2004) 'Isis Capitolina and the Egyptian cults in late Republican Rome'. In *Isis en Occident. Actes du IIème Colloque International sur les études Isiaques, Lyon III, 16–17 Mai 2002*, ed. L. Bricault, 421–48. Leiden and Boston

Vervaet, F. (2004) 'The *lex Valeria* and Sulla's empowerment as dictator (82–79 BCE)', *CCGG* 15: 37–84

    (2006) 'The scope of the *lex Sempronia* concerning the assignment of the consular provinces (123 BCE)', *Athenaeum* 94: 627–56

Virlouvet, C. (1994) 'Les lois frumentaires d'époque républicaine', in *Le ravitaillement en blé de Rome et des centres urbains des débuts de la République jusqu'au Haut-Empire*, 11–29. Rome

Viscogliosi, A. (1993) s.v. Bellona, aedes in Circo, *LTUR* I: 190–2

    (1995) s.v. Diana, aedes in Circo, *LTUR* II: 14

    (1996a) s.v. Hercules Musarum, aedes, *LTUR* III: 17–19

    (1996b) s.v. Iuno Regina, aedes in Campo, ad Circum Flaminium, *LTUR* III: 126–8

    (1999a) s.v. Porticus Metelli, *LTUR* IV: 130–2

    (1999b) s.v. Porticus Octavia, *LTUR* IV: 139–41

Vishnia, R. F. (1996) *State, society, and popular leaders in mid-Republican Rome, 241–167 BC*, London and New York

Vollmer, F. (1892) *Laudationum funebrium Romanorum. Historia et reliquiarum editio*, Leipzig

Wachsmuth, D. (1975) s.v. *Victoria, Der Kleine Pauly*, V: 262. Munich

Walbank, F. W. (1941) 'A note on the embassy of Q. Marcius Philippus, 171 BC', *JRS* 31: 82–93

    (1949) 'Roman declaration of war in the third and second centuries', *CPh* 44: 15–19

    (1957) *A commentary on Polybius*. Vol. 1, Oxford

Waldstein, W. (1975) s.v. *duoviri, Der Kleine Pauly*, II: 177. Munich

Walsh, P. G. (1996) 'Making a drama out of a crisis: Livy and the Bacchanalia', *G&R* 43: 188–203

Ward, A. M. (1977) *Marcus Crassus and the Late Roman Republic*, Columbia and London

Warrior, V. M. (1996) *The initiation of the Second Macedonian War: an explication of Livy Book 31*, Stuttgart

Watson, A. (1974) *Law making in the later Roman Republic*, Oxford

Weigel, R. D. (1982–3) 'The duplication of temples of Juno Regina in Rome', *AncSoc* 13–14: 179–92

(1992) *Lepidus: the tarnished triumvir*, London and New York

Weinstock, St. (1937a) s.v. Penates, *RE* XIX.1: 417–57

(1937b) 'Clodius and the lex Aelia Fufia', *JRS* 27: 215–22

Welch, K. (2003) 'A new view of the origins of the basilica: the Atrium Regium, Graecostasis, and Roman diplomacy', *JRA* 16: 5–34

(2006) 'Art and architecture in the Roman Republic'. In *A companion to the Roman Republic*, ed. N. Rosenstein and R. Morstein-Marx, 496–542. Oxford

Werner, Chr. (1888) *De feriis Latinis*, diss. Leipzig

Werner, R. (1963) *Der Beginn der römischen Republik*, Munich and Vienna

Weynand, R. (1935) s.v. Marius, *RE Suppl.* VI: 1363–1425

White, K. D. (1970) *Roman farming*, London

Will, W. (1991) *Der römische Mob: soziale Konflikte in der späten Republik*, Darmstadt

Willems, P. (1883) *Le sénat de la république romaine*, Louvain

Williamson, C. (2005) *The laws of the Roman people: public law in the expansion and decline of the Roman Republic*, Ann Arbor, MI

Wiseman, T. P. (1970a) 'Roman Republican road-building', *PBSR* 38: 122–52

(1970b) 'Pulcher Claudius', *HSPh* 74: 207–21

(1979) *Clio's cosmetics: three studies in Greco-Roman literature*, Leicester

(1993) 'Rome and the resplendent Aemilii'. In *Tria lustra: essays and notes presented to John Pinsent*, ed. H. D. Jocelyn, 181–92. Liverpool

(1994) 'Caesar, Pompey, and Rome'. In *Cambridge Ancient History*, 2nd edn., 9: 368–423. Cambridge

(1998) 'Two plays for the Liberalia'. In *Roman drama and Roman history*, ed. T. P. Wiseman, 35–51. Exeter

Wissowa, G. (1901) s.v. *dedicatio*, *RE* IV: 2357

(1904) 'Die Überlieferung über die römischen Penaten'. In G. Wissowa, *Gesammelte Abhandlungen zur römischen Religions- und Stadtgeschichte*, 95–128. Munich = *Hermes* 22, 1887, 29–57

(1912) *Religion und Kultus der Römer*, Munich

Wolff, H. (1979) 'Caesars Neugründung von Comum und das sogenannte *ius Latii maius*', *Chiron* 9: 169–87

Wülcker, L. (1903) *Die geschichtliche Entwicklung des Prodigienwesens bei den Römern*, Leipzig

Wulff, F. (1991) *Romanos e Itálicos en la Baja República. Estudios sobre sus relaciones entre la Segunda Guerra Púnica y la Guerra Social (201–91 a.C.)*, Brussels

(2002) *Roma e Italia de la Guerra Social a la retirada de Sila (90–79 a.C.)*, Brussels

Yakobson, A. (1999) *Elections and electioneering in Rome: a study in the political system of the late Republic*, Stuttgart

Zecchini, G. (2006) 'Ambasciatori e ambascerie in Polibio', in *Diplomacia y autorrepresentación en la Roma antigua*, ed. E. Torregaray and J. Santos, 11–24. Vitoria

Zevi, F. (1996) s.v. Mars in Circo, *LTUR* III: 226–9

Ziehen, J. (1898) 'Ein Ciceronianum zur Geschichte des Isiscultes in Rom', *Hermes* 33: 341–2

Ziolkowski, A. (1988) 'Mummius' Temple of Hercules Victor and the Round Temple on the Tiber', *Phoenix* 42: 309–33

(1992) *The temples of mid-Republican Rome and their historical and topographical context*, Rome

Index of Subjects

ager publicus: 6, 169, 170, 172, 186, 209
Allotment of provinces; 19, 20, 67, 68, 69, 98, 112, 213
Auspices: 17, 22, 29, 69, 250, 318

Bacchanalia: 27, 89, 90, 105, 122, 124, 125, 126, 127, 134, 177, 210, 211

Capitolium: 17, 18, 21, 22, 37, 68, 85, 208, 216, 217, 218, 253, 258, 259, 264, 269, 270, 271, 316, 318
clavus annalis: 36, 37, 38, 39, 57
Colonization: 173, 174, 175, 176, 177, 178, 180, 181, 187, 209, 222, 330
Comitium: 74, 75, 76, 89
consul prior factus: 193, 194, 197, 206, 288
Consular elections: 50, 70, 88, 90, 91, 93, 98, 99, 125, 130, 169, 173, 177, 192, 193, 194, 197, 198, 199, 200, 201, 202, 203, 204, 205, 206, 218, 221, 250, 283, 284, 285, 286, 287, 288, 316, 324, 330
Consular legislation: 101, 110, 117, 118, 119, 120, 246, 249, 250, 268, 290, 295, 307, 330, 331
Consular year: 13, 14, 15, 16, 18, 19, 22, 26, 27, 41, 43, 52, 61, 62, 63, 64, 66, 68, 69, 73, 74, 81, 82, 84, 86, 87, 98, 102, 107, 108, 112, 115, 125, 126, 130, 153, 158, 175, 193, 198, 202, 203, 204, 207, 210, 211, 218, 219, 221, 229, 236, 243, 245, 321, 330, 331
contio: 83, 84, 85, 86, 89, 90, 91, 92, 93, 94, 95, 96, 97, 98, 115, 123, 126, 209, 215, 220, 240, 245, 249, 250, 276, 277, 278, 279, 280, 281, 282, 289, 308, 316, 319, 320, 321, 323, 325, 330, 331, 333
Courts: 309, 316, 333

Declaration of war: 102, 103, 104, 105, 106, 107, 108, 110, 118, 119
dedicatio: 142, 146, 147, 148, 150, 155, 157, 158, 159, 160

Edicts: 83, 84, 85, 86, 87, 88, 98, 205, 206, 209, 250, 276, 277, 281, 316, 330, 333

fasti consulares: 1, 15, 38, 193, 196, 197, 288
feriae Latinae: 22, 30, 31, 32, 33, 34, 35, 43, 46, 57, 97, 118, 208, 210, 213, 214, 220, 251, 254, 255, 256, 257, 316, 321, 329
Fora: 169, 181, 182, 183, 184, 185, 186, 187, 209, 330
Foreign embassies: 58, 59, 60, 63, 64, 65, 66, 67, 68, 69, 70, 71, 72, 74, 75, 76, 77, 78, 80, 82, 112, 209, 257, 261, 262, 263, 269, 321, 329

Graecostasis: 75, 76

imperium: 2, 3, 4, 5, 17, 22, 37, 39, 40, 43, 46, 47, 51, 58, 122, 128, 133, 137, 153, 154, 178, 217, 225, 227, 228, 247, 329

lex Cornelia de provinciis ordinandis: 7, 225, 226, 227, 228, 242, 243
lex Pompeia de provinciis: 241, 298
locatio: 135, 142, 145, 146, 148, 150, 155, 156, 157, 159, 160, 162, 163, 164, 275
ludi: 22, 44, 45, 46, 47, 48, 50, 51, 52, 57, 86, 209, 251, 329

paludamentum: 6, 216, 217, 220, 234, 237
pax deorum: 21, 22, 26, 37, 52, 57, 250, 253, 329
pomerium: 4, 5, 78, 80, 88, 100, 150, 217, 225
praetor maximus: 36, 37
Prodigies: 22, 23, 24, 25, 26, 27, 28, 29, 31, 32, 46, 49, 57, 67, 68, 70, 87, 112, 118, 208, 213, 251, 252, 253, 254, 257
profectio consularis: 215, 216, 217
Public buildings: 160
Public roads: 136, 137, 139, 140, 141, 330

quaestio: 122, 123, 127, 128, 129, 130, 131, 132, 133, 134, 210, 330

Recruitment: 84, 85, 98, 112, 118, 215, 220

sacra of Lavinium: 40, 42, 43, 57, 209

Index of Ancient Sources

Index of Ancient Personal Names

Acilius Glabrio, M'. (cos. 191): 29, 48, 49, 69, 86, 103, 112, 156, 213
Acilius Glabrio, M'. (cos.suff. 154): 50, 148
Acilius Glabrio, M'. (cos. 67): 233
Aebutius, P.: 123, 125
Aelius Lamia, L. (aed. 45): 277
Aelius Paetus, P. (cos. 201): 66, 177
Aelius Paetus Catus, Sex. (cos. 198): 126, 200
Aelius Tubero, Q. (tr.pl. 193): 178
Aemilius, M. (pr. 217): 47, 53
Aemilius, T. (cos. 339): 71
Aemilius Lepidus, M. (cos. 187 and 175): 50, 66, 131, 134, 138, 146, 157, 185, 218, 271
Aemilius Lepidus, M. (cos. 78): 230, 254, 265, 271, 284, 300, 301, 302, 312
Aemilius Lepidus, Mam. (cos. 77): 239, 277
Aemilius Lepidus Paullus, L. (cos. 50): 239, 260
Aemilius Mamercus, L. (cos. 341 and 329): 70
Aemilius Paullus, L. (cos. 219 and 216): 95
Aemilius Paullus, L. (cos. 182 and 168): 33, 46, 87, 96, 97, 212, 216, 217, 260
Aemilius Paullus, M. (cos. 255): 162, 163
Aemilius Regillus, L. (pr. 190): 59
Aemilius Regillus, M. (pr. 217): 91, 149
Aemilius Scaurus, M. (cos. 115): 113, 167
Afranius, L. (cos. 60): 289, 309
Ampius Balbus, T. (pr. 59): 311
Annius Milo, T. (pr. 55): 286, 294, 314
Antiochus: 28, 48, 59, 68, 86, 103, 109, 148, 221
Antonius, C. (cos. 63): 230, 234, 240, 318, 320, 321, 325, 327
Antonius, M. (IIIvir r.p.c.43–38): 257
Appuleius Saturninus, L. (tr.pl. 103): 94, 181, 246, 310, 323
Aquillius, M' (cos. 129): 74, 140
Asclepiades of Clazomene: 264
Atilius, C. (IIvir.aed.dedic. 216): 149
Atilius, M. (cos. 294): 71
Atilius, M. (IIvir.aed.dedic. 216): 149
Atilius Calatinus, A. (cos. 258 and 254): 150
Atilius Regulus, M. (cos. 294): 149

Atilius Regulus, M. (cos. 267 and 256): 150
Atilius Serranus, A. (cos. 170): 32, 203, 204
Atilius Serranus, Sex. (cos. 136): 110
Atinius Labeo, C. (pr. 195): 178
Attalus: 68, 76
Aufidius Orestes, Cn. (cos. 71): 318
Augustus: 40, 44, 228
Aurelius Cotta, C. (cos. 252 and 248): 139, 140
Aurelius Cotta, C. (cos. 200): 29, 172
Aurelius Cotta, C. (cos. 75): 231, 265, 281, 292, 301, 302
Aurelius Cotta, L. (cos. 144): 139, 140
Aurelius Cotta, L. (cos. 65): 239, 292
Aurelius Cotta, M. (cos. 74): 231, 232, 236, 266
Aurunculeius, L. (pr. 190): 173, 221

Baebius Tamphilus, Cn. (cos. 182): 212
Baebius Tamphilus, M. (cos. 181): 112, 118, 201

Caecilius Metellus, L. (cos. 251 and 247): 146
Caecilius Metellus, L. (cos. 68): 229, 233
Caecilius Metellus, Q. (dict. 205): 92, 191
Caecilius Metellus Celer, Q. (cos. 60): 239, 306, 309, 321
Caecilius Metellus Creticus, Q. (cos. 69): 232, 301
Caecilius Metellus Delmaticus, L. (cos. 119): 146
Caecilius Metellus Diadematus, L. (cos. 117): 141
Caecilius Metellus Macedonicus, Q. (cos. 143): 164
Caecilius Metellus Nepos, Q. (cos. 98): 115
Caecilius Metellus Nepos, Q. (cos. 57): 234, 274, 281, 287, 303, 307, 314, 327
Caecilius Metellus Numidicus, Q. (cos. 109): 289
Caecilius Metellus Pius, Q. (cos. 80): 231, 289, 305
Caecilius Metellus Pius, Q. (cos. 52): 229, 239, 273, 286, 287
Calidius, C. (pr. 79): 289
Calpurnius Bestia, L. (cos. 111): 81
Calpurnius Bestia, L. (tr.pl. 62): 327
Calpurnius Bibulus, M. (cos. 59): 239, 241, 276, 278, 281, 285, 299